Trent Freeman

168 - 300

A SURVEY OF
ISRAEL'S
HISTORY

A SURVEY OF
ISRAEL'S
HISTORY
LEON WOOD

ZONDERVAN
PUBLISHING HOUSE
OF THE ZONDERVAN CORPORATION
GRAND RAPIDS, MICHIGAN 49506

A SURVEY OF ISRAEL'S HISTORY
Copyright © 1970 by Zondervan Publishing House
Grand Rapids, Michigan

Library of Congress Catalog Card Number 70-120041

Eleventh printing   December 1978
ISBN 0-310-34760-2

Printed in the United States of America

CONTENTS

FOREWORD

The view had been prevalent for some years that the traditional conservative position regarding the Bible is unacceptable to the modern mind. It is held that one is uninformed if he believes that the autographs of the biblical books were free from error. In keeping with this view is the fact that liberal works have long dominated the scene of scholarship, making it sometimes difficult to find acceptable texts for a conservative class in Bible. The number of scholars who disagree with this viewpoint, however, has been growing in recent years, and some volumes have appeared to make a change. It is with the intention of aiding in that change that this book has been written.

A knowledge of Israel's history is important if one is to understand the message of the Old Testament. Both message and history are inseparably intertwined. This is especially true for the student who accepts the supernatural origin of the Bible, for then Israel's history is seen to be divinely ordained as preparatory for the coming of Christ. One cannot understand Him without knowing of those events which called for and led to His coming.

This book has been written especially with the undergraduate theological student in mind, but its language and level of content should make it useful to a much wider range of readers. One does not need to have a wide background in ancient history to follow the thought. No attempt to give full documentation has been made, but it is hoped that sufficient references have been included to lend credence to positions taken and direction to students interested in further study.

The reader may be surprised that all of one chapter (chapter five) is devoted to a discussion in chronology, and so includes details of a kind and quantity not found elsewhere in the book. The reason is that this chronology has long been a matter of discussion, being basic in importance. It is my conviction that the viewpoint held traditionally by conservatives remains as defensible as ever, and a presentation of the matter in sufficient detail to support this conviction was thought appropriate.

Biblical references have been included with the history, and the student is urged to make use of them. The chapter and verse references are taken from the English translation and not the Hebrew text, where differences exist. The name "Yahweh" has been used for God instead of the more common "Jehovah," because it represents more closely the original pronunciation of the sacred name. Scripture quotations are taken from the American Standard Version.

A word of gratitude is due to Professor David Egner, a former student and now a faculty member of the English department of the Grand Rapids Baptist Bible College, who read the entire work and made helpful suggestions; to Mrs. Joyce VanderMeer, who gave so much of her time to typing the manuscript; and to my wife and family for patience as well as assistance in various ways.

LIST OF MAPS

ABBREVIATIONS

AASOR Annual of the American Schools of Oriental Research
AB   G. A. Barton, *Archaeology and the Bible* (7th ed.; Philadelphia: American Sunday School Union, 1937)
ABH   J. P. Free, *Archaeology and Bible History* (8th ed.; Wheaton: Scripture Press Publications, Inc., 1964)
AJSL   American Journal of Semitic Languages and Literatures
ANE   Cyrus Gordon, *The Ancient Near East* (3d ed.; New York: W. W. Norton & Co., Inc., 1965); formerly issued as *The World of the Old Testament* (Garden City: Doubleday & Co., Inc., 1958)
ANEP   J. B. Pritchard, *The Ancient Near East in Pictures* (Princeton: Princeton University Press, 1954)
ANET   J. B. Pritchard, ed., *Ancient Near Eastern Texts Relating to the Old Testament* (2d ed.; Princeton: Princeton University Press, 1955)
AOOT   K. Kitchen, *Ancient Orient and Old Testament* (Chicago: Inter-Varsity Press, 1966)
AOT   M. F. Unger, *Archaeology and the Old Testament* (2d. ed.; Grand Rapids: Zondervan Publishing House, 1954)
AOTS   D. Winton Thomas, ed., *Archaeology and Old Testament Study* (Oxford: At the Clarendon Press, 1967)
AP   W. F. Albright, *The Archaeology of Palestine* (Penguin Books, Inc., 1949)
ARI   W. F. Albright, *Archaeology and the Religion of Israel* (3d ed.; Baltimore: The Johns Hopkins Press, 1953)
ASV   American Standard Version
AV   Authorized Version (King James Version)
BA   The Biblical Archaeologist
BAR   G. E. Wright, *Biblical Archaeology* (rev. ed.; Philadelphia: The Westminster Press, 1962)
BASOR Bulletin of the American Schools of Oriental Research
BETS   Bulletin of the Evangelical Theological Society
BHI   J. Bright, *A History of Israel* (Philadelphia: The Westminster Press, 1949)
BJRL   Bulletin of the John Rylands Library
BP   W. F. Albright, "The Biblical Period," in L. Finkelstein, ed., *The Jews, Their History, Culture and Religion* (New York: Harper & Brothers, 1949), pp. 3-65; reprinted, The Biblical Colloqium, 1950

BS	Bibliotheca Sacra
DOTT	D. Winton Thomas, ed., *Documents From Old Testament Times* New York: Harper & Brothers, 1958)
FSAC	W. F. Albright, *From the Stone Age to Christianity* (2d. ed.; Garden City: Doubleday Anchor Books, 1957)
GTT	J. Simons, *The Geographical and Topographical Texts of the Old Testament* (Leiden: E. J. Brill, 1959)
HDB	Hasting's Dictionary of the Bible
HIOT	R. K. Harrison, *Introduction to the Old Testament* (Grand Rapids: William B. Eerdmans Publishing Co., 1969)
ISBE	The International Standard Bible Encyclopedia
JAOS	Journal of the American Oriental Society
JBL	Journal of Biblical Literature
JCS	Journal of Cuneiform Studies
JETS	Journal of the Evangelical Theological Society
JNES	Journal of Near Eastern Studies
JTVI	Journal of Transactions of the Victoria Institute
KDC	Keil and Delitzsch Commentaries
LAP	J. Finegan, *Light From the Ancient Past* (2d ed.; Princeton: Princeton University Press, 1959)
LB	Yohanan Aharoni, *The Land of the Bible*, trans. A. F. Rainey (Philadelphia: The Westminster Press, 1962, 1967)
MNHK	E. R. Thiele, *The Mysterious Numbers of the Hebrew Kings* (rev. ed.; Grand Rapids: William B. Eerdmans Publishing Co., 1965)
NBD	The New Bible Dictionary
NHI	M. Noth, *The History of Israel* (2d ed.; Eng. trans.; London: A. & C. Black, 1958)
OHH	J. B. Payne, *An Outline of Hebrew History* (Grand Rapids: Baker Book House, 1954)
OTS	S. Schultz, *The Old Testament Speaks* (New York: Harper & Row, 1960)
PBW	Claire Epstein, *Palestinian Bichrome Ware* (Leiden: E. J. Brill, 1966)
PEQ	Palestine Exploration Quarterly
RB	Revue Biblique
SE	W. C. Hayes, *The Scepter of Egypt* (Cambridge: Harvard University Press; Part I, 1953; Part II, 1959)
SOTI	Gleason Archer, *A Survey of Old Testament Introduction* (Chicago: Moody Press, 1964)
TH	John Van Seters, *The Hyksos* (New Haven: Yale University Press, 1966)
WTJ	The Westminster Theological Journal

A SURVEY OF
ISRAEL'S
HISTORY

CHAPTER ONE

INTRODUCTION

Though the beginning of Israel as a nation must be placed at her exodus from Egypt, an account of her history must start with Abraham.[1] Only when Israel moved across Egypt's border did she have size and identity with which other nations would have to reckon; but she already had a history, a history which stretched back through the time of residence in Egypt to her patriarchal fathers, Jacob and Abraham. To Jacob had been born the twelve heads of the respective tribes, and to Abraham had been given God's promises concerning this unique posterity.

A. SOURCE MATERIAL

Source material for Israel's history is found mainly in the Old Testament. Because of this rich treasure of information, her history can be written in greater detail than that of her neighbors. In fact, an area of advantage exists over even the great countries of her day, for, though archaeological research has filled out their stories in remarkable detail, none boast a document comparable to the Old Testament. This invaluable book tells of Israel's ancestral background; her period of development in the foreign land of Egypt; her beginnings as separate tribes in her own promised land; the uniting of these tribes in a monarchy with the names, reign-durations, and main activities of all the kings who ruled; the imposition of punishment by God for her sin in the form of captivity to eastern countries; and the return from that captivity by many of her people with consequent experiences. Not only is history contained herein, but law, philosophy, dissertation, and sermon. One learns not only what the people did, but how they thought,

---

[1] Liberal scholars commonly begin their treatments of Israel's history with the Exodus, giving only cursory remarks concerning the patriarchal periods. For instance, M. Noth, *NHI*, or B. Anderson, *Understanding the Old Testament* (Englewood Cliffs, N.J.: Prentice-Hall, Inc., 1957).

spoke, and behaved. One becomes acquainted not only with activities, but the people who acted.

This wealth of information is provided even though the main purpose of the Old Testament is other than to present a history. The Old Testament is not a history book as such. Its purpose is to portray God's interest in, and preparation for, His redemptive provision for sinful man. When man in his representative head, Adam, sinned in the Garden of Eden, need for such a provision came into existence. The Old Testament is God's record of how He prepared for and affected that provision as culminated in Jesus Christ, working particularly through the nation of Israel. The history involved is what is narrated in the Old Testament. Accordingly, that historical material which was pertinent to this preparation was included, and that which was not pertinent was normally omitted. For this reason, though the history is remarkably complete in many respects as noted, omissions occur which a book of history would include.

Happily there is another source of information which helps to fill in these omissions and supply general background. That source is archaeological research. Diligent and fruitful work by excavators has gone on in the Bible lands for many years, a work which continues and grows more productive with each new season. The information contributed is of the greatest value, and we shall make constant use of it.

B. IMPORTANCE OF ISRAEL

Israel was one of the smaller countries of the pre-Christian era, but her history has had a major impact on the world. It is correct to say that the history of no other nation has had more influence. In Israel's law, given through Moses, God's own pronouncements as to suitable and just law for a country of Israel's size and situation were laid down. Basic principles observed have provided guidelines for lawmakers since. Among Israel's prophets are the greatest thinkers and writers of their day. Some parallels to their productions have been sought in the words of Ipu-wer[2] or Nefer-rohu[3] of Egypt, the communication of the "prophet" of Mari in Mesopotamia to his king,[4] or the "Oracles of Arbella"

---

[2] Dated by most about 2000 B.C., prior to the rise of the strong Twelfth Dynasty. He stands before the king, denounces him, points out social deficiencies, and recommends improvements. Cf. J. Breasted, *The Dawn of Conscience* (New York: Chas. Scribner's Sons, 1935), pp. 197-98; for text, *ANET*, pp. 441-44.

[3] Also dated about 2000 B.C. He predicts the downfall of the current regime and even names the next. Cf. Breasted, *op. cit.*, and *ANET*, pp. 444-46. Recently Van Seters (*The Hyksos*, 1966, p. 103) has dated both Ipu-wer and Nefer-rohu to the Thirteenth Dynasty.

[4] For text and discussion, see A. Lods, "Untablette inedite de Mari, interessante pour l'histoire ancienne du prophetisma Semitique," *Studies in Old Testament Prophecy*, ed. H. H. Rowley (Edinburgh: T. & T. Clark, 1950), pp. 103-110.

in Assyria,[5] but none really rival the brilliant writings of Israel's representatives in kind, variety, and power. In Israel's wisdom literature, the view of this unique people as to God, the world, and life in a more philosophical vein is presented. Here is found dialogue, drama, psalm, and proverb, with appeal to feeling and volition as well as thought. The message for social justice and the supreme place of a life of commitment to God, in both this wisdom literature and the prophets, has continued to be as significant in history since their writing as they were then.

The abiding value of the Old Testament is mainly religious and moral, but its artistic merit must not be overlooked. It contains the finest literary pieces of the day. In fact, the book of Job, the Psalms, or Isaiah's brilliant chapters are among the finest of any day. They have inspired writers everywhere since. Not only writers have experienced this inspiration, but musicians, painters, sculptors, and artists in most every field have thrilled to these books. How much of the world's fine music, how much painting, how much statuary finds its theme in the pages of the Old Testament. How many volumes have been penned with its story in view. The Christian sector of the world has been dominant since the days of the Roman Empire, and the influence of the Old Testament in fashioning that dominance has been enormous.

C. Israel's Strategic Location

Contributing also to Israel's importance was her strategic location. Wedged between the Mediterranean on the west and the Arabian desert on the east, her narrow sixty miles afforded the only caravan routes for north-south traffic. To the south lay Egypt, a continuing world power throughout the Old Testament period, dependent on the Nile River. The Nile, flooding annually, gave water to an otherwise arid desert and brought fertile soil for productive farming. It also provided convenient transportation for both people and merchandise. Because of the Nile, Egypt prospered and called for extensive trade with countries to the north.

To the north lay the countries of what is often called the Fertile Crescent. This area also was dependent on the benefits of rivers,[6]

[5] A. Guillaume, *Prophecy and Divination Among the Hebrews and Other Semites* (London: Hodder & Stoughton, 1938), pp. 42-43, finds parallels to Hebrew prophecy in these oracles as follows: "Like the Hebrew prophets, the priestesses employed the first person in speaking on behalf of Ishtar. The frequent injunction to 'fear not,' the promise of help, and of the overthrow of the king's enemies, the assertion of the goddess's greatness, are all suggestive of Hebrew prophecy."

[6] Reflected in the names given to the region by the Greeks; the name Mesopotamia meaning "the land between the rivers."

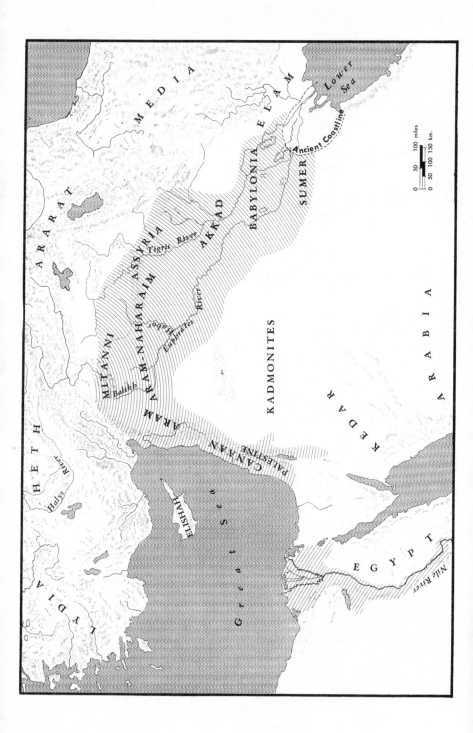

especially the Euphrates and the Tigris. Both rise in the Armenian mountains, with a distance of 450 miles separating them at one point. And both flow southeastward by different routes gradually approaching each other until near the Persian Gulf they join.[7] The shorter Tigris descends more rapidly. Both of Assyria's capitals, Assur and later Nineveh, lay on its banks and were dependent upon it. The Euphrates flows more leisurely. It provided a main avenue of travel to the west for Babylonians, Assyrians, Armenians, and Mitanni in their respective periods. All of these countries wished to trade with prosperous Egypt to the south. Their caravans joined with those of Northern Canaan, and even of Anatolia farther to the north, employing the much-used line of travel through the length of Israel.

D. Geography of Palestine

The name "Palestine"[8] is derived from "Philistia," meaning "land of the Philistine." Philistia originally included only the southwest portion of the land, the area where the Philistines dwelt. But the name, in its slightly different form, came to be applied to all the land of Israel.

Palestine was not a large country. It lay along the southern portion of the east Mediterranean coastline and extended little more than 150 miles north to south and 60 east to west. Natural limitations confined it on three sides. On the east was the vastness of the Syrian-Arabian desert; on the south the desert-like Negeb; and on the west the great Mediterranean. Only on the north did similar arable land continue, where, for much of Old Testament time, lay the two countries, Phoenicia along the Mediterranean, and Aram-Damascus farther inland. Phoenicia became a leading maritime power, and the benefits of her merchandising were in some part shared by Israel, because of peaceful relations continuing between the two countries most of the time. Aram-Damascus, on the other hand, was a poorer country, made so in large part by extensive areas of desert waste within her border, and she was frequently at war with Israel, apparently trying to better her position.

1. *The Jordan rift.* The most distinctive feature in Palestinian topography is the remarkable rift in the earth's surface constituting the Jordan Valley. Through this great fissure, averaging ten miles in width, runs the Jordan River, falling from an altitude of about 300 feet near the base of Mt. Hermon to a depth of more than 1,200 feet below sea level at the Dead Sea, the lowest place on earth. The valley is lined

---

[7] It is believed that they entered the Persian Gulf separately in Abraham's day. However, the great burden of silt they carry has filled the Gulf to its present shoreline over 100 miles from where it was then, within which distance they now join.

[8] For good geographical discussion, cf. Y. Aharoni, *LB*, pp. 3-57.

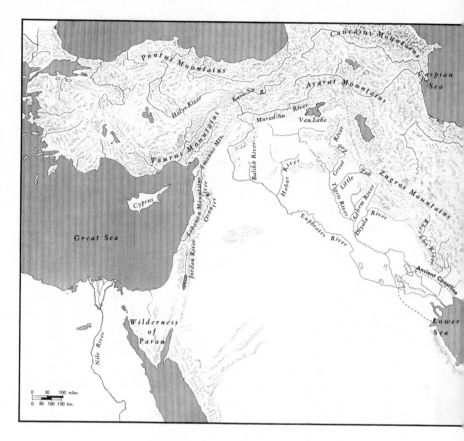

Map 2. Ancient World — Physical Features

by slopes which are generally sudden and steep, sometimes forming sharply rising cliffs.

The Jordan River is formed by four small tributaries,[9] joining just north of nearly drained Lake Huleh[10] where the surface is 210 feet above sea level. Ten miles farther south the Jordan empties into the Sea of Galilee, 13 miles long, 7 wide, and 630 feet below sea level. This sweet water lake is unusually blue in color, abounds in fish today as it did in Bible times, and is famous for its sudden storms which transform its normally placid surface into a boiling cauldron. The Jordan Valley proper runs approximately 70 miles from the Sea of Galilee to the Dead Sea. The Jordan River, winding and twisting for this distance, averages between 90 and 100 feet in width and from 3 to 10 feet in depth. Flood season has seen it flow over its banks, however, for a width of up to a mile. Extensive irrigation projects of recent years have reduced the flow of water measurably.[11]

The Dead Sea is one of the most remarkable bodies of water in the world. Its concentrated chemical content[12] gives it great buoyancy but makes it fatal for any form of marine life. Potash, extracted from it, provides Israel with a source of revenue today. The Sea is approximately 47 miles long and 6 to 9 wide, its northern two-thirds being very deep, up to 1,200 feet. The two parts are divided by the *Lisan,* a boot-shaped peninsula extending from the eastern shore leaving only a two and one-half mile expanse remaining at one point. Across this expanse a passable ford was employed for centuries.

South of the Dead Sea the great rift continues in what is called the Arabah.[13] It runs to the Gulf of Aqabah about 110 miles distant. Sealed off by the mountains of the Negeb to the west and the high peaks of old Edom to the east, this narrow stretch is hot and arid, receiving only sporadic rainfall. It carried economic importance, especially after the time of Solomon, for its fine copper mines. Solomon developed these and built efficient smelters to refine the ore. Then he

[9] The Bareighit, the Hasbany, the Leddan, and the Banias. These vary from 5½ to 24 miles in length.

[10] Work was completed in 1957 in straightening and deepening the Jordan which served to drain most of Lake Huleh as well as extensive marshy areas, thus reclaiming many acres of fertile farm land.

[11] Both Jordan and Israel take water, Jordan especially from the Yarmuk River before it flows into the Jordan and Israel directly out of the Sea of Galilee.

[12] This concentration is 25%, made up of salt, potash, magnesium, and calcium chlorides and bromide.

[13] This name is limited today to this southern portion of the rift. However, the Bible uses it in reference to the rift as far north as the Sea of Galilee (cf. Deut. 3:17; Josh. 3:15; II Sam. 2:29).

employed Elath as a port nearby on the Gulf of Aqabah from which to ship ore for trade with countries south.

2. *Transjordan.* On the east of the Jordan rift lies Transjordan. This is rolling plateau land, long known for its grazing value. Little farming is done there because hot winds (siroccos) burn it in the spring and fall, and cold desert winds sweep across it quite unhindered in the winter. The high ridges running up from the Jordan, arresting and cooling the air, do cause substantial rainfall, however. This water drains mainly back into the Jordan through four principal river systems: the Yarmuk just below the Sea of Galilee, the Jabbok, at the approximate midpoint between the Sea of Galilee and the Dead Sea, the Arnon emptying directly into the Dead Sea, and the Zered at the southern extreme of the Dead Sea.

The area north of the Yarmuk was known as Bashan, a fertile table-land highly prized by, and a source of contention between, Israel and Aram-Damascus for many years. Gilead extended from Bashan as far south as Moab. This region attains altitudes of over 3,000 feet both north and south of the Jabbok River, which bisects it. Fine forests covered many of its slopes in ancient time. Moab lay south of Gilead, and at times was confined between the Zered and Arnon Rivers, but more often controlled as far north as a latitudinal line approximately even with the northern tip of the Dead Sea. North of the Arnon, the land averages 2,000 to 2,400 feet high, but south it rises to peaks of over 4,000 feet. South of the Zered River stretched Edom, long and narrow, confined mainly to the mountain ridge east of the Arabah called Mt. Seir ("the hairy mountain"). These mountains, formed of red Nubian sandstone, exceed 5,000 feet. Nestled among them is one of the world's most unusual cities, old Petra, a city carved from the cliffs and entered only by a long narrow defile called the Sik.

3. *The central mountains.* On the west of the Jordan runs what is often called the backbone of Palestine proper, a series of three blocks of mountain country. The northern block was called Galilee, separated from the central block by the expansive Esdraelon Valley, a fertile farming region of Bible days and even more today. Elevations in Upper Galilee reach more than 3,000 feet, while in Lower Galilee they attain about 2,000 and the peaks are more widely separated by valleys suitable for farming. The middle block was early called Mount Ephraim and later Samaria. The name "Ephraim" came from the Tribe of Ephraim which occupied its southern half. The mountains of its northern half are not as high as those of the southern half and again are separated more by valleys. Here the two mountains, Ebal and Gerizim, with the important city Shechem between, were especially significant. The southern block was Judea. Though its slopes are steep, they

were well farmed through Bible times by employing the principle of terracing. As one moves toward the Dead Sea, however, these slopes become arid and bare and form what is called the Judean Desert. Apart from the oasis of En-gedi and a few less significant settlements, this wilderness region never knew permanent habitation. It was in this area near the Dead Sea that the invaluable discoveries of the so-called Dead Sea Scrolls were made.

4. *The coastal region.* Between the mountains of Palestine proper and the Mediterranean run the coastal plains. The shore line itself is marked by shifting sand dunes, but inland only a short distance is good farming land. The coastal plains are cut at one point all the way to the Mediterranean by the ridge of Carmel, which forms a jutting irregularity into the Mediterranean on a latitudinal line about even with the Sea of Galilee. North of this ridge, running angularly east and west, is the splendid Esdraelon Valley. South, all the way to modern Tel Aviv, extends the beautiful Sharon Plain, dotted today by fine orchards. Below the Sharon was the excellent land controlled so long by the Philistines. Here the Mediterranean begins to sweep westward and makes the plain wider. Here, too, heavy alluvial soil predominates making excellent crops possible. Rainfall becomes less toward the south, but is still sufficient at Gaza for agriculture. Old Gaza appears to have been the metropolis of the region, with Ashkelon, slightly north, the main port. The name "Shephelah" is given to the gradually rising ground between the coastal plain and the central mountains. It, too, is well suited for farming.

Though the Mediterranean extends along the entire length of Palestine on the west, it has never had the influence on the lives of Palestinians one might think. The reason is found in a lack of natural harbors. The shore is remarkably straight, so that only at Ashkelon, Joppa, Dor, and Acco was there any appreciable shipping, and this was limited. Little fishing and trading by water was done by the Israelites, who depended rather on the Phoenicians to the north, who did have fine harbors at Tyre, Sidon, and Byblos.

5. *Climate.* Palestine is located in a sub-tropical zone. Its temperatures are suited, for instance, to growing the citrus fruits, oranges, lemons, and grapefruit. A split year of rainfall is experienced, the wet season extending from about November to April. The early rains come in November, the heavier winter rains in December, January, and February, and the latter rains taper off through March and early April. About the time the rains cease, the hot desert winds (siroccos) begin to blow and bring rapid drying conditions to soil which will not experience rainfall again for six months. Vegetation soon becomes brown. The amount of rainfall varies in different parts of the land. The coastal

region and the northern highlands receive the most. Many streams carry water only when rain falls. Only the larger streams are perennial such as the Yarmuk, Jabbok, Arnon, Zered, and Jalud all flowing into the Jordan rift, or the Yarkon flowing into the Mediterranean at Tel Aviv. Even these fall to low levels during the dry season.

E. HISTORY DIVISIONS

Israel's history may be divided into seven periods: first, the patriarchal, running from Abraham to Jacob's twelve sons, the heads of the respective tribes; second, the Egyptian, covering the period from Jacob's descent into Egypt until the Exodus; third, the time of wilderness travel and Palestinian conquest; fourth, the period of the Judges, when the tribes lived as quite separate entities unified by their common faith in God, their ancestral heritage, and the central sanctuary at Shiloh; fifth, the time of the united monarchy from Saul to Solomon; sixth, the years of the divided monarchy, with these closing for Israel at the fall of Samaria in 722 B.C. and for Judah at the fall of Jerusalem in 586 B.C.; and seventh, the exilic and postexilic period running until the close of the fourth century.

CHAPTER TWO

PATRIARCHAL BACKGROUND

A. HISTORICAL ACCURACY

Evidence from archaeological research has caused numerous liberal scholars to change in their respect for historical accuracy in the Old Testament. This is true regarding the patriarchal period probably more than any other. Until recent time, not only were the actions of Abraham, Isaac, and Jacob doubted, but even their existence as persons.[1] Today the latter is readily accepted, and their actions are believed to agree in large part with those presented in the Genesis account.[2] The evidence which has prompted this new respect is extensive. Only a part can be noted here.

1. *Names.* One aspect concerns the existence of names in ancient texts like those used in Genesis. The name, Jacob, for instance, has been found in the form *Ya'qob-el* designating a person in an eighteenth century text from Chagar-bazar in Upper Mesopotamia, and designating a place in Palestine in a list of Thutmose III; also in the form *Ya'qob-har* as the name of a Hyksos chief.[3] The name, Abraham, has been found in Babylonian texts of the sixteenth century in the form *Abamram,* and in other forms at Mari.[4] A Mari text uses the name of Abraham's brother, Nahor, in the form *Nakhur,* as the name of a city in the vicinity of Haran. Mari texts speak further of a people called *Banu-yamina* (Benjamin),[5] and use names built on the same

[1] For instance, J. Wellhausen, *Prologomena to the History of Israel,* trans. Black and Menzies (Edinburgh: A. & C. Black, 1885), pp. 318f.

[2] Cf. Bright, *BHI,* pp. 82-83; also Albright, *ARI,* pp. 145, 176. For helpful surveys of recent trends in Old Testament studies, cf. H. H. Rowley, ed., *The Old Testament and Modern Study* (Oxford: At the Clarendon Press, 1951). Recently a slightly contrary note has been sounded by Van Seters, *JBL,* 87(Dec., 1968), pp. 401-408.

[3] Cf. Albright, *JAOS,* 74(1954); p. 231; R. DeVaux, *RB,* 72(1965), p. 9.

[4] For three such texts, cf. G. Barton, *AB,* pp. 344-45. On names generally at Mari, cf. H. B. Huffmon, *Amorite Personal Names in the Mari Texts* (1965).

[5] Cf. Gelb, *JCS,* 15(1961), pp. 37-38; and H. Tadmore, *JNES,* 17(1958), p. 130, n. 12.

roots as Gad, Dan, Levi, and Ishmael. Later Assyrian texts speak of two cities, *Til-turakhi* and *Sarugi,* the equivalents of *Terah* and *Serug,* father and prior ancestor of Abraham respectively. These names, and others that might be added, all appear in texts from the first half of the second millennium. Though evidence is lacking that any refers to a specific biblical person or place, they do indicate that the names employed in the Genesis record are those of the nomenclature of the day.[6]

2. *Customs.* Further evidence concerns customs of the period. Some of the actions of the patriarchs seem strange in view of Mosaic law and later practices, but are understandable in the light of customs of the early second millennium as shown especially by texts from Nuzi.[7] For instance, Abraham was concerned lest his servant, Eliezer, be his heir instead of a son (Gen. 15:1-4). The Genesis record implies that this manner of inheritance was normal when there was no son. Nuzi texts show that this was the case. They reveal that childless parents would adopt a servant as a son who would then serve them for their lifetime and become heir at their death unless a natural son should be born.[8] Again it seems strange that Sarah should give her slave, Hagar, to Abraham as second wife (Gen. 16:1-4), but Nuzi texts tell of this practice also as something quite normal for the day. These texts indicate too that, should a son then be born, neither the slave nor the son were to be put out of the home, which gives an added reason for Abraham's reluctance to expel Hagar and Ishmael when Sarah requested it (Gen. 21:9-11).[9] Later both Rachel and Leah gave their maids to Jacob in similar fashion (Gen. 30:1-13). That Rachel should take her father's teraphim, the family idols, also finds explanation at Nuzi (Gen. 31:19, 34, 35). Such idols signified right of heirship. Laban had natural sons, apparently born after Jacob's arrival as a member of the family (Gen. 31:1). Rachel by her action was attempting to maintain Jacob's right to be principal heir. Nuzi texts further reveal that oral blessings were considered binding. A discovered court record contains the blessing of a father for his sons which the court held binding. This explains Isaac's refusal of Esau's entreaty to change the bless-

---

[6] For further discussion generally and references, cf. M. Unger, *AOT,* pp. 127-28; J. Bright, *BHI,* pp. 70f; C. H. Gordon, *ANE,* pp. 113-33; and K. A. Kitchen, *AOOT,* pp. 48f, 153f.

[7] Nuzi texts date from the 15th century and represent Hurrian customs, many of which were adopted from prior Amorites; cf. C. H. Gordon, *BA,* 3(1940), pp. 1-12; G. E. Wright, *BAR,* pp. 43-44. Gordon's assumption that these parallels imply a date for the patriarchs in the fifteenth century does not hold, for similar parallels exist in tablets from Ur of the nineteenth and eighteenth centuries; cf. D. J. Wiseman, *JTVI* 88(1956), p. 124.

[8] Cf. Nuzi tablet H. 60; E. A. Speiser, *AASOR,* 10(1930), p. 30.

[9] Cf. Nuzi tablet H. 67; *ibid.,* p. 32.

ing given to Jacob even though deceit had been involved. This is in keeping, too, with the prominent place given to blessings generally in Genesis, as pronounced by Noah (9:25-27) and Jacob (49:1-29).

3. *Conditions in Palestine.*[10] A third area of evidence concerns general conditions in Canaan, of the patriarchal time, coinciding with those reflected in the patriarchal stories. Abraham was able to move about in the land with remarkable freedom, pitching his tent without interference, unhindered in using the land for pasturing his flocks. He did not find it necessary to purchase land until Sarah died, at which time he bought the cave of Machpelah for a place of burial.[11] At one time he found it necessary to separate from his nephew Lot to find adequate pasture (Gen. 13:5-12), but this was not due to pressure from native inhabitants. The implication is that the region in which Abraham moved, from Shechem in the north to Beersheba in the south, was sparsely populated. Both archaeological research in Palestine and the Execration texts of Egypt[12] testify that this was the situation particularly in the twenty-second to the nineteenth centuries B.C., the exact period when Abraham, Isaac, and Jacob lived.[13] Also the Tale of Sinuhe[14] of the twentieth century depicts persons like Abraham moving freely about in the Canaanite region with large flocks and herds in a semi-nomadic type of existence. Archaeology reveals further that cities mentioned in the patriarchal stories (Dothan, Shechem, Bethel, Jerusalem, et al.) all existed then, and further that the Jordan Valley near the Dead Sea was a region of many cities, as indicated in the story of Lot (Gen. 13:1-12).

4. *Extensive travel.* The last area of evidence concerns the existence of extensive travel in the Near East of patriarchal times. This is shown to be the same as that reflected in the patriarchal stories. Abraham traveled more than 1,000 miles in moving from Ur of the Chaldees to southern Canaan (Gen. 11:31 - 12:9). Later he sent his chief servant, Eliezer, more than 400 miles north to Haran in Upper Mesopotamia to acquire a bride for his son, Isaac (Gen. 24:1-10). Then Jacob traveled to the same area in flight from Esau, acquired a family and possessions, and returned to southern Canaan (Gen. 28 - 33). Numerous texts from archaeological research show that travel of this kind was not uncommon for the time. Letters from Mari indicate that her envoys visited all the way from Hazor in Palestine to southern Mesopotamia and even Elam.[15] Somewhat earlier, the Cappadocian Texts from Kan-

---

[10] Cf. *infra*, pp. 32-33.
[11] Cf. *infra*, chap. 3, pp. 61-62.
[12] Cf. *infra*, p. 33, n. 28, and chap. 3, p. 48, n. 5.
[13] Cf. *infra*, pp. 30-38.
[14] Text in *ANET*, pp. 18-22.
[15] Cf. K. A. Kitchen, *AOOT*, p. 50, for references.

ish in Asia Minor tell of extensive trade relations between the Hittites and Assur. Assyrian trade colonies existed among the Hittites, where Assyrian wares were exchanged for native merchandise.[16] Earlier still, both Sargon and his grandson, Narim-sin, of the Akkadian period in southern Mesopotamia, conducted military campaigns as far distant as the Mediterranean coast and held, at least intermittently, an empire that extended from there all the way to central Persia.[17]

B. SIGNIFICANCE OF ABRAHAM'S CALL

God's call of Abraham instituted a variation in the divine manner of dealing with mankind. Until this occasion God had dealt with all men in a general way. There had been no select nation, chosen in distinction from others. Accordingly, when mankind did not obey, mankind was punished in the Flood. But with the call of Abraham, this world-wide approach was changed. No longer did God address Himself generally, but particularly. He chose one man alone. He separated him from others and gave him individual instruction. The intention was to rear a new, select nation, with Abraham as the father. People at large had refused God's way and so had for a time forfeited their opportunity. God would now make a special people through whom to work in effecting His plan of redemption. Through them now the written Word, the Scriptures, would come to existence, and through them too the Living Word, Jesus Christ, would be born in due time. In this manner the redemptive provision would be brought to reality in spite of the wickedness of the world at large. When complete and ready, however, it would be made available to all the world and God would once more work with all men generally.

C. DATE OF ABRAHAM

Both biblical and extra-biblical materials bear on the date of Abraham. Considerable difference in evaluation of these materials exists among scholars, especially between conservatives and liberals. The conclusions of liberal scholars vary from a date in the latter half of the fifteenth century[18] to sometime in the twentieth.[19] Conservative schol-

[16] The texts date from the nineteenth century, but the colonies existed from the last of the third millennium; cf. W. Albright, *BASOR*, 139(1955), p. 15. Cf. Kitchen, *AOOT*, for references describing colony activities.

[17] Cf. *infra*, chap. 3, pp. 51-53.

[18] So Cyrus Gordon who argues from reflected Nuzi customs, from Egypt being called "land of Rameses" in Jacob's time (Gen. 47:11), and from his belief that there were only four generations from Moses back to Joseph (Gen. 15:16; Ex. 6:16-20), with Moses dating in the thirteenth century; Gordon, *ANE*, pp. 115-116. H. H. Rowley argues for the seventeenth century, *From Joseph to Joshua* (London: Oxford University Press, 1948).

ars favor an earlier date, many placing Abraham's birth at the middle of the twenty-second century.[20] The matter depends on three determinations: the date of Israel's Exodus from Egypt, the duration of Israel's stay in Egypt, and the length of time between Abraham's birthdate and Jacob's descent into Egypt with his family.

1. *Biblical evidence.* The Bible has much to say on all three matters. It answers the third in a way to leave no question for the conservative scholar. Abraham was 100 years old when Isaac was born (Gen. 21:5), Isaac was 60 when Jacob was born (Gen. 25:26), and Jacob was 130 when he went down into Egypt (Gen. 47:9), giving a total of 290 years.

a. Date of the Exodus. The first matter, the date of the Exodus, receives an answer also nearly as certain for the conservative;[21] namely, that the Exodus occurred shortly after the middle of the fifteenth century. This date, commonly placed c. 1446 B.C., is called the "early" date in contrast to one advocated for some time during the thirteenth century called the "late" date.[22] Extensive evidence, both biblical and extra-biblical, which is evaluated in a later chapter,[23] bears on this determination. Suffice it now simply to list four biblical items which favor the early date: first, a statement in I Kings 6:1 that the Exodus preceded the time when Solomon began to build the Temple (c. 966 B.C.) by 480 years; second, Jephthah's word in Judges 11:26 that by

[19] So Albright who believes Abraham's move to Canaan could have been part of the Amorite migration and Jacob's to Egypt part of the Hyksos occupation there; Albright, *AP*, p. 83. So also N. Glueck, *BA*, 18(1955), pp. 4, 6-9; and G. E. Wright, *BAR*, p. 50.

[20] So J. B. Payne who holds to the early date of the Exodus with Israel's sojourn in Egypt lasting 430 years and so finds Abraham born 2166 B.C.; Payne, *OHH*, pp. 34-36; cf. M. Unger, *AOT*, pp. 106-107, and G. L. Archer, *SOTI*, pp. 203-205. However, S. Schultz, *OTS*, pp. 30-31, 48-49, holds to a date more in keeping with Albright, apparently believing that Israel's sojourn in Egypt lasted less than 430 years; and K. A. Kitchen, *AOOT*, pp. 41-56, generally agrees, only he finds his evidence in a late date for the Exodus.

[21] There are a few conservative writers who take a contrary position. For instance, F. F. Bruce, *Israel and the Nations* (Grand Rapids: Wm. B. Eerdmans Publishing Co., 1963), pp. 13-14; C. Pfeiffer, *Egypt and the Exodus* (Grand Rapids: Baker Book House, 1964), pp. 84-88; K. A. Kitchen, *AOOT*, pp. 57-75; or R. K. Harrison, *HIOT*, pp. 174-77.

[22] Often placed early (c. 1290 B.C.) in the reign of Rameses II (1304-1238; cf. *infra*, chap. 5, p. 90, n. 30, for discussion of these dates). A former popular view that Merneptah (1238-1228) was the Pharaoh of the Exodus has been generally abandoned with the finding of Merneptah's inscription claiming to have defeated Israel in the land of Palestine. However, Cyrus Gordon still favors the "third quarter of the thirteenth century," *ANE*, p. 115; and cf. H. H. Rowley, "Israel's Sojourn in Egypt," *BJRL*, 22(1938), p. 263, for a date of c. 1225 B.C.

[23] Cf. *infra*, chap. 5, pp. 88-109.

his day Israel had been in possession of the land for 300 years; third, an analysis of the duration of the Judge's period which requires more years than possible with the late date; and fourth, the sequence of events in Egyptian history involved with the Exodus which fits the biblical story well in the fifteenth century but not in the thirteenth.

b. Duration of Egyptian sojourn. As to the second matter, the duration of the Egyptian sojourn, greater difference of opinion among conservative scholars exists, but here too a rather certain conclusion can be reached: namely, that the sojourn lasted 430 years. An alternate view sees it as 215 years. Once again several matters, which are discussed in a later chapter,[24] bear on the question. We here only list the main arguments for the longer period: first, the statement of the Hebrew text in Exodus 12:40 that the period lasted 430 years; second, God's prediction to Abraham (Gen. 15:13) that his posterity would be afflicted in a foreign land "four hundred years" (a round number); third, Stephen's similar statement in Acts 7:6 using again the figure 400; and fourth, the high improbability of Jacob's family multiplying in size to a nation of over 2,000,000 people in a period substantially less than 430 years.

In the light of these three determinations, Abraham's birthdate is easily calculated. To 966 B.C., the date when Solomon began construction on the Temple, is added 480 years, the intervening time after the Exodus according to I Kings 6:1; to this 430 years, the time Israel sojourned in Egypt; and to this 290 years, the time between Jacob's descent to Egypt and Abraham's birth. The resultant date is 2166 B.C.[25]

2. *Extra-biblical evidence.* Extra-biblical evidence also lends substantial testimony. Three areas call for attention.

a. Conditions in Canaan. If Abraham was born c. 2166 B.C., the date of his arrival in Canaan was c. 2091 B.C., for he was seventy-five years old at the time (Gen. 12:4). Do conditions in Canaan as reflected in the Genesis stories agree with indications of archaeological research for this date? The answer is that they do.[26]

For one thing, there is agreement as to sparseness of population in

[24] Cf. *infra*, chap. 5, pp. 83-88.

[25] This date cannot be pressed within a possible variation of a few years due to possible roundness of number in the biblical figures. This still leaves the date near the middle of the 22nd century, however.

[26] Besides the two items listed here, K. A. Kitchen mentions the matter of "seasonal occupation of the Negeb region on the south-west border of Palestine" as attested by archaeology for the "twenty-first to nineteenth centuries B.C." but "*not* for a thousand years earlier or for eight hundred years afterwards," citing many references from especially Albright and N. Glueck in evidence; Kitchen, *AOOT*, pp. 49-50. Both Abraham and Isaac spent time in this area (Gen. 20:1; 24:62).

Canaan at the time. It has been observed that the Abraham stories do indicate this situation, especially in that Abraham was able to move freely between Shechem and Beersheba, pitching his tent and grazing his flocks almost as he pleased. Archaeology testifies similarly,[27] particularly as to the inland region, the very section through which Abraham moved. This sparse condition did not last long, since many cities west of the Jordan came again to be occupied during the nineteenth century.[28] This too is significant because both Isaac and Jacob[29] also enjoyed comparative ease of movement in the land, which means that Abraham must have lived well before this rebuilding time. The twenty-first century, indicated in the above chronology, fits well.

Further, there is agreement as to the existence yet in Abraham's day of a vigorous population in the region of Sodom and Gomorrah.[30] Though Abraham moved freely through a sparse area in the highlands of Palestine, Lot found numerous cities in the Jordan plain (Gen. 13: 12; 14:2-7; 19:29). But the research of Nelson Glueck[31] has shown that these cities were destroyed sometime in the twentieth or nineteenth century. He points out that they, along with other population centers of Transjordan and the Negeb generally, were still occupied when the "Amorite" destruction was experienced in Palestine proper, but that they were all abandoned for some reason at this slightly later time.

This means that Abraham and Lot must have lived in the land sometime following the general destruction in the highland region and prior to the destruction of the cities in the Jordan plain; in other words, sometime between c. 2100 B.C. and c. 1900 B.C. According to our chronology, Abraham lived in Canaan from c. 2091 B.C. to c. 1991 B.C.

b. Conditions in Egypt. The second area of evidence concerns whether or not Egyptian history of the early nineteenth century (c.

---

[27] Cf. discussion, infra, chap. 3, pp. 47-48.

[28] Evidenced especially by the Egyptian Execration Texts which mention many more Palestinian cities for the nineteenth century than for the twentieth; cf. Wright, BAR, p. 47; Aharoni, LB, pp. 131-35. Van Seters, TH, pp. 9-19, finding confirmation from Kenyon (Archaeology in the Holy Land, New York: Praeger, 1960, pp. 158f), recently argues that this condition existed 2200-1950, which still fits our dating and requires it to be as early as indicated.

[29] Isaac remained mostly in the south (Hebron, Beersheba, Gerar), but Jacob, after his return from Padan-aram, moved freely to Shechem, on to Bethel, and then further south to Hebron, from where his sons later took the family flocks back north for pasture, first to Shechem and then on to Dothan (Gen. 35:1-8; 37:12-17).

[30] For discussion of the destruction, cf. infra, chap. 3, p. 56.

[31] Cf. Glueck, "The Age of Abraham in the Negeb," BA, 18(Feb., 1955), pp. 2-9; also his The Other Side of the Jordan (New Haven: American Schools of Oriental Research, 1940), p. 21. Van Seters, op. cit., places this destruction at 1950 B.C.

1876 B.C.)[32] fits conditions reflected in the biblical story regarding Jacob's descent there. The answer again is in the affirmative. Two matters are worthy of note.

One concerns freedom of travel between Canaan and Egypt. Jacob's sons experienced no difficulty in crossing the Egyptian border two different times to buy corn, and later Jacob himself went to Egypt with his whole family (Gen. 42 - 46). Prior to this, Abraham too had traveled to Egypt in time of famine (Gen 12:10-20). These occasions suggest that movement between the two countries was common for the time. Evidence from archaeology testifies similarly. Particularly significant is an Egyptian tomb painting, dated c. 1900 B.C., which pictures a group of Semitic semi-nomads entering Egypt as Jacob and Abraham must have. There are thirty-seven of them, dressed in colored garments in contrast to the plain white of the Egyptians.[33] Pictured thus in a tomb, this type of movement is indicated to have been well known in Egypt.[34]

The other matter concerns the existence of a Pharaoh who, as the biblical account says, "knew not Joseph" (Ex. 1:8); one who arose sometime after Joseph and enslaved the Israelites. The Genesis story implies that, whoever he was, he began a new line of kings from those who had befriended Israelites previously. Does Egyptian history of this general time reveal such a king? The answer is that it does; in fact two. One was the first king of the foreign, semitic rulers, the Hyksos.[35] These outsiders drove the native dynasty from the throne sometime prior to 1700 B.C. (c. 1730), and so did establish a new line that could easily have taken a new attitude toward multiplying Israelites. The other was the first king of the Eighteenth Dynasty, Ahmose, who was able, in turn, to drive these foreign Hyksos back out of the land and

[32] Jacob entered Egypt 430 years before the Exodus (Ex. 12:40). Adding 430 to c. 1446 B.C. (Exodus date) gives c. 1876 for Jacob's entry.

[33] Tomb of Khnum-hotep III from the Twelfth Dynasty Period (cf. infra, chap. 6, p. 110) at Beni Hasan. For picture, cf. ANEP, fig. 3.

[34] G. E. Wright, BAR, p. 56, cites two inscriptions from the thirteenth and fourteenth centuries which show that similar ease of entrance to Egypt by Asiatics continued for several centuries.

[35] A Semitic people who gradually infiltrated Egypt and finally took over the rule. Their names suggest a Northwest Semitic background, but their exact origin is still unknown. Manetho, as quoted by Josephus, says that the name, Hyksos, means "king-shepherds," evidently relating the element hyk to an Egyptian word for "ruler," and the element sos to a word meaning in the later stages of the language "shepherd." However, this explanation may be only a later popular idea. The name more likely comes from the Egyptian heku shoswet (later pronounced hyku shose) meaning "rulers of foreign lands." Cf. Steindorf and Seele, When Egypt Ruled the East (2d ed.; Chicago: University of Chicago Press, 1957), p. 24; R. M. Engberg, The Hyksos Reconsidered (Chicago: University of Chicago Press, 1939); and Van Seters, TH, pp. 181-90.

reestablish the native line. He could also have inaugurated new attitudes toward Israelites who were ethnically related to the hated Hyksos just expelled.[36]

c. Pharaoh identity. The third area of evidence concerns the specific identity of this Pharaoh "who knew not Joseph." We have observed that two rulers fit the general pattern, but can a choice be made between them? There is reason to make the choice if possible, for if the earlier of the two, the Hyksos ruler, should be the more likely, then further evidence is supplied in favor of the early nineteenth century B.C. for Jacob's entrance to Egypt. This follows in view of the amount of time needed between the rise of this ruler and the descent of Jacob to allow for Joseph to have died[37] and Jacob's descendants to have multiplied to a place where the new ruler felt it necessary to enslave them (Ex. 1:8-11). The century and a half existent between Jacob's entrance and the accession of the Hyksos ruler would be adequate but none too much for this development. If, on the other hand, the second of the two rulers, Ahmose, who expelled the Hyksos from Egypt, were the one, then Jacob's entrance could have been correspondingly later, even during the Hyksos period itself.[38] Four factors show evidence in favor of the earlier ruler.[39]

First, the Egyptian cities, Pithom and Raamses, which were built by enslaved Israelites for the unfriendly Pharaoh (Ex. 1:11), must have been constructed either before or after the period of the Eighteenth Dynasty, when Ahmose lived, for archaeological evidence indicates that they were not constructed during that time. Excavation at old Raamses (identified with Avaris, capital of the Hyksos) has revealed "not a single object of the Eighteenth Dynasty."[40] G. E. Wright uses this

[36] A possible objection to a nineteenth century entry to Egypt that Egyptians (strong Twelfth Dynasty then ruling) considered shepherds an "abomination" (Gen. 46:34) and so would not have been likely to give choice farm land to Jacob's family, who were shepherds, may be answered as follows. The Pharaoh's willingness to bestow this favor was prompted by his gratitude toward Joseph for his excellent work in time of famine. Further, the amount of land given would not have been extensive, for the days of great multiplication for Jacob's family were yet future.

[37] Joseph was 39 years old when Jacob entered Egypt (Gen. 41:46, 53, 54; 45:6) and lived to be 110 (Gen. 50:22); hence he died 71 years after c. 1876 B.C. or c. 1805 B.C.

[38] Cf. *supra*, n. 19. With the first Hyksos ruler dating at c. 1730 B.C. and Ahmose at 1584 B.C., the entrance could have been up to a century and a half later.

[39] Cf. John Rea, "The Time of the Oppression and the Exodus," BETS, 3(Summer, 1960), pp. 58-59; also Archer, SOTI, pp. 205-208.

[40] G. E. Wright, BAR, p. 60; cf. J. Finegan, LAP, pp. 118-19. The identification of Raamses with Tanis, as held by Wright, is widely accepted. The site,

fact as evidence for the late date of the Exodus, believing that the city was built by Rameses II (1304-1238) of the Nineteenth Dynasty, but it can be used just as well in favor of the Hyksos time preceding the Eighteenth Dynasty. At that time the city, Raamses, was even the capital of the country, and so the Hyksos kings, especially the first, would certainly have been interested in building and enlarging it. The fact that nothing from the Eighteenth Dynasty has been found in the city argues strongly against Ahmose or any of his successors in that dynasty having built it. In fact, Wright observes that the city was destroyed by Ahmose,[41] and not occupied again until the close of the fourteenth century.

Second, a statement in the book of Exodus attributed to this Pharaoh "who knew not Joseph" is more easily understood if he were a Hyksos ruler rather than one of the Eighteenth Dynasty:

> Behold, the people of the children of Israel are more and mightier than we: come, let us deal wisely with them, lest they multiply and it come to pass that, when there falleth out any war, they also join themselves unto our enemies, and fight against us, and get them up out of the land (Ex. 1:9-10).

One matter to notice is that this king spoke of Israel as being "more and mightier than we." The statement was made long before Israel grew in size to her eventual number of 2,000,000 at the Exodus, and so would have been a gross exaggeration if said in comparison to all Egyptians, who would have been the ones compared if this was said by Ahmose. However, if said by the first Hyksos ruler it would not have been an exaggeration, for he would have been comparing only with Hyksos people who never were numerous in Egypt. The Hyksos ruled by holding key positions, not by force of numbers. Another matter is that this ruler feared that the Israelites might join with an enemy against his people. Once more this is understandable if the speaker was a Hyksos, for the enemy was always close at hand, namely the Egyptians, whose native rulers still held sway in the southern part of the land. But if the speaker was Ahmose, who would then have just driven the enemy, the Hyksos, out of Egypt and well up into Palestine,[42]

Qantir, is favored by some, for instance, Hayes, *SE*, II, p. 339, and Van Seters, *TH*, pp. 128-49. However, no Eighteenth Dynasty remains have been found there either.

[41] *BAR*, p. 60.

[42] Ahmose pursued the Hyksos as far as Sharuhen in southern Palestine (cf. Josh. 19:6), then besieged this city for six years, and finally destroyed it. This decisively ended any relation of the Hyksos with Egypt. A direct account of these events is available from the pen of a naval officer under Ahmose; cf. *Ancient Records of Egypt*, II, secs. 1-16.

this is not so understandable. The enemy had just been thoroughly defeated and driven far away.

Third, a statement made by God to Abraham is more in keeping with Israel's enslavement having been earlier, with the Hyksos, rather than later, with the Eighteenth Dynasty. The statement is, "Know of surety that thy seed shall be a stranger in a land that is not theirs, and shall serve them; and *they shall afflict them four hundred years*" (Gen. 15:13; cf. Acts 7:6; italics mine). During the first years of Jacob's descendants dwelling in Egypt, they were not afflicted. This hardship started only when the Pharaoh "who knew not Joseph" came to the throne. But if this Pharaoh was Ahmose, then the enslavement condition would have lasted only about a century and a third,[43] a period far short of four centuries and out of keeping with the above statement. However, if he was the first of the Hyksos kings, this enslavement would have lasted nearly three centuries and be quite suitable.

Fourth, it is difficult to understand why the Eighteenth Dynasty, in driving the Asiatic Hyksos from Egypt, would not have driven the Asiatic Israelites out also at the same time. Those who believe that the Eighteenth Dynasty was the first to enslave Israel commonly argue that, because the two groups had been ethnically related, therefore Israel was enslaved after the Hyksos were expelled. One group was driven out and the other made bondmen. But would it not have been more likely for both groups to have been expelled? Why would Ahmose have wanted to chance a new rebellion by leaving a group the size of Israel (very likely more numerous than those put out) yet in the land? Further, if the two groups had been friendly, intermarriage would likely have occurred and it might have been difficult to distinguish one Asiatic group from the other to be able to treat them separately. However, if the two groups had been enemies, as true on the basis of the enslaving king having been Hyksos, then a clear distinction between them, and a different treatment for each, is understandable.

As an argument in favor of Ahmose of the Eighteenth Dynasty having been Israel's enslaver, it is asserted that such an action by a foreign people, like the Egyptians, is more easily understood than if by a related people, like the Hyksos. However, it is understandable that also Hyksos, whether related or not, would have wanted to enslave Israel under the circumstances then existent. As has been observed, the Hyksos were not themselves very numerous. Consequently they could well have considered this closeknit, separated, rapidly growing group of Is-

---

[43] This is on the basis of the Exodus having occurred at the early date of c. 1446 B.C., evidence for which will be developed in chapter 5. With Ahmose coming to the throne in 1584 B.C., this leaves only 138 years intervening.

raelites, located in the choice farming land of Goshen,[44] a threat to their reign, and, at the same time, a potential source of valuable labor if enslaved.[45]

D. ABRAHAM'S COUNTRY

The words of God's initial call to Abraham were, "Get thee out of thy land, and from thy kindred."[46] The question rises as to what sort of land this was from which God called this man. The call was given at Ur of the Chaldees,[47] which is still generally recognized as the well-known Ur of the lower Mesopotamian Valley.[48] The possibility that it was an Ur in upper Mesopotamia has been suggested in recent years, but supporting evidence is meager.[49] It is likely that Abraham came from the site traditionally accepted, and so we look for information concerning conditions in Ur, and lower Mesopotamia generally, at the close of the twenty-second century when Abraham would have grown to adulthood and still lived in this country.

[44] Goshen is best identified with the region of Wadi Tumilat, a valley over 30 miles long extending from the Nile River to Lake Timsah. It has long been considered one of Egypt's richest farming areas; cf. Wright, *BAR*, p. 56.

[45] Cf. *supra*, p. 35, n. 36 for answer to a further objection that free acceptance into Egypt accorded Jacob's family is more easily understood if granted by ethnically related Hyksos than by foreign Egyptians (an objection voiced often by those who hold that the Egyptian sojourn lasted only 215 years, thus placing Jacob's entry well into the Hyksos period). Then, even favoring the idea that Joseph's Pharaoh was Egyptian rather than Hyksos are two other factors: first, that this Pharaoh gave a wife to Joseph (Gen. 41:45) from the priests of On (Heliopolis), and these priests served particularly the sun-god Ra who was disfavored by many of the Hyksos (cf. Anderson, *The History and Religion of Israel*, London: Oxford University Press, 1966, p. 25); and second, the requirements of this Pharaoh appear Egyptian in that Joseph shaved (Gen. 41:14) before going to see him.

[46] Acts 7:3. The similar words of Gen. 12:1 are given in reference to God's call later at Haran.

[47] Because it was after 1000 B.C. that Chaldeans became dominant in lower Mesopotamia and finally even established the Neo-Babylonian Empire, many scholars hold that the name used in Genesis, Ur *of the Chaldees*, must be anachronistic. M. Unger explains it as "a later scribal gloss to explain to a subsequent age, when Ur and its location had utterly perished, that the city was located in southern Babylonia"; *AOT*, p. 108.

[48] Excavation was first carried out at Ur by J. E. Taylor in 1854, more extensively by H. R. Hall in 1918, and with care by C. L. Woolley between 1922 and 1934. For description, cf. Woolley, *Ur of the Chaldees* (Penguin Books, 1940).

[49] Cyrus Gordon, "Abraham and the Merchants of Ura," *JNES*, 17(1958), pp. 28-31, advocates an Ura somewhere in western Mesopotamia as Ur. A text from Ugarit speaks of merchants to Ugarit from this Ura. Gordon's reason is that Haran was somewhat out of the way for Abraham if he traveled from Ur in lower Mesopotamia on his way to Canaan; also that Abraham later speaks of his home territory as being the Haran region (Gen. 24:4, 7, 10). However, it

1. *Third Dynasty of Ur.* In making the inquiry we are in the fortunate situation of having a period involved which is well known from extra-biblical sources. This is the political period known as the Third Dynasty of Ur,[50] lasting 108 years, when the city of Ur was the capital of all lower Mesopotamia.

The time covered by this period either included or just followed the close of the twenty-second century, the time of our interest. The exact determination depends on the much discussed date of Hammurabi, back from which this period can be fixed. Three main dates are suggested by scholars for the beginning of Hammurabi's reign: a "low" date of 1728 B.C., a "middle" date of 1792 B.C., and a "high" date of 1848 B.C.[51] To any of these dates must be added approximately 340 years to arrive at the beginning of the Third Dynasty of Ur. This places that period on the basis of the low date at c. 2070-1962, the middle date at c. 2130-2022, and the high date at c. 2190-2082.[52] With Abraham born c. 2166 B.C., and migrating c. 2100 B.C.,[53] this means that, on the basis of the low date, he left Ur about thirty years before this period began, and, on the basis of either the middle or the high date, he lived and left during that period. It is difficult to choose which position is best, but fortunately it is unnecessary for our purpose, for even if the period began a few years after Abraham left, conditions would not have greatly changed in this length of time.

What were conditions during the Third Dynasty of Ur? This was the classical time of Sumerian civilization, the era when Sumerian cul-

is likely that this Ura was also out of position for Haran to have been a logical stopping place, for it seems to have been further west than Haran, more in the Ugarit area. From there a traveler would have gone straight south to Canaan. Further, Abraham's "homeland" references may have been only in view of the family of his one living brother, Nahor, who had apparently moved from Ur to Haran (Gen. 24:10, 15; 28:2). Abraham's interest was not in a particular land, but in blood relatives where a wife might be found.

50 For a brief summary of this period, cf. J. S. Schwantes, *A Short History of the Ancient Near East* (Grand Rapids: Baker Book House, 1965); or Finegan, *LAP*, pp. 49-53; or for summary of cultural conditions, G. Childe, *What Happened in History*, (rev. ed., Penguin Books, 1954), pp. 89-112.

51 For discussion of the complex evidence, cf. M. B. Rowton, "The Date of Hammurabi," *JNES*, 17(1958), pp. 97-111; for a brief summary, cf. Archer, *SOTI*, p. 204. Rowton himself favors the middle date.

52 P. Van Der Meer, *The Chronology of Ancient Western Asia and Egypt* (Leiden: E. J. Brill, 1963), p. 46, argues to a beginning date for the period of 2044 B.C., still some later than the low date given. Albright follows the low date, which he gives as 2060-1950; *BASOR* 88(1942), pp. 28-33, and *ibid.*, 144(1956), pp. 26-30.

53 With Abraham 75 years old when leaving Haran (Gen. 12:4) and not likely having remained there more than a very few years, it is likely he was at least 70 when he left Ur, making the date for his departure just after the turn of the century.

ture reached its highest development. Sumerian culture had progressed toward this peak during all the Early Dynasty Period preceding,[54] but then suffered eclipse approximately two centuries before with the rise to power of the city of Agade (Akkad) and its Semitic culture. This eclipse had come when Sargon, capable ruler of Agade, had defeated powerful Lugal-zaggisi, king of Erech (Uruk), who had only recently enjoyed success himself in unifying lower Mesopotamia. Sargon was a Semite, speaking the Akkadian language in contrast to Sumerian. A few Semitic names had appeared in the king list of lower Mesopotamia during the prior Early Dynastic Period, indicating the presence of some Semitic influence, but for the most part Sumerian civilization had dominated until Sargon's rise. The period he instituted continued for more than a century. The area he controlled extended for a time from central Persia to the Mediterranean, the first true empire in history.[55] This Akkadian period was brought to an end by a barbaric people called Guti who invaded the region apparently from the Zagros Mountains. A dark age resulted, but it paved the way for the resurgence of Sumerian culture in the Third Dynasty of Ur. It was actually the king of Erech, Utu-hegal, who broke the hold of the Guti, but Ur-nammu, king of Ur, in turn defeated him and began the period of our concern.

2. *Rulers.* Ur never controlled as much land as Agade. Her kings claimed to perpetuate Sargon's empire, however, styling themselves as "Kings of Sumer and Akkad," and "Kings of the Four Parts of the World." They likely did control as far north as Ashur and certainly over all lower Mesopotamia. The names of the five successive rulers are known: Ur-nammu, who ruled eighteen years; Shulgi, forty-eight years; Amar-sin, nine years; Shu-sin, nine years; and Ibbi-sin, twenty-five years. Power waned during the reign of Ibbi-sin and finally the city was sacked by Elamites, who came down from the mountains to the east.

Ur-nammu, the first ruler, is probably best known for his fine code of laws. This code is the oldest found, antedating the better known and more complete code of Hammurabi. A brief text accompanies the code and states that Ur-nammu had been appointed by the god Nanna to rule over the land. It says that he had removed dishonest practices in respect to weights and measures and had shown concern that orphans

[54] Cf. Bright, *BHI,* pp. 27-28 for a brief survey of conditions during this lengthy period.

[55] Military expeditions ranged even farther, at least into Asia Minor and southeastern Arabia and possibly Egypt. Trade contacts extended as far as the Indus Valley eastward. A victory stele of Naram-sin, grandson of Sargon, who rivaled his grandfather in power, was found at Susa and is a beautiful work of art showing high cultural progress; cf. J. Finegan, *LAP,* pp. 47-48 for picture and description.

and widows not be exploited by the wealthy. Many of the laws themselves are not legible, but those that are, manifest a marked similarity with those of Hammurabi.[56] They show an understanding of basic problems in society and a concern for justice. The desire to have them recorded in the form found would have also provided for their enforcement. Apparently Abraham lived in a well controlled society.

3. *Religion.* The society of Abraham's day was religious. The remains of fine religious structures so testify. The best preserved example of an ancient ziggurat dates from this period. Ur-nammu's name and title are stamped on its bricks, showing that he directed much of its construction. It seems to have been built on the top of a smaller ziggurat, doubtless constructed earlier, and its upper part was the work of Nabonidus of the much later Neo-Babylonian era. The completed structure measured 200 feet by 150 feet by 70 feet high, and had the shape now know as customary for ziggurats of the day, square and pyramidal. The religious shrine at the top no longer existed at the time of excavation, but there remained a number of the blue-glazed bricks which apparently covered it. C. L. Woolley, mainly responsible for laying bare the massive structure, believes that trees and shrubs were planted on its various levels.[57] It was a masterpiece of workmanship and testifies to high skills of the day.

Around the ziggurat lay numerous other sacred structures, one a splendid temple to Ningal, a moon-goddess and wife of Nanna. Other buildings provided living quarters for priests and storehouses for ceremonial materials. These surrounded a brick-paved open court stretching 225 feet in front of the ziggurat. One can imagine the busy coming and going of both official personnel and visiting worshipers in such a complex.

4. *Living conditions.* Regarding general living conditions, as much or more is known from artifacts left by one Gudea, *ensi* at Lagash, as from any of the main rulers at Ur. Gudea apparently held greater power than the average sub-ruler, claiming 216,000 subjects. He left numerous hymn and prayer texts which show the Sumerian language at its highest point of development.[58] One of these texts tells of instructions given to Gudea by the god, Ningirsu, for restoring the Lagash temple, Eninnu. We are told that Gudea proceeded quickly to the task, bringing wood from as far away as the Amanus Mountains in northern

[56] Cf. S. N. Kramer, *Archaeology,* 7(1954), p. 143f.

[57] Woolley, *op. cit.,* pp. 114-29.

[58] Not long after this period, the Akkadian took its place as the common language, but Sumerian continued as the classical language of the whole Mesopotamian area until the Akkadian itself disappeared in the first century A.D.; cf. Cyrus Gordon, *ANE,* p. 17.

Syria, a part of the same general range from which Solomon later brought cedar for the Jerusalem Temple (I Kings 5:6).[59] Gudea also left many statues, often of himself, sculptured in the round, revealing remarkable artistic ability for skilled craftsmen of the day.

The times generally were prosperous. Some 100,000 business documents discovered in the general area, most of which concern this period, give helpful insight.[60] Concerning transactions in grain, vegetables, fruit, cattle, slaves, and other commodities, they show prices and general methods of doing business. Economic conditions appear to have been mainly stable, though inflation was not unknown. They reveal too that, in spite of the large place religion held in people's lives, the main power still lay with the civil ruler and not the religious leader. Further evidence of prosperity and cultural advance is depicted by an impressive number of cylinder seals, all excellently carved, and a host of finely worked metal trinkets indicating that the science of metallurgy was unsurpassed here in antiquity

All of this comprised the world of Abraham when he was called by God. It was a progressive world, where cultural advantage was notable. Artists were skilled, builders competent, business active, and times good. Religion, centering in the worship of the moon-god Nanna, was extremely important. Writing was comparatively common, and schools where this art and various subjects might be learned apparently existed.[61] We may believe that Abraham, clearly a capable person, would have availed himself of educational opportunities. He may have learned to write and so been able to record some of the early stories later put in Holy Writ by Moses. Certainly he had gained an appreciation for cultural niceties when he found it necessary to leave and go where standards could only be lower. But he had been able to profit from these advantages before leaving.

5. *Abraham's call to leave.* It should be realized that such advantages would have made Abraham's leaving more difficult. The picture of him portrayed in Genesis is not one of an adventuresome spirit, easily given to moving. He was a staid person, thoughtful, a man of judgment and foresight, who calculated before he acted. We may be sure that he would have much preferred to remain in surroundings he knew and where he could continue to enjoy old friends and comfortable living conditions. But he responded to God's call, and this response is an indication of remarkable faith on his part.

[59] Cf. ANET, pp. 268-69 for texts.

[60] Cf. ANET, p. 217 for texts.

[61] Cf. J. P. Free, ABH, pp. 49-50. Foundations of what appears to have been a school were uncovered, and clay tablets for learning the cuneiform signs were found. Some tablets show reading lessons of hymns and others of multiplication and division tables.

The question rises as to why God asked him to leave. Could not the nation of Israel have come to existence in lower Mesopotamia as well as Canaan? The answer would seem to involve three considerations. The first is that Abraham needed to be removed from old friends and situations which might hinder his full obedience to God. The second is that this departure provided a definite step of faith which contributed of itself to his further spiritual development. If he could obey God in leaving Ur, he would be able to do so in still more difficult matters later on. The third is that there was a need at this historical juncture to shift the center of God's working from lower Mesopotamia to strategically-located Canaan. Abraham's posterity should inhabit this narrow neck of land which would soon become the crossroad of the Near East for trade.

E. DEPARTURE

In Genesis 11:31, we read that "Terah took Abram his son,"[62] and departed "from Ur of the Chaldees," suggesting that Terah, the father, was the one who led in the departure rather than Abraham. However, Stephen (Acts 7:2) speaks of Abraham as the one to whom God appeared, not mentioning Terah. Likely the son persuaded the father to accompany him, and the father, then, according to patriarchal propriety, became the official leader of the party.

Question rises too as to whether or not Abraham knew his destination when he left Ur. In Genesis 11:31 again, we read that the party left "to go into the land of Canaan." But Hebrews 11:8 states that Abraham left Ur "not knowing whither he went." It is likely that the latter passage carries reference to the specific place, and the former to the general area. Abraham knew that he should go to Canaan, which to him at the time would have meant a country in the West near the Mediterranean,[63] without knowing the exact location of that large area.

With Terah and Abraham went Sarai, Abraham's wife, and Lot, the son of Abraham's brother, Haran. Abraham had two brothers, Haran and Nahor, but Haran seems to have died prior to this departure (Gen. 11:28), and Nahor did not join the party, though apparently he moved north to the city of Haran at some later time (Gen. 24:10, 15).

1. *Stop at Haran.* The four travelers did not get to Canaan, how-

---

[62] Abraham's name was changed from Abram ("high father") to Abraham ("father of a multitude") at the time of God's announcement to him regarding Isaac's birth (Gen. 17:4-5).

[63] The region was known in general terms. Lugal-zaggisi (c. 2360 B.C.) claims to have marched troops to the area and both Sargon and Naram-sin ruled as far as the Mediterranean; cf. *supra*, p. 30 and chap. 3, pp. 51-53. Naram-sin calls the area, "The land of the Amorites." Cf. Finegan, *LAP*, pp. 44, 47, 48; and Bright, *BHI*, p. 30.

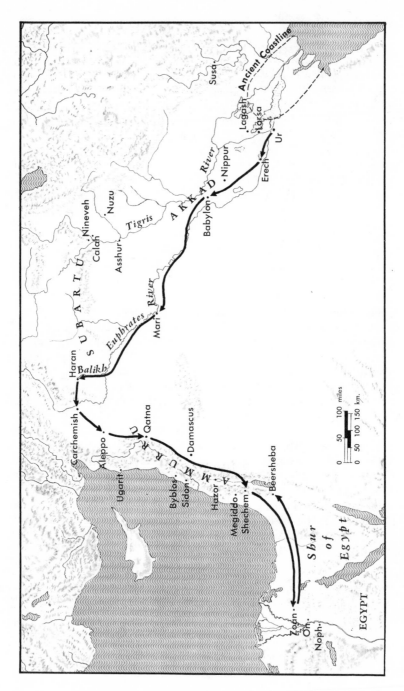

Map 3. Route of Abraham

ever, before they stopped. The city of Haran, nearly 700 miles along the way, or about two-thirds of the total distance, attracted them and they set up residence. Haran lay on the Bilikh River about sixty miles north of where the Bilikh empties into the Euphrates. The name, Haran, means "road," and the city was located on a main caravan road connecting cities of the East with Damascus and Egypt. It was considered a strategic location by successive nations that controlled it, and it is accordingly mentioned often in contemporary letters and documents. Excavations since 1951 indicate that it was occupied at least from the third millennium. It was a center of moon-god worship in common with Ur. Abraham remained there as long as Terah lived (Acts 7:4).

2. *Reason for stopping.* Since Abraham's destination was Canaan, and Haran, being sixty miles north of Abraham's normal line of travel along the Euphrates, was out of his way,[64] the question arises as to why Abraham stopped and then remained for a substantial period of time. A common answer is that his father found affinity in Haran and its moon-god[65] worship being practiced as in Ur and simply persuaded his son, whose faith too may have waned because of the long trip, to interrupt their journey at this point. This explanation rests on the assumption that Terah worshiped this god, Nanna. Adherents find support for the assumption in Joshua 24:2 which states that Israel's "fathers," naming Terah specifically, "served other gods." Among these gods, it is asserted, would have been Nanna.

However, there are reasons to question this explanation. Abraham himself was devoted to Yahweh[66] which means that somehow he had been instructed regarding the true God. This is not easy to understand if his father worshiped the false deity, Nanna. Neither does it fit that Terah would have been willing to listen to his son in leaving culturally-advanced Ur if he did not himself give allegiance to the God whose orders Abraham was obeying.

Another explanation is needed. One which fits the biblical story better is that Terah suffered ill health on the journey and could go no further than Haran. Abraham, knowing that Haran held at least a religious kinship with Ur, and so might present an atmosphere more fa-

---

[64] It may be that Abraham traveled up the Tigris, however, rather than the Euphrates, and if so, would have taken the normal road west which did lead directly to Haran.

[65] The name used for the moon-god in this northern, Semitic area was Sin, the equivalent of the Sumerian Nanna.

[66] Because the personal name of God was not pronounced by the Jews after their return from Exile, no one knows for sure how the name was pronounced originally. *Yahweh* is generally accepted as the nearest we know, certainly much closer than *Jehovah;* and so this form is used in this book.

miliar to the aged man, detoured from his intended route the sixty miles to find a place where his father might either regain his strength or else live out what might be only a few remaining days. In favor of this explanation is the fact that Terah was very old when he left Ur,[67] and that he did die while Abraham was still with him at Haran, and so not very long after his arrival there.[68] Also, this explanation gives reason for Abraham being willing to remain with his father. It is doubtful that Abraham would have even made the detour, much less remained any length of time, if his father had only wished to worship at the shrine of Nanna. As an explanation of Joshua 24:2, it may be that Terah earlier in life had given allegiance to Nanna and other deities as well as Yahweh, but later changed. He may never have arisen to Abraham's truly monotheistic belief, but at least he had come to a place where he had introduced his son to the worship of Yahweh and been willing to respond to Abraham's urging to leave Ur when Yahweh called.

In keeping with this explanation, we may think of Abraham remaining with his father through months of illness. He would have been aware that he was not yet where God had called him, but accepted the filial responsibility toward his father. He had persuaded this loved one to go with him, thinking no doubt that it would be good for him to leave former religious associations and be with him where they might worship Yahweh together. But now he had to tarry while his father passed his closing days. Abraham may have been anxious, but he properly stayed. The few months, and possibly years, slipped by, and then, when Terah died, Abraham was ready to hear God's further call to move on to the land of His choice.

---

[67] Terah died at 205 (Gen. 11:32) when Abraham was 75 (Gen. 12:4), and so was 130 at Abraham's birth (the Gen. 11:26 mention of 70 is in reference only to the eldest son, likely Haran). Abraham was a married adult when the party left Ur which means that Terah must have been near 200 at the time. Marriages do not seem to have been made early: Isaac was 40 (Gen. 25:20) and Jacob 77 (Gen. 47:9; 41:46, 47, 54; 45:11; 31:41; 30:25) when they married.

[68] It is not likely that Abraham would have remained long and extensively interrupted his trip to Canaan. However, for Abraham later to refer to the Haran region as his homeland calls for him to have stayed at least several months and maybe even a few years. This follows, too, in that it was appropriate for God again to call him from there (Gen. 12:1-3).

Chapter Three

ABRAHAM

Genesis 12:1–25:18

A. The New Land

The destination intended by God for Abraham proved to be the land of Canaan, named after the son of Ham of the same name who settled in the region.[1] In its broader sense,[2] Canaan included Syria-Palestine, defined in Genesis 10:19 as extending from Sidon south to Gaza, east to Sodom and Gomorrah, and north to Lasha (location unknown). In the Amarna Letters (14th century B.C.),[3] references are made to "Canaan" as equivalent to Egypt's Syro-Palestinian territories at the time, which would include land also well north of Sidon. The land to which Abraham came, however, was southern Canaan, later called Palestine.

1. *Canaan.* The third millennium, known as the Early Bronze Age in Canaan, was drawing to a close when Abraham arrived. Canaan had been a progressive land during the prior centuries. Excavation reveals that Early Bronze people had effected remarkable urban development, no doubt under a city-state form of government. Cities like Megiddo, Bethshan, Shechem, Ai, Jericho, and Lachish, later to be important in biblical events, already existed and were well built, boasting strong fortifications. The people were predominantly Canaanite, with their own language from which Hebrew was to develop.

Late in the third millennium, however, still before Abraham's appearance, Canaan experienced a major change at the hands of a semi-nomadic people pushing into the land. Many of the fine Early Bronze cities (Megiddo, Jericho, Ai, etc.) were destroyed and abandoned,

[1] According to Gen. 10:15-18 and a native tradition preserved by Philo of Byblos.
[2] A narrower sense confines Canaan to the coastland, especially Phoenicia proper: cf. Num. 13:29; Josh. 5:1; 11:3; Judg. 1:27-33.
[3] Cf. *infra*, chap. 5, pp. 104-107.

beginning about 2200 B.C.[4] Those first affected lay west of the Jordan, but later (after 2000 B.C.) the same happened on the east. Cities thus became few in number and population scarce, as witnessed by both direct excavation in Palestine and the Execration texts of Egypt, which date in the twentieth and nineteenth centuries.[5] The people who brought the change clearly were Amorite, indicated by their pottery and their names. Amorites are known to have moved similarly in other parts of the Near East at this time. For some years the new inhabitants were content to live merely as semi-nomads, moving freely about in the area, but gradually came to settle down[6] and rebuild many of the cities they earlier had destroyed.[7]

The cultural level of Palestine before Abraham's arrival had been high, comparing favorably with that of any part of the world with the exception of Abraham's native Sumeria or Egypt. The incoming Amorites, who would still have been in their semi-nomadic state on Abraham's entrance to the scene, in time brought changes to this culture, but still a basic continuity was maintained and no lessening in level was experienced. Abraham would have found the cities that remained well made, boasting fine houses. Pottery would have manifested numerous shapes and sizes, displaying intricate, attractive decoration. Canaanites he encountered would have been deeply religious, as witnessed by temples and altars uncovered in various excavations;[8] but if their religion was like that represented later at Ugarit,[9] which is likely, it was morally base in employment of fertility rites.

2. *Egypt.* Some notice must be taken of Egypt at this juncture also, for her influence was felt in Canaan during the patriarchal day, and Abraham was himself soon to make direct contact there. During the

---

[4] Cf. Wright, BAR, pp. 41-42; Albright, FSAC, pp. 118-20; Aharoni, LB, pp. 125-26.

[5] These texts, inscribed on vases and statuettes, contain names of actual or potential enemies of the Pharaoh, both within Egypt and in neighboring lands including Palestine. The idea was that the Pharaoh could bring harm on any such person simply by breaking the vase or statuette, on which the name was inscribed, to the accompaniment of magical ceremony. Considerable information on conditions in these lands is implied. Cf. Albright, AP, pp. 82-83.

[6] For this reason, Amorites, along with Canaanites, are regularly mentioned in biblical passages: Gen. 15:16; 48:22; Ex. 3:17; Josh. 24:15, 18.

[7] Cf. for references, *supra*, chap. 2, p. 33, n. 28.

[8] For instance, a giant altar, 26 feet in diameter, was discovered at Megiddo running through Levels XVII to XIV, showing existence from 2500 to 1800 B.C., and as many as three temples at one time there in Level XV, dating 1950-1850 B.C.; cf. G. Loud, *Megiddo II: Seasons of 1935-39* (University of Chicago Press, 1948), pp. 70-85.

[9] For discussion, cf. *infra*, chap. 9, pp. 207-208.

third millennium, Egypt too had experienced marked progress.[10] From 2600 to 2200 B.C., the Third to the Sixth Dynasties ruled in the Old Kingdom Period, when came the first flowering of Egyptian culture, shown especially by the giant pyramids. Sozer, founder of the Third Dynasty, built the first, the Step Pyramid, and Khafre, Khefren, and Menkure of the Fourth Dynasty built the three largest. Other pyramids built during the Fifth and Sixth Dynasties were smaller, but were important for in these the so-called Pyramid Texts were found, consisting of incantations for assuring safe passage of the Pharaoh into the life to come.

But Egypt too fell upon difficult days between 2200 and 2000 B.C., in what is called the First Intermediate Period. Rival Pharaohs claimed the throne, provincial administrators became feudal lords, and numerous cities came to act quite independently of any outside authority. Asiatic semi-nomads came here, possibly the same as invaded Palestine, and added to the confusion. Economic hardship and famine became widespread, and this resulted in a gloom of hopelessness and depression among the people. From this condition arose an appealing literature, however, among which are found *The Eloquent Peasant, The Admonitions of Ipuwer,* and *The Instruction for King Merikare.*[11] Religion played a dominant role in people's lives, but it was never a unitary whole in Egypt overall. Every community had particular local gods, with the identities of national deities varying with political changes. Priests held great power, and people generally were kept in a state of fear.

B. SHECHEM, BETHEL, EGYPT, BETHEL (Genesis 12:4–13:18)

1. *Arrival at Shechem (Genesis 12:4-9).* Abraham's journey into Canaan took him to Shechem,[12] located about thirty-five miles north of Jerusalem. Here God informed him that he had arrived at the intended destination, saying, "Unto thy seed will I give this land" (Gen. 12:7). Abraham thus learned that his journey was ended. He was

[10] For discussion of both Egypt's Old Kingdom and First Intermediate periods, cf. Hayes, *SE,* Part I, pp. 58-131; or A. Gardiner, *Egypt of the Pharaohs* (Oxford: At the Clarendon Press, 1961), pp. 72-106.

[11] For these and other Egyptian texts, see Erman and Blackmann, *Literature of the Ancient Egyptians,* 1927; and for numerous selections, *ANET.*

[12] Shechem lay between the twin peaks, Mt. Ebal and Mt. Gerizim. Toward the east stretches a small plain in which later Joshua heard Abraham's posterity respond to blessings and curses of the law (Josh. 8:30-35), and here also Jesus met a woman of Samaria at Jacob's well and led her to faith in Himself (John 4). For an account of the significant discoveries made at Shechem by the Drew-McCormick Expedition, cf. G. Wright, *Shechem: The Biography of a Biblical City* (New York: McGraw-Hill Book Co., 1965).

where God had planned for him to come. Reassured at the good news, he built an altar. Shortly, he moved south in the land, stopping for a time between Bethel and Ai where he built another altar, and then on to the southern part of the land.

2. *Down to Egypt (Genesis 12:10-20).* When a famine developed, apparently soon after his arrival, Abraham journeyed southeast to Egypt. We may believe that he was puzzled at the coming of the famine. Was this the sort of country God had chosen for him? The strain on his faith may have been in part responsible for his lapse on reaching Egypt in telling a half-truth concerning his wife Sarai, a form of subterfuge devised actually when he had first left Ur (Gen. 20:13).[13] He presented her to the Egyptians as his sister (she was his half-sister, Gen. 20:12), for he feared that the Pharaoh, seeing the attractiveness of Sarai, might so desire her for himself that he would take the life of any husband to get her. Pharaoh[14] did want her and did take her to the palace, but God intervened in her behalf by bringing plagues on Pharaoh's house. This served to bring Abraham's deception to the ruler's attention, and he then dismissed Abraham from the land, though he bestowed gifts on him beforehand.

Abraham must be critcized for his action at this time. He should have trusted God, who certainly would have prevented his death at the hand of an Egyptian, having so recently brought him all the way from Ur to be the head of a new nation. Further, if Abraham had feared that the situation might be this dangerous in Egypt, he should have remained in Canaan in the first place, trusting God to provide for him there (cf. Gen. 26:2).

3. *Separation from Lot (Genesis 13:1-18).* When Abraham returned to Canaan, a new problem faced him (Gen. 13:1-18). He and Lot owned too much livestock between them to find adequate pasture. Both had inherited from Terah, whose property evidently had been considerable, and now Abraham had been further enriched by gifts from Pharaoh (Gen. 12:16). Separation was necessary and Abraham magnanimously gave his nephew first choice as to which part of the land he would choose. Lot took the valley region of the Jordan which at

---

[13] R. Laird Harris, *The Seminary Review,* 16(Fall, 1969), pp. 8-9, following Speiser, explains Abraham's action as observing a Hurrian custom in which a husband might adopt his wife as his sister to give her added status. Such an act signified nobility for both parties and helped to guarantee protection for both wherever Hurrian law was recognized, which apparently was not true in Egypt at this time, nor later with Abimelech at Gerar (Gen. 20:1-13; 26:6-11).

[14] With the date here c. 2090 B.C., the ruler in question would have been from the First Intermediate Period. The strong Twelfth Dynasty came to power just a century later.

the time thrived with cities and farming.[15] Lot was selfish in this choice, taking the area he thought best. Actually he not only was wrong in so choosing, but he should have insisted that his uncle, senior to him, have first selection. But Lot, wanting the best for himself, was not as gracious as his uncle. Later he found how foolish he had been. The valley region, though prosperous, was inhabited by people of low morality, and Lot came to be influenced (Gen. 13:13). He was finally even to lose his family as a result (Gen. 19:14-38). Abraham remained in the highland region, relatively free from outside influence, and there he continued in the favor of God. He took up residence in the plain of Mamre.[16]

C. RESCUE OF LOT (Genesis 14)

1. *Abraham's courageous rescue (Genesis 14:1-16).* Lot had not spent many months in his new surroundings before he needed Abraham's assistance. A confederacy of four kings from lower Mesopotamia, far to the east, led by Chedarlaomer, King of Elam, attacked Sodom, Gomorrah, and other cities of the area, taking many people captive including Lot and his family. News soon came to Abraham who, with 318 of his own servants, plus help from his neighbors, Mamre, Aner, and Eschol, gave pursuit. This smaller force overtook and defeated the imposing enemy[17] at Dan, set free those taken captive, and recovered a large amount of booty. Abraham displayed outstanding courage, resourcefulness, and especially faith in God in this action.

2. *Extra-biblical evidence.* This story, perhaps more than any other from patriarchal times, was challenged by liberal scholars for its historical value until recent years. The thinking was that kings as far away as lower Mesopotamia did not make military expeditions this far from home. However, archaeological research has prompted marked change in the viewpoint today. The facts of the story are now found to fit conditions of Abraham's time. For instance, as observed earlier,[18] both Sargon and his grandson, Naram-sin, conquered all the way to the

[15] One would not choose the southern Jordan Valley today, for it is hot and arid. But N. Glueck's explorations reveal numerous cities having been there until c. 1900 B.C. (cf. *supra,* chap. 2, p. 33) which means it was then highly attractive; cf. Glueck, *The Other Side of the Jordan* (New Haven: American Schools of Oriental Research, 1940), pp. 114f.

[16] Mamre was where Hebron later was built, but which existed now only as a smaller city called Kirjath-arba (Gen. 23:2; 35:27; cf. Josh. 14:15; Judg. 1:10). Num. 13:22 states that Hebron was founded "seven years before Zoan in Egypt." Zoan is identified with Avaris, the capital of the Hyksos, who rebuilt it about 1730 B.C. Likely Hebron as such was built about 1737 B.C., then.

[17] Coming this far, the enemy forces would have been somewhat limited, but still much greater in number than Abraham's group.

[18] *Supra,* chap. 2, p. 30.

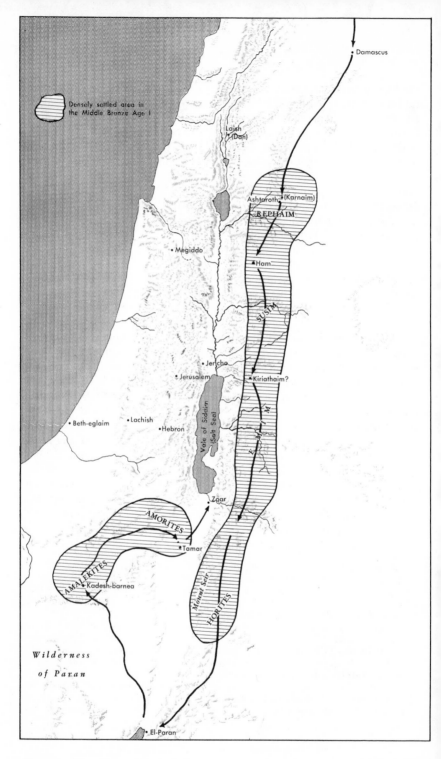

Map 4. The Campaign of Genesis 14 and main areas of population

Mediterranean and held substantial territory along its coast[19] three centuries before Abraham. One Akkadian text from the time, concerning a condition for renting a wagon, is particularly significant for indicating frequency of travel to the west. The condition was that the renter not drive the wagon "unto the land of Kittim," meaning the Mediterranean coastland.[20]

Further, the names of the kings involved, as well as the places mentioned, suit the nomenclature of the time. Some scholars have even suggested possible identification of at least two kings with known personalities of Babylonian history: Amraphel with the great law-giver, Hammurabi, and Arioch with an Arriwuk, contemporary with Hammurabi mentioned in texts from Mari.[21] However, there is difficulty in making an exact equation of the names, and there is a clear time differential when one accepts the early date for Abraham set forth above. But the general suitability of the names to the nomenclature of the day is beyond dispute.[22] Some have pointed out that the mention of Dan as the place where Abraham caught the retreating kings must be anachronistic, and so, in this sense, an exception. It is true that the name Dan was not given to the city formerly called Laish until the migration of the Danites in the days of the Judges (Judg. 18:29), but the reference may be to another Dan. In II Samuel 24:6, a Dan-jaan in the Gilead area is mentioned, and Gilead is more likely to have provided the path these eastern kings would have taken as they headed home than Coele-Syria where the better known Dan was located.[23]

[19] Naram-sin claims to have conquered even Magan (used in later texts for Egypt). Most scholars doubt this, but agree that he did control substantial areas along the Mediterranean. Cf. Wright, *BAR*, p. 34; Bright, *BHI*, p. 30.

[20] For the text, cf. Barton, *AB*, pp. 346-47.

[21] Until comparatively recent time, when Hammurabi's date was found to be in the eighteenth century rather than the twentieth, this identification was held as valid by numerous scholars, such as Pinches, Hommel, Sayce, Clay, et al. It may be added too, that Chedorlaomer, king of Elam, held a name of excellent Elamite type, having the likely spelling, *Kudur-lagamar*. A parallel name, *Kudur-mabug*, has been found for a king of West Elam, *Yamutbal;* the element *Kudur* being the family name, and *mabug* the name of a deity. The element *lagamar* is also a deity name. Further, the name Tidal is recognized as equivalent to Tudkhula, the name of several Hittite kings. Cf. T. G. Pinches, *The Old Testament in the Light of the Historical Records of Assyria and Babylonia* (3d ed.; London: Society for Promoting Christian Knowledge, 1908), pp. 209-33; Barton, *AB*, pp. 347-53.

[22] As to names of places also fitting, both Ashteroth Karnaim and Ham (Gen. 14:5) have been identified as having existed at the time; cf. M. Unger, *AOT*, p. 117.

[23] The Anti-Lebanon range was also a factor, for it would have had to be crossed if the better known Dan was the city involved. It is not likely either that Abraham would have had to give chase as far north as the better known Dan, making a Dan somewhere in Gilead more likely in terms of distance.

The likely reason for these kings wanting to campaign in this territory, when it was so far from home, is also known today.[24] It is that valuable natural resources were to be found there. Both Edom and Midian held fine copper and manganese deposits. The kings may have been interested also in the asphalt of the Dead Sea. Also related was the existence of a convenient access to the region via the "King's Highway" (Num. 20:17), so-called by N. Glueck,[25] running down the eastern edge of Gilead, south through Moab and on to the Gulf of Aqabah. Glueck points out that many of the old cities of Transjordan, which belonged to this general time, lay along the likely route which these eastern armies would have taken.

3. *Kings of Sodom and Salem (Genesis 14:17-24)*. When Abraham returned from his remarkable victory over these armies, two kings of his own country met him. One was the king of Sodom who urged Abraham to retain the booty recovered and return only the people to their King and city. Abraham, however, refused the generous offer on the basis that people might say this earthly king had made him rich, and Abraham desired that all credit be rendered to God. The other was Melchizedek, king of Salem (Jerusalem). His name is well known because he is made typical of Christ in the book of Hebrews. His name means "king of righteousness." Melchizedek brought bread and wine to Abraham's weary troops, and Abraham in turn gave him, as "priest of the most high God," a tenth of the booty. This gracious gesture was made apparently before Abraham returned the remainder of the spoil to the Sodom ruler. By this gesture Abraham recognized Melchizedek to be a priest of the true God, which is significant in illustrating that there did exist in the world a few beside God's chosen line who continued to worship Him. Abraham's act also demonstrated that the principle of tithing was recognized this early as a proper basis for giving to God.[26]

D. DESTRUCTION OF SODOM (Genesis 18:1–19:38)

1. *Abraham intercedes for Lot (Genesis 18)*. Several years had passed[27] when Lot needed assistance again. The occasion concerned

---

[24] Since the cities they conquered (Gen. 14:5-11) were all in the Transjordan area, apparently they did not cross the Jordan at all.

[25] Glueck takes the term from its biblical use. For discussion, cf. Glueck, *op. cit.*, pp. 15-16; 114-25; and Finegan, *LAP*, pp. 152-53.

[26] Note also Jacob's promise, Gen. 28:22. The Mosaic law later established this principle clearly e.g. Lev. 27:30f; Num. 18:21f.

[27] If we knew how long a time had intervened between Lot's choice to go to Sodom and the military attack by the four kings, we could know exactly how many years elapsed here. We know the time when Sodom was destroyed, namely when Abraham was 99 (Gen. 18:10; 21:5), and Lot chose Sodom likely when

God's destruction of Sodom and surrounding cities. Three "men" came to Abraham as he sat at the entrance to his tent in Mamre. As the story later indicates, two were angels (Gen. 18:22; 19:1) and one the "Angel of Yahweh."[28] The Angel of Yahweh, indicated here directly as "Yahweh" (Gen. 18:1, 13, 17, 20, etc.), told Abraham regarding the portending destruction, which prompted the patriarch to intercede for the city (Gen. 18:23-33). He urged that if there were even only a few righteous in the city—"bargaining" with the Angel as to how few—the city might be spared. He was assured that if there were only ten his request would be granted. We may believe that this assurance gave Abraham relief, for the fact that he used the expedient of intercession at all shows that he believed there must be some others beside Lot who could be classified as righteous.

2. *Lot delivered from Sodom (Genesis 19).* While Abraham made this intercession, the two angels, who earlier had departed, were making their way toward Sodom and were eventually received by Lot into his house. After a night in which men of the city gave shocking witness to the grave wickedness of Sodom,[29] Lot, his wife, and two daughters were persuaded to leave the city.[30] There were not ten righteous there, as Abraham had hoped, and so the city had to be destroyed. But God showed favor toward Abraham's entreaty in at least having these four led to safety. The city was consumed as the four moved away, and Lot's wife, in a gesture of longing and regret, turned to look back for which God brought death by changing her into what is called a "pillar of salt" (Gen. 19:26). Later, Lot's two daughters, showing the influence of the sinful life of Sodom, had incestuous relations with their father which issued in the births of Moab and Ben-ammi.[31] Lot's earlier choice of the cities of the plain, which had seemed so attractive at the time, indeed worked to his regret in these closing days of life.

Abraham was 76 (about one year after entering Canaan). But where during the intervening 23 years this episode of the four kings fell is not indicated, though probably in the first half.

[28] The "Angel of Yahweh" is not called by that name here as elsewhere, but corresponds in description to other places where the name is used, being called both a "man" (18:2) and "Yahweh." This is a pre-incarnation appearance of Christ. Cf. Josh. 5:13 - 6:5; Judg. 6:11-22; 13:2-21; etc.

[29] The extent of desire on the part of these men to "know" Lot's guests is accentuated by the number involved, their insistence, and Lot's expedient of offering his two daughters to them in an attempt to spare the guests (Gen. 19: 4-9).

[30] Lot could not persuade his sons-in-law. The Hebrew is not clear whether these were only betrothed to the two daughters, who did escape, or whether they had married other daughters otherwise unknown, who then also refused to accompany their parents (Gen. 19:14).

[31] These became fathers of the Moabites and Ammonites respectively, enemies of Israel in later years.

3. *Destruction of Sodom (Genesis 19:24-25, 27-28).* The destruction of Sodom was effected by a rain of "brimstone and fire." In examining the meaning of this expression, scholars have ruled out volcanic action on the basis of negative geological indications. Many believe that it refers to an earthquake resulting in an enormous explosion.[32] Several factors are pointed out as favoring the view. The idea of brimstone and fire suggests incendiary materials raining upon the city as the result of an explosion. Another descriptive word used is "overthrew" (Gen. 19:29), and this fits the thought of an earthquake. That Abraham saw smoke rising in the direction of the city indicates that there was fire. Inflamable asphalt has long been known in the area. Records from ancient writers speak of strong sulphuric odors which suggest that quantities of sulphur were there in past time.[33] Further, the whole Jordan Valley constitutes an enormous fault in the earth's surface, given to earthquake conditions. It is possible, then, that God did see fit miraculously to time an earthquake at this precise moment, which could have released great quantities of gas, mixed sulphur with various salts found in abundance, and measurably increased the flow of asphalt seepage. Lightning could have ignited all, and the entire country been consumed as indicated. The Bible is clear that God does use natural means to accomplish His purpose when and to the extent that they are available. He may have done so here.

Whatever the method employed, God did bring the destruction. The results are still to be seen.[34] When one views the Jordan Valley near the Dead Sea today, he is immediately impressed that Lot never would have chosen the area if it had been then like it is now. Barren wastes meet the eye in every direction. This great change came too, just after the beginning of the second millennium, the very time of Abraham and Lot.[35] The ruins of Sodom and Gomorrah have not been found, but they are believed to lie beneath the shallow southern end of the

[32] For discussion, cf. J. Penrose Harlan, "The Destruction of the Cities of the Plain," *BA*, 6(Sept., 1943), pp. 41-52.

[33] Harlan quotes Strabo of the first century B.C., Josephus his successor, and Tacitus of about A.D. 100. All testify to severe odors, asphalt seepages, and a general burned complexion of the area now called the southern end of the Dead Sea. This area, identified by Harlan as the "vale of Siddim" (Gen. 14:8), was not under water at that time. Writes Tacitus, "Not far from the lake (Dead Sea) is a plain which, according to report, was once fertile and the site of great cities, but which was later devastated by lightning; and it is said that traces of this disaster still exist there; and that the very ground looks burnt and has lost its fertility"; Book V, chap. 7 of his *Histories*.

[34] Harlan agrees that the desolate condition seen yet today does date from this severe time of destruction; *ibid.*, p. 52.

[35] Cf. *supra*, n. 15.

Dead Sea, which has been formed since that time by gradually rising water.[36]

E. COVENANT

God gave promises to Abraham several times, which, taken together, constitute what is called the Abrahamic covenant. The first instance of giving promises fell prior to Abraham's arrival in the chosen land (Gen. 12:1-3), the second after Lot's separation from Abraham (Gen. 13: 14-17), the third after Abraham's deliverance of Lot from the four kings (Gen. 15:1-21), the fourth when Abraham was ninety-nine just prior to the Sodom destruction (Gen. 17:1-22), and the fifth several years later following God's command to sacrifice Isaac (Gen. 22:15-18). Analyzing what God said these five times, three principal areas of promise can be distinguished: first, that Abraham's posterity would grow to the size of a nation and be His special people (Gen. 12:2; 13:16; 15:2-5; 17:4-6; 22:17); second, that the country to which God had brought Abraham would be this nation's homeland (Gen. 13:14-17; 15:19; 17:8); and third, that his posterity would be a blessing to the world, to the extent that all nations would be blessed (Gen. 12:2-3; 18:18; 22:18).[37] Genesis 15:6 states that Abraham "believed in Yahweh; and he reckoned it to him for righteousness" (cf. Rom. 4:1-4). That is, Abraham believed that God would perform what He promised. The promises were great, but so was Abraham's faith. He believed that God could and would do what He said. The additional element—that God then reckoned this faith to Abraham for righteousness—indicates that God's declared principle of salvation by faith alone, and not by works, was in effect at the time. Abraham's righteous standing before God was established by his belief in the promises of God.

F. WAITING THE PROMISED CHILD (Genesis 16:1–18:15)

God's promise to Abraham that he would have a large posterity came the first time just before he entered the chosen land at the age of seventy-five. No doubt he thought in terms of a child being born very soon. He and Sarah had no children at the time and both were already advanced in years with Sarah only ten years younger than he.

---

[36] Cf. Harlan, "The Location of the Cities of the Plain," *BA*, 5(May, 1942), pp. 17-32. In this earlier article, Harlan gives a discussion of factors bearing on the question. He states, for instance, that the Dead Sea rises between 2½ and 3½ inches per year, and that a Roman road once crossed from the peninsula, el-Lisan, to what is now the west shore of the Dead Sea. Tying in further with this location is the fact that asphalt seepage, true of the Dead Sea, fits the description of Gen. 14:10 that the area was full of "slimepits."

[37] Such detailed aspects as, "I will bless thee, and make thy name great," or, "I will bless them that bless thee, and curse him that curseth thee," are part to these three main promises.

But no child was born. After waiting ten years (Gen. 16:3)—a period which must have seemed long — Sarah suggested the expedient that Abraham take Hagar as a secondary wife to beget a child (Gen. 16: 1-4). Abraham did so, likely reasoning that this must be God's way of accomplishing what He had promised, since no child had been born through Sarah. But Abraham was out of God's will in this, for the seed was to come through Sarah in God's own time. Abraham's actions, however, wrong as they were, must be understood and judged in terms of customs of the day.[38] A son, Ishmael, was now born to Hagar, but God indicated that he was not the one through whom the promised posterity should come (Gen. 16:7-16; 17:20-21).[39] After the birth, Sarah became bitter and wanted Abraham to drive Hagar with her son from the household, causing severe distress for the patriarch, who did not wish to compound the error already committed.[40]

Abraham thought that he had waited a long while by the time Ishmael was born, but he had fourteen more years to wait before the son of promise arrived. Finally when Abraham was ninety-nine (Gen. 17:1), God specifically told him concerning Isaac (Gen. 17:15-19; 18:10-15). By this time so many years had passed that both Abraham (Gen. 17:17) and Sarah (Gen. 18:12-15) laughed in their hearts. Apparently their faith had waned. But Isaac was indeed born when Abraham was one hundred and Sarah ninety. Twenty-five years had passed since God's first promise. God signalized the occasion in both their lives by changing the name of each. Abraham's name was changed from Abram (Gen. 17:5) and Sarah's from Sarai (Gen. 17:15). The significance was that now Abraham became in truth a "father of many nations" and Sarah a "princess" before God as mother of this posterity.[41] At this time too, God directed that every male of Abraham's household should be circumcised as a "sign of the covenant made with Abraham."[42] The propriety of inaugurating the sign at this time is

[38] *Supra*, chap. 2, p. 28.

[39] God did promise a plenteous seed to Hagar, however; though not the seed of the covenant promise.

[40] Hagar was actually driven away twice, and the second time Abraham's displeasure at the act was more pronounced (Gen. 21:9-12). Custom, as noted in the prior chapter, was against driving her away; as was also, of course, moral obligation.

[41] Abram means "high father"; Abraham means "father of a multitude" (cf. *supra*, chap. 2, p. 43, n. 62). Sarai is obscure in meaning, with the idea "contentious" perhaps being the most likely, from the root *sarah*. Sarah means "princess."

[42] Circumcision was not unique to Israel. Arabians, Moabites, Edomites, Ammonites, and Egyptians practiced it; cf. G. L. Robinson, *The Bearing of Archaeology on the Old Testament* (New York: American Tract Society, 1941), p. 26 for a tomb picture of a circumcision operation. Circumcision was unique, however, in being used as a sign of God's covenant with His people.

found in that Isaac's birth was the first tangible fulfillment of the several promises of the covenant. As it were, the covenant now began in tangible form.

The question presses as to why it was necessary for Abraham to wait twenty-five years for Isaac's birth. What was accomplished by this lapse of time? At least two matters seem to bear on the answer. One is that this delay constituted a major test of Abraham's faith. Could Abraham yet believe God would fulfill His promise after so long a time? The Scriptures give frequent illustration of similar tests of faith brought by God into the lives of His children that He might stimulate further growth in that faith.[43] Abraham's faith would be stronger for meeting new challenges if he could continue to believe God here. His faith did wane to a degree, as we have observed, but in view of over-all developments, it did not suffer serious decline. The other matter is that this delay forced Abraham to realize that the nation to be raised from him was to be of God alone and not of Abraham. God waited until Sarah was past her natural time of bearing children so as to demonstrate that Abraham's promised posterity would truly be of supernatural origin. Isaac was to be uniquely God's child, though born to Abraham and Sarah.

G. ABIMELECH AND PHILISTINES (Genesis 20–21)

1. *Second half-truth regarding Sarah (Genesis 20).* Between the time of the announcement of Isaac's birth and the happy event itself, Abraham was again guilty of telling a half-truth regarding his wife; this time to Abimelech, king of Gerar, a city west of Beersheba. About twenty-five years had elapsed since the similar occasion in Egypt and perhaps Abraham's memory had dimmed regarding the reprimand and humiliation then experienced. Abimelech took Sarah to his palace, as had Pharaoh at the earlier time, but God once more intervened to protect her. God revealed to Abimelech her true relationship to Abraham through a dream.

2. *Early Philistines.* In Genesis 21:32, 34, the land where Abimelech lived is called "the land of the Philistines." Also, later when Isaac had further dealings in the area, the people themselves are called Philistines (Gen. 26:1, 8, 14, 15, 18). Were these people indeed the ancestors of those of the same name following Israel's conquest? Liberal scholars commonly answer negatively, taking these mentions as anachronistic.[44] But reason exists for believing that this was the case, at

---

[43] A prime example is Job, tried so severely by Satan to make him curse God.
[44] For instance, Wright, *BAR*, p. 40; Burrows, *What Mean These Stones?* (New Haven: American Schools of Oriental Research, 1951), p. 277. Another item said to be anachronistic is the mention of camels (e.g. Gen. 24:10, 11, 14,

least in part. It is true that the major number of Philistines came to Palestine as a member group of the Sea Peoples repulsed by Rameses III of Egypt c. 1190 B.C.[45] But this does not preclude the possibility that some ancestors came many years before. Archaeological evidence testifies that they did. Caphtorian type pottery, like that which Philistines left later in Palestine, since their earlier home had been the region of Caphtor, has been found both in Philistia proper and as far inland as Bethshan and Jericho dating at least to 1500 B.C. Also, that there was communication in patriarchal times between Canaan and Caphtor has been evidenced: first, by discovery of Middle Minoan II pottery at both Hazor and Ugarit; and second by a document from Mari of the 18th century mentioning the king of Hazor sending gifts to Kaptara (Caphtor).[46] Flinders Petrie years ago suggested the rationale for this early coming of Philistines; namely, that there was a desire to export grain back to the rocky, non-self-supporting homeland.[47] Petrie's discovery of sickles in the Philistine region from the early period indicates that grain was grown.

H. NEAR SACRIFICE OF ISAAC (Genesis 22)

1. *Birth of Isaac (Genesis 21:1-21).* Shortly after Abraham's encounter with Abimelech, the wonderful promise regarding Isaac's birth was fulfilled (Gen. 21:1-8). The long-awaited child was born. This was certainly a memorable day for both Abraham and Sarah. It led Sarah, however, to request a second time that Hagar and Ishmael be sent away, Ishmael now being fourteen years old. The "Angel of God"

19), asserting that "the camel had not been generally domesticated as yet" (Wright, *BAR*, p. 40). However, J. Free, *ABH*, p. 55 (cf. his article, "Abraham's Camels," *JNES*, July, 1944, pp. 187-93; also Kitchen, *AOOT*, pp. 79-80; and R. DeVaux, *Theology Digest*, 12, 1964, p. 233) says that camels were known in Egypt even before Abraham, listing as evidence "statuettes and figurines of camels, plaques bearing representations of camels, rock carvings and drawings, camel bones, a camel skull, and a camel hair rope" all dating "from the seventh century B.C. to the period before 3000 B.C."

[45] The Sea Peoples were constituted of at least five ethnic groups, who moved from the Aegean area, particularly Crete, perhaps pushed in turn by European migrators. The *prst* group is identified with the Philistines, the hieroglyphic script using "r" for "l," a change not uncommon; cf. Albright, *AASOR*, 12(1934), pp. 53-58; Wright, *BAR*, pp. 87-88; D. N. Freedman, *BA*, 26(Dec., 1963), pp. 145-49.

[46] C. Gordon calls the Philistine migration of 1200 B.C. only a late migration "in a long series of migrations that had established various Caphtor folk in Canaan long before 1500 B.C."; *ANE*, pp. 121-22. Gordon believes that the name Caphtor is a name for the whole "Aegean and Minoan sphere"; *ibid.*, p. 85.

[47] Petrie, *Palestine and Israel* (London: Society for Promoting Christian Knowledge, 1934), p. 62, as cited by J. Free, *ABH*, p. 6.

found the mother and son in the desert suffering from lack of food and provided for their need (Gen. 21:9-21).

2. *Abraham's most severe test (Genesis 22:1-14)*. A few years later[48] God brought Abraham his most severe test. He called upon him to sacrifice this promised son. No other request could have been quite so difficult to fulfill. The boy meant much to Abraham in terms of personal affection, in view of his miraculous birth, but even more in terms of the fulfillment of God's promise. How could a nation be formed through him if he were now sacrificed? But still Abraham was able to obey. He had grown in faith as God had led and blessed him, and was able now to meet even this challenge. God had designated the place for the sacrifice as Mt. Moriah,[49] and Abraham took three days to get there. This means that he traveled slowly, perhaps with the thought that God might give him counter-orders. But none came; that is, not until the boy had been bound and the knife raised by Abraham to perform the actual sacrifice. Then God did intervene. He told Abraham that he should substitute for Isaac a ram caught in a nearby thicket. God let Abraham go this far, to prove his sincerity of faith. One can hardly think of a greater test. At no time did Abraham's faith shine more brightly. The book of Hebrews says in explanation that Abraham believed that God would even raise Isaac from the dead in order to fulfill the promise regarding the nation (11:19).

I. DEATH AND BURIAL OF SARAH (Genesis 23)

Sarah died at the age of one hundred twenty-seven. Isaac was thirty-seven at the time; Abraham still had thirty-eight years to live. Sarah had been married to Abraham while they were yet in Ur of the Chaldees (Gen. 11:29-31). She was Abraham's half-sister, the daughter of his father, but not of his mother (Gen. 20:12). She had been an obedient wife to Abraham, even acceding to his sinful request that she pass herself off as his sister, first to the Egyptian Pharaoh and later to Abimelech. She had displayed a vindictive spirit, however, in turning against Hagar when the latter bore her son Ishmael to Abraham.

---

[48] The story does not say how many, but likely Isaac was not more than ten years old. He goes with his father quite as a matter of course, even permitting himself to be bound without apparent protest. His question, "Where is the lamb for a burnt-offering?" indicates that he was old enough to reason, but also shows that he was young enough not to have asked the question prior to arrival at the mountain or for the father to have shared such information with him.

[49] The designation, "Moriah," occurs only twice in the Old Testament: here in the form, "land of Moriah," and in I Chron. 3:1 as "in mount Moriah," where the reference is to the mountain where Solomon built the Temple. Some scholars have objected that the distance is not great enough from Beersheba to this Moriah of Solomon for Abraham's three days travel. However, he was in no hurry. The identification is likely.

As a burial place for Sarah, Abraham purchased the cave of Machpelah at Kirjath-arba (Hebron) from a Hittite named Ephron. The business transaction is briefly described (Gen. 23:3-16) and reveals the possible influence in Ephron's thinking of a law of the Hittites to which apparently he felt bound.[50] The law was that the owner of any property obligated himself to the state for military duties as long as he owned it. When Abraham asked to buy only the cave of Machpelah, Ephron urged him to take the whole field in which it was located. If he was to be rid of a part of his property, he apparently wanted to be rid of it all and so avoid this military obligation. Abraham finally did buy the whole field, paying 400 shekels for it, weighing the money to Ephron.[51] The transaction was effected before the "children of Heth," and so made public and binding. This was the only real estate that Abraham purchased of the total land God had promised to give him for his posterity.

J. A BRIDE FOR ISAAC (Genesis 24:1–25:11)

1. *Rebekah is found (Genesis 24).* Three years after Sarah's death, when Isaac was forty years old (Gen. 25:20), Abraham sought a bride for his son. He did not want Isaac to marry a daughter of the Canaanite neighbors. Guided by God, he apparently recognized that marriage with the Canaanites—now by his son and later by future generations—could only lead to amalgamation. A distinction had to be maintained if Abraham's posterity was to develop into a separate nation.[52] Abraham thus thought of his relatives[53] who lived north in Mesopotamia[54] where Abraham had stopped years before with his father,

---

[50] For discussion, cf. Cyrus Gordon, "Abraham and the Merchants of Ura," *JNES*, 17(1958), p. 29; also C. Pfeiffer, *The Patriarchal Age* (Grand Rapids: Baker Book House, 1961), pp. 115-16.

[51] Coinage was not yet practiced, and money was valued in terms of weight. Earliest evidence of coinage (striking of a piece of metal with a seal authenticating its title and weight) comes from the Lydians of Asia Minor perhaps as early as the late eighth century B.C. By the late seventh century, coined money was plentiful in the Aegean region. Probably Cyrus the Great introduced the practice to the Persian world about 540 B.C.

[52] Abraham's example was followed by Isaac in his direction to Jacob that he take his wife from elsewhere (Gen. 28:1-5). Esau, knowing that Canaanite wives displeased his father, married a daughter of Ishmael, though he had previously married two Hittite girls (Gen. 26:34), which was "a grief of mind unto Isaac and to Rebekah."

[53] Persons indicated as living there are those of Nahor's family, particularly his son Bethuel and two children of Bethuel, Rebekah and Laban. Nahor had either accompanied Terah and Abraham in going there or else made the journey from Ur himself later.

[54] The term used here for the area is Aram-naharaim (Gen. 24:10), also employed in Deut. 23:4 and Judg. 3:8. It means "Aram of the two rivers," refer-

Terah. Isaac's wife should come from these. So decided, Abraham sent his senior servant, probably Eliezer (Gen. 15:2), on the long journey to find the one whom Abraham believed God Himself would select (Gen. 24:7). The servant went and arrived at the "city of Nahor" (likely Haran), so called in the story because Nahor, Abraham's brother, now lived there.[55] Under the blessing and guidance of God, he met Rebekah, granddaughter of Nahor, at a well on the edge of town as she came to draw water. Displaying kindness and hospitality, Rebekah drew water not only for the servant, but also his camels, an action which served as a confirming sign to the servant that this was the person whom God had selected. Highly encouraged, the servant went with the young lady into the city, met her family, including the father, Bethuel, and brother, Laban (Gen. 24:29-50), told of his mission, and received consent for Rebekah to accompany him to become Isaac's wife. Rebekah was agreeable and went with him to meet and begin her life with Isaac.

2. *Abraham's marriage to Keturah (Genesis 25:1-11).* Abraham still lived thirty-five years after Isaac's marriage. He married Keturah of whom nothing is known before this time. Six sons were born to them: Zimran, Jokshan, Medan, Midian, Ishbak, and Shuah,[56] all of whom became ancestors of various Arabian peoples. Nothing is known of Abraham's life during this period. He died at the advanced age of 175 (Gen. 25:7), and Isaac and Ishmael buried him next to Sarah in the cave of Machpelah. Isaac alone was designated as heir, though Abraham set aside certain gifts for Ishmael and Keturah's six sons.

K. Abraham, Man of Faith

Abraham was truly one of the great men of the Old Testament. He was a man of outstanding faith, demonstrated especially in his willingness to leave Ur of the Chaldees for an unidentified land, and to sacri-

ring to the Euphrates and Tigris, and so speaks of all northern Mesopotamia. Another term used in the story is Padan-aram (Gen. 25:20; 28:2; 31:18), meaning "Field of Aram." This term seems to have more specifically designated the region near Haran.

[55] It could mean a city named Nahor, too, for a Mari text speaks of a city of this name; cf. *supra*, chap. 2, p. 27. Its mound has not been identified with certainty, but is commonly believed to be near Haran; cf. Wright, *BAR*, p. 41.

[56] To account for Abraham here having children when previously said to be "dead" (Rom. 4:19) in this respect, Keil suggests that he had married Keturah well before Sarah's death (*KDC*, Genesis, p. 261). This is difficult to understand, however, in view of his reluctance even to take Hagar while Sarah lived, and the clear implication of the Genesis story. It is better to think either of his rejuvenation in begetting Isaac as continuing on, or else that his "deadness" had been only in connection with Sarah being incapable of having children rather than with his own body.

fice his own son, even believing God would raise him from the dead to fulfill the promise of a great nation. He was magnanimous, giving Lot first choice of the land he desired. He was forgiving, willing to aid Lot after the selfish choice he made, first by delivering him from invaders, and then by interceding for him on learning that the wicked city of Sodom, Lot's chosen home, was to be destroyed. He was courageous, daring to pursue a much superior army to effect Lot's deliverance. His one weakness was prevarication in connection with his wife on coming in contact with foreign kings. How to assess or understand this weakness is not easy to know. It does not fit the pattern of his life otherwise. But one should not let this deficiency cloud the other splendid characteristics of the man. He was one who loved God, for which reason the high accolade is accorded him that he was the "friend" of God (II Chron. 20:7; Isa. 41:8; James 2:23).

CHAPTER FOUR

ISAAC, JACOB, JOSEPH

Genesis 25:9–50:26

In this chapter, our interest remains with the partriarchal period, but now as centered in the three descendants of Abraham: Isaac, Jacob, and Joseph. They represent three successive generations which intervened between Abraham and the period of sojourn for Abraham's posterity in Egypt. Isaac and Jacob differ from Joseph in that, for their generations, they alone lived as members of the line of promise. Joseph, however, had eleven brothers in that line, each one to be head of a respective tribe. But Joseph stands out among them for special consideration, for he was easily the most significant, the one upon whom God had chosen to place special favor, and the one, accordingly, of whom more is said in the sacred record.

A. ISAAC (Genesis 25:9–26:35)

Isaac[1] is the least known of the three. Considerably more is related in Genesis regarding Jacob and Joseph. Because of this, one tends to think of Isaac more as either the son of Abraham or the father of Jacob, rather than an individual in his own right. It is true that Isaac was the least conspicuous of the patriarchs. He was not given to daring action or unusual exploits. But still he constituted an important link in the ancestral chain of Israel, and is honored throughout Scripture in parallel with Abraham and Jacob. He was granted longer life than either.

We have noted earlier aspects in Isaac's life in our consideration of Abraham. We now take up matters which followed the death of his father.

[1] The name, Isaac, means "one laughs." The reference is to the fact that both Abraham and Sarah laughed (Gen. 17:17-19; 18:9-15) in incredulity at the promise of a child at their age.

65

1. *Jacob and Esau born (Genesis 25:21-34).* The first matter recorded is the birth of his twin sons, Jacob and Esau. These were born only when Isaac had reached the age of sixty (Gen. 25:26), twenty years after his marriage to Rebekah. Abraham had waited twenty-five years for Isaac, and now Isaac had waited twenty years for Jacob and Esau. Isaac's faith was tried even as Abraham's, but he, like his father, continued to believe God. It is stated that he "intreated Yahweh for his wife, because she was barren" (Gen. 25:21). It must have been difficult, however, to understand why God should tarry so long in fulfilling the promise of a large posterity. But finally God heard Isaac's prayer, and Rebekah conceived.

Even before birth, the twins struggled within the womb of Rebekah. She inquired as to the significance and God told her that this was a sign that the two, followed in turn by their respective posterities, would struggle with each other in years to come, with the elder being made to serve the younger. Esau was born first, with Jacob grasping his heel.[2]

Growing up, the twins little resembled each other. Jacob was fair, a man of the house, beloved of his mother. Esau was rugged, a man of the outdoors, favored by his father. In keeping with God's prediction, they did clash (Gen. 25:27-34). They had grown to be young men when Jacob one day took advantage of his home position to persuade Esau to sell him his birthright. Having been born first, Esau enjoyed the inheritance rights of the eldest son. Jacob wanted these rights and persuaded Esau to exchange them for a portion of food Jacob was preparing.[3] Esau, having been in the field, was hungry and foolishly made the trade urged by Jacob. Jacob is to be criticized for coveting something not his own, but Esau gave up a legal right of lifelong value for the satisfaction of a moment. The birthright secured for its owner the headship of the family, the possession of a major share of family property, and the right to the parental blessing. How poorly Esau measured relative values!

2. *Relations with Philistines (Genesis 26:1-33).* A famine in the land prompted Isaac to move, as an earlier famine had caused a similar action on the part of his father. God warned him not to go to Egypt, however, but only to a place He would designate. The location proved to be near the city, Gerar,[4] where Philistines[5] lived, an area where Abraham had similarly sojourned (Gen. 20:1-18).

[2] The name, Jacob, means "heel grasper" from which the idea, "supplanter," is derived. The name, Esau, means "hairy" in description of him at birth.

[3] Nuzi tablets give instances of similar negotiation in inheritance rights between brothers. In one, a brother sells a grove, which was his inheritance, to another brother for three sheep; cf. C. Gordon, *ANE*, p. 126; also Wright, *BAR*, p. 43.

[4] Formerly identified with Tell Jemmeh, 8 miles south of Gaza, but now

Here Isaac followed in the sin which his father had twice committed; telling an untruth regarding his wife. Rebekah was fair, as Sarah had been, and Isaac feared for his life. He spread the word that Rebekah was his sister, a deception still more serious than Abraham's, for Sarah at least had been Abraham's half-sister. Isaac must be severely blamed, though he did have the poor example of his father to influence him. It was sometime later that Abimelech,[6] the Gerar ruler, learned of the deception, properly warned his people against familiarity with Rebekah, and graciously permitted Isaac to remain in his land.

Isaac accepted this hospitality, planted crops, and reaped a fine harvest. His wealth, inherited and now increased, made Abimelech's people jealous, and Abimelech finally asked him to leave. Isaac did so, but went only as far as a valley still in the general vicinity. Here he reopened wells which Abraham had dug and which the Philistines had later refilled. Isaac experienced the results of continued ill-will by the people in having them claim water he found each time of redigging. At last he moved back to Beersheba and there received a visit from Abimelech, who now wished to make a covenant with him regarding land rights; and this was done.

A bright aspect in this otherwise unhappy period is that God confirmed His covenant with Isaac, as He had with Abraham; in fact, this happened two different times. The first was just before Isaac went to Gerar, when God not only told him not to go to Egypt, but promised him great seed and possession of the land in which he lived (Gen. 26: 2-5); and the second was just after his return from Gerar when God promised to be with him, to bless him, and to multiply his seed for Abraham's sake (Gen. 26:24).

3. *The stolen blessing (Genesis 27:1-46).* At the age of 137[7] Isaac took steps to bestow the parental blessing on his eldest son. In spite of Esau's having bargained away the right to this blessing, as well as God's clear indication at the birth of the two boys that the elder should serve the younger (Gen. 25:23), Isaac determined to perform the rite in favor of Esau. However, Rebekah wanted it for Jacob. She persuaded Jacob, who at first was reticent, to disguise himself as his brother to procure it. She placed hairy goat skin on his hands and neck, and dressed him in his brother's clothing. Isaac, who was nearly blind,

thought to be Tell Abu Hureira, 11 miles southeast of Gaza; Albright, *BASOR,* 163(1961), pp. 47-48.

[5] Cf. *supra,* chap. 3, pp. 59-60.

[6] Descendant of the Abimelech visited by Abraham.

[7] Dying at 180 (Gen. 35:28) Isaac still had 43 years to live but he could not know this. His age here is figured on the basis that Jacob was now 77 (cf. *infra,* n. 11) and he was born when Isaac was 60.

had to depend on touch and smell for identification, and so was deceived. Thinking the person was Esau, he bestowed the blessing, calling for the recipient to receive abundant material provisions and rulership over both his mother's posterity and surrounding nations.

Jacob had scarcely left his father's presence when Esau came expecting to receive the blessing. When both father and son realized the deception that had been perpetrated, each experienced remorse and anger. But what had been done, even though in this manner, was binding,[8] and all Isaac could do for Esau was grant a secondary blessing; promising material provisions but stating also that he would be subservient to his younger brother. Bitter hatred stirred in Esau's heart, and he resolved to kill Jacob as soon as the father died. Accordingly, at Rebekah's urging, Jacob made ready to flee north to the home country of Rebekah in Haran.

4. *Isaac the man.* Isaac as a person is not easy to understand. He is accorded a high place in Scripture, as an important member in Israel's lineage, and yet there is comparatively little in the record for which to admire him. It is true that he showed commendable faith when he continued to trust God for children after twenty years of waiting. And earlier he had properly submitted before the sacrificial knife of his father, though he then may have been too young to have had much to say in the matter. But many of his actions and omissions otherwise call for criticism. He followed his father in the sin of telling an untruth regarding his wife. His two sons seem not to have been properly instructed and disciplined in religious matters: Jacob coming to be known as a deceiver and demonstrating little understanding of the greatness of God (Gen. 28:16-22); and Esau marrying pagan girls (Gen. 26: 34; 36:1f). Even Isaac's wife exhibited little fear of God and less respect for her husband as she schemed with her son to steal a blessing intended for another.

Clearly Isaac was not a man of action, as Abraham and Jacob had been. This must be borne in mind in evaluating him. Almost never is he seen in situations which called for initiative or a display of faith. He left the matter of choice of wife entirely to his father and readily accepted the one whom he provided. When Philistines successively claimed wells he had reopened, he did not greatly protest but moved on to dig others. He seems never to have traveled outside the confines of southern Canaan in all his 180 years.[9] And never is he said

---

[8] Cf. *supra*, chap. 2, pp. 28-29.

[9] Most references show him near either Beersheba or Gerar (Gen. 24:62; 25: 11; 26:1, 23; 28:10), though he was at Hebron when Jacob returned from Haran (Gen. 35:27-29).

to have been asked by God, as was Abraham, to perform actions calling for great faith. One reason may be that he had been dominated in early life by an outstanding father, and later was simply content to bask in the greatness Abraham had displayed. No doubt, too, he was naturally one of more retiring personality, not given to aggressive, outward demonstration, a characteristic which in itself can be commendable. In fact, one can admire Isaac for being willing to receive his chosen wife, Rebekah, so readily, and also to give up wells to enemies without serious protest. Certainly meekness is high on the list of godly virtues. But still one would expect more evidence than exists, particularly in good influence on those near him, if Isaac were truly a great man of God. He knew God, and was a worthy member of the patriarchal line, but certainly he fell short of the measure of either Abraham or Jacob.

B. Jacob (Genesis 28:1-36:43)

Jacob, the third patriarch, contrasts markedly with his father. He was again a man of action, more like Abraham, though unlike him in the manner of those actions, especially during his early life. He is known then for his deceptions. We have already noted his schemes against his brother and father; and he was yet to work the same against his Uncle Laban in the northland. In later life, however, God changed him, and he became truly devoted. Much more is said regarding him than Isaac.

1. *The flight to Haran (Genesis 28:1-29:13).* Before Jacob departed for Rebekah's homeland, Isaac summoned him. Though Jacob had wronged his father, Isaac loved him and had his best interest in mind. Isaac bestowed further blessing on him and then charged him not to take a wife from the Canaanites, but rather from his mother's relation in Haran.[10] It should be realized that Jacob at this time was no longer young. A comparison of Scriptures reveals that he was seventy-seven years of age.[11]

Jacob departed and had proceeded as far as Bethel when, resting for the night, he had a dream of a ladder reaching to heaven, with

[10] Isaac's urging of Jacob to seek a wife in the north does not contradict Rebekah's interest that he flee north to escape from Esau. The prime reason for his going was to escape from his brother, but in addition Isaac wanted him to find a wife. Rebekah and Isaac were agreed on this as shown by their mutual anxiety that Esau had married local girls (Gen. 26:34-35).

[11] When Jacob was 130 at his descent to Egypt (Gen. 47:9), Joseph was 39 (41:46, 47, 54; 45:11), which means that Jacob was 90 when Joseph was born. Joseph was born 14 years after Jacob's arrival in Haran (31:41; 30:25), which, subtracted from 91, leaves 77.

angels ascending and descending upon it (Gen. 28:10-22).[12] In the morning, properly impressed that God was with him, he poured oil on the stone that he had used for a pillow, called the place Bethel (house of God), and made solemn promises to God. His pouring oil on the stone was a symbolic way of giving religious importance to the place, for God had here reassured him of His abiding presence. Jacob needed this reassurance because he was carrying a deserved guilty conscience for his action toward Esau. Also, all that we know of him points to spiritual immaturity on his part at the time, and we may believe that little thought of God had crossed his mind as he had left home. His response to the dream, accordingly, was one of amazement, appreciation, and then determination to reciprocate with proper conduct of life. This new thinking was to be of great importance for him as he would soon enter a land where false deities were worshiped (Gen. 31:19, 30) and where he would encounter an uncle who would work treachery against him.

Jacob met Rachel, his bride-to-be, as she came to water her flock of sheep at a well near Haran. Jacob had arrived somewhat sooner and found shepherds awaiting removal of the well's covering stone. He now proceeded to move the stone himself, so that he could water Rachel's flock. Jacob apparently was physically strong and not one to wait long for others, or to be hindered by local customs. No one objected to the brusque action, and Rachel's flock was watered early that day. Jacob told her who he was; she in turn called her father, Laban, who came and greeted Jacob; and then all went to the uncle's house. Here Jacob was to spend twenty unusual years.

2. Twenty Years in Haran (Genesis 29:14–31:20)

a. Jacob's two wives (Gen. 29:14-31). Jacob loved Rachel from the beginning and agreed with Laban to serve him seven years for her hand in marriage. When the seven years were completed, Laban showed his deceitfulness by giving to Jacob Leah, his eldest daughter, in place of Rachel. Laban explained that the custom of the country was that the elder sister should marry first.[13] He could have told Jacob this seven years before but had not, and now Jacob found it necessary to work another seven years for the one he loved. To be deceived in terms of seven years employment is not a small matter.

---

[12] The significance of this God-sent dream was to show Jacob that God was maintaining a constant means of communication between Jacob and Himself. In other words, Jacob was important to Him and could know that God was with him to help as he would look to Him.

[13] This custom seems to have been only local for no other evidence of it exists. Jacob, however, acceded in apparent recognition of it.

Jacob could not have helped but remember the similar deceptions he had perpetrated against his brother and father.

Jacob did not have to wait seven years before Rachel was given to him, however.[14] He waited only one week, apparently while wedding festivities for Leah were completed (Gen. 29:27-28). He was then permitted to marry Rachel also, but he was expected to work seven additional years in payment for her, which he did.[15]

b. Jacob's children (Gen. 29:32-30:24). It was at this point that the promise to Abraham of more than a century and a half earlier[16] began to be fulfilled in greater degree. Jacob was now given a large family (Gen. 29:31-30:24). Though Jacob favored Rachel, it was through Leah that God gave Jacob his first and most children. Leah bore in succession Reuben (*see, a son*), Simeon (*hearing*), Levi (*joining*), and Judah (*praise*). Rachel, who continued to be barren, now urged Jacob to raise up children unto her through her handmaid, Bilhah.[17] Jacob did so and Bilhah gave birth to Dan (*judge*) and Naphtali (*wrestling*). Leah then countered by giving her handmaid, Zilpah, to Jacob; and to her were born Gad (*troop*) and Asher (*gladness*). At this point, God again blessed Leah with children, and she bore Issachar (*he brings wages*) and Zebulon (*dwelling*). She also gave birth to a daughter, Dinah (*judgment*). Finally God gave conception also to Rachel and she bore Joseph (*adding*). This gave Jacob eleven sons and one daughter. The twelfth son, Benjamin (*son of my right hand*), was born to Rachel too, but not until the family had moved back to Canaan (Gen. 35:16-20).

c. The last six years (Gen. 30:25-31:21). Following Joseph's birth, and with the completion of the fourteen years of service owed, Jacob asked permission of Laban to leave the land; but Laban persuaded him to remain longer (Gen. 30:25-34). Apparently Jacob had been a good worker and his employment thus far had cost Laban little. Laban wanted more of this advantageous relationship.

Jacob set as his new wage all Laban's sheep and goats that were other than solid white or solid black (or dark brown), including those

[14] Evidenced both by the story as told (Gen. 29:27-30) and that strife existed between Leah and Rachel from the first in respect to bearing Jacob children (Gen. 29:31 - 30:24).

[15] What would have happened had Jacob left for Palestine before completing these additional years (which normal reaction to Laban's treachery could have indicated) is not made clear. It is to Jacob's credit that he paid what he owed. Sometimes Jacob's deficiencies in character are over-emphasized.

[16] Adding 25 years until Isaac's birth, 60 until Jacob's, and then Jacob's age here of 77 gives 162 total years.

[17] Cf. *supra,* chap. 2, p. 28.

living and those to be born while he worked. Laban agreed, since he knew that normally few animals were born spotted. Jacob now sought to better his own interests through selective breeding measures (Gen. 30:40) and devices for pre-natal influence.[18] Jacob's attitude was wrong but understandable in the light of Laban's previous actions. God prospered Jacob in spite of the moral deficiency, and the spotted animals became unusually numerous. Laban, probably pressured by his sons,[19] countered by changing the agreement, as Jacob later says, ten times (Gen. 31:7, 41), but still Jacob prospered. His flocks and herds became very large; indeed, so large that, when he later left for home, after working for this wage only six years, he could afford a gift of 580 animals[20] at one time to his brother Esau (Gen. 32:13-16).

Jacob's prosperity at his father-in-law's expense did not endear him to the Haran relation, the recognition of which prompted him to leave after six years (total of twenty) of this arrangement (Gen. 31:1-20). His own desire to this end was reinforced by a dream from God giving direct instruction. Even his wives, daughters of Laban that they were, did not object. Jacob waited until a day when Laban was away for sheepshearing, apparently lest his uncle try to hinder or make matters unpleasant by claiming a substantial portion of Jacob's property. Then Jacob took his two wives, twelve children, servants, and abundant livestock, and departed for home. Unknown to Jacob, Rachel took also the family idols, which were significant for symbolizing inheritance rights,[21] in a desire thus to have evidence of Jacob's right to all he possessed. As he left, Jacob recognized that God had been good to him. Jacob had come to Haran as one person alone and now was departing after only twenty years as a wealthy man with a large family (Gen. 32:10).

3. *Return to Canaan (Genesis 31:21–33:20)*

a. Pursuit of Laban (Gen. 31:22-55). Laban was angry when he discovered Jacob's secret departure. Immediately he pursued Jacob's slower moving company, but was unable to catch the group until it

---

[18] Gen. 30:37-39 says that he peeled white stripes on tree branches and set these before the animals as they bred. He believed that these would effect spotted offspring. Many spotted animals did result, but only because God blessed to that end.

[19] Gen. 31:1 suggests this thought. It may be that these sons had been born since Jacob's arrival, for none are mentioned earlier and apparently they were still too young to be a factor when the bargain was first made with Laban.

[20] Mostly sheep and goats. However, also camels, asses, and cattle were included, indicating that Jacob had been able to accumulate these from Laban as well.

[21] Cf. *supra,* chap. 2, p. 28.

had reached Mt. Gilead, at least 275 miles from Haran.[22] He was especially interested in recovering the family idols which Rachel had taken, for, as Rachel had wished by these to establish Jacob's inheritance rights, he desired otherwise. In fact, this appears to have been the real reason why he put forth the great effort of giving chase so far. For all the effort, however, Laban accomplished little. God warned him in a dream not to speak harshly to Jacob, and his own daughter tricked him so that he was unable to locate the idols (Gen. 31:32-35). The matter ended with an agreement that neither he nor Jacob would impose on the other again.

b. A wrestling match (Gen. 32:24-32). As Jacob now continued his journey, he feared an inevitable meeting with Esau; but before that meeting could occur, he experienced another confrontation of much greater significance. This came in the form of a wrestling match with none other than the Angel of Yahweh. Jacob was alone on the north bank of the Jabbok River. He had sent his family and possessions across the stream the prior evening, and had remained by himself apparently for a time of private devotion. During the night the Angel drew near and began to wrestle with him. Jacob was now ninety-seven years old but evidently still in good physical condition. He realized as the match progressed that his opponent was more than human, and accordingly he asked for a blessing. He remembered well the dream of twenty years before when he had left the land and the resulting benefit in his life. He wished now for a renewed blessing. He wanted to be assured that God would continue to be with him. The Angel gave this assurance. As tangible evidence, he changed Jacob's name to Israel[23] and touched his thigh so that it shrank in size. From now on, Jacob would limp, but it would be a constant reminder of both God's gracious favor and his own responsibility for proper life conduct. From this time on, Jacob is not seen again scheming or deceiving.

c. Meeting with Esau (Gen. 32:1-23; 33:1-17). The next day Jacob received clear evidence that God indeed was blessing him. He met Esau, and no bitterness was shown (Gen. 33:1-17). Jacob had dreaded this meeting, especially after having learned that Esau, accompanied by four hundred men, was coming to meet him (Gen. 32: 3-6). Jacob had sent three droves of animals as presents to appease his brother's anticipated anger, but they had not been needed. Some-

[22] It is this distance to the northernmost fringes of Mt. Gilead which was likely the region. To travel this far in seven days (Gen. 31:23) is fast travel. Jacob had started three days earlier and had moved quickly also, particularly since he had to drive sheep and goats.

[23] The name Israel comes from the verb, *sarah*, meaning "to strive," from which also the noun, *sar*, meaning "prince" or "striver" comes. The last element of the name, *'el*, means "God." The full name means "prince (striver) with God."

how Esau's heart had mellowed through the intervening twenty years. He too possessed material wealth and at first refused Jacob's gifts, but Jacob urged him to accept, and he did. The brothers embraced each other warmly, exchanged pleasantries, and parted with all former barriers removed. Jacob's heart was now much lighter for moving on. Esau returned to his chosen territory of Mt. Seir, south of the Dead Sea, and Jacob continued across the Jordan to Shechem.[24]

4. *Back in Canaan (Genesis 34–36)*. Arriving at Shechem, Jacob was unable to remain very long as a result of a perfidious slaying of Shechemites by his sons, Simeon and Levi (Gen. 34:1-31). They sought revenge for gross misconduct toward Dinah their sister. A young man, Shechem, son of Hamor, leader in the city of Shechem, had taken her, violated her, and requested permission of Jacob to marry her. Jacob's sons devised a plan for reprisal. All Shechemites would have to be circumcised if the request were granted. All Shechemites were, and then while they were yet sore and incapacitated for physical defense, they were killed by Simeon and Levi wielding swords. Dinah was brought home. Jacob, fearing reprisal in turn from other inhabitants of the area, quickly moved on south in the country.

Jacob now came again to Bethel where he had experienced his memorable dream (Gen. 35:1-10). Once more God appeared to him, this time renewing the promises given to both Abraham and Isaac concerning a large posterity and the land of Canaan as an inheritance (Gen. 35:11-13). He traveled farther south. When he drew near Bethlehem, Rachel died while giving birth to Benjamin (Gen. 35:16-20), and Jacob set a monument on the grave[25] of this one whom he dearly loved. He then moved on to Hebron where he found his father yet living. Jacob now seems to have lived with, or at least near, his father for the remainder of Isaac's life.[26] When Isaac died, Esau came to join Jacob for his burial (Gen. 35:27-29).

At this point in the record, Esau's generations are enumerated, closing with the words, "This is Esau, the father of the Edomites"

---

[24] Jacob here purchased a tract of land from Hamor (Gen. 33:18-20). Today one can view Jacob's well just outside old Shechem, supposedly located on the tract that Jacob bought. Here Jesus met the woman of Samaria years later (John 4). For discussion of the well, cf. Wright, *Shechem* (New York: McGraw-Hill Book Co., 1965), pp. 215-217. It is not known when the well was dug, but very likely it was in Old Testament time.

[25] A grave for her is still marked today by a small Moslem mosque on the northern outskirts of Bethlehem, but the actual site is probably farther north (cf. I Sam. 10:2).

[26] Isaac far outlived expectations; cf. *supra*, n. 7. Esau had said 20 years earlier that he would kill Jacob when his father was dead (Gen. 27:41), but Isaac had lived all during Jacob's 20 years absence and still was to live 23 more until he reached the age of 180 (Gen. 35:28).

(Gen. 36:1-43). In later years, Edom proved to be a perennial enemy of Israel.

5. *Jacob, a transformed man.* Jacob presents the picture of a man who has been transformed by the power of God. In his early life, he was a schemer and deceiver, but in later days he became a devout follower of God. Before the change he bargained for his brother's birthright, deceived for his father's blessing, and schemed for his uncle's flocks; after the change, he lived a life of quiet meditation, was grieved at his sons' sinful activities, and was a proper recipient for God's further revelation regarding covenantal blessing. One should not judge him too harshly for his early wrong actions, however, for it was his mother who persuaded him as to the deception of his father, and surely his uncle gave him severe provocation for the retaliation while in Haran; but still Jacob found it easy to fit into these roles, and it should be remembered that the first bargain with his brother was of his own doing alone. The great change in Jacob's life came at two points: first, at Bethel on his way to Haran, where he encountered God in a way never experienced before, but after which he could still engage his uncle in their standoff of wrongdoing; second, at the brook Jabbok on his return from the North, where he wrestled with the Angel of Yahweh. That Jacob did experience change at this time was important for the rearing of his sons, who by this time were growing old enough to experience his influence. His life as they knew him after the return to Palestine was highly exemplary.

C. JOSEPH (Genesis 37-50)

The story continues with the life of Joseph. As noted earlier, he was the outstanding son of Jacob's twelve. He was a person of remarkable gifts and sense of dedication. He had the faith of Abraham, the gentleness of Isaac, and the courage of Jacob. Above all, he was a man of obedience to God, and one of the most admirable persons in all the Old Testament. The closing chapters of Genesis center mainly on his experiences.

1. *Sold into Egypt (Genesis 37).* At the age of seventeen,[27] Joseph was sold by his brothers into Egypt. Their ill will toward him had been prompted by his father's favoritism and his own unwise action of relating dreams that predicted his superiority over both them and his parents (Gen. 37:5-11). His exemplary life could also have played a part in making them resentful. The treachery occurred at Dothan. Father Jacob had sent Joseph from Hebron to the area where the

[27] Gen. 37:2. Joseph was born when his father had served Laban 14 years (Gen. 30:23-26) and so was 6 when Jacob returned to Canaan. This means 11 years had elapsed since his return.

brothers were pasturing the family flocks. They had gone north some fifty miles to Shechem for the purpose, but, when Joseph came there, he found that they had now moved on another fifteen miles to Dothan. Pasture apparently was scarce in southern Canaan. The brothers recognized Joseph while he was still some distance off and immediately plotted against him. Most wished to take his life, but Reuben, the oldest, and Judah, who often assumed leadership, urged in different ways that his life be spared. The matter was settled when a caravan of Midianites[28] traveling to Egypt passed by, and Joseph was sold as a slave for the price of twenty pieces of silver.[29] The emotional shock to Joseph must have been severe, not only for being sold as a slave into a foreign country, but for being rejected and treacherously treated by his own brothers, whom he had only come to help. The brothers worked further villainy in deceiving their father into thinking that Joseph had been killed by a wild beast, when they presented to him Joseph's fine specially made robe, which they had dipped in the blood of a goat, as evidence of his death.

2. *Judah and Tamar (Genesis 38)*. Joseph's story is interrupted at this point by a sad episode in the life of Judah, involving Tamar, his daughter-in-law. When Judah's son Er died without progeny, Tamar, wife of Er, was given to Onan, the younger brother, in keeping with the levirate principle.[30] When Onan also died childless, Tamar waited for still a younger brother, Shelah, to reach maturity that she might marry him and still have hope of children. Judah did not give Shelah to her, however, and when some time had passed, Tamar took a bold step in posing as a prostitute to have a child by Judah himself. Her scheme worked and twins were born to her.[31] The influence of Hittite law may be reflected in Tamar's action, for it held that, when no brother-in-law existed to fulfill the levirate duty, the father-in-law was responsible.[32] Accordingly, Judah said to Tamar, even though she had tricked him, that she was more righteous than he (Gen. 38:26). Ugarit sources attest the custom also of showing three different items to prove

[28] Called both Midianites and Ishmaelites (Gen. 37:28). As Midianites they were descendants of Abraham by Keturah, and as Ishmaelites, descendants of Hagar; cf. Judg. 8:1, 24.

[29] Twenty shekels was the average price of a slave at this time. In prior centuries the price had been less, averaging 10 to 15 shekels, and by the 15th century, 30 to 40 shekels. This is further confirmation of this story occurring in the early centuries of the second millennium. For references, cf. Kitchen, *AOOT*, pp. 52-53.

[30] Indicating that the principle of levirate marriage was recognized at this period in history.

[31] One of them, Pharez, apparently became ancestor to David (Ruth 4:18), thus giving this episode, sad in itself, unusual historical significance.

[32] For discussion, cf. Gordon, *ANE*, p. 136.

identification in such a situation, as Tamar did in presenting Judah's signet, cord, and staff as evidence that Judah indeed was the father of her twins.[33]

3. *Joseph in Egypt (Genesis 39–41).* Joseph's trials did not end when he reached Egypt. The betrayal of his brothers had been enough to bear, but more injustices awaited him.

a. Injustice in Egypt (Gen. 39–40). He was sold by the Midianites to one Potiphar,[34] officer of Pharaoh. Joseph suffered a major wrong while working for him (Gen. 39:1-20). The young man worked diligently for the new master and was rewarded at first by being elevated to a place of trust. But in this position, Potiphar's wife became attracted to him, sought to entice him, and, when he properly and commendably resisted her, she had him consigned to prison.[35] Young in life and away from home restraints, Joseph must be highly admired for this fine behavior in a tempting, difficult situation. Even more must he be commended for not becoming bitter and morose when thrown into prison. Instead he distinguished himself and was once more rewarded with a position of trust (Gen. 39:21-23). But again disappointment came (Gen. 40:1-23). He favored two of Pharaoh's servants, a butler and baker, by interpreting their respective dreams.[36] Appreciation was expressed to Joseph at the time, but when the butler was reinstated to his position, according to the interpretation Joseph had given, he promptly forgot Joseph's favor, though Joseph had specifically requested that he try to effect his release.

b. Honored in Egypt (Gen. 41). However, God intervened. Pharaoh himself was made to dream, and the butler, made aware of the ruler's desire that the dream be interpreted, remembered the prisoner who had interpreted his dream (Gen. 41:1-37). He told Pharaoh of Joseph, who was immediately summoned. Joseph's interpretation of Pharaoh's dream was that Egypt would soon experience seven years of unusual abundance followed by seven years of terrible famine. He then advised the ruler to procure an able superintendent who should store great quantities of food during the plentiful years in preparation for the lean. Pharaoh followed this advice and promptly placed Joseph

---

[33] *Ibid.*

[34] Some scholars consider the name Potiphar to be of late origin (cf. Wright, *BAR*, p. 54), but for refutation of this view, cf. Free, *ABH*, pp. 77-78.

[35] A parallel story is found in the Egyptian Tale of Two Brothers. A younger brother, Bitis, resisted the advances of the wife of his older brother Anubis. Like Potiphar's wife, she then charged mistreatment by the younger brother, who had to flee for his life. For text, cf. Barton, *AB*, pp. 365-67.

[36] The interpretations were that the butler would be reinstated to his former position within three days, while the baker would be killed within that time (Gen. 40:12-23). Both predictions came true.

himself in that position, reasoning quite correctly that a man through whom God would give this kind of information would be one also able to perform the important task involved (Gen. 41:38-44). Joseph was given authority next to that of Pharaoh himself.[37] What a remarkable elevation this was! One day a prisoner and the next a virtual prime minister! Of course, this was the high position God had predicted for Joseph years before in his dreams. Other people were now to bow before him; even his brothers and father. We may believe that Joseph had wondered how those dreams could ever come true, particularly after being sold into slavery. But now God had shown him. God had rewarded faithfulness in a manner far surpassing what he could have imagined!

Joseph immediately addressed himself to the new work (Gen. 41: 45-57), being first given an Egyptian name, Zaphenath-paneah,[38] and an Egyptian wife, Asenath, daughter of a priest of the god Ra.[39] Joseph was thirty years old at the time. During the seven plentiful years, he gathered an immense store of food, and during the seven lean years he dispensed it to the people for a price. News of this possible source of supply reached outside Egypt, and people from other countries came.

During the plentiful years, Joseph's two sons, Ephraim (*fruitful*) and Manasseh (*causing to forget*), who later took Joseph's place as heads of Israelite tribes, were born to Asenath (Gen. 41:50-52).

4. *Extra-biblical matters.* Corroboration of details in this over-all story with contemporary Egyptian practices and customs illustrates the accuracy of the biblical record.[40] The titles, "chief of the butlers," and "chief of the bakers," occur both in Genesis (40:2) and extant Egyptian texts.[41] Famines were known in Egypt and the idea of persons being assigned to dispense food during these famines is borne out in tomb inscriptions. One inscription speaks even of a seven-year famine at the time of the Third Dynasty (c. 2700 B.C.).[42] Indication is made on the Rosetta Stone that the Pharaoh had a custom of releasing prisoners on his birthday, as he did the butler (Gen. 40:20). Joseph shaved before seeing Pharaoh (Gen. 41:14), and shaving was a dis-

[37] The degree of his authority is revealed by the freedom he exercised in making decisions, apparently without consulting the Pharaoh. For instance, he set the price the people were to pay for the food, even telling them they could pay in animals when their money was gone and later in land when the animals were gone (Gen. 47:14-26).

[38] Best taken to mean, "The one who furnishes the sustenance of the land."

[39] Cf. *supra*, chap. 2, p. 38, n. 45.

[40] Cf. Gordon, *ANE*, pp. 139f for discussion.

[41] Cf. Wright and Filson, *The Westminster Historical Atlas to the Bible* (Philadelphia: The Westminster Press, 1945), p. 28b.

[42] *Ibid.*

tinctive custom of Egypt. Pharaoh gave Joseph a signet ring, linen clothing, and a gold chain (Gen. 41:42), all three of which are mentioned in Egyptian texts for similar use. Some scholars have objected to the idea of Joseph, a Semite, being elevated to such a high position in Egypt; but a letter dating from the Amarna period has been found written to a person in similar position having the Semitic name Dudu (David).[43] It fits, too, that the Twelfth Dynasty, ruling at this time,[44] had now moved the capital back from Thebes to the northern site of Memphis.[45] Joseph was thus more accessible to his brothers coming down from Canaan, as the continuing story indicates, and also to them living later in Goshen after Jacob's arrival.

5. *Jacob moves to Egypt (Genesis 42:1–47:11)*. The Scriptures frequently indicate that God effects His program in ways man little understands or recognizes at the time. Joseph's being sold into Egypt, the following distressing years of famine, and the resulting visits by his brothers in search of food, which we now consider, all served to bring about the descent of Jacob's family to Egypt and the consequent sojourn there where its number would increase to the size of a nation. It was no doubt difficult at the time to see the good in these respective developments, but God saw them working together to bring about His plan for Israel (Gen. 45:7-8).

a. Joseph and his brothers (Gen. 42–45). The story of the visits to Egypt is told in some detail. The brothers came twice, both times to get food in the only country where it was available, a distance of more than 200 miles one way. Both times they spoke with Joseph personally, but because of the many intervening years since they had last seen him, his Egyptian dress and speech, and the "impossible" position he now held, they did not recognize him. Joseph treated them harshly both times, not in retaliation but apparently in an effort to discover their present attitudes toward their father and younger brother Benjamin.

At the first visit (Gen. 42), Joseph accused them of being spies, demanded that they prove their integrity by returning to him with Benjamin, kept Simeon as hostage until they should, and effected consternation among them by giving back the money they had paid for the food, placing it in the mouths of their sacks of grain. At the second visit (Gen. 43–45), when Benjamin was duly brought along in spite of Jacob's first protestation, Joseph further startled the brothers by dining with them in his own home where he seated each according to his respective age. He released Simeon since they had brought Ben-

---

[43] Cf. Barton, *AB*, pp. 368-69.
[44] Cf. *supra*, chap. 2, pp. 35-38.
[45] Cf. Bright, *BHI*, p. 46.

jamin, asked regarding the father at home, and then sent them away, once again placing their money in the sacks. In Benjamin's sack, he also placed his own silver cup. Soon after they left, he ordered apprehension of the one with the cup. This brought further remorse and an extreme show of humiliation on the part of all, as they returned and again appeared before Joseph. Finally Joseph could refrain himself no longer and revealed himself to them. He told them that he was indeed their brother and asked once more regarding the father at home. Then he urged that the entire family be brought to Egypt because of the famine. Pharaoh, informed of the situation, himself gave his signal approval by even supplying wagons to facilitate the move.

b. Jacob's move (Gen. 46–47:11). Back in Palestine, Jacob rejoiced at the news regarding Joseph. He immediately decided to heed Joseph's invitation and to set out for Egypt. On the way he stopped in Beersheba to sacrifice, and there God indicated His divine approval and restated the promises first given to Abraham over two centuries before. With this reassurance, the aged father, now 130 years old, moved on to Egypt with all his family.[46] There Joseph presented him to Pharaoh, whom Jacob blessed. Pharaoh in turn assigned the family a home in Goshen.[47]

The divine wisdom in Jacob's family moving to Egypt is apparent. Egypt was a country in which his descendants would have to remain a separate, distinct people, for Jacob and his sons were shepherds, and shepherds were an abomination to Egyptians (Gen. 43:32; 46:34). The fact would remain a natural barrier to intermarriage. In Canaan there had already been some intermarriage with the inhabitants[48] and

[46] Gen. 46:27 says their number totaled 70, and Gen. 46:8-27 tells who they were: 32 descendants of Leah (vs. 15 says 33, but in this figure Jacob is included, and it should be realized that both figures count Dinah, the daughter, and do not include Er and Onan who had died, vs. 12), 11 of Rachel (vs. 22 gives 14, but this includes Joseph and his two sons already in Egypt), 16 of Zilpah (vss. 16-18), and 7 of Bilhah (vss. 23-25), for a total of 66 (vs. 26), which plus Jacob, Joseph, and Joseph's two sons totals 70. Stephen, in Acts 7:14, gives the total figure as 75, apparently following the Septuagint rendition of both Gen. 46:27 and Ex. 1:5, where the additional persons in mind are the 5 (total) sons and grandsons of Ephraim and Manasseh (cf. Num. 26:28-37; I Chron. 7: 14-21).

[47] Cf. *supra*, chap 2, p. 38, n. 44.

[48] In Gen. 46:10, Simeon's son Shaul is called "the son of a Canaanitish woman." Gen. 38:2 tells of Judah having children with Shuah, a Canaanite. And if Shechem wanted Dinah for his wife (Gen. 34), though he did not get her, other Canaanites could have desired the same. On the other hand, in that Gen. 46:10 does single out Shaul as the son of a Canaanite, the implication is that this was not common. If it were not, this means that most of Jacob's sons had taken wives from Haran (returning for them, then, for the oldest could only have been about 12 when Jacob left) or other areas outside Canaan.

continued living there would certainly have brought more. This could only have led to serious amalgamation with the Canaanites, rather than distinctness as a nation. Further, Egypt afforded excellent living conditions for necessary rapid growth in numbers. The land of Goshen was fertile and regularly watered by the flooding Nile for adequate food supply. Still further, Egypt was now the world leader in cultural advances.[49]

6. *Death of Jacob and Joseph (Genesis 47:27–50:26)* Jacob lived yet 17 years after coming to Egypt, dying at the age of 147 (Gen. 47: 28). These were probably the happiest years of his life. His family was together again, and living conditions were fine. Certainly he took great pride in Joseph, whom he had favored in early life anyway and who was now next in power to the Pharaoh. We may be sure that Joseph, in turn, saw to it that his family, and especially his father, lacked for nothing that wealth and position could provide.

One day Joseph brought his two sons, Ephraim and Manasseh, to Jacob for his blessing (Gen. 48:1-22). Joseph so brought the boys that Jacob's right hand, the one of highest blessing, would rest on the head of Manasseh, the oldest, and the left on Ephraim. But Jacob, guided by God, crossed his hands so that the right rested on Ephraim. Joseph objected, but Jacob told him that the younger would indeed be the more favored of the two. Jacob blessed each and then gave similar pronouncements regarding each of his twelve own sons (Gen. 49:1-28). In this he experienced divine guidance, for what he said constituted the future history of each.

When Jacob died, his sons embalmed his body[50] and took it back to Canaan for burial in the cave of Machpelah, according to the directions of Jacob beforehand (Gen. 49:29–50:14). Joseph accompanied them, and a large group besides, ordered by Pharaoh in his respect for Jacob. Upon returning to Egypt, Joseph's brothers feared reprisal by Joseph with Jacob now dead, but Joseph reassured them that no revenge was intended (Gen. 50:15-21).

Joseph died at the age of 110 (Gen. 50:26), 54 years after Jacob. His body also was embalmed but remained in Egypt until the Exodus, when Israel took it along for final burial in Canaan (Ex. 13:19).

7. *Joseph, man of integrity.* Joseph stands with Abraham as a person to be admired. He was a man of the highest integrity. Few in Scripture compare with him for righteous conduct in tempting, trying circumstances. Sold treacherously by his own brothers, he did not react with bitterness or a defeated life of sin. Tempted by a woman of Egypt, he did not deviate from what he knew was right. Betrayed

---

[49] Cf. Bright, *BHI*, pp. 46-47 for description of life under the Twelfth Dynasty.
[50] For description of embalming, cf. Free, *ABH*, pp. 80-81.

by her so wrongly, he did not become morose and moody when cast into prison. Joseph also was capable. Not only was he given a high position in Egypt, but he was able to hold it and distinguish himself in it. Joseph remained in high position apparently for the rest of his life. The main reason for this manner of blessing was that he might prepare the way for Jacob's coming to Egypt. Had not Joseph been prime minister, Jacob would not have thought of bringing the family to the foreign land, nor would Pharaoh have received him or given him the fine land of Goshen if he had. Joseph was God's instrument to go before so that the chosen family might have this fine country in which to grow to nation-size.

8. *The patriarchal period.* The patriarchal period closed with the death of Joseph. Religiously, it was a time of simple faith in God. All four of its principals, Abraham, Isaac, Jacob, and Joseph, displayed this faith, though in different ways and degrees. All four were unusual men, each making his respective contribution. God required of them a consistent, godly life. The patriarchs built altars and offered sacrifices, which suggests that God had given general directions as to what constituted acceptable sacrifice,[51] even though the Mosaic Law had not yet been revealed. The patriarchal head of the family acted as priest for the family.[52] Prayer was offered in a simple direct manner. Abraham spoke face to face with the Angel of Yahweh (Gen. 18). Abraham's servant felt free to request directly an indication as to whom God would have as Isaac's bride (Gen. 24:12-24). Revelation was given to the patriarchs upon many occasions: God using dreams, visions, and appearances of the Angel of Yahweh for the purpose. By various means, the covenant promises were repeated to Abraham, Isaac, and Jacob. Tithing seems to have been practiced, as witnessed by Abraham's act in respect to Melchizedek. The principal requirement in all this was true obedience to God's revealed will. In contrast merely to ritualistic requirements among neighboring peoples, the patriarchs knew their responsibility consisted in proper ethical conduct. God told Isaac that because "Abraham obeyed my voice, and kept my charge, my commandments, my statutes, and my laws," the blessings of the covenant would come on his posterity (Gen. 26:5).

---

[51] Some indication must have been given even prior to Abel's sacrifice (Gen. 4:4) to make his experience understandable.

[52] Job's intercession for his children provides a clear illustration (Job 1:5). Job is best dated about the time of Joseph.

CHAPTER FIVE

SOJOURN AND EXODUS CHRONOLOGY

While in Egypt Jacob's posterity grew to a size that could class them as a nation. Until this time of foreign sojourn, growth in numbers in fulfillment of God's promise to Abraham had been very slow; but during this period it became very rapid. When Moses led Israel across Egypt's border at the time of her Exodus, Jacob's seventy had become more than two million.

Coming now to study this period of growth, it is first necessary to determine the approximate dates involved: when the period began and when it ended. This is essential in order to correlate the biblical and Egyptian histories. The determination depends on two major matters: how long Jacob's descendants remained in Egypt, and the date of the Exodus. Both matters were discussed earlier when Abraham's date was considered, but briefly then in anticipation of the fuller study now to be undertaken.

A. DURATION OF EGYPTIAN SOJOURN

Indication was made at the earlier time that there are two main views as to the duration of Israel's sojourn in Egypt: that the sojourn lasted 430 years, or that it lasted only 215 years. Some of the principal reasons favoring the longer period were pointed out but without discussion or consideration of evidence set forth by adherents of the shorter time.[1]

1. Evidence for 430 years

a. Exodus 12:40. The first reason listed in favor of the longer period was that Exodus 12:40 in the Masoretic Hebrew text gives 430 as the number of years involved. It reads, "Now the time that the children of Israel dwelt in Egypt was four hundred and thirty years." However, a textual problem exists. The reading in both the Septuagint

[1] *Supra,* chap. 2, p. 32.

83

and Samaritan Pentateuch indicates that the 430 years included the sojourning of the patriarchs in Canaan as well as the posterity in Egypt.[2] This reading favors the 215-year position for it requires that the time of the patriarchal activity in Canaan, which lasted 215 years,[3] be subtracted from the total 430 years. A decision, therefore, has to be made as to which reading represents the original. A well known rule in textual criticism is that the Masoretic Hebrew text should be favored unless the evidence from other testimony is strong. In this instance the strength of that evidence is lessened in that the Septuagint and Samaritan Pentateuch do not reflect the exact same original, and also that neither reading is supported by the Syriac or Vulgate versions, both of which are primary in value. It may be added that the affirmation of Exodus 12:41, that at the end of 430 years, "on that very day," the people went out of Egypt, is more impressive if it was the anniversary of the beginning of life in Egypt only.[4] For these reasons, a decision in favor of the Hebrew rendition is best.

b. Genesis 15:13. The second reason listed was that God predicted to Abraham that his posterity would be "sojourners in a land" that was "not theirs," and that this land would "afflict them four hundred years." One matter to notice is that the land for this sojourn of Abraham's posterity would be one "not theirs"; but this does not fit the situation if Canaan was included in God's mind, for Abraham was happily dwelling in Canaan at the time and had already received God's promise that this land would be the home of his descendants. Another matter is that affliction would be involved in this land, but the patriarchs were not afflicted in Canaan. Quite the contrary, they were treated well for strangers, being permitted to move freely through the land and they were even extended courtesies and favors. Affliction came later in Egypt. As to the figure used here being 400, rather than the more exact 430 of Exodus 12:40, this is an employment of a round number, something not uncommon in Scripture. The mention in Genesis 15:16 that the return would be "in the fourth generation,"[5] may be explained in terms of the length of a generation in Abraham's experience. God

---

[2] The Septuagint (Codex Vaticanus) reads, "And the sojourning of the children of Israel, while they sojourned in the land of Egypt and the land of Canaan, was 430 years." The Samaritan Pentateuch is the same in thought though not entirely in words.

[3] Abraham had been in Canaan 25 years when Isaac was born (Gen. 12:4; 21:5), Isaac was 60 when Jacob was born (Gen. 25:26), and Jacob was 130 when he went down to Egypt (Gen. 47:9).

[4] Finegan, *LAP*, p. 72, makes a similar observation.

[5] This mention has been related by some scholars to the four listed generations of Ex. 6:16-20 and taken as evidence for an even shorter period than 215 years. See discussion, p. 86.

knew that Abraham would be one hundred at Isaac's birth and here employed this length of time in a multiple of four to stress how long Abraham's posterity would remain in Egypt.

c. Acts 7:6-7. The third reason listed was that centuries later Stephen used language similar to Genesis, when he spoke before the Sanhedrin, and referred to God's warning that Israel would be treated ill in a strange land four hundred years. Since Stephen said essentially the same thing as in the Genesis passage, similar arguments may be drawn from his words. The foreign land is called a "strange" (*allotria*) land, hardly proper for Canaan as noted; and Israel would be placed in "bondage" there and be treated "ill."

d. Population increase. The fourth reason listed concerned the high improbability of Jacob's family multiplying to a nation of over 2,000,000[6] in a period substantially less than 430 years. Jacob's grandsons had been born when he descended to Egypt. They numbered 41,[7] excluding those of Levi whose descendants are not numbered in the final count. Doubling this number to include wives, we have 82 individuals from whom resulted the 2,000,000. It may be that to these 82 should be added numerous servants whose descendants would also have come to be counted as Israelites in time.[8] How many servants Jacob's family had is not known, but even if as many as 2,000 total persons are conjectured, the increase to reach 2,000,000 is still 1,000 times. Never in history otherwise has anything like this rate of growth transpired, even if we think in terms of 430 years for the time involved.[9] The reason for the rapid growth was God's unusual blessing. There was need that the population develop to a size that, when the people returned to Canaan in due time, they might do so as a full-fledged nation; and so God simply provided accordingly. Mathematically this increase in 430 years is possible under such blessing, the birth rate being kept high and the death rate low. However, the same can hardly be said for 215 years. An increase of this size in so brief a time is quite unthinkable.

e. "Children of Israel" sojourned. Still a fifth reason may be taken

---

[6] Cf. discussion, *infra*, chap. 7, pp. 154-55.

[7] For discussion of this number, cf. *KDC*, Pentateuch, II, pp. 28-29.

[8] Certainly Jacob's family, being wealthy, did have servants, and it is likely (especially in view of shepherds being an abomination to Egyptians) that intermarriage occurred between their descendants and Jacob's. Some scholars have thought in terms of "several thousand" servants, but this seems unlikely. Even the near 2,000 here suggested is probably too high.

[9] Speaking comparably, if Israelites had continued to multiply 1,000 times in each succeeding period of 430 years, they would have numbered two billion by the time of David, two trillion by the captivity, and over two quadrillion by the time of Christ.

from Exodus 12:40, which uses the phrase, "children of Israel" (*bene yisra'el*), for those who sojourned the 430 years. Adherents of the 215-year view must accept this as a suitable designation for Abraham, Isaac, and Jacob as single persons, prior to the birth of Jacob's children. Evidently the transcribers of the Samaritan Pentateuch saw difficulty in this, however, for they wrote, "and the sojourning of the children of Israel *and of their fathers*" (italics mine),[10] a reading which must be rejected otherwise for lack of supporting textual evidence. If one takes "children of Israel" in its normal meaning, he is limited to subtracting at most 33 years[11] from the total 430 as the sojourning time in Egypt, for Jacob's children lived in Canaan no longer than this before moving to Egypt.

2. Evidence for 215 Years

a. Four generations. Those who favor the shorter period of time often point to Exodus 6:16-20, where the genealogy of Moses as there given makes him the great grandson of Levi. The names listed are: Levi, Kohath, Amram, and Moses. These are commonly spoken of as the four generations anticipated in Genesis 15:16, as noted earlier. Since generations really did not last 100 years, it is asserted that this listing makes the 430-year position impossible.[12] In response, it need only be pointed out that this genealogy is not complete, something not unusual in Israelite genealogies.[13] This is shown by a comparison with a parallel genealogy, running from Ephraim to Joshua as given in I Chronicles 7:22-27, which lists no less than ten generations.[14]

[10] Codex Alexandrinus carries a similiar thought: "which they and their fathers sojourned in Egypt and in Canaan."

[11] Evidence for 33 years: Joseph was 39 when the family joined him in Egypt (Gen. 41:46, 47, 54; 45:11), and he had been 6 (born when his father had served Laban 14 years, Gen. 30:23-26, and all came to Canaan after 20 years) when Jacob left Haran.

[12] Indeed, it would argue for less than 215 years. The exact average length of generations at this time is difficult to determine, but was certainly much less than 50 years.

[13] For instance, Ezra (7:1-5) gives 16 generations for his genealogy back to Aaron, a period of 1,000 years, which calls for at least twice that many, and Matt. 1:8 lists "Ozias" as son of "Joram," but from both II Kings and II Chronicles we know that Ahaziah, Joash, and Amaziah intervened.

[14] Further evidence may be taken from Num. 3:27-28, which shows that the Amram of Ex. 6:20, indicated as the father of Moses, cannot have been the Amram of Ex. 6:18, indicated as the son of Kohath, which this reasoning assumes. This passage indicates that Kohath's descendants, divided into four groups (Amramites, Izeharites, Hebronites, and Uzzielites), numbered no less than 8,600 men and boys by the time of Moses. About one-fourth would have descended from Amram, or 2,150, which means that Moses would have had this many immediate brothers and nephews, which is impossible. In other words, a period of no less than 430 years is called for to account for this extent of growth.

b. Church fathers. Sometimes early church fathers, like Tertullian,[15] are quoted in support of the 215 year position. However, another, Hippolytus,[16] favored 430 years. Josephus speaks in one place as though he held to 215 years[17] and in another as though he held to 430.[18] All that is established by such quotations is that both views were held in the early church, even as now. The reason for both views existing then is probably to be found in the variant reading of Exodus 12:40 in the Septuagint, the Greek Bible of the day.

c. Galatians 3:17. The strongest evidence for the 215-year position is taken from Galatians 3:17, where Paul says, "A covenant confirmed beforehand by God, the law, which came four hundred and thirty years after, doth not disannul, so as to make the promise of none effect." Paul has been speaking in prior verses of the covenant given to Abraham, and seems to say here that the Law came 430 years later. Since the promises of that covenant were given to Abraham first at his entry into Canaan (Gen. 12:1-3), which was 215 years before Jacob took his family to Egypt, it would appear that the actual time in Egypt could only have been the remaining 215 years. It is often pointed out as well that Paul was likely referring here to the Septuagint reading of Exodus 12:40, and so in this indirect way showing his approval of it.

It should be brought to mind, however, that Paul, while familiar with the Septuagint, would also have known the Hebrew text. He had been educated in the rabbinical schools of Jerusalem. This means that he would have known the chronological difference involved with the reading of the two texts. Therefore, any figure employed by him, whether 430 or 645 (430 plus 215), would have been well pondered and the result of careful choice.

Factors influencing that choice certainly would have included the following. First, Paul's main point was not one in chronology. It was that the Law could not disannul the covenant given many years prior

[15] Tertullian writes, "For thus, after the above mentioned patriarchs, was the law given to Moses, at that well known time after their exode from Egypt, after the interval and space of four hundred years. In fact it was after Abraham's 'four hundred and thirty years' that the law was given"; "An answer to the Jews," *Ante-Nicene Fathers*, III, p. 153.

[16] Hippolytus says, "That means that they may be slaves to the nations, not four hundred and thirty years as in Egypt, nor seventy as in Babylon, . . ."; "Expository Treatise Against the Jews," *Ante-Nicene Fathers*, IV, p. 220.

[17] Josephus says, "They left Egypt . . . four hundred and thirty years after our forefathers Abraham came into Canaan, but two hundred and fifteen years only after Jacob removed in Egypt," *Antiquities*, II, xv, 2.

[18] He says again, "And four hundred years did they spend under these afflictions; for they strove one against the other which should get the mastery, the Egyptians desiring to destroy the Israelites by these labors, and the Israelites desiring to hold out to the end under them," *Antiquities*, II, ix, 1.

to it. Really, the number of those years, so long as it was large, was quite unimportant. Paul included a specific number likely because this made his argument more concrete. Second, there was reason to employ a number which would bring the least chance of detracting readers from the main point, and to use 645 could do this for those who knew only the Septuagint. And third, the covenant had been given not only to Abraham, but repeated to Isaac and even Jacob,[19] the last time, indeed, just before Jacob moved down to Egypt (Gen. 46:1-4). This made any chronological conclusion by Paul's readers necessarily indefinite, and allowed him to use a figure that would at the same time not be detracting and yet historically accurate.

B. DATE OF THE EXODUS[20]

The former discussion of Abraham's date set forth the year c. 1446 B.C. as the date of the Exodus. The main reasons favoring this early date were cited without discussion or consideration of arguments set forth by adherents of the late date, of approximately two centuries following.[21]

1. Direct biblical evidence

a. I Kings 6:1. The first reason listed for the early date is the statement of I Kings 6:1 that the Exodus preceded the time when Solomon began to build the Temple (c. 966 B.C.) by 480 years. Adding 480 years to 966 B.C. gives the date 1446 B.C. To offset this evidence, adherents of the late date assert that the number 480, being the twelfth multiple of forty (forty is said to represent a generation[22]), is indicative of twelve generations,[23] and that, since a generation was really much less than forty years, one is justified in reducing 480 by as much as 200 years,[24] bringing it into agreement with the late date.

[19] Significantly, in the prior verse, Gal. 3:16, Paul speaks of the promises having been made not only to Abraham but to "his seed"; cf. Ps. 105: 9, 10. M. Kline, "Law Covenant," WTJ, 27(1964), p. 7, n. 11, holds a similar view.

[20] Material here contained is largely dependent on a paper read at the annual meeting of the Evangelical Theological Society, December 26-28, 1968.

[21] Supra, chap. 2, pp. 31-32.

[22] This is argued from the many times that the number 40 is used in the Old Testament. For instance, Israel was 40 years in the wilderness, Moses was 40 years old when he fled to Midian and then remained there for 40 years, Saul ruled 40 years, and so did both David and Solomon. However, many other numbers appear along with these and in parallel with them which argues that these, too, must be taken as exact numbers.

[23] Cf. Finegan, LAP, p. 121; Wright, BAR, pp. 84-85.

[24] The exact amount of reduction varies with the date for the Exodus respectively favored. Most late date scholars favor a time in the early part of the reign of Rameses II (1304-1238), but H. H. Rowley, for instance, favors c. 1225 B.C.; cf. supra, chap. 2, p. 31, n. 22 for references.

This explanation, however, must be rejected by one who holds to a high view of inspiration. The text in no way states or implies the thought of twelve generations. It refers merely to the definite number 480, which means that any idea of generations must be read into the text. One is minded to say that if this plain number can be reduced so drastically by this manner of analysis, then many other biblical numbers can be similarly adjusted by parallel methods, making Scriptural numbers very uncertain indeed.

b. Jephthah's statement. The second reason listed is that Jephthah speaks of Israel as having possessed the land of Palestine by his day for a period of 300 years (Judg. 11:26).[25] Jephthah was the eighth judge of Israel. Following him came four other judges,[26] Samuel's time of leadership, the kingships of Saul and David, and four years of Solomon's reign, all prior to the beginning of the building of the Temple. The total years represented by these successive leaders[27] must be added to the date c. 966 B.C., when the construction of the Temple began, to arrive at Jephthah's date. This works out to approximately 1100 B.C., which is just 300 years after 1400 B.C., the time of the conquest on the basis of the early date. There is simply no way to harmonize Jephthah's statement with the late date, apart from a denial of its historical accuracy.

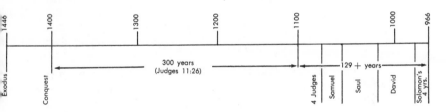

c. Length of the Judges Period. The third reason listed is that an analysis of the length of the Judges Period requires a total time longer

[25] His words are, "While Israel dwelt in Heshbon and its towns, and in Aroer and its towns, and in all the cities that are along by the side of the Arnon, three hundred years."

[26] Cf. Judg. 12:8-15, listing Ibzan for 7 years, Elon 10 years, and Abdon 8 years. After this came Samson for 20 years (Judg. 16:31), but he was contemporary with Samuel.

[27] The reigns of Saul, David, and four years of Solomon add to 84 years. Samuel's time (Samson contemporary) may be figured as about 25 years (cf. chap. 9, p. 231, n. 93). The three judges overlap, but their years plus Jephthah's six, after he made the statement, add to more than 20 (cf. chap. 9, p. 222, n. 63; p. 225, n. 72), making a total of more than 129. Cf. chap. 9, p. 222 for suggested exact date of 1096 B.C.

than possible with the late date. The Judges Period occupied a major part of the time between the Exodus and the establishment of Israel's monarchy in c. 1050 B.C., but not all. Not included were the years of the wilderness journey, of Joshua's leadership, and of the period between Samson's demise and Saul's inauguration: totalling about sixty-one. Therefore, between the date of the Exodus and 1050 B.C., enough time must be allowed for both these sixty-one years and the Judges Period. On the basis of the early date, this leaves about three and one-third centuries for the Judges Period,[28] but, with the late date, less than a century and a half. Admittedly, some overlapping of judgeships and times of rest existed in the period, but only enough to suit the three-century allotted time of the early date.[29] Again there seems to be no way to harmonize the late date and the biblical indication of the length of this period.

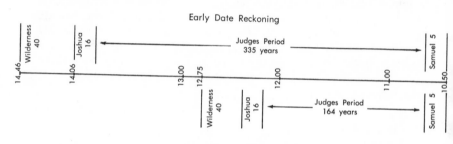

d. Historical correlations. The fourth reason listed concerns a better correlation between the events of Scripture and Egyptian history on the basis of the early date. The biblical story of the Exodus fits Egyptian history well if the Exodus transpired in the fifteenth century, but not if in the thirteenth. Two aspects of the story call for particular notice.

One concerns the order by an Egyptian Pharaoh for the building of Pithom and Raamses (Ex. 1:11) by enslaved Israelites. Late date adherents commonly identify Rameses II (1304-1238)[30] as both the one

---

[28] From 1446 B.C. to 1050 B.C. is 396 years, less 61 leaves 335. For greater detail, cf. infra, chap. 9, pp. 211-31.

[29] When added together, all the judgeships and periods of rest of the Judges Period total 410 years, which is 75 more than the 335 available even on the early date basis. Cf. infra, chap. 9, p. 207 for discussion of hints in the book of Judges itself that overlapping existed.

[30] The date of Rameses II is determinative for the 18th and 19th dynasties. From the mention of a new moon in his 52nd year, astronomical calculations make his accession year either 1304 or 1290 B.C. In an article, "Comparative Chronology at the Time of Dynasty XIX," JNES, 19 (Jan., 1960), pp. 15-22,

who gave the order[31] and the Pharaoh of the Exodus. But if he were, then the order could not have preceded the Exodus by more than a few years, thirty at the most.[32] The biblical account, however, implies a much longer time. The mention of the order falls in a context showing that it was part of Egypt's initial afflictions of the Israelites.[33] It was following this order that other methods for curtailing their population growth were taken: first ordering Hebrew midwives to kill Hebrew male babies (Ex. 1:15-21) and later directing that all Hebrew male children be cast into the Nile (Ex. 1:22). Then to the years implied for these measures must be added eighty more, for Moses was only born at the time of the last directive and he was that old by the time of the Exodus. The total number of years implied is in keeping with the conclusion made in chapter two,[34] that the Pharaoh who gave the order to build these two cities was the first of the Hyksos about 1730 B.C., but not with any suggestion of late date adherents.

The other aspect concerns the identity of the king who died while Moses was in Midian (Ex. 2:23-25). The rationale for the mention of his death in the biblical record is that the death made possible Moses' return to Egypt, which strongly suggests that the one who died was the same as the one from whom Moses fled forty years before (Ex. 2:15). Whenever the Exodus occurred, then, a Pharaoh who had ruled at least forty years must have just died. On the basis of the early date, such a death had just occurred; namely of Thutmose III, who died in 1450 B.C., just four years before our accepted date for the Exodus of

M. B. Rowton reverses his former opinion in favor of the earlier year. E. Hornung, *Untersuchungen zur Chronologie and Geshichte des Neuen Reiches*, 1964, however, still argues for the later. Herein, dates in keeping with the earlier year are followed.

[31] Sometimes Seti I (1316-1304), predecessor of Rameses II, is suggested as the one who gave the order, but still this does not allow enough time as indicated.

[32] Most late adherents place the Exodus no later than c. 1275 B.C. Merneptah (1238-1228), successor of Rameses II, defeated Israelites in Canaan (cf. Kitchen, *AOOT*, 1966, pp. 59-60 for good discussion of evidence) which means the Exodus had to precede this time by at least the 40 years of the wilderness wanderings.

[33] Kitchen, *AOOT*, p. 57, n. 3, defending the late date, argues that Ex. 1:7-14 provides merely a general summary of Egypt's total oppression of Israel, so that events listed later need not be taken as necessarily having followed chronologically. He believes the very fact that the Pithom and Raamses matter is mentioned at all argues that it came last when it would have been best remembered. However, two questions come quickly to mind on this basis. Why, if Ex. 1:7-14 is such a general summary, was the specific matter of Pithom and Raamses mentioned within it when other events are listed later? And why, if the Pithom and Raamses matter came last in the over-all story, was its mention made rather early in the summary rather than last where one would expect it?

[34] *Supra*, chap. 2, pp. 35-38.

1446 B.C. Also, he had ruled alone since 1482 B.C., and before this jointly with his famous aunt-stepmother Hatshepsut (1504-1482),[35] long enough to be the one from whom Moses had fled. For the late date, however, there is no death of a long ruling Pharaoh which fits. Seti I (1316-1304) was the ruler who immediately preceded Rameses II, but he reigned only twelve years. Furthermore, late date adherents normally place the Exodus well into the reign of Rameses II,[36] which locates the death of Seti I too many years prior to the Exodus to suit the rationale for the reference of Exodus 2:23. At one time, late date adherents identified the successor of Rameses II, Merneptah (1238-1228), as the Exodus Pharaoh, thus making Rameses II as the one who died permitting Moses to return to Egypt, and Rameses II did rule long enough to qualify as the one from whom Moses could have fled. Very few make this identification today, however, due to the discovery of the so-called "Israel Stele" which commemorates a victory by Merneptah in his fifth year (c. 1234 B.C.) over the Libyans, and lists places and peoples in the Canaan region, significantly including Israel, claimed by Merneptah as conquered.[37] If Israel was defeated by Merneptah in Canaan, she must have left Egypt at least forty years before.[38]

2. *Extra-biblical considerations.* Numerous scholars believe that matters thus far discussed, all involving direct biblical evidence, are sufficient to settle the question in favor of the early date, in view of the Bible's authority and the clarity of the evidence given. However, there are other matters, more extra-biblical in nature, which have bearing and must be considered. Among these are items which other scholars present as evidence for the late date.

a. Pithom and Raamses. The first we notice concerns further the matter of Pithom and Raamses being built by enslaved Israelites. In spite of the chronological difficulty in harmonizing the biblical statements with Egyptian history in the thirteenth century, as just seen, many late date adherents find evidence for their position from this building order of Exodus 1:11. It is pointed out that at Pithom, gen-

[35] This most unusual person was likely the Pharaoh's daughter who found Moses in the Nile and adopted him; cf. *infra.*, chap. 6, pp. 117-20 for discussion regarding her and the nature of the joint rule between herself and the younger Thutmose III.

[36] If Rameses II was the one who gave the order for Pithom and Raamses to be built, as commonly held, there is need to put several years between this order and the actual Exodus.

[37] Found in Merneptah's mortuary temple at Thebes. The stele has 28 lines of closely spaced writing. Cf. *supra*, p. 91, n. 32.

[38] Israel was 40 years in the wilderness. By greatly reducing this 40 year time, however, Rowley still finds place for the Exodus under Merneptah; *From Joseph to Joshua* (London: Oxford University Press, 1950), pp. 133f. This suggestion is correctly rejected by most scholars.

erally identified today with Tell er-Retabeh,[39] the oldest royal building uncovered was a temple claimed to have been built by Rameses II. Hence, if the Israelites built for royalty in this city, it could not have been earlier than his time.[40] Then it is pointed out that it was this same ruler who gave the name Pi-Ramesse (House of Rameses) to the old Hyksos' capital Avaris; and so, since Exodus 1:11 uses the name Raamses for the city ordered built by the Pharaoh, this one must have been Rameses II.

This is impressive evidence, not so much respecting Pithom, the identification of which with Tell er-Retabeh is not certain, but with Raamses. For wherever the site of the ancient Hyksos capital Avaris,[41] Rameses II seems to be the ruler who first named it Pi-Ramesse, and at this time there does not appear to be any other old Egyptian city called Raamses to correspond to the mention of Exodus 1:11.

The most likely explanation[42] is that the name Raamses had already been used by the Hyksos kings many years before the Nineteenth Dynasty.[43] It has been shown earlier[44] that the Hyksos were the likely ones to have forced the Israelites to build Pithom and Raamses. Several matters make their use of the term highly plausible; matters which show ties between the Nineteenth Dynasty and these earlier rulers. For instance, it is known that the Nineteenth Dynasty traced its ancestry back to the Hyksos line.[45] Then, as indicated earlier, the old Hyksos city Avaris was once again made capital in the North by the Nineteenth Dynasty.

[39] In 1883 the Swiss archaeologist Naville suggested that Tell el-Mashkuta (also in wadi Tumelat, six miles east of Tell er-Retabeh) was Pithom. Naville found the word, Pi-Tum meaning ".House of the god Tum," on certain inscriptions there. General acceptance, however, has now switched to Tell er-Retabeh.

[40] Wright, BAR, p. 58.

[41] Cf. supra, chap. 2, p. 35, n. 40.

[42] M. Unger's explanation is that the name is "a modernization of an archaic place name" by a later writer (AOT, p. 149). This writer wanted to make the original name more easily identified by later readers. However, this explanation, though possible, fits the rationale for change in Exodus 1:11 better than for a similar use of the name in Gen. 47:11, where the phrase "land of Rameses" is used for the area still better known as Goshen.

[43] Held by J. Rea, "The Time of the Oppression and the Exodus," BETS, 3(Summer, 1960), p. 63, and G. Archer, SOTI, pp. 207-208.

[44] Supra, chap. 2, pp. 35-38. Note that Gen. 47:11 gives evidence that the term Rameses was used in the Goshen area even before the Hyksos time.

[45] Albright, FSAC, p. 223, writes, "The Ramesside house actually traced its ancestry back to a Hyksos king whose era was fixed 400 years before the date commemorated in the '400-year Stele' of Tanis. The great-grandfather of Rameses II evidently came from an old Tanite family, very possibly of Hyksos origin, since his name was Sethos (Suta) . . . Rameses II established his capital and residence at Tanis . . . where he built a great temple to the old Tanite, later Hyksos, god Seth."

Further, Rameses II built there a temple to the Hyksos deity Seth, adopted as deity earlier by the Hyksos from the Egyptians. Still further, the father of Rameses II took his official name from this Hyksos deity, calling himself Seti I. It is in keeping too that the name Raamses (Egyptian, *Ra'amessu*), meaning "begotten of Ra," was a suitable Hyksos name since the Hyksos recognized the god Ra as well as Seth, as is evidenced by the occurrence of the element Ra in various Hyksos personal names.[46] If one of the Nineteenth Dynasty took his royal name from the Hyksos god Seth, then another might have taken his from the Hyksos god Ra; and, more significant, the name Raamses might have been used for the capital city at the earlier time as well as later.

b. Jericho. Another matter concerns the date of Jericho's fall. At one time a majority of scholars believed that evidence from Jericho favored the early date of the Exodus. The same is not true today, but it may be that the evidence has been too easily dismissed. There is need to consider the matter with some care.

i. Conclusions of John Garstang. John Garstang, while professor at the University of Liverpool, directed an expedition for the Institute of Archaeology of the University to excavate old Jericho (Tell es Sultan), working from 1930 to 1936. His principal conclusions were as follows:[47] first, that Jericho fell to Joshua during the reign of Amenhotep III (1414-1378), since both pottery and scarabs were found still existing for his time but none for that of his successor, Akhenaton; second, that a small amount of pottery found in one lone building dating toward the close of the fourteenth century was from the brief occupation of Eglon, king of Moab (Judg. 3:12-14), a view supported by the fact that none of this same pottery was found in the tombs nearby, showing that whoever lived there at the time did not bury in Jericho's cemetery; and third, that a few pieces of still later pottery (including imitation Mycenaean), dating to Late Bronze II and Early Iron I, were from a few sporadic residents, since the pieces were so few in number, intrusive in nature, and appeared in only two of forty-three tombs examined, with none from the tell itself.

For several years scholars accepted Garstang's conclusions.[48] Grad-

---

[46] The name "Rameses" for an Egyptian male has actually been found on a tomb painting at Thebes from the time of Amenhotep III (14th c.); *The World of the Bible* (Yonkers, N.Y.: Educational Heritage Inc., 1964), III, pp. 118-119.

[47] John Garstang and J.B.E. Garstang, *The Story of Jericho* (2d ed.; Marshall, Morgan & Scott, Ltd., 1948), see especially pp. 120-29, 177-80.

[48] For instance, Albright did; cf. his *The Archaeology of Palestine and the Bible* (New York: Fleming H. Revell Co., 1933), p. 234; or F. Kenyon, father of K. Kenyon, *The Bible and Archaeology* (New York: Harper & Bros., 1949), p. 189.

ually, however, doubt arose,[49] not because of declining value in the Jericho evidence, but because Garstang's date for Jericho's fall did not agree with evidence arising that other cities taken by Joshua showed a layer of destruction dating nearly two centuries later.[50] It was believed that the two areas of evidence should agree, and desire existed to have more work done at Jericho.

ii. Excavations and conclusions of Kathleen Kenyon. Miss Kathleen Kenyon of the British School of Archaeology now headed an expedition to Jericho, excavating from 1952 to 1958.[51] But, though her effort was rewarding relative to early Jericho, she found little to add to Garstang's evidence regarding Joshua's Jericho.[52] Her interpretation of the evidence was quite different, however, concluding: (1) that Garstang's well-known "double-wall,"[53] which he believed was the wall which fell before Joshua, was not a double wall at all, but two separate walls, dating at different times and both more than 500 years before Joshua;[54] (2) that the city mound was severely denuded of all remains of Late Bronze occupancy (i.e. after 1500 B.C.), except on the mound "above the spring," which, she believed, minimizes the strength of evidence regarding this period;[55] (3) that the pottery, found by Garstang either on this portion of the mound or else in tombs, which he said was continuous into the reign of Amenhotep III at 1400 B.C., actually ceased with Middle Bronze II probably about 1550 B.C.; meaning that a layer of ash found by Garstang in connection with this pottery does not represent Joshua's destruction, but probably one effected by Egyptians shortly after the Hyksos expulsion;[56] (4) that the few pottery pieces Garstang found in the lone building above the spring,[57]

---

[49] Aware of this doubt, Garstang writes in the preface of the second edition of *The Story of Jericho;* "We are aware that varying opinions have appeared in print which conflict with our interpretation," but he continues to say that he has found no evidence to change his former views.

[50] For discussion regarding these other cities, cf. *infra,* pp. 99-101.

[51] Admittedly undertaken, in large part, to clear up this seeming conflict; cf. A. Tushingham, *BA,* 16(Sept., 1953), pp. 49-60.

[52] Kenyon, *Digging Up Jericho* (New York: Frederick A. Praeger, 1957), pp. 51-102. Her reports appeared in *PEQ,* 1952, pp. 62-82; 1954, pp. 81-95; 1954, pp. 45-63; 1955, pp. 108-117; 1956, pp. 67-82.

[53] Garstang believed that he had located a double wall as that which fell when Joshua destroyed the city. Though this wall really did not enter into his evidence for Jericho's date of fall, he made quite a little of it, and Miss Kenyon reacts in stressing his apparent error.

[54] Garstang, *op. cit.,* pp. 112-14; Kenyon, *op. cit.,* pp. 45-46.

[55] Kenyon, *ibid.,* pp. 44-47; 261-62. This denudation was due to the mound lying unoccupied from Joshua's destruction to the time of Ahab (I Kings 16:34; cf. Josh. 6:26).

[56] Kenyon, *ibid.,* p. 229.

[57] Kenyon found one more in a room of a house nearby; cf. *ibid.,* p. 261.

which he ascribed to the occupation of Eglon, king of Moab, are actually the only evidence of the city Joshua devastated; a city, then, apparently small and destroyed c. 1325 B.C.;[58] and (5) that the few pottery pieces Garstang found in two tombs are of the same date as the pottery of the city Joshua overthrew and not of Late Bronze II and Early Iron I as Garstang thought.

Notice should be taken that, though these conclusions do not agree with Garstang's view, neither do they support the position of late date adherents. Their thinking has been that, since at least some habitation existed at Jericho for the fourteenth century, of which a little evidence remains, there could have been a city there which Joshua destroyed also in the thirteenth century, even though almost no evidence remains.[59] But Miss Kenyon's view is that "the latest Bronze Age occupation" must be dated "to the third quarter of the fourteenth century";[60] and, speaking directly regarding the thirteenth-century position, she says, "It is impossible to associate the destruction of Jericho with such a date."[61]

iii. Evaluation. With the evidence and conclusions of both archaeologists before us, an evaluation is called for. First, as to items (1) and (2) of Miss Kenyon's conclusions, she is certainly correct. The evidence she gathered regarding the "double wall" is convincing that Garstang was wrong. It is true also that the city mound was severely denuded. However, neither item makes any difference as to Garstang's real evidence. The section of the wrongly dated wall found is well removed from the area where he located his significant material. Also, Garstang realized too, as did Miss Kenyon, that the city mound was denuded, though he did not make as much of it. Both based their conclusions on materials found on the mound above the spring.

As to item (5), Miss Kenyon conflicts with late date adherents more than with Garstang; for, in assigning the few pottery pieces, found by Garstang in only two of forty-three tombs, to the fourteenth century, she removed the only evidence they had for a thirteenth-century city.

As to item (4), it may be fairly stated that the explanation of Garstang fits the evidence measurably better than that of Miss Kenyon. This item concerns the several pottery pieces found mainly by Garstang in or near the lone building above the spring. Both Garstang and Miss Kenyon date these pieces to the latter half of the fourteenth

58 Kenyon, *ibid.*, p. 262.
59 For instance, Finegan, *LAP*, p. 159. K. Kitchen indeed argues, following Albright, *BP*, p. 100, n. 59, "Positive evidence that a settlement existed in the thirteenth century B.C. comes from the tombs, these yielding Mycenaean pottery and imitations of such"; *AOOT*, p. 63, n. 22.
60 Kenyon, *op. cit.*, p. 262.
61 "Jericho," *AOTS*, p. 273.

century;[62] but Miss Kenyon believes they represent the city of Joshua's destruction, while Garstang attributes them to the temporary occupancy of Eglon, king of Moab. Miss Kenyon's reason is only that this is the one occupancy that can date to Joshua's time, the former one having closed at c. 1550 B.C., with a long gap intervening. She admits that the idea of a small (apparently wall-less) city for the time is out of keeping with the biblical story, but argues that evidence for the city having been larger and walled may have simply washed away in the general denudation. Garstang's explanation, however, fits well. That the city was small fits, for Eglon, occupying Jericho only temporarily, would not have rebuilt extensively; and that none of the pottery, found in the city, was located in the tombs also fits, for Eglon, being king of Moab, would not have buried at Jericho.

The most significant item is (3). This concerns the extensive pottery[63] found on both the mound above the spring and in the tombs which Gartsang contends represents occupancy until c. 1400 B.C., but which Miss Kenyon says terminated before 1500 B.C. A thick burned layer of ash lies below this pottery representing a major destruction, which Garstang takes as the destruction of Joshua, while Miss Kenyon ascribes it to Egyptians. She defends her view on the basis that Late Bronze I pottery is better known now than when Garstang made his evaluation, particularly since the publication of the Megiddo excavations.[64]

Garstang did not change his position, however, in view of Megiddo,[65] and with seemingly adequate reason. For one thing, along with the pottery he had dated to c. 1400 B.C., he had found scarabs, and these dated to, and ended with, the reign of Amenhotep III at c. 1400 B.C. Of these Miss Kenyon only remarks that scarabs are not safe as evidence for dating, for they "are the sort of thing liable to be heirlooms."[66] Though one would not disagree with this statement generally speaking, one cannot help but wonder at the remarkable coincidence of these scarabs ceasing exactly at the time of Jericho's fall on the early date basis. Furthermore, if they were heirlooms, they would have had

[62] It is noteworthy that both Albright and Wright agree with this dating; cf. Wright, *BAR*, p. 79.

[63] In contrast to only eight pieces dating, according to Garstang, to LB II or EI I, Garstang identifies 320 pieces for this time (also 419 to MB III and 1012 to MB II); Garstang, *op. cit.*, p. 128 and 129, n. 3.

[64] Kenyon, *op. cit.*, p. 260; cf. her *Archaeology in the Holy Land* (New York: Frederick A. Praeger, 1960), p. 198.

[65] Garstang, *op. cit.*, preface, p. xiv, written in 1947, eight years after completion of work at Megiddo.

[66] Kenyon, *Digging Up Jericho* (New York: Frederick A. Praeger, 1957), p. 260.

to be this sometime after c. 1400 B.C., and those found seem to appear in context only with pre-1400 B.C. pottery.[67]

Another aspect of evidence presented by Garstang, which appears as valid as ever, concerns imported Cypriot pottery, especially well-known wishbone milk bowls and pipe-necked bilbils found as part of the pottery he dates to c. 1400 B.C. At Megiddo, the site Miss Kenyon believes is determinative, the same were found in Levels X to VII, with the major number in Levels VIII and VII which date 1479 to 1150 B.C.[68] Since Jericho was well inland, in contrast to Megiddo, it is to be expected that this imported ware would have reached Jericho later than Megiddo and quite possibly only after it had become plentiful there, which means after 1479 B.C.[69] If so, it supplies significant evidence that this pottery context did indeed extend to c. 1400 B.C.[70] And

[67] Garstang reports none with the small amount of pottery from the fourteenth and thirteenth centuries, and Miss Kenyon states that she found nothing in tombs she excavated after "the end of the Middle Bronze Age," *op. cit.*, p. 260, and only one pottery piece on the mound, *ibid.*, p. 261.

[68] Cf. G. Loud, *Megiddo II: Seasons of 1935–39*, Vol. Plates (University of Chicago Press, 1948), plates 45, 54, 58, 61, 65, 69, 72, 130, 133-34, 137-141. Garstang includes a picture of the four principal types he found, *op. cit.*, p. 121.

[69] Kenyon herself states, "Cypriot imports during the Middle Bronze Age are rare. . . . But in the transitional period covered by Megiddo IX they become much more numerous, until during the Late Bronze Age almost as much pottery of Cypriot connections is found as that in the native tradition"; *Archaeology in the Holy Land*, p. 200.

[70] The particular type of pottery lacking at Jericho, on which Miss Kenyon seems to base her conclusion mainly, is a bichrome ware using red and black geometric lines enclosing stylized figures of fish, birds, and animals (cf. Epstein, Palestinian Bichrome Ware, Leiden, Brill, 1966). The pottery is attractive, distinctive, and attributed by some to the genius of an itinerant artist (Cf., Kenyon, *op, cit.*, p. 200; Thomas, *AOTS*, p. 317; Epstein, however, arguing for its introduction to Palestine by the Hurrian migration). Found in both north and south Palestine, it is commonly taken as marking the transition point between MB and LB periods. However, the use of this pottery was really quite limited, which gives reason to doubt that simply because it is lacking at Jericho, one may conclude that Jericho was then uninhabited. Its duration is generally agreed not to have exceeded a century (c. 1575-1475 B.C.), and its extent of coverage was not over all the land. It seems to have spread out from Megiddo east in the Esdraelon Valley to Ta'anach and north to Hazor, in respect to the North; and from Tell el-'Ajjul to numerous sites but only as far east as the foothills of Judah, in the South. It has not been found in the mountain region of central Palestine, nor in the Jordan Valley (cf. Epstein's map, *ibid.*, facing p. 188). It should be noted also that numerous sites in the areas where it has not been found have been worked sufficiently to show it, if there. Even Bethshan, located on the quite accessible crossroad of the Esdraelon and Jordan Valleys, though still 50 miles north of Jericho, has revealed no bichrome ware proper, and the uninterrupted occupancy of Bethshan during this time is generally asserted (Epstein, *ibid.*, p. 118).

if this is true, the layer of ash below this pottery may fairly be attributed to the thorough burning of the city by Joshua (Josh. 6:24).

c. Lachish, Debir, and Hazor. Since scholars have been reluctant to accept the date of c. 1400 B.C. for Jericho's fall, due in substantial part to alleged conflicting evidence regarding the dates for the destruction of other cities captured by Joshua, it is well now to turn our attention to this matter. Three principal cities are involved: Lachish, Debir, and Hazor.[71] Lachish and Debir were captured by Joshua in his southern campaign (Josh. 10:32, 38, 39) and Hazor in his northern (Josh. 11:10).

i. A thirteenth-century destruction. Lachish has been well identified with modern Tell ed-Duweir.[72] Besides scarabs from Amenhotep III and Rameses II, also found here was a broken bowl generally accepted as dating to the "year four" of Merneptah (1238-1228), successor of Rameses II. The fragments of the bowl were discovered in a burned layer of destruction, and particularly date this layer to the latter half of the thirteenth century.[73] Debir (Kiriath-sepher, Josh. 15:15) is thought to be modern Tell Beit Mirsim,[74] though without conclusive or unchallenged evidence. A burned layer of destruction was found also

[71] Bethel and Eglon are commonly included in this list (cf. Wright, BAR, pp. 80-85). Evidence respecting Bethel, however, is largely dependent on identifying it as the city captured by Joshua in Josh. 8, rather than Ai. But this is doubtful (as an answer to the problem of Ai) if only because Josh. 7:2 says specifically that Ai, as attacked by Israel, lay "on the east side of Bethel." Thus the burned layer at Bethel, dating to the thirteenth century could well represent only its capture by the "house of Joseph" (Judg. 1:22-25). Also, Bethel's pottery, being superior to that of Lachish and Debir at the time of destruction, suggests a different date for Bethel's fall. It should also be added that Bethel's identification with Tell Beitin is now being challenged. Eglon suffers in evidential value both because its identification with Tell el-Hesy is not certain and because the evidence for the date of destruction of this Tell, excavated already in the last century by Petrie and Bliss, is not clearly determinative.

[72] Excavated 1932-38 by the Wellcome-Marston Archaeological Expedition led by J. L. Starkey. Lachish was formerly thought to be Tell el-Hesy. H. Torczyner, Lachish I; The Lachish Letters, 1935; O. Tufnell, et al., Lachish II: The Fosse Temple, 1940; Lachish III: The Iron Age, 1953; Lachish IV: The Bronze Age, 1957.

[73] Cf. J. Finegan, LAP, pp. 161-63. A scarab of Rameses III (1195-1164) found there, however, has suggested a date even in the twelfth century which does not fit the late date view so well; cf. O. Tuffnel, Lachish IV, p. 97, and her article, "Lachish," AOTS, p. 302.

[74] Excavated in 1926 and following years by a joint effort of the Pittsburgh-Xenia Theological Seminary and the American School of Oriental Research, M. G. Kyle and W. F. Albright directors. It is located twelve miles southwest of Hebron. Cf. Kyle, Excavating Kiriath-Sepher's Ten Cities, 1934; Albright, AASOR, 12 (1930-31); 17 (1936-37); 21-22 (1941-43); and Albright, "Debir," in Thomas, AOTS, pp. 207-19 for recent treatment.

here, and it is dated to the same general time since it was found at the cessation point of Late Bronze material.[75] Neither Tell ed-Duweir nor Tell Beit Mirsim show a similar burned layer for c. 1400 B.C.[76]

Hazor has been well identified with Tell el-Qeday, nine miles north of the Sea of Galilee.[77] The site boasts an oval-shaped tell of about twenty-five acres and a much larger plateau next to it of about one hundred seventy-five acres, indicating that Hazor was by far the largest city of ancient Palestine.[78] There is evidence of violent destruction sometime in the thirteenth century, so that nearly all habitation ceased on the plateau, and life on the main tell was able to continue only in a poor and modest way. Such a change in living pattern speaks of a major defeat, and late date adherents take the enemy to have been Israel, thus linking the date of Hazor's destruction with that of Lachish and Debir. Once more an exact time in the thirteenth century for the destruction cannot be determined, but a date is assumed which fits the Lachish information. Some observations regarding this evidence are pertinent.

ii. Earlier burning at Hazor. First concerning Hazor, Yadin found no indication of burning regarding the destruction of the thirteenth century (Stratum I on the plateau), whereas Joshua 11:11 states definitely that the city destroyed by Joshua was burned. However, at Stratum III below, Yadin did find evidence of burning, stating that this level "was effectively destroyed by fire, most probably by one of the Egyptian Pharaohs of the New Kingdom, Amenophis II or more probably Thutmose III."[79] Since it is at this level where burning is indicated, and since a destruction by Amenhotep II or Thutmose III[80] is less than half a century prior to the early date time for Joshua's destruction, the suggestion is in order that this city of Stratum III was really the one Joshua destroyed and not that of thirteenth-century Stratum I. In keeping, too, is the fact that Hazor still appears strong at the time of Deb-

[75] The Late Bronze Age closes c. 1200 B.C. However, this city may have lain waste for several years so that it cannot be dated precisely.

[76] Thomas (AOTS, p. 215) believes a non-occupancy period which began c. 1564 B.C. at Tell Beit Mirsim continued after 1400. However, the following C1 level probably began already at 1475 B.C. (cf. Epstein, op. cit., p. 185). Even if not, it is very possible that Tell Beit Mirsim is not ancient Debir (cf. Simons, GTT, p. 282).

[77] Excavation began in 1955 under direction of Yigael Yadin who gives summaries in BA, 19-22(1956-59). As many as 200 laborers and 45 technicians worked on this major project.

[78] This size of 200 acres compares with Lachish at 18 acres, Megiddo at 14, and Jericho at 8.

[79] Yadin, BA (1957), p. 44.

[80] The spelling of names of various Egyptian Pharaohs varies among scholars as indicated in Yadin's quotation.

orah and Barak later in the Judges Period. Though Deborah and Barak fought their battle with Sisera, this man was only a military underling of "Jabin, king of Canaan, that reigned in Hazor" (Judg. 4:2, 17), which means that Hazor was still the leading city of the north. If so, a time for Joshua's destruction well before the thirteenth century, and the condition of semi-demise for Hazor then existent, is far more suitable.[81]

iii. Lachish and Debir not burned by Joshua. Concerning Lachish and Debir, contrary to the case with Hazor, the Bible does not say that these cities were burned by Joshua. This omission cannot be considered insignificant either, for when Joshua did burn cities, as Jericho (Josh. 6:21) and Ai (Josh. 8:28), the fact is mentioned. Further, Joshua 11:13 states specifically that the cities that "stood on their mounds, Israel burned none of these, save Hazor only, that did Joshua burn." Admittedly the primary reference in this passage is to cities of northern Palestine, but there is no reason to think that the general practice differed greatly in the South, and both Lachish and Debir did stand on "mounds." [82] Regarding these cities, it is stated only that Joshua "took" (*lakadh*) them, smiting them with "the edge of the sword," which could well mean merely that the people were thoroughly subdued, without doing great material harm. After all, Israel could use these cities and so reason existed not to destroy more than necessary. The point to notice is that, if Joshua did not burn Lachish and Debir, the burned layers found must represent some other destruction,[83] and the fact that no such layer is found for c. 1400 B.C. is only as should be expected on the early date basis.

[81] K. Kitchen, *AOOT*, pp. 67-68, argues against this conclusion stating that the stress in the biblical account of Deborah and Barak's battle is elsewhere than on Hazor. However, this is because the battle took place elsewhere, namely further south near Megiddo.

[82] The Hebrew word used is the very word, "tell," which has come to be employed as the technical designation for such mounds. O. Tufnell agrees that Israel did not cause the burned layer at Lachish; cf. her "Lachish," *AOTS*, p. 302.

[83] There is no difficulty in finding other possible destroyers. Simply inter-city warfare, known to have been common, could have been responsible. Or Merneptah of Egypt, who campaigned in the area c. 1234 B.C., could have burned both. Or, perhaps even more likely, the Sea Peoples, in their destructive migration, could have done this. These people swept down the eastern Mediterranean coast and destroyed cities from Ugarit to Ashkelon (cf. *supra*, chap. 3, p. 60, n. 45, for references). They moved on to Egypt and there were repulsed, one group by Merneptah in his fifth year (1234 B.C.) and another by Rameses III from his fifth to eleventh years (c. 1190-1184). If these migrating peoples destroyed other coastal cities, why not Lachish and Debir; indeed, why not thirteenth-century Hazor? M. Noth, *NHI*, p. 82, agrees: "These destructions were more probably due, . . . circa 1200 B.C. to the warlike emergence of the 'Sea Peoples' in the regions of the city-states of Palestine."

d. Transjordan evidence. Another reason cited frequently in favor of the late date concerns an alleged absence of sedentary occupation in the Transjordan and Negeb regions between c. 1900 and c. 1300 B.C.[84] Nelson Glueck's presentation of evidence to this effect is well known.[85] The biblical story tells of Israel being refused a travel route through the land of Edom by the king of that country (Num. 20:14-21); of defeating great nations east of the Jordan ruled by the kings, Sihon and Og (Num. 21:21-35); and of being the object of a plot by Balak, king of Moab, who had called for a prophet Balaam to "curse" Israel (Num. 22–25). All these occasions transpired in the Transjordan-Negeb region, which suggests that there was a sedentary habitation there at the time of Israel's wilderness experiences. Glueck and others have concluded from this that Israel, therefore, must have traveled through this region on her way to Palestine sometime after 1300 B.C., when a sedentary occupation did exist.

Concerning this evidence, however, it must be said that Glueck's assertion, regarding absence of settled living conditions in this area, is being challenged today. Scholars have admired the long and painstaking efforts of Glueck, but some have reserved full acceptance of his conclusions since they have been based almost solely on surface exploration. Recently, other discoveries have borne out the wisdom in this reservation. Lancaster Harding, for instance, points out that in the district of Ammon there was sedentary occupation during the Hyksos period, since tombs found there from that time were well stocked with burial objects.[86] He asserts that such tombs "are not the work of nomads." He speaks also of a small temple, found while the Amman airport was being built, which held considerable pottery and other objects, "including much imported Mycenaean and Cypriot pottery and Egyptian stone vases, which are typical of the period 1600 to 1399 B.C." Lastly he notes a large tomb found at Madaba dating from the "end of the Late Bronze to the Early Iron periods." In the light of these items, and others which can be anticipated to be found in view of them,

---

[84] Glueck states that occupation of Transjordan did not start again until "the beginning of Iron Age I"; BA, 18(Feb., 1955), p. 9. Iron Age I is normally dated as beginning c. 1200 B.C. However, Glueck and others regularly use the date c. 1300 B.C. in reference to Transjordan, perhaps because Israelite travel cannot be placed, even on the late date basis, after c. 1250 B.C. Is the archaeological evidence being forced here, however?

[85] Glueck, ibid., pp. 8-9; BA, 10(1947), pp. 77-84; also The Other Side of the Jordan (New Haven: American School of Oriental Research, 1940), pp. 125-47.

[86] The Antiquities of Jordan (New York: Thomas Y. Crowell Co., 1959), p. 17. In defense of his position, Glueck has stated recently that these tombs could still be the work of "nomads and semi-nomads"; "Transjordan," AOTS, p. 444.

Harding suggests that the sherds found in the surface exploration be re-examined, particularly since it is now known that Transjordanian pottery differed somewhat from that in Palestine proper during these "empty" centuries.

e. Egyptian capital location. A further reason cited in favor of the late date concerns the location of the Egyptian capital. During the period of the Eighteenth Dynasty, ruling at the time of the Exodus on the early date basis, the capital was at Thebes, nearly 400 miles south of the Delta. But during the reign of the Nineteenth Dynasty, involved with the late date, a northern capital was established once more at the old Hyksos site, Avaris. Since the biblical story implies that the Pharaoh concerned was near the northern area of Goshen, when Moses was able to make his frequent contacts during the period of the plagues, it is asserted that the capital can only have been in the North at the time and that the general date, then, must have been that of the Nineteenth Dynasty.

However, good evidence exists that, though the Eighteenth Dynasty did maintain its capital in the South, still some of the rulers, particularly Thutmose III and his son, Amenhotep II, the two most concerned in the early date position, did conduct extensive operations in the North and even resided there for substantial periods of time. Speaking first of the father, it is known that he appointed a vizier for the northern area at Heliopolis, beside the vizier who continued at Thebes. This can only mean that he had unusually important interests there, which called for this kind of supervision. Further, Thutmose III had himself called "Lord of Heliopolis," on two red granite obelisks which he erected in the city of Heliopolis,[87] indicating particular attachment for this northern center of Ra worship. Again, a scarab was found stating that his son Amenhotep II was born at Memphis, the ancient northern capital. This is especially significant, for the mother at least must have resided there for several months, and likely the father, too, who would have been interested in the birth of the crown prince. Indeed, that he permitted his son to be born in the ancient capital carries important implications. Lastly, the general fact that Thutmose III campaigned extensively against the Hittites and the kingdom of Mitanni far to the north, a matter well known,[88] argues that he must have maintained substantial supply bases in northern Egypt. These military forays could

[87] Cf. W. C. Hayes, SE, II, p. 118, and John Rea, "The Time of the Oppression and the Exodus," BETS, 3(Summer, 1960), p. 65. One of these obelisks now stands in Central Park, New York City, and the other on the Thames embankment in London.

[88] Thutmose III is considered the greatest of the Egyptian Pharaohs. In 16 campaigns during 18 summers he pushed the Egyptian boundary even across the Euphrates, thus fashioning the Egyptian Empire.

hardly have started from Thebes, far to the south. In fact, they probably constituted a prime cause for the other matters noted. Thutmose III had to maintain a strong interest in the North in order to conduct these ambitious Asiatic endeavors.

As for Amenhotep II, the son, pertinent discoveries were made at Tell Basta, the ancient city of Bubastis (Pi-beseth of Ezek. 30:17) by the Swiss archaeologist Naville, as early as 1887-89. On a red granite slab of two carved panels, this king is shown in worship before Amon-Ra, "he who dwells in Perunefer."[89] Amenhotep II had been appointed as a youth to serve as commandant at Perunefer, a dockyard near Memphis, and there exists evidence that he spent much time there. W. Hayes states that he "seems to have maintained large estates" in the vicinity of Perunefer, where not only he but "his successors appear to have resided for extended periods of time."[90] This is substantiated further by the discovery of a temple which his grandson Amenhotep III had erected at the same site. All of this indicates that Amenhotep II, the Pharaoh of the Exodus on the early date basis, could have been residing in the north at the time Moses needed to contact him relative to the plagues.

f. The Amarna Tablets. Now to be considered is the matter of the Amarna Tablets[91] and their mention of Habiru invading Canaan. This is admittedly a complex question. At one time it was commonly believed that these Tablets constituted good evidence for the early date of the Exodus, but the opinion of many scholars has changed in recent years.

i. The evidence. The Tablets are letters written between c. 1400 and 1367 B.C. to the Egyptian courts of Amenhotep III and of Akhenaton, mostly by Canaanite city-kings. The letters reveal a chaotic condition of plot, counterplot, and contradictory accusations among Canaanite rulers. Particularly pertinent is the frequent mention of trouble from a people called Habiru.[92] Since there is possible equivalency in

[89] John Rea, op. cit., p. 65, who referes to Naville, Bubastis: (London: Kegan Paul, Trench, Trubner & Co., 1891), p. 30.

[90] Op. cit., p. 141.

[91] The first of them were found by an Egyptian peasant woman in 1887, at Tell el-Amarna, Akhenaton's capital. Total collection now numbers 378 of which about 300 were written by Canaanite scribes in Palestine, Phoenicia, and southern Syria. They are written in a conventional vulgar Akkadian filled with Canaanitisms. Cf. S. A. B. Mercer's two-volume work, The Tell el-Amarna Tablets (Toronto, 1939) for full treatment; ANET, pp. 483-90 for translations by Albright and Mendenhall of 28 representative letters; or F. F. Bruce, "Tell el-Amarna," AOTS, for recent brief discussion.

[92] Also called 'Apiru, especially in Canaan, the frequently occurring idiogram, SA.GAZ, being used interchangeably.

name between "Habiru" and "Hebrew" (*'ibri*),[93] and since the disturbances wrought by these people are approximately at the time of the Israelite conquest on the basis of the early date, there is attraction toward identifying these Habiru with Joshua's invading forces.

In recent years, however, this attraction has been measurably reduced by the discovery that Habiru are mentioned also in many other texts, found as far distant as Boghazkoi, Mari, Nuzi, and Babylon, and dating back as early as the Third Dynasty of Ur. Also, scholars have come to recognize more fully that the letters speak of Habiru causing trouble in northern Canaanite cities (where Joshua did not campaign) as well as southern. Still further, it has been learned that the term "Habiru" carried a social and descriptive connotation rather than ethnical: namely, of a person without citizenship, an undesirable, a migrant, even a bandit or raider. As a result, many late date adherents today believe that there is no connection between the Habiru of the Tablets and the Hebrews of Joshua and see no bearing of the letters on the date of the Exodus.

ii. One explanation: Hebrews were Habiru. Numerous early date adherents, however, believe they do still carry evidence. Among these scholars, many directly identify the Habiru with the Hebrews, as formerly commonly held.[94] That is, they identify those Habiru involved in southern Canaan with the Hebrews. Other Habiru in other places and at other times obviously were not; but it is believed that those who invaded southern Canaan could have been, for the disturbed city-kings of that area could have classed Joshua's forces as Habiru in type, since they were without country and seeking to seize Canaanite land. This view considers the Canaanites to have used the name quite as an epithet, a derogatory term, at least at first.[95] Supporting this viewpoint

[93] For discussion on name equivalency and other matters, as well as listing of significant works, cf. M. Greenberg, *The Hab/piru* (New Haven: American Oriental Society, 1955). Cf. also H. H. Rowley, *From Joseph to Joshua* (London: Oxford University Press, 1950), pp. 46-56 for good discussion and many references.

[94] Cf. M. Unger, *AOT*, pp. 124-25, 145-46; also G. Archer, *SOTI*, pp. 164, 214, 253-59. It is believed that this view makes an observation of J. W. Jack, *The Date of the Exodus* (Edinburgh, 1925), p. 128, still pertinent: "Who were these invaders of southern Palestine? . . . Who could they be but the Hebrews of the Exodus, and have we not here the native version of their entry into the land?"

[95] The term is not always used derogatorily, however. At Alalakh, for instance, Habiru held official positions in the city government, and were among the chariot owning *maryannu* (highest warrior class). Abraham was already called a Hebrew (Gen. 14:13) and certainly not derogatorily. The name continued on after the conquest too (I Sam. 4:6, 9; 13:3, 7; 29:3, etc.; though never used frequently) and not with the derogatory connotation. However, the Canaanites could have so used it while being divested of their land.

is the fact that the southern Canaanite Amarna letters were written only from cities late in being captured by Israel, among them Megiddo, Gezer, Ashkelon, and Acco, and not from cities captured early, like Jericho, Bethel, Gibeon, and Hebron. Since the letters date after Joshua's initial conquests, this is the way it would have had to be if the view is correct.[96]

iii. Second explanation: Hebrews preceded the Habiru. There is also a second viewpoint as to a relation between Habiru and the Hebrews, espoused by Meredith Kline.[97] It does not identify the two but places Joshua's conquest just prior to the time of the Habiru notices,[98] rather than many decades later as with the late date view.

Kline argues against identification by showing first that the term "Hebrew" is not used in the Old Testament with a social connotation (true for the term "Habiru"), but ethnical, harking back to Eber, ancestor of Abraham; second, that there is difficulty in etymologically equating the two terms "Habiru" and "Hebrew" (asserted also by numerous late date adherents, though not all); and third, that there are a few difficulties in completely harmonizing the activities of the Habiru in the Amarna letters and those of the Hebrews in Joshua's conquest.

Further, to show that the conquest preceded the Habiru references,

[96] Arguments are raised against this view, but they can be satisfactorily answered. It is asserted (Wright, BAR, pp. 75-76) that the Habiru are represented in the letters as resident within Canaan, often even serving Canaanite princes, whereas the Hebrews were invaders; but, in answer, it should be realized that the Hebrews were already in the land by the time the Amarna letters were written, with Joshua's initial campaigns completed and the various tribes active in occupying their allotted areas. Again, it is pointed out (Finegan, LAP, p. 118) that correspondence from the ruler of Jerusalem, Abdi-Hiba, indicates that Jerusalem was in imminent danger of falling to the Habiru, whereas the city does not appear to have been a real objective of Joshua; but, since Joshua's campaigns were past, the concern of Abdi-Hiba could have been due simply to all the country around Jerusalem having been occupied and his city now having to survive alone. Thirdly, it is commonly argued that the names of persons in the letters do not correspond to those in the text of Joshua, with the king of Jerusalem, for instance, being called Abdi-Hiba and in Joshua 10:3 Adoni-zedec; but it should be realized that Joshua's nomenclature is earlier than that of the letters, and in a troubled time, such as represented in this correspondence, local rulers rise and fall with marked rapidity. It may be added, however, that one correlation in name does exist, namely for Japhia of Josh. 10:3, said to be king of Lachish; and also a letter from Megiddo refers to a Benenima and Yashuya which could be Benjamin and Joshua.

[97] Kline, "The Ha-Bi-Ru — Kin or Foe of Israel? — II," WTJ, 20 (Nov., 1957), pp. 54-61.

[98] If the conquest began in 1406 B.C. (40 years after 1446), it likely was completed in its initial stages by c. 1400 B.C., the date of the first of the Amarna letters. The letters indicate that the main Habiru threat came about two decades later.

Kline develops an attractive historical reconstruction. He states that Joshua's main campaigns had been completed by the time Habiru raiders entered southern Canaan. Then he suggests that these southern raiders were sent by a larger group of Habiru already established in northern Canaan, and that, coming into the South, where Joshua's people had recently arrived, they did not at first take notice of them since they were new and not yet settled. He continues to suggest that later, upon becoming stronger themselves, they did recognize them and then proceeded to force them into subjection, which occasion Kline identifies with Israel's oppression at the hands of Cushan-rishathaim of Mesopotamia (Judg. 3:8-10). This last point lends measurable credence to Kline's view, for otherwise there is real problem in harmonizing this first oppression of Israel with the Habiru mentioned, for they date at the same time.[99]

It is unnecessary to choose which of these two views is best. Perhaps there is more to commend the second at the present time. What is significant is that either view gives a satisfactory explanation in keeping with the early date position. It should be observed further that either position sees the letters as contemporary with Israel's early years in Canaan and finds in them helpful commentary on conditions Israel encountered.

g. Military campaigns of Seti I and Rameses II. The last matter to notice concerns the military campaigns through Palestine by the Egyptian Pharaohs Seti I and Rameses II. Late date adherents argue that, if Israel were in Palestine at the time of these campaigns, which would have been true on the early date basis, the campaigns of each should be mentioned in the book of Judges, a book given largely to military activities; and, since they are not, Israel must not yet have been there.

i. The evidence. Seti I campaigned northward already in his first year (1316 B.C.), encountering enemy forces in northern Palestine and slightly beyond. In a later campaign he pressed as far as Kadesh on the Orontes River, where he made a treaty with the Hittite king, Muwatallis.[100] Rameses II followed with other campaigns, notably in his fifth and twenty-first years, in the last of which he made his famous treaty with the Hittite, Hattusilis III (1283 B.C.).[101] In each of these

[99] The first oppression lasted 8 years and is best dated c. 1375-67 (cf. *infra,* chap. 9, p. 212), exactly during the years of Akhenaton (1384-1367) when the Habiru seem to have been the most active.

[100] Cf. W. C. Hayes, *SE,* II, p. 327. This agreement continued to place all Palestine under Egyptian control. The main intention of both Seti I and Rameses II was to restore the northern borders of empire days, but in this they did not succeed.

[101] Copies of this treaty have been found both in cuneiform and hieroglyphic writing, respectively at Boghazkoi and Karnak. Cordial relations followed this

campaigns, the Egyptian army had to march through the length of Palestine, and must have come in contact with Israelites, if indeed they were there. Then, besides, both Seti I and Rameses II appear to have engaged in actual warfare in Palestine itself. At least both left a stele at Bethshan;[102] and Seti I tells of his clashing with Apiru near that city, a reference certainly to the Hebrews in which the term "Habiru-Apiru" is used again. These Palestinian activities do make the question pertinent as to why, if Israel was in the land at the time, the book of Judges gives no record of them.

ii. The explanation. Two observations may be made in giving answer. The first is that later military inroads into Palestine by Merneptah (1238-1228) and Rameses III (c. 1195-1164)[103] are not mentioned in the book of Judges either, and the campaigns of each did follow the time of Israel's entrance into Canaan, even on the late date basis. Merneptah, as already noticed,[104] claims to have wrought extensive havoc in Palestine, stating that "Israel is laid waste, his seed is not; Hurru is become a widow for Egypt."[105] Rameses III of the Twentieth Dynasty boasts of having reduced both the "Tjeker and the Philistines" to ashes.[106] He even had scenes of the campaign he conducted into Palestine depicted on the walls of his famous temple of Medinet Habu. He seems to have had a major interest in the Bethshan area, even as Seti I and Rameses II, for he rebuilt the city, including a fine temple, and made the city a sort of Egyptian frontier post.[107] It is clear that both Pharaohs centered attacks on the Palestine sector itself and did not merely pass through, as was true mainly for both Seti I and Rameses II. But the books of Judges omits their activities too. One may conclude from this that, if their campaigns are not mentioned, when Israel surely was in the land, then that the earlier campaigns are not mentioned need not be evidence that Israel was not in the land at this time.

treaty, with Rameses II even marrying the eldest daughter of Hattusilis in Rameses' 45th year of reign. Cf. Hayes, SE, II, pp. 344-45; and ANET, pp. 201-203 for copy of the treaty.

[102] Cf. ANET, p. 255 for text of each. Cf. G. M. Fitzgerald, "Beth-Shean," AOTS, pp. 185-96, for recent brief treatment of discoveries at Bethshan.

[103] Date uncertain, Albright, FSAC, p. 289, prefers 1175 as first year of Rameses III.

[104] Supra, p. 91, n. 32, and p. 92.

[105] Cf. ANET, pp. 376-78 for text. "Hurru" is Syria, here no doubt including Palestine.

[106] Cf. ANET, p. 262 for text. "Tjeker" (tkr) is the name of one of the Sea Peoples who in part, along with the Philistines (prst), took up residence in Palestine. The Egyptian Wenamon (1100 b.c.) speaks of the tkr occupying the coastal town, Dor, just south of Mt. Carmel; cf. ANET, p. 26, n. 5.

[107] Cf. Wright, BAR, p. 95, and ANET, p. 262, n. 21.

The other observation concerns the reason for this omission in the book of Judges, whether of the earlier or the later campaigns. The book does not constitute a history as such of the period of time covered. It is rather an accounting of Israel's deviant behavior and corresponding punishments. In keeping with this idea, those military encounters with other nations, which served as means of punishment or correction, are mentioned, and those which did not, are omitted. An outside power would strike, Israel would be defeated and then suffer a period of oppression, and finally a delivering Judge would often arise to bring relief. Several outside powers were so involved,[108] but Egypt was not among them. Her military encounters did not lead to servitude and punishment for Israel.

---

[108] Mesopotamians (Judg. 3:8), Moabites (Judg. 3:12), Canaanites (Judg. 4:2), Midianites (Judg. 6:1), Ammonites (Judg. 10:7), and Philistines (Judg. 10:7).

CHAPTER SIX

LIFE IN EGYPT

Exodus 1–14; Psalm 105:17-39; Acts 7:15-36; Hebrews 11:22-29

A. FOUR PERIODS OF EGYPTIAN RULE

The second millennium B.C. in Egyptian history was marked by four distinctive periods of rule. First came the powerful Twelfth Dynasty, lasting from c. 1991 to c. 1786 B.C.[1] During this time the country was stabilized, following a period of divided feudal lordship, and the Pharaoh ruled once more with full authority. Lower and Upper Egypt were united. The capital was located at Ith-taui, south of the great capital of the Old Kingdom, Memphis. The country prospered and conditions for the most part pleased the people. Egyptian pottery found in neighboring countries indicates that trade relations existed. The period was one of Egypt's strongest and her influence in the world extended far beyond her borders.[2]

The second period was that of the Hyksos,[3] a foreign people who now came into Egypt and took over the throne. Though their exact origin still remains a mystery, it is quite clear that they were Asiatics who gradually infiltrated Egypt during the latter half of the eighteenth century. The strong Twelfth Dynasty had been succeeded by much

[1] These dates are from R. A. Parker, *The Calendars of Egypt* (Chicago: University of Chicago Press, 1950), pp. 63-69, with which Albright, *BASOR*, 127 (1952) pp. 27-30, agrees. Cf. W. F. Edgerton, "The Chronology of the Twelfth Dynasty," *JNES*, 1(1942), pp. 307-14, who differs slightly. For general discussion, cf. H. E. Winlock, *The Rise and Fall of the Middle Kingdom* (New York: The Macmillan Co., 1947).

[2] This period is known as Egypt's Middle Kingdom. The fascinating story of Sinuhe occurred at this time. He fled from Egypt, traveled through the East and returned, the story giving valuable information regarding life of the day; cf. *ANET*, p. 418.

[3] This period is called the Second Intermediate. Cf. R. M. Engberg, *The Hyksos Reconsidered* (Chicago: University of Chicago Press, 1939); W. C. Hayes, *SE*, II, pp. 3-8; J. Van Seters, *TH*.

110

weaker kings of the short-lived Thirteenth and Fourteenth Dynasties,[4] in whose days the infiltration took place. About 1730 the new comers took over rule in the northeastern Delta, establishing their capital at Avaris;[5] and about 1680 they succeeded in displacing the Egyptian ruler at the main capital, Memphis, and so assumed control over all Egypt, even including Nubia to the south for a time.[6] The Hyksos were not really numerous during these years, but remained dominant by holding key positions. They adopted Egyptian ways[7] and appear to have been accepted by the Egyptian people at first, though being hated later. There is no evidence of extensive warfare even when they made conquest of the country. They left few records, however, and not much is known of them for sure.

The third period was that of the strongest dynasty of all, the Eighteenth.[8] During this time Egypt enjoyed her most influential role in world affairs. A first endeavor was ridding the land of the hated Hyksos. This was begun already by the Seventeenth Dynasty;[9] but it was Ahmose (1584-1560), first ruler of the Eighteenth, who captured the Hyksos capital, Avaris, and drove the foreigners far north into Palestine. With him, too, native rule became solidified, and with his grandson, Thutmose I (1539-1514), came the beginning even of empire status for Egypt. This Pharaoh's army campaigned as far south as the Third Cataract of the Nile and as far north along the Mediterranean coast as the Euphrates River. Later his grandson, the great Thutmose III (1504-1450), generally considered Egypt's most capable ruler, sur-

[4] These dynasties, so designated by Manetho, apparently ruled contemporaneously.

[5] This occasion is commemorated on a New Kingdom stele stating that it took place 400 years prior to the reign of Horemhab, the last king of the Eighteenth Dynasty. For discussion, cf. Van Seters, *TH*, pp. 97-103.

[6] Manetho names the ruler who took Memphis in 1680 as Salutis and says the Fifteenth Dynasty began with him. Manetho assigns both the Fifteenth and Sixteenth Dynasties to the Hyksos, though these were likely contemporary like the Thirteenth and Fourteenth.

[7] The rulers used Egyptian titles and throne names, writing them in the Egyptian hieroglyphics. They admired Egyptian art, for they made copies of Middle Kingdom originals of statues, reliefs, and other works. That they took over the Egyptian gods, Seth and Ra, shows that they even accepted much of the Egyptian religion.

[8] Cf. Steindorff and Seele, *When Egypt Ruled the East* (rev. ed.; Chicago: University of Chicago Press, 1957); also Hayes, *SE*, II, pp. 42-325.

[9] The Seventeenth Dynasty dates from about 1660 B.C. It took over in Thebes from the Thirteenth which had continued in the Thebes area after the Hyksos conquest. The last ruler of the Seventeenth, Kamose, already took back much Egyptian territory from the Hyksos, pushing at least as far as the Delta. Ahmose, first of the Eighteenth Dynasty, was his younger brother; cf. Hayes, *SE*, II, pp. 8-9.

passed him in marching yet farther and establishing recognized boundaries. The son of Thutmose III, Amenhotep II, was also gifted as a military commander. At this time, Egypt's army was the strongest in the world, spearheaded by the chariot corps. With good crops at home, advantageous trade relations with neighbors near and far, and now rich booty from successful conquests, Egypt reached a zenith of prosperity. The country also enjoyed the finest in educational and cultural advantages.

The fourth period was that of the Nineteenth Dynasty,[10] nearly as strong in world influence as the Eighteenth. The period lasted one hundred nine years, of which sixty-six were under the rule of Rameses II (1304-1238).[11] He and his predecessor, Seti I, sought to reestablish the northern boundary of Thutmose III, and, though they fell short of this goal, did secure full control once more over all Palestine and southern Syria.[12] Rameses II was a builder as well as military strategist, as witnessed by structures he erected or enlarged in nearly every major city of both lower and upper Egypt.[13] Throughout the Nineteenth Dynasty prosperity continued and Egypt remained the dominant world power.

B. Egyptian Life

Egyptians lived near and depended greatly on the Nile River.[14] Annual flooding by this long waterway brought new fertile soil and initial deep wetting so that continued irrigation through the growing season produced excellent crops. Without the Nile, Egypt would have been mere desert. The country was long and narrow, with most of the people living within a few miles of the Nile's banks. A delta, formed by the Nile fanning out into numerous branches as it neared the Mediterranean, provided broader areas for farming. The land of Goshen, given to Jacob's family, lay on the east of the Delta. Present day Cairo lies at its southern end just over a hundred miles from the Mediterranean. The Delta region was called Lower Egypt and the area south, Upper Egypt, these terms given in view of the Nile flowing from south to north.

Religion played a major role in Egyptian life.[15] The people believed

[10] Cf. Hayes, SE, II, pp. 326-434 besides general works. It should be realized that the Eighteenth, Nineteenth, and Twentieth Dynasties constituted Egypt's New Kingdom period.

[11] For discussion of this date, cf. *supra*, chap. 5, p. 90, n. 30.

[12] Cf. *supra*, chap. 5, p. 107, n. 100.

[13] Hayes, SE, II., p. 342.

[14] For a recent popular study, cf. Bruce Brander, *The Nile River* (Washington, D.C.: National Geographic Society, 1966).

[15] Hayes, SE, I, chap. vi, "The Religion and Funerary Beliefs in Ancient Egypt," pp. 75-83.

in many gods, often identifying them with birds and animals. Every community had gods which were particularly venerated. The will of these gods, thought to be discernible in a variety of ways, governed decisions of life. In addition to the local gods there were national deities, thought to be higher in rank, though actually not influencing personal life patterns as much as the local gods. Horus, the falcon god, rose from local to national status when Lower and Upper Egypt were first united under King Menes.[16] During the old Kingdom, the god Ra was honored as chief deity. For most of the second millennium, however, Amon (sometimes identified with Ra as Amon-Ra) carried this distinction. Thebes was his main center of worship, and immense temples, particularly Karnak and Luxor, were erected to him there. His priesthood wielded enormous power, controlling vast tracts of land and insisting on contributions from people already poor. The priests exerted extensive influence politically. Amenhotep IV (1384-1367), of the Eighteenth Dynasty, sought to break from their hold and establish a revolutionary monotheistic cult to the god Aton (changing his own name to Akhenaton, accordingly) in a new capital at Tell el-Amarna; but when he died all reverted to the established pattern.

A major feature in Egyptian religion was the belief in life after death. People believed that a record of their deeds was weighed after death to determine their continuing status in the after life. People desired adequate material provisions for the future existence, thus giving stress to burial preparation. Bodies were embalmed and fine tombs constructed. Pharaohs of the Old Kingdom built the immense pyramids as their places to be buried. Food, drink, furniture, and other necessities of life were included in the tombs. In earlier days, even servants were slain and placed beside their masters' bodies. Poor people could not prepare as lavishly as rich, but still they did as much as they could.

C. Jacob's Descendants in Egypt

On the basis of the chronology established in the prior chapter, Jacob and his family arrived in this Egyptian milieu during the first period of rule in the second millennium, that of the Twelfth Dynasty. Since the date of the arrival was c. 1876 B.C.,[17] the Pharaoh would

[16] Manetho identifies Menes as the first king of permanently united Egypt, the first of the First Dynasty. Cf. Alan Gardner, *Egypt of the Pharaohs* (London: Oxford University Press, 1961), pp. 66-67; Finegan, *LAP*, pp. 82-83.

[17] *Supra*, chap. 2, p. 34, n. 32. It is of interest that considerable evidence exists in Egyptian papyri that a large Asiatic slave population lived in Egypt during the latter part of the Twelfth and especially the Thirteenth Dynasty. This cannot reflect Israel's enslavement as a nation, however, for this did not ensue until the Hyksos' time. Some Israelites may have been taken earlier as slave-

likely have been Senusert (Sesostris) III (1878-1871), one of the most aggressive of the Dynasty. He made conquest as far south as the Second Cataract and north through all of Palestine. He dug a canal from the Delta to the Red Sea and reopened another at the First Cataract. His predecessor, Senusert II (1894-1878), would have been the man whose dream Joseph interpreted and who made Joseph his vizier.

Given the fertile land of Goshen, and being unusually blessed by God, Jacob's descendants prospered. God gave Jacob seventeen years to see this prosperity, and the satisfaction he experienced must have been gratifying, after suffering so much disappointment earlier in life. Crops grew and the population increased until "the land was filled" (Ex. 1:7) with the children of Israel. This does not mean that they spread throughout all the land, in both Lower and Upper Egypt. This would not have occurred for the reason especially that every shepherd was "an abomination unto the Egyptians" (Gen. 46:34). The Egyptians would not have permitted this kind of intermingling. For the most part, the sons of Jacob remained together, but, doing so, expanded their holdings to fill the Goshen area completely.

Joseph lived seventy-one years after the coming of his family to Egypt.[18] This means that he died c. 1805 B.C., during the reign of Amenemhet III (1841-1797), approximately twenty-five years prior to the end of the Twelfth Dynasty. Apparently Joseph continued in high office even after the famine and, if so, would have been able to do much for the benefit of his loved ones. It is easy to believe that the finest in irrigation equipment, farming tools, and home conveniences were provided. Life would have been good for Israelites as long as Joseph lived.

D. Oppression Instituted (Exodus 1:8-22)

Prior discussion has revealed that the King who arose and "knew not Joseph" was the first of the Hyksos.[19] This one likely was the very first of these rulers, who, in the initial stages of their control, ruled only northeastern Egypt and established Avaris as capital. Goshen was in the area and no doubt was included in this first stage of conquest. If so, the year was about 1730 B.C.,[20] some seventy-five years after Joseph's death. These intervening years likely had continued as years of prosperity for the Israelites. The Egyptian Pharaohs would have per-

servants, but probably most of these were Asiatics of other origins. Cf. Van Seters, *TH*, pp. 90-92 for discussion and references.

[18] *Supra*, chap. 2, p. 35, n. 37.

[19] *Supra*, chap. 2, pp. 35-38.

[20] The alternative is that this one was Salutis, the Hyksos who took over all Egypt about 1680 B.C. He was likely a still more aggressive person.

mitted them to live quite as before, both because of respect for the memory of Joseph and because there was no urgent reason to change. It is probable that the special benefits provided by Joseph ceased, but these would not have been so needed by this time, with a position of strength having already been attained.

1. *Slavery imposed (Exodus 1:8-14)*. But now matters changed. A rigorous servitude was imposed on the dwellers of Goshen. Exodus 1:8-10 records the reasons. First, the new Hyksos ruler "knew not Joseph"; that is, he did not have historical knowledge of Joseph, nor did he have reason to respect it if he had. He headed a new dynasty of a foreign rule, so that former allegiances or obligations were of little consequence. Second, Israelites were seen to be "more and mightier" than the Hyksos. As has been pointed out, the Hyksos were never of great number, and Jacob's family could have easily outnumbered them by this time. The new ruling family would not have wanted a strong, unified, foreign group to continue unchecked as a potential source of trouble. Third, a military alliance with the former regime was seen as a possible way in which this trouble might come. The deposed rulers, whose dynasty had befriended this group of people, might now call upon them for support in re-establishing the old *status quo*.

Accordingly, a decision was made to enslave the people. Their potential for trouble would be removed both by taking away freedom to move about and work as they wished and by placing "taskmasters" over them to make sure that all energy was expended in hard labor. Further, not only would this keep them in control, but also provide valuable labor for building projects such as the cities of Pithom and the new capital Raamses (Avaris).[21]

The Hyksos did gain in labor contributed and also prevented any alliance between the deposed Egyptians and Israel — if indeed such a possibility really existed — but they did not succeed in curtailing Israelite population growth. Exodus 1:12 states that "the more they afflicted them, the more they multiplied and grew." Population growth was necessary if Israel was to become nation-size by the time of the Exodus, and God blessed them to that end. The rapid rate of increase[22] continued as before.

2. *Male babies ordered killed (Exodus 1:15-22)*. In time another measure to hinder this growth was instituted: all male children were ordered to be killed. This order was not given by the Hyksos, however, but by one of the Eighteenth Dynasty.[23] This follows from the fact

[21] *Supra,* chap. 2, p. 35, n. 40.

[22] *Supra,* chap. 5, p. 85.

[23] Any Egyptian dynasty now would have desired such a controlling measure for several reasons: first, the historical tie with Israelites would now have been

that Moses was born while the order was in effect. Since Moses was eighty years old[24] at the time of the Exodus (1446 B.C.), his birth-date may be figured as c. 1526 B.C., during the reign of Thutmose I (1539-1514), the third ruler of that dynasty.

The order came in two stages, which may have been separated by several years. The first stage was a directive to Hebrew midwives[25] to kill every male Hebrew child at the moment of birth (Ex. 1:15-21). It was probably issued by either Ahmose (1584-1560) or Amenhotep I (1560-1539), the first two rulers of the Eighteenth Dynasty. It was a vicious order and would have been very effective had it been obeyed. However, thanks to courageous midwives, it was not, the excuse being given that the Hebrew women were quick in giving birth so that mid-wives could not arrive in time to do the evil deed.

The second stage of the order was issued, as observed, by Thut-mose I, the first great empire builder of Egypt. It was a public order, directed to every Egyptian, that all male children of the Hebrews be thrown into the Nile to drown (Ex. 1:22). This was surely one of the most inhuman directives ever issued by a public official; but it is, in a measure, understandable in view of the circumstances. The Israelites were becoming very numerous, now that three and one-half centuries of rapid growth had elapsed. Thutmose I was involved in enlarging Egypt's borders, which meant that most of his army was out of the country for extensive periods of time. He did not want this foreign people to increase and become still a greater threat while his home force was so small.

E. MOSES[26] (Exodus 2:1-10)

While the new order was more effective than the first,[27] it did not keep one very important person from entering Israelite history. That was Moses, the one whom the king, had he known his destiny, would

forgotten; second, instead would have existed an awareness of Asiatic kinship between these who remained and the hated, departed Hyksos; and third, the numbers of the Israelites would now have grown much larger than at any time prior to the Hyksos period.

[24] Ex. 7:7. Moses spent 40 years in the wilderness and was 120 at his death (Deut. 34:7).

[25] Only two midwives are named, Shiphrah and Puah (Ex. 1:15), but these may have been the superintendents. Likely there were more than two to serve the number of Hebrew families then living.

[26] The name, Moses, finds meaning both in Hebrew and Egyptian. In Hebrew *mosheh* means "drawn out" (Ex. 2:10), and in Egyptian *mos* means "child," it being the same element as found, for instance, in Thutmose, which means "child of Thot."

[27] At least Moses' parents found it advisable to hide the baby and then make an ark to place him in the river.

have been the most interested in disposing. God's special protection was over him, however, for he was planned as Israel's great deliverer.

1. *Early home (Exodus 2:1-10).* Moses' father, Amram,[28] and his mother, Jochebed, were both descendants of Levi (Ex. 6:16-20). They already had two children: Aaron, three years old, and Miriam, perhaps about seven.[29] It is certain that the home was a center of godly instruction, for Moses, there only during his beginning years, was still highly influenced by it years later in the Egyptian palace. At that time he admirably chose to identify himself with his own people and so "share ill treatment with the people of God," rather than enjoy "the pleasures of sin for a season" (Heb. 11:25). Other homes among the Israelites, after so many years since Joseph, probably had become cold toward the God of their fathers, but not that of Amram and Jochebed. Their piety, no doubt, was a factor in God's selection of them to be the parents of Moses.

Moses is described as a "goodly" child, a matter which would only have intensified the parents' desire to have his life spared (Ex. 2:2-10). They hid him at home three months, in defiance of the King's commandment, and then, when this was no longer possible, laid him in a basket of bulrushes (papyri) which they placed in the river, leaving his sister to watch. Under God's providential care, the daughter of Thutmose I came to bathe,[30] found the baby crying, and, at the sister's suggestion, hired Jochebed to care for the child until he should be weaned, apparently not knowing that Jochebed was the baby's own mother. Jochebed thus had her son back, now legally safe, and was even to be paid for caring for him, all of which certainly prompted great thanksgiving in her heart. In perhaps four or five years,[31] however, she had to give him up to the palace where he became the legal son of Pharaoh's daughter.

2. *Hatshepsut, Pharaoh's daughter.* This daughter may have been the renowned Hatshepsut, who in time came to declare herself supreme ruler in Egypt. For a woman to assume such a position in that day

---

[28] Cf. *supra,* chap. 5, p. 86, n. 14 for evidence that Moses' father was not the same Amram as the grandson of Levi (Ex. 6:16-18).

[29] Ex. 7:7 gives Aaron's age. Miriam is probably correctly identified with the older sister who watched Moses when he was placed on the river. If so, she was old enough to assume this responsibility.

[30] With the capital then at Thebes, this princess must have been visiting in the north near the Goshen area. Such trips were not unusual, however, cf. *supra,* chap. 5, pp. 103-104.

[31] Moses would hardly have been younger than this, for he certainly was influenced by early home instruction years later in his choice to go to his own people, and also the princess would not likely have wanted to care for him much younger.

was most unusual, but Hatshepsut was a most unusual person.[32] She had a strong personality and remarkable gift for leadership, which she used in advantageous circumstances to claim the throne.[33] She proclaimed herself ruler of both Lower and Upper Egypt and took a special king's name, Kamare, as well as most of the normal royal titles.

Hatshepsut was the only living child of Thutmose I and his official wife, Ahmose.[34] Four children had been born: two sons, Wadmose and Amenmose, and one daughter besides Hatshepsut, Nefruibity. It is all but certain, however, that each of the others died early in life, leaving Hatshepsut as sole lawful heir to the throne; as well as the only one who could really be identified as the daughter of Pharaoh who found Moses.[35]

Because she was not male, Hatshepsut could not directly accede to the throne. Thutmose I had a son by a lesser wife, and he was now married[36] to Hatshepsut so that her legal title might work in his behalf. He took the name, Thutmose II (1514-1504). This man was weak both in body and personality, quite in contrast to the robust Hatshepsut; and he was dominated in his rule by her and the queen-mother, Ahmose, also a woman of strength. To Hatshepsut's advantage in this was the fact that she held the people's favor, since her birth was royal on the part of both parents. One daughter only, Nefrure, was born to Thutmose II and Hatshepsut, and so once again a son of the Pharaoh by a lesser wife was brought forward as successor. He too may have been married to the daughter, royal in blood from both parents, though no certain evidence has been found in this instance.[37] This successor assumed the name Thutmose III (1504-1450). It was when Thutmose II had died and this young Thutmose III was about ten years of age that Hatshepsut took the daring step of assuming full control of the

[32] Two prior queens in Egypt's history had assumed supreme headship, but neither had posed and dressed as a man as did Hatshepsut; cf. Gardner, *Egypt of the Pharaohs* (London: Oxford University Press, 1961), p. 183.

[33] Since the Egyptian word for *king* is written the same as *queen*, it cannot be said for sure that she applied the masculine term to herself. However, her reliefs and statues depict her often in masculine clothing, wearing the ceremonial beard.

[34] Cf. Steindorff and Seele, *When Egypt Ruled the East* (rev. ed.; Chicago: University of Chicago Press, 1957), pp. 36-46; Hayes, *SE*, II, pp. 78-83.

[35] It is possible that this daughter may have been of a lesser wife, of course. However, it seems more than coincidental that one of Hatshepsut's stature, who could provide every advantage for Moses, lived at this very time. Also, it would have taken someone of her strength and daring to rescue a Hebrew baby and even rear him right at the palace in defiance of the king's command.

[36] Brother-sister marriages were accepted in ancient Egypt where it was believed that even the god, Osiris, had married his sister, Isis.

[37] Cf. discussion by Hayes, *SE*, II, pp. 81-82; 105-106.

kingdom. Thutmose III clearly had been crowned before she did so and reigned perhaps a year.[38] But then she did seize his crown; and it was not until her death twenty-two years later (1503-1482), following a most impressive reign,[39] that he was finally able to take the headship back again. That he harbored great bitterness toward her as a result is witnessed by his multiple defacements of her name and representation from monuments and temples.[40] He clearly wished to obliterate her memory from the minds of the people. This same man went on to become the greatest ruler Egypt ever knew.[41]

3. *Moses at the palace.* We may safely think of Moses, then, as having been reared by this remarkable woman. It was she who found him in the river and later received him into the palace at Thebes as her adopted son. Thebes was a city of splendor at the time and offered the finest in cultural benefits. Being the center of Amun worship, great religious buildings abounded and educational advantages were the best the world afforded. Hatshepsut, intellectually endowed herself, would not have been satisfied with anything less than the finest education for her son. Her own daughter, Nefrure, died while still little more than a child,[42] which left Moses to receive all Hatshepsut's attentions.[43] He would have been provided the finest in tutors, and his own mental capacity would have been able to absorb all that was taught. That he

[38] During this year, Hatshepsut permitted herself to be represented on public monuments standing behind her stepson, bearing only titles which were hers as wife of the deceased Thutmose II.

[39] During her reign, Egypt enjoyed the highest economic prosperity since the Twelfth Dynasty period. She built extensively in Thebes, particularly her magnificent temple, Deir el Bahri, as well as in other cities. Sanctuaries, destroyed or neglected by the Hyksos, were restored. She was devoted to Amon, adding courts and halls to his immense temple of Karnak and erecting there two giant obelisks each about 97 feet high. She gave attention to trade and also mining ventures in the copper and turquoise mines of Sinai.

[40] For instance at Hatshepsut's great funerary complex at Deir el Bahri, though the buildings were spared, the names and figures of Hatshepsut were methodically obliterated wherever found. This involved destruction of much relief sculpture and more than 200 statues and sphinxes, which adorned the courts and colonnades.

[41] Hayes describes him as "Incontestably the greatest Pharaoh ever to occupy the throne of Egypt," *SE*, II, p. 116. Steindorff and Seele state, "If any Egyptian ruler deserves to be honored by being designated 'the great,' he is a far more fitting candidate than any other"; *op. cit.*, p. 66.

[42] If she married Thutmose III, it was when both were still ten years of age or less.

[43] Moses was older than the daughter too. Born c. 1526 B.C., he would have been 22 years old when Thutmose III was made king in 1504 B.C. Hatshepsut was married to Thutmose II probably just before his accession in 1514 B.C. which makes their daughter something less than 10 at this time.

did profit greatly was verified years later by Stephen saying, "Moses was instructed in all the wisdom of the Egyptians" (Acts 7:22).

F. MOSES' CHOICE (Exodus 2:11-25; Acts 7:23-29; Hebrews 11:24-27)

1. *A commendable decision (Hebrews 11:24-27).* In view of these matters, the words of Hebrews 11:24 carry deep meaning: "Moses, when he was grown up, refused to be called the son of Pharaoh's daughter." That is, he turned down opportunities this high position afforded. This occurred particularly when he was forty years old. He chose to aid his own people in their plight of bondage. Had he not done so, he might have commanded a fine office in Egypt. Some have suggested that Hatshepsut might even have tried to make him Pharaoh to succeed her, especially in view of the bitterness between herself and the young deposed Thutmose III. This is hardly likely, however, for Thutmose III had already been given this position before Hatshepsut's assumption of it, and he was extremely capable and strong-willed in his own right. He would certainly have done everything possible to prohibit such a move. Moses' Hebrew origin, a fact Hatshepsut probably sought to hide, would have given the young man a strong weapon to use in a struggle. Moses, however, with his ability and advantageous position, may well have had most other offices open to him.[44] But when he chose to identify himself with his people, the enslaved Hebrews, all this was forfeited. Hatshepsut certainly had warned him of the result, but Moses would not be deterred. For this we can only admire him.

2. *Unwise procedure (Exodus 2:11-22; Acts 7:23-29).* Having made the commendable choice, however, Moses did not carry it out wisely. He went out among his kindred Hebrews, saw one abused by a taskmaster, and directly killed the cruel fellow.[45] He hid the body, thinking no one had seen him. The next day he attempted to settle a difference between two struggling Hebrews, and in doing so learned that his action of the previous day was known. Hearing this, he immediately fled from the country, thus giving up in a moment what he had achieved through nearly forty years. But the reason is not difficult to see. He knew the danger from Thutmose III if he stayed. This rival[46] of many

[44] Indeed, he may already have held office, here at the age of 40. Thutmose III, on returning to the throne, would likely have left him alone, too, so long as he was himself Pharaoh. Moses by then could have been courting high favor with the people and so to depose him would have been to stir up unnecessary trouble.

[45] This event too would have had to occur in Goshen, far north of Moses' usual home in Thebes. However, Moses may have spent much of his time in the north on significant government business.

[46] The animosity existing between Thutmose III and Hatshepsut would have

years would now have all the excuse necessary to take his life. Moses would not be able to defend himself, having shown his identity with the enslaved foreigners. He saw safety only in flight, and that as quickly as possible.[47]

Moses' escape led him eastward into the Sinaitic peninsula to the home of one Jethro,[48] a priest of Midian (Ex. 2:15-22). He married this man's daughter, Zipporah, and, for employment, tended his sheep. Forty years passed in quietness and solitude, much in contrast to the bustling court activity of Egypt. Moses' area of work seems to have been near the Gulf of Aqaba and Mt. Sinai, the very region through which he would lead Israel not many years hence. No doubt geographical information gained aided significantly in the later day.

3. *Thutmose III.* Most of Moses' forty-year period in the desert had elapsed when finally the great Thutmose III died (Ex. 2:23-25). By this time the mighty king had ruled thirty-two years since his return to full control. These had been years of great accomplishment.[49] He excelled as a statesman and administrator, and was one of the accomplished horsemen, archers, and all-around athletes of his day. He was a patron of the arts. But it was as a military strategist that he distinguished himself. Immediately upon Hatshepsut's death, he was faced with a major revolt by northern Palestine and Syria. This he put down decisively with a brilliant victory at Megiddo. In later campaigns he pushed Egypt's northern border once more beyond the Euphrates, even farther than his grandfather had. Then two quick campaigns south along the Nile fixed this boundary as far as Napata below the Fourth Cataract. Egypt's borders were now brought to their maximum limits, a true empire. Gold, silver, and valuable merchandise of all kinds poured into the land, both in the form of seized booty and products of trade. Egypt flourished as seldom in her history. But finally the great ruler died, and Moses was able to return to Egypt.

G. Moses Returns to Egypt (Exodus 3:1–4:31)

The idea of returning to Egypt, however, did not originate with Moses. He even resisted the thought. God called him as Moses tended sheep on Mt. Horeb, the very mountain where God later would im-

been shared by the two young men. Thutmose would now have been about 28 years old, right at his prime and ever becoming stronger as Hatshepsut grew older. Her death about 4 years later may even have been unnatural.

[47] Unless Thutmose III was also in the North, Moses would have had ample time to get away, however, before news reached the young ruler in Thebes.

[48] Also called Reuel (Ex. 2:18; cf. 3:1). Reuel, meaning "friend of God," may have been his personal name, and Jethro, meaning "excellence," his title.

[49] Cf. Hayes, *SE*, II, pp. 114f; Steindorff and Seele, *When Egypt Ruled the East* (rev. ed.; Chicago: University of Chicago Press, 1957), pp. 53f.

part Israel's law (Ex. 3:1–4:17). Using the miracle of a non-consumed, burning bush as a sign of authentication, the Angel of Yahweh[50] brought the call, informing Moses that he was indeed to go back to Egypt and there lead Israel out from her long-extended bondage. He also gave Moses the name of God which he was to tell to the Israelites (Ex. 3:13-14).[51] Translated "I AM," it is the first person form of the verb *hayah* ("to be") from which in the third person the name Yahweh comes. The thought of the name, whether in the first or third person form, is that God is the self-existent One, responsible for all existence, including His own. He would not fail Israel in any of His promises for He knew no contingencies. Nothing could hinder Him in His faithfulness for He controlled all existence, and nothing could exist to effect a hindrance unless He permitted it. When Moses protested that the people would not believe him if he returned to them after so many years, God gave him two miracles to perform as credentials.[52] Again Moses protested, this time claiming inability to speak well enough, and to this God replied that Aaron would act as his spokesman.[53]

Moses bade farewell to his father-in-law and departed for Egypt with his wife Zipporah and two sons (Ex. 4:18-31). On the way a dispute arose concerning the circumcision of one of the boys, and Zipporah, after performing the operation, was sent back home by Moses with both sons.[54] It was not until Moses came back to Horeb much later with the Israelites that the family rejoined him. Now Moses went on alone and was met by his brother, Aaron, whom God had previously instructed to go to Sinai for this meeting. Moses shared God's instructions with him, and the two then made their way to the land of Israel's bondage. Their first act on arrival was to assemble

[50] *Supra*, chap. 3, p. 55, n. 28.

[51] The name, Yahweh, had been known to the patriarchs, but, according to Ex. 6:3, had not been understood in its full meaning. Critics assert that the name only now came to be used, but this must be rejected.

[52] The first was having his staff turn into a live serpent, when cast upon the ground; and the second, having his hand made leprous when placed within his clothing, followed by removal of the leprosy when placed within it a second time (Ex. 4:2-7).

[53] In view of Moses' early experience in the palace and later abilities to communicate with Israel, it is not likely that his speech was seriously impaired. His forty years of solitude may have given him a sense of insecurity in meeting Pharaoh. Aaron apparently was known for his greater ease in oral communication.

[54] It is stated that God "sought to kill" Moses in this instance. Apparently Moses had been lax in circumcising one of the boys, probably the younger, Eliezer (Gershom likely circumcised earlier properly). Zipporah had clearly opposed the idea but here circumcised him herself to save Moses' life.

Israel's elders, as representatives of the people, and relay to them God's words, along with displaying the confirming signs. Happily, Moses and Aaron were well received at this time, and their words and signs were believed.

H. THE CONTEST WITH PHARAOH (Exodus 5:1–12:36)

This done, Moses and Aaron went to see the Pharaoh, now Amenhotep II, son of Thutmose III. A ruler of valor and strength in his own right, Amenhotep II had been carefully trained by his outstanding father. Ascending the throne at the age of eighteen, he prided himself in his horsemanship and claimed to be a better handler of ships and more expert with the bow than any other.[55] He conducted at least three successful military campaigns north in Syria, maintaining his father's holdings there, and was able to continue Egypt's southern boundary at Napata near the Fourth Cataract. Moses and Aaron would have encountered this man when he was yet young in life and in the early years of his reign.[56]

Moses first requested of Pharaoh only that Israel be permitted to go "three days journey into the wilderness and sacrifice unto Yahweh" (Ex. 5:1-3). Apparently Moses desired to test the King and observe his reaction before presenting the request for complete release of the people. The reaction was immediate and decisive (Ex. 5:4-11). The King flatly refused the request and moreover imposed increased hardship on the Israelites. The Israelites had already been laboring diligently in making a large toll of bricks, but now they would have to do so without straw being provided. They would have to gather their own in the form of stubble.[57] The Israelites, angered at this, blamed Moses and Aaron for adding to their burden (Ex. 5:12-21). The effect on Moses and Aaron, now resented by both Pharaoh and the people, was one of crushing discouragement and a sense of need for a fresh revelation from God.

God knew the need and did bring the revelation, outlining further instructions (Ex. 5:22–6:13; 6:28–7:9). Moses and Aaron were renewed in spirit and returned to Pharaoh to effect the first step indicated. They performed one of the miracle-signs that God had given as a credential: that of turning the rod into a serpent (Ex. 7:10-13). Pharaoh's magicians, however, appeared able to duplicate the miracle

[55] Hayes, *SE*, II, pp. 140-41; cf. Steindorff and Seele, *op. cit.*, pp. 67-71, and J. Breasted, *A History of Egypt* (New York: Chas. Scribner's Sons, 1912), p. 326.

[56] Coming to the throne at the age of 18 in 1450 B.C., he would have been about 22 in 1446 B.C. and in his fourth year of rule.

[57] Cf. Free, *ABH*, pp. 91-92 for discussion of Egyptian manufacture of bricks with and without straw.

which left the king unconvinced regarding the credential,[58] and he refused to comply with the request to let Israel go.

1. *The ten plagues (Exodus 7:14–12:33)*. With the king having been given this much opportunity to grant the request without use of force, Moses now proceeded with the second step in which force indeed was employed. Ten severe plagues were brought upon the country. God gave particular instruction regarding each as the time came to bring it. The ten plagues were: (1) water turned to blood (Ex. 7: 14-25); (2) frogs (Ex. 8:1-15); (3) lice[59] (Ex. 8:16-19); (4) flies (Ex. 8:20-32); (5) cattle disease (Ex. 9:1-7); (6) boils (Ex. 9:8-12); (7) hail (Ex. 9:13-35); (8) locusts (Ex. 10:1-20); (9) darkness (Ex. 10:21-29); and (10) death of firstborn (Ex. 12:29-33).

An examination of these plagues reveals an increasing degree in capacity to inflict suffering and loss on the Egyptians. The first four would have been extremely unpleasant, but none would have brought great suffering or material loss. The fifth (cattle disease), however, would have caused real material loss in the death of livestock. The sixth (boils) would have inflicted severe human suffering. The seventh (hail) and eighth (locusts) would have brought great material loss again in severe destruction of crops. The ninth (darkness) would have dealt a serious psychological blow. The tenth (death of firstborn) would have been the worst of all, taking the lives of family heirs. God thus gradually increased pressure on Pharaoh to accede to Moses' request.

2. *Pharaoh's magicians*. Pharaoh's magicians were able to convince Pharaoh that they could duplicate the first two of the plague-miracles,[60] in addition to the miracle-sign of the rod turning into a serpent. It is definitely stated that they did turn the river to blood and brought frogs onto the land (Ex. 7:22; 8:7). The explanation for this apparent duplication must be sought in one of two directions. One is trickery. Ancient magicians were highly skilled in trickery. It may be that they performed the first trick by making the serpents immobile and then bringing them back to normal functioning. It is known, for instance, that the Egyptian cobra can be rendered immobile by first charming

---

[58] Magic and religion were closely linked in Egypt. There were two patron deities of magic: the god Thoth and the goddess Isis. In all areas of mystery, whether involving man and man, or god and man, magic was employed to obtain answers and ends. Magicians attained great skill in their art.

[59] The Hebrew word here used, *kinnam*, means some type of insect which may have been lice, gnats, mosquitoes, or some other.

[60] Though most of the plagues involved phenomena natural to Egypt, they were still miraculous in several ways: (1) intensification of the natural phenomena; (2) prediction as to exactly when each would occur; (3) distinction between Goshen and the rest of Egypt as to where each would occur; and (4) the over-all plan and purpose involved with them. Cf. Free, *ABH*, p. 95.

the reptile and then applying pressure at the nape of the neck.[61] The other is by demon power. These Egyptian magicians were religious personnel, devoted to the temple and to the false gods. This means that they were apt subjects for demon empowerment. History records many remarkable acts by similar "holy men" in the propagation of false religions, all apparently in the pattern of the "lying wonders" of Satan mentioned in II Thessalonians 2:9. It should be observed, however, that the inadequacy of these magicians, in comparison with God, was displayed in three clear respects: first, the serpent of Moses and Aaron swallowed their serpents (Ex. 7:12); second, they could not duplicate any miracle after the second, being stopped by their inability to bring lice to life, even admitting that this was "the finger of God" (Ex. 8: 18-19); and third, they were themselves afflicted by the boils of the sixth plague (Ex. 9:11). It is of interest that the names of these magicians are given in II Timothy 3:8 — Jannes and Jambres.

3. *Goshen exempted.* With the fourth plague (flies), God made a distinction between Goshen and the rest of Egypt: the last seven plagues, by far the more serious, affecting only the latter. This relieved God's people from major suffering, but, more significantly, it provided additional evidence that Israel's Yahweh was indeed sending the plagues. With the third plague, as noted, the magicians admitted the existence of a supernatural power, but there was need yet to prove that this God was Yahweh. The distinction made regarding the fourth plague demonstrated that this was so. It is noteworthy, too, that with the fifth plague (cattle disease) Pharaoh specifically sent to Goshen to ascertain if this distinction really existed (Ex. 9:7).

4. *Pharaoh's gradual change of mind.* The continued increase in severity of the plagues caused Pharaoh gradually to become more inclined toward acceding to Moses' request. He made a series of promises to let the people go — promises he broke each time when the plague was removed — which became more and more in keeping with Moses' petition. As early as the second plague (frogs) he made a general promise to let the people go if the frogs should be withdrawn (Ex. 8:8); though, in view of the later promises being more specific, this one likely was not seriously intended. No promise was given with the third plague (lice); but with the fourth (flies), he promised again (Ex. 8:25-28): this time more specifically and no doubt more seriously, that the people could go a little distance for the sacrificing if the flies were removed. Once more no promise came with the fifth (cattle disease) or sixth (boils), but with the seventh (hail), eighth (locusts), and ninth (darkness) he went much farther than before. Twice he ad-

---

[61] Cf. K. Kitchen, "Magic and Sorcery," *NBD,* pp. 769-70, for discussion and references.

mitted sin on his part (Ex. 9:27-28; 10:16), even naming Yahweh as the one sinned against; and with the eighth he promised that all Israelites with their animals could go (Ex. 10:8-11), though with the ninth again he retracted to speaking only of the people departing (Ex. 10:24). The significance is that, though he remained adamant in never keeping a promise, he was being psychologically conditioned for granting the full request with the tenth.

5. *Duration of plagues.* A few clues exist for determining the length of time between the first and last plagues. While no certain conclusion can be reached, the probable time is just under six months. The first clue is one of limitation. Amenhotep II, the Pharaoh concerned, would certainly have had to be in the Delta region during the period, and, since the capital was at Thebes far south, he would hardly have been there an extensive time. The other clues all suggest, however, that the period covered at least a few months. One concerns the time of year when it ended: in the Spring, on the fourteenth of Nisan (March/April), the date of the Passover. This was the time of the tenth plague. Another is equally sure in identifying the time of the seventh plague (hail), for it destroyed the barley and flax crops when they were mature.[62] These crops ripen in the first half of February, six to eight weeks before Passover. A third clue is less certain, but suggests that the first plague was timed near the height of the Nile's flood stage. The Nile did flood each year, reaching its maximum depth in September and slowly receding through October.[63] To have timed the turning of its water to blood at a moment when the water was covering much of the country would have brought the greatest impression on the people.[64] A fourth clue is that since the second plague (frogs) is said to have come only seven days after the first (Ex. 7:25), and a situation of muddy conditions such as would result from a flood drying up would suit this type of plague, it is likely that the specific time of the first plague was just after the height of the high-water period, which means sometime in October.[65] All this argues for a total period from sometime in October to the latter part of March.

[62] The need for the eighth plague (locusts), in destroying more crops, is to be found in the wheat and spelt not being mature as early as the barley and flax and not being destroyed by the hail.

[63] The Nile was at its lowest in May, gradually began to rise in June, true flooding came through July-August, with maximum height reached in September.

[64] It is not likely, however, that this plague involved merely flood-stage reddening due to red silt, as some have suggested. Such reddening does not normally kill fish (Ex. 7:20-21) nor does it occur suddenly as at the precise command of Moses on a particular day.

[65] The mention in Ex. 7:19 of so many different types of bodies of water being affected (rivers, streams, pools and ponds) suggests that the flood had started to decrease, leaving these.

6. *Purpose of the plagues.* God's purpose in the plagues was not only to persuade Pharaoh to let Israel depart from Egypt, important as that was,[66] but also to demonstrate His reality and power in this foreign country. Pharaoh had significantly asked Moses, when first approached, "Who is Yahweh, that I should hearken unto his voice to let Israel go?" (Ex. 5:2). This question is understandable in terms of standards of deity evaluation accepted in that day. Since Yahweh's people had no land of their own, no army, and no independent status,[67] Pharaoh thought that Egypt's gods were much greater. But God would not let this thinking stand; Pharaoh and the Egyptians should be forced to recognize who Yahweh really was before Israel left the land. He even stated this clearly to Moses before bringing the first plague, foretelling that Pharaoh would refuse the request so that God's hand might be on Egypt to reveal to them that He was Yahweh (Ex. 7:4-5; cf. 9:14). Later God declared further that Pharaoh's very rule was to the end that God's power might be demonstrated and that God's name might be made known throughout all the earth (Ex. 9:16).

This means that every time Pharaoh changed his mind and broke his promise, rather than demonstrating his own personal authority, as he thought, he was actually helping to fulfill God's purpose.[68] It was in keeping with God's over-all plan that all ten devastating plagues be wrought and a maximum impression of God's power made. That this purpose was truly accomplished, even to the extent of God's name being made known in foreign countries, finds significant witness in the Philistines' repeated mention of these plagues some 400 years later, far north from Egypt in Palestine, at the time that they captured Israel's Ark (I Sam. 4:7-9; 6:5-6).

7. *The tenth plague (Exodus 12:29-30).* The tenth and final plague was the slaying of Egyptian firstborn. The eldest male child[69] of every Egyptian household was killed (Ex. 11:5) during the night of the fourteenth of Nisan. Only the firstborn of Israel escaped.

Even Pharaoh's son was included in the slaughter, a fact interestingly

---

[66] Had this been the only purpose, God could have used fewer plagues, or some other means entirely, to accomplish it in a much shorter time.

[67] People believed that the domain of the gods of a country extended as far as the borders of that country, and measured their strength by the size of it, the victories of its armies, and the degree of its prosperity.

[68] Pharaoh's refusal is said twice (plagues 2 and 4) to have been the result of Pharaoh hardening his own heart; three times the result of God hardening his heart (plagues 6, 8, and 9), and five times the result simply of hardening of heart without specifying the agent (plagues 1, 3, 5, 7, and the initial sign). This is a remarkable illustration of human responsibility and divine sovereignty working together to accomplish God's will.

[69] Even the firstborn of animals were killed (Ex. 11:5).

confirmed by an extra-biblical text. A curious "dream" inscription was left by the successor of Amenhotep II, Thutmose IV. Since the eldest son of Amenhotep II would have died on that night, Thutmose IV must not have been the eldest. This "dream" inscription suggests indeed that he was not. Written on a granite stele placed between the paws of the great Sphinx of Gizeh, the inscription states that the god Harmakhis, with whom the Sphinx was identified, had promised the young man in a dream that the kingship would be his if he uncovered the Sphinx from the desert sand. The point is that, in order for the young man to have been emotionally conditioned to have such a dream, and to record it in this way, he must have been fearful that he would not receive the throne. But he would not have been fearful if he had been the eldest son, for heirship to the crown then was all but automatic.[70]

The tenth plague, serious as it was, brought quick results from Pharaoh (Ex. 12:29-36). He called for Moses and Aaron that same night and told them that Israel could leave the land as requested. No exceptions nor variations were now stated.

Moses must have given careful directions ahead of time to the Israelites regarding preparations for departure, for, according to Numbers 33:3, the people were able to leave on the fifteenth of Nisan, the very next day. Much packing and loading of wagons would have had to be done beforehand.[71] Moses did relay the message to his waiting couriers, and they in turn took it to the people. The next day all Israel began the long awaited move out of the land of bondage.

8. *The Passover (Exodus 12:1-28).* The occasion of the last plague was eventful, not only for the Egyptians, but also for the Israelites. They escaped death in their homes because they observed the Passover prescribed at the time by God. Moses had delivered the prescription a few days before (Ex. 12:1-23), when he no doubt also had given the directions for departure. Every Israelite household was to select an unblemished year-old male lamb or goat on the tenth day of Nisan, and kill it on the fourteenth in the evening.[72] The blood from this lamb was to be sprinkled on the two sideposts and lintel of each

[70] The comment of Hayes (SE, II, p. 147) is noteworthy: "This fanciful tale, . . . suggests that Thut-mose IV was not his father's heir apparent, but had obtained the throne through an unforeseen turn of fate, such as the premature death of an older brother."

[71] The people must also have done their "borrowing" (Ex. 12:35-36) from the Egyptians before the fifteenth, for there would have been little time then. The Hebrew word translated "borrowed" in AV is simply the word "to ask" (*sha'al*). They asked gifts from the Egyptians, and the Egyptians, now highly respectful of them after the plagues, gave what they asked. Really, the Egyptians owed them far more than this for the many years of slave labor by the Israelites.

[72] The Hebrew says, "between the evenings" (*ben ha'arbayim*), which likely means between sunset and complete darkness.

doorway, using a sprig of hyssop as an applicator. Then the roasted flesh of the lamb was to be eaten by the family along with unleavened bread and bitter herbs. While eating, the family members were to be ready to leave quickly, for the order to march might come at any time.

When the designated days arrived, the Israelites followed these instructions, and their firstborn were spared. They killed the lambs, applied the blood to the doorways, and ate the roasted flesh. When the death-cry arose from all the homes of Egypt, their homes, identified by the applied blood, were silent, having been spared the terrible loss. Lambs had died in place of sons. God instructed that an annual Passover Feast should be observed in memory of this significant occasion (Ex. 12:14-28).[73]

I. DEPARTURE FROM EGYPT

1. *Route through Egypt (Exodus 12:37; 13:20; 14:2).* Israel's assembly point on the fifteenth of Nisan was the city of Raamses (Ex. 12:37). If the common identification of Raamses with ancient Tanis is correct,[74] the people assembled well north of their main area of dwelling, for old Tanis was at the northern extreme of Goshen.[75] The route taken from Raamses led through Succoth (Ex. 12:37; 13:20) which commonly is identified with Tell el-Maskuta. This Tell lies thirty-two miles southeast of ancient Tanis, in the likely direction of Israel's march. Israel then came to Etham, which is unknown, but may be the name of a district lying along both sides of the northern end of the Red Sea.[76] Here some change in direction of travel occurred as instruction came to "turn"[77] and "encamp before Pi-hahiroth,

---

[73] The significance was more than commemorative. It was also predictive in that the slain lamb was typical of Christ, as the Lamb of God who would in due time die in the place of sinners.

[74] Some favor Qantir, however (*supra,* chap. 2, p. 35, n. 40), which is 16 miles southwest of Tanis and so within the Goshen area, though still in the northwest portion.

[75] This fact in itself argues against the identification and more in favor of Qantir, for the rationale of assembling to the north, when the route lay southeast, is not apparent. J. Simons, *GTT,* pp. 245-46, n. 209, makes the observation that a significant part of the people may have started from Raamses, as stated, but that a major portion joined the march as it proceeded through Goshen proper, which idea could apply for either Tanis or Qantir.

[76] The area through which Israel traveled south for three days after crossing the Red Sea is also called Etham (Num. 33:6-8).

[77] Wright, *BAR,* pp. 60-62, follows Albright, *BASOR,* 109(1948), pp. 15-16, in arguing that the "turn" at Etham was back north several miles, so that the eventual crossing of water was not far from Raamses where they had started. The evidence given deserves notice, but is hardly sufficient to offset the unreasonableness of such retracing of steps. J. Simons, *GTT,* p. 247, argues against such a turn back north, which would have been toward the center of enemy power, in favor of a more southwesterly route around the Bitter Lakes.

between Migdol and the sea, before Baal-zephon" (Ex. 14:2), these places being unknown.[78]

At this point they were on the shore of an extensive body of water which barred further progress. This body of water is called *yam suph,* meaning literally "Sea of Reeds" (Ex. 13:18). Though it is said that the Red Sea did not have reeds (from which fact it is often argued that *yam suph* could not mean Red Sea),[79] still this term is clearly used elsewhere to designate the Red Sea, being employed in reference both to the Gulf of Suez (Ex. 10:19; Num. 33:10-11; western arm) and the Gulf of Aqaba (Num. 14:25; Deut. 1:40; eastern arm). However, three matters argue that the body of water here concerned was not the Red Sea proper (Gulf of Suez): first, the Gulf of Suez is too far south to have provided a logical place of exit from the country; second, the biblical account (Ex. 13:20–14:3; Num. 33:6-8) implies that the *yam suph* divided between productive Egyptian soil and the desert, while, if the people first went as far south as the Gulf of Suez, they would have encountered much desert before reaching it; and third, when they had crossed this body of water, they found themselves in the "wilderness of Shur" (Ex. 15:22), which was in the northern part of the Sinaitic peninsula, hardly as far south as the Gulf of Suez.[80] A more likely identification for *yam suph,* then, is the water of the Bitter Lakes, which may even have been an extension of the Gulf of Suez in that day. This identification in no way militates against the miraculous character of the crossing, for the water here too is deep.[81]

[78] Both Pi-hahiroth and Migdol are found mentioned in Egyptian inscriptions, but have not been identified. On the basis of a Phoenician letter, which indicates that a temple to the god Baal-zephon was located at ancient Tahpanhes (modern Tell Defneh, where Jeremiah was brought, Jer. 43:7-9), Wright, *BAR,* pp. 60-62, argues that the mention of Baal-zephon here is a reference to this temple. This constitutes one of his arguments for the retraced northern route (cf. n. 77). The rationale for the biblical account mentioning a temple in a city, however, rather than the city itself, Tahpanhes, is hard to see, particularly when this temple was to a pagan deity. Baal-zephon is better thought of as a place farther south. Cf. further, Albright, "Baal-Zephon," *Festschrift Alfred Bertholet* (Tubingen: J. C. B. Mohr, 1950), pp. 1-14. For concise treatment and references in respect to various proposed routes, cf. C. de Wit, "Encampment by the Sea," *NBD,* pp. 368-69; for more detail, J. Simons, GTT, pp. 234-41; also Aharoni, *LB,* pp. 179-81.

[79] Jonah 2:5 uses *suph* to mean "(sea)weed," and certainly the Red Sea had plenty of this.

[80] Shur is mentioned five other times in the Old Testament and always as located just south of Canaan or on the way to Egypt: Gen. 16:7; 20:1; 25:18; I Sam. 15:7; 27:8.

[81] Liberal scholars argue for an area merely marshy in order to avoid the miraculous. It may be added that Lake Timsah, also deep, still farther north is another possible identification.

2. *The people.* The number of people who moved out from Egypt was very large. Several biblical references give the approximate figure 600,000 as the number of men twenty years and above (Ex. 12:37; 38:26; Num. 1:46; 2:32; 11:21; 26:51).[82] This means a probable total figure of more than 2,000,000.[83] Most all of those were descendants of the household of Jacob. They had remained a people distinct from the Egyptians through the 430 years.

At least three factors would have contributed to the maintenance of this distinctness. One factor, which would have tended to keep Israelites from marrying Egyptians, was a sense of heritage from, and corresponding loyalty to, the patriarchal fathers. Many Israelites would have simply wanted to keep the line of descent pure. The other two, which would have tended to keep Egyptians from marrying Israelites, were, first, that shepherds were an abomination to Egyptians, and, second, that Israelites had been despised slaves of the Egyptians now for two and one-half centuries. The last two certainly would have been unpleasant in the minds of God's people, but would at least have served this good purpose.

There was also a minority group which accompanied the Israelites proper. They are called by the term, "mixed multitude" (*'erebh rabh,* Ex. 12:38; *'asaphsuph,* Num. 11:4).[84] These people were other than Israelites, doubtless mostly Egyptians and made up of two basic types: a helpful, welcome group who had been influenced by the plague-miracles to go with a people whose God could wield such power; and a critical, undesirable number who were dissidents of Egypt looking for what might have more appeal elsewhere. No doubt it was the second group who led in much of the complaining by the people during the wilderness experiences (Num. 11:4).

A multitude this size could not have traveled very fast, particularly when they had flocks and herds (Ex. 12:38). It would have taken nearly a week to travel the approximately sixty miles to the *yam suph.* Their path was directed by a miraculous, moving cloud which at night

---

[82] This repetition of the 600,000 figure, in different contexts, is clear evidence that it is not a copyist error as liberal writers so often assert. This number is very large, and certainly immense problems existed in view of it for the wilderness journey. But it must be accepted in view of the evidence. God, working through Moses, was able to work out the problems.

[83] The 600,000 must be doubled to include women, and to this number the children under 20 years must be added. Cf. *infra,* chap. 7, pp. 154-55 for further discussion.

[84] The word, *'erebh,* means "mixture." It is used again in Neh. 13:3 to refer to a similar group who returned with Jews from Babylon. It is translated "mingled people" in Jer. 25:20; 50:37; Ezek. 30:5 and means "foreigners" each time. The word, *'asaphsuph,* means "collected," a similar idea.

became a "pillar of fire" providing light (Ex. 13:21-22). They moved when it moved, followed the direction of its leading, and stopped when it stopped.

3. *The plight at the* YAM SUPH *(Exodus 14:1-12).* On reaching the *yam suph,* the people found themselves in a serious plight. They were barred from further progress by this extensive body of water. In addition, they learned that they were being pursued. Pharaoh, hearing of the direction in which they were headed and calculating that they would encounter the water, had changed his mind[85] and sent his elite chariot corps after them (Ex. 14:6-10). The chariot corps had become a major factor in the world-feared Egyptian army, and here, coming against the defenseless Israelites, would have struck fear into their hearts (Ex. 14:11-12). Certain return to bondage, if not death, seemed inevitable. All their diligent preparation and flight appeared to have been fruitless.

4. *Three great miracles (Exodus 14:14-31)*

a. Moving the cloud (Ex. 14:19-20). At this point, God intervened to deliver His people with three distinct and impressive miracles. The first was a shift in position of the cloud which had been leading. From standing out over the water before the camp, it now moved directly overhead to stand behind it. This accomplished two things: it stopped the Egyptians, as it settled down on them like a fog so that they could not see,[86] and it provided light on the Israelite side so that the people there could see better. The cloud's normal lighting property was at this time confined to one side only. This illumination enabled the people to make preparations for crossing the water and allowed them to witness the second miracle God performed.

b. Opening the water (Ex. 14:21-22). The second miracle was the dividing of the water so that the people could cross to the other side. We are told that as a part to the miracle, God "caused the sea to go back by a strong east wind all the night" (Ex. 14:21). The wind is said to be particularly effective on the Bitter Lakes in changing water levels, but certainly wind alone did not do all that was necessary in this instance. God had to intervene with additional, supernatural power.[87] We know that the water involved was deep, and not merely

---

[85] That Pharaoh had been so reluctant to let Israel go before and now here changed his mind again, even after so many terrible plagues, shows how valuable Israelite labor had been to Egypt.

[86] Fog is quite unknown otherwise in Egypt. These men were not accustomed to this type of interference, which fact itself contributed to their frustration and decision to stop entirely.

[87] A study of biblical miracles reveals that God normally employs natural law when, and to the extent that, it is available to do His work; and that He only

that of a marshy area, for later the Egyptians were drowned in it (Ex. 14:27-28). Moreover, the soil was made sufficiently dry (Ex. 14:22, the Hebrew using *yabbashah*) so that Israelites could drive their wagons over it. Still further, the path had to be very wide, perhaps as much as a mile, to permit the more than 2,000,000 Israelites to cross during a part of one night.[88] To push back water for a half mile on one side and a half mile on the other would indeed take the miraculous power of almighty God. The path was made as the startled Israelites watched under the blaze of the illuminating cloud; then they moved into it on the broad front now possible. The statement that the waters were a wall on both their right hand and on their left (Ex. 14:22) is meaningful in terms of so much water having been pushed back on both sides.

Since there is no way to know exactly where the crossing was made, the length of this miraculous path is uncertain. Three factors have a bearing on the matter, however. The first is that the length could not have been greater than the distance the people could travel in perhaps five or six hours. Darkness apparently had fallen by the time the first of the people started, since the light from the cloud was already needed; and it was "in the morning watch" (Ex. 14:24; between three and six o'clock) that all were across, because by then the Egyptians were already in the path pursuing. A second factor concerns the length of the Israelite line going through the path. Numbering so many, even on a front of up to a mile wide, the column would have extended close to two miles, which means that an hour or more would have been consumed in merely passing over its own length, or in entering the path. Still a third factor is that progress would have been slow, with wagons having to be driven, and flocks and herds shepherded. These matters together suggest that the distance was not more than three or four miles.

c. Closing the water (Ex. 14:23-31). The third miracle was the closing of the water, so that the pursuing Egyptians were drowned. As the last of the Israelites moved into the dried path, the cloud began to move ahead of the Egyptians so that they could once more see to take up the chase. They found the footprints and wheelmarks of the Israelites leading down to where the water had been, and they directly followed. They thought, no doubt, that if the Israelites had been able to go through, so could they. When all were well between the great

uses supernatural force when the natural is insufficient. It should be realized that as much divine power is required to effect natural processes as supernatural interventions.

[88] A marching line of 2,000,000 people, walking ten abreast with an average five feet separating each rank, would be 190 miles long. Had this path been only as wide as a modern highway, the first Israelites through would have been in Canaan before the last started, and several days would have elapsed.

walls of water, however, God intervened to bring trouble. Chariot wheels began to come off. The Egyptians, remembering the plagues, realized that again Yahweh was fighting for His people (Ex. 14:24-25). But as they started to flee back to the shoreline, God released the pent-up waters, enormous in amount as they were, and they rolled down upon the helpless Egyptians with speed and crushing power. In the resulting maelstrom, neither man nor animal had a chance to survive. Israelites, watching in the planned, opportune light of morning, saw the mighty, awesome elite of Egypt go down to complete destruction.

It is not likely that Pharaoh himself was in this group. The story does not say so,[89] and Amenhotep II did not die at this time. He lived twenty-two years after this, and his mummy has been found in the Valley of the Tombs of the Kings along with those of the many other Pharaohs buried there.[90]

d. Reason for the experience. The question rises as to why God led His people to a place where they would be trapped between water and pursuing Egyptians. A slightly different route, really no longer in distance, would have missed the Bitter Lakes entirely.[91] The answer is clear that there was need for just this sort of experience by the Israelites at the beginning of their long weary march through the wilderness. They needed a strong impression of the greatness of Yahweh's power, for they had been long in the land of Egypt where false gods were worshiped. They had forgotten how great in power the true God really was. The demonstrations of power in the plagues had helped, but most

[89] Ex. 14:6 suggests that Pharaoh did personally assemble the army and possibly even accompanied them at the start, but no indication is made that he was involved in the closing waters. He is not mentioned after Ex. 14:10, and the drowning is not described until the following verses 26-27. Psalm 136:15 is poetical, with a figure of speech to be expected.

[90] His mummy was found in 1898 by Loret. The discovery was unusual for the mummy was found yet in its own coffin and tomb, whereas most royal tombs had been robbed and the mummies taken elsewhere. In one of the side rooms of his tomb, indeed, were found nine other royal mummies, including those of Thutmose IV, Amenhotep III, and Merneptah, which had been brought here from their tombs. Cf. Owen, Archaeology and the Bible (Westwood, N. J.: Fleming H. Revell, 1961), pp. 214-17.

[91] It has been suggested that the need for Israel coming to this water was to avoid Egyptian fortifications elsewhere. Seti I, in inscriptions at Karnak, does speak of fortifications along the eastern approaches to Egypt. One is known to have been at Zilu (Thel) north, and one toward the southern end of the Bitter Lakes, which seems to have been there also during the eighteenth Dynasty; cf. J. Simons, GTT, p. 248. However, not enough is known regarding either location or purpose of these "forts" (mktl) to make certain conclusions. Furthermore, it is doubtful if a small garrison would have done much to stop 2,000,000 people or would have been a necessary reason to detour.

of these had occurred, intentionally, only in the Egyptian area. Israelites certainly had heard of them, but hearsay is never as impressive as direct experience. The people needed to see for themselves God's power, and here they did. They saw most vividly what their God could do in controlling and redirecting forces of nature, and then employ them in turn to overthrow the world-renowned, mighty Egyptian army. The memory would have fortified the Israelites for meeting days of trial that lay ahead during the forty years of wilderness travel.

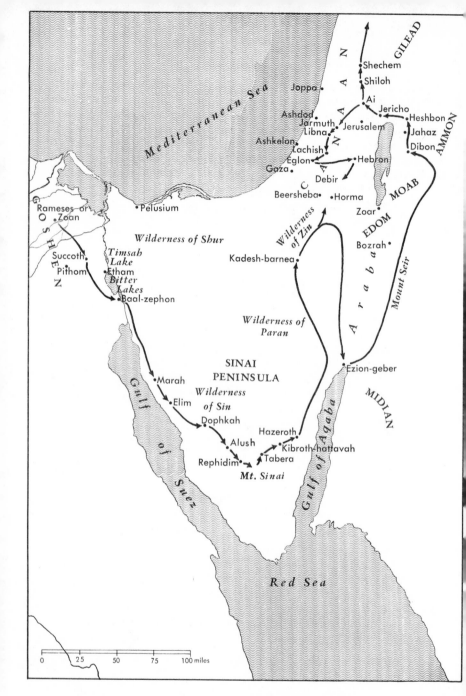

Map 5. The Route of the Exodus and the Conquest of Canaan

CHAPTER SEVEN

ISRAEL IN THE WILDERNESS

Exodus 15:22–40:38; Leviticus 8–10; Numbers 1–4; 10:11–14:45; 16–17; 20–27; 31–36; Deuteronomy 1–4; 34

Israel's task, now that she was out of Egypt and across the *yam suph,* was to make her way to Canaan. The 430-year sojourn in Egypt had served to fulfill one of God's promises to Abraham: that of a nation-size posterity. It was time now for the second to be fulfilled: that of a homeland. The shortest way to Canaan lay northeast. From Israel's present location on the east side of the *yam suph* to southern Canaan was approximately 150 miles. Had the people gone directly they could have been in the land in less than a month. However, God did not so lead them, one reason being that they would have encountered Philistines and been wearied by battle with them (Ex. 13: 17).[1] The route God did select has been the subject of considerable discussion.

A. ISRAEL'S ROUTE OF TRAVEL

The route of Israel (held traditionally and by most scholars today[2]) runs south along the Red Sea for over one hundred miles and then diagonally inland toward modern Jebel Musa (Mt. Sinai) nearly fifty miles. From this point, where Israel remained for nearly a year, it leads north to Kadesh-barnea at the southern extremity of Canaan.

The key to determining the route is the location of Mt. Sinai. The traditional view identifies it with Jebel Musa, in the southern Sinai peninsula. Some scholars believe, however, that it must be found somewhere east of the Gulf of Aqaba. Their reasoning is that Mt. Sinai

---

[1] For existence of Philistines here at this time, cf. *supra,* chap. 3, pp. 59-60.
[2] Held for instance by Bright, *BHI,* pp. 114-15; Wright, *BAR,* pp. 62-64; *Westminster Historical Atlas to the Bible* (1956), pp. 38-39; Anderson, *Understanding the Old Testament* (Englewood Cliffs, N.J.: Prentice-Hall, Inc., 1957), p. 46.

137

apparently was a volcano, because of the fire, smoke, clouds, and sound which issued from it as the people one day stood at its base (Ex. 19:16-18); and no volcanos are found in the Sinaitic peninsula. The nearest is beyond the Gulf of Aqaba. In reply, it must be observed that these phenomena, fearfully witnessed by Israel, were supernatural in origin; and the mountain itself need not have produced them. Another view is that Mt. Sinai must have been in the north of the Sinaitic peninsula, because Amalekites waged battle with Israel there (Ex. 17: 8-16), and Amalekites were never otherwise found as far south as Jebel Musa (Num. 14:43-45; I Sam. 15:7; 27:8). In reply to this, it may be pointed out that, though Amalekites did normally remain farther north, in this instance they had apparently followed Israel south for the purpose of preying on them (Deut. 25:18). A roving tribe, they lived by looting wherever there was opportunity; and it is not surprising that they should here have left their ordinary territory in pursuit of Israel as a likely victim.

Several matters favor the traditional location. For one thing, it has been held as correct for many centuries; in fact, from early Christian times and probably before. For another, Mt. Sinai must have been some distance from the point of Israel's exodus from Egypt, for a number of stopping places are listed between the two locations (Num. 33: 2-18), some of which can be identified with a degree of probability. For a third, Mt. Sinai must have been well south of Canaan, for it was an eleven-day journey from there to Kadesh-barnea (Deut. 1:2), and years later Elijah even took forty days to make the trip from Beersheba, though he likely moved slowly and indirectly (I Kings 19:8).[3] For a fourth, it may be pertinent that Moses' father-in-law is called a Kenite, meaning "smith," for near Jebel Musa lay the copper mines of Serabit el-Khadim which could have prompted smiths to live in the vicinity.

B. To Mt. Sinai (Exodus 15:22–18:27)

1. *Marah, Elim, Wilderness of Sin (Exodus 15:22–16:36)*

a. Water provisions (Ex. 15:22-27). Israel watched the overthrow of the Egyptian army from the eastern shore of the *yam suph,* paused to give praise to God (Ex. 15:1-21), and proceeded to follow the directing cloud southward. Three days they traveled without finding water.[4] They finally came to a small oasis called Marah, but its water

---

[3] He is said to have traveled to Mt. Horeb, but Mt. Sinai and Mt. Horeb were identical, except that the former may have been the entire mountain of which the latter formed only one peak.

[4] J. Simons, *GTT,* p. 251, states that Israel must have moved inland for some distance here or else they would have found water in several places near the Red Sea before coming to Hawarah.

was bitter. Marah has been commonly identified with Modern Hawarah, where the water is still bitter.[5] Moses, at God's direction, cast a piece of wood into the water, and it immediately became sweet and drinkable. The people moved on to Elim, believed to be present day Wadi Ghurundel,[6] about six miles south of Hawarah, where plenty of sweet water is still to be found. Israel discovered here twelve wells and seventy palm trees, which made it a place of welcome refreshment for both water and shade. This location is yet a favorite stop for travelers, and Israel may have remained for several days. Then the people moved on to a region called "wilderness of Sin" (Ex. 16:1). This is best identified with a sandy, easily-traveled plain along the shore of the Red Sea, since the terrain just inland is rugged. They arrived in this plain "on the fifteenth day of the second month" (Ex. 16:1), exactly one month after departure from Raamses.

b. Manna (Ex. 16:1-36). It was here that Israel's food supply ran out. The people had brought considerable provisions, but one month had depleted them. The Israelites became anxious and cried to Moses. With so many people, besides flocks and herds, and with the wilderness barren, their anxiety is understandable. Where would adequate food be found in such a desolate region?[7] However, the people should have realized that God, who had already miraculously delivered them at the *yam suph,* would also be able to meet this need. They should have trusted rather than doubted.

God's provision turned out to be a nourishing food in the form of "a small round thing,"[8] described as "like coriander seed, white" and sweet, which the people called "manna"[9] (Ex. 16:14, 15, 31). It lay on the ground fresh each morning except the Sabbath. The people were instructed to gather as much as they needed for one day, and on the sixth day to gather a double portion to last over the Sabbath. They

[5] Described as a basin some five feet wide and eighteen inches deep, containing water disagreeably bitter and salty; cf. W. G. Blaikie, *A Manual of Bible History,* rev. C. D. Matthews (New York: The Ronald Press, 1957), p. 65; also J. Simons, *GTT,* p. 252, n. 218.

[6] *Westminster Historical Atlas to the Bible* (1956), pp. 38-39.

[7] A modern city of 2,000,000 by comparison calls for hundreds of food markets. The Israelites needed an enormous amount of food.

[8] This was not the honeydew excretion of scale-insects sucking sap from the tamarisk thickets of Sinai, as suggested by some scholars (Wright, *BAR,* pp. 64-65). Such excretion would not have sufficed for so many and, furthermore, is seasonal.

[9] Hebrew *man,* meaning "what?" The people asked "What is it?" and from this question took the name, "manna."

were told that unused food gathered on normal days would spoil, but not when gathered on the sixth.[10]

c. Quail (Ex. 16:12-13). In the evening prior to the first morning on which the manna appeared, another provision of food was made, though only for one day. It was meat and was supplied through a great flight of quail. It is stated that "the quail came up, and covered the camp." Perhaps the birds were caused to fly near enough to the ground for the people to strike them in flight, as seems to have been the case approximately one year later in a similar instance.[11] Whatever the method of capture, the people were provided abundant meat from these quail that night. The next morning the manna first appeared. Certainly no one hungered in camp that day! God had marvelously supplied. It should be added that the provision of manna continued daily, from this time until the Jordan had been crossed forty years later (Ex. 16:35; Josh. 5:11-12).

2. *Rephidim and Mt. Sinai (Exodus 17:1–19:3)*. From the wilderness of Sin, Israel turned inland, perhaps moving up Wadi Feiran which leads toward Jebel Musa, and came to a place called Rephidim, sometimes identified with Wadi Refayid. Rephidim was near Mt. Sinai, for it was here that God told Moses to smite the "rock in Horeb" to bring water for the people; Horeb being identical with, or at least inclusive of, Sinai.

a. Water from the rock (Ex. 17:1-7). At Rephidim the people found their water depleted. The region boasts a few springs, but these apparently were not flowing strongly this year. The people complained bitterly to Moses, who brought the need to God. Following instructions, Moses struck[12] the rock of Horeb, and water in great quantity

[10] God could have kept the manna over other days, too, of course, but did not, no doubt, to make each day a fresh experience of trusting God to supply. Jesus taught the disciples to pray, "Give us this day our daily bread" (Matt. 6:11). God's people are to trust Him for each day's provision.

[11] On the second occasion, the quail flew about three feet above the ground; cf. Free, *ABH*, p. 116. Wright's suggestion, *BAR*, p. 65, that both instances may have involved an annual crossing of the Mediterranean by quail must be rejected for two reasons: the Israelites were not near the Mediterranean either time; and this annual migration today comes in September and October, while both these instances for Israel were in the Spring.

[12] The suggestion of Wright, *BAR*, p. 65, and others, that Moses merely opened a vein of water in the rock must be rejected. Such a small amount could not have satisfied 2,000,000 people. Actually, Moses' action in striking the rock was unnecessary for making this water flow, for it was produced supernaturally. The only reason for the act was to provide a typical picture of Christ who in due time would be smitten on Calvary to provide spiritual water for lost sinners (I Cor. 10:4). Cf. Num. 20:8.

gushed forth.[13] The people's thirst was satisfied. It is very possible that this stream so started continued to flow all the time that the people were at Sinai.[14] There are sources of water near Jebel Musa today,[15] but, in view of the water-lack at Rephidim, this particular year had evidently seen little rainfall, and so there was need for such a special stream. Rephidim and the plain before Sinai were not so far apart but what the stream could have flowed by natural course near enough to the plain to make its water available to the encampment there.

b. Amalekite battle (Ex. 17:8-16). Also at Rephidim, the Israelites encountered a roving band called Amalekites in battle. This band may have descended from Esau[16] (Gen. 36:12), even as the Edomites (Gen. 36:1). The Amalekites moved about, preying on others,[17] in distinction from many tribes of the day which were more sedentary. Though not directly stated, the Amalekites apparently had been attacking the weak and stragglers of Israel since the crossing of the *yam suph* (Deut. 25:17-18), but now had become bolder in their hit-and-

[13] In Psalm 105:41, the amount is called a "river" (*nahar*). It would have taken a river to satisfy the needs of so many people and animals.

[14] Some matters suggest this. Deut. 9:21 speaks of the brook, on which Moses later spread ashes from the burned golden calf, as "the brook that descended out of the mount." The descriptive phrase used here is unnecessary if this was a natural brook. Also I Cor. 10:4 speaks of the rock from which the water flowed at Rephidim as the "spiritual rock that followed them," which could mean that the water from this rock followed them by natural course the short distance to the plain before Mt. Sinai. Further, since the people ate food supplied supernaturally while at Sinai, it would be in keeping if God desired them to drink water supplied supernaturally and so be daily reminded of their continual dependence on Him in these two basic ways.

[15] C. Conder, *ISBE*, IV, p. 2804, quotes F. Holland, *Recovery of Jerus*, p. 524, as follows: "With regard to water-supply there is no spot in the whole Peninsula which is nearly so well supplied as the neighborhood of *Jebel Musa*. Four streams of running water are found there: one in *Wady Leja;* a second in *Wady et Ti'ah* which waters a succession of gardens extending more than 3 miles in length, and forms pools in which I have often had a swim; a third stream rises to the N. of the watershed of the plain of *er Rahah* and runs W. into *Wady et Ti'ah;* and a fourth is formed by the drainage from the mountains of *Umm 'Alawy,* to the E. of *Wady Sebaiyeh* and finds its way into that valley by a narrow ravine opposite *Jebel ed Deir.* In addition to these streams there are numerous wells and springs, affording excellent water throughout the whole of the granitic district."

[16] One problem exists in this identification, however, in that eastern kings are said to have devastated "all the country of the Amalekites" already in Abraham's day (Gen. 14:7). If this is not proleptic speech, Amalekites must have existed before Esau. If so, his descendants probably joined with them.

[17] Clearly illustrated in their attack years later on the Philistine city of Ziklag in the time of David (I Sam. 30).

run tactics.[18] Consequently, Moses instructed Joshua, one in whom he had learned to place confidence,[19] to choose men for engaging the raiders in battle.

This was not an easy task for Joshua, for the people, fresh from Egyptian slavery, were not trained for warfare and would not have had many weapons. Certainly Joshua could not have expected many to volunteer for fighting in these circumstances, especially when the enemy lived by his very expertness in combat. However, some did respond, probably in large part out of respect for Joshua. The battle was fought the following day, and God gave a most unusual victory. Moses, on a nearby hill observing, raised his arms toward God in a gesture of supplication, and, as long as his arms were held upright, Joshua's troops advanced; but, when his arms tired and were lowered, his men were forced to retreat. Finally, Aaron and Hur,[20] standing on either side of Moses, assisted their leader in maintaining his arms upright until full victory was achieved. In this way, the Israelites were given an impressive lesson that victory was not won through their own abilities but through trust in God's might.

c. Organization (Ex. 18:1-27). Also at Rephidim, Moses was visited by his father-in-law, Jethro. This was Jethro's home country, and he did not have far to come to make the visit. He brought with him Moses' wife, Zipporah, and Moses' two sons, Gershom and Eliezer, whom Moses had earlier sent home when on his way back to Egypt (Ex. 4:24-26; 18:2). Upon arriving in the camp and making some observations, Jethro offered counsel to Moses.[21] He suggested that Moses appoint assistants to aid in superintending the host of Israel. Moses followed the counsel and did appoint "rulers of thousands,

---

[18] Moses probably had hoped that Israel's journey southward, directly away from the Amalekites' natural habitat, would dissuade this enemy from continuing to pursue. From the fact that Joshua seemingly knew when and where to expect their attack at the time of the battle, it is clear that the raids had been increasing in frequency, however.

[19] This is the first mention of Joshua in the biblical story. To cause Moses so to entrust him now means that Joshua had already been found capable and dependable.

[20] Aaron we know was Moses' brother, and Hur may have been his brother-in-law, the husband of Miriam, as Josephus states (*Antiq.* III, 2, 4). Later Hur was given responsibility, along with Aaron, in superintending Israel while Moses was absent receiving the Law (Ex. 24:14). He may have died soon after this, however, for he is not mentioned in the story again.

[21] Jethro here voiced praise to Yahweh and even performed sacrifice to Him (Ex. 18:10-12), which means that Moses had strongly influenced him during the prior forty years. He also said: "Now I know that Yahweh is greater than all gods." The view of liberal scholars that Moses had learned of Yahweh from Jethro (cf. H. H. Rowley, *The Rediscovery of the Old Testament*, Philadelphia: Westminster, 1946, chap. 5) must be rejected.

rulers of hundreds, rulers of fifties, and rulers of tens" (Ex. 18:25). This means that at least several hundred, if not a few thousand,[22] persons then became official personnel in the camp of Israel. Without question, this action proved of great value to Moses. The work of these assistants appears to have been mainly judicial, for it is stated that "hard cases they brought unto Moses," but "every small matter they judged themselves." In addition, the divisions of the people thus formed would have provided natural lines of organization for dispensing information and effecting regulations.

d. Arrival at Mt. Sinai (Ex. 19:1-2). The next stop was at Mt. Sinai itself, best identified with one end of a mountain ridge about two miles long and one mile wide.[23] Only the southern peak of this mountain is Jebel Musa (7363 feet high), while the northern peak is called Ras es-safsafeh (6540 feet). Before each peak stretches a plain adequate for the Israelite encampment, but scholars generally favor the one before Jebel Musa as the one used. Here Israel arrived in the third month of the journey (Ex. 19:1) on what is called "the same day"; likely meaning the same day of this third month as that of the first month on which the journey had started from Raamses, which was the fifteenth. The people were to be here eleven months and five days, for they departed finally on the twentieth day of the second month, a year later (Num. 10:11). During this time the all-important Law was to be given and the central Tabernacle built.

C. GIVING THE LAW (Exodus 19:3–24:18; 32:1–34:35)

As Israel had been making her way from Egypt to Sinai during the prior sixty days, she had been only a vast host of people with little order or organization. Except for size, she could scarcely be called a nation. Slavery conditions while in Egypt had prohibited anything like self-government. Certain persons, who had held the title "elder," had no doubt been used by the Egyptians to keep contact and control; but, when Israel left Egypt, she had no law of her own nor any real identity as an organized people. Neither did she have a true consciousness of God or the manner of life He required.

This needed to be corrected before entrance was made into the Promised Land. God planned this correction to be effected at Sinai. In fact, it is not too much to say that a prime reason for the long detour through the peninsula is to be found in this intention.[24] Sinai

[22] It is impossible to figure the exact number, for insufficient information is given regarding the particular units over which these officials ruled. They likely were family units, but these could be figured either larger or smaller.

[23] Cf. *supra*, n. 3.

[24] There was little reason to go this far south merely to avoid Philistines (Ex. 13:17).

offered an advantageous setting. Here the people would be quite un-
disturbed by others, for population was scarce. Here, too, the people
would be entirely dependent on God's physical provisions, certainly in
respect to food and likely water, which should cause hearts to be more
receptive to God's spiritual ministrations. Here, then, God did choose
to weld them into a true nation; to give them a law and organization;
to unify them as a people with a sense of identity and mission; and
above all to make them a people of faith and confidence in their God.

1. _Giving the Decalogue (Exodus 19:3–20:17)_. The first aspect of
God's communication to Israel at Sinai was His oral speaking of the
Decalogue or Ten Commandments (Ex. 20:1-17). To ready the people
to receive these ten principles in a proper spirit, God gave instructions
regarding two days of preparation (Ex. 19:3-15). The people were
to realize the importance of what God was about to impart to them.
Effecting these opening instructions, Moses initially called for the
people to declare their willingness to obey the laws God was about to
give; and the people responded that they would (Ex. 19:3-8). Then
he drew a boundary line at the foot of the mountain beyond which
both people and animals were not to pass, or else they would die.
Further, the people were to wash themselves physically and sanctify
themselves spiritually and so be "ready against the third day." The
washing was necessary both as physical cleansing, in view of many days
of dusty walking, and as a symbol of the spiritual cleansing needed.
The spiritual sanctification consisted in this inner cleansing, so symbolized, as the people brought their minds and heart-attitudes to a
state befitting the occasion.

The anticipated third day began with an awe-inspiring display on
Mt. Sinai (Ex. 19:16-25). A thick cloud rested on the mountain, from
which came thunder, lightning, and an increasing sound of a blowing
trumpet. Smoke ascended as from a great furnace. An earthquake
shook the mountain. This demonstration was to prepare the people
further. They were to be impressed with the great might and authority
of Him who was about to speak. During the display, Moses once
more, at God's command, instructed the people not to cross the
boundary line.

At the proper moment, God began to speak audibly from the mountain so that all could hear.[25] Probably these spoken words now took
the place of the trumpet sound, but the other phenomena apparently
continued to make the setting awesome. Certainly the emotional effect
on the people was marked, as out from this fearful, majestic back-

[25] Cf. Ex. 20:1, 19; Deut. 5:4, 22. This miraculous, oral declaration, and then
permanent recording on tables of stone, of the Ten Commandments should have
impressed the people with their great importance.

ground oral words were heard without the appearance of a human speaker.

That which was communicated was the Decalogue. One by one ten basic principles of life were delineated. The people listened and were afraid. When the Voice ceased, the people urged Moses to act as their mediator, so that they would not have to hear more in this direct, fearful manner (Ex. 20:19). After this, Moses did "draw near unto the thick darkness where God was" (Ex. 20:21), so that he alone could hear, and God continued His communication.

2. *The Book of the Covenant (Exodus 20:22–24:4).* That which Moses now received from God is called the "book of the covenant" (Ex. 24:7). Its record covers more than three chapters. All of it was apparently revealed to Moses that same third day, after which Moses returned to the people[26] and relayed it orally to them.[27] In response, the people once more declared that they would obey what God commanded. This response was more meaningful than the first, for now there was content to what God demanded. Still that same day Moses recorded the material in writing (Ex. 24:3-4). The hour must have been late when Moses retired.

3. *The ratification ceremony (Exodus 24:4-8).* The following day was one of Israel's most important. It was the occasion of ratification of God's covenant. If one were to pick out a particular day when Israel became a true nation, this would be the day. For here God's covenant with Israel went into effect, being ratified by a formal ceremony. It is true that all the Law had not yet been revealed—in fact, only a small part of the total[28]—but enough so that this could represent the remainder. Since nearly three months would be occupied in giving the remainder, and it was now that the people had been duly prepared in mind and heart for the ratification, this was the day most opportune for it.

Moses first built an altar and placed twelve stone pillars around it; the altar clearly representing God and the pillars the twelve tribes of Israel. Then young men were appointed to kill oxen for sacrifice. Half of the blood was caught in containers and half was applied to the altar.[29] This done, Moses read aloud the entire "book of the cove-

---

[26] There was hardly time for Moses to climb all the way to the top of Sinai either this time or the ones previous. He may have gone that far only later when he was to be there for forty days.

[27] A great feat of memory. God may have especially gifted him, or perhaps Moses had been instructed to take notes.

[28] In that it included the Moral Law, however, it was the most important part and that on which the remainder was based.

[29] With more than one animal killed, there would have been sufficient blood to cover this altar completely. This blood so applied symbolized purification of

nant,"[30] recorded just the night before as noted, and the people responded for the third time that they would obey.[31] With this proper response given, Moses took the blood in the containers and sprinkled it out toward the people in a gesture representing the covering of their sin. The people's sin thus covered, and their promise to keep God's law formally declared, the covenant was made binding and Israel became God's chartered nation.

In representation of this new intimate relationship, Moses, Aaron, and Aaron's two eldest sons, Nadab and Abihu, besides seventy elders, ascended Mt. Sinai the same day and ate in God's presence, a presence symbolized to them by a majestic vision (Ex. 24:9-11).

4. *The Law given and broken (Exodus 24:12-18; 32:1-34:35)*

a. First forty days (Ex. 24:12-18). God now called Moses up into the mountain to begin a period of revelation lasting forty days. Moses took Joshua with him, leaving Aaron and Hur in charge of the camp. For six days Moses stayed at a point only part way up the mountain, apparently still with Joshua, but on the seventh day God called him on alone.[32] He remained in God's presence continuously for forty days as God revealed the Law to him.[33] At some point during this time, God also inscribed the Ten Commandments on two hewn tables of stone.

b. Golden calf (Ex. 32). On the fortieth day, God interrupted proceedings by telling Moses that the people had sinned in making a golden calf as an image of worship. Moses immediately returned to camp, meeting Joshua again on the way. On arrival there, Moses, in a display of righteous indignation, broke the two inscribed stone tables in the sight of the people,[34] utterly destroyed the golden calf, repri-

the altar, as did the blood which came to be sprinkled on the "mercy seat" and brazen altar on the Day of Atonement (Lev. 16:14-20). Representing God, this altar had to be symbolized as perfectly pure.

[30] Likely Moses had recorded also what God had said orally, the Ten Commandments, which means that he here read what is now in Ex. 20-23.

[31] This third time counted much more than the first two. The first time the people had only assented to what they thought God would command. The second time was more meaningful, in that they now knew what God commanded. But this third time was in full ceremony, which constituted their formal pledge to obey. The first two had been more preliminary, giving them occasion to reflect before making the formal promise.

[32] Joshua remained on the mountain while Moses was gone, for Moses found him there on returning (Ex. 32:17), and Joshua knew no more about the people's sin than did Moses at that time.

[33] This first period of forty days was probably occupied mainly with plans for the Tabernacle, in view of these plans being included in the immediately following chapters (Ex. 25-31).

[34] Deut. 9:17 implies that this action was deliberate on Moses' part, as he symbolized before the people their sin in breaking God's covenant.

manded a flustered Aaron who had consented to the sin, and instructed Levites to slay guilty Israelites, which they did to the number of 3,000. The next morning, Moses, in a praiseworthy demonstration of selflessness, pleaded with God that no more Israelites be destroyed in punishment for the sin, but instead, if more retribution were necessary, that Moses himself be blotted out of the "book" which God had "written"[35] (Ex. 32:30-32).

Why Israelites, within forty days of ratifying the covenant, should have sinned so seriously in breaking that covenant is not easy to explain. Apparently they believed that Moses, who had now been gone from them for several days,[36] had died on the mountain in the fearful presence of God (Ex. 32:1). So believing, they thought themselves leaderless, and this prompted the idea of returning to Egypt. This in turn somehow led to the thought of a bull image, no doubt influenced by memories of Egyptian bull worship.[37] It may be that Aaron thought to stop the movement by demanding that the people contribute their gold earrings as material to make the image, and was caught by his own demand when the people complied. Whatever the details, the image was made and the great sin committed.

c. Moses' commendable spirit (Ex. 32:11-14, 30-33). But if the people are to be severely condemned, Moses, in contrast, is to be highly applauded. On the mountain, at the time of first notice to Moses concerning the sin, God had really given Moses a choice: either not intercede in behalf of guilty Israel and have himself honored in being made head of a new nation; or intercede for them and spare them, which in turn would negate this attractive evaluation for himself. In other words, all Moses needed to do to become head of a new nation was refrain from interceding in Israel's behalf. But Moses chose to intercede, and did so on the basis of God's reputation, thus putting his own interest below that of God's and of the people's. Then, after returning to camp and effecting considerable retribution, Moses went still further and asked to be destroyed himself, even eternally, rather than have Israel be further punished. Aside from Christ, only one other per-

[35] This "book" is the book of life (Ps. 69:28; Dan. 12:1). The figure is taken from the practice of the time in maintaining registers of accepted people in a community or tribe.

[36] Very likely Moses had not absented himself from them for any extended length of time before this. Even when he had received the "book of the covenant" he had been gone only a part of one day.

[37] Egypt had Apis bull worship at Memphis and Mnevis bull worship at Heliopolis, but both of these were at some distance from Goshen. Nearer, and no doubt more influential, were bull-cults connected with Horus worship. The bull was a symbol of fertility and strength. Cf. Steindorff and Seele, *When Egypt Ruled the East* (Chicago: University of Chicago Press, 1957), pp. 140-41.

son demonstrated this degree of selflessness: the Apostle Paul, who wrote, "I could wish that I myself were anathema from Christ for my brethren's sake" (Rom. 9:3). God's response to Moses was that only those who had sinned would experience punishment.

d. Two further actions (Ex. 33:7-23). Before returning to the mountain to continue receiving the Law, Moses did two more things. First, he pitched a tent[38] outside the camp for himself, and, when he entered it, the pillar of cloud moved to stand at its door. The intention was to show the people how displeased God was with them, for the cloud left them to move where Moses dwelt, and to encourage full repentance toward God for their sin. Moreover, it demonstrated that God's approval was on Moses, and the people should again rally to his leadership, if they were to be blessed.

Second, Moses requested that he be permitted to see God's own glory. Moses, discouraged by Israel's serious disobedience, needed reassurance. God promised that His own "presence" would surely go with Moses, but Moses still wanted tangible evidence. God graciously acceded by hiding His servant in a "cleft of the rock," somewhere on Sinai, and allowing him to see what is called the "back" of God.[39]

e. Second forty days (Ex. 34:1-35). Moses was now bidden to hew two more tables of stone and return to the top of Sinai. He did so the following morning, and for forty more days God revealed the Law to him. When Moses descended this time, his face shone with the brightness of God's presence, and he had to cover himself with a veil that he might converse with others. It was likely soon after this return to camp that Moses recorded all that God had told him on the mountain, while it was still fresh in his mind.[40]

D. THE LAW

The Mosaic Law includes the Ten Commandments given orally to all the people, the "book of the covenant" given to Moses alone later the same day, and the lengthy, detailed regulations revealed to Moses, again alone, during the two forty-day periods on Mt. Sinai. The total content may be divided into moral, civil, and ceremonial law.

1. *Moral law.* The moral law is the Decalogue, or Ten Command-

---

[38] This tent is called "tent of meeting" (*'ohel mo'edh*), the same name given to the later Tabernacle. However, that structure had not yet been built and so should not be confused with this simple tent.

[39] This language is highly anthropomorphic. God is pure spirit (John 4:24) and cannot be seen by physical eyesight; and if He could, the man that should see Him would die, as God Himself says (Ex. 33:20). What Moses saw, however, was real and represented God in His glory.

[40] For discussion as to when Moses wrote the Pentateuch as such, cf. *infra*, pp. 166-67.

ments. It supplies the broad moral principles for conducting life generally, and it presents the basis for the more specific civil and ceremonial regulations. Its importance was stressed in that it was orally
proclaimed by God and then inscribed supernaturally on stone tables.
It is of two parts:[41] the first concerning man's duties to God, regarding God's being, His worship, His name, and His day; the second
concerning man's duties to man, regarding honoring parents, not mur-
dering, not committing adultery, not stealing, not bearing false witness,
and not coveting.[42] It is likely that every person was expected to
memorize these precepts and esteem them of the highest importance.

2. *Civil law.* The civil law gives specific instruction about daily
social relationships. It concerns administration of justice, rights of
property, care of the poor, training of children, punishment of criminals,
and many other matters. Numerous laws deal with personal interrela-
tionships: fathers and children, husbands and wives, masters and servants, and kindness to strangers. Nearly all of the "book of the covenant" concerns civil laws, many of which can be rightly understood only
in the light of contemporary cultures. Regulations were especially
needed that many Egyptian customs and practices might be avoided.

3. *Ceremonial law.* The ceremonial law has to do with religious
matters, with much of it concerning priestly functions at the Tabernacle. Specifications are given for the Tabernacle itself, the dress and
duties of the priests and Levites, and the various sacrifices and offerings.[43] The great annual feasts are prescribed, and every male was required to celebrate the three main ones[44] annually at the central sanctuary. The ceremonial law is the longest of the three divisions. It
should be added that many of the ceremonial and civil laws were only
temporary in nature, being valid for as long as conditions made them
appropriate, whereas the moral laws were designated to be permanent.

4. *Comparison with other laws.* The Mosaic Law has often been
compared with other legal codes of early time. Six are known: (1) the
Ur-nammu code, c. 2050 B.C., from the Third Dynasty of Ur; (2) the
code of Bilalama, c. 1925 B.C., from Eshnunna; (3) the code of Lipit-
Ishtar, c. 1860 B.C., from Isin; (4) the code of Hammurabi, c. 1700

---

[41] This twofold division was recognized by Christ in speaking of the two great
commandments of the Law (Matt. 22:34-40).

[42] Another division combines the first two (God's being and worship) and
divides the last (not coveting) into two (not coveting a neighbor's house and
not coveting a neighbor's other property or wife).

[43] For discussion, cf. *infra*, chap. 8, pp. 193-201.

[44] The Feast of Passover in the spring (Ex. 12:1-28; Num. 28:16-25; Deut.
16:1-8); the Feast of Pentecost fifty days later (Ex. 34:22; Lev. 23:15-22; Deut.
16:10); and the Feast of Tabernacles in the Fall (Lev. 23:34-42; Num. 29:
12-40).

B.C., from Babylon; (5) the Hittite code, c. 1450 B.C., from Boghaz-koi; and (6) the Assyrian code, c. 1350 B.C., from Assur.[45]

Comparison has revealed several parallels between these codes and Israel's law, but no more than common needs and situations would require. On the other hand, several basic differences significantly indicate the uniqueness of Israel's Law. There is difference: (1) in form, for Israel's law is constituted both of casuistic and apodictic law,[46] while other codes are constituted almost solely of casuistic;[47] (2) in general character, for Israel's law is religious in motivation while other codes are only legal and secular; (3) in moral tone, for other codes show no control of lust, no limitation of selfishness through regard for others, no postulate of charity, or no recognition of ethical sin as the cause for the destruction of a people;[48] and (4) in social distinctions, for at least the Hammurabi code establishes the place of three classes of people, the free men, the semifree, and the slaves, whereas Israel's law has nothing parallel, recognizing slavery only for the purpose of giving protection to this underprivileged group.

E. THE TABERNACLE (Exodus 25–31; 35–40)

One of the main subjects in God's communication to Moses was the Tabernacle. In contrast to Egypt and other countries where many temples existed, Israel was to have only one place of worship. For the period of wilderness travel, and also for many years after occupying Palestine, this place was to be a portable sanctuary called the Tabernacle. God gave Moses the plan for it, which was to be followed exactly since it involved numerous symbolisms of spiritual truth. Bezaleel of the tribe of Judah and Aholiab of the tribe of Dan, both skilled by special enablement of the Spirit of God, were to lead in the construction (Ex. 35:30-35). Freewill offerings of the people quickly provided ample building material, though the amount needed was large and of great value (Ex. 35:4-29). The importance of this struc-

---

[45] Mendenhall, "Ancient Oriental and Biblical Law," BA, 17(May, 1954), p. 23, n. 18. For discussion, cf. his Law and Covenant in Israel and the Ancient Near East (Pittsburgh: Biblical Colloquim, 1955); also for texts and discussion, cf. ANET, pp. 159-98.

[46] Casuistic laws, often called "judgments" or "case laws," begin with an "if" and set up a specific situation. Apodictic laws, often called "statutes," cover a general area of conduct. The Ten Commandments are good examples of the latter.

[47] Mendenhall has pointed out a very few apodictic laws in the Hittite code, "Ancient Oriental and Biblical Law," BA, 17 (May, 1954), pp. 29-30 and T. J. Meek in the Assyrian laws, ANET, p. 183, n. 24.

[48] A. Jeremias, The Old Testament in the Light of the Ancient Near East, trans. C. L. Beaumont (London: Williams & Norgate, University of Wales Press Board, 1911), II, p. 112.

ture was stressed by the large place given to it in the Law and its assigned central location among the tribes. There was need for it to be central, for, being God's own sanctuary, it represented His presence among the people.

1. *Description.* The Tabernacle consisted of a portable building located within a rectangular court. The court measured 150 feet[49] by 75 feet, and was enclosed by linen curtains hung from silver hooks on silver-covered rods, attached to posts of acacia wood. Entrance was from the east through a gate of curtains. Two articles of furniture were located in the eastern half of the court. Nearest the entrance was the brazen altar where the priests offered sacrifices for the people (Ex. 27:1-8; 38:1-7). It measured seven and one-half feet square and four and one-half feet high, was made of acacia wood covered with bronze, and had horns at each corner. Beyond the altar was the laver (Ex. 30:17-21; 38:8; 40:30). This was made of bronze and was the place where priests washed prior to engagement in ceremony.

In the western half of the court stood the Tabernacle proper, a rectangular building, forty-five feet long, fifteen feet wide, and fifteen feet high, constructed of forty-eight frameworks[50] of acacia wood covered with gold (Ex. 26:1-37; 36:8-38). It consisted of two compartments: the first, called the Holy Place, comprising two-thirds of the area and containing the seven-light lampstand, the table of showbread, and the altar of incense; and the second, called the Holy of Holies, containing the Ark of the Covenant,[51] which supported two golden cherubim with outstretched wings. The building had four layers of covering: the first of linen, the second of goats' hair, the third of dyed rams' skins, and the fourth of dugong[52] skins.

[49] Figuring the standard cubit as approximately 18 inches (more precisely, 17:51 inches); cf. R. B. Y. Scott, *JBL*, 78(1958), pp. 210-12.

[50] "Frameworks" (*qerashim*; Ex. 26:15f; 36:20f) is better than "boards" of KJV because: (1) a plank 15 feet by 27 inches would be extremely heavy and very difficult to obtain, whereas a framework of this dimension would be lighter and easily constructed; (2) frameworks would have let one see through to the beautiful covering curtain; and (3) the best analysis of the Hebrew word favors "frameworks." Cf. A. R. S. Kennedy, "Tabernacle," *HDB*, pp. 559-661.

[51] The Ark was the most sacred object. The high priest alone was to enter the Holy of Holies where it was, and this only once a year on the Day of Atonement. Made of acacia wood, overlaid on the inside and out with gold, and with a solid gold plate for a lid, called the mercy seat, the Ark represented the presence of God among His people. The Decalogue forbade any image of God, and this Ark in a way took the place of one without the element of attempted physical resemblance. The Ark contained the two inscribed tables of stone representing the Covenant, a golden pot of manna, and later Aaron's rod that budded (Heb. 9:4; Num. 17:1-13).

[52] The dugong is a marine animal, averaging 5 to 9 feet long, which lives in the seas around Egypt and Sinai. It was likely the skin of this animal which

2. *Location.* God directed that the Tabernacle be located in the exact center of the tribes, when encamped during the wilderness journey. On the east were to be the tribes of Judah, Issachar, and Zebulon; on the south, Reuben, Simeon, and Gad; on the west, Ephraim, Manasseh, and Benjamin; and on the north, Dan, Asher, and Naphtali

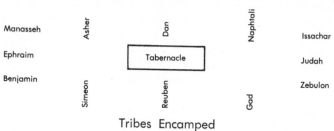

Tribes Encamped

(Num. 2).[53] When marching, the three eastern tribes were to go first, followed by the Levitic families of Gershon and Merari bearing the dismantled Tabernacle material;[54] then the three southern tribes, followed by the Levitic family of Kohath bearing the Tabernacle furniture;[55] then the three western tribes, and finally the three northern tribes (Num. 3–4; 10:11-28). Even when marching, the Tabernacle furniture was to be kept in the center, though the Tabernacle itself was

Judah		Reuben		Ephraim	Dan
Ark	Issachar	Tabernacle Material (Gershon Merari)	Simeon	Tabernacle Furniture (Kohath)	Manasseh	Asher
	Zebulon		Gad		Benjamin	Naphtali

Tribes Marching

was used, rather than that of the badger; the Hebrew word employed being properly so rendered and badgers are not known to have lived in this part of the world; cf. Free, *ABH*, pp. 106-107.

[53] This grouping is according to mother ancestry: Leah's posterity, Reuben, Simeon, (Levi removed as priestly tribe), Judah, Issachar, and Zebulon, are on the east and south; Rachel's posterity, Ephraim, Manasseh (sons of Joseph), and Benjamin, are on the west; Bilhah's (maid of Rachel) posterity, Dan and Naphtali, are on the north; and Zilpah's (Leah's maid) posterity, Gad and Asher, are divided, one on the north and one on the south.

[54] The Gershonites transported the fabrics of the Tabernacle (Num. 4:21-28) in two wagons drawn by four oxen (Num. 7:7); and the Merarites the wood and metal items (Num. 4:29-33) in four wagons drawn by eight oxen (Num. 7:8).

[55] The Kohathites did not need wagons, for the furniture was carried on poles inserted through supporting rings (Num. 4:1-15).

to go earlier so that it might be erected in time for the furniture to be set in place on arrival (Num. 10:21). One item of furniture went before all, the Ark of the Covenant, which led the way, with the priests carrying it as they followed the pillar of cloud moving overhead.

3. *Service instituted.* A main task for the approximate year that Israel remained at Sinai was the construction of this Tabernacle. Presumably work began shortly after Moses returned from the mountain, which would have been about three months after the people's first arrival at Sinai.[56] The date of completion is given as the first day of the first month in the second year (Ex. 40:17), which means about five and one-half months later. On the day of completion, the cloud, which otherwise led the people, settled over the Tabernacle and the glory of God filled it (Ex. 40:34).

The next matter was the consecration of Aaron and his sons, Nadab, Abihu, Eleazar, and Ithamar, to act as priests for ministering at the Tabernacle (Ex. 29:1-37; 40:12-15; Lev. 8:1-36). All five were washed with water, clothed in the prescribed priestly garments, and anointed with oil. A series of offerings was presented to God, with blood from a slain ram applied to the right thumb, right ear, and large toe of the right foot of all five persons. Wave offerings followed, and lastly a sacrificial meal eaten by Moses and the priests. The ceremony was repeated on seven successive days.

After this week of consecration, the priests began their ministry (Lev. 9:1-24). The inaugural day was most impressive. Several offerings were presented to God, both for the priests and the people, before Aaron was escorted by Moses into the Tabernacle for general orientation. When the two came out, miraculous fire appeared on the brazen altar, apparently consuming the offerings that were on the altar in an instant. This was not the initial kindling of altar fire, however, as sometimes believed, for offerings had been made all during the prior week of priestly consecration. This fire served more to climax the eight days of festivities, showing God's approval, both of all that had been done and what would be done in days and years to come.

4. *Sin of Nadab and Abihu (Exodus 10:1-7).* This happy atmosphere was now saddened, however, by unexpected, serious sin on the part of Aaron's two older sons, Nadab and Abihu. They had just been highly honored by inclusion in Israel's priesthood, but now offered what is called "strange fire" on the altar of incense. The implication is that they used coals of fire not taken from the prescribed place, the brazen altar. The fire on the brazen altar was never to go out (Lev. 6:13),

---

[56] Besides Moses' 80 days on the mount, there had been 4 days spent prior to his going there and a few days at the mid-point when the golden calf had been made, for a total of nearly 90 days.

for one reason that there would always be coals available for burning the incense. Nadab and Abihu certainly knew this, and should have been particularly conscious of the altar as the place to get coals, after the miraculous fire had so recently burned upon it. But somehow they were negligent, or else deliberately rebellious, and took coals from elsewhere. It seems evident as well that they offered the incense at an unprescribed time; that is, other than at the morning or evening sacrifice. Perhaps their new position had made them proud, and spoiled them for obeying orders carefully, or perhaps they had partaken of too much wine: a possibility which finds support in God's immediate warning to Aaron (Lev. 10:9) that wine and strong drink should be avoided at the time of Tabernacle service. Whatever the full reason, the sin of the two was serious. God in judgment sent forth fire again, this time to take the lives of each, both as punishment on them and as warning for those observing.

F. The Number of People

The need for organization of the people gave reason for a census. One was taken early in the second month of the second year, beginning on the first day, exactly one month after completion of the Tabernacle (Num. 1:1).[57] Twenty days later, Israel broke camp (Num. 10:11), which means that the census was one of the last matters undertaken at Sinai. In this activity, Moses' knowledge from Egypt would have benefited, for Egypt is known to have had good methods in census taking.

Those numbered were the men available for military service, from twenty years of age and above. Their total proved to be 603,550 (Num. 1:46). Others were not counted, but the grand total can be approximated. To the number of military men should be added an equal number of women, making then over 1,200,000; and to this the number of young people under twenty. This last group is difficult to estimate. In the United States, those under twenty number approximately sixty percent of those over.[58] If this had been the ratio for Israel, there would have been 720,000 young people, making the total figure 1,920,000. In view of the rapid growth rate while in Egypt, how-

[57] This may have been the completion of a census actually begun 9 months before, when the offering was taken for the Tabernacle. Every male then had to give one-half shekel and the number who did is given the same as here (603,550; Ex. 30:11f; 38:25-28). The count may have been taken then and the formal registration made here for the purpose of military availability.

[58] The 1960 census gave 113,974,000 twenty and over, and 66,009,000 under twenty, for 58%. In the author's own city, Grand Rapids, Michigan, it was 125,804 to 75,863, for 60%. Some countries with higher birth rates, show a figure of 80%.

ever, the family size in Israel was probably larger[59] which would have increased the number of young people to a 1,000,000 or more, making a grand total of between 2,000,000 and 2,500,000 people.

Liberal critics commonly object to the idea of this large number of people living in the wilderness. Wright[60] and Albright[61] do, and believe that these large figures really come from the later time of David, and were misplaced in the records. This explanation finds difficulty, however, in that the misplacement would have had to occur in no less than six different biblical texts,[62] and that the census for David's day is given in its appropriate place and is much larger.[63] The census figures must be accepted as correct. In doing so, however, one must not minimize the enormity of Moses' task in superintending a host so large. This was a vast number of people to keep together and control, especially in the unpleasant conditions of desert travel, for no less than forty years. Probably no other person ever carried greater responsibility. It is pertinent to remember that Moses had been well trained, that he had the tribes well organized following the year at Sinai, that there was a general signal for travel in the pillar of cloud which all could see, and, most important, that the supernatural provision and blessing of God was attendant at all times.

G. SINAI TO KADESH-BARNEA (Numbers 10:11–17:13; 33:16-19)

Eleven months and five days had elapsed at Sinai (Num. 10:11) when the pillar of cloud lifted, leading Israel north in the direction of Canaan. A covenant had been made between God and people, an organization established, and the Tabernacle built. The people were ready to move on to the Promised Land.

1. *The route (Numbers 10:12, 34, 35; 33:16-19)* The route north led to Kadesh-barnea,[64] a city located at the southern extremity of

---

[59] It should be borne in mind, however, that the birth rate may well have slowed by this time, this especially in view of actual loss in population during the wilderness journey (cf. Num. 26).

[60] *BAR*, p. 66. Wright argues also that an army of 600,000 could have crushed any opposing army by "sheer weight of numbers." However, these 600,000 were only the available men, not any real army. The numbers employed in actual battle would have been comparable to those of the enemy.

[61] Albright, *ARI*, p. 123.

[62] Ex. 12:37; 38:26; Num. 1:46; 2:32; 11:21; and 26:51. It is significant, too, that the figures of Num. 1:46, the first census, and 26:51, the second, are not the same, and this not only in the totals, but for all the separate tribes, some varying considerably.

[63] This census gives 1,300,000 men of army age which means more than 4,000,000 total population (II Sam. 24:9).

[64] Earlier at Kadesh the four eastern kings of Gen. 14 defeated Amalekites (Gen. 14:7). Hagar was found by the angel between Kadesh and Bered on the way to Shur (Gen. 16:7-14). Kadesh is associated with Shur also in Gen. 20:1.

Canaan. Its location is reasonably sure. Two sites in close proximity, lying about fifty miles southwest of Beersheba, qualify for general position and water supply, Ain Qudeis and Ain Qudirat. The first retains the basic name Kadesh, and the second boasts the best springs. Lying only five miles apart, both sites may have contributed water to the large encampment.

The path by which Israel came to Kadesh, however, is less certain. The names of only two places enroute are given: Kibroth-hattaavah and Hazeroth (Num. 11:34-35; 12:16; 33:16-18).[65] Hazeroth has been suggested as modern 'ain hudrah, a site about thirty miles northeast of Mt. Sinai, which would make Kibroth-hattaavah to be modern el-ebeirig, an oasis between the two.[66] Little evidence exists in support of these suggestions, however, and Numbers 12:16 is opposed, for it implies that Hazeroth was really much nearer Kadesh than modern 'ain hudrah, in that it lists the "wilderness of Paran," which included Kadesh, as having been reached next after Hazeroth.[67] Two matters suggest that the route was not direct between Sinai and Kadesh, but veered to the east. In Numbers 11:31, it is stated that quail were brought "from the sea" as food for Israel, which is likely a reference to the Gulf of Aqaba to the east; and Deuteronomy 1:2, 19 implies that at some time the people were in the vicinity of Mt. Seir, also to the east.

2. *Four incidents enroute (Numbers 11:1-33; 12:1-15).* Though the time of travel for this leg of the journey was not long,[68] four events are recorded from it. The first was a time of severe complaint by the people after only three days of travel from Sinai (Num. 10:33; 11:1-3). It apparently was hard for them to adjust again to the rigors of desert travel, and three days were enough to bring strong discontent. God

[65]Num. 33:16-36 gives 21 names of places between Sinai and Kadesh. However, these include names not only from this early trip from Sinai to Kadesh, but also from the later wanderings as the people left Kadesh and finally returned there again. This is clear from the places and events cited after Num. 33:36 which are all from the last year of the wilderness journey. The most likely place in the listing of the 21 cities for the break between the two portions of the total journey is with Rithmah (v. 19), making Rithmah the same as Kadesh and leaving only the two names given, Kibroth-hattaavah and Hazeroth, as stopping places on this earlier leg of the trip.

[66] Simons, GTT, p. 255.

[67] Also Kibroth-hattaavah is where the people ate the quail, and this incident transpired after the people had traveled at least three days and probably longer (Num. 10:33; 11:31-34).

[68] Deut. 1:2 calls it a journey of eleven days. However, since the distance is nearly 150 miles, it is doubtful if Israel made it in this time. Eleven days may have been a normal time of travel, but Israel went much slower. It would seem that three weeks would have sufficed, however.

effected discipline in the form of fire which burned in one section of the camp. Moses called the place "Taberah" (tab'erah, "burning") because of the punishment.

The second was the appointment of seventy elders of Israel to act as Moses' assistants in bearing "the burden of the people" (Num. 11: 4-30). This action resulted because Moses despaired after hearing further complaint from the people. The objection this time, initiated by the "mixed multitude,"[69] concerned food, for the people had become weary of manna. They wanted fish, cucumbers, melons, leeks, onions, and garlic, which they remembered from Egypt. When Moses cried to God that he was unable to bear alone the burden of such a difficult people, God gave the directive that seventy elders be appointed to help him. God "took of the Spirit that was upon" Moses "and put it upon the seventy," to enable them for the task.[70] As a concomitant to this enablement, the seventy joined in a chorus of praise[71] to God. When two of the seventy, Eldad and Medad, continued to sing longer than the others, Joshua was disturbed and questioned their behavior before Moses, but Moses approved their action. The relationship in office between these seventy and those priorly appointed as rulers of thousands, hundreds, fifties, and tens (Ex. 18:25), is not indicated, but likely these were higher in authority, helping Moses solve problems which the earlier appointees, as lesser officials, brought to him.[72]

The third event was another provision of quail (Num. 11:31-34), brought about because of the complaint regarding the manna. God told Moses that the people, because of their sinful attitude, would now eat meat for "a whole month, until it" came out of their "nostrils" (Num. 11:20). Moses found this difficult to believe, but God indeed brought quail in immense number. The best interpretation of the description given, as to how so many were killed, is that the quail were caused to fly about three feet above the ground at a level where Israelites could hit them easily in flight. The striking continued for two days and a night and extended for a "day's journey" on either side of the

[69] *Supra,* chap. 6, p. 131.

[70] The Holy Spirit came upon persons in the Old Testament particularly for the purpose of enablement for some task, as with Bezaleel (Ex. 35:30) and such later judges as Othniel (Judg. 3:10), Gideon (Judg. 6:34), Jephthah (Judg. 11:29), and Samson (Judg. 13:25; 14:6, 19; 15:14).

[71] The text says that they "prophesied," but since the idea of a spoken message does not fit the occasion, and according to I Chron. 25:1-3 a proper meaning for "prophesy" (*yithnabbe'*) is "praise," it is best to take this meaning here since it fits very well.

[72] Based on the fact that this group was much fewer in number, and also that they were especially endowed with the Holy Spirit in distinction from the others.

camp, resulting in an average take of more than ten homers.[73] When the people began to eat in a greedy manner, thus displaying their belief that God had not been supplying adequately before, God smote them "with a severe plague," bringing death to many.

The fourth event was an act of insubordination by Aaron and Miriam, Moses' brother and sister (Num. 12:1-15). The immediate occasion was Moses' marriage to a Cushite woman,[74] but clearly the true reason was jealousy. These two, already enjoying places of honor,[75] wanted greater authority, claiming that God had spoken by them as well as by Moses. God called all three before the Tabernacle, and, speaking out of the pillar of cloud, made known His appointment of Moses, saying that Moses had been honored above even the prophets in being privileged to speak with God "mouth to mouth." He then brought punishment on Miriam, who apparently had led in the brief rebellion, by smiting her with leprosy for one week.

3. *Refusal to enter the land (Numbers 13–14).* When the people arrived at Kadesh, the first matter of business was a reconnaissance of Canaan, the land to be conquered. To that end God directed the appointment of twelve men, one from each tribe, to act as spies. These were instructed to investigate both the land, in terms of food production, and the people, in terms of strength for self-defense. The twelve spent forty days traversing the land, going as far north as Rehob.[76] All agreed in their report. The land was good for food supply, but would be very difficult to conquer because the people were strong, giants lived in the land, and the cities were walled (Num. 13:27-28). They differed, however, in their evaluation. Ten said that the difficulties were too great, which meant returning to Egypt (Num. 13:31-33), while two, Caleb and Joshua, asserted that God could give victory in spite of the difficulties, pleading that the people not rebel against God by refusing to enter the land (Num. 13:30; 14:6-9). The people, erringly, heeded the ten, even threatening to kill the two, and began planning to return to Egypt under new leadership if need be.[77]

[73] P. B. Y. Scott, *BA*, 22(1959), pp. 22-40, states that the homer was equal to 6¼ bushels, which means that the average take here was more than 60 bushels. For other discussion and references, cf. *supra*, p. 140, n. 11.

[74] Probably not Zipporah, who could have been Cushite true enough, but Moses' marriage to her had taken place over 40 years earlier. Probably she had died and Moses had married again. The marriage was not contrary to the Law which forbade marriage only to Canaanites (Ex. 34:16).

[75] Miriam is called "the prophetess" and seemingly held a leading position among Israelite women (Ex. 15:20). Aaron of course had been made high priest.

[76] Located near the city of Laish, later called Dan (Judg. 18:28-29).

[77] This action was inexcusable. It is difficult to see why the people would have thought that God, who had led and provided so miraculously thus far, had

As a result, God threatened to annihilate Israel in punishment, but again Moses interceded[78] for the people, on the basis of God's own reputation (Num. 14:11-20). God then stipulated the nature of the punishment that would be inflicted, now milder in view of Moses' prayer but still severe. He said that the entire nation, rather than entering the land, would remain in the desert wilderness for a total of forty years, one year for each day of the spies' search; and that every Israelite twenty years and older (hence, responsible for this rebellious decision), with the exception of Caleb and Joshua, would die during this time and never enter the Promised Land (Num. 14:20-35). Following this, all ten of the faithless spies died immediately in a plague (Num. 14:36-38). The people, witnessing these events, now reversed their thinking and wanted to storm the land immediately. But this no longer was pleasing to God, and, when they made an attempt, they were sorely defeated by the Amalekites and Canaanites (Num. 14:39-45).

H. Thirty-seven Years and Six Months of Fruitless Wandering (Numbers 15–19; 33:19-36)

At this point, Israel began approximately thirty-seven and a half years[79] of fruitless wandering in the Sinai desert. Very little is recorded from these years, for clearly this was a time intentionally devoid of profit or progress for a disobedient people. The nation had been given opportunity to move into the land of blessing, but had refused. Now the people should wander in unpleasant conditions, with nothing positive accomplished, until all over twenty years of age had died.[80]

During these years, the people did move about some, within a confined area, going from Kadesh as far southeast as Ezion-geber at the tip of the Gulf of Aqaba (Num. 33:36), about eighty-five miles distant. Sixteen other stopping places are listed, all probably between these two extremes, though none can be identified. Likely much of the time was spent at Kadesh, since there really was little reason to travel elsewhere,

brought them all the way to Canaan's southern border only now to fail in the original objective.

[78] Similar to the occasion in connection with Israel's sin with the golden calf (Ex. 32:11-13).

[79] The length of this period is figured as follows. The time spent in the journey until the rebellion at Kadesh had been something less than 18 months. Then, beginning with Num. 20:1, all events concern the fortieth year of travel (Num. 20:1, 28; 33:38), thus leaving 37½ years intervening between Numbers 14 and 20, the chapters concerned with this period.

[80] Figuring 1,200,000 (600,000 of both men and women) as having to die in 14,508 days (38½ years), gives 85 per day. Figuring 12 hours per day maximum for funerals, gives an average of seven funerals per hour for all 38½ years, a continuous foreboding reminder of God's punishment upon them.

except for change of scenery. They were back at Kadesh again at the close of the intervening period, for it was there, in the first month of the fortieth year, that Miriam died (Num. 20:1, 28; 33:38).

Only one incident is recorded from all these years. That was a revolt of 250 people, led by the Levite Korah and two Reubenites, Dathan and Abiram (Num. 16–17). Jealousy again seems to have been the reason. These leaders desired places of authority along with, or in place of, Moses and Aaron. God demonstrated His power in vindication of Moses and Aaron by opening the earth to swallow Korah and Dathan and Abiram, along with their households;[81] then bringing fire to consume the 250 supporters; and, when many Israelites complained at this harsh treatment, even sending a plague through the camp, which took the lives of 14,700 of these (Num. 16:23-35, 41-50). Further, to show Aaron's approved position, God caused Aaron's rod,[82] placed at God's direction in the Tabernacle, to bud, in contrast to the rods placed there by other tribal heads (Num. 17:1-11). Then God instructed Moses to continue to keep Aaron's budded rod in the Tabernacle as a constant reminder and evidence that he had been divinely chosen as the religious leader of Israel (cf. Heb. 9:4).

I. KADESH-BARNEA TO THE JORDAN (Numbers 20–21; 33:37-48; Deuteronomy 2:1–3:14)

1. *Death of Miriam (Numbers 20:1)*. About the time of Israel's final arrival in Kadesh, following the years of fruitless wandering, Miriam died. The date is given as the "first month," and the year clearly was the fortieth of the sojourn, for it was the same year of Aaron's death five months later (Num. 20:23-29), which is definitely designated as the fortieth (Num. 33:38). It should be realized that even the head family of Miriam, Aaron, and Moses had to die before Canaan could be taken, for God had excepted only Caleb and Joshua in His earlier pronouncement of judgment (Num. 14:30). The three were allowed to live, however, until this closing year of wandering.

2. *Water again from a rock (Numbers 20:2-13)*. On arriving back in Kadesh at this time, the people lacked water once more. Since the

---

[81] The "men that appertained unto Korah" (Num. 16:32), indicated here as among those swallowed by the earth, must mean Korah's servants, for Num. 26: 11 says that "the sons of Korah died not." This was in contrast to the children of Dathan and Abiram, and was no doubt for the purpose of continuing this priestly line, which may have later contributed celebrated singers (I Chron. 6: 18-22; 9:19; Ps. 42, 44, etc.).

[82] Rods (*matteh*), undescribed in kind, were here labeled with the names of heads of each of the tribes, apparently symbolizing the authority of each. When Aaron's budded, representing life, his divinely appointed supremacy over the others was demonstrated.

area normally boasted good springs, the people may have looked forward to getting back. But apparently the springs were running low this year. The people complained, and Moses brought the matter to God. The reply was that Moses should bring water from the rock,[83] as he did formerly at Rephidim (Ex. 17:1-7). This time, however, God instructed Moses only to "speak" to the rock,[84] saying nothing about smiting it. But Moses smote it, even twice, and cried to the people, "Shall we bring you forth water out of this rock?" Water came forth, but Moses' action and words made it appear as though his human effort had helped to produce it. God was displeased and pronounced punishment on Moses, stating that now he would not be permitted to enter the Promised Land (Num. 20:12; 27:12-14; Deut. 32:48-52), a matter implied long before, as just observed, but here definitely stated in the context of God's particular reason.[85]

3. *Request to pass through Edom (Numbers 20:14-21)*. While at Kadesh, Moses sent messengers to the king of Edom requesting passage through his land. The plan now was to skirt the southern end of the Dead Sea, march north on its east side, and enter Canaan heading west. But Edom lay in the way, stretching in its narrow width from the Dead Sea south to the Gulf of Aqaba. Moses promised to stay strictly to the "King's Highway" enroute. Many scholars believe that, using this term, he referred to an ancient, well-known, north-south road, identified in recent times and traced as far north as Syria.[86] It had been used by the four eastern kings of Genesis 14, was later paved by the Romans, and is today followed closely by a modern Jordanian highway. But even though Moses promised not to stray from this "highway," the Edomite king refused passage. This meant a tedious journey south to Ezion-geber again (Deut. 2:8),[87] where the people had been only shortly before (Num. 33:35), and then a return on the eastern side of Edom.

4. *Death of Aaron (Numbers 20:23-29; 33:38)*. Enroute Aaron died

---

[83] The article is used with "rock," showing that the rock must have been one well known at Kadesh. The idea that it was the same as the one struck in Rephidim, having been carried along since, however, is not correct; cf. *KDC, Numbers*, p. 131, n. 1.

[84] Typology is involved here. Christ as the Rock (I Cor. 10:4) was smitten only once at Calvary. One need only speak to Him since to receive water of life. When Moses struck the rock, he spoiled the type.

[85] Apparently Moses, in view of his work and position, would have merited entrance to Canaan along with Caleb and Joshua had he not sinned here.

[86] Cf. *supra*, chap. 3, p. 54, n. 25. This road, however, does not cross from east to west through the mountains of Edom. Israel would only have reached it after traversing Edom.

[87] From Jebel Madeira (cf. n. 88) south to Ezion-geber is approximately 90 miles. This means that Israel had about 180 miles extra to walk because of this refusal.

on Mt. Hor at the age of 123. Since Mt. Hor is best located roughly on an east-west parallel with Kadesh nearer Edom,[88] it is possible that until this time Moses still hoped to pass through Edom. It may be that a return message from the Edomite ruler did not reach him until his arrival at Mt. Hor. Aaron died the first day of the fifth month of the fortieth year (Num. 33:38), just five months after Miriam's passing. Instructed of God, Moses accompanied Aaron, with Eleazer, Aaron's son and successor, to the top of the mountain and placed Aaron's clothes on the son before Aaron's life was taken. The people remained in mourning at Mt. Hor for thirty days.

While they were there, a brief battle occurred (Num. 21:1-3). Arad, king in south Canaan, led an assault against Israel. Initially defeated, Israel looked to God for help and then thoroughly routed the foe, even pressing on to destroy several of Arad's cities.

5. *Edom detour (Numbers 21:4-20; 33:41-49)*. Israel now began the long southern detour around Edom. Several unidentified stopping places are listed,[89] but only one event is described.

God again punished Israel for complaint concerning food and drink (Num. 21:5-9).[90] Apparently the people had found little water as they had marched south through the barren Arabah valley, and also had grown weary of eating manna. God brought punishment by sending "fiery serpents" among them so that many died.[91] This brought a repentant spirit to the people, and God instructed Moses to provide a remedy for those bitten, in the form of a brazen serpent placed high on a pole where it might be easily seen.[92] This he did, and when any

[88] Exact location uncertain, but either Jebel Madeira or Jebel el-Hamrah, both roughly parallel with Kadesh (though slightly north) are the most likely. A traditional site, Jebel Nebi Harun ("mountain of the prophet Aaron"), near Petra, must be rejected, for it is east of the Arabah and too far out of position to fit the story. Cf. J. Simons, *GTT*, p. 258.

[89] Some scholars believe that Israel reversed direction shortly after leaving Mt. Hor and actually marched around the north end of Edom rather than the south. The view is based largely on identifying Punon and Oboth (Num. 33: 42-44; 21:10-11) with modern Feinan and el-Weibeh both of which are on Edom's west side rather than the east. However, these identifications should be rejected, since little evidence exists for them. Deut. 2:8 says that the "turn" was made at Elath and Ezion-geber which are at the head of the Gulf of Aqaba. Cf. Aharoni, *LB*, p. 51 for opposing view.

[90] This is the first recorded incident of complaint regarding food since the time of quail provision 38 years before, though numerous incidents could have occurred during the silent years.

[91] Perhaps "fiery" due to color or due to a resulting sore on the one bitten. Reddish, poisonous snakes are known in the Arabah today.

[92] This brazen serpent was later worshiped by the people, and finally Hezekiah had to destroy it (II Kings 18:4).

who were afflicted looked upon it, they were instantly healed.[93]

6. *Return north and victory over Sihon and Og (Numbers 21:10-35).* Following God's instructions not to interfere with the Edomites (Deut. 2:4-5), Israel skirted their territory on the east and again made her way northward. Coming to the brook Zered,[94] Moab's southern boundary, God forbade interference with Moab also (Deut. 2:9). Israel obeyed and followed a path well to the east.

However, interference was unavoidable with the kingdom of Sihon, next encountered. King Sihon's land stood between Israel and the Jordan River. Moses requested permission of Sihon to cross his country, but was refused, even as by the king of Edom (Num. 21:21-32). Sihon mustered his army at Jahaz, and Moses met and defeated him. Then Israel occupied all Sihon's territory to the Jabbok River.

With this victory Israel's forces were not far from the country of Og, king of Bashan,[95] who ruled from the Yarmuk River as far north as Mt. Hermon. Now Moses took the offensive and defeated this powerful ruler at his important city, Edrei (Num. 21:33-35),[96] before moving on to occupy his land. Israel now controlled most of the land from the Arnon River in the South (Moab's northern boundary) to Mt. Hermon in the North, a distance of 130 miles. The defeat of these kings was really the beginning of the conquest, for God had in mind that His people should dwell on both sides of the Jordan. These victories were important, too, in impressing the Canaanites across the Jordan with Israel's might as led by her God (Josh. 2:9-11; 9:8-10).

J. AT THE JORDAN (Numbers 22–27; 31–32; Deuteronomy 31, 34)

1. *Balaam and the Moabites (Numbers 22-25; 31).* With these significant victories won, Moses assembled the host near the Jordan River opposite Jericho. Here Balak, king of Moab, viewed Israel as a menace to his country[97] and, in cooperation with elders of Midian, sent mes-

[93] Used by Christ as an illustration of how a sinner is saved: by looking in faith to Him as the Israelite looked to the serpent (John 3:14-15).

[94] The Zered is a small stream which flows into the southern extremity of the Dead Sea from the southeast. In Deut. 2:14 it is stated that Israel crossed this stream just 38 years after the Kadesh rebellion.

[95] This was a man of large stature, perhaps a descendant of the Rephaim mentioned in Abraham's time (Gen. 14:5; 15:20), having an iron bed over 13 feet long and 6 feet wide (Deut. 3:11). His country boasted many cities, of which 60 were walled (Deut. 3:4-5).

[96] It should be realized that Moses in bringing the army here, was about 60 miles north of where the Jordan was later crossed.

[97] Balak was here north of his Arnon border. Perhaps with Sihon recently defeated by Israel, he had thought to reoccupy land formerly taken from him by Sihon (Num. 21:26).

sengers far north to Pethor on the Euphrates River[98] to bring Balaam, a prophet whose reputation had reached this far south,[99] to place a curse on Israel (Num. 22–24).[100] At first Balaam refused to accompany the messengers, but a second visit persuaded him. However, once with Balak, Balaam only blessed Israel instead of cursing her, much to the frustration of the Moabite king. Balak took him to three different vantage points from which to view the Israelite encampment, hoping that the prophet would change his pronouncement, but to no avail. In each place, Balaam spoke words of blessing desired by God. Then, after dismissal by Balak in disgust, Balaam uttered yet a fourth message (Num. 24:14-25), in which he gave a remarkable prediction regarding the coming Messiah and future blessings of Israel. Finally, however, the strange prophet did work in Moab's favor. He gave advice[101] for enticing Israelite men to take part in the impure cult activities of Baal-peor (Num. 25:1-18).[102] The counsel was followed and many Israelites were ensnared, resulting in God sending a punishing plague, which took 24,000 Israelite lives. The plague was stopped only when Phinehas, son of the high priest Eleazar, slew an Israelite man and a Midianite woman who had walked openly into the Israelite encampment together. Moses then dispatched an army of 12,000 to punish Midian, which had been partner with Moab from the start, and here apparently had assumed leadership. The Midianites were soundly defeated, and "all the males," the "kings of Midian," and Balaam himself were killed (Num. 31:1-54). All the married women were slain later, and a great amount of booty was divided among the Israelites.

2. *A request granted (Numbers 32).* With the land east of the Jordan conquered and found to be well adapted for pasture, the tribes of Reuben, Gad, and later half of Manasseh, all having extensive flocks, asked permission to make this region their home. Moses' first reaction

[98] Pethor was in Mesopotamia (Deut. 23:4) and is commonly identified with Pitru of Assyrian texts (cf. *ANET*, p. 278) located 12 miles south of Carchemish. These messengers had a trip of over 400 miles each way.

[99] Balaam was a strange combination of prophet-diviner. His spiritual condition was such that God could communicate with him and even impart remarkable predictions relative to Israel and Christ (Num. 24:17-19). Still Balaam was willful in wanting his own way and finally in bringing great harm to Israel. He is severely condemned in Scripture (II Pet. 2:15; Jude 11; Rev. 2:14).

[100] It was thought that such a curse would weaken the one cursed; cf. Egyptian execration texts, *ANET*, pp. 328-29.

[101] That this idea was indeed Balaam's is not indicated until later when Moses had sent the army to punish the offenders (Num. 31:8, 16).

[102] Two matters suggest that the tribe of Simeon was involved in this defection more than other tribes: first, the one man named was a leading Simeonite; second, the census taken just after this shows Simeon's number greatly reduced, as if by such a plague as here sent (Num. 26:14; cf. 1:23).

was unfavorable. However, these tribes assured Moses that their men of military age would accompany the other tribes in conquest of the west side of the Jordan, too, and would not return to their families until that task had been completed. Moses finally acceded, but made it clear that indeed this would have to be done. When agreement was reached, those requesting set about repairing cities and building sheepfolds for use of their families while the men were away (Num. 32:34-42).

3. *Anticipatory matters (Numbers 26–30; 33:50–36:13).* Moses now did several things in anticipation of Israel's soon crossing into the land. First, he had another census taken (Num. 26). Thirty-nine years of wilderness wandering, with deaths of 1,200,000, had transpired since the census at Mt. Sinai. There was need to know Israel's present manpower as she faced the challenge of Canaan. The number counted this time was 601,730 men twenty years and older, in comparison with the earlier 603,550 (Num. 1:46).[103]

A second matter concerned a problem regarding inheritance rights raised by the daughters of one Zelophehad, who had died leaving no sons (Num. 27:1-11). The directive from God was that daughters should inherit their father's possessions, if there was no son, so that family claims might be maintained.

A third and very important matter was the appointment of a new leader. Someone had to be selected to take the place of Moses, rejected earlier, for crossing the Jordan. God's choice was Joshua (Num. 27:15-23), certainly a logical replacement. He and Caleb were the only older men who could enter the land, for all others their age either had or would die before that time.[104] Joshua had led in battle against the Amalekites (Ex. 17:8-14). He had accompanied Moses part way up Mt. Sinai at the time of receiving the Mosaic Law (Ex. 24:13). He had assisted Moses following Israel's repentance regarding the sin with the golden calf (Ex. 33:11). He had served as one of the twelve spies of Canaan and urged advance into the land along with Caleb (Num. 13:8; 14:6-9). In all these instances Joshua had acquitted himself well, demonstrating responsibility and leadership. By these expe-

---

[103] Seven tribes grew (Judah, Issachar, Zebulon, Manasseh, Benjamin, Dan, and Asher); five lost (Reuben, Simeon, Gad, Ephraim, and Naphtali). The biggest gainer was Manasseh which grew 20,000 (32,200 to 52,700) and the biggest loser Simeon which lost 37,000 (59,300 to 22,200).

[104] At the crossing, no other persons could have been more than 58 years old, for all 20 and above 38½ years earlier had now died. Caleb at this time was 79 (Josh. 14:7) and Joshua likely older. Joshua had been entrusted with more leadership than Caleb and also is said to have been "old and stricken in years" (Josh. 13:1) when Caleb speaks of himself as being yet strong and vigorous. Joshua was probably more than 90 at this time (cf. *infra,* chap. 9, p. 212).

riences, too, good preparation for the great task now being assigned had been provided. God revealed the selection of Joshua to Moses, who then made proper announcement to the people and gave appropriate charge to the new leader.

Finally, Moses relayed closing instructions, which the people would need when they entered the land. As given in Numbers 28–30, these concerned regular offerings, periodic feasts, and keeping of vows; and in Numbers 33:50–36:13, destruction of idolatrous inhabitants of Canaan, description of certain borders of the land, identification of persons who should determine divisions of the land among the respective tribes, establishment of forty-eight Levitic cities which should include six cities of refuge, and further matters pertaining to inheritance rights.

K. DEUTERONOMY

At the very close of Moses' last days,[105] he orally delivered the great messages of Deuteronomy and then wrote the book. He reviewed for the new generation what God had done for His people since leaving Egypt, including a resume of the laws revealed at Sinai. Then he set forth new regulations, given by God, relative to Canaan's soon entrance and the more sedentary life there to be experienced.

It had been sometime prior to this that Moses had penned the first four books of the Pentateuch,[106] though how long before is impossible to state. It is clear that Moses had been writing a book of some kind (Ex. 17:14), perhaps a type of daily record (Num. 33:2), from the time of the journey's first stages, and probably had used this as a historical basis for the more formal production. We know, too, that he had recorded the Book of the Covenant immediately after its revelation (Ex. 24:4-7), and likely had done the same with the more extensive regulations of the two forty-day periods on Sinai, as observed earlier. But the material in the form now found in Genesis, Exodus, Leviticus, and Numbers was probably not recorded until shortly before the Deuteronomic messages.[107] It certainly had been completed by the time

---

[105] According to Deut. 1:3, Moses began these messages on the first day of the 11th month of the 40th year, which was only two months and ten days before the Jordan was crossed.

[106] Then as one continuous document, however.

[107] Contrary to the view of higher critics, there is good evidence that Moses did write the Pentateuch : (1) writing was advanced, with even an alphabet in existence which Moses could employ; (2) Moses was capable, both in terms of education and accessibility to necessary information; (3) six times the Pentateuch states that he wrote some respective part of it; (4) the remainder of the Old Testament gives testimony in various ways implying his authorship of it; and (5) Christ and the New Testament writers give yet clearer testimony to this end, even equating the name Moses to the *torah* (Pentateuch) division of the Old Testament.

he gave and recorded them, however, and so with Deuteronomy complete, the Pentateuch was finished. The Israelites thus had their all-important guidebook ready for the eventful days when they would have crossed the Jordan.

With the work both of leadership and writing complete, and a replacement now appointed, Moses, at the age of 120 years, was ready for God's call to heaven. Few men in all history could claim to have had so rich an experience; few so used of God. He was gifted and trained as perhaps none other of his day, and he was entrusted with a task probably greater than any other person of any day. But now his work was done. According to God's instruction, he climbed "to the top of Pisgah, that is over against Jericho," surveyed the Promised Land, heard God remind him that this was indeed the land which had been promised long before, and then was taken in death by God. He was buried in an unknown grave of a nearby valley (Deut. 34:1-7).

Chapter Eight

THE CONQUEST

Joshua 1–24

A. The Land of Canaan

1. *Israel's task in conquest.* Canaan, across the Jordan from encamped, waiting Israel, was a land of city-states. There was no central government, but many cities, each with its own king. To conquer the land meant to defeat each city in turn. Egypt was nominal overlord. Thutmose III, Moses' archenemy and principal founder of the Egyptian empire, had added the region to Egypt's domain. His son, Amenhotep II, Pharaoh of the Exodus, had continued strict control. But his son Thutmose IV, Pharaoh while Israel was in the wilderness, who had married the Asiatic daughter of Artatama, king of Mitanni,[1] was more favorable toward foreign powers and less interested in military dominance. Then his son Amenhotep III, who now ruled, gave little attention to foreign control, concerning himself rather with home interests. He did make boasts of conquest, but these were largely empty, for, as Hayes remarks, his "indolent neglect of his Asiatic provinces paved the way for the collapse of Egypt's northern empire."[2] The Tell el-Amarna letters depict him as turning only a deaf ear to Canaanite pleas for help against invaders.[3] The individual cities of Canaan were left to themselves as prizes of conquest for Israel.

This does not mean, however, that Israel's task was to be easy. The

[1] Founded late in the sixteenth century, the kingdom of Mitanni came to extend across most of northern Mesopotamia, with capital at Wasshugani (site uncertain). The population was mainly Hurrian, but the rulers were Indo-Aryan. Their zenith of power came about this time. The kingdom ceased about 200 years later.

[2] Hayes, *SE*, II, p. 233; cf. Steindorff and Seele, *When Egypt Ruled the East* (2d ed.; Chicago: University of Chicago Press, 1957), pp. 72-75.

[3] For discussion and references, cf. *supra,* chap. 5, pp. 104-107.

spies thirty-nine years before had given a true report in speaking of Canaanites as vigorous people and their cities as strongly walled. The people fought frequently among themselves and with outside foes, which kept their warriors in fighting trim and well equipped. The cities were built to withstand siege for months at a time.[4] These cities, too, could band together against a common enemy, as later they did against Joshua, in both a southern (Josh. 10) and northern confederacy (Josh. 11). Besides this, the land was mountainous. Once past Jericho, Israel would be in rugged country most of the time, difficult in which to travel and maneuver for war.

2. *Canaanite culture advanced.* Canaan was advanced in material culture. Cities were well laid out, and houses showed good design and construction. Floors of buildings were often paved or plastered. Drainage systems had been developed. Workers were skilled in the use of copper, lead, and gold. Pottery was among the finest anywhere in the world. Extensive trade was conducted with foreign countries, including Egypt, Northern Mesopotamia, and Cyprus. In technical knowledge, Canaanites were much in advance of Israelites who had spent the past forty years in nomadic conditions of the desert.

In this cultural disparity lay grave danger for Israel: a danger which soon issued in sad reality. History shows that less developed cultures are normally absorbed by those more advanced. In years which followed, Israel did not become absorbed by Canaan, but she did experience pronounced influence. Had this involved only material culture, such as pottery manufacture, city construction, or methods of farming, there could even have been benefit; but when it came to include ways of thinking, ideas, and especially religious belief and practice, the harm was great. Many of the people were led actually to accept the worship of Canaanite Baal rather than Yahweh. The attraction was that Baal was held to be god of rainfall and good crops. No doubt Canaanites advised their new farming neighbors that technical skill was not enough to insure full larders, but that worship of the right deity was still more important. Such counsel by native inhabitants would have been most influential on incoming Israelites who desired bountiful harvests. Without question, it was this danger which God sought to avert by commanding that all Canaanites be destroyed or driven from the land (Num. 33:51-56; Deut. 7:1-5). Canaanites who had been dispossessed could not give such counsel. Had Israel complied, all would have been well, but she did not. Many Canaanites were allowed to remain, and

---

[4] Samaria withstood the siege of Assyria for more than fourteen months (II Kings 17:5); and Gaza withstood even the mighty Alexander the Great for five months, in 332 B.C.

Israel suffered the wide-reaching effects of their influence, with consequent loss of God's all-important blessing (Judg. 2:11-15).[5]

3. *Plan of attack.* Moses' strategy for taking Canaan, no doubt revealed to him by God, clearly had been to attack the land at its approximate midpoint, coming in from the east, and divide it into a south and north section, that each might be conquered separately. We may assume that Moses had shared this thinking with Joshua, so that the new leader had the plan in mind as the people prepared for crossing the Jordan.

B. Entrance to the Land (Joshua 2:1–5:12)

1. *Reconnaissance of Jericho (Joshua 2:1-24).* As Joshua contemplated the task of conquest, he recognized Jericho as a first and principal objective. It was a strong city and could not be safely by-passed. It stood as an imposing challenge to be met almost immediately.

He desired more knowledge of the city and sent a team of two spies to make reconnaissance, likely remembering the similar tactic of thirty-nine years before when he had played a vital role himself. The two crossed the Jordan and came to the city where they were protected by a harlot, Rahab, whose house was located on the city wall.[6] When the men were detected, she hid them beneath drying stalks of flax on the roof and then sidetracked pursuers on a false trail. Convinced that Jericho would fall to Israel, she requested safety for herself and family in return for her favor. The men gave their promise and then, with her further help, succeeded in escaping back to Joshua and the camp. Though the mission of the men likely became known in Jericho too soon for them to observe much detail concerning the city, they did learn from Rahab that the people greatly feared Israel. News of victories over Sihon and Og had reached Canaanite ears. Joshua thus had reason for encouragement.

2. *Crossing the Jordan (Joshua 3–4).* The next morning after the spies' return,[7] Joshua ordered the people to move to the bank of Jordan. Shittim,[8] where they had been encamped,[9] apparently was not

---

[5] *Infra*, chap. 9, especially pp. 211-31.

[6] Here their visit would not be questioned so soon, and also the house, being on the wall, afforded easy escape if necessary.

[7] The spies had been gone longer than expected, being forced to hide in a mountain for an extra three days to avoid pursuers. Joshua may have become somewhat impatient and so here moved immediately after they returned.

[8] The name Shittim (with the article, literally "The Acacias"), probably refers to a small region rather than a town. Its exact location, though frequently conjectured, remains unknown.

[9] Numbers 33:49 mentions their first arrival here. While here, Moses delivered his final instructions, probably including the Deuteronomy messages. Moses be-

immediately at the river, and so the first step in crossing was to move to it. The river was at flood stage here in the Spring.[10] At its bank, three days were occupied in final preparations and instructions. We may believe that during these three days the people wondered how all Israel could possibly cross the wide expanse of water flowing by them, but they were soon to learn.

When all was ready, the priests carrying the Ark moved toward the river, the people remaining behind at a distance of 3,000 feet by divine command (Josh. 3:4). This insured a maximum number seeing the Ark as the guiding signal. When the feet of the priests touched the water, it miraculously separated. That which flowed toward them "rose up in one heap" as if stopped by a dam; the other continued its course to the Dead Sea leaving a wide space for the people to cross. During the time consumed as the people then did cross, the water backed up as far as the city Adam, approximately fifteen miles up-river.[11] The priests bearing the Ark stopped and remained at the mid-point (riverbed proper) of the river as the people moved past. This gave testimony to each person that God, represented by the Ark, was restraining the water to make the crossing possible. The previous days of wonderment at the river's edge would have only heightened their appreciation now of the power displayed.

Two memorials of this crossing were created; one in the Jordan and one across at Gilgal where the people encamped (Josh. 4:1-24). Twelve chosen men, one from a tribe, took a stone each from the Jordan, near where the Ark-bearing priests stood, and brought the stones to the place of encampment. Then Joshua in turn "set up twelve stones in the midst of the Jordan," as a pillar at the place from which the other stones had just been removed. Both acts were done after all the people had crossed and just before the priests moved on with the Ark to where the people waited. As soon as all were beyond the path of the water, the river once again flowed, moving downstream

gan to give these on the first day of the eleventh month, more than two months before crossing.

[10] Joshua 3:15 and 4:18 speak of the Jordan now being "over all its banks" (*'al-kol-gedhothaw*). This could mean merely "upon all its banks," indicating that the water only filled the banks without spilling over. The same phrase, however, is used in Isa. 8:7 where it must mean "over its banks." This and the context argue that Jordan was now at flood stage.

[11] Adam is identified with *ed Damieh* about 20 miles from the Dead Sea. Since Israel crossed the Jordan opposite Jericho (Josh. 3:16) about 5 miles from the Dead Sea, they were 15 miles from Adam. Since rock slides have occurred near Adam temporarily stopping the Jordan (once in A.D. 1267, in 1906, and July, 1927), the suggestion is often made that God used this means here. This is possible, but the story suggests that the waters separated immediately before the priests, which would not have been true if 15 miles of water had yet to pass.

now with greater force than before, due to the extra water which had backed up. When all the people had arrived at Gilgal, Joshua made the second pillar from the twelve stones brought out of the Jordan. The two pillars were to remind future generations that God had miraculously opened the Jordan so that His people might enter their land of promise.

3. *Encampment at Gilgal (Joshua 5:1-12).* Gilgal now became a continuing center of Israelite activity. Its exact location is still uncertain,[12] but clearly it was somewhere in the Jordan Valley between Jericho and the Jordan River (Josh. 4:19). From here, Jericho and Ai soon were taken. To Gilgal later came the Gibeonites seeking a peace treaty (Josh. 9:6). From Gilgal Joshua led his army by forced march to help the Gibeonites against the southern confederacy (Josh. 10:6-7). From here, too, he went north to meet the northern confederacy (Josh. 11:6-14). And here the first allotment of tribal territories was made (Josh. 14:6). While the army was in the field fighting, the people remained at Gilgal as home base.

Three important events transpired soon after encampment. One was the circumcision of all the men (Josh. 5:2-9). This mass observance was necessary because Israelites now living were of a new generation, and apparently children had not been circumcised during the wilderness journey. But God had commanded the rite and wanted it effected as a badge of separation for His people from their new neighbors. Accordingly, He ordered its observance and later stated that it here also symbolized the removal of Egypt's reproach.[13]

A second event at Gilgal was a special observance of the Passover (Josh. 5:10). This may have been only the third Passover kept;[14] at least none others are mentioned as having been observed since the occasion at Mt. Sinai (Num. 9:1-5). Having now arrived in the land, however, with all males properly circumcised, the people were minded to follow God's order also in regard to this feast, and the Passover was kept on its appointed day, the fourteenth of Nisan. It should be realized that this was exactly the fortieth year for the annual Passover (whether kept ,or not) since the Egyptian departure, in accordance with God's

---

[12] Muilenburg, *BASOR*, 140(1955), pp. 11-27, suggests identification with Khirbet el-Mefjir, which perhaps is the most likely; though Simons, *GTT*, pp. 269-70, rejects it.

[13] This symbolism gave Gilgal its name. "Gilgal" is from the Hebrew root *galal*, meaning "to roll away."

[14] The first was in Egypt and the second at Sinai. That no others are mentioned could, of course, be due only to a silence in the record. Since circumcision, however, was not observed, which according to Ex. 12:48 was reason alone to prohibit one from the Passover, it seems best to believe that the Passover was not either.

word of punishment at Kadesh, declaring that the people would spend one year for each day of the spies' reconnaissance in Canaan (Num. 14:33-34). God brought them across the Jordan on the tenth day of Nisan (Josh. 4:19) just in time for preparations for this on the fourteenth. Not even the Jordan at flood stage had been reason to miss this appointed occasion in the new land,[15] exactly forty years after leaving Egypt.[16]

The third matter of note at Gilgal was the cessation of manna. God had continued to supply this miraculous food since early in the first year of travel (Ex. 16:14-22). Nearly forty years of this special provision had now elapsed; but, having crossed into the land of promise, the people had no further need for it. The day after the Passover observance, the people no longer found it on the ground. Instead, they ate "the produce of the land," which was now available.

C. CONQUEST OF CENTRAL PALESTINE (Joshua 5:13–9:27)

1. *Defeat of Jericho (Joshua 6:13-27).* With the land entered and preliminary matters accomplished, Joshua turned his attention to the main task of military conquest. The first objective, anticipated already in the mission of the spies, was Jericho. The city was near at hand as a constant danger to Gilgal if not taken, and, as noted, was too important as a Canaanite stronghold to be by-passed in any case.

a. The city. Old Testament Jericho is well identified with Tell es-Sultan, five miles west of the Jordan and seven miles north of the Dead Sea. The mound covers about eight acres, though, due to extensive erosion, it is not certain how much was occupied by the city Joshua captured. If, however, a conclusion made in chapter five is correct,[17] that the city of Joshua's conquest was the city Miss Kenyon says was taken by Egyptians about 1550 B.C., then it probably did cover most of the mound. This means that it was about average size for the day, though smaller than large sites like Megiddo at fourteen acres, Lachish at eighteen, or especially Hazor at two hundred. What-

---

[15] There was reason to cross the Jordan now, too, in the further impression of God's power this would give Canaanites.

[16] Frequently scholars take these forty years as only approximate, standing for a generation of time. But these years are exact. Aaron died the first day of the fifth month of the fortieth year (Num. 33:38) and the people mourned for one month. Since Moses began the Deuteronomic messages the first day of the eleventh month (Deut. 1:3), which followed the Sihon and Og conquests, Israel had taken five months for the remaining journey and these two campaigns. This left two months and ten days for Joshua to assume leadership and for the Jordan to be crossed by this tenth day of the first month.

[17] Cf. *supra*, chap. 5, pp. 96-99.

ever its size, frequent biblical reference to it[18] shows that it had a major importance in the land.

Miss Kenyon's description of the walls of this city is of significance.[19] The walls were of a type which made direct assault practically impossible. An approaching enemy first encountered a stone abutment, eleven feet high, back and up from which sloped a thirty-five degree plastered scarp reaching to the main wall some thirty-five vertical feet above. The steep smooth slope prohibited battering the wall by any effective device or building fires to break it. An army trying to storm the wall found difficulty in climbing the slope, and ladders to scale it could find no satisfactory footing. The normal tactic used by an enemy to take a city so protected was siege, but Israel did not have time for this, if she was to occupy all the land in any reasonable number of months.

b. The conquest. God had quite other plans for taking Jericho, however, and these were revealed to Joshua in an unusual manner (Josh. 5:13–6:5). One day while Joshua was in the vicinity of the city, perhaps pondering how it might be taken, he was met by one called the "prince of the host of Yahweh"[20] and told those plans. The plans were to have "men of war,"[21] led by seven priests carrying the Ark, walk around the city once each day for six days and seven times on the seventh. At the close of the thirteenth circuit, the priests should blow trumpets and the people shout with a loud voice. When they did, the walls of the city would collapse and the army could enter.

The plan was executed as given. Those assigned to the daily marching took their places with the Ark in their midst.[22] Thirteen times the city was encircled and then the walls did fall as the trumpets sounded and the people shouted. The army now took the city with ease, no doubt aided by great fear engendered in the hearts of Jericho's inhabitants. Rahab had testified that they were already fearful at the

[18] For example, Num. 22:1; 26:3, 63; 31:12; 33:48-50; 34:15; 35:1; 36:13; Deut. 32:49; 34:1, 3; Josh. 4:13; etc.

[19] Kenyon, *Digging Up Jericho* (New York: Frederick A. Praeger, 1957), pp. 214-20. She dates these walls only to c. 1550 B.C.; but cf. contrary conclusion, *supra*, chap. 5, pp. 97-99.

[20] Another Old Testament appearance of Christ as the Angel of Yahweh. This "Prince" called the ground "holy" (Josh. 5:15) as with Moses at the burning bush (Ex. 3:5), and used the personal pronoun "I" as giving Jericho into Joshua's hand.

[21] All 2,000,000 people did not encircle Jericho. Critics are right in saying this would have been quite impossible. These "men of war" represented the others and likely were not numerous themselves as they accompanied the priests with the Ark.

[22] The important object in the marching column was the Ark which represented God. As the Ark had earlier held back the Jordan, now it would bring down Jericho's walls.

time of the spies' visit, and now Israel's strange daily encirclement of the city would have added to this emotional state. All the people of the city were killed, with the exception of Rahab[23] and her family, whose lives were spared in keeping with the spies' promise, and the city was leveled by fire. No Israelite was permitted to enrich himself by spoil, however; God having placed a ban on the city, declaring that it was "devoted"[24] to Himself (Josh. 6:17-18). The valuable metals, gold, silver, bronze, and iron were placed in God's treasury. Joshua further pronounced a curse on any who should rebuild the city, the reality of which was experienced much later in the reign of King Ahab by Hiel the Bethelite (I Kings 16:34).

2. *Defeat and victory at Ai (Joshua 7:1–8:29)*

a. Defeat. This case of victory at Jericho, however, may have contributed to a tragic defeat at Ai shortly after (Josh. 7:1-26). The city of Ai was the next objective before Israel. A reconnaissance party sent by Joshua was not impressed by Ai's strength and, apparently overconfident, advised that merely "two or three thousand" would be sufficient to take the city. Joshua sent the larger number, 3,000, but still they were defeated by the men of Ai, who killed 36 men as Israel's army fled.

The main reason for the defeat, however, was not the fewness of Israelite soldiers. It was the existence of sin in Israel's camp. Achan of the tribe of Judah had sinned in disregarding God's ban on the "devoted" items from Jericho, and took for himself a Babylonian garment, two hundred shekels of silver, and a fifty-shekel bar of gold.[25] Following the defeat, God revealed to Joshua that such a sin had been committed and told him to make inquiry as to the identity of the guilty party. This was done,[26] and Achan was the one indicated. The man confessed to having taken the items and hidden them in his tent. These were recovered from their hiding place, and then Achan, his family, and all his possessions were stoned and later burned. This punishment was necessary, both in view of the serious offense and as a warning to other Israelites.

b. Victory. With the sin punished, Israel was now enabled to con-

[23] Here spared, Rahab came to be included in the ancestral line of David and so of Christ (Matt. 1:5).

[24] The Hebrew word is *cherem*, used five times in Josh. 6:17-18. The idea, "curse," sometimes ascribed to the word is appropriate only in the sense of the thing involved being banned from employment by any other than God.

[25] The common shekel weighed about four-tenths of an ounce, thus making the silver here about eighty ounces and the gold twenty ounces.

[26] Probably by using the official provision for such an inquiry, the Urim and Thummim (Ex. 28:30; Num. 27:21). This revelational device was to be used solely by the high priest.

quer Ai (Josh. 8). By night, Joshua sent an ambush to hide in a valley between Ai and nearby Bethel. The next day Joshua led another force in frontal attack on the city similar in tactic to the earlier time of defeat. This time, however, when the men of Ai came out from the city to countercharge, with Joshua's force again retreating as if defeated, the ambush arose and pressed upon the army of Ai from behind. Joshua's force then turned and the enemy was trapped. The result was that all 12,000[27] of the male inhabitants of Ai were killed, the king hanged, and the city reduced to rubble. This time God permitted Israelites to take of the spoil. It should be observed, too, that Joshua employed many more troops in the second attempt on the city, apparently assigning 30,000 to the ambush alone (Josh. 8:3).[28] He and the people clearly had learned two lessons: the costliness of sin, and the error of overconfidence.

c. Location. The exact location of Ai is still uncertain. The traditional site is et-Tell,[29] about one and one-half miles southeast of Bethel, excavated in 1933-35 by Mme. Judith Marquet-Krause and in 1964 by Joseph A. Calloway. Their work revealed, however, that this mound was not inhabited between c. 2200 and c. 1000 B.C., and so not in Joshua's day. Various solutions have been suggested,[30] but the most likely is that et-Tell is not the right location. Some matters even favor this explanation. For instance, et-Tell is rather far from Bethel whereas Joshua 12:9 (cf. 7:2) states that Ai was "beside (*mitsad*) Bethel"; also et-Tell is a comparatively large mound whereas Joshua's reconnaissance party described Ai's inhabitants as few.[31] Future ex-

[27] Either among these, or perhaps additional to them, may have been men of Bethel. It is stated (8:17) that Bethelites did go with those of Ai in pursuit of Joshua's decoy group.

[28] The relationship between the 30,000 of vs. 3 and the 5,000 of vs. 12 is not clear. Possibly the 30,000 refers to the total force and the 5,000 to those set in ambush. Even so, 30,000 is still ten times the number used in the first attack.

[29] The name et-Tell means "the hill" or "heap of ruins" (Josh. 8:28) which is the approximate meaning of Ai (*ha'ay*). This is one reason for the identification, on the assumption that the meaning has carried over to modern time. Simons (*GTT*, p. 270) argues against this, however, pointing out that several sites are today called et-Tell, and also that the name Ai need not carry the thought of "ruin" at all, but only of a "heap of stones."

[30] Albright, followed by Wright (*BAR*, p. 80), believes that this story of Ai's fall is really the story of Bethel's conquest, which later became attached to Ai to explain the existence of the continuing ruin near Bethel. But this must be rejected as inconsistent with the veracity of Scripture. More plausible is Vincent's explanation that Ai had become a military outpost of Bethel, which left no permanent remains for the excavator. But Wright counters this idea by observing correctly that Joshua 8 speaks often of the "king of Ai" (*ibid*).

[31] Simons gives two other arguments: "Et-Tell was not a ruin in the post-conquest period, whereas Joshua indicates that Ai was (8:28)"; and "There is

cavations will likely bring more light. At least Ai was near Bethel; and Bethel clearly was located (though its common identification with Tell Beitin is now being challenged) about fourteen miles northwest of Jericho, the approximate distance, then, that Joshua's troops had to march for this battle.

d. Bethel. No indication is given as to a conquest of Bethel in Joshua's day.[32] Her king is listed as having been killed by Joshua's forces (Josh. 12:16), but no record is given of a direct attack on the city. The reason probably is that her power was broken at the time of Ai's defeat. It was only logical for her to join in assisting Ai against an enemy which she could expect would confront her next, and Joshua 8:17 states directly that she did. Bethel's king may have been killed at this time, though the story mentions only Ai's ruler (Josh. 8:23, 29). Joshua's employment of so many more troops the second time of attack may have been in part due to his expectation that Bethel would join with Ai.

3. *Ceremony at Shechem (Joshua 8:30-35; Deuteronomy 27:1-26).* With Jericho, Ai, and Bethel controlled, Joshua took the people, according to God's instruction (Deut. 27:1-26), north to Shechem to renew God's covenant. The intention was to repeat in picture what had been done forty years before at Sinai in reality, when the covenant had been officially ratified (Ex. 24:4-8).[33] The people were now actually in the land, with many years having elapsed and a new generation living, and it was fitting that there be a reminder of God's requirements and a renewal of the people's promises. Near Shechem, at the foot of Mt. Ebal,[34] Joshua built an altar, and the priests made burnt offerings and peace offerings. On prepared stones, Joshua wrote a "copy of the law of Moses" (Josh. 8:32),[35] apparently as a concrete

no broad valley to the north of et-Tell, whereas Joshua 8:11 indicates the existence of a valley near Ai"; summarized in "Archaeological Digest" of the *American Journal of Archaeology,* July-September, 1947, p. 311, as cited by Free, *ABH,* p. 134. Further, as to fewness of inhabitants, the 12,000 of Joshua 8:25 may have included people of Bethel (cf. n. 27).

[32] Either in Scripture or by excavation. Excavation reveals a general destruction of Tell Beitin (Bethel?) in the thirteenth century, too late for Joshua's day, but possibly that of Judg. 1:22-26.

[33] *Supra,* chap. 7, pp. 145-46.

[34] Mt. Ebal and Mt. Gerizim lie north and south from each other with Shechem between their eastern ends. Before Shechem to the east a plain opens up, in the middle of which Joshua may have stood as he later read the law to the people on both sides of him.

[35] This can hardly have been all the Mosaic Law, which would have taken very long to inscribe. Various views are held as to how much was included: only the Decalogue; the Decalogue plus the blessings and curses here read by

representation of God's Law among His people. Then half the tribes moved over toward Mt. Gerizim, with half remaining near Mt. Ebal, and these in turn gave respective response to the blessings and curses of the Law as read by Joshua. Near Joshua as he read was the Ark of the Covenant representing God's presence. The ceremony must have been impressive, and the people[36] would have remembered it well in succeeding days.

A matter of interest, of which little is known, concerns Israel's conquest of this northern, central region where Shechem was a principal city (Gen. 12:6; 33:18-20). The biblical account speaks of the Israelites being able to move north to it, apparently without difficulty, but does not explain how this was possible. Shechem was more than thirty miles north of Ai, and her people would not have considered themselves under Israelite domination simply because the more southern city had fallen. The most likely explanation is that Israelite forces had moved north to subjugate the area ahead of time, though after Ai's fall. Certain matters suggest this. One is that the account of the Ebal-Gerizim ceremony (Josh. 8:30) begins with the word "then" ('az not merely the simple conjunction waw), which could imply lapse of sufficient time for such an intervening conquest. Another is that Joshua 11:19 states that no city other than Gibeon (Josh. 9) capitulated to Israel peacefully, which means that Shechem must have been taken forcibly. And a third is that Joshua 12:17, 18, 24 lists kings of the Shechem area who were killed by Joshua's troops sometime and so probably here at this logical juncture. It should be realized that the biblical account is not explicit on numerous details in the over-all conquest.

4. *Peaceful homage (Joshua 9)*. Returning to Gilgal, the Israelites received unexpected peaceful homage from another important group of people of central Palestine. These were Hivites,[37] representing four

---

Joshua; the legal portion of Deuteronomy; the 613 commandments of the whole law (according to Jewish reckoning); a running gist of the whole law.

[36] The number of Israelites brought from Gilgal the approximate 40 miles to Shechem is hard to determine. Josh. 8:35 speaks of women, little ones, and sojourners besides the men. Certainly the women and children of the two and one-half tribes still across the Jordan were not there, and it is not easy to think of nearly 2,000,000 others making such a trip, though it is possible. If only a representative group went, at least all ages and both men and women were represented.

[37] One of the seven listed (sometimes only six) national groups of Canaan at the time of the conquest: Amorites, Perizzites, Canaanites, Hittites, Girgashites, Hivites, and Jebusites (Deut. 7:1; Josh. 3:10; 24:11). Little is known of their origin unless they are the same as Horites, for which identification some evidence exists. They are represented as located in a variety of places (Gen. 34:2; 36:2; Josh. 11:3; Judg. 3:3; etc.) thus suggesting little homogeniety.

major cities generally northwest of Jerusalem a few miles: Gibeon, Chephirah, Beeroth, and Kirjath-jearim, sometimes called the Gibeonite tetrapolis. News of Israel's early successes had spread through the land (Josh. 9:1), and these people saw wisdom in peaceful capitulation. Doubting acceptance by warlike Israel if known to be from the land proper, they contrived a trick, wearing worn-out clothing and bearing moldy bread, to make themselves appear to have traveled from a distant country. They asked that Israel make a treaty of peace with them, and it was granted. This was contrary to God's instruction (Ex. 23:32; 34:12; Deut. 7:2), however, and the Israelites were held responsible, though tricked, because they had not asked counsel "at the mouth of Yahweh" (Josh. 9:14).[38] When three days later the ruse was known, Joshua and the elders kept the treaty (properly now that it had been made, cf. II Sam. 21:1-19), but forced the Gibeonites to serve as "hewers of wood and drawers of water unto all the congregation" (Josh. 9:21). On the good side for Israel, of course, though not excusing the sin involved, was the fact that Israel thus acquired further important control in the central portion of the land, and this without effort on her part.

D. CONQUEST OF THE SOUTH AND THE NORTH (Joshua 10–12)

At this point Israel had succeeded in making a significant division of the land. Jericho, Ai, Bethel, Beeroth, Gibeon, Chipherah, and Kirjath-jearim formed a continuous, slightly curving line across southern central Palestine; and, as we have seen, the fact that Israel had been able to assemble peaceably at Shechem indicates control had been gained in the northern central area as well. The general strategy was working. The South and North were now separated and remained to be taken each by itself.

1. *Defeat of the southern confederacy (Joshua 10:1-11)*. Contact with the South came soon after the treaty with the Hivite tetrapolis. Among the four capitulating cities, Gibeon carried the leading reputation for strength (Josh. 10:2);[39] and, when news of her action reached the king of Jerusalem, he initiated work to form a counter confederacy. Four leading cities joined with him: Hebron, Jarmuth, Lachish, and Eglon.[40] These confederates began their general resistance to Is-

---

[38] This was the type of inquiry for which God had given the Urim and Thummim, but it was not employed here.

[39] Excavation at Gibeon (el-Jib, some 7 miles northwest of Jerusalem) during 1956, 57, and 59 has given corroboration; cf. J. B. Pritchard, *Gibeon Where the Sun Stood Still* (Princeton: Princeton University Press, 1962).

[40] These five cities in their geographical interrelation formed an approximate right triangle. Jerusalem and Hebron formed an eastern north-south leg of about 20 miles. Lachish lay approximately on the southern east-west leg about

rael by first attacking Gibeon, apparently to force her out of the new alliance with Israel. Gibeon quickly appealed to Joshua in Gilgal, and Joshua brought his troops by forced march the twenty-four-mile distance to Gibeon in one night. He took the attackers by surprise, routed them, and pursued them toward the heights near Beth-horon to the west.[41] Near Beth-horon the fleeing troops turned south in an apparent attempt to reach home cities,[42] but on the way suffered from a storm of stones (likely hailstones) sent from Yahweh, so that more died from the pelting than from Israel's swords. The five kings, staying close together, succeeded in getting to the vicinity of Azekah[43] and Makkedah, but then sought shelter in a cave.

The pursuing Israelites found the kings in a cave, but, in passing, merely sealed the opening with stones and continued after the fleeing soldiers. Joshua wanted the troops themselves caught and killed before they could get to the safety of their walled cities. This was accomplished in major part (Josh. 10:18-20), and then attention was again given to the trapped kings. Joshua commanded his military leaders to place their feet on the necks of these rulers while he slew them, thinking, no doubt, that this would bolster their confidence for future battles. Then Joshua had the lifeless bodies of all five hung on trees for his men to see during the remainder of the day (Josh. 10:21-27).

2. *A prolonged day (Joshua 10:12-14).* It was earlier that same day, as Joshua stood on a commanding height near Gibeon, likely watching the fleeing enemy outrun his tired troops, that he voiced a poetic call which has caused considerable discussion: "Sun, stand thou still upon Gibeon; and thou, Moon, in the valley of Ajalon" (vs. 12).[44] These

7 miles from Eglon, which was at the east end of the southern leg, and Jarmuth lay about on the hypotenuse roughly half way between Eglon and Jerusalem. All are well identified with the possible exception of Eglon.

[41] Beth-horon the upper lay about five miles west and slightly north of Gibeon. Beth-horon the nether was about two miles farther. One should think here merely of the general area.

[42] Since the enemy had not fled south at the first toward Jerusalem, the nearest of the five allied cities, it is evident that Joshua had cut off this avenue of escape. Apparently the enemy out-stripped Joshua's tired men, however, and so was able to swing south at Beth-horon.

[43] Azekah was located at the head of the valley of Elah where David later fought Goliath (I Sam. 17:1), about fifteen miles southwest of Beth-horon. Jarmuth, one of the allied cities, was only about three miles west from here. As to Makkedah, cf. n. 48 following.

[44] The first words of this poetic call and later words of vs. 13 which say that the "sun stayed in the midst (*chatsi*, "half") of the heavens" suggest that the time of day was noon with the sun directly over Gibeon where Joshua stood. The remainder of the cry, "And thou, Moon, in the valley of Ajalon," suggests that the moon then lay close to the horizon in this valley. Since the valley lies

words and the description following have traditionally been taken to mean that this day was miraculously prolonged. Numerous scholars take exception to the view, however, including some conservatives. A few have thought that Joshua merely appealed for added strength for himself and troops. Others have believed that a miracle in refraction of light occurred, so that, though the position of the sun itself did not change in relation to the earth, it appeared to do so and indeed lengthened the day in some amount. Still others have suggested that Joshua only requested relief from the burning heat of the noonday sun, which God answered by sending clouds and storm.[45]

The traditional view must be maintained, however, for these alternate explanations do not do justice to the language of the text. Though it is true that the verb *dum* (translated "stand still" in Joshua's call) means basically "be silent," and so could refer to being silent in other ways than retardation of movement,[46] still the verb *'amadh* is also used (twice in vs. 13) and it definitely indicates a change in pattern of movement. Further, verse 13 closes with the expression, "and hasted not to go down," where the word "hasted" (*'uz*) again speaks of motion, and the phrase "to go down" (*labho'*) is normal in reference to the sun setting. Still further, verse 14 states that this day was unique in history which suggests a major miracle occurred such as the prolonging of a natural day. The extent of this prolongation can also be estimated. Since the hour was at noon when Joshua voiced the call, and it is stated that the sun did not go down for "about a whole day (*keyom tamim*)," it is likely that the afternoon hours until sunset were prolonged twice their normal length. In other words, the total daylight hours of the day were one and one-half times normal.[47]

There was good reason for Joshua wanting this day prolonged. The five strong kings had brought their armies out from their fortified cities to do battle with Israel in the open. Their thinking likely had been

17 degrees north of west from Gibeon, the time of year can be figured as July, and the relative positions of the sun and moon indicate that the moon was at third quarter, half full.

[45] For a helpful summary of these and other views, cf. B. Ramm, *The Christian View of Science and Scripture* (Grand Rapids: Wm. B. Eerdmans Publishing Co., 1955), pp. 156-61. Ramm himself favors the "clouding over" view, but cf. Payne, *BETS*, 4(1960), p. 95 for refutation.

[46] For instance, as one explanation holds, to be silent in shining with such heat.

[47] As to how this was effected, the closing words of vs. 13 "and hasted not to go down about a whole day," suggest that the relative positions of the sun and earth did not hold still but merely slowed in their change. This means that the earth simply slowed, in its speed of rotation on its axis, approximately to half that of normal. This did not affect the speed of movement around the sun or the rest of the solar system, which complicating factors have been mentioned in criticism by those advocating other explanations.

that, since the walls of Jericho and Ai had not helped those cities, it would be better to try a new method. But this left them without their best means of defense, and Joshua knew it. He did not want them now to get back behind those walls if he could help it. With the enemy fleeing as they were, however, and with his own troops tired, more time was needed to catch them, and so prevent this return, than normal hours of remaining daylight afforded. Accordingly, he asked God to supply added hours, and God did so, graciously responding to the commendable faith of His servant.

3. *Subjugation of southern cities (Joshua 10:28-43).* With this crucial battle won, Joshua pressed on to subjugate cities in all the southern area. He had planned to do this anyhow, following the conquest of central Palestine, and now the opportunity was most propitious with the armies of the principal cities decimated.

The first assaults were against Makkedah and then Libnah, both close to the cave where the kings had been killed.[48] Each city was taken, apparently without difficulty, with the respective kings and many people killed. Little physical harm seemingly was done to the cities,[49] however, a pattern of operation followed for all this southern campaign. Joshua then moved south to three of the cities of the confederacy: Lachish, Eglon, and Hebron. Jarmuth, another, had been very near Joshua when he took Makkedah, but no mention is made of fighting there. Perhaps the city, being so near and her king killed with the others, capitulated without sufficient fighting to call for mention. Lachish,[50] about ten miles southwest of Azekah, was probably the strongest of the three and was attacked first. The city fell on the second day of fighting and the people were killed as at Makkedah and Libnah, though this time the king had been dispatched already at the cave near Makkedah. While Israel was so engaged, the King of Gezer,[51] who for some reason felt obligated to Lachish, though his city was some twenty miles north, came with his army to aid Lachish, but he and his men all perished before Joshua in the attempt. Joshua might then have turned to take Gezer, but he did not, probably because it

[48] Though each is uncertain, Makkedah is best identified with Khirbet el-Kheishum, two miles northeast of Azekah at the head of the Elah valley, and Libnah with Tell es-Safi four miles west.

[49] At least no mention of general destruction is made. For discussion of significance, cf. *supra*, chap. 5, p. 101.

[50] A large city of 18 acres. Cf. *supra*, chap. 5, p. 99, n. 72 as to excavation and references.

[51] Identified with Tell Jezer; excavated by R. A. S. Macalister in 1902-05; 1907-09; cf. his report, *The Excavations of Gezer*, 1912. Hebrew Union College began excavations in 1964; cf. *BA*, 30(Feb., 1967), pp.47-62.

was well out of his way. Instead, he moved on to Eglon,[52] the farthest west of the southern three confederate cities, and then to Hebron,[53] the farthest east. Both fell and were treated as Lachish. After these earlier and more major conquests, Joshua continued south to subdue all the lower part of the land. His army even reached Kadesh-barnea, where Israel had spent so much time during the wilderness journey. Debir[54] was probably the most important prize in this lower southern area. Finally Joshua returned to Gibeon where the whole effort had started.

Several months must have been occupied in making this extensive campaign. The distances covered were long and the cities taken numerous. Had the cities not fallen with comparative ease, the time would have been yet much longer, of course. In fact, Joshua then would likely have had to make several campaigns. That he was able to subdue the entire region in this one great effort shows that indeed the cities did capitulate without long periods of siege. A main reason for this little resistance was no doubt a paralyzing fear which had gripped the inhabitants. They had heard of Israel's victories: first when she had yet been beyond the Jordan, and, after crossing, at Jericho and Ai, and now over the five confederate kings. They had been impressed, too, by the prolonged, miraculous day and also by the unusual storm that had killed so many of the confederate forces. The God who could perform such works must be great indeed! There was little use in trying to withstand Him! So thinking, they had quickly sued for peace, and Joshua was able to sweep through the land in this single grand campaign.

One main city, however, was not taken. That was Jerusalem, one of the five confederates.[55] It had been out of the way as Joshua had pursued the fleeing enemy on the way south, and perhaps his troops were too weary to attempt the difficult task on the return. It remained a tiny island, not incorporated into Israelite territory, until David seized it much later; then making it, however, even the capital.[56]

4. *Defeat of the northern confederacy (Joshua 11)*. News of Joshua's remarkable conquest of the South traveled north and reached the ears

[52]Commonly, though uncertainly, identified with Tell el-Hesi; Albright, *BASOR*, 17 (1925), p. 7.

[53] Hebron still continues as an important city in the midst of the hills of old Judea at its highest point (about 3,000 feet). The exact site of the biblical city lies probably east at Gebel er-Rumeidi.

[54] If correctly identified with Tell Beit Mirsim, it lay some 13 miles southwest of Hebron. Cf. *supra*, chap. 5, p. 99, n. 74 as to excavations and references.

[55] Cf. Josh. 15:8, 63; 18:28. Jerusalem had led the confederacy.

[56] Cf. II Sam. 5:7. Jerusalem was taken once by Judah, but apparently only temporarily, Judg. 1:8.

of Jabin, powerful king of Hazor. Hazor[57] was the great metropolis of the North and her monarch quite automatically found himself to be leader. Jabin, fearing similar attack on his region, now formed a confederacy. He apparently planned to do better than the southern alliance by gathering a greater force. The kings he assembled are listed as representing all parts of northern Palestine: the mountain region still above Hazor, the plain "south of Chinneroth,"[58] the "lowland" (perhaps Valley of Esdraelon), the western region as far as Dor,[59] and three cities mentioned in particular, Madon, Shimron, and Achshaph.[60] The assembly included Canaanites, Amorites, Hittites, Perizzites, Jebusites, and Hivites. The gathering point was the waters of Merom,[61] and the host numbered like "the sand that is upon the seashore" (Josh. 11:4).

Instructed of God, Joshua brought his battle-tried troops north to meet this formidable enemy. He did not hesitate in making attack, and probably achieved thereby an element of surprise. God used the move to give his smaller force complete victory. The huge enemy army was routed and chased far to the west. Joshua followed up this triumph by smiting "with the edge of the sword" all "the cities of those kings, and all the kings of them" (Josh. 11:12). Then he returned to the city of Hazor itself and burned it; something he did not do to the other cities. As noted in chapter five, most cities were spared, no doubt for the future use of Israelites; but Hazor was apparently seen by Joshua as a prize of psychological value for burning. People would be forced to recognize that any city could have been burned had Israel so chosen, if great Hazor could not escape.

These matters make clear that Joshua effected the same thorough conquest of the North as he had of the South. Actually, the fact that Jabin made an alliance to withstand Israel aided Joshua in this full conquest, even as the alliance of the South had helped there. If Joshua had not been able to defeat the strength of the North in one major blow, the individual subjugation of each city would have occupied

[57] *Supra*, chap. 5, pp. 100-101.

[58] Chinneroth probably means the Sea of Galilee. The plain would be the Jordan where many fine cities existed.

[59] Dor lay on the Mediterranean, 8 miles north of later Caesarea.

[60] Listed separately, these three cities were likely the strongest. Little is known of them, however; cf. Josh. 12:20; 19:15 (Shimron of the tribe of Zebulon); 19:25 (Achshaph, farther west, of Asher). Madon is often, though uncertainly, identified with modern Qeren Hattin, west of Tiberias, near Khirbet Madjan which preserves the ancient name.

[61] Waters of Merom may refer to Lake Huleh, recently drained. Some believe, however, the place is better identified with large springs near the modern village of Meiron, ten miles west and slightly south.

a much longer time. As it was, the northern campaign appears to have taken even less time than the southern.

5. *Summary of conquest.* A summary statement of Israel's total conquest is made in Joshua 11:16-23. Joshua gained victory from the extreme south, near "mount Halak, that goeth up to Seir,"[62] to the extreme north "in the valley of Lebanon under mount Hermon." The only people who made peace without being attacked were the Hivites of the Gibeonite tetrapolis. It is expressly stated that among those slain were the feared giants, the Anakim, of whom the spies had particularly spoken years before (Num. 13:33). The total number of kings killed was thirty-one, the names of their cities being given in Joshua 12:10-24.

This means that, when Joshua returned to Gilgal from the northern campaign, the military strength of the major part of the land had been broken. Included was the area on the east of the Jordan from the Arnon River in the south to Mt. Hermon in the north, and on the west from below the Dead Sea in the south to Mt. Hermon again in the north. The cities had been overcome and a large number of the people, including leaders, killed. No record is given that Joshua left controlling garrisons in these cities (probably lacking sufficient men to leave); but the defensive strength of the cities had been broken, and Joshua had reason to believe that actual occupation by the respective tribes should not be difficult.

One principal region had escaped Joshua's might. That was the Mediterranean coastline (Josh. 13:1-6). Even there, Gaza is mentioned as having been affected by Joshua's presence in some respect (Josh. 10:41), and farther north the king of Dor had been defeated and killed as a member of the northern coalition (Josh. 12:23). But for the most part, the coastal territory had remained untouched, with fighting having occurred only more inland. Joshua's thinking, no doubt, was that the tribes would be able to subdue their own respective portions of it at the time of occupation[63] (something, however, which did not occur until the time of David much later).

E. The Land Divided (Joshua 13–22)

Before the respective tribes could begin occupation, there was need for assignment of land portions. Since there was reason to begin occupation rather soon, while psychological and material advantages from

[62] "Mount Halak" means smooth or bald mountain. This is likely the ridge mentioned in Num. 34:3, 4; Josh. 15:2, 3 as Ascent of Akrabbim. It is located southeast of the Dead Sea.

[63] Josh. 13:1 implies too, that Joshua's age was a factor in God not directing him personally to lead against this coastal area. Joshua had done well to lead as he had and likely now was very tired.

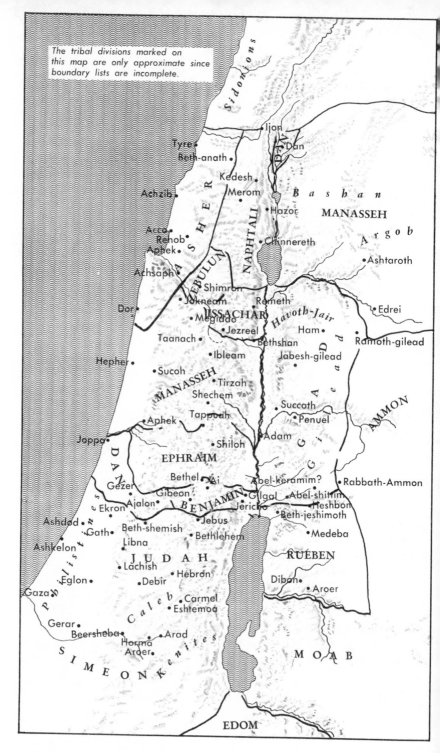

Map 6. The Tribal Divisions

the main campaigns still lingered, there was wisdom in assigning these portions as soon as possible. This was the task to which Joshua set himself on returning to the people still encamped at Gilgal. The method of procedure had already been indicated when the people were still east of the Jordan; namely, by lot, which placed the decision with God rather than men (Num. 26:55-56; 33:54).

1. *Allotments east of the Jordan (Joshua 13)*. Reuben, Gad, and half the tribe of Manasseh had already received their allotted portions. Moses had supervised in this prior to the Jordan crossing (Num. 32:1-42; Deut. 3:13-17; Josh. 13:8-33). The land then assigned stretched from the Arnon River north to Mt. Hermon, though how much of this was actually occupied north of the Yarmuk River is uncertain.[64] The line of division between Reuben, assigned the southern section, and Gad, the middle, is quite clear as having run east from the northern tip of the Dead Sea. The division between Gad and half of Manasseh to the North, however, is not clear. The principal boundary certainly was the Jabbok River, since this stream had been Sihon's northern boundary, and it was his kingdom that was divided between Gad and Reuben (Josh. 13:27). Two northern extensions across the Jabbok, however, also seem to have existed, one near the east bank of the Jordan running as far north as the Sea of Galilee (Josh. 13:27), and one nearer the desert running as far north at least as Ramoth-gilead (Josh. 13:24-28; 20:8).

2. *Allotments of Judah, Ephraim, and Manasseh (Joshua 14:1-17:11)*. While preparations were being made for allotting portions on the west of the Jordan, Caleb, the other senior citizen besides Joshua, interrupted proceedings with a remarkable request (Josh. 14:6-15). He asked that he might personally be granted the Hebron area, where the giant Anakim had been found, when he, Joshua, and the other spies had surveyed the land years before. Joshua had broken the strength of these people in the southern campaign, but apparently some of them still remained and Caleb wanted to achieve complete extermination. He reminded Joshua that Moses had promised him the region (cf. Deut. 1:36). Caleb at this time was eighty-five years old, an age when people normally think of easy tasks; but Caleb asked for a hard one, and Joshua, no doubt long an admirer of his close friend, granted the request. Caleb moved at once to the challenging work and did drive the Anakim from the land assigned him (Josh. 15:13-19).

The tribe of Judah, Caleb's tribe, received the first regular allotment of land, which included the area already granted to Caleb. The ter-

[64] North of the Yarmuk the states of Geshur and Maachah took up much of the territory, and express statement is given that neither came under control of Manasseh (Josh. 13:13).

ritory was very large (Josh. 15:1-12). Its eastern border was the
Dead Sea, and its western the Mediterranean. Its southern border
angled south from the Dead Sea so that Kadesh-barnea was included,
and its northern border ran irregularly from the northern tip of the
Dead Sea west to the Mediterranean just skirting Jerusalem on the
south. Its main cities, as named in Joshua 15:20-63, make a long list.

The next lot was for Ephraim, Joshua's tribe (Josh. 16:1-10). Judah
and Ephraim were the two most influential tribes and continued to be
until the time of the exile.[65] Both headed their respective kingdom
divisions following the reign of Solomon.[66] Ephraim was given a smaller section than Judah, north of Judah and with room left between for
Benjamin. The third lot was for the remaining half tribe of Manasseh
(Josh. 17:1-11).[67] This portion bordered Ephraim on the north, stretching again, like Judah and Ephraim, from the Jordan to the Mediterranean. The two Joseph tribes thus were located side by side at the
center of the land. The northern boundary of Manasseh was the
southern edge of the Esdraelon Valley.

3. *Allotting interrupted (Joshua 17:12–18:9).* At this point allotting was interrupted. For some reason the people, before allotting for
the remaining seven tribes, gave themselves to the task of moving camp
from Gilgal to Shiloh, where they then erected the Tabernacle in the

---

[65] The man Judah had assumed leadership among the brothers (Gen. 43:3;
46:28) and was promised leadership for his tribe by Jacob (Gen. 49:8-12).
Ephraim was a son of Joseph and given preference over Manasseh when blessed
by grandfather Jacob (Gen. 48:1-22), and also Joshua was from this tribe.

[66] Ephraim assumed a prestige position already in the Judges Period, challenging Gideon for not calling its people to fight the Midianites (Judg. 8:1-3),
and similarly challenging Jephthah sometime later (Judg. 12:1-6). Bitterness
against Judah broke out when Ishbosheth, succeeding son of Saul, ruled Ephraim
and the northern tribes, and David ruled Judah (II Sam. 2:1-11); and later
again when David returned to Jerusalem following Absalom's rebellion (II Sam.
19:41-43). After the kingdom's division, Ephraim is identified frequently with
all ten tribes: Isa. 7:2, 5, 8, 9, 17; 11:13; Jer. 7:15; 31:9, 18, 20; Ezek. 37:16;
Hos. 7:8; etc.

[67] Comparing Num. 26:28-34; Josh. 17:1-3 and I Chron. 2:21-23, the rationale
for the division of Manasseh appears as follows. The half tribe which settled on
the west of Jordan descended from Manasseh's grandson through Machir, namely
Gilead, the father of six sons. Zelophehad, the son of one of the sons had only
daughters to inherit, and by special decision (Num. 27:1-11; cf. *supra*, chap. 7,
p. 165) they were permitted to inherit with the sons, with the result that of
the ten portions allotted to Manasseh on the west, five were given to these
daughters (Josh. 17:3-6). The half tribe on the east of Jordan apparently descended from two grandsons of Manasseh, one through a marriage between
Machir and Maacah (I Chron. 7:15-16) and the other through a marriage between a granddaughter of Manasseh through Machir, whose mother is unknown,
and Hezron, from which last marriage came Jair, definitely said to have lived
within the Transjordan area (I Chron. 2:21-23).

place it was to occupy for many years (Josh. 18:1). They had been at Gilgal between six and seven years, during the time of Joshua's campaigns.[68] Now they moved up into the land that had been conquered, and to a city which had just been allotted to Ephraim.

One reason for the interruption certainly was the people's desire to locate the Tabernacle in its continuing place as soon as possible, and this possibility was realized with the assignment of Ephraim's territory, in that it included Shiloh.[69] Since, however, there was need to avoid unnecessary delay in allotting, before the advantage of Joshua's campaigns had worn off, there must have been another reason also.

The text suggests one. The remaining tribes suddenly displayed a surprising lack of interest in receiving their portions. This change of attitude seems to have resulted from objections which both Ephraim and Manasseh made to their allotments.[70] These two tribes complained that their portions were too small, especially since they contained large wooded areas[71] and that the Canaanites living there were hard to dislodge (Josh. 17:12-18). Joshua wisely responded that they should solve their own problems by cutting the trees and driving out the Canaanites, whether strong or not, matters certainly which they should have undertaken without being told. Their objections, however, wrong as they were, evidently were enough to influence the other tribes and these now hesitated to receive their allotments at all; reasoning, perhaps, that if it was this difficult to occupy the land it might be better to retain their nomad type of life to which they had become accustomed. Apparently recognizing the seriousness of the situation, Joshua chose to give the tribes time to reflect while all moved to the vicinity of Shiloh.

[68] This length of time is based on Caleb's statement that he had been 40 years old at Kadesh-barnea and was now 85 (Josh. 14:7, 10), and the fact that over one year of the total 40 in the wilderness had elapsed by the time the people were at Kadesh. That this much time had been employed in Joshua's campaigns is not surprising in view of all he had done. Joshua himself was probably near 100 years old when he finished the northern campaign (cf. *infra*, chap. 9, p. 212).

[69] What had led to Shiloh's selection is not stated. Probably any site in Judah had been rejected as too far south to serve all the tribes, and Ephraim was next in importance. Some relation may exist to the much-discussed passage Gen. 49: 10, but this is not clear.

[70] From this it appears that Joshua had directed each tribe, on receiving allotment, to move immediately to occupy it before allotting another. Likely Joshua had figured a time schedule so that this could be done and still complete the process in reasonable time.

[71] Almost no trees exist in the area today, but clearly did then (cf. II Kings 2:24). Heavy woods in this middle region could indicate that few people had lived in these mountains (the offending Canaanites would have been in the valleys) which may have been a factor in Joshua apparently having experienced little fighting in the area prior to this (cf. *supra*, p. 178).

With the people settled at Shiloh, however, Joshua waited no longer but gave clear orders for reinaugurating and facilitating the allotting procedure (Josh. 18:2-9). He gave instructions that three representatives from each of the remaining seven tribes should form teams to survey the land left to assign. The teams should return with descriptions of the land, which would form a basis for the next allotments. From these descriptions, the location of dense woods, the nature of soil, and the density of Canaanite population could be determined, which would help in making proper divisions of the land and also let people know ahead of time what they would find. The decision as to which section, so prescribed, was to be received by a particular tribe was still to be revealed by lot. Joshua's directions were carried out, and allotting began once more.

4. *The seven remaining allotments (Joshua 18:10–19:51).* The first tribe now to receive territory was Benjamin (Josh. 18:10-28). Benjamin's allotment was small, squeezed between large Judah to the south and the important Joseph tribes, north. Further, it extended only about half-way to the Mediterranean from the Jordan. It did include the important cities, Jericho and Jerusalem.

The next allotment was for Simeon. This time no land area as such was assigned but only cities within the large territory of Judah. Seventeen cities are named (Josh. 19:1-9) which included small population centers near them.[72] One reason for this change in type of allotment was that Judah had been given more land than it needed (Josh. 19:9). Another was that Simeon was now the smallest of the tribes, numbering only 22,200 men at the second census (Num. 26:14)[73] and so could fit into smaller quarters than others. A third, and most important reason, was that its ancestor, Simeon, along with Levi, had received as his "blessing" from Jacob the prediction that he would be scattered in Israel,[74] a consequence clearly of the indiscretion of these two brothers many years before in tricking and brutally slaying the inhabitants of Shechem.[75]

Zebulun received allotment next (Josh. 19:10-16), followed by Is-

[72] Apparently Beersheba and Sheba listed in vs. 2 are the same city, otherwise the cities listed add to one more than the total figure indicated in vs. 6; also a parallel list in I Chron. 4:28-31 does not list a Sheba separately.

[73] *Supra,* chap. 7, p. 164, n. 102.

[74] Levi was scattered in that only individual cities were assigned through all the tribes (this, of course, due to being the priestly tribe, Josh. 21:1-41), and Simeon in being given these cities. It is of interest that later a number of Simeonites moved north near to Ephraim and Manasseh (II Chron. 15:9; 34:6) for which reason the northern kingdom could be called a ten-tribe kingdom when originally only 9 tribes were geographically so located.

[75] Gen. 34:1-31; cf. *supra,* chap. 4, p. 74.

sachar (Josh. 19:17-23). Both territories were small, about the size of Benjamin, but constituted mainly of fine level land of the fertile Esdraelon Valley. Canaanites, however, were strong in the region, and courage was needed to drive them out. Neither tribe succeeded well in doing this for many years. Zebulun bordered on Issachar's northwest.

Asher received the fifth allotment, a larger section again (Josh. 19:24-31). It lay along the Mediterranean, from Manasseh on the south to Israel's border on the north. The sixth allotment was for Naphtali, the last of the northern tribes (Josh. 19:32-39). Her area was again large, extending from north to south beside Asher, splitting the northern region with her. She bordered both Zebulun and Issachar on the south.

The last tribe to receive allotment was Dan, whose land was again in the south (Josh. 19:40-48). This division once more was small, pressed between Judah and Ephraim, like Benjamin, which bordered it on the east. Eighteen cities are listed in the division, indicating a prior heavy population, which promised difficulty for them in occupation.[76] Because Dan was one of the larger tribes numerically,[77] and also because of this difficulty in occupation, many Danites soon migrated[78] without divine approval. They went far north to Laish, which city they then renamed Dan (Josh. 19:47; Judg. 18).

5. *War narrowly averted (Joshua 22:1-34).* A tragic war was narrowly averted at the time when the men of Reuben, Gad, and half of Manasseh returned to their own homes. According to Moses' directive (Num. 32:16-32) seven years earlier, these men had faithfully remained with the main camp on the west of Jordan until the conquest had been completed and the land allotted; but now they properly returned to their own assigned lands. On the way they erected a memorial altar at the Jordan River. This action appeared strange to people of the other tribes. Thinking the altar had been erected as a place of sacrifice, and so a substitute for the Shiloh altar, they objected strongly, fearing punishment from God for all the tribes due to what seemed like blatant disobedience.[79] Wisely, however, before instituting

[76] The Canaanites there would be pressed too by the Philistines, later to arrive in large numbers along the immediate coast; cf. Josh. 19:47; Judg. 1:34; 18:1.

[77] There were 62,700 in the first census (Num. 1:39) and 64,400 in the second (Num. 26:43), making Dan the second largest after Judah.

[78] Not all migrated. The story as given in Judg. 18 indicates only 600 men went at first to seize the land, though likely many others followed. Samson's family, however, were Danites and still lived in the allotted section (Judg. 13:2); and so likely others did too.

[79] This incident gives clear evidence that altars were not permitted indiscriminately in the land. Altars, other than at the Tabernacle, are found used only in unusual religious situations (Judg. 6:24; II Sam. 24:25; I Kings 18:30) and not by people generally for offering regular sacrifices.

punitive war against the transjordan tribes, they sent Phinehas, son of Eleazar the High Priest, and ten companions to give the offenders opportunity to explain their action. The transjordan tribes explained that this altar had not been erected for sacrifice at all but as a fitting object of memorial. These eastern tribes, separated from the others by the Jordan, did not want successive generations to think themselves any less a part of Israel than those on the west of the Jordan, and they believed this memorial altar would help. Phinehas and his committee were satisfied with the answer and returned with it to relieve the disturbed minds of the western tribes.

F. INSTITUTIONS

1. *Civil government.* Upon settlement in the land, Israel's Twelve Tribes lived with a minimum of government. There was no king and no central ruling body. Each tribe lived quite to itself. The tribes themselves did not have central administrative bodies either. There were few officials at any level to whom people had to render obedience.

The situation was according to God's plan, however. God desired that His people render obedience directly to Him. He would be their Ruler; and if they would live as He directed, they would not need many earthly officers. He had given them His revealed laws so that they would know what He wanted. If they would obey these, they could live together meaningfully and peacefully. Also they would avoid the expense of supporting a human administration. Above all, they would please God, who then would prosper them in their earthly pursuits.

Some government, of course, was necessary to take care of details. This consisted mainly of appointed elders. These persons held jurisdiction over local communities. Elders had carried responsibility since the days of Egypt (Ex. 3:16-18; 19:7; 24:9; Num. 11:16-17), and the office still continued. They are said to have served as judges of persons who had killed someone (Deut. 19:12), conducted inquests (Deut. 21:2), heard family problems (Deut. 21:18f), settled matrimonial disputes (Deut. 22:15; 25:7), and settled cases of controversy in the gate of the city (Ruth 4:2).

Courts also existed, many local and one supreme. Each community had "judges and officers" for its local court. These sat in the gate of the city (Deut. 16:18), apparently sharing cases with elders.[80] When cases were "too hard" for the local court, they could be sent to the

---

[80] The Lachish ostraca were discovered in the gate of Lachish, for they were part to the evidence in a trial in progress at the time of the city's destruction. Cf. Deut. 21:19; Prov. 22:22; Amos 5:15. For the ostraca, cf. H. Torczyner, *The Lachish Letters*, 1935; or *DOTT*, pp. 212-17.

supreme court (Deut. 17:8f). This court sat at the central sanctuary in Shiloh, and was composed of priests and lay judges. The latter conducted the investigations (Deut. 19:18), and the former served as legal counsels. Court decisions required at least two witnesses (Deut. 19: 15). If a witness proved false, he received the punishment that the accused would have suffered had he been found guilty (Deut. 19:16-19). Punishment was executed without delay (Num. 15:36; Deut. 22:18) and was sometimes carried out in the presence of the judges (Deut. 25:2f), even at times by the officials themselves (Deut. 22:18). If the sentence was stoning, many people assisted (Num. 15:36; Deut. 22:21), and the witnesses had to cast the first stones (Deut. 13:9).

2. *Central sanctuary.* In keeping with the idea of theocracy, with God as chief Ruler, the main unifying instrument among the tribes was the central sanctuary at Shiloh, the Tabernacle. As in the wilderness, the Tabernacle represented God's presence among His people. This religious center was for all the people of every tribe, with no tribe favored over another. Ephraimites, in whose midst it was located, carried no priority for its ministration over Asherites, Reubenites, or any other far away. To the Tabernacle all could come, and on occasion were commanded to come, for their religious expression.

The Tabernacle served as the place of sacrifice. Here the priests and Levites ministered in the offerings and ceremonies prescribed in the Law. Offerings were made every day, with more on sabbaths and still more on feast days. All sacrifice was to be made at the Tabernacle, private altars not being permitted except in most unusual religious situations.[81] At the Tabernacle too the prescribed annual feasts were celebrated. To attend at least three of these every male of each tribe was expected to come to Shiloh (Deut. 16:16).

This situation of the Twelve Tribes, finding their one bond of unity in a central religious sanctuary, has a parallel in the later leagues of Greece and Italy. Greece called these leagues amphictyonies.[82] Two of the better known were the Delphic League and the Estuscan League of Voltumna, both consisting of twelve member states. Most leagues were composed of either twelve or six members. No central government bound the member states but only, as in Israel, a central religious sanctuary. Usually each individual state had more self-government than

---

[81] Cf. note 79.

[82] Awareness of the existence of such amphictyonies has influenced numerous liberal scholars to recognize that Israel did have a true central sanctuary. M. Noth's writings have been particularly important; cf. *NHI*, pp. 87f. On the basis of lists of 12 descendants in Gen. 22:20-24, in Gen. 25:13-16, in Gen. 36:10-14, and of 6 in Gen. 25:2, Noth suggests that similar amphictyonic organizations may have existed among the Aramaeans, Ishmaelites, Edomites, and Keturah's descendants respectively.

Israel's separate tribes, however; and their concept of the god (gods) worshiped at the central place differed greatly from Israel's belief in Yahweh.

3. *Priests and Levites.* Religious personnel were important to the manner of worship that God had instituted in Israel. One entire tribe was devoted by God to provide this personnel, the tribe of Levi.[83] This tribe was considered by God as a substitution for the male first-born, spared on the night of the initial Passover, and so otherwise claimed by God[84] (Ex. 13:1-15; Num. 3:40-51). Levites numbered 23,000 males one month and older at the time of the conquest.[85]   Among them, descendants of Aaron were declared to be priests,[86] and the eldest son of the continuing family was designated high priest.[87] Priests and Levites administered the Tabernacle ceremonies. Priests did the sacrificing and Levites assisted. By David's time there were so many priests and Levites that twenty-four divisions were made (I Chron. 24:1-31), with each division serving in turn for one week. A similar division must have been made at least among Levites already in the

[83] To maintain the number of tribes at twelve, when one was thus removed, the tribe of Joseph was divided into two, Ephraim and Manasseh. Some liberal scholars believe that the term, Levites, never designated a family but only an office; cf. Oesterley and Robinson, *Hebrew Religion* (New York: Macmillan Co., 1930), p. 164. But, as T. J. Meek, *Hebrew Origins* (New York: Harper & Bros., 1950), p. 121, himself a liberal, says, "The unequivocal testimony of the Old Testament" is that the "Levites were originally a tribe."

[84] At Sinai, Moses numbered Israel's first-born males older than one month (22,273) and, finding them more than Levites (22,000) by 273 he paid a five-shekel redemption tax for those extra (Num. 3:40-51).

[85] Some scholars question that to be a priest one had to be a descendant of Levi; cf. G. B. Gray, *Sacrifice in the Old Testament* (Oxford: Clarendon Press, 1925), p. 240. This questioning is based largely on the following texts: Judg. 17:5; II Sam. 6:17-18; I Kings 3:4; 8:62-64; and especially II Sam. 8:18. Each text, however, finds an interpretation fully in keeping with the traditional view that priests had to be Levites; cf. an unpublished thesis, L. J. Wood, *The Relationship of the Priests and Prophets in Pre-Exilic Israel as to Their Respective Teaching Functions*, pp. 146-49.

[86] The view of many higher critics that no distinction existed between priests and Levites until the time of Ezekiel must be rejected. The view holds that Ezekiel broached the idea of limiting the term "priests" to descendants of Zadok, and then that later writers broadened the number by assigning Aaron as the progenitor. For discussion, cf. S. R. Driver, *Introduction to the Literature of the Old Testament* (Edinburgh: T. & T. Clark, 1894), pp. 146-50.

[87] Aaron's two eldest sons, Nadab and Abihu, had died at Sinai (without children, Num. 3:4) for improper ceremonial observance, which left Eleazar and Ithamar, of whom Eleazar was the oldest and so he became high priest. His oldest son in turn was Phinehas, and his son Abishua, etc., who were successive high priests. How many other sons Eleazar and Ithamar may have had, to help as priests at the time when service at Shiloh began, is not known.

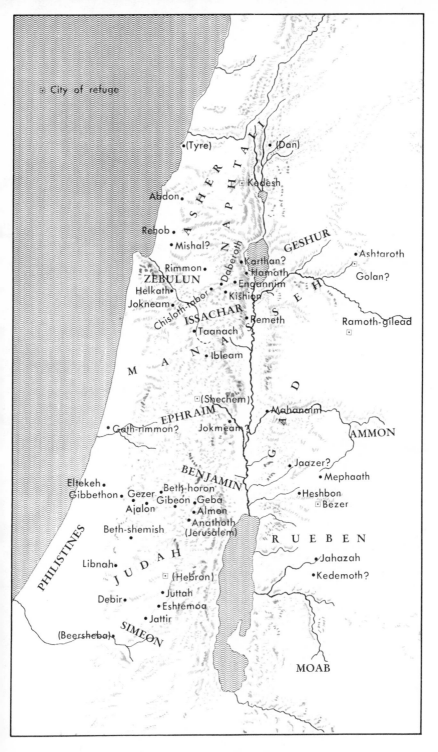

□ City of refuge

(Tyre) • • (Dan)

• Kadesh

Abdon •

Rehob •
• Mishal? GESHUR

Rimmon • Karthan? • Ashtaroth □
ZEBULUN • Hamath
Helkath • • Engannim Golan?
Jokneam • • Kishion

Chisloth-tabor Ramoth-gilead □
ISSACHAR • Remeth

• Taanach

• Ibleam

□ (Shechem)

• Mahanaim
EPHRAIM
• Gath-rimmon? • Jokmeam? AMMON

• Jaazer?
BENJAMIN • Mephaath

Elfekeh • • Heshbon
Gibbethon • Gezer Beth-horon □ Bezer
Ajalon Gibeon • Geba
• Almon
Beth-shemish • Anathoth
(Jerusalem) R U E B E N

• Jahazah
Libnah • • Kedemoth?
JUDAH
□ (Hebron)
Debir • • Juttah
• Eshtemoa
• Jattir

(Beersheba) • SIMEON
MOAB

Map. 7. The Levitical Cities

Judges Period, for even then too many existed for all to serve at one time.[88]

a. Levitic cities. When at home, priests and Levites lived in specially assigned cities. They were not allotted tribal territory because they had lost tribal significance in being designated for religious service (Josh. 13:14; 21:1-3). These special cities were evenly divided among the tribes, averaging four to a tribe, for a total of forty-eight (Num. 35:1-8; Josh. 21:1-41).[89] Among these forty-eight, six, also evenly distributed, were designated as "cities of refuge."[90] To these any slayer of some person could flee and be protected by the priests or Levites living there, until determination could be made as to his guilt or innocence (Num. 35:9-28; Josh. 20:1-9). If judged innocent, he could remain in safety from any avenger of blood by staying in the city until the death of the current high priest, after which he could return home and apparently still be safe.

b. Teaching. Since priests and Levites lived most of the year in their own cities rather than at the Tabernacle, and since they were supported by tithes of the people (Num. 18:20-28), which freed them from manual labor, they had time for another important religious function. That was teaching the people the Mosaic Law. Moses had received the Law and recorded it. The two stone tables engraved with the Decalogue were housed in the Ark (Ex. 25:16, 21; Deut. 10:1-5), and the copy of the whole Law certainly was kept in or near the Tabernacle. It told of Israel's covenantal relation with Yahweh and contained the civil and religious rules by which the people were to live. God had graciously revealed this vital information but it needed to be communicated throughout the land, if people were to respond. Some persons had to act as teachers, and those persons were the priests and Levites. God had commanded them to fill this need (Lev. 10:11; Deut. 33:10), and provided time and opportunity for it.

c. Urim and Thummim. In addition to the revealed, recorded Law,

[88] If 23,000 were one month and older (Num. 26:62), at least 10,000 must have been 25 years and older, the age when service began (Num. 8:24). Even to divide this group into 24 divisions would have given over 400 to serve in any one week.

[89] There were thirteen cities from Judah, Simeon, and Benjamin designated for priests (Josh. 21:13-19), all of which were not needed until some years had elapsed and priests had become more numerous; and thirty-five cities from the other tribes for Levites (Josh. 21:20-41). The only tribes with other than four cities were Judah and Simeon with nine between them, and Naphtali with three.

[90] On the west of Jordan were Kedesh in Naphtali, Shechem in Ephraim, and Hebron in Judah; on the east, Bezer in Reuben, Ramoth in Gad, and Golan in Manasseh. With this distribution of cities north, central, and south on both sides of the Jordan, no place in the land was more than thirty miles from a city of refuge.

God supplied the priests and Levites with a special device for receiving further information from Himself. This was the Urim and Thummim, apparently consisting of objects (probably two) which could be contained in the pocket-type[91] linen "breastplate" of the high priest worn on the front of his ephod (Ex. 28:30; Lev. 8:8; Num. 27:21; Deut. 33:8; I Sam. 28:6; Ezra 2:63). The exact method by which God intended these objects to give the revelation is not stated.[92] Whatever it was, when so used, the Urim and Thummim did provide a way whereby God's will might be known, though perhaps limited to a "Yes" or "No" type of communication.[93] The question could be voiced and God would use this means to give answer. Only the high priest could use the objects, a limitation which safe-guarded against improper use.

There was good reason for this device. Though the Law gave guidance for many areas of Israelite life, it did not, nor could not, serve all areas. Occasional questions were certain to arise, both of national[94] and local significance, which would not be answered there. A way was needed whereby direct revelation might be received from God. This was all the more true in Israel's theocratic form of government. There was need to be able to hear from God as King in regard to significant decisions. As to questions of local nature, these could be heard by priests and Levites living in the area, who then, if deeming the questions of sufficient importance, could bring them to the high priest for the inquiry. God might not answer the question. Saul, asking regarding his pending, final battle with the Philistines, was refused (I Sam. 28:6). This means that God kept full command in respect to Urim and Thummim inquiry. He did not have to give the revelation simply because man placed a question. But the Urim and Thummim did give God's people a way by which inquiry could at least be inaugurated, and God might then respond and uniquely fill the role of King of His people.

4. *Offerings.* The Law prescribed five types of offerings to be made

[91] Ex. 28:15-16 describes the "breastplate" as made of linen "foursquare . . . and double (passive participle of *kaphal*)." Since no need existed for this doubling to give added strength, it must be that it was to form a pocket-like pouch.

[92] For discussion of suggested methods, cf. L. J. Wood, "Urim and Thummim," *Theolog* (Winter, 1964), pp. 25-32.

[93] Even if so limited, considerable information could be gained by voicing repeated questions. Identifications were actually made in this way, as, for instance, in the case of Achan (Josh. 7:16-18) and later Saul (I Sam. 10:17-24). Some scholars, however (for instance, Payne, *Theology of the Older Testament*, Zondervan, 1962, p. 48), believe God communicated directly to the mind of the high priest.

[94] For instance, as to the request of the Gibeonites, who wished for a treaty with Israel (Josh. 9:14). This time an inquiry should have been made and was not.

at the Tabernacle. Each symbolized a distinctive religious truth. Some were offered regularly and for the people collectively; others only on occasion and by an individual for himself.

a. Burnt offering (Lev. 1:5-17; 6:8-13). The burnt offering symbolized complete consecration of life to God, being consumed entirely on the altar. It was the principal regular sacrifice offered for the people collectively, and it was also made by individuals for themselves. As a collective sacrifice, a lamb was offered every morning and evening, two lambs on sabbaths, and still more on feast days (Ex. 29: 38-46; Num. 28:3–29:39). For the individual, a lamb, goat, bullock, or ram might be used, and was brought as simply an act of consecration to God. Certain occasions or situations required it: when priests were consecrated (Ex. 29:15; Lev. 9:12); when women were purified (Lev. 12:6-8); when lepers were cleansed (Lev. 14:19); when ceremonial uncleanness was removed (Lev. 15:14-15, 30); and when the Nazarite vow was broken (Num. 6:11, 14).

b. Meal offering (Lev. 2:1-16; 6:14-23). The meal offering symbolized full dedication of one's material possessions to God. It was unique from others in being bloodless, not involving any animal. Instead, grain was offered, and this might be presented in different forms, but always with oil, frankincense, and salt. The meal offering regularly acompanied the burnt offering, and was also entirely consumed. It might be brought by an individual, like the burnt offering, and, if so, the priest then took only a handful of the presented grain for burning and kept the rest for Tabernacle use. Every meal offering was accompanied by a drink offering of wine. The burnt, meal, and drink offerings were those most frequently made.

c. Sin offering (Lev. 4:1-35; 6:24-30). The sin offering was to atone for sins of ignorance.[95] Collective sin offerings were presented regularly on days of prescribed feasts. Individuals were expected to bring sin offerings to cover their own sins at any time. The type of animal prescribed varied partly with the life status of the offerer (the higher his position, the more valuable the animal) and partly with the nature of the offense. The most valuable animal designated was a young bullock, and the least a turtledove or young pigeon, which might be substituted in turn even by a "tenth of an ephah of flour" in case of extreme poverty.

d. Trespass offering (Lev. 5:1–6:7; 7:1-7). The trespass offering was for a similar purpose as the sin offering, except that it atoned for particular sins whereas the sin offering carried reference more to the

---

[95] Sins of ignorance were sins committed without deliberation. The person who committed deliberate sin, called presumptuous sin or sin with a high hand, was to be "cut off from among his people" (Num. 15:30-31).

person himself as sinner. Certain sins were specified as requiring the trespass offering (Lev. 5:15, 17; 6:1f; 14:12; 19:20-22; Num. 6:12), with these usually calling in addition for money compensation to the person offended. The animal prescribed was normally the ram. The offering was always individual in kind; never collective.

e. Peace offering (Lev. 3:1-17; 7:11-34; 19:5-8; 22:21-25). Peace offerings were of three types: the thank offering rendered when unusual blessing had been experienced; the votive offering given in payment of a vow; and the freewill offering presented simply as an expression of love to God. Collective peace offerings were customary on festive occasions (I Sam. 11:15; II Sam. 6:17), and were prescribed for the Feast of Pentecost (Lev. 23:19). Individual peace offerings were given voluntarily and the person might bring any of several types of animals. A primary feature was the sacrificial meal in which portions of the slain animal were eaten in symbolism of fellowship between God and the person.

5. *Three great feasts.* The Israelite calendar called for three main annual feasts. Every male citizen was expected to come to Shiloh for these occasions.

a. Passover and Feast of Unleavened Bread (Ex. 12:1–13:10; Deut. 16:1-8). This twofold feast was the first of the religious year and the most important. It began on the fourteenth of Nisan (first religious month, March/April) with the observance of Passover, when a prescribed meal was eaten in commemoration of the first Passover in Egypt; and then continued seven days with the Feast of Unleavened Bread, named from the kind of bread eaten. On the day of Passover, a central feature was the slaying of a perfect lamb, selected four days before, quite as at the first Passover time. On the seven following days, numerous sacrifices were offered each day, and the first and seventh were days of rest and convocation for the people.

b. Feast of Weeks (Ex. 23:16; Lev. 23:15-22; Num. 28:26-31; Deut. 16:9-12). This feast came at the close of wheat harvest (thus sometimes called, Feast of Harvest, Ex. 23:16), when the first loaves made from the current harvest were offered (thus sometimes called, Feast of Firstfruits, Lev. 23:17), and exactly fifty days after Passover (thus sometimes called, Feast of Pentecost, Lev. 23:15-16; Deut. 16:9). It was observed one day only, with no work allowed and numerous offerings made, including the presentation of two loaves baked from the new harvest.

c. Feast of Tabernacles (Ex. 23:16; Lev. 23:34-43; Deut. 16:13-15). This feast lasted one week during which celebrants lived in booths or tents, in commemoration of Israel's manner of life during the wilderness journey from Egypt. The feast began on the fifteenth of Tishri, the seventh month (September/October), at the close of the harvest season (thus sometimes called, Feast of Ingathering, Ex. 34: 22). Many animals were sacrificed each day of the week, for a total of 71 bullocks, 15 rams, 105 lambs, and 8 goats, more than for any other festival.

6. *Other religious occasions.* Besides the three main feasts, other religious occasions also were observed.

a. Sabbath (Ex. 20:8-11; Num. 28:9-10; Deut. 5:12-15). Foremost and most frequent was the Sabbath, falling on every seventh day of each week, patterned after God's rest on the seventh day of the creation week, and serving as a reminder of God's deliverance of Israel from Egypt. No work was done, and the daily morning and evening sacrifices were doubled.

b. New Moon (Num. 10:10; 28:11-15). Every new moon was celebrated by the blowing of trumpets and a further increase in the daily offerings.

c. Feast of Trumpets (Lev. 23:23-25; Num. 29:1-6). The new moon of the seventh month (Tishri, September/October) was especially celebrated with yet more trumpet blowing and increased number of animals sacrificed. This day marked also the beginning of the civil year.

d. Day of Atonement (Lev. 16:1-34; 23:26-32; Num. 29:7-11). This day, the tenth of the same seventh month, was one of the most important of the year. An elaborate ceremony at the Tabernacle displayed in symbolism the necessity of atonement for sin. On this day, the high priest, for the only time of the year, entered the Holy of Holies as a part to the ceremony in which atonement was made for the priesthood, the Tabernacle itself, and the people collectively. No person was to labor, and all were to fast.[96]

e. Sabbatical Year (Ex. 23:10-11; Lev. 25:1-7; Deut. 15:1-11). Every seventh year the people were to refrain from working their land or pruning their vines. Spontaneous growth was to be shared by the poor, servants, and strangers. Debts of fellow Israelites were to be cancelled.

f. Year of Jubilee (Lev. 25:8-55; 27:16-25). After seven consecutive sabbatical years (forty-nine years), a special Year of Jubilee (fiftieth year) was to be observed. Again the land was to rest, meaning that at this time there would be two consecutive rest years (forty-ninth and fiftieth), God promising that the sixth year preceding would be so abundant that all needs would still be supplied. On this year, all family

---

[96] "To fast" is the apparent meaning of to "afflict your souls" (Lev. 16:29; cf. Ps. 35:13, Isa. 58:3). The Day of Atonement was the only day of the year on which fasting was commanded.

inheritances, somehow lost, were to be restored, and all slaves who wished were to be freed.

7. *Prophets.* Besides priests and Levites, Israel's religious personnel included prophets. Prophets had no prescribed responsibility with the central sanctuary, the offerings, or the festivals,[97] but held a vital mission of their own. The mission consisted of two basic functions: preaching and being recipients of revelation.

a. Preachers. First and foremost, they were preachers of God's message. As noted, the priests and Levites were communicators also, but more in the role of teachers, instructing the people in God's Law, "line upon line, precept upon precept" (Isa. 28:9-13). Prophets were more preachers, addressing their message to the heart and will. The priests and Levites told the people what God desired; the prophets urged conformity to God's standards. Their preaching was frequently in a reformation role, after people demonstrated that they would not follow what priests had taught them.

b. Recipients of revelation. They were also recipients of God's revelation; that is, revelation in addition to that recorded in the Mosaic Law. The one official recognition of prophets in the Law (Deut. 18:9-22)[98] concerns their place in this capacity. Israelites were not to resort to divination practitioners for divine communication, as in other countries, but they were to go to the prophet in whose mouth God would place His word. There was a difference between this prophetic revelation and that given through the priestly Urim and Thummim. The latter was a device by which the human instrument might initiate the revelation, as we have seen, but which was limited in type of answer to mere affirmation or negation. In contrast, the prophet could only wait for God to speak; but then, when the revelation came, he received a full propositional message. Messages so given constituted basic portions of what the prophets preached.

c. Called to service. Prophets differed from priests and Levites also in that they did not receive their office by inheritance, but through a special call of God. Prophets thus were fewer in number than priests and Levites, but also, being particularly selected, they were men of unusual gift, vision, and dedication. God's assignments led them to many places and situations, often difficult and even dangerous. They needed to be resourceful, courageous, and especially, men of faith.

[97] The view as held by Haldar, *Associations of Cult Prophets Among the Ancient Semites* (Uppsala: Almquist and Wiksells Boktrycheri, 1945), or Johnson, *The Cultic Prophet in Ancient Israel* (Cardiff: University of Wales Press Board, 1944), that prophets were cultic persons, finds no biblical basis and must be rejected.

[98] The Law recognized the prophets, but did not give formal, legal standing or prescription as with priests and Levites.

d. Number. Though prophets were never as numerous as priests and Levites, clues exist in Scripture that probably Israel was never without prophets and most of the time had a substantial number. This was true even during the Judges Period. Deborah is called a prophetess (*nebhi'ah;* Judg. 4:4), and an unnamed prophet is depicted as coming to warn the people of sin just prior to Gideon's call (Judg. 6:8-10). The casual manner in which each is mentioned suggests that these were in no way the only members of their kind then living. More significant is the indication of I Samuel 9:9 that before prophets were called "prophets" they were called "seers." To have reason for such name-development, there must have been many representatives then living.[99] It is likely that from the time of Moses, Israel was never without prophets, and that during the early monarchy and especially the divided monarchy they became very numerous. Their influence for good in Israel should never be minimized.

[99] It may be added also that Moses' promise of Deut. 18:15-19 suggests that numerous prophets would always be available to fill the task there described.

Chapter Nine

THE JUDGES

Judges 1–21; Ruth 1–4; I Samuel 1–8

With the Promised Land conquered and allotted to the respective tribes, a day long anticipated was at hand for God's chosen people. Six centuries earlier God had promised that Abraham's seed would become nation-size and possess this land. Now the fulfillment of that promise had been realized. While the people had been in Egypt, they no doubt had longed for the day when they would have their own land. In Egypt they had been foreigners and even slaves, and then in the wilderness they had been restless transients. But now they were in a land of their own. They could plan for the future and carve out their own manner of life.

It was also a day of great promise. In that Israel had been raised up by God to be His special people, and in that God would desire such a people to be a fine witness to His glory, there was reason for Israel to anticipate success and prosperity. God indeed had clearly promised unusual blessing, stating that if the people followed Him faithfully, they would be "the head, and not the tail" in their world community, and so be "above only" and "not beneath" (Deut. 28: 1-14; 30:1-10). All that the Israelites needed to do was obey their heavenly Ruler and the most attractive future ever enjoyed by a nation awaited.

This grand future did not result, however, because the people did not meet the condition. They did not remain true to their God or obey His laws. These wonderful blessings, therefore, were forfeited.

A. Background Matters

1. *Book of Judges.* The book of Judges is the main source of information for the period of time now to be considered, the so-called Judges Period. But if one is correctly to evaluate the information it

203

gives, the basic nature of the book must be understood. Its record as history is from a particular point of view. That view is the failure, deficiency, and sinfulness of Israel during this time. A key verse, written twice (Judg. 17:6; 21:25) sounds this note: "Every man did that which was right in his own eyes." The book shows how this was tragically true. The rationale for this type of historical report is found in the need to tell why Israel was not blessed by God as she might have been. She, who had owned such attractive prospects, did not realize them because she did not obey her God. The book depicts the many ways she failed.

Chapter one describes Israel's failure to drive the Canaanites from the land. Chapter two tells of her consequent acceptance of Canaanite Baal worship. Chapters three through sixteen depict successive periods of oppression, brought as punishment, by Mesopotamians, Moabites, Canaanites, Midianites, Ammonites, and Philistines. Each period involved a cycle of Israel sinning, being invaded and severely oppressed, and then delivered by a judge raised up by God. Finally, chapters seventeen through twenty-one narrate two sad episodes which illustrate the manner of misbehavior which generally characterized the period.

Since this failure motif is dominant in the book, the manner of life depicted must not be taken as normative or legally proper, as is often done by liberal scholars. For instance, because a certain Levite happened to be walking through the country looking for employment when hired by the Ephraimite Micah (Judg. 17:7-13), one must not conclude that Levites generally were transient opportunists. Without question, most Levites were living properly in their assigned cities, with only a few recalcitrants pursuing such a deviant manner of life.

2. *The oppressions*

a. Brought by local enemies. Most of the record in the book of Judges, and most of the time involved in the period concerned, are occupied with the six successive foreign oppressions. It should be observed that none of these came from large, national powers of the day. The period of the judges was a time in world history when large powers were not engaged in an active domination of the area. Egypt's Eighteenth Dynasty rulers after Amenhotep III were all weaker than he and no longer interested in Canaanite control.[1] Both Seti I and his son, the great Rameses II, of the early Nineteenth Dynasty, did campaign north against the Hittites, but for the most part only passed through the coastal areas of Palestine.[2] Bethshan was occupied by both these rulers, but the valley region in which the city lay was yet under Canaanite control, and Israel still was little affected. Nineteenth Dynasty

[1] *Supra,* chap. 8, p. 168.
[2] *Supra,* chap. 5, pp. 107-108.

rulers, after these two, were again weaker, though Merneptah and later Rameses III of the Twentieth Dynasty did make temporary invasions of the region.[3]

Great powers to the north did not invade southern Canaan during this period at all. The Hittites, against whom Egypt particularly battled, were strong, but were kept in check by these battles. The country of Mitanni of northern Mesopotamia was still vigorous in Joshua's time but shortly after was seriously curtailed in strength by the rising Hittites under the great Shuppiluliuma.[4] Both Assyria and Babylonia lay further to the east and at this time did not play any significant role in the West. Southern Canaan, thus, was left quite to itself. Israel's enemies were the peoples of the area, small like herself.

b. Philistines, the most serious. The most serious menace of these local enemies was the last faced during the period, the Philistines. This people, as we have seen,[5] had been in the land to some extent from the days of Abraham but, during the Judges Period, came in far greater number. They were part to the vast movement of the Sea Peoples, some of whom had been repelled already by Pharaoh Merneptah (1238–1228), but came in larger number against Egypt in the rule of Rameses III (c. 1195–1164),[6] between his fifth and eleventh years. They were kept from infiltrating Egypt, but not from retreating to and occupying land which Egypt yet claimed along the southern Canaanite shoreline. Here, in an area previously assigned to Judah and Dan, the Philistines established a pentapolis, in which the five main cities were Ashkelon, Gaza, Ashdod, Ekron, and Gath, each of which had its own ruler (*seren*). After a period of adjustment, assimilating much of the Canaanite culture and religion, the Philistines made their presence known by vigorous military activity, which resulted in Israel's sixth oppression. One of the Philistines' chief sources of strength in their military success was a local monopoly on the manufacture of iron (I Sam. 13:19-22), the secret of which they had probably learned from the Hittites.[7]

[3] For discussion as to why these inroads are not mentioned in Judges, cf. *supra*, chap. 5, pp. 108-109.

[4] Shuppiluliuma (c. 1375-1340) was mainly responsible for the rise of the Hittite empire. He made conquest as far south as the Lebanon mountains; cf. O. R. Gurney, *The Hittites* (Penguin Books, Inc., 1925).

[5] *Supra*, chap. 3, pp. 59-60.

[6] Dates uncertain, cf. *supra*, chap. 5, p. 108, n. 103.

[7] Though meteoric iron was known as early as the Third Millennium B.C., the art of smelting iron appears to have been developed by the Hittites, who accordingly held a monopoly through most of the Second Millennium. Being much harder than bronze, it gave a monopolizing country enormous advantage over enemies. Cf. Albright, *AP*, p. 110.

3. *The Judges.* The book of Judges is named from the persons God selected to give leadership among His people during this period. Judges 2:16 says that God "raised up judges who saved them." Of most of these persons, it is stated that they "judged Israel" for a specified number of years. Twelve names are normally included in the honored group.

Name	Oppression	Reference
1. Othniel	Mesopotamians	3:7-11
2. Ehud	Moabites	3:12-30
3. Shamgar		3:31
4. Deborah with Barak	Canaanites	4–5
5. Gideon	Midianites	6–8
6. Tola		10:1-2
7. Jair		10:3-5
8. Jephthah	Ammonites	10:6–12:7
9. Ibzan		12:8-10
10. Elon		12:11-12
11. Abdon		12:13-15
12. Samson	Philistines	13–16

To this list sometimes are added Abimelech, Eli, and Samuel. Abimelech, son of Gideon, however, was more a renegade king, during his three years of leadership, than a judge, and both Eli and Samuel, though spoken of as "judging" Israel (I Sam. 4:18; 7:15-17), were respectively more high priest and prophet.

For most of the judges, work was both military and supervisory in kind. Though not all were involved in the military, this is the aspect for which judges are best known, since much of the biblical record concerns this aspect. Rather detailed descriptions are given of the military activities of six of these persons. These stories will be noted later in the chapter. No military involvement is mentioned for four judges (Jair, Ibzan, Elon, and Abdon), however, and only brief notice for two (Shamgar and Tola).[8] But all twelve seem to have been occupied for a varying number of years[9] with supervisory activity. This aspect of their work no doubt arose as a consequence of the first, the people recognizing leadership ability in the new deliverer and continuing to look to him for general civic management. The name "judge"[10] comes

---

[8] Of Shamgar it is stated merely that he killed 600 Philistines and of Tola that he arose "to save Israel."

[9] The number is indicated for 7 Judges: Tola 23 years, Jair 22, Jephthah 6, Ibzan 7, Elon 10, Abdon 8, and Samson 20. The exact years for the others are not mentioned, though succeeding periods of rest are: Othniel 40 years, Ehud 80, Deborah 40, and Gideon 40. No figure is given for Shamgar.

[10] This name is the participial form of the verb *shaphat,* meaning "one who judges." No doubt matters of general civic interest were judged as well as those commonly associated with a court room.

from this part of the work. Though the office of judge was not prescribed in the Law, it was approved by God. It is regularly stated that the persons filling it were "raised up" of God (Judg. 3:9, 15, etc.) and also that at least four[11] were especially enabled by the Holy Spirit.

4. *A chronological problem.* The book of Judges presents a problem in chronology. The number of years indicated in the book for the numerous periods of oppression or peace, including the time of Samson, add to 410.[12] But even when the Exodus is placed at the early date, insufficient time exists to allow 410 years for these events.[13] First Kings 6:1 states that only 480 years elapsed between the Exodus and Solomon's fourth year, when he began to build the Temple. That leaves only 70 years in which to locate the wilderness period of 40 years, Joshua's time of leadership of possibly 16 years, the period between Samson's demise and Saul's inauguration of perhaps five years, Saul's rule of forty years (Acts 13:21), David's reign of forty years, and Solomon's first four years, all of which total 145 years. In other words, the 410-year total for the events of Judges is about 75 years too long.

The book of Judges itself, however, suggests the solution, implying that certain of these events overlapped in time. For instance, Judges 3:30–4:1 implies that Shamgar judged during the 80 years of peace following Ehud's deliverance from the Moabites. Judges 10:7 implies that Jephthah, occupied with the Ammonites east of the Jordan, and Samson, concerned with the Philistines on the west, were contemporary in activity. Certain of the lesser judges, because they were active in particular, separated areas of the land, could well have worked at the same time; as, for instance, Tola, who judged in Issachar (Judg. 10: 1-2), and Jair, who judged across the Jordan in Gilead (Judg. 10:3-5). Careful study reveals that sufficient years may be properly accounted for to solve the problem, without doing injustice to the text.

5. *Canaanite religion.* The main area in which Israel displeased

[11] Othniel (Judg. 3:10), Gideon (6:34); Jephthah (11:29); and Samson (13: 25; 14:6, 19; 15:14).

[12] Mesopotamian oppression, 8 yrs. (Judg. 3:8); Othniel's deliverance and rest, 40 yrs. (3:11); Moab oppression, 18 yrs. (3:14); Ehud's deliverance and rest, 80 yrs. (3:30); Canaanite oppression, 20 yrs. (4:3); Deborah and Barak's deliverance and rest, 40 yrs. (5:31); Midianite oppression, 7 yrs. (6:1); Gideon's deliverance and rest, 40 yrs. (8:28); Abimelech's rule, 3 yrs. (9:22); Tola as judge, 23 yrs. (10:2); Jair as judge, 22 yrs. (10:3); Ammonite oppression, 18 yrs. (10:8); Jephthah's deliverance and rest, 6 yrs. (12:7); Ibzan as judge, 7 yrs. (12:9); Elon as judge, 10 yrs. (12:11); Abdon as judge, 8 yrs. (12:14); Philistine oppression, 40 yrs. (13:1); and Samson's exploits, 20 yrs. (15:20), totalling 410 yrs.

[13] Cf. discussion, *supra*, chap. 5, pp. 89-90.

God, thereby forfeiting the abundant blessing otherwise promised, was that of religion. Many Israelites came to adopt Canaanite religious practices.

The most significant deity of the Canaanites was Baal, for he controlled rain and storm. Canaanites believed that economic prosperity in good crops and large flocks depended directly on pleasing this god. Though El[14] was theoretically chief deity, Baal received the greater homage. The extensive epic literature found at Ras Shamra sets forth many other gods also,[15] with Baal being always central in importance. Mot, god of death, is described as annually effecting Baal's death, but Anath, goddess of war and both sister and consort of Baal, is able as often to effect his resurrection.[16] Asherah, though presented as wife of El at Ras Shamra, in lower Canaan appears as consort of Baal; and her carved pole is mentioned in the Old Testament as standing beside his altar (Judg. 6:25-28; I Kings 15:13).[17] Ashtaroth, goddess of fertility, love, and war, is also frequently linked with Baal in the Old Testament (Judg. 2:13; 10:6; I Sam. 7:3-4; 12:10). The concepts of all three female deities, Anath, Asherah, and Ashtaroth, were somewhat fluid, tending to change and merge into one another, so that clear distinctions were not always maintained. Prescribed worship of these deities involved religious prostitution, and the mythology includes stories of extreme brutality and immorality. Child sacrifice and snake worship were also observed. The religion was decadent, and Israel sinned greatly in being enamored by it. The attraction was basically economic. Israelites wanted to be prosperous in their new agricultural pursuits, and they believed erroneously that adherence to the Baal cult was the way to accomplish this (cf. Hos. 2:5, 8).

B. Failure to Occupy the Land Fully (Judges 1:1-3:7)

The prior chapter has shown that Joshua broke the strength of the Canaanites, but the individual tribes were expected to occupy their respectively assigned portions.[18] In this responsibility came the first fail-

[14] This El is a Canaanite deity, not the El of the Old Testament, though the name is basically the same.

[15] Cf. Wright, *BAR*, pp. 106-16; Albright, *ARI*, chapters III and IV; Unger, *AOT*, pp. 168-77.

[16] C. Gordon, however, disputes this commonly accepted viewpoint, denying the death-resurrection cycle. Cf. his *Ugaritic Literature* (Rome: Pontifical Bible Institute, 1949), pp. 4-5; or *ANE*, p. 40.

[17] Some scholars believe that this was an image of the goddess, others that it was merely symbolic of her. Cf. Albright, *ARI*, pp. 77-79; M. Burrows, *What Mean These Stones?* (New Haven: American Schools of Oriental Research, 1941), pp. 212-13.

[18] Liberal scholars have alleged a discrepancy between Joshua's record and that of Judges on this count, saying that Joshua presents the conquest as swift

Map 8. Area Actually Settled by Israelites

ures of the period. Not one tribe succeeded in occupying all the territory allotted.

Judah, with the help of Simeon whose assigned cities lay in Judah's territory, pressed the attack first. In comparison with other tribes later, they did well, but still "could not drive out the inhabitants of the valley, because they had chariots of iron" (Judg. 1:19). The "valley" here mentioned is likely the flat land toward the Mediterranean into which the Philistines were shortly to come. Canaanites were yet strong there, and apparently had adopted the chariot[19] for warfare, an effective weapon in this level terrain. Benjamin, we are told, failed to "drive out the Jebusites that inhabited Jerusalem" (Judg. 1:21). Jerusalem was a stronghold, and the Benjamites, though not having much land on which to expend occupation efforts, did not succeed in taking it. Dan, directly to Benjamin's west, was forced like Judah to stay in the mountains, not being permitted to enter the better low land. As a result, many of them, as noted in the prior chapter,[20] migrated north of Naphtali (Judg. 18). Ephraim, who had already complained about her portion at the time of allotment, failed to take Gezer on her west (Judg. 1:29). If Gezer is the only place Ephraim failed to take, she did comparatively well, perhaps profiting from Joshua's earlier admonition (Josh. 17:14-18). It is likely, however, that Gezer only stands for rather extensive land in its vicinity, again the better flat land of the allotment. Manasseh, next north, had problems in level areas too. She failed to take Bethshan, Taanach, Dor, Ibleam, and Megiddo, with their respective regions (Judg. 1:27), all located either near the Mediterranean or in the Esdraelon or Jordan valleys. Issachar and Zebulun both found much of their assigned portions in the Esdraelon valley, an area held by the Canaanites. Strangely, the fortunes of Issachar remain unmentioned in Judges, but she probably fell short as well. Cities of the Esdraelon valley do not evidence Israelite occupation this early, and the same valley saw the Egyptian Pharaohs Seti I and Rameses II make their inroads as far east as Bethshan less than a century later, apparently without greatly disturbing Israelites.[21] Zebulun failed to take Kitron and Nahalol (Judg. 1:30), neither of which has been well iden-

and complete, while Judges shows it as slow and partial. But Wright, *BAR*, p. 69, himself liberal, observes that "It has now become necessary to modify the common scholarly view" in recognizing that Joshua, too, particularly in chapter 13, indicates that much land remained to be occupied after the first successes.

[19] Probably from the Egyptians, who had used the chariot effectively in establishing their empire earlier (cf. *supra*, chap. 6, pp. 111-12). Southern Canaan was well within the Egyptian orbit of influence.

[20] *Supra*, chap. 8, p. 191.

[21] Bethshan, at the border of Manasseh and Issachar, was probably occupied by both Pharaohs; cf. *supra*, chap. 5, pp. 107-108.

tified but were probably in this valley. Asher failed regarding Acco, Sidon, Achzib, and Aphik, all well identified near the Mediterranean, and also Ahlab, Helbah, and Rehob, less well identified but again probably in the level area (Judg. 1:31-32). Naphtali, the last to notice, did not dislodge the Canaanites from Bethshemesh or Bethanath, the latter being rather well identified with modern el-Ba'neh on the western edge of Naphtali.

In summary, the tribes were reasonably successful in the hill country, but not in the more attractive level regions. In those areas, Canaanite population would have been larger and opposition greater. The Israelites took the less valuable hills and left the valleys to the former inhabitants. This was directly contrary to God's specific command (Deut. 7:1-4). Canaanites were to be exterminated lest they turn Israelite hearts away from Yahweh to serve their false gods. This is what did happen in many localities. Accordingly, severe reprimand for unfaithfulness to God came early in the Judges Period, even from the "Angel of Yahweh" (Judg. 2:1-4), but while briefly prompting a repentant attitude, the rebuke did not significantly change the course on which the people had embarked. Consequently, disciplinary measures in the form of the severe foreign oppressions were necessary.

C. The Period of Mesopotamian Oppression
(Judges 3:8-11; 17–21)

The first punishing oppressor came from the far north, Mesopotamia. In addition to considering the suffering and deliverance which resulted from this enemy, it is necessary to look here also at two representative stories included at the close of the book of Judges (chaps. 17–21), for they transpired at this same general time.

1. *The oppression and deliverance (Judges 3:8-11)*

a. Identity of Cushan Rishathaim. The leader of this Mesopotamian invasion bears the name Cushan Rishathaim. His country is called Aram Naharaim, meaning "Aram of the two rivers," a designation for Mesopotamia, which lies between the Tigris and Euphrates. Since this is the only oppressor who came from such a distant land, and since the Mesopotamian region did not otherwise have military contact as far south as Israel at this time in history, considerable discussion has ensued as to the man's identity. Some have thought that the spelling of "Aram" (*'rm*), his home country, is a copyist's mistake for "Edom" (*'dm*), so that the attack really came from this nearby southern country; especially since Othniel, the Judge who opposed it, was himself a member of the southern tribe of Judah.[22] Garstang suggests differently

---

[22] Cf. G. Ricciotti, *The History of Israel* (2nd ed.; Milwaukee: The Bruce Publishing Co., 1958), II, p. 244.

that Cushan Rishathaim may have been the Hittite king who is known to have conquered Mitanni and later penetrated southward as far as Palestine about this time, leaving traces at Bethshan and elsewhere.[23] But M. Kline's suggestion, noted in chapter five,[24] is perhaps likely. He believes that Cushan Rishathaim was a Habiru leader, who had entered the land primarily to crush Canaanites and who now, seeing Israel become strong, proceeded to subjugate her as well.

b. Conquest and deliverance. The record does not tell how this conquest was affected, nor how many tribes were involved. None of the other oppressions affected all of the tribes, and so likely this one did not either. The duration is given, however, as eight years. Toward the close of this time the people cried to God for relief, and He gave it through Othniel, younger brother of the renowned Caleb. Othniel had already distinguished himself in seizing Debir (Kiriath-sepher) at a former occasion, when his uncle had promised his own daughter Achsah as wife to the man who would accomplish the feat. Probably his abilities were remembered now, and he was called upon to lead against the Mesopotamians. No record is given of how he won the victory. It is significantly stated, however, that "the Spirit of Yahweh came upon him" in achieving it. After the victory, the land had rest forty years before the next oppression.

c. Date. This first oppression is best dated in the early second quarter of the fourteenth century. It cannot have immediately followed Joshua's death, for Judges 2:7 states that the people continued faithful to God during his time and that of the elders who outlived him. Since the oppression was permitted because of unfaithfulness, there had to be time for these elders to die and the declension to occur. Joshua could hardly have died before 1390 B.C.,[25] which means this oppression cannot be placed much before 1375 B.C., fifteen years later.[26]

2. *Two representative stories (Judges 17–21).* Two representative stories at the close of the book of Judges fall into this period. One concerns the movement of Danites from their allotted territory to an area north of Naphtali (Judg. 17–18). The other concerns the violation of a concubine of a certain Levite by men of Gibeah, and the resultant war with Benjamin by the other tribes (Judg. 19–21). The first story must be placed this early in the Judges Period because the book

---

[23] Garstang, *Joshua, Judges* (London: Constable & Co., Ltd., 1931), p. 62.

[24] *Supra*, chap. 5, pp. 106-107.

[25] He lived to the age of 110 (Judg. 2:8) and likely was not much over 90 when the Jordan was crossed in 1406 B.C.

[26] Fifteen years may seem like a rather short time, but it is adequate since the declension likely started before all elders died. Time must be used sparingly from the Judges Period since chronological compression is needed, as noted earlier.

of Joshua (19:47) mentions this Danite move, and that book was written while Rahab, rescued from Jericho, yet lived (Josh. 6:25). The other story must be placed this early because Phinehas, son of Eleazar, active during and even before the time of the conquest (Num. 25:7, 11; Josh. 22:13, 31f), was still high priest (Judg. 20:28). Both stories are narrated to illustrate the extent of declension in the land, and certainly represent many others that might have been included.

a. Danite movement (Judg. 17–18). The first illustrates the seriousness of religious defection at this time. The Ephraimite Micah was given money by his mother, used it to make a private sanctuary, and established his own son as priest. When a wandering Levite, who should have been active in his own Levitic city, passed by, Micah hired him as his personal priest. About this time five Danites, looking for new and less hazardous land for their tribe, happened by Micah's house, saw this private religious arrangement, and were attracted by it. Later, when leading a contingent of six hundred Danites to seize the new northern area they had selected, they again passed Micah's dwelling and urged the Levite to accompany them. The young man, clearly an opportunist, accepted the invitation and then took several of Micah's religious articles with him. Micah's strong protestations did not avail to stop the man or the theft.

The episode involved several factors contrary to the Law. Micah erred in making his own sanctuary, when Shiloh alone was to be recognized. The Levite was wrong for not remaining in his assigned city and for engaging in illegal priestly activity with a private party. The Danites were in error for moving from their allotted territory, for establishing their own private sanctuary, and for stealing the property of another to do it.

b. Gibeah outrage (Judg. 19–21). The second incident reveals the extent of moral degradation in the land, caused in large part certainly by the influence of the Baal cult. A Levite stopped with his concubine at Gibeah of Benjamin for the night. During the evening, men of the city came to the house where he stayed and demanded to have improper relations with him. The Levite offered them his concubine instead, and she was taken and abused. The Levite found her dead on the doorstep the following morning. In shock and anger, he divided her body into twelve parts and sent a part to each tribe, demanding reprisal against Gibeah for the deed. The other tribes then called for the Benjamites to deliver to them the guilty persons, but they refused. Civil war ensued, and, though Benjamin's force was much smaller,[27]

[27] The other tribes had 400,000 men (Judg. 20:17), about two-thirds of their potential fighting force (Num. 26:51). Benjamin had only 26,000 (Judg. 20:15) slightly less than two-thirds of its tribal strength (Num. 26:41). Cf. *KDC*, Joshua, Judges, Ruth, pp. 449-51 for good discussion.

she defeated the other tribes two times. The third time, however, she was defeated, Gibeah was leveled, and all Benjamites were killed, with the exception of 600 men who fled to the rock of Rimmon. Four months later, the other tribes realized that now one tribe would be exterminated if wives were not provided for these 600 who had escaped, and unusual measures were taken to do so.[28]

The main sin involved this time was the moral outrage committed by the people of Gibeah, first in their desire toward the Levite himself and then toward his concubine. This shows that serious degradation had developed among God's people, similar to that of Sodom in the days of Lot. With sin of this magnitude occurring so soon after Joshua's day, the necessity for God's repeated punishments through the oppressions is easily understood.

D. THE PERIOD OF MOABITE OPPRESSION (Judges 3:12-31)

1. *The oppression and deliverance (Judges 3:12-30).* The second oppressing nation, Moab, lived close at hand. Moab lay immediately across the Dead Sea from Judah, south of the Transjordan tribes. It had been their king, Balak, who years before had brought the strange prophet Balaam to curse Israel when she was yet encamped east of the Jordan.

Now the Moabites, assisted in some part by Ammonites and Amalekites, crossed the Jordan and occupied Jericho. Since Joshua had pronounced a curse on any who should rebuild this city (Josh. 6:26), and since I Kings 16:34 states that such rebuilding was done only much later by one Hiel the Bethelite, it is not likely that the Moabites had to dislodge any inhabitants here at this time. Probably the invaders simply moved on to the bare, unoccupied mound, erected a minimum of buildings for their temporary purpose,[29] and brought the Israelites of the area under their control. Eglon, a fat man, was their king. Using Jericho as a center, he kept the Israelites in servitude for eighteen years.

Finally Israel cried once more to God for relief, and God raised up a second deliverer, Ehud of Benjamin. Since the date here was certainly not long after the civil war of Benjamin and the other tribes just noted, this new deliverer may have been one of the 600 Benjamites who escaped to the rock of Rimmon. The deliverance Ehud effected

---

[28] First, by seizing 400 unmarried young women from Jabesh-gilead (the city had not sent soldiers to help in the civil war) and giving these to the 600; second, by having some of the 600 lie in ambush near the dancing area of "daughters of Shiloh" and taking wives from among these young women.

[29] According to Garstang's calculations, the "Middle Building" (so named by him) above the spring could be the main building erected at this time; cf. *supra,* chap. 5, pp. 94, 96-97.

was not through warfare, but through an act of deception in which he succeeded in slaying King Eglon. Ehud presented himself to Eglon to extend a gift from the subjugated Israelites. But having delivered the present, with all servants removed from the room, he drew near the king and plunged a sword into his body, killing him. Leaving the blade enclosed in the fat which engulfed it, he quietly left the room, locked the door after himself, and moved safely away while the deed remained undiscovered. Then Ehud quickly assembled Israelites at the fords of the Jordan where the Moabites, who could now be expected to retreat, would cross. The Moabites did retreat, and Ehud's men killed 10,000 of them. This brought a lengthy peace of eighty years to the land.

2. *The eighty years of peace (Judges 3:30).* A contributing reason for this eighty-year extension of peace, the longest such time in the Judges Period, may be found in the renewed activity of Egypt during this era. These eighty years bring us past the middle of the thirteenth century.[30] A correlation of dates shows that these years fell during the influential rule of the strong Nineteenth Dynasty of Egypt, a time in which power was exerted once again by Egypt in Palestine and southern Syria, particularly by Seti I (1316-1304) and Rameses II (1304-1238). Both rulers extensively campaigned north through Palestine against the Hittites, effecting some conquest in northern Palestine itself.[31] Such a display of power would have been well observed by small nations of the region, who, in reaction, would have refrained from undue overt activity that might call attention to themselves. All would have desired to avoid the displeasure of Egypt toward them. Consequently, local wars would not have been waged so long as Egypt was in the area, thus making for the period of peace.[32]

3. *Shamgar (Judges 3:31).* It was probably during this same eighty-year span that Shamgar lived as third judge. His brief story is recorded directly following the above account; and Deborah, the next judge, mentions Shamgar in her victory song (Judg. 5:6) as at least having preceded her. He is called "the son of Anath," which suggests that his home town was Bethanath, a southern city of Judah (Josh. 15:59). He later fought Philistines of the south, indicating that he did not come from a similarly named city in Naphtali to the north (Judg. 1:33).

---

[30] The forty-year rest period after the Mesopotamian oppression (c. 1375-1367) brings us to c. 1327-1309 for the eighteen years of Moabite oppression, placing this 80-year peace period c. 1309-1229.

[31] *Supra,* chap. 5, pp. 107-108.

[32] Garstang, *op. cit.,* pp. 51-56, believes that there was correspondence between Egyptian activities and all of Israel's peace periods during the time of the judges. He has difficulty making the correspondences, however.

Shamgar is not called a judge, nor is he said to have done the work of one. He did, however, win a remarkable victory over Philistines, bringing deliverance to Israelites; and so, since he is listed in the over-all story in parallel with other judges, he is best taken as one. His victory is described as a personal one, in which he demonstrated enormous strength and courage, killing no less than 600 Philistines with nothing but an ox-goad.[33] That this wooden stick was his only weapon likely reflects the lack of iron in Israel, known from other sources as having been true for this time.[34]

E. THE PERIOD OF CANAANITE OPPRESSION (Judges 4–5)

1. The oppression and deliverance (Judges 4–5)

a. Oppression (Judg. 4:1-3). The third oppression came from Canaanites within the land of Palestine, whom the Israelite tribes should have driven from the land years before. Jabin,[35] king of Hazor, was the leader, and Sisera[36] his general. The city of Hazor, soundly defeated by Joshua some 170 years before,[37] had again become strong in the land. Sisera employed 900 chariots of iron[38] and made Harosheth,[39] about 11 miles northwest of Megiddo on the Kishon River, his center of activity. He was able to assert dominance and maintain control over Israelite tribes of the area for 20 years.

b. Deborah and Barak (Judg. 4:4-9). Israel's principal deliverer this time was a woman, Deborah, unique among the twelve judges, not only because she was a woman, but also because she was acting as judge even before her victorious battle. She is called a prophetess (nebhi'ah), and people are said to have come to her for counsel, which no doubt included judicial decisions. She received people under a palm tree located between Ramah and Bethel, some sixty miles south of where the battle with Sisera later took place. Already recognized for leadership, she was the logical one to initiate any deliverance from

---

[33] The ox-goad was merely a stout stick, often bronze-tipped, used to guide and impel oxen at work.

[34] Note especially I Sam. 13:19-22; cf. supra, p. 205, n. 7.

[35] Same name as that of the king Joshua defeated; but this does not mean that this story and that found in Joshua 11 are mixed accounts, as held by some liberals; cf. Myers and Elliott, Interpreter's Bible, II, pp. 12-24.

[36] The name "Sisera" has made some scholars think of this general as one of northern origin, who had allied himself with Jabin; cf. Simpson, The Composition of the Book of Judges (New York: The Macmillan Co., 1957), pp. 12-24.

[37] Joshua's defeat was c. 1400 B.C. and the date here c. 1230.

[38] Canaanites had employed chariots for some time (cf. ANET, p. 237), but Israel, confined mainly to mountains, had little use for them. They are first mentioned as used by Israelites with Absalom, II Sam. 15:1.

[39] Probably modern Tell el-Harbaj, a six-acre site on the south bank of the Kishon River, at the foot of Mt. Carmel.

the Canaanites. Being a woman, she did not wish to lead in battle, and requested Barak to do this. He lived far north in Kedesh [40] of Naphtali. He consented, provided she would aid him. When she agreed, he gathered an army of 10,000 men from Zebulun and Naphtali, apparently the two tribes most affected by the oppression.

c. Deliverance (Judg. 4:10–5:31). Barak brought his army south to Mt. Tabor and joined battle with Sisera west of Megiddo (Judg. 5:19) on the banks of the Kishon. From Deborah's later song (Judg. 5:21), it is learned that during the conflict the Kishon overflowed and mired Sisera's chariots. This made victory by Deborah and Barak possible, and they pursued the fleeing enemy back to Haroseth. Meanwhile, Sisera personally fled northward, in an apparent attempt to reach Hazor. On the way, he took refuge in the tent of a Kenite named Jael, who lived near Barak's home town of Kedesh (Judg. 4:11); and she, under guise of friendship, killed him by driving a tent peg through his skull. Forty years of peace followed.

2. *Inroads of Merneptah and Rameses III.* Two instances of Egyptian inroads into Palestine in this general time, not mentioned in the book of Judges, call for notice. The first was by Merneptah (1238–1228) in his fifth year,[41] and the second by Rameses III (c. 1195–1164).[42]

Merneptah's main activity lay close to the Mediterranean, where he claimed victories at Ashkelon, Gezer, and Yanoam.[43] His contact, therefore, was principally with Canaanites, though he states in general terms that "Israel is laid waste." This last may be something of a boast, however, for he lists no Israelite cities as plundered, and, when he refers to Israel, he does so using the determinative of people and not land.[44] From this it would appear that he defeated Israelite people in battle, but did not gain control of any significant portion of their land.

The fighting of Rameses III seems also to have been limited mainly to the Philistine area, with later battles conducted south of Israelite territory below the Dead Sea.[45] At least he does not list battles fought within Israelite territory proper. He did reach and carry on building

---

[40] Identified with Tell Qades, northwest of drained Lake Huleh.

[41] *Supra*, chap. 5, pp. 91-92, 108.

[42] *Supra*, chap. 5, p. 108.

[43] *ANET*, p. 278. Yanoam was in northern Palestine.

[44] In this inscription otherwise, he uses the "determinative of land" for those conquered. Cf. *ANET*, p. 378, n. 18 for a different interpretation regarding this change in the determinative.

[45] Regarding Philistines, he boasts of having reduced both the "Tjeker and the Philistines" to ashes; *ANET*, p. 262. *Supra*, chap. 5, p. 108, n. 106. Regarding Edom area, cf. *ANET*, p. 262, n. 21.

activity at Bethshan in the Jordan Valley, but does not mention any conflicts with Israelites in doing so. The occupation of Bethshan, a bastion earlier of Seti I and Rameses II,[46] appears to have been relatively peaceful.[47] Apparently he had marched his army on north after the Philistine action and then turned to move eastward the length of the Esdraelon Valley to Bethshan,[48] all without major conflict.

These two invasions relate in date to the Judges Period in the following manner. Merneptah's campaign, dating c. 1234 B.C., would have come at the close of the eighty-year period of peace, which followed Ehud's deliverance from the Moabites, and preceded the Canaanite oppression. As the dominance of Egypt's Nineteenth Dynasty had served to maintain this eighty-year period of peace earlier in its duration, this further Egyptian influence could have served to prolong it at its close.[49] The invasion of Rameses III would have followed the Canaanite oppression, falling in the forty-year peace period that then ensued. It may have played a role in prolonging this season of peace. Why the book of Judges makes no mention of either invasion has been discussed in chapter five. There simply was no reason to mention foreign campaigns that did not bring punishing oppression on Israel, in a book designed to describe Israel's deviant behavior and resulting punishments.

F. THE PERIOD OF MIDIANITE OPPRESSION
(Judges 6:1–10:5; Ruth 1–4)

The close of this forty-year period of peace saw the invasion of Palestine by a Midianite horde. The oppression which resulted must now be considered as well as three tragic years following, when the renegade king, Abimelech, set up rule. Some mention is necessary also regarding two lesser judges who succeeded Abimelech, Tola and Jair, and further of the story of Ruth, which transpired during this general time.

1. *The oppression and deliverance (Judges 6–8)*

a. Oppression (Judg. 6:1-6). The fourth oppression was brought by Midianites, aided by Amalekites and "children of the east."[50] This

---

[46] *Supra*, chap. 5, pp. 107-108.

[47] Cf. Wright, *BAR*, pp. 95-96.

[48] Bethshan, modern Tell el-Hosn, gives indication of almost continuous Egyptian control from the time of Thutmose III to Rameses III. Manasseh had been allotted Bethshan and had found it too difficult to occupy (Josh 17:16; Judg. 1:27). Opposition to Egyptian occupation, then, would have been from Canaanites, not Israelites. Cf. C. C. McCown, *The Ladder of Progress in Palestine* (New York: Harper & Bros., 1943), pp. 151-70.

[49] For dates involved, cf. *supra*, n. 30.

[50] "Children of the east" seems to have been a general designation for desert tribes, much like the term "Arabs" today.

combined enemy came again from the east, crossing the Jordan to reach the fine grain growing areas of Israel, principally the Esdraelon Valley and the Mediterranean coastlands as far south as Gaza (Judg. 6:4). For six years the invaders were quite unhindered in annually depleting these areas of both livestock and grain. The Israelites became so fearful that they took refuge in caves.

b. Warning (Judg. 6:7-10). When the people cried for relief this time, God first sent an unnamed prophet to warn them concerning their sin. That a prophet was available suggests that prophets were indeed active during the Judges Period.[51] There is little evidence that his preaching brought repentance; but, even so, God still graciously provided a deliverer, Gideon. God called this one to service through an honored appearance of the angel of Yahweh.

c. Gideon, the deliverer (Judg. 6:11-7:6). Gideon lived in Ophrah, a village of Manasseh, likely located in the Esdraelon Valley[52] where the Midianite attacks had been centered. The people of Ophrah had accepted Baal worship so completely that they had built their own Baal altar and Asherah symbol.[53] God's first directive to Gideon was to destroy these objects, which he did at great personal risk, showing true courage and faith (Judg. 6:25-32). This act, so unpopular at first that the townspeople wanted to kill Gideon, later served to inspire the people to accept him as leader.[54] Some 32,000 responded from the tribes of Manasseh, Asher, Zebulun, and Naphtali when he called for troops to fight the invading Midianites.[55]

As Gideon saw the enemy host appear, numbering some 135,000 (Judg. 8:10), he believed his 32,000 were too few to do battle. He immediately sought reassurance from God by means of the well-known sign of the fleece (Judg. 6:33-40). God did graciously reassure him, but then said that the 32,000 were really too many, rather than too few. Gideon should reduce the number in order that God might receive credit from the people for the victory when it had been won. Gideon obeyed, first by permitting all who were fearful of heart to return home and then testing to see which men would drink from a

[51] *Supra*, chap. 8, p. 202.

[52] The location of Ophrah is uncertain, with modern et-Tayibeh, eight miles northwest of Bethshan favored. The Esdraelon Valley no doubt had come under Israelite control increasingly after the defeat of the Canaanites by Deborah and Barak.

[53] Cf. *supra*, n. 17.

[54] When Gideon experienced no harm from Baal (Judg. 6:31), he emerged as victor over Baal and received the name Jerubbaal, meaning "let Baal contend" (Judg. 6:32).

[55] The date was c. 1169 B.C. The Canaanite oppression had lasted 20 years, c. 1229-1209, and the peace period 40 years, c. 1209-1169; cf. *supra*, n. 30.

brook in a manner showing readiness for battle. This left him only 300 men, an unbelievably small number to face 135,000. Certainly Gideon's faith was challenged in view of such odds, but God had commanded the reduction, and Gideon prepared for the encounter. No doubt he wondered, however, as to how the battle could possibly be won.

d. Deliverance (Judg. 7:7–8:32). The battle scene found the enemy encamped in the Esdraelon Valley, at a point between Mt. Gilboa on the south and Mt. Moreh on the north. Gideon's men were grouped near the well of Harod at the foot of Mt. Gilboa. Gideon armed his men with strange weapons: trumpets and empty pitchers containing lamps.[56] The he divided them into three sections and attacked the enemy at night. All blew the trumpets and broke the pitchers at the same time, thus revealing the lighted lamps simultaneously. The enemy was taken by surprise and fled in panic, thinking that a great host had come upon them. They headed for the Jordan River and home.

Gideon, desiring to inflict the greatest defeat, quickly sent word to the people of Ephraim to cut off escape by the enemy at the Jordan. The Ephraimites responded and were able to kill two Midianite leaders, Oreb and Zeeb (Judg. 7:24-25).[57] At this time too, some of Gideon's troops, who had previously gone home when given the chance, returned to help in the chase (Judg. 7:23). Gideon pursued the enemy even to their home country, where he achieved complete victory and killed two main leaders Zebah and Zalmunna. Enroute, Gideon had requested food for his troops from the people of Succoth, south of the Jabbok (Gen. 33:17), and also nearby Penuel, but had been refused by both cities, each time in fear of reprisal from the enemy (Judg. 8:6-8). On returning, after winning the final victory, he punished both cities.

Following his return home, Gideon was pressed to accept kingship over the people, but he properly refused, knowing that God had reserved all rule to Himself. He did err, however, in accepting gold earrings, taken as spoil, with which to make an ephod, presumably like that worn by the high priest.[58] Gideon sinned in thus presuming to

---

[56] Chosen likely for two reasons: they were weapons to effect surprise, and probably Gideon had few if any normal weapons in view of enemy dominance for the past seven years.

[57] Timewise this was possible, for the Midianites could have moved only slowly with their flocks and herds. The places mentioned to which they fled near the Jordan, Beth-shittah and Abel-meholah, are best identified south of the original battle area near to the Ephraimite territory. Ephraimites did not have far to go to intercept them.

[58] This was not an image as advocated by some scholars. Gideon, knowing that God had been revealing His will through him, and knowing of probable

enter upon the prerogative of the priesthood, and the wrong was amplified when later the object came to be worshiped by the people (Judg. 8:24-27). The country had quietness for forty years while Gideon lived.

2. *The renegade king, Abimelech (Judges 9).* At Gideon's death, peace was again broken, now not by an outside enemy, but by three years of treachery and bloodshed at the hand of the renegade Israelite Abimelech, who had himself proclaimed king. He was a son of Gideon by a concubine in Shechem (Judg. 8:31), but he did not share his father's love for peace or humility. Instead, he actively sought the kingship. Supported by his mother's family in Shechem, he proceeded to slay all but one of his seventy brothers, whom he considered to be potential rivals. Only Jotham, the youngest, escaped. Abimelech was crowned by the Shechemites, who were glad to have a king from their own number. He reigned for three years, though the extent of his actual control may have been quite limited. After three years, the Shechemites had experienced enough of his arbitrary ways and revolted, seeking leadership from one Gaal, head of a roving band. In the resulting war, Abimelech was able to crush Gaal's force at Shechem, even burning many of the people alive when they took refuge in the temple of Baalberith[59] (Judg. 9:23-49). Moving on to Thebez[60] to crush further resistance, however, he was killed when a woman dropped a millstone[61] on his head (Judg. 9:50-57).

3. *Judgeships of Tola and Jair (Judges 10:1-5).* Two minor judgeships now followed, which probably were contemporaneous.[62] The two judges served in widely separated parts of the country and so could have been active without mutual interference. Tola, of the tribe of Issachar, judged in Shamir, Ephraim, for twenty-three years. Jair judged in an unidentified city of Gilead across the Jordan for twenty-two years. Little is know of either person. Tola is said to have defended Israel, though without explanation; and Jair is said to have had thirty sons, riding on thirty ass colts, living in thirty cities, which suggests that he was an individual of unusual position and wealth.

4. *The story of Ruth (Ruth 1-4).* The well-known story of Ruth transpired in the last half of the twelfth century, during the time of

deficiency in the priesthood in using the true ephod for revelation, somehow improperly believed that he should now assume this "mantle" for himself.

[59] Following Gideon, the people sadly had returned to the old Baal worship (Judg. 8:33-34).

[60] Modern Tubas, about ten miles north of ancient Shechem toward Bethshan.

[61] Likely the upper small millstone, which in grinding grain was moved back and forth on the lower larger one. It was usually about ten inches long and of a size easily gripped.

[62] Cf. *supra,* p. 207. The words "after him" of Judg. 10:3 need refer only to Jair beginning after Tola began and not necessarily after Tola finished.

Gideon's judgeship. The general date is ascertained from the fact that Ruth was the great-grandmother of David (Ruth 4:17), who began his rule at Hebron in 1010 B.C. She was a Moabitess and had married into the Israelite family of Elimelech and Naomi, who had migrated to Moab from Bethlehem-judah in time of famine. Elimelech died in Moab, leaving his wife, Naomi, and two sons, Mahlon and Chilion. Ruth married Mahlon (Ruth 4:10), and another Moabitess, Orpah, married Chilion. Then both sons died, leaving all three women now as widows. At this point, Naomi returned to Bethlehem. Both daughters-in-law left with her, but only Ruth continued, vowing never to leave Naomi and to accept Naomi's people as her own. At Bethlehem, Ruth gleaned grain in the field of a wealthy relative of Elimelech, Boaz, who then married her. To them was born Obed; to Obed, Jesse; and to Jesse, David.

G. THE PERIOD OF AMMONITE OPPRESSION (Judges 10:6–12:15)

The four punishing oppressions of Israel thus far considered did not cause the people to change their ways. In fact, their sin seemingly increased as they came to serve, not only the false gods of Canaan, but also of Syria, Sidon, Moab, Ammon, and the Philistines (Judg. 10:6). Consequently, God now brought oppression from two quarters simultaneously: from the Ammonites east of the Jordan, and from the Philistines to the far west (Judg. 10:7). The date was c. 1096 B.C.[63] The biblical story narrates the Ammonite oppression first.

1. *The oppression and deliverance (Judges 10:6–11:33).* The Ammonite oppression was experienced mainly on the east of the Jordan, though somewhat also in Judah, Benjamin, and Ephraim on the west (Judg. 10:9). God's deliverer this time was Jephthah, the son of a Gileadite named Gilead and a harlot (Judg. 11:1-3). Gilead's younger, proper sons had driven their older half-brother from home because of his illegitimacy, and Jephthah had since demonstrated military ability in leading a roving band[64] in the land of Tob[65] north of Gilead. When Ammon now invaded the land, elders of Jephthah's home territory found him and asked him to return and lead against this enemy. He agreed, but only upon their promise that he could continue as leader after Ammon had been defeated. Jephthah, rejected earlier, did not want to be insulted again.

[63] Since the beginning of the Midianite oppression in 1169 B.C. (cf. *supra,* n. 55), 73 years had elapsed: Midianites 7, peace under Gideon 40, Abimelech 3, and Tola and Jair 23.

[64] Perhaps after the pattern of David's later band who served to protect people from marauders; cf. I Sam. 22:2; 25:14-16; 27:7-12; 30:1-31.

[65] An area east of the Sea of Galilee. From here soldiers were later hired by Ammon in the Israel-Ammon conflict to fight against David (II Sam. 10:6-8).

Jephthah first tried to effect settlement with the Ammonite king by negotiation but did not succeed. The foreign ruler would not accept Jephthah's argument that the land now rightfully belonged to Israel, since she had held it for 300 years. Then Jephthah, especially enabled by the Spirit of Yahweh, prepared for open conflict by raising troops from Manasseh and Gilead.[66] Establishing his headquarters at Mizpah in Gilead, he moved against the Ammonite army and won a decisive victory, seizing no less than twenty cities located between Minnith and Aroer[67] in an area formerly allotted to Reuben.

2. *Jephthah's vow (Judges 11:30-31, 34-40)*. Eager for divine approval as he entered battle, Jephthah vowed that, if he were victorious, he would offer to God whatever first came from his house to meet him on returning home. When he did return, that which first came was his daughter and only child. Jephthah lamented deeply, for apparently he had not seriously contemplated this eventuality. He resolved, however, still to keep his vow. The way he did this was probably not by taking her life in human sacrifice, as many suggest, but by devoting her to the service of God for the rest of her life, in perpetual celibacy at the Tabernacle. Several reasons point to this conclusion.

First, for Jephthah to have offered his daughter as a human sacrifice would have been contrary both to Mosaic Law (Lev. 18:21; 20:2-5; Deut. 12:31; 18:10) and Israelite practice. Prior to the wicked reigns of Ahaz and Manasseh much later (II Kings 16:3; 21:6) no record of human sacrifice by Israelites is found, even by those who greatly sinned in following Baal. Second, Jephthah held respect for God, which would have kept him from going against the Law and Israelite practice. This respect is demonstrated both in his manner of making covenant with the Gileadite elders and in his very desire to make the vow at all. Third, if he did sacrifice his daughter, his piety would have led him to do so at the proper place of sacrifice, the Tabernacle, but no priest would have been willing to officiate. If he had tried to prepare the sacrifice himself in his home country, certainly elders there, as well as people generally, would have strongly objected. Fourth, that Jephthah permitted his daughter to bewail her virginity (Judg. 11:37-38) for two months suits well the idea of her soon being devoted to God in perpetual celibacy. Fifth, the notice that the daughter "knew no man"

[66] Gilead included land even north of Gad, but since Manasseh (half-tribe on the east of Jordan) is also specified here, it must mean primarily Gad in this instance.

[67] Aroer is well identified on the north bank of the Arnon River about 14 miles east of the Dead Sea. Minnith is believed to have been located directly north about even with the north end of the Dead Sea.

(Judg. 11:39), given as a result of Jephthah having carried out his vow, has particular point if her offering concerned the matter of celibacy. Sixth, a reason for believing that such service for devoted women did exist at the central sanctuary is found in Exodus 38:8; I Samuel 2:22; and Luke 2:36-37. Seventh, the pivotal statement of Jephthah in Judges 11:31, "It shall be Yahweh's, *and* I will offer it up for a burnt-offering" may be translated with the conjunction "or" and so make the first part a reference to what Jephthah would have done if a human first met him, and the second if an animal.

3. *Ephraimite complaint (Judges 12:1-7).* Following Jephthah's fine victory over the Ammonites, the men of Ephraim complained at not having been asked to assist,[68] showing again that they thought their tribe was of prime importance.[69] Jephthah tried to appease them with words, but to no avail. Their feelings had been hurt, and they intended to make Jephthah realize this by force. They joined in battle against Jephthah on the east of the Jordan. Their army, however, was no match for Jephthah's well-trained troops, who then not only won a decisive victory but moved quickly to control the fording places of the Jordan, which retreating Ephraimites would have to use. The victors tested all who wished to cross by making them pronounce the word *shibboleth.* All who said *sibboleth,* using the "s" sound in place of the "sh," were taken as Ephraimites and killed.[70] A total of 42,000 Ephraimites lost their lives either in the battle proper or at the Jordan.

These events completed, Jephthah continued as judge for six years. The promise of the Gileadite elders was kept, for the people did recognize him as leader after the Ammonite vitcory.

4. *Judgeships of Ibzan, Elon, and Abdon (Judges 12:8-15).* Following Jephthah came three minor judges, perhaps somewhat contemporaneous again.[71] Ibzan judged in Bethlehem for seven years, and had thirty sons and thirty daughters. Elon judged in Ajalon of Zebulun to the north for ten years. Abdon judged in Ephraim, half-way between, for eight years. Abdon's wealth and position are attested in that he had forty sons and thirty grandsons (sons of sons).

---

[68] This was the second time of such a complaint, the first having been regarding Gideon following the Midianite victory (Judg. 8:1-3).

[69] Cf. *supra,* chap. 8, p. 188, n. 66.

[70] Apparently Ephraimites were accustomed to pronouncing the letter *shin* like the *samech.* "Shibboleth" means "flowing stream," a reference here to the Jordan.

[71] Whether they were or were not does not have significance now for the overall chronology, for the Philistine oppression next considered was contemporary with all three either way.

H. THE PERIOD OF PHILISTINE OPPRESSION (Judges 13–16)

1. *The oppression (Judges 10:7; 13:1)*. The sixth and last great oppression was brought by the Philistines. According to Judges 10:7, the time was roughly contemporary with the oppression of the Ammonites.[72] The Philistines had come into the land in force during the first quarter of the twelfth century, which would have been in the forty-year peace period following Deborah's victory over the Canaanites. It was now approximately one century later, and the Philistines had become firmly entrenched and strong. Their designs relative to Israelite land differed from those of prior oppressors, who seem to have thought mainly in terms of temporary exploitation. These desired permanent occupancy. The others were members of groups of long standing in the region, but the Philistines were newcomers and ready to challenge old residents for all they could seize. They had a war-like tradition, having been one division of the migrating, rampaging Sea Peoples, and they were prepared in both knowledge and temperament to press their challenge vigorously and long. It should be realized, too, that Canaanites were as much an object of this aggression as Israel,[73] and there is reason to believe that the Philistines did in time seize land from them as far north as the Esdraelon Valley, and then through the Valley east all the way to the Jordan.[74] At the time now concerned, the Philistines were able to impose their will on Israel for forty years, the longest of any of the oppressions; and they later continued to do so periodically throughout the reign of Israel's first king, Saul.

2. *Samson (Judges 13:2–16:31)*. God's man to counter the Philistines was Samson. His father's name was Manoah, a Danite who apparently had not migrated north with others of his tribe. Importance was lent to Samson's birth by a prior announcement through the Angel of Yahweh (Judg. 13:3-23). The son to be born would be a Nazarite, which means, among other things, that his hair was not to be cut (Num. 6:1-13). Samson's place of birth was Zorah, located at the boundary line between Israelite and Philistine land. Samson's contact with the enemy was different from that of other judges. He did not lead an army to battle, but went alone among the Philistines, working havoc

[72] This contemporaneousness fits other factors too. With Saul beginning to reign c. 1050 B.C., the battle of Mizpah (I Sam. 7:7-14) could not have been after c. 1055 B.C., which means the forty-year Philistine oppression (Judg. 13:1) must have begun c. 1095 B.C. The Ammonite oppression came c. 1096 B.C. (*supra*, p. 222, n. 63).

[73] This would have tended to make allies of Canaanites and Israelites, something giving further reason for God's original order that Canaanites should be driven completely from the land.

[74] Cf. *infra*, p. 231, n. 95.

by feats of enormous strength. This strength was not the result of an unusually large stature (at least no hint is given in the biblical account to this effect) but of special enablement by the Spirit of God,[75] symbolized particularly in Samson's uncut hair. Through this strength he was able to kill many of the enemy; but his greatest contribution in Israel's behalf was to make the Philistines see the greatness of Israel's God, who was able so to empower a human individual. Numerous stories concern Samson's feats, and these may be only representative of others of like kind that could have been included.

3. Samson's feats of strength (Judges 14–15)

a. Wedding incidents. Samson's first demonstrations of strength came in connection with his marriage to a Philistine girl of Timnah.[76] He wished to marry the girl and persuaded his parents to arrange the wedding, in spite of their disapproval.[77] On the way to visit her on one occasion, Samson encountered a lion and killed it with his bare hands. On a later visit he found the lion's carcass holding a swarm of bees and honey, from which fact he propounded a riddle to the Philistine guests at the seven-day feast of his wedding. They were able to solve it only by forcing his bride to deceive Samson into telling her the answer, so that she could tell them. Realizing what they had done, Samson paid the agreed-upon reward, thirty changes of clothing, by slaying thirty Philistines at Ashkelon[78] and taking theirs.

b. Wheat harvest feats. The second demonstrations occurred within a year, during wheat harvest (Judg. 15:1-19). Samson returned to claim his bride, having had time to assuage his first anger, but he was told that she had been given to another. In retaliation, he caught 300 foxes, tied firebrands to pairs of them joined by their tails, and released them to burn Philistine crops. The Philistines reacted by burning to death Samson's one-time bride and her father. Samson avenged their death by effecting another slaughter among the enemy. Then he moved back to Israelite territory taking up a position on "the top of the rock Etam,"[79] where he was soon apprehended by 3,000 of his own people,

[75] This is stressed by mention four times (Judg. 13:25; 14:6, 19; 15:14). Of no other Judge is similar mention made more than once.

[76] Rather well identified with Khirbet Tibneh, only four miles southwest of Zorah. Originally allotted to Dan (Josh. 19:43), it was at this time controlled by Philistines and later changed hands more than once (II Chron. 28:18).

[77] Though Israelite marriage was expressly prohibited only with Canaanites (Deut. 7:3-4), the reasons for this prohibition were as true regarding Philistines. Samson's parents, therefore, were right in believing the marriage improper.

[78] Ashkelon was the port city of the Philistine pentapolis, located about 23 miles southwest of Timnah.

[79] The site is unknown but may be the same as an Etam later rebuilt by Rehoboam (II Chron. 11:6). It must have been in western Judah.

pressured by the Philistines whom they recognized as their overlords. Not wishing conflict with his countrymen, who promised not to hurt him themselves, Samson permitted himself to be bound and delivered to the Philistines in Lehi.[80] But once among them, he easily burst his binding ropes, and killed 1,000 of the enemy with the use of a "new jawbone of an ass." Extremely thirsty after this effort, he experienced God's gracious provision in water supplied miraculously from the rock where he stood.

c. Twenty-year judgeship. After these experiences Samson remained content to assume a more peaceful mode of life and served as judge in Israel for a period of twenty years (Judg. 15:20). These years may have been spent in Hebron (Judg. 16:3), and were certainly contemporary with Samuel's judgeship[81] prior to the battle of Mizpah (I Sam. 7:3-11).[82] Though Samson had experienced the disapproval of his own people, who lived close to Philistine territory, illustrated by the incident just considered, his exploits could have made him quite a champion in an area farther removed, like Hebron. Apparently people there were willing to consult with him as judge.

d. Closing events. Toward the close of these twenty years, Samson again visited Philistine territory, stopping at Gaza[83] where he fell victim to lust and sinned with a harlot (Judg. 16:1-3). Rising at midnight, and finding the city surrounded by waiting Philistines, he inflicted marked humiliation on Gaza by breaking away defensive gates and carrying them to a nearby hill on his return to Hebron.

Not long after, Samson once more submitted to lust, becoming infatuated with a scheming woman of the Philistines name Delilah, who lived in the Sorek Valley not far from his place of birth, Zorah. Given promise of reward by the Philistine leaders, Delilah sought to entice Samson to reveal the secret of his strength. He gave her false answers three times, but finally told her the truth regarding his uncut hair. She cut it off while he slept, and the Philistines were able to put out his eyes and make him labor sightless in their prison in Gaza, controlling him at last. When his hair had grown again, however, Samson had his

---

[80] The site of Lehi is unknown, but clearly was somewhere between Etam and Philistine land proper.

[81] Samson's 20-year judgeship fits history between the battle of Aphek (I Sam. 4:1-11) and that of Mizpah (I Sam. 7:7-14), 20 years later (I Sam. 7:2). Cf. discussion regarding Samuel which follows.

[82] Mizpah is best identified with Tell en-Nasbeh, 8 miles north of Jerusalem. Samuel's activity likely centered in this vicinity, well north, then, of Samson's likely area near Hebron.

[83] Identified with Tell el-'Ajjul, some 40 miles west of Hebron and 12 miles south of Ashkelon. Perhaps Samson came here to fight some giant-sized descendant of Anak (Josh. 11:22; II Sam. 21:15-22).

last revenge. Taken to entertain assembled Philistines in the temple of Dagon, he called upon God for a return of his strength, and he was enabled to dislodge two central supporting columns of the temple from their bases, destroying the building and killing more of the enemy in this time of his own death than in all his prior years.

4. Evaluation of Samson

a. Characteristics. Samson is one of the perplexing persons of the Old Testament. Numerous commendable things may be noted regarding him, but some very blameworthy. Among those calling for, or suggesting commendation, are the following: that his birth, alone among the judges, was fore-announced by no one less than the Angel of Yahweh,[84] implying unusual divine favor in respect to him; that more description is devoted in the biblical record to his life than to any other judge except the honored Gideon; that he is said to have been especially enabled by the Holy Spirit for his work no less than four times, when this is said of other judges no more than once; that he called on God for supernatural provision at two different times, and God was pleased to grant it on each occasion (Judg. 15:18-19; 16:28-30); and that he is included in the honor role of faith of Hebrews 11 (vs. 32). Among his blameworthy characteristics, the most notable was his lust for women, from which weakness, in turn, stemmed the violation of his Nazarite standing and his general coldness of heart toward God. It should be realized, however, that the two principal episodes depicting this weakness came at the close of his life, near the end of his twenty years of service as judge.[85] It may be that the majority of his years serving as judge were lived quite free from similar occasions.

b. Divine assignment known. It is quite clear that Samson knew from the first that God had assigned him to combat Philistines. The Angel had so instructed his mother (Judg. 13:5), and certainly she would have passed the information along to him. Also it is directly stated that, in spite of the wrong involved in marrying the Philistine girl, Samson did seek thereby an occasion to quarrel with the Philistines [86] (Judg. 14:4). It follows, then, that his consequent contacts

---

[84] In fact, Samson was here honored along with Isaac (Gen. 18:1-16) and John the Baptist (Luke 1:5-25).

[85] He was likely about 40 years old at his death. His birth announcement seems to have been given after the Philistine oppression had started (Judg. 13:5), and the oppression lasted 40 years (Judg. 13:1). He was about 20, then, at his wedding which just preceded the 20-year judgeship.

[86] That Judg. 14:4 does mean that Samson sought this occasion, rather than Yahweh as some suggest (though in keeping with Yahweh's pleasure as the verse indicates), follows from the idea of "quarrel" being implied by its use of *tho'anah* (cf. II Kings 5:7), and also that Samson directly sought a way to prompt this quarrel in propounding the riddle. Apparently Samson had a two-

with the Philistines were similarly calculated (though perhaps unwisely) and not merely outbursts of temper. The reason that he did not proceed as other judges in raising an army to defeat the enemy is probably twofold: first, God did not direct him to do so, which is clear from the statement of the Angel to the mother that Samson would only "begin" to deliver Israel (Judg. 13:5); and second, his fellow Israelites were not of a mind to fight the Philistines, apparently having accepted a co-existence policy which gave the enemy the upper hand (Judg. 15: 9-13).

c. Effectiveness. In spite of Samson's decline into sin, his overall work was beneficial for Israel. He did much to confuse and hinder the Philistines in their designs on the people of Yahweh. Philistine plans were disrupted, and the citizenry was made to respect the God who could so empower a man. They could hardly press on to complete their subjugation of Israel until they had solved the puzzle of this one person. His final slaughter of Philistines in the Dagon temple likely had a direct bearing on the defeat the Philistines experienced shortly after at Mizpah (I Sam. 7:7-14). Further, the presentation by the Philistines of their own champion, Goliath, about a half century later, may well have been a retaliatory gesture in remembrance of Israel's champion. Certainly Samson could have accomplished far more had he not fallen prey to the sin of lust, and for this he must be sharply criticized. He affords a strong lesson of warning to others on this count. But this weakness should not cause one to forget his commendable points nor overlook the benefits he achieved for his people.

I. SAMUEL (I Samuel 1–8)

During the entire period of Samson's judgeship and feats among the Philistines,[87] one of Israel's great personalities was active in Israel proper. This was Samuel, whose general date is determined by the fact that he had sons old enough to act as judges in Beersheba (I Sam. 8:1-2) before Saul began to reign in 1050 B.C. This places Samuel's birth hardly later than 1100 B.C.,[88] which was just prior to the outbreak of the Ammonite and Philistine oppressions and the birth of Samson.[89]

fold purpose in mind for the wedding: to marry a girl attractive to him, and to arrange an occasion for quarrel.

[87] Also while Jephthah was involved with Ammonites across the Jordan and later judged Israelites there for six years.

[88] This agrees with the fact that Ahimelech, high priest in Saul's time, was a grandson of Phinehas, one of the wicked priests in this period (I Sam. 14:3; 22:9).

[89] Samson was born just after the start of the Philistine oppression c. 1095 B.C.; cf. *supra*, ns. 72 and 85.

Samuel is also called a judge (I Sam. 7:15-17), as these others before him, but he was more than a judge. He was primarily a prophet, so recognized from Dan to Beersheba (I Sam. 3:20), and he even acted as a priest (I Sam. 9:12-13; 13:8-13). In these capacities he filled a vital need in a crucial time of Israel's history. His work in correcting religious malpractice, maintaining national morale in the face of major disaster, promoting return to faith in God, and even establishing the new Israelite monarchy was of the greatest importance. He stands as one of the more significant persons in the Old Testament (Jer. 15:1).

1. *Early life (I Samuel 1–3).* Samuel was the son of a Levite, Elkanah of Ramathaim-zophim (Ramah).[90] Samuel's mother was named Hannah, one of two wives of Elkanah, and she had been barren prior to Samuel's birth. She had prayed for a son and had promised him to God if her prayers were answered. Accordingly, when Samuel was weaned, he was brought to the Tabernacle and devoted to service there.

Conditions at the Tabernacle were not good at the time and they were getting worse (I Sam. 2:12-17). Eli, descendant from Aaron through Ithamar,[91] was high priest. His two sons, Hophni and Phinehas, were priests. Eli, himself an earnest follower of Yahweh, was old, and the two sons were in charge of ceremonies. They were wicked men, sorely perverting the ritual and profaning the sanctuary, in a debauchery similar to that of Canaanite temples. As a result, people abhorred to come to worship. Eli was held responsible by God and was rebuked for permitting this abuse by his sons. Reprimand came first through an unnamed prophet, and later through the lad Samuel (I Sam. 2:27–3:18). The experience of Samuel when the reprimand came through him, must have been both gratifying and fearful. God honored him by speaking to him audibly during the night, and Samuel had to relay the serious message to Eli, Samuel's own teacher, the next morning. Certainly this was a maturing event for so young a boy. The message he conveyed concerned grave punishment for Eli's house, and this took on tangible form within approximately fifteen years.[92]

2. *The tragic battle of Aphek (I Samuel 4).* Punishment came through a disastrous battle with the Philistines. Twenty years of Philistine op-

[90] Ramah is best identified with Er-Ram, 5 miles north of Jerusalem in Benjamin. Elkanah was an Ephraimite (I Sam. 1:1) because his family had formerly lived in Ephraim, but he was a Levite by tribal descent (I Chron. 6:33-35).

[91] The family of the high priest had formerly descended from Eleazar (Num. 20:25-29), but now with Eli there had been a change to Ithamar's descendants (cf. II Sam. 8:17; I Kings 2:27; I Chron. 24:3).

[92] If Samuel was about 10 years old at the time, which seems reasonable, the date was about 1090 B.C., 15 years before the battle of Aphek c. 1075 B.C.

pression had passed,[93] and Israel attempted to end it by a direct engagement in war. The encounter was at Aphek,[94] well north of Philistine territory in the Sharon plain, which signifies that the enemy had already been making sizeable gains against the coastal Canaanites.[95] In the battle that ensued, Israel was badly defeated and lost some 4,000 men.

Wrongly thinking that the presence of the Ark at the battle front would help in a renewed conflict,[96] the people, finding the degenerate Hophni and Phinehas agreeable, took the Ark from Shiloh, contrary to God's will, and brought it the twenty-three miles to camp. But God could not bring favor in the presence of such flagrant disobedience, and again defeat was experienced. This time 30,000 of Israel fell, including Hophni and Phinehas; and the all-important Ark was captured. When news of the major catastrophe reached Shiloh, confusion reigned; and Eli, old and obese, fell from his seat backward and died of a broken neck.

Excavation has revealed that the Philistines now moved directly into Israelite territory, even as far as Shiloh which they destroyed (Jer. 7:12; 26:6).[97] Probably it was now, too, that they first placed controlling garrisons in the country (I Sam. 10:5; 13:3) and, in a move to protect their own iron monopoly, destroyed what metal industry the Israelites may have had, making them completely dependent on Philistine smith services (I Sam. 13:19-22).

At such a time, obviously, Israelite morale could only have been extremely low. It had seriously declined before this because of the deficient religious condition, but this would have reduced it still more, crushing people's spirits to the point of despair. Israel twice had been severely defeated, losing many men and now the Ark. The Philistines controlled vast areas of the land. No doubt it seemed to many that the days of Israelite independence were at an end. This foreign power would swallow them completely.

[93] The oppression began c. 1095 B.C. (cf. supra, n. 72), making the date here c. 1075 B.C. The oppression lasted 40 years (Judg. 13:1) until c. 1055 B.C., about 5 years before Saul became king.

[94] Best identified with later Antipatris, modern Ras el-'Ain, some 23 miles west of Shiloh.

[95] Eventual Philistine occupation has been evidenced as far north as the Esdraelon Valley, all through that plain, and even south in the Jordan Valley a short distance.

[96] They were influenced in this by the belief of their neighbors that a physical image insured the presence of the deity. Israel erroneously thought that God's presence could thus be assured.

[97] Shiloh was excavated by Danish expeditions in 1926-29 and 1932, showing that the city was leveled during the 11th century, no doubt at this time; cf. Albright, *BASOR*, 9 (Feb., 1923), pp. 10f.

3. *The man Samuel (I Samuel 7)*. This was the situation that Samuel faced as he found himself now, at the age of about twenty-five, thrust into the position of Israel's leader. Until this time he had been under Eli's supervision, but now the high priest and his sons were dead. Samuel had already achieved a reputation as a prophet of God among the people (I Sam. 3:20) and could expect to be looked to for leadership. Prospects for the country were extremely dismal, but the task of bringing order out of near chaos was clearly his.

a. Good preparation. God had prepared Samuel well for the task. There had been the early influence of a godly mother and the careful instruction of the learned Eli, the latter of whom may even have given him greater attention in view of his own sons' profligacy. Also, Samuel, having been raised in the corrupt atmosphere of the Tabernacle, knew the dire religious need of the people. He certainly knew, too, the low morale existent everywhere, for Shiloh would have been a center of such information. And Samuel had been divinely granted a courageous heart, full of faith in God. Many strong men would have despaired at the task, but Samuel moved into it with ability and strength.

It is clear that his efforts were remarkably productive, for twenty years later, Israel, rather than being yet weak and miserable as a vassal of the Philistines, had become a vigorous people, who could and did bring major defeat on the oppressors (I Sam. 7:3-14). Change of this kind does not happen without due cause, and the only human instrument who could have effected it was the man Samuel putting forth enormous effort to bring it about.

b. Type of work. The biblical record is silent on how Samuel accomplished so much, indicating only the results. But conjecture is possible, for certain activities would have been necessary. He would have had to give attention to reestablishment of the Tabernacle, now that the Ark had been taken and Shiloh destroyed. In fact he must have lent immediate effort on this count in order to spare the structure from the oncoming enemy. It was moved to Nob.[98] Once there, its rightful sacrifice and ceremony would have had to be renewed, after the years of perversion under Hophni and Phinehas, a task complicated certainly by the absence of the Ark. Then priests and Levites, in their widely distributed cities, would have had to be encouraged, especially in taking up their teaching ministries anew, which doubtless had lagged under the example of the Eli regime. Careful instruction by them was important, for the priests and Levites could contact people directly and

---

[98] Cf. I Sam. 21:1-9. Samuel is not mentioned as having had contact with the Tabernacle at Nob, but it is unthinkable that he would not have been concerned to save the sanctuary at Shiloh and do all possible to move it to another location like this.

do much in bringing change of outlook and heightening of morale.[99]
We may think of Samuel traveling extensively to make the necessary
contacts, always urging people everywhere to a renewal of faith in God.

c. Training schools. Samuel seems to have pioneered a new idea,
too, no doubt related to the same endeavor: that of training schools
for young prophets. We know of these schools only from notices which
come later in the time of Saul (I Sam. 10:5-12; 19:19-24),[100] but
they clearly had been existent for some time. The best explanation as
to why Samuel started them is that he saw a need for helpers in this
time of crisis. He could not be everywhere himself, and required assistants. If well trained,[101] these persons could multiply his efforts,
covering much of the ground he could not. Instructing them would
have taken valuable time, but Samuel may have conducted school enroute on his travels.[102]

4. *The victorious battle of Mizpah (I Samuel 7:5-14).* After twenty
years of this effort (I Sam. 7:2), Israel was at last enabled to win a
decisive victory over the Philistines. Morale had been raised so that
the people found courage for another encounter; but, more important,
renewal of faith in God had been engendered so that Yahweh could bless
them with a triumph. In fact, the battle occurred as the people were
gathered for a time of spiritual revival before God at Mizpah.[103] The
Philistines heard of the assembly and, no doubt thinking that it was
for the purpose of war, decided to attack directly themselves. At first
the Israelites were afraid when they heard of the enemy's approach,

[99] A prime tendency of the people that would have had to be averted at this
time was to align themselves with Canaanites against the common Philistine
enemy. It would have taken strong exhortation and careful detailing of dangers
involved to offset this natural inclination.

[100] Such a phrase as "training school" is not used in these passages, but only
the phrase, "company of prophets." This group, however, is not mentioned before this and Samuel is said to have been "standing as head over them" (I Sam.
19:20). This suggests a training situation, perhaps not formal, but at least in-
formal.

[101] The liberal view that these prophets were ecstatics must be rejected. Saul's
strange action of "prophesying" with them and then lying all night minus his
outer garment (I Sam. 19:24) cannot be attributed to sympathetic participation
in such ecstasy. To be a participant requires due preparation of mind and desire for it, besides efforts to induce the state. But Saul came in anger, because
of ineffectiveness on the part of three contingents of policemen, and then began
"to prophesy" even before arriving where the "company of prophets" was located. His lying all night in this manner is better explained as a fit of emotional despair caused by seeing David in Samuel's approving company.

[102] Naioth in Ramah may have been the headquarters. Naioth means "habi-
tations," and Samuel was there standing head over the young prophets (I Sam.
19:18-24).

[103] Cf. *supra*, n. 82.

but Samuel called on God for help and God heard. A violent thunderstorm was sent and struck fear into the hearts of the advancing Philistines, and then the Israelites were enabled to inflict severe defeat, after which they pursued the enemy as far as Beth-car.[104]

It should be brought to mind too, as noted earlier, that Samson's efforts could have played a role in this victory. His slaughter of 3,000 Philistines in the temple of Dagon, which likely had just preceded this battle, would have rekindled respect among the Philistines for Israel's God, and thereby contributed to the fear experienced in the thunderstorm.

Following this victory, Philistine inroads into Israelite territory ceased, until after Saul had been made king (I Sam. 13). This battle brought the forty-year oppression mentioned in Judges 13:1 to a close.

5. *The Ark returned (I Samuel 5–6).* The Ark of the Tabernacle had been captured in the battle of Aphek twenty years earlier. God had caused a series of events, catastrophic for the Philistines, to bring about its return to Israel just seven months after its capture. First, the image of Dagon,[105] beside which the Ark had been placed, had twice been made to fall to the floor before it; next, painful tumors had been inflicted on the people, which in some instances brought death; and finally, the land had been overrun with mice.[106] In determining how to send the troublesome Ark home, the Philistine priests had tried to save face by employing trickery, whereby the Ark would be thrown from the wagon on which it was placed; but God had intervened so the young heifers drawing the wagon, unbroken and with their calves taken from them, had wondrously moved straight along the road to Beth-shemesh[107] in Israelite territory (I Sam. 6:1-18).

Back in the land, however, the Ark still was not returned to the Tabernacle at Nob. At Beth-shemesh, it was desecrated when curious people looked into it,[108] and God took the lives of many in punishment (I Sam. 6:19-20). Then, instead of sending it back to the Tabernacle,

[104] Beth-car must have been a high point, for the reference here is to "under Beth-car," but its location remains unknown.

[105] The name Dagon may be from *dagh*, meaning "fish," but more likely from *daghan*, meaning "grain," hence, an agricultural deity. Temples to Dagon found at Mari, Ugarit, Bethshan, etc., show that this deity was borrowed from the Canaanites.

[106] This plague of mice is not so described, but the idea is implied in that images of mice were made by the Philistines, as well as of tumors (I Sam. 6:5).

[107] Beth-shemesh, identified with modern Tell er-Rumeileh and located in an east-west valley leading from Philistine land, was the first city back within Israelite (Judah) territory.

[108] The Ark represented God's presence among His people and was to be respected accordingly. These Israelites should have known better than to use it as an object of curiosity.

the Beth-shemites sent for men of Kirjath-jearim[109] to come and get it. Apparently these people handled it properly, because they experienced no harm, but still did not return it to the Tabernacle. It remained with them for more than seventy years[110] until David brought it to Jerusalem. Question exists as to why at least Samuel did not insist that it be brought to the Tabernacle. He must have known of its return to the land, for news of so important an event could not have been kept secret. One would think, too, that he would have desired this as a further means of encouraging the people. Since he did not, all one can say is that there must have been some significant factor, unstated in the biblical record, which caused him to decide against it.

6. *The people request a king (I Samuel 7:15–8:22)*. Samuel's activities following the Mizpah victory, with priests and Levites now doing their work with reasonable effectiveness once again, became considerably curtailed. It is stated that he covered a relatively small circuit in his work of judging, touching only Bethel, Gilgal, Mizpah, and Ramah his home town (I Sam. 7:16-17). To help in the south near Beersheba, he installed his own sons, Joel and Abiah, as judges. In the pattern of Hophni and Phinehas, however, they did not follow the godly example of their father, but took bribes in a perversion of justice.

Their poor conduct stirred the people to make a request of Samuel which disappointed him greatly. They asked that they be given a king (I Sam. 8:4-6). The failure of these sons was not the main reason for the request, however: the people had seen how nearly they had come to complete disaster under the present governmental system; and now that the situation was improved, wanted a change. The Philistines, or another enemy,[111] might come again. They wanted a king with an organized army "like all the nations."

Samuel took the request as a personal affront, however. He had worked hard for Israel, and rightly believed that the country was now in relatively strong condition. The request seemed an indication of a lack of confidence in him. God, however, told him that this was not so, but that really the affront was against Himself, God; the people no longer wanting the theocratic forms of government He had given them. Likely at this point Samuel expected God to tell him to reprimand the people and deny the request, but this God did not do. In-

---

[109] Commonly identified with Kuriet el-'Enab. (Abu Ghosh), a village 9 miles west of Jerusalem on the road to Tell Aviv. It had been one city of the Gibeonite tetrapolis (Josh. 9:17).

[110] The battle of Aphek occurred c. 1075 B.C., and David began to rule in Jerusalem c. 1003 B.C., with the Ark being brought there shortly after.

[111] Nahash, King of Ammon, seems to have been quite in their mind also; cf. I Sam. 12:12.

stead, God told him to comply with the people's request, implying that what they wanted was really best.[112] What God had first designed would have been best had the people obeyed His Law, but they had not. God further instructed Samuel to warn them that, along with the king they requested, they would receive heavy burdens in taxation, which they had not experienced under God's theocratic rule. If they had followed God's way, it would have been much better for them, as well as pleasing to God; but now that they had not, it was best that they have what the other nations had, with all its disadvantages.

[112] It should be realized that also earlier indications had been given regarding a coming monarchy: Gen. 49:10; Num. 24:17; Deut. 17:14; I Sam. 2:10.

CHAPTER TEN

KING SAUL

I Samuel 9–31

Palestine was less disturbed by outside world powers during the time of Israel's united monarchy than during the Judges Period. Even Egypt did not interfere while Saul, David, and Solomon ruled. After Rameses III (c. 1195–1164), no Egyptian king crossed the border of Palestine until the time of Rehoboam, Solomon's son.[1] Assyria was the rising power in the world, but had not yet advanced as far as Israelite territory.[2] Prior to the monarchy, there had been only one significant extension of Assyrian conquest into the west-land, and it was temporary. Tiglath-pileser I (1116–1078) had brought his army as far as the Mediterranean, still far north of Palestine, but other interests kept him from maintaining a hold. No other ruler advanced as far for two centuries following.[3] This means that Israel's first three kings were quite unaffected by large powers,[4] making possible in part the wide expansion of boundaries under King David.

When Saul came to office, his major task was to unify the tribes into a true nation. Samuel's efforts had contributed significantly, for he had rescued the tribes from complete disaster, restored morale, and renewed their faith in God. The tribes, however, were still separate

[1] Shishak (Sheshonq I), who founded Egypt's XXII Dynasty, did so in Rehoboam's 5th year (I Kings 14:25-26). Earlier, he had given refuge to Jeroboam fleeing from Solomon.

[2] Assyria did so for the first under Shalmaneser III (859–824); cf. *infra*, chap. 13, p. 323. King Ahab, a few years earlier, had joined a coalition against this Assyrian at Qarqar; cf. *infra*, chap. 13, p. 312.

[3] Cf. *infra*, chap. 13, p. 308.

[4] After 1240 B.C., the Hittites were engulfed in a flow of race migration (Sea Peoples) that brought an end to their nation. Boghazkoi, their capital, was completely destroyed. Earlier the Hittites had brought an end to the Mitannian power in the process of establishing their own empire under the powerful Shuppiluliuma (1375–1340).

entities, with deep-seated differences between them. Jealousies of the past and even inter-tribal warfare were not easily forgotten. Even more serious was the capture of the Ark, the ruin of Shiloh, and the necessary transfer of the Tabernacle to Nob. The central sanctuary had been intended as a principal unifying factor, where people could meet and be reminded of their common heritage as they joined in worship. But Shiloh was no more. The Ark had been returned to the land, but not to the Tabernacle at Nob. Without it, the Tabernacle exerted little of the centralizing influence intended. A strong hand was required if differences were to be forgotten. Saul's task, to weld these twelve long-standing units into one nation, would not be easy.

A. Anointing of Saul (I Samuel 9–12)

1. *Anointing at Ramah (I Samuel 9:1–10:16)*

a. Anointed by Samuel (I Sam. 9:1-27). Not long after God revealed to Samuel that the tribes should have a king, He identified who that person should be: Saul, son of Kish, of the tribe of Benjamin. That a member of small Benjamin should receive this honor is significant. Judah and Ephraim were the two leading tribes, with Benjamin lying between. A man chosen from this tribe would prevent the two leading tribes from mutual jealousy, an important consideration when the great need was for unification.

Saul was tall and of striking appearance; none in Israel being a "goodlier person than he" (I Sam. 9:2). He apparently was humble prior to his anointing too. At least he was timid, for only after repeated urging by a servant was he persuaded to seek advice from the prophet Samuel at Ramah concerning his lost asses. Samuel first told him that the animals had been found and then the astonishing fact that he was actually to be Israel's first king. What a turn of events for a young man! He had hesitatingly come for the purpose of learning the location of lost animals, and now had been informed that he was to be the chief ruler of all the tribes! Samuel even anointed him with oil in symbolism of this honor the following morning.

b. Confirming signs (I Sam. 10:1-12). Before Saul left to go home, Samuel also told him of three confirmatory signs that Saul would experience as he traveled. He would meet two men who would tell him that the lost asses had been found and that his father was now seriously concerned about him. Then he would come upon three men, having goats, bread, and wine, who would give him two of the loaves of bread. Thirdly, and most important, he would encounter a company of prophets[5] playing musical instruments as they rendered praise to God.[6]

[5] These were likely young trainees of Samuel's school; cf. *supra*, chap. 9, p. 233.

He should join with this last group in giving praise himself, at which time he would experience the "Spirit of Yahweh" coming upon him.

These events took place just as Samuel had predicted, which no doubt served to confirm Samuel's remarkable announcement in Saul's mind. Confirmation would have been needed, for Saul had surely wondered, as he walked along after leaving Samuel, how so great a future could possibly be his. But when these less important matters happened just as foretold, the greater would have become easier to believe. That he did come to believe in a substantial degree follows from his then joining in praise with the prophets as instructed. People who knew him were amazed that he did so, for clearly they were not used to seeing the timid Saul engaged in such overt activity. He seemed to be a new person to them, something Samuel also had foretold. It should be noted that Saul had need for this manner of change in personality if he was to become an effective king. He could not then be timid as before, but aggressive for leadership.[7]

2. *Identified at Mizpah (I Samuel 10:17-27)*. With Israel's first king now chosen, it remained for Samuel to identify him to the people. Samuel did so at Mizpah, the site of the great victory over the Philistines, an event still reasonably fresh in Israel's memory. He summoned representatives of all the tribes to meet with him there. He did not tell them directly whom God had already chosen, but proceeded to make inquiry, probably by the Urim and Thummim,[8] as though no prior information had been given. Apparently Samuel wished the people to witness God's selection firsthand rather than through himself as intermediary. An identification procedure was followed much like that involving Achan years earlier (Josh. 7:16-18). First Saul's tribe, Benjamin, was identified, then Saul's family, Matri, and finally Saul himself. When the people looked for Saul, whom Samuel apparently had instructed beforehand to be present, they could not find him. Further inquiry revealed that he had hidden himself among the traveling wagons and baggage, another indication of natural timidity. Saul was now summoned, seen to be kingly in stature, and accepted with shouts of approval by those assembled.

[6] The text says that they "prophesied" (I Sam. 10:10). But this was not in a spoken message. They prophesied in the sense given the term in I Chron. 25:1-3, where Levites "prophesied in giving thanks and praising Yahweh." Samuel's trainees were praising God in song as they came down from the high place.

[7] This is a better interpretation of his being "turned into another man" (I Sam. 10:6) than that he became an ecstatic as believed by some. Samuel would not have associated himself with ecstatic activity taken from the Canaanites.

[8] Though the Urim and Thummim device is not mentioned in the text, it was the normal method of inquiry in such circumstances; cf. Num. 27:21; and *supra,* chap. 8, pp. 196-97.

3. Established as king (I Samuel 11–12)

a. **A period of waiting.** It is one thing to be approved by representatives, but another to be accepted by people at large. Saul's actual coronation as king was not to follow now as a matter of course. The people had to give their voluntary acceptance, and Saul was still quite unknown to them. There was need that he have public exposure before acceptance could be expected. Also, the tribes were still autonomous units and would naturally hesitate to join such a common venture, no matter the identity of the prospective ruler. Further, there was no capital, palace, staff, or governmental machinery to use. Saul needed an opportunity to prove himself so that he would be accepted and admired by all, which in turn would make efforts possible toward removing the other hindrances.

b. **Distinguished at Jabesh-gilead (I Sam. 11:1-15).** Such an opportunity arose soon after the Mizpah identification. The Ammonites, defeated by Jephthah some forty years earlier, now attacked the city of Jabesh-gilead[9] across the Jordan, led by King Nahash. The inhabitants of this city sent for help from all the tribes, apparently not knowing that Saul had been chosen king. Their appeal came to Saul's attention, nonetheless; and he immediately saw it as both a responsibility for him and the opportunity he needed. In a dramatic gesture, he butchered a yoke of oxen and sent pieces to all the tribes. Messengers taking them declared that all who did not respond to Jabesh-gilead's call by joining Saul would have their own oxen treated in similar fashion. The response was excellent. A total of 30,000 presented themselves from Judah, and 300,000 from the other tribes, here collectively called Israel.[10] From this group[11] Saul selected three army contingents, which he led against the Ammonites, winning a decisive victory. The result was as Saul desired. The fancy of the Israelites was caught, and they now did accept him as king. The formal ceremony was conducted at Gilgal, with Samuel again leading the proceedings. Saul was crowned as first king, amidst an offering of sacrifices and general rejoicing.[12]

---

[9] Identification is uncertain, but Glueck argues rather convincingly, *BASOR*, 89 (Feb., 1943) and 91 (Oct., 1943), for Tell Abu-Kharaz on Wadi Yabis, two miles from the Jordan and nine miles from Bethshan.

[10] In this twofold division, there is an early hint of the basic conflict between Judah and the other tribes, which was to break out fully after Solomon. Probably representatives of Simeon were with Judah, but the rest would have been with Israel.

[11] We need not think of all 330,000 as an army, but as those who expressed approval of Saul's action and who responded. From these Saul could choose the actual fighting force.

[12] The date was c. 1050 B.C. Saul ruled 40 years (Acts 13:21), and David's period following is generally accepted as c. 1010–970.

c. Samuel's word of exhortation (I Sam. 12:1-25). Following the coronation, Samuel delivered a parting exhortation to the people.[13] It was an emotional moment for the great prophet and retiring leader. He had acceded to the people's request for a king, at God's own direction, and now he voluntarily served in crowning him. Samuel, who had worked so well and to whom the people owed so much, was now stepping down. But further, Samuel knew that the sin which had caused the former system of rule to fail could also affect the new one. Exhortation was needed, because the people must be made to realize that change of heart was more important than change of rule.

Samuel began by soliciting the people's acknowledgment of his own righteous activity before them. Then he reminded them of their past failures and strongly urged them to obey God's Law. This they must do if they were to experience God's blessing. Further, as a way of impressing the importance of his words, he called for God to send a thunderstorm in this time of wheat harvest, normally the dry season.[14] God did so, and the people cried out in fear as the thunder rolled and the rain fell. He closed with brief words of further exhortation, promising in addition that he would himself pray unceasingly for them.

B. THE RULE OF SAUL

1. *Simple and inexpensive.* The government Saul established was simple—no doubt, purposely so. There had been time for Saul to plan, and he had evidently recognized that the people were in no mood for elaborate government. It would not be easy to impose rigid controls when the people had never had them; and, though Samuel had warned that taxes would come, it was apparent that time and education would be necessary before the people would accept them. Accordingly, the government was kept simple and inexpensive.

The capital Saul established was at Gibeah,[15] his own home town. He may even have built the palace on his own property to reduce expense. The palace itself was of simple design. Excavation has revealed that it was more of a fortress than a lavish residence.[16] There is no

[13] Though Samuel would live many more years, and continue to be influential in the government (even anointing David in time, I Sam. 16), this was his last act as chief. From now on a king would be the main leader.

[14] The dry season lasts from about mid-April to the first of November. Wheat harvest comes in June.

[15] Well identified as Tell el-Ful, located at the northern outskirts of present-day Jerusalem. The serious crime of the Judges Period, when civil war followed, had occurred here.

[16] Excavated by W. F. Albright in 1922-23. For recent study, cf. L. A. Sinclair, "An Archaeological Study of Gibeah (Tell el-Ful)," *AASOR*, 34 (1960); also Wright, *BAR*, pp. 122-24.

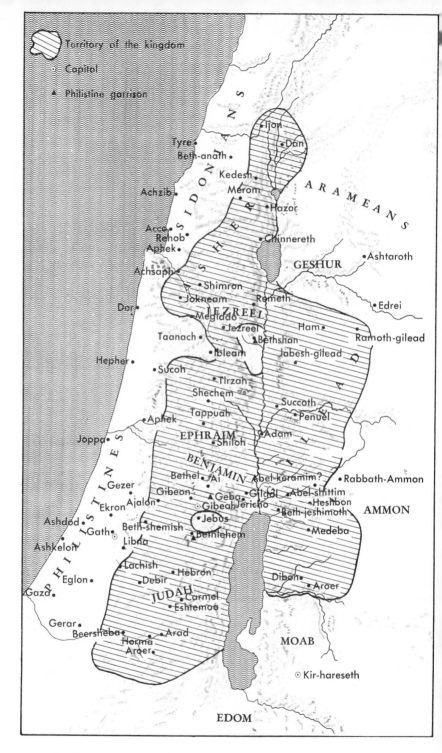

Map 9. The Kingdom of Saul

suggestion that he gave the capital city any special privilege in the land, something which, if done, could have stirred criticism among people unaccustomed to the ways of royalty. Still further, no elaborate court was created. Indeed, the biblical record only names one officer, Abner, captain of the army and cousin of Saul[17] (I Sam. 14:50). Monthly meetings at the time of new moon may have been the set occasions for discussing problems and planning strategy (I Sam. 20: 24-27).

2. *Little basic change.* It is clear, too, that Saul instituted few policies which caused appreciable change in the life patterns of people. For instance, old tribal borders continued to be observed. Saul did not do away with them or seek to change them as a measure of achieving unity, though the people were no longer to think of themselves as separate entities. No doubt Saul realized that any new central form of government could only be truly this if it won voluntary allegiance on its own merits. Tradition-defying orders might stir rebellion.

Likely the people were pleased that Saul instituted this manner of rule. They had the satisfaction of a king like other nations, and still did not suffer irritating interference in their private lives. Radical new laws, systems, or institutions had not been imposed and taxes had not been greatly increased.[18] It was good to know that a chief ruler was in charge to lead in battle, which seemed important after years of repeated oppressions. There was a sense of a security, too, in having a standing army ready to fight in their behalf. They were quite willing to fill army quotas if they could avoid the fearful invasions of past years. All this Saul apparently realized and acted accordingly. His manner of beginning the rule showed wisdom and foresight.

C. The Rejection of Saul (I Samuel 13–15)

Saul's manner of continuing the rule, however, did not show the same good judgment; for though reasons existed for not starting with strong government, he should have begun to institute policies and measures toward unification before many years had passed. If the tribes were to be welded into a nation, these were needed. But no evidence exists that Saul ever tried to effect them. Saul's lack of discernment in such matters likely stemmed in part from two causes: first, his personal deficiency in self-control, of which more will be seen presently; and second, his serious wrong of harboring a rebellious heart

---

[17] Since the biblical record speaks only of Abner, Saul himself, Jonathan his son, or David his son-in-law as leading the army, it may be that Saul intentionally kept military leadership confined to his own family.

[18] The biblical record gives no hint that any of these were instituted, but rather implies that they were not.

toward God. Because of these matters, Saul did not rule long before God told him, through Samuel, that he had been rejected as king. This rejection was voiced in connection with two military episodes, spaced somewhat apart.

1. *The first rejection (I Samuel 13–14)*. The first was a renewed conflict with the Philistines, which occurred at Michmash. The Philistines had been quiet since their sound defeat at Mizpah; but now, only two years after Saul's inauguration (I Sam. 13:1),[19] they again entered the land and encamped at Michmash,[20] just four miles northeast of the capital, Gibeah.[21] They had come to revenge a victory wrought by Jonathan over a garrison of Philistines left in the land (I Sam. 13:2-3). Their forces may have included 30,000 chariots,[22] 6,000 horsemen, and a host of foot soldiers. The presence of such an army caused terror among Israelites of the vicinity, many fleeing to caves and thickets to hide, and others crossing the Jordan. Saul quickly assembled a force at Gilgal to withstand them, and waited for Samuel to come and offer sacrifice prior to the impending engagement. It was at this point that he committed the particular sin which prompted the first rejection. Having waited seven days, the impatient Saul assumed the priestly office, which in turn demonstrated that he had a proud, self-sufficient, rebellious heart. In this respect, considerable change in character had taken place since the day he had been first anointed.

God still prospered Saul in this battle, however, mainly through the effort of his able son, Jonathan. Prospects were dark until Jonathan achieved a minor but brilliant victory. The Israelite forces were much smaller than the Philistines, and the only swords were those held by Saul and Jonathan themselves.[23] Saul's own army, too, was apparently suffering from daily desertions (I Sam. 13:15; cf. 13:2), while the Philistines remained capable of sending foraging troops in three directions at the same time (I Sam. 13:16-18). But then came Jonathan's daring triumph. Accompanied only by his armorbearer, he crossed from Geba,[24] on the south of Wadi Suweinit, to Michmash on the north,

---

[19] About five years elapsed between the Mizpah battle and Saul's inauguration, which means that the land had been quiet about seven years.

[20] Present-day Mukhmas, on the northern ridge of Wadi Suweinit, east of Bethel on the way to Jericho.

[21] Usually the Philistines liked to fight in level areas where they could use their chariots best. They had come, however, to retaliate for Jonathan's victory and also, no doubt, seize Saul's capital if possible.

[22] Numerous scholars believe this number is too large, the result of a corruption of the text; cf. *KDC*, Samuel, p. 127 for discussion.

[23] Due to the Philistine iron monopoly; cf. *supra*, chap. 9, p. 205, n. 7.

[24] Identified with Modern Jeba, located opposite old Michmash. Geba must be distinguished from Gibeah, Saul's capital, three miles southwest.

descending and climbing steep ridges enroute, and attacked and defeated an entire Philistine garrison (I Sam. 14:1-14). News of so courageous an exploit spread rapidly, bringing new hope to the Israelites and resulting in the return of many deserters to Saul's army. At this time, too, God intervened to bring an earthquake, which resulted in more confusion among the enemy. Saul took advantage of the quick change of events to attack, and was enabled to defeat the frightened Philistines and drive them as far west as Aijalon.

Saul almost defeated his own cause in the course of the victory, however. He foolishly imposed a restriction on the men of his army, forbidding any to eat food for all of one day (I Sam. 14:24-46). He apparently hoped to give more incentive and time to pursue the enemy, but what he accomplished was to deprive his men of badly needed nourishment for the chase. Further, Saul nearly took the life of his son because of the order. Jonathan, who had not heard the command, did eat; and Saul, believing his word must be maintained even at the cost of his son, would have killed him but for the pleas of the people.

2. *The second rejection (I Samuel 15).* The second instance of disobedience came with Saul's battle with the Amalekites, approximately twenty years later.[25] During the intervening years, Saul had been militarily active, and had not experienced censure. Among his opponents had been the countries of Moab, Ammon, Edom, and Zobah,[26] besides the Philistines in an ever-continuing struggle. He appears to have been relatively successful. Then came the Amalekite battle. Samuel gave Saul specific instruction regarding it. Saul was to initiate this encounter as a retaliatory measure for the hit and run raids on Israel by Amalek years before, during the wilderness journey (Ex. 17:8-14),[27] and completely destroy the people and all their livestock. Saul carried out the mission, defeated the foe, and in large part obeyed in slaying all the people and their animals. He disobeyed, however, in sparing King Agag and some of the finest sheep and oxen. When Samuel asked the

[25] This 20-year span is determined as follows. David was anointed soon after the Amalekite battle (I Sam. 16:1-13). Since he was 30 years old at his inauguration to kingship (II Sam. 5:4) in 1010 B.C., he was born in 1040 B.C. He could hardly have been less than 15 years old when anointed (he had been left to attend sheep alone) which means about 1025 B.C., and the earlier battle of Michmash had occurred about 1047 B.C., 2 years after Saul's inauguration.

[26] A rather large state located just north of Damascus, hence much farther from Saul's home base than his other opponents.

[27] God speaks more strongly against the Amalekites than any other foe Israel encountered. In Ex. 17:14 He promises complete annihilation, and in Deut. 25:17-19 Moses reminds the people of this promise. Here Saul is told to carry it out. Apparently it was the manner of their attack on Israel (hitting and running, taking advantage of Israel's weak position) which prompted the severe censure.

reason, he explained that the animals were for sacrifice. Samuel, however, sternly replied that God desired obedience more than sacrifice. Samuel rebuked the king and told him once more that God had rejected him as the head of Israel's ruling family. Samuel then killed King Agag with his own hands.

Israel's first king failed in the sight of God. He would not obey divine commands. God had not given His people a king to act according to his own will, but to be God's intermediary. Saul, having started well, was affected by his role as chief, and forgot that God was the supreme Head. It may be assumed, too, that these two crucial occasions were not the only instances of disobedience on his part, but rather were representative of many others and of a general rebellious attitude. Because these were particularly pointed, the official rejection was voiced only regarding them.

The rationale for the permitted lapse of twenty years between these two times seems to be as follows. The first rejection was more of a warning than a final pronouncement.[28] That is, Saul might have made amends had he taken heed. For this reason he continued to experience success in other military endeavors. He did not, however, profit from the warning, but continued in disobedience, which was climaxed in the Amalekite encounter. This brought the final rejection, with God's enabling Spirit then being taken from him (I Sam. 16:14).[29]

D. SAUL AND DAVID (I Samuel 16–20)

1. *David's divine selection (I Samuel 16:1-13)*. With Saul now rejected by God, there was need for one to take his place. Accordingly, God soon instructed Samuel regarding procedure in locating such an one. He was to go to Bethlehem[30] and anoint there a son of Jesse. Samuel went to Bethlehem and had Jesse bring his sons before him. Seven were brought, but each was refused by God. David, the eighth and youngest, had been left to care for the family's sheep. Samuel insisted that he be brought, and God indicated him to be the one. As the father and brothers watched, Samuel then anointed the young man, who was probably about fifteen years of age, as Israel's second

---

[28] It is true that Samuel's words to Saul the first time sound final, but this does not mean that there was no provision for repentance. Jonah's words to Nineveh sound final also, but God was ready to change the order when repentance was shown (Jonah 3:4, 10).

[29] With no mention of the Spirit since the time of His coming on Saul prior to the Jabesh-gilead battle (I Sam. 11:6), the assumption is valid that the Spirit had remained on him after that time to enable him for ruling and had remained until this instance about 22 years later.

[30] Not a long distance, for only about 10 miles separate Ramah, Samuel's home town, from Bethlehem south; cf. *supra,* chap. 9, p. 230, n. 90.

king. He was not destined actually to rule for a few years, but already at this time the Spirit of God came upon him for special enablement, in anticipation of that day (I Sam. 16:13). Though not stated, Samuel very likely also warned the family not to let information regarding this anointing be made public to protect David from possible reprisals by Saul.[31]

2. *Saul's emotional instability*. Saul had imposing stature and did not lack in courage, but he was emotionally unstable. This weakness came to the fore soon after his second rejection as king. As long as the Spirit of God remained upon him for special empowerment, he was able to maintain self-control. But with the Spirit departed, periods of severe depression came upon him, prompted in large part, no doubt, by the divine rejection.[32] Consequently, a person was sought as court musician, whose music might aid in soothing the king during these attacks. In God's providence, the one chosen was David, who was skilled with the harp. His music did help, but it was not a cure. Saul became jealous very easily. David, who at first was a favorite of the king, soon experienced this jealousy as the people came to give him higher plaudits than the king. Saul also at times became extremely angry, even to the point of insanity. In this state he twice attempted to strike David with his spear. Further, Saul was subject to paranoid tendencies, thinking himself to be persecuted by all around him. At one time this tendency led to the slaughter of eighty-five innocent priests (I Sam. 22:7-19). Such a man could not command the respect of his people. Actions so abnormal and frequent would have become widely known, with people losing confidence accordingly. What gains he may have made in achieving good-will early in his reign were no doubt lost in his later years.

3. *David's rise to prominence (I Samuel 16:14–18:7)*. Under God's blessing, though David did not soon become king after his anointing, he did quickly rise to prominence in the land. The first step was being made court musician to Saul, as just observed. David was a man of many talents, of which musicianship was one.[33] He must have dis-

---

[31] Secrecy must have been maintained, for no intimation is made that anyone else ever knew of this original anointing. Though the brothers were jealous of David, they would not have wanted to talk to others about him having been so honored over themselves.

[32] These periods were the result of "an evil spirit from Yahweh" troubling Saul. Apparently this was God's way of showing His rejection rather than immediate dismissal from office.

[33] Few could match him: a trusted shepherd; a skilled harpist; an oustanding poet, writing many of the Psalms; an expert with the sling; a man of strength, dexterity, and courage to kill both a lion and bear with only his hands; a military genius who did not lose battles; an outstanding statesman when he became king; and above all a man of great faith in God.

played military ability before the king as well, for he was soon made a royal armorbearer (I Sam. 16:21).

The next step, and a big one, was David's victory over the Philistine giant, Goliath (I Sam. 17:1-58).[34] The Philistines had attempted to enter Israel through the Elah Valley, a natural approach into the mountains of Judah. They assembled for battle between Shochoh and Azekah.[35] Saul led his army to meet them, while David for some reason was at home. For forty days a Philistine over 9 feet tall, named Goliath, dared any Israelite to meet him in personal combat and so decide the whole contest;[36] but no one accepted the challenge. David came to the camp at the end of the forty days, on a mission for his father, to inquire about the welfare of three of his brothers who were there as soldiers. When he realized the shameful situation, he quickly volunteered to meet the giant. Saul at first doubted the wisdom of this but, seeing David's earnestness and faith, let him go. David refused normal armor, but took only weapons to which he was accustomed, a sling and five suitable stones. Goliath met him, covered with armor from head to foot and with a shield-bearer before him. When Goliath first saw David approaching, he disdained him, thinking himself humiliated by such an unlikely opponent. David, however, came not in his own strength, but in the name of Yahweh, God of Israel. One stone was all that David needed. It struck Goliath in the one vulnerable place, his forehead, and he fell stunned to the ground. David quickly ran to him and, using Goliath's own sword, for David had none, cut off his head. A brilliant victory was won for Saul and Israel by this display of great courage and faith.[37]

News of such an achievement spread rapidly among the people. Soon David found himself known and honored on all sides (I Sam. 18:1-7).

[34] II Sam. 21:19 attributes Goliath's death to one of David's men, Elhanan. I Chron. 20:5, however, says that Elhanan killed Lahmi, brother of Goliath. The apparent conflict is best resolved in terms of a textual error in the Samuel passage. The view of some that the Chronicler sought deliberately to maintain David's right to the honor by changing the truth must be rejected, for this assumes a fallible text.

[35] This places the battle about four miles south of Beth-shemesh or seventeen miles southwest of Jerusalem in modern Wadi es-Sant.

[36] This type of two-warrior contest was not unknown in the ancient world. Several examples are related from the Greco-Roman time. One is found regarding the Near East in the "story of Sinuhe," cf. ANET, p. 20, for the text.

[37] Because Saul asked regarding David's identity after this exploit (I Sam. 17:55-58), some scholars believe that David could not have been court musician prior to this. It is doubtful, however, if Saul would have let him fight Goliath at all if he had not known him beforehand. Probably the inquiry concerned David's family and background which had not seemed too significant before; cf. I Sam. 17:25. The biblical order of events must be maintained.

The people sang his praises, and Saul himself now rewarded him by making him commander of the army, though David was still a young man.[38] About this time, too, Jonathan, Saul's able and eldest son, developed a deep friendship for David. The mutual respect and love between the two lasted for the remainder of their lives, and provide one of the beautiful stories of the Bible. As army commander, David continued to achieve outstanding success, adding to his growing reputation throughout the land.

4. *Saul's jealousy (I Samuel 18:8–20:42)*. Soon David came to be ascribed higher honor than Saul, and Saul's emotional weakness showed itself by intense jealousy. He could not accept the people singing that David had slain his "ten thousands" and Saul only his "thousands." He attempted to take David's life, numerous times and ways.

a. Attempts to kill David (I Sam. 18:8–19:24). The first attempts were direct, for Saul tried twice to kill David with his spear (I Sam. 18:8-11). These attempts came as David continued to play the harp in the king's presence. David was able to avoid both attacks, and then Saul sought to work more indirectly. As a seeming reward for David's service,[39] Saul promised him Michal, his daughter, as wife. But he asked David supply one hundred foreskins of Philistines as dowry, hoping that David would be killed in acquiring them. David delivered two hundred safely, however (I Sam. 18:20-27). Saul next attempted to work through his servants, commanding that they take David's life, but Jonathan intervened to have the order changed (I Sam. 19:1-7). Shortly after, another signal victory wrought by David over Philistines prompted a further direct attack by Saul to strike David with the spear, but once more David avoided the king's effort. Saul quickly ordered servants to follow David to his home and kill him the next morning, but Michal worked against her father by letting David down from an outside window (I Sam. 19:8-17). David fled from the palace area, realizing the intensity of Saul's hatred, and came to Samuel at Ramah about two miles north. Saul sent three different companies of men there to seize David for execution. When all three failed, Saul himself went. When he found David, however, in the approving company of Samuel and his young prophets (besides the three companies Saul had earlier sent, all engaged in rendering praise to God),[40] Saul did not apprehend him,

---

[38] Probably in his early twenties since he started to rule in Hebron at thirty (II Sam. 5:4).

[39] In that Saul had promised his daughter (besides riches and tax-free status, I Sam. 17:25) to whoever would kill Goliath, David should have been given Saul's eldest daughter, Merab (of whom Saul did speak to David, though then gave her to another, I Sam. 18:17-19), and this without dowry.

[40] *Supra*, p. 239, n. 6.

but fell into a fit of despair and lay all night in a deep stupor (I Sam. 19:18-24).[41]

b. David's flight from the palace (I Sam. 20:1-42). These repeated attempts to take David's life made the young man realize that living any longer at the palace was too hazardous. Though Saul had been shamed at Ramah, there was good reason to believe that he would soon forget and try again. David accordingly sought the counsel of Jonathan, and the two planned a final test to determine the continuing intention of the king. The test was planned in connection with a regular feast of new moon where David's presence would be expected.[42] He would intentionally not appear, however; and the test would concern the attitude displayed by the king in view of his absence, which Jonathan would then report to his friend. The next day at the feast Saul demonstrated his attitude to be no different than before, and so Jonathan, regretfully but faithfully, brought the word to David. Both agreed that David would have to leave the palace area, and they parted with great emotion. David began the life of a fugitive.

E. SAUL'S LAST YEARS (I Samuel 22:6-19; 28:1-25; 31:1-13)

1. *Further degeneration of conduct (I Samuel 22:6-19).* How many years of life remained for Saul after the flight of David is not clear. No definite clues exist. It is not likely, however, that David's fugitive experiences lasted more than a few years, perhaps four or five at the most. Certainly the greater part of Saul's reign had elapsed by this time.[43]

What years did remain were spent in continued frustration and wasted effort. Most of the time seems to have been occupied in trying further to apprehend David. Saul's principal motivation in this was his recognition that David was the divinely chosen successor to the throne. He did not have to be told about the official anointing ceremony at Bethlehem to realize this. God's evident blessing on the young man, as well as the general approval of the people, were all too significant. Saul was intent on forcing a change in the divine plan

[41] *Supra,* chap. 9, p. 233, n. 101.

[42] Since this feast lasted two days (I Sam. 20:5, 27), it was considered important. The new moon was a religious feast time; but this feast at the palace was something additional, for it took place in civil surroundings with apparently only civil personnel present (I Sam. 20:25). It was probably a regular monthly meeting, which was scheduled at new moon time, to determine affairs of state.

[43] Something over 22 years had elapsed by the time of David's anointing (*supra,* p. 245, n. 25), which means that about 13 years had been consumed in David's coming to the palace as musician, experiencing life as army commander when high plaudits were rendered by the people, and suffering Saul's numerous attacks on his life.

if possible and lent strong effort to that end. Further rebellion of heart toward God was manifested in this, of course.

At one time Saul cruelly took the lives of eighty-five defenseless priests in retaliation for really no crime at all (I Sam. 22:6-19). As David had fled from Gibeah, he had stopped at Nob,[44] then site of the Tabernacle, to ask for food, a weapon, and apparently advice.[45] Ahimelech,[46] then high priest, had cooperated,[47] while Doeg, chief herdsman of Saul who happened then to be present, observed. Not long after, Doeg, an opportunist interested in royal favors, told Saul what he had seen. Saul immediately summoned Ahimelech and the priests attendant in Nob, numbering eighty-five, to answer for assisting David. Ahimelech gave his answer, and Saul then ordered Doeg, after refusal by guards standing by, to kill Ahimelech and all eighty-five priests. Doeg did so and, after this, Saul also had the city of Nob itself destroyed, including women, children, and all animals. Certainly this was one of Saul's most despicable actions.

2. *Final Philistine conflict (I Samuel 28:1-25; 31:1-13).* When David fled from Saul, Israel lost her ablest military leader. The Philistines had been kept in check so long as David led against them, but Saul had no one of equal ability to replace him.[48] Nothing is heard from the Philistines for a time after David's departure, but their thrusts into the land gradually became more pronounced, as revealed by two particular incidents. One occurred when fugitive David went to the town of Keilah, located well within the hill country of Judah southwest of Bethlehem,[49] to assist in withstanding a Philistine attack there. On this occasion, Saul did not attempt to defend territory belonging to him

[44] Site uncertain, but apparently within viewing distance of Jerusalem (Isa. 10:32; Neh. 11:32). Best suggestion is Ras Umm et-Tala on the eastern slope of Mt. Scopus, northeast of Jerusalem. If correct, David had only about two miles to get there, heading southeast.

[45] That advice was given is not indicated in the story proper (I Sam. 21:1-9), but is in the reports later of both Doeg (vs. 10) and Ahimelech (vs. 15).

[46] Ahimelech was a son of Ahitub, grandson of the wicked Phinehas, and great grandson of Eli, descendant of Ithamar. Earlier, Ahimelech had aided Saul in making inquiry for him at the battle of Michmash (I Sam. 14:3, 36-42, where he is called Ahijah).

[47] Though David did not tell Ahimelech that he was fleeing from Saul, it is clear that Ahimelech suspected the fact; first by his question in I Sam. 21:1 and then by his defense of David here before Saul (I Sam. 22:14-15). He had taken a chance in helping David and is to be commended for his courage.

[48] Though Abner was still captain of the army, he is never seen leading in victory. Jonathan is (Michmash battle), but not Abner, who may have been a better administrator than military strategist (cf. I Sam. 17:55-57; 20:25; 26: 5, 7, 14, 15; II Sam. 2:8, 12-31; 3:6-37).

[49] Identified as Khirbet Qila, six miles east of modern Beit Guvrin, eighteen miles southwest of Jerusalem, three miles south of Adullam.

(I Sam. 23:1-5). The other was an instance, not long after, when Saul did quickly pull back from pursuit of David on being informed of a Philistine inroad into the country, and apparently did make a defense (I Sam. 23:27-28). The particular place of Philistine penetration this time is not indicated.

The decisive and final battle for Saul with the Philistines came at Mt. Gilboa (I Sam. 28:1-25; 31:1-13). The Philistines first gathered at Aphek, the site of their important victory over Israel some sixty-five years earlier.[50] Then they marched in force through the Esdraelon Valley and encamped at Shunem[51] near Mt. Gilboa. Saul moved to meet them and took up quarters in that mountain. Fearing the coming encounter, he sought information on its outcome from God, but was not answered "by dreams, nor by Urim, nor by prophets" (I Sam. 28:6). He longed to consult Samuel who was now dead (I Sam. 25:1), and in desperation broke a Mosaic ordinance (Lev. 20:27), and his own regulation (I Sam. 28:9), by visiting a witch who lived at Endor[52] (I Sam. 28:7-25). Through what was apparently a resulting supernatural appearance of Samuel, at which the witch herself was terrified, Saul was warned of tragic defeat on the morrow.

The battle was joined, and the prediction came true (I Sam. 31:1-13). Israel was severely defeated, and Saul's three sons, Jonathan, Abinadad, and Melchi-shua were killed. Saul was sorely wounded and, not wanting to be captured alive, fell on his own sword.[53] The Philistines found the four bodies of the royal family and hung them for public viewing on the wall in the nearby city of Bethshan. The men of Jabesh-gilead, hearing of the tragedy and remembering their debt to Saul (I Sam. 11:1-13), then came by forced march at night and rescued the bodies for decent burial. Several years later, David likewise showed grace toward his predecessor by transferring his bones, as well as Jonathan's, from Jabesh-gilead to Saul's homeland, Benjamin, for permanent interment (II Sam. 21:12-14).

3. *Estimate of Saul.* Sad indeed was the end of Israel's first king. He had started well but ended shamefully. His tragic death on Mt.

[50] Cf. *supra*, chap. 9, p. 231, n. 93.

[51] Identified with modern Solem in the territory of Issachar at the eastern foot of "Little Hermon" (hill of Moreh, Judg. 7:1), about eight miles from where Saul would have camped in Mt. Gilboa. This is doubtless the town where the Shunammite later provided a special room for Elisha (II Kings 4:8-10).

[52] Endor, modern 'En-dur, was located about nine miles straight north of where Saul encamped. The Philistines were far enough east at Shunem to permit him access to the city.

[53] The later story told by the Amalekite to David (II Sam. 1:2-10), that he had killed Saul, was very likely a fabrication. At the most, he only finished what Saul had already done in falling on his own sword.

Gilboa suited the perverted manner in which he had ruled during his last years. Saul is an example of what can happen to a man of promise who does not obey God. He had good potential and even was selected by God for his task. He had an attractive appearance. He had the certainty of God's blessing, if he would only follow God's will. But his reign proved to be one of almost continual frustration and lack of accomplishment. In their initial request, the Israelites had wanted one like him to rule so that their country might be strong against enemy attack; but when Saul died, after forty years of rule, the country had actually become weaker than when he began.

Saul was plagued with an emotional problem from the beginning. He probably fought continually to overcome his timidity. This inborn lack of confidence may have influenced him, for instance, in not imposing strong unifying regulations on the people, a policy which was wise at first, as observed, but should not have been continued. Saul's main problem, however, was his pride and rebellious spirit toward God. Fame apparently affected him, and he did not control his actions. He forgot that God was still Head of His people. For this reason he was rejected by God.

The country was probably as disunited at his death as at his inauguration. Whatever may have been gained during early years was likely lost during the latter. Waning confidence in Saul as a man would have soon led to loss of confidence in the united nation for which he stood. This distrust on the part of the people no doubt played a significant role in Saul's final defeat on Mt. Gilboa. Few men responded to his call to serve in the army, and this left him quite incapable of meeting the Philistine challenge. He had ample reason to fear, which is why he resorted to the witch of Endor.

For this reason the Philistines won an easy victory. Israel's army was destroyed and the king killed, leaving the country helpless before the enemy. There is little doubt that the Philistines now moved into the land in strength. This is reflected in the fact that when Ishbosheth, Saul's son and successor, set up his capital, he did so, not at Gibeah, but at Mahanaim across the Jordan (II Sam. 2:8-9). It is reflected also by the panic experienced in Gibeah when news of the Gilboa disaster was received—panic which, for instance, caused the nurse of Mephibosheth, Jonathan's son, to flee with him in her arms, and drop him in her anxiety (II Sam. 4:4). As Saul fell on his sword he must have realized that such a situation would now result. What a picture with which to die! He had been promised much when young, but ended with little. Favored above all of his day, he had failed in his great opportunity.

F. DAVID AS FUGITIVE (I Samuel 21–27, 29–30; II Samuel 1)

1. *David's situation.* When David fled from Saul, the change in his relation to the king presented difficulties. For one thing, he had to face a new kind of life, requiring a psychological adjustment not easy to make. He had been the favorite in the land, leader of Israel's victorious army, and applauded on every hand. Now he was a fugitive, legally an outlaw, hunted by the king. Such an adjustment is hard, but David had to make it if he was to keep a clear mind in his new role.

Another matter concerned his relation to the people as their future king, for which he had been anointed by Samuel. How would this new life affect the people's opinion of him? Until now he had enjoyed excellent prospects, with good public exposure and even marriage to the king's daughter. Would his new role change this thinking regarding him?

Still a third matter concerned his own protection from Saul. Certainly the king would pursue him, and David would be forced to seek safety somewhere. How should he proceed and where should he go? Two possible avenues confronted him. One was to move outside the land, where Saul could not follow; but this would involve risk, for he had been leader of Israel's army and might be recognized. The other was to remain in the country, gather a substantial protective band of men, and remain mostly in sparsely populated areas where pursuit would be difficult. This, however, had the drawback of requirements for food and shelter, and he could not really hope to gather a force sufficiently large to withstand Saul's army. The events now to be traced show him trying both avenues.

2. *David's course of action (I Samuel 21–26).* When David left the capital, Gibeah, after bidding farewell to Jonathan, he went, as we have seen, first to Nob, where Ahimelech served as high priest at the Tabernacle.[54] Here David received some of the sacred bread for food, Goliath's sword for a weapon, and, most important, an indication through Ahimelech of God's will (I Sam. 21:3-9; 22:10-15).[55] With a few personal servants,[56] David then directed his steps to the Philis-

---

[54] The Tabernacle was probably intact here yet, minus only the Ark. It seems to have been in good condition still later when at Gibeon (II Chron. 1:3).

[55] No indication is given as to the nature of the communication, but only that it was given, probably by the Urim and Thummim. A likely guess is that it was an approval for the flight.

[56] Ahimelech's indication that David was alone (I Sam. 21:1) is in terms of David having no army with him, which apparently was unusual. It is clear, however, that a few attendants were there (I Sam. 21:4-6).

tine city, Gath,[57] apparently determined to try the foreign alternative first. However, he was soon recognized there by the servants of King Achish, and he quickly feigned madness that he might escape harm.

David then tried the second alternative. He returned to his homeland and took up residence in a cave near Adullam,[58] where he began gathering a protective force of men. Since he was within ten miles of his home in Bethlehem, he was near enough for his father and brothers to visit him. Somehow David was able to make known, perhaps in part through help of his family, his desire that men join him. Four hundred responded—men described as in distress, in debt, and discontented (I Sam. 22:1-2; I Chron. 12:8-15). Many may have been political refugees in common with David, having fled from the capricious Saul. It is not likely that David would have harbored persons guilty of gross crimes.

With the band assembled, David again tried the foreign expedient, this time moving east to Moab.[59] He took his parents with him now, no doubt fearing reprisals against them by Saul. For some reason, however, Gad, a prophet who had joined David's band, soon counseled him to leave this country; and David moved once more back to Judah, this time to an area called "the forest of Hareth," unknown today.

Here Abiathar, son of Ahimelech, fleeing from Saul, came to David (I Sam. 22:20-23). The time was soon after Saul's slaughter of the eighty-five priests of Nob, from which Abiathar had escaped. He was high priest now, since his father had just been killed. He brought the priestly ephod with him, apparently including the Urim and Thummim for divine inquiry.[60] We can imagine David's grief at news of the atrocity, but also joy that Abiathar had been able to reach him, especially bringing the Urim and Thummim.

It was not long before David had opportunity to put this divine means of inquiry to use. He learned that the Philistines were preying on the inhabitants of Keilah;[61] and, desiring to make friends wherever possible, and wanting to help these people, he sought God's will as to giving them assistance (I Sam. 23:1-13). The answer to the in-

---

[57] Often identified with Tell el-'Areini, but better with Tell es-Safi, about 23 miles southwest of Gibeah; cf. A. F. Rainey, "Gath of the Philistines," *Christian News From Israel* 17 (Sept., 1966), pp. 31-38.

[58] Identified with modern Tell esh-Sheikh Madhkur, Adullam was about nine miles east of Gath, half-way between Gath and Bethlehem.

[59] Moab had been defeated by Saul a few years earlier (I Sam. 14:47) and perhaps David reasoned that they would be friendly with one who was now fugitive from Saul. Too, David's ancestress, Ruth, had come from Moab, and it held natural ties for him.

[60] *Supra*, p. 239, n. 8.

[61] *Supra*, p. 251, n. 49.

quiry was affirmative, and David came to the relief of Keilah and helped defeat the Philistines. In spite of the benefit given, however, further inquiry revealed that the people of Keilah would now turn him over to Saul if he remained, and he soon left.

At this point David moved southward, to the region of Ziph and Maon below Hebron.[62] Here Saul made his first attempt to seize David, for the Ziphites had informed him of David's position. He was unsuccessful, however, for from here he had to return to fight Philistines (I Sam. 23:14-28). David then moved east to En-gedi[63] on the shore of the Dead Sea where Saul again pursued him after the Philistine encounter (I Sam. 24:1-22). It was here that David spared Saul's life for the first time. Saul had entered a cave where David was hiding, and David could have killed him, but instead he merely cut off part of Saul's clothing for evidence of his proximity. When Saul learned of David's gracious sparing of his life, as David later showed him the severed cloth from a distance, Saul outwardly repented and asked for David's continued mercy.

David next moved back once more to the region of Maon. Now he sought food for his men from a wealthy landholder, named Nabal, who lived near his camp (I Sam. 25:2-42). David believed that he had a right to ask for assistance, since his men had been giving protection to Nabal's flocks from Bedouin robbers (I Sam. 25:7, 14-17). But Nabal, a surly person, was of no mind to accede, and David prepared to punish him. Nabal's wife, Abigail, however, of a different temperament, intervened to supply the food needed. Nabal died ten days later, perhaps in part from shock in learning from his wife what David had planned to do. David then took Abigail as his own wife.

Not long after, the Ziphites once more tried to curry Saul's favor by telling him of David's hiding place (I Sam. 26:1-25). Saul came, and for a second time David spared his life when he could have killed him. David, accompanied by Abishai,[64] went to where Saul slept under the guard of Abner and the army, and took away Saul's own spear and jug of water. Once again, the following day, Saul, shown the articles by David, repented and promised not to pursue David any longer.

[62] Ziph, identified with modern Tell Zif, is 3½ miles southeast of Hebron and 14 miles southeast of Keilah. Maon, identified with Khirbet Ma'in, is 5 miles south of Ziph.

[63] En-gedi is still called by the same name, after a fresh flowing spring. It is 16 miles straight east from Ziph.

[64] Abishai was a brother of Joab, and became David's general. They were sons of David's sister, Zeruiah (possibly half-sister, cf. I Chron. 2:16; II Sam. 17:25). This is the first mention of either, and both may have first associated themselves with David at this time.

3. David at Ziklag (I Samuel 27, 29–30; II Samuel 1)

a. To Ziklag (I Sam. 27:1-4). Following this second instance of sparing Saul's life, David went once more to the foreign area of the Philistines, for he feared that he could not always escape these attempts by Saul. There was no doubt another reason for this move, too: one suggested by the fact that he had recently requested food from Nabal. David's troops now numbered 600 (I Sam. 27:2; cf. I Chron. 12:1-7, 19-22), and it would not have been easy to keep them in provisions. The Philistines, like many peoples of the day,[65] employed mercenary troops; and, if they would now accept his band as such, this problem would be solved. Saul would not follow him here either. With these advantages in mind, David made the move, chancing another unfavorable reception, and offered his services to Achish, king of Gath. Achish accepted David this time, no doubt persuaded by David's being a proven refugee from his enemy, Saul, and also by the 600 men David now led, whom Achish apparently could use. He gave David the city of Ziklag,[66] well south in Philistine territory, as a base of operations.

b. Precarious activity at Ziklag (I Sam. 27:5-12). David played a dual role at Ziklag. Pretending to serve Achish as a good mercenary, he attacked southern foreign tribes which had been perennial enemies of Israel, particularly the Geshurites, Gezrites, and Amalekites.[67] He let Achish believe that he was distressing southern Judah, thus maintaining standing with him, but all the while distributing booty among cities of southern Judah (I Sam. 30:26-31) to keep their favor toward the day when he would need support in becoming their king. This was a precarious path to tread, but David apparently did it with success. This is not to say, however, that God was pleased. It seems clear that David's time of sojourn among the Philistines was not one of high spiritual standing.

c. Spared from fighting Israel (I Sam. 28:2; 29:2-11). After sixteen months of this activity (I Sam. 27:7), the final Philistine battle

---

[65] Mercenary troops were not uncommon. Ittai, the Gittite (of Gath), had a band of 600 men (II Sam. 15:18-22) and later joined himself to David at the time of Absalom's rebellion. Hanun, king of Ammon, hired 20,000 Syrians and 1,000 Macathites to help fight Israel (II Sam. 10:6).

[66] Tentative identification has been made with Tell al-Khuwailfa, 23 miles nearly straight south of Gath and 12 miles north northeast of Beer-sheba. Ziklag had been one of the cities allotted to Simeon (Josh. 19:5), but apparently had been taken by the Philistines, though far from the center of Philistine activity.

[67] The Geshurites were of Geshuri, south of Philistine land (Josh. 13:2), not of Geshur in Syria (II Sam. 15:8). Gezrites are unknown, but were not of Gezer to the north. Amalekites are well known as inhabitants of the northern Negeb.

with Saul drew near, and David found himself in difficulty. He apparently had committed himself to Achish to a degree where he could not remain uninvolved without endangering his own position. Consequently, he purported to go along with the Philistine plans. It is unthinkable that he really wished to participate,[68] however, even though he did accompany Achish on the way to battle as far as Aphek, the place of general assembly. Accordingly, he must have been greatly relieved when other Philistines objected to his presence and he was sent home to Ziklag.[69]

d. Amalekite encounter (I Sam. 30:1-25). Catastrophe met David on his return to Ziklag. The Amalekites, perhaps in retaliation for David's earlier raids, had ravaged the town and taken his wives and the wives of all his men, besides much booty. David's men, ordinarily faithful to him, now came near mutiny. It may be that they had earlier disagreed with David regarding the whole Philistine policy, and so blamed him here for this. But David was quick to act, and set out in pursuit of the captors. Learning the location of the Amalekites from a captured Egyptian, left behind because of illness, David stormed the camp and recovered both wives and booty. This alleviated the wounded feelings of the men, and peace was restored. The booty he took exceeded what had been lost, and there was even enough to distribute elsewhere. He did so in thirteen listed Judean towns, where he had received friendly assistance in recent months, and whose friendship he wished to maintain in view of his coming kingship (I Sam. 30:26-31).

e. News of Saul's death (II Sam. 1:1-27). It was on the third day after returning from this pursuit that he received word of Israel's tragic defeat at Mt. Gilboa and the death of Saul and his sons. The news was brought by one who had escaped the slaughter and who now thought he might obtain favor from Israel's next king by claiming to have killed the prior one. He told the story that Saul, realizing that the battle was lost and that the enemy was pressing hard upon him, had called to the young man and asked that he kill him; which the young man, who was an Amalekite, said he had done. He carried Saul's crown and bracelet as evidence to support his story. This was

[68] David's words to Achish never directly indicate that he wanted to go, but are carefully phrased to have made Achish think so. Had David really found it necessary to go he may have defected to aid Saul, even as the Philistine captains suspected. Certainly he would not have fought against Saul, whom he recognized as God's anointed.

[69] It is about 48 miles straight south from Aphek to Ziklag, a distance which took David sometime into the third day to cover (I Sam. 30:1).

convincing to David, who had no reason to doubt his testimony,[70] and he responded by weeping and fasting until the evening of that day. Then he returned to see the young man once again, but not to honor him, as the man had hoped, but to order his death for having put his hand on the anointed of Yahweh. This gesture was in keeping with David's own earlier refusal to touch the king's life. David's sincere and touching words of lamentation for both Saul and Jonathan are recorded in II Samuel 1:17-27.

David's mourning came from his heart, but at the same time he was aware that this news sounded the note for his time to return to Israel. David would have no part in bringing about Saul's death, but at the same time it was what he had been waiting for since the long-past day of his personal anointing. The way was now clear for him to move home and receive the kingship.

[70] The crown and bracelet were evidence that the man had been on hand at least shortly after Saul's death. However, they were not evidence that he had actually killed Saul, and he probably had not in view of the story in I Sam. 31: 4-5. Cf. *supra,* p. 252, n. 53.

CHAPTER ELEVEN

DAVID

II Samuel 1–24; I Kings 1:1–2:11; I Chronicles 12–29

In contrast to the rule of Saul, David's reign was one of unification and development of the kingdom. He brought the tribes together, established an efficient government, organized the priesthood, and maintained an army that scarcely lost a battle. He inherited a divided, wartorn land and, when he died, left an empire. David was not only a strong king in contrast to his predecessor; he was the strongest king Israel ever had. He was the measure of others. To be a king like David came to be the highest accolade a successor could have.

A. DAVID AT HEBRON (II Samuel 1:1–5:5)

Though Saul was dead, David was still not to rule all twelve tribes for a few years. He was readily accepted as king by Judah, but not by the tribes of the north. They crowned Ishbosheth, a remaining son of Saul. In this division of loyalties, a basic separation among the people was evidenced, which has been noticed earlier[1] and which came to fruition after Solomon. David ruled over Judah for seven and one-half years and later over all Israel for thirty-three, making a total reign of forty and one-half years (1010–970; II Sam. 5:5).

1. *David made king of Judah (II Samuel 2:1-4)*. At the time of Saul's death, David was better known by the people of Judah than of the other tribes. He was from Bethlehem of Judah, and most of his activity had been south of Saul's capital, Gibeah. This had been true during the time when he had led Saul's army against the Philistines, who lived southwest, and also during his life as a fugitive. It was logical for him, therefore, as he returned to his own people,[2] to go first

[1] Regarding the time Saul called for volunteers to go against Ammonites in behalf of Jabesh-gilead; *supra,* chap. 10, p. 240, n. 10.
[2] Returning from Ziklag (cf. *supra,* chap. 10, p. 257, n. 66) he would have had only 17 miles to travel northeast to get there.

260

to Hebron, a central, principal city of Judah, and for the people there to proclaim him king. He had been their champion for many years, and his gifts and favors had been distributed among their cities. Moreover, he had proved his ability in leadership, especially warfare, much in contrast to the prior regime. No doubt a large majority were glad for the opportunity at last to make him king, giving them one in whom they could place confidence. Accordingly, when David arrived at Hebron with his own household, plus the households of all his 600 followers (II Sam. 2:3), the men of Judah promptly assembled and anointed him "king over the house of Judah."

2. *Ishbosheth made king of Israel (II Samuel 2:8-10)*. The situation was different for the other tribes,[3] because they did not know David so well. Stories would have circulated among them regarding his prowess against the Philistines, when he was still Saul's army commander; but, after he fled from the king, he probably dropped from their attention. Consequently, on learning of Saul's death, logic led them to think first of Saul's surviving son, Ishbosheth.[4] Three sons had died with Saul, but this one remained, along with two daughters, Merab and Michal. Abner, who somehow had survived the slaughter on Mt. Gilboa, was instrumental in establishing him as king, choosing Mahanaim[5] across the Jordan as the new capital. This change in location of capital was caused by the Philistine domination of Israel since the Gilboa rout. At Mahanaim the young man was proclaimed king of both sides of the Jordan, though the extent to which people west of the river either benefited or felt responsible is questionable. Their main concern was with the threatening presence of the Philistines.

How did the Philistines react to the crowning of David and Ishbosheth over their respective countries? Did they consider them dangerous enemies, helpful vassals, or were they unconcerned? Regarding the Israelite king, they probably were quite unconcerned. His influence

[3] From here on in Scripture, the term, Israel, is used with some regularity to mean the tribes north of Judah; for instance I Sam. 2:9, 10, 17. When David eventually comes to reign over all 12 tribes, he is said to reign over "all Israel and Judah" (II Sam. 5:5:).

[4] Ishbosheth was formerly called Ishbaal (I Chron. 8:33; 9:39). Similarly, Gideon's later name, Jerrubbaal (Judg. 6:32), was afterward changed to Jerubosheth (II Sam. 11:21). The element "baal," meant "master" or "possessor" but came into disrepute because of the foreign god, Baal. The element, "bosheth," chosen as substitute (cf. also Mephibosheth, II Sam. 9:6) meant "shame," referring to shameful Baal.

[5] The site of Mahanaim is not certain. It is commonly identified with Khirbet Mahneh, 12½ miles north of the Jabbok, but is better placed nearer the Jabbok, for it was at Gad's northern border (Josh. 13:26-30). It was some distance east of the Jordan in view of II Sam. 2:29.

at most would be minimal west of the Jordan where they were interested. Regarding David, they may have thought of him yet as only a vassal. He had been among them and served well under Achish, and should not be difficult to control as ruler over small Judah. Certainly they were pleased that Israel was now divided, and no doubt thought in terms of soon taking over the entire country anyway.

3. *Struggle between David and Ishbosheth (II Samuel 2:12–4:12)*

a. Early conflict. Conflict between Judah and Israel was almost inevitable from the beginning. It broke out first in a minor skirmish at Gibeon[6] of Benjamin, six miles northeast of Jerusalem (II Sam. 2: 12-32). There Abner met David's chief, Joab,[7] by the pool of Gibeon.[8] At first only twelve men of each side fought, but the conflict widened and a small war ensued. Finally David's force emerged victorious. Following the main struggle, Asahel, younger brother of Joab, was killed by Abner as he fled from the battle scene, a deed Joab was not to forget.

b. David's increase in strength. As months passed, David continually grew stronger in his rule, while Ishbosheth became weaker. Abner, who had been the true ruling voice in Mahanaim from the first, finally quarreled with his king and offered his services to David (II Sam. 3:7-16). In this, Abner was showing his recognition of inevitable developments. He had gained respect for David's ability long before, when both had been active in Saul's inner circle. Now that David was definitely becoming stronger in his position, Abner could see that any future for him lay with David. Sending a message to David, he agreed to deliver all Israel into David's hands in return for his own safety and, no doubt, an honored position. David first made him agree, however, to return Michal, David's former wife. She had married one Phaltiel after David became a fugitive, and David now wanted her back. Apparently his love for her had not waned; and, further, the marriage tied him with the house of Saul, which should help gain the allegiance of the northern tribes. Abner gave assent and brought about Michal's return, much to the sorrow of her present husband, who followed her weeping as far as Abner would permit. Abner also communicated with elders from the various tribes, urging that they now turn their allegiance to David, apparently with some success. Before

---

[6] Cf. *supra*, chap. 8, p. 179, n. 39.

[7] Abishai, brother of Joab, was mentioned earlier (*supra*, chap. 10, p. 256, n. 64), but this is the first mention of Joab, himself. Asahel was the youngest of the three.

[8] A pit identified with this pool has been excavated. It was dug to a depth of 35 feet in the rock with a descending stairway. Further steps were found to lead another 40 feet down a tunnel to a water chamber.

he could really effect this change of allegiance, however, he was killed by Joab (II Sam. 3:17-27). This wanton act by David's leader was committed in retaliation for the death of Asahel; though one wonders how much Joab's fear of a rival for his position may also have contributed. David, desiring to court favor with the northern tribes, now did all he could to disassociate himself from the deed, showing true sorrow that it had happened (II Sam. 3:28-39).

c. Ishbosheth assassinated. With Abner's control gone, two of the lesser officers of Ishbosheth assassinated their king in his palace and carried his head to David, thinking they would be rewarded (II Sam. 4:1-12). But, as with the messenger of Saul's death, David again reacted in a way unexpected, having both immediately killed. Probably two reasons accounted for this reaction: first, David's respect for one who had been duly appointed king of Israel, particularly since he was a son of Saul; and second, David's desire once more to disassociate himself from a deed which could bring disfavor of the northern tribes toward him. The image of one who schemed and killed to attain his goals was undesirable. He wanted to be known as he truly felt, and he did have personal revulsion against such actions. Similar thinking had earlier caused him to extend his appreciation to the inhabitants of Jabesh-gilead for their act in giving Saul and his sons an honorable burial (II Sam. 2:4-7).[9]

4. *David made king of all Israel (II Samuel 5:1-5; I Chronicles 12: 23-40).* Seven years and six months of ruling at Hebron (II Sam. 5:5) had passed when David was formally anointed king over all Israel.[10] By this time, people spontaneously desired him. Leaders from all the tribes, accompanied by sizable armies,[11] came to Hebron to make the formal request and reach an agreement. Since the biblical record specifically states that a "covenant" was made at the time, it

[9] David had been told of this kindness of Jabesh-gilead immediately after arrival in Hebron. Years later he went further and brought the bones of Saul and Jonathan back to Gibeah for burial (II Sam. 21:12). He could not do this now, for Benjamin was not yet in his jurisdiction.

[10] In II Sam. 2:10, Ishbosheth is said to have ruled over Israel only two years, some 5½ less than David over Judah. This difference may be accounted for as follows. With confusion reigning and Philistines dominant, Abner may have waited many months before proclaiming Ishbosheth king; a brief time elapsed between Ishbosheth's death and the northern leaders getting together (with Abner also dead and so not able to give leadership) to ask David to rule them; and several months again elapsed after their request and the actual move of David to Jerusalem, during which time he had to make plans and fight Philistines in two battles.

[11] The numbers in these armies are listed in I Chron. 12:23-40. The total adds to 339,600. If all these came, as seems indicated, this was a great showing of enthusiasm for David to accept the Israelite throne.

is likely that some negotiation transpired. The people wanted David as king, but he would have wanted some commitments in return, guarantees that would insure a true central government. He had seen enough laxity during Saul's rule to realize that regulation, organization, and taxation were necessary if unity was to be achieved. He recognized too, apparently, that the time to procure promises was before the rule started. Negotiation also would have been necessary between Judah, who was present as well (Simeon too, I Chron. 12:24-25), and the northern tribes. The people of Judah would have had to agree to share their king, perhaps demanding some concession in return, and also to accept the same regulations that David now demanded of the other tribes. The thinking of all the tribes in weighing such demands is not difficult to conjecture. They needed a king, and they needed a strong one; indeed, one with the kind of ability David had earlier shown as head of Saul's army. If David could lead them out of their present subjection to the Philistines, any terms, at all reasonable, would not be too high to meet. Agreement was reached, the terms were accepted,[12] and David was anointed for the third time in his life.[13]

B. DAVID ESTABLISHES THE KINGDOM OF ISRAEL
(II Samuel 5:6-8:18; 10:1-19)

David's genius for rule was apparent from the first. His initial problem concerned the Philistines. Though the northern tribes had accepted him as their king, the Philistines still were dominant there. Before David could fully rule, this dominance had to be removed. David succeeded brilliantly in the task.

1. *Struggle with Philistines (II Samuel 5:17-25).* David did not have to ponder the problem long before it was thrust upon him, for the Philistines themselves initiated military action. They had remained quiet while David was king of Judah only; but, with the kingdom now united, their policy changed. It was clear that David was no longer a vassal. He was once again a chief enemy and should be dealt with accordingly.

a. First battle. The Philistines made their attack in the Valley of Rephaim, just south of Jerusalem. The strategy is apparent. They already had a garrison in Bethlehem (II Sam. 23:14), probably established after the Mt. Gilboa victory, and they wanted to supplement it and divide the country, making it impossible for David to effect the

---

[12] Evidence that they were is seen in the manner of strong rule that David did establish, much in contrast to that of Saul.

[13] The first had been by Samuel in anticipation, the second by the people of Judah 7½ years before, and now over all the land.

union to which agreement had been given. David, no doubt recognizing the intention, established his headquarters northeast of Hebron at the cave of Adullam[14] (II Sam. 23:13-14), where he had first assembled his band when a fugitive. His army still consisted mainly of the faithful group gathered during fugitive days. It was a closely-knit band of men, willing to risk their lives if their leader wished for as much as a drink from a spring behind enemy lines (II Sam. 23:15-17). God assured David of victory, and David attacked at Baal-perazim (location unknown), defeating the Philistines, though his force must have been much smaller. The victory was so complete that the enemy left images of their gods behind as they fled, apparently in panic. These images were burned by David.[15]

b. Second battle. The Philistines were not through, however. They regrouped, probably with a still larger force, and came again into the same valley, attempting a similar devisive tactic. This time God's instruction was for David to change the direction of his attack and come at them from the rear at an opportune moment, which God Himself would signify by a sound in nearby balsam trees. This strategy made use of the mobility of David's small, disciplined band to effect surprise on the enemy. The result was that the ensuing attack brought decisive victory once again, and David this time drove the Philistines as far as Gezer.[16] This major triumph ended the domination of the Philistines over Israel.[17] What further contacts there were in later years occurred on Philistine soil and were relatively minor in significance (II Sam. 21: 15-22; I Chron. 18:1; 20:4-8).

David's beginning as king, thus, was most auspicious. In two brief encounters, with only a minimum of troops, he had solved the problem of the Philistines. The impression on the northern tribes, which had long been oppressed by this formidable enemy, must have been very great. These tribes had sought David as their king, especially that he might rid them of this oppression, and here he had done so already, with apparent ease. Without question, his role as true monarch, which required imposing necessary regulation and organization upon them, was made much easier because of this signal achievement.

[14] *Supra*, chap. 10, p. 255, n. 58.
[15] David's burning these images is directly opposite to the action of the Philistines, when years earlier they had captured the Ark at Aphek (I Sam. 4: 11). They had taken the Ark in parade as symbolic of victory, but David burned these images in disdain.
[16] Cf. *supra*, chap. 8, p. 182, n. 51. Gezer, at the northeast boundary of Philistine territory, was at least 15 miles from the point of this battle.
[17] That David had lived and fought with the Philistines helped him to know their ways and plan his own strategy. This certainly helped also to break their monopoly on iron.

2. *A new capital (II Samuel 5:6-12; 6:1–7:29; I Chronicles 13, 15–17).* With the Philistine menace disposed, David could think in terms of an appropriate capital.[18] Hebron was central for Judah but too far south to serve all the country. A city like Shechem was central for Israel, but too far north for Judah. Gibeah, Saul's former capital, had been destroyed by the Philistines and had not been a particularly good location anyhow. Its water supply apparently had been only by cistern, excavation having found no trace of a spring.[19]

a. Jerusalem made capital. David's choice fell on Jerusalem, a city still held by Jebusites.[20] It lay exactly on the border between Judah and Israel, had a good water supply in the Spring of Gihon,[21] and its position was readily defensible. To occupy it would also eliminate a Canaanite stronghold within the country; so David captured it, apparently without difficulty,[22] and fortified it. There is no indication that he destroyed the former inhabitants, which means that a majority of the city's population may have been foreign for some time.[23]

b. Religious capital too. David desired to make Jerusalem also the religious capital. It was not long, therefore, before he sought to bring the Ark, which had been at Kirjath-jearim for seventy years,[24] to the city (II Sam. 6:1-11; I Chron. 13). However, David did not transport it correctly, using an open cart rather than poles as prescribed by God. As a result, one of the attendants, Uzzah, son of Abinadab in

[18] Though II Sam. 5:6-9 records David's taking Jerusalem before telling of the Philistine battle, the intention cannot be to indicate that this transpired first. II Sam. 5:17 says that the Philistine encounter came as soon as the Philistines heard of the agreed union. Also, if David had then already taken Jerusalem, the Philistine attack at Rephaim to divide the country would not have made sense. Further, I Sam. 23:13-14 indicates that David made his headquarters at the cave of Adullam, which would have made no sense at all if he already had the stronghold of Jerusalem.

[19] For discussion, cf. references *supra,* chap. 10, p. 241, n. 16.

[20] Jebusites were Canaanites who had continued to live in Jerusalem. Jerusalem even carried the alternate name, Jebus (Josh. 18:16, 28; Judg. 19:10). The name Zion is introduced in II Sam. 5:7 and probably referred to the hill on which the city stood, which later was only one of other hills occupied as the city grew. Cf. also *supra,* chap. 8, p. 183, n. 56.

[21] A fine flowing spring in the Kidron Valley east of Jerusalem, from which Hezekiah later had a tunnel cut; cf. *infra,* chap. 14, p. 359.

[22] II Sam. 5:8 suggests that some strategy involving a water-way was used to take the city. Since the Jebusites already had a slanting tunnel to the Spring of Gihon, it may have been this tunnel that David's men employed.)

[23] That Jebusites did continue to live in the area is indicated also by the fact that Araunah, at whose land a plague in David's latter days was stopped, was a Jebusite (II Sam. 24:16f). There is even reason to believe that he was the former deposed King (II Sam. 24:23).

[24] *Supra,* chap. 9, p. 235, n. 110.

whose house the Ark had resided, was struck dead when he attempted to keep it from falling from the cart. David then left the Ark at the nearby home of one Obed-Edom, whose household was greatly blessed by God as a result. Three months later David returned to finish the task, this time proceeding according to divine direction (II Sam. 6:12-23; I Chron. 15:1-29). He placed the Ark in a tent which he had prepared in Jerusalem amidst great rejoicing and offering of sacrifices.

David desired to build a fine temple for the Ark, but was refused permission by God (II Sam. 7:1-17; I Chron. 17:1-15). The prohibition came through Nathan, a prophet active throughout David's reign, but first mentioned here. He told David that God would greatly bless him, that his family would never be replaced on the throne by another, but that, since he was a man of war, he should not build a temple himself. His son, who would be a man of peace, would be the man to do so. David's admirable reaction to these disappointing words was to voice a prayer of submission and thanksgiving before God (II Sam. 7:18-29; I Chron. 17:16-27). He then proceeded to gather substantial quantities of material toward the day when his son would build it (I Chron. 22:1-5, 14-16).

The contrasting attitudes between David and Saul toward the Ark and the priesthood would not have escaped the people. Saul had not only neglected the Ark, but he had killed many of the priesthood. David, on the other hand, had here brought the long-displaced Ark to the new capital early in his reign; and he now further installed the priests, Abiathar and Zadok,[25] along with assisting Levites, to minister before it (II Sam. 8:17; 15:24-36; I Chron. 15:11). David's concern for the Ark and priesthood would have pleased the people, endearing him yet more to their hearts.

3. David's conquests (II Samuel 8; 10; 12:26-31; I Chronicles 18–20)

a. Consolidation of the tribes. The biblical record includes little information regarding David's consolidation of the Israelite tribes into a centralized government. Much more is stated regarding his foreign wars. Since these, however, could not have been waged without a strong nation at home, it is certain that he did achieve true unity, something which Saul never did. Several factors would have contributed to this unification. For one thing, David had made the initial agreement

---

[25] Zadok is first mentioned at this time. He probably is the one who is listed with others as having come to David in Hebron, as head of 22 captains of his father's house (I Chron. 12:28). He was a descendant of Eleazar, third son of Aaron while Abiathar was descendant of Ithamar, the fourth son (I Kings 2:27; I Chron. 24:3). Since he came with others from the northern tribes, he must have been recognized there as high priest, which suggests that Saul had so appointed him following the flight of Abiathar after the Nob slaughter.

with the people as to regulations and organizations, as already noted. For another, he had earned the good-will of the people—something of immense importance in itself—especially by his early success against the Philistines. Also, he had ability to work with people and bring them to agree with his thinking. Still further, he was a man of conviction and confidence, which would have inspired others to follow. These matters would have prompted the people to accept his program for unification; and his own good judgment, as well as experience gained while a member of Saul's government, would have determined the best measures to employ.

This tribal consolidation would also have involved the acquiring of land originally allotted but never occupied. Until now Israelites had been confined mostly to the hills, with the Philistines and Canaanites yet holding the better lowlands. But this situation changed as well. Excavation has corroborated the implication of Scripture[26] that Canaanite holdings along the Mediterranean to the north, across the Esdraelon Valley, and through the Jordan Valley were now brought under Israelite control. The Philistines were not entirely driven from the land to Israel's southwest, true enough, but they too were confined to a much restricted territory. No longer did pockets of non-occupation remain (other than Philistia), but David ruled continuously from north of the Sea of Galilee to Beersheba in the south and on both sides of the Jordan River. As a result, Israelites could know for the first time that they did exist as a true nation. The tribes had become genuinely united, controlled almost all their allotted land, and had a fine king of whom they could be proud.

b. David's army. To make extensive conquests beyond home borders, David needed a strong army. Again, little information is available as to its constituent parts; but certain facts may be pieced together from various intimations. In general, the army consisted of three sections: the original faithful 600 from David's fugitive days, a group to which probably some replacements and additions were made; troops levied from the people, constituting a sort of revolving standing army; and foreign mercenaries.

The core at all times seem to have been the 600, likely the group referred to as Gittites (from Gath) in II Samuel 15:18 and as *gibborim*, "mighty men"[27] in several places. This term appears to be used for

[26] Evidenced by the continuous route taken by David's census people somewhat later (II Sam. 24:5-8), and also by the description of the land which later was passed along to Solomon (I Kings 4:7-19).

[27] The term *gibborim* is used for armies other than David's, but almost always with an added term, such as *hayil*, "of valor." This is never true for David's group. Also, when used of David's army, the term, especially in I Kings

them, for instance, when a group is mentioned as being with David in his flight from Absalom (II Sam. 16:6); also when his supporters are listed at the revolt of Sheba (II Sam. 20:7); later when supporters of Solomon are named at the attempted rebellion of Adonijah (I Kings 1:8, 10); and still later when attendants are listed on the occasion of David's closing admonitions (I Chron. 28:1). It was probably from this 600 that the special "mighty men" were selected (II Sam. 23:8-39; I Chron. 11:10-47), all perhaps commanders. A recorded list of "thirty" may be of captains over divisions of twenty each; and another five named may have served over them.[28] The high caliber of these troops is indicated both by described exploits (II Sam. 23:8-39) and by the exemplary conduct of one of them, Uriah the Hittite, who, when called back from battle by David, would not even go to his own home, since this comfort would be out of keeping with his duty as a soldier (II Sam. 11:11; 23:39).

David also kept 24,000 in service as a regular standing army, changing the personnel once every month (I Chron. 27:1-15). This means that he had 288,000 trained men, prepared at all times for immediate call to service as needed. At the time of Absalom's revolt, this group turned against David when Absalom called on them, and their number is then described as "the sand that is by the sea" (II Sam. 17:11).

Then David kept foreign mercenaries, who appear to have served as his private bodyguard, made up of Cherithites and Pelethites[29] (II Sam. 8:18; 15:18; 20:7; I Kings 1:38, 44). They may not have gone to war frequently with the regular army but stayed with the king for his personal protection.

c. Foreign conquests. With the home country firmly consolidated and controlled, and with an effective army available, David was in a position to wage war on foreign soil as need arose. There is no suggestion that he intentionally sought conquest, however, or that he gave himself to creating an empire. For the most part, he simply entered

1:8, 10 and I Chron. 28:1, seems to carry a particular reference rather than general as at other times.

[28] The elite five are listed in two classes: first, Jashobeam, Eleazar, and Shammah; second, Abishai (brother of Joab, with Joab himself not named) and Benaiah, each listed with corresponding exploits. The "thirty" (actually thirty-two are named, probably indicating later additions) are listed without exploits. I Chron. 11:41-47 adds sixteen additional names, suggesting further additions.

[29] Believed to be Cretans and Philistines on the basis of name comparisons. They remained loyal to David in the rebellion of Absalom (II Sam. 15:18; cf. II Sam. 20:7). They were present and last heard from at Solomon's anointing to kingship (I Kings 1:38, 44). There is no intimation of how David obtained the service of such a group.

battle situations as they arose and sought to win them. He was victorious, which did result in the country's borders continually enlarging.

i. Moab and Edom. The first war listed[30] was with Moab, on the east of the Dead Sea (II Sam. 8:2; I Chron. 18:2). David had found refuge there for a time when pursued by Saul, but now he inflicted a complete defeat upon the country. The cause of the war is not indicated, but David's harsh measures point to serious provocation. The result was that Moab became a vassal state, apparently keeping her own king, but having to pay tribute.

Sometime later, David fought and defeated Edom, located south of the Dead Sea (II Sam. 8:13-14; I Chron. 18:12-13). Again little description is given. The battle occurred in the "valley of salt;[31] severe reprisals once more were effected;[32] and Israelite garrisons were installed, signifying that Edom also was made a vassal state. These two victories gave David sovereignty on the east and south of the Dead Sea to the Gulf of Aqaba, an important water-way for trade.

ii. Damascus, Zobah, Hamath. In the north, David achieved victory over strong Zobah,[33] from whose king, Hadadezer, he seized 1,000 chariots, 700 horsemen, and 20,000 foot soldiers (II Sam. 8:3-12; I Chron. 18:3-11). David killed the horses except enough for 100 chariots. Evidently he did not believe that he had use for more in his own army, probably because much of his fighting was done in mountain areas where chariots were of little value. When Aramaeans of Damascus came to assist Zobah, apparently arriving after the main battle, David further defeated them, demanded tribute, and received it. Also, voluntary tribute was now extended by Hamath, located further north on the Orontes River. No details are given regarding these interchanges either. David placed garrisons in Damascus as he had in Moab and Edom, indicating that this region, too, became a vassal state, though how far north of Damascus this degree of control extended is not clear. Certainly it did not reach Hamath, which only acknowledged David's sovereignty; and the status of Zobah, between Damascus and Hamath,

---

[30] Both II Sam. 8:1 and I Chron. 18:1 list a preceding engagement with the Philistines. This was a minor battle, however, for only a few towns were taken.

[31] A part of the Arabah (cf. II Kings 14:7) and not the Wadi el-Milh (valley of salt) near Beersheba. An offensive war with Edom is not likely to have been waged that far into Israelite territory.

[32] This severity is brought out especially in I Kings 11:15-18, where Joab is said to have killed "every male," likely meaning the men of the Edomite army, remaining in the land six months to do so. I Chron. 18:12 indicates that 18,000 were killed. Likely the royal household was also killed, with only Hadad and some servants escaping to Egypt.

[33] An Aramaean state north of Damascus and east of the Anti-Lebanon mountains, which controlled nomadic tribes as far north as the Euphrates. It was the most powerful of the Aramaean states at this time.

is not certain. As for the coastal region along the Mediterranean, David had already made a treaty with Hiram, King of Tyre, respecting material and labor for building David's palace (II Sam. 5:11), which issued in peaceable relations in that direction, rather than conquest and control.

iii. Ammon and Zobah. An important war with Ammon, again to the east, is described in greater detail (II Sam. 10; I Chron. 19). Chronologically, this engagement probably preceded the northern struggle just noticed,[34] though its record follows in the biblical account. David's kindness toward Hanun, a new king of Ammon, had been misunderstood; and messengers sent by David had been insulted. Ammon, fearing reprisal from David, immediately prepared for war with good reason. King Hanun hired mercenaries to assist from the Aramaean states, Bethrehob (in Coele-Syria, north of Dan; cf. Judg. 18: 28), Zobah, and Maacah (south of Mt. Hermon).[35] David sent Joab with Israel's army to meet this combined force, and Joab displayed marked ability in effective deployment of troops to win a decisive victory.

Joab returned to Jerusalem, but Hadadezer, king of defeated Zobah, wanting to save face for his defeated army, came again with fresh troops for a return battle. David's army moved across the Jordan to meet him at Helam[36] and once more won a complete victory. The opposing army, now sorely depleted in numbers, retired from the scene acknowledging Israelite supremacy.

Joab then laid siege to Rabbah,[37] capital of Ammon, evidently in a continuation of the struggle begun earlier by Ammon (II Sam. 12:26-31; I Chron. 20:1-3). It was during this siege that David sinned with Bathsheba and had her husband, Uriah, placed at the point of heaviest fighting to insure his death (II Sam. 11:1-27). Rabbah was finally taken and David assumed the crown of Ammon, thus annexing this country, making it a part to his own kingdom.

d. David's empire. This was the extent of David's conquests. The breadth of his authority was now most impressive. As for the kingdom proper, this included all land originally allotted to the twelve tribes (less reduced Philistia), plus the kingdom of Ammon. As for vassal

[34] Because Zobah is involved at this time, too, and actively engaged against Israel, whereas in the northern struggle she was fully subdued and so no longer in a position to assist should Ammon or any other have called.

[35] For discussion of the location of each, cf. M. Unger, *Israel and the Aramaeans of Damascus* (London: James Clark & Co., Ltd. 1957), pp. 42-45.

[36] Helam is best identified with modern 'Alma, 30 miles east of the Sea of Galilee, considerably north of Ammon where the previous battle was fought.

[37] Rabbah is well identified with modern Amman, present capital of Jordan, 22 miles east of the River Jordan.

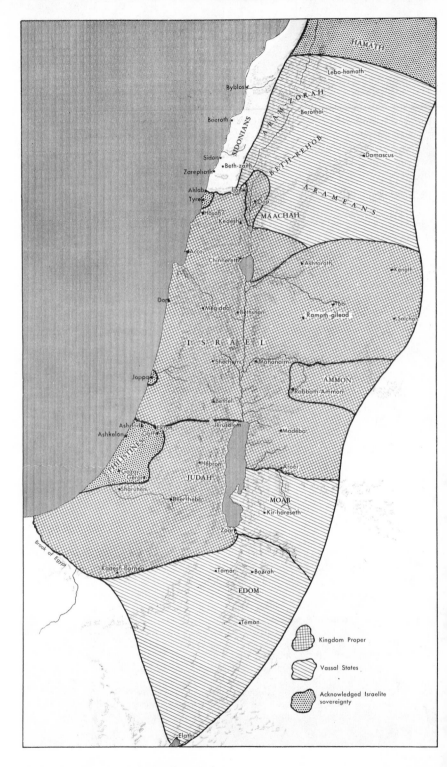

Map 10. The Kingdom of David

states, keeping their own kings but controlled by David's troops, these included Moab and Edom, east and south of the Dead Sea, and the area around Damascus northeast, which may have involved even all Zobah. As for territory which at least acknowledged Israelite sovereignty, this included the region still further north of which Hamath was capital. Since its boundary reached northeast to the Euphrates, and since this country at least acknowledged Israelite sovereignty, David's authority extended from the Gulf of Aqaba and the River of Egypt[38] in the south all the way to the Euphrates in the north. This was the area which God had promised to Abraham for his posterity centuries before (Gen. 15:18). It did not rival the vast territories of Egypt, Assyria, Babylonia, et al., in their empire days; but in David's time it was one of the larger land areas held, and David was no doubt the strongest ruler of the contemporary world.

C. DAVID'S GOVERNMENT

1. *The state.* The world view of Israelites could not have helped but change radically during the reign of David. Before his rule, they had been the object of attack, for they had been weak and other nations, especially the Philistines, had been strong. But now matters were reversed. They had become the dominant nation, and those nearby feared them. Never before in history had it been this way. God's promise to their father Abraham had at last come true.

King David was the central figure in this new status of power. He was responsible for it. The Israelite people had only followed and marveled as he led the way. To him belonged the honor. Israel was David's kingdom more than David was Israel's king.

Little information is given as to the administrative measures David enacted. There is indication that he placed general supervisors over each tribe, with the exceptions of Gad and Asher, though their duties are not described (I Chron. 27:16-22). He also appointed heads over treasuries, storehouses, and various agricultural departments (I Chron. 27:25-31). Certainly high taxes had to be imposed to support the program, though considerable foreign tribute was received, which would have helped.

2. *The court.* Two similar lists of leading members of David's court are recorded (II Sam. 8:15-18; 20:23-26). Serving in a military capacity were Joab, commander of the army, and Benaiah, commander of the two foreign divisions, the Cherethites and Pelethites.

---

[38] River of Egypt (*nahal misrayim;* Num. 34:5) is best taken to mean Wadi el-'Arish, reaching the Mediterranean 45 miles southwest of Gaza and 80 miles east of the Pelusiac mouth of the Nile. For discussion, cf. K. Kitchen, "Egypt, River of," *NBD*, pp. 353-54.

Superintending civic duties were Jehoshaphat, the *mazkir* ("one who reminds"), whose task likely was to keep records and remind the king of appointments and responsibilities; Seraiah, the *sopher* ("scribe"), who carried on official correspondence; and Adoram, minister over the *mas* ("tribute labor"),[39] probably composed of foreign laborers serving on public works. Leading in religious matters were Zadok and Abiathar, the two high priests. Besides these, the chronicler (I Chron. 27: 32-34) lists four others high in rank: Jonathan, an uncle of David, as counselor; Jehiel as governor of David's children; and Ahithophel and Hushai as two other counselors.

David's own family was large. In various lists taken together (II Sam. 3:2-5; 5:13-16; I Chron. 3:1-8; 14:4-7; II Chron. 11:18), the names of eight wives and twenty-one children are revealed. Besides the wives named, other "wives and concubines" unnamed were added when David assumed his rule in Jerusalem. The number of these is not given, but, at the time of his flight from Jerusalem before Absalom, at least ten concubines were left to keep the palace (II Sam. 15:16). It was customary in that day for powerful kings to keep large harems, and David apparently followed the practice to some extent.

Besides these persons mentioned, others too, sat at the king's table. Mephibosheth, to whom David showed unusual kindness because he was a son of Jonathan (II Sam. 9:1-13), did so. Barzillai, a rich Gileadite who befriended David in his flight from Absalom, was invited; and, though he refused, he was represented by Chimham, likely a son. David's select "mighty men," noted above, being highly honored by him, also probably ate at the palace with some regularity.

3. Religious personnel

a. Gad and Nathan, prophets. Among David's religious personnel, the prophets Gad and Nathan were outstanding in significance. Gad had been with David when he was a fugitive (I Sam. 22:5), and later in David's reign he was the one who offered David the choice of three punishments from God for his sin in census-taking (II Sam. 24:10-15). Nathan told David that God would not permit him to build the Temple (II Sam. 7:2-17). Later he rebuked David for his sin with Bathsheba (II Sam. 12:1-15), and finally he played a prominent role in Solomon's acclamation as king (I Kings 1:11-45).

b. Zadok and Abiathar, high priests. As noted, David recognized

---

[39] Probably the same man as called Adoniram in Solomon's day (I Kings 4:6; 5:14), whose task was essentially the same. Since his name appears in only the second of the two lists (II Sam. 20:24) from David's rule, it is likely that he was not needed until late in David's reign when this type of conscript labor had come to be used.

two high priests, Zadok and Abiathar, contrary to the Law which allowed for only one. The circumstance, however, was unusual. Abiathar had escaped Saul's slaughter of the eighty-five priests of Nob (I Sam. 22:20-23) and come to David. He had been with David ever since, certainly high in David's honor and affection. On assuming the rule of all Israel, however, David had found Zadok also recognized as high priest, probably appointed by Saul following the slaughter.[40] Both were descendants of Aaron, Abiathar through Ithamar and Zadok through Eleazar, and so both had inheritance rights to the title. Zadok appears to have been favored by David over Abiathar by being placed in charge of the Ark (II Sam. 15:24-29). Later, he helped in the anointing of Solomon as king when Abiathar supported Adonijah (I Kings 1:7f). As a result Zadok and his family continued in the office of high priest after David's rule, whereas Abiathar was expelled (I Kings 2:26-27).

c. Organization. Under these two high priests, the priests and Levites were reorganized into specific courses.[41] The priests were divided into twenty-four courses, with each designated to serve at the central sanctuary for a week in turn, giving each normally two weeks total service during any one year (I Chron. 24:1-19).[42] He also divided the Levites, previously sectionalized into "singers," "gatekeepers," "officers and judges," and general priestly assistants.[43] Of these, at least the "singers" were divided into twenty-four courses (I Chron. 25:1-31) as were the priests, and probably the other sections as well.[44] David

[40] *Supra*, p. 267, n. 25.

[41] The main reason being that priests and Levites numbered too many to serve at one time. Since this condition would have existed also in the Judges Period, David may have had precedent for what he did. When the Ark was away from the Tabernacle, this system could have fallen into disuse, with David now reviving and strengthening it.

[42] Until the Temple was built by Solomon, this service presumably was conducted at the Tabernacle located in David's time at Gibeon (II Chron. 1:3) and at the special tent David erected for the Ark in Jerusalem. An altar requiring priestly service was located at this tent as witnessed by Joab running there for safety (I Kings 2:28). Certain Levites were assigned to the tent (I Chron. 16:4-6). Zadok and others were assigned to Gibeon (I Chron. 16:39).

[43] When these distinctive Levitic groups came into existence is not indicated. I Chron. 9:17-26 shows that at least the "gatekeepers" had their distinction from the time of Moses. The "singers" were the religious musicians; the "gatekeepers," the guardians of the sanctuary (with gates assigned, I Chron. 26:13-19); and the "officers and judges" (*shoterim, shophetim*), seemingly special recorders and court judges assigned to various tribes (I Chron. 26:29-32). Most Levites conducted the more normal Levitic duties, as described in I Chron. 23:28-32.

[44] David's census revealed 38,000 Levites of service age, of which 4,000 were "singers," 4,000 "gatekeepers," 6,000 "officers and judges," and the remaining 24,000 for general service (I Chron. 23:3-5).

was rightly concerned with the religious life of the people, and believed that efficient service by the priests and Levites, as enhanced by this manner of organization, would be crucial in making it the highest possible. David himself contributed to religious emphasis and growth by his own exemplary life and the numerous psalms he wrote, some of which came to be used in the official religious services.[45]

D. SIGNIFICANT DEEDS

Several significant deeds of David while king are narrated in the biblical record. Some are commended by God; others are condemned.

1. Commended deeds (II Samuel 9; 21:1-14)

a. Kindness to Mephibosheth. One of David's finest actions was his gracious gesture toward Jonathan's lone surviving son, Mephibosheth. As noted above, David granted him a place of honor in the kingdom (II Sam. 9:1-13). Early in his reign, David took the initiative in looking for a descendant of Saul, whom he might so honor in memory of Jonathan. When informed of Mephibosheth, he immediately instructed that he be brought to the palace. Mephibosheth, made lame by a fall in the midst of panic in Gibeah following the Mt. Gilboa disaster, came with much fear, for a summons to a member of a deposed royal family could mean death. But David quieted his fears, and then rejoiced his heart by giving him all the land which Saul, his grandfather, had owned, besides granting him a place to eat at the royal table. David further assigned Ziba, a previous servant of Saul, who had informed David concerning Mephibosheth, to become overseer for Mephibosheth. In this action, David showed a great heart. Supplanting monarchs of the day normally disposed of all members of rival families; seldom did they honor them. There was benefit for David in being thus gracious, however, for he would have further endeared himself to those northern subjects who still felt loyalty to Saul's departed house.

b. Justice to Gibeonites. A later commendable deed was his rectification of a wrong committed by Saul against the Gibeonites (II Sam. 21:1-11), who years before had tricked Joshua into making a league with them (Josh. 9:1-27). Though the pact never should have been

---

[45] Superscriptions attribute 73 psalms to David. His musical ability is witnessed by his early appointment as court musician to Saul. Some of his poems are recorded outside the Psalms (II Sam. 1:18-27; 3:33-34; 23:2-7). Psalm 18 is given also in II Sam. 22:2-51 and attributed to him. He is called the "sweet psalmist of Israel," II Sam. 23:1. Even Amos, 300 years later, refers back to him as a musician (6:5). I Chron. 16:7 tells of David giving parts of Psalms 105, 96, and 106 to Asaph for use in rendering thanksgiving to God.

made, God still held His people responsible to respect it. Saul had not done so, but had killed many of the Gibeonites, appropriating their possessions for himself and family. A famine of three years prompted David to inquire of God concerning some possible wrong, and the misdeed of Saul was cited. David immediately sought to make amends. He asked the Gibeonites what they would like him to do, and they requested that seven sons of Saul be delivered to them for hanging. David carried out the request,[46] sparing Mephibosheth; and the Gibeonites then hanged the seven in Gibeah, Saul's old home town. It may be that all seven had earlier benefited from spoils Saul had taken from these people and so were justly punished.

2. *Disapproved deeds (II Samuel 11:1–12:25; 24:1-25; I Chronicles 21)*

a. Sin with Bathsheba. Two disapproved deeds of David are recorded. The first occurred toward the first of his reign, while his army under Joab was in battle with the Ammonites laying siege to the capital, Rabbah. It was his sin with Bathsheba and consequent murder of her husband, Uriah (II Sam. 11:1-27). David, upon seeing Bathsheba washing herself as he looked from a palace window, sent for her and committed adultery with her. When she informed him later that she was pregnant, he had Uriah brought home from the battlefront so that he might be with his wife. But Uriah would not go to his home, on the basis of noble principles, and David in desperation had him assigned a deadly position in the battle. There he was killed as David planned, and David took Bathsheba as his wife. For this serious sin, David was severely reprimanded by God through Nathan the prophet, and David rightly repented (II Sam. 12:1-23). In keeping with Nathan's prediction at the time of the rebuke, Bathsheba's baby when born died, and David displayed touching grief at this punishment from God.[47] The death of this little one was only the beginning of continuing family difficulties for David, also in keeping with Nathan's forewarning.

b. Sin in census taking. The other disapproved deed of David,

---

[46] II Sam. 21:8 states that five of these were sons of Michal. If so, they must have been born when she was married to Phaltiel, for she was barren with David as a result of her criticism of him for dancing before God (II Sam. 6:20-23). However, there is textual evidence of a copyist error involved in which "Michal" was substituted for "Merab." Also, the husband cited in II Sam. 21: 8 is Adriel, whom Merab, Saul's older daughter, married (I Sam. 18:19), not Michal. It is, of course, possible that Michal raised these children for Adriel (Merab perhaps having died). If so, David's action in taking them from her would have been difficult for David as well as for her; for, though they had quarreled, she likely still lived in the palace.

[47] Psalm 51 and likely 32 were written at this time, as expressions of David's grief and repentance.

coming many years later in his reign,[48] was the taking of a census of the people (II Sam. 24:1-25; I Chron. 21). The nature of the real sin involved, which certainly was more than merely counting numbers, is not clear, but must have been very serious. Even cold-hearted Joab urged the king to refrain in the action, and the degree of God's displeasure is indicated by the severity of the punishment inflicted as a result. The real sin may have concerned intended imposition of high taxes, and possibly even conscription of labor.

Other countries used the hated corvee principle for construction of public works, and David may have thought to do the same. We know at least that a second list of David's officers (II Sam. 20:24), as observed above, did include the name of one Adoram who was supervisor of "tribute labor." The phrase here used normally refers only to foreign labor, but David may have now decided to add to it levies from his own people, such as Solomon did later on (I Kings 5:13-14), much to the dislike of the people then (I Kings 12:4). Whatever David's full purpose, he insisted that the census be taken, clearly in an act of pride (cf. Ps. 30:6),[49] and Joab obeyed in directing the work. The census, which revealed 800,000 men of military age in Israel and 500,000 in Judah,[50] took more than nine months to complete. When the work was done, Gad the prophet was sent by God with three choices of punishment, from which David was to choose one. David selected "three days of pestilence," which resulted in 70,000 of David's newly counted people dying. The plague which killed them was stopped just outside Jerusalem at the threshing floor of Araunah the Jebusite, where Solomon later built the Temple. In repentance, David purchased the floor and also oxen from Araunah, and offered sacrifices to God.

---

[48] However, not at the very close of David's rule as one might think from the story being recorded at the end of II Samuel. The sacred writer sometimes groups his subject matter more in terms of content than chronological order. Such a census as here conducted would have had a goal in view such as a king would set in his years of strength. Perhaps the place of reporting it in I Chronicles (ch. 21) is significant, between the Ammonite battle and David's organization of the priests and Levites.

[49] Psalm 30, for "the dedication of the house," may have been composed at this time; cf. I Chron. 22:1.

[50] Counting women and children, the total population was about 4,000,000, approximately double what it had been at the time of Joshua's conquest (Num. 26:1-65). That Judah's number is so large in comparison with that of all the other tribes combined shows that Simeon's number was probably included, and also much of Dan's, since not all of Dan had migrated to the north. Danites who remained in the south likely amalgamated with Judah. The Chronicler adds that this number did not include the people of Levi or Benjamin, for Joab did not complete the count since the whole matter was so offensive to him (I Chron. 21:6).

E. Last Years of David (II Samuel 13–20; I Kings 1:1–2:11; I Chronicles 22; 28–29)

David's final years were marked by continual problems within his own family. These came as further punishments for David's sin, and carried overtones of repeated struggle for succession to the throne.

1. *The succession problem.* As David's outstanding reign drew to a close, the problem of who should succeed him became increasingly acute. There was no question but that the people wanted the monarchial form of government to continue, for David's benefit to them had been great; but it was not clear who should take his place. In that Saul had been the first king, and the ruling family had changed following him, no pattern of succession had been established. Since the general rule followed in neighboring countries—observed too when Ishbosheth had been anointed after Saul—was that a family should continue to rule until overthrown, and since David was an excellent king, it was to be expected that one of his sons would be the successor. But which son was not clear, nor how he should be designated.

With David so strong, certainly most expected him to make the selection, but no public announcement was made. Actually, David did make his choice, designating Solomon at his birth,[51] but for some reason he did not make this generally known, perhaps since the time was yet early in his reign. But with no announcement made, people were left to wonder who the selection might be. If David's other sons knew, they sought to circumvent it, perhaps taking it merely as a passing whim of the king.[52] In any event, a serious struggle for the throne ensued; involving especially the two sons, Absalom and later Adonijah.

2. *Absalom's revolt (II Samuel 12–19).* Absalom made the more concerted effort of the two. He was David's third son, born of an Aramaean princess of Geshur[53] named Maacah (II Sam. 3:3). On

[51] This designation by David is not recorded directly in the story, which states at the time only that God loved Solomon (II Sam. 12:24). However, when Adonijah attempted much later to seize the throne, Nathan, who knew of the designation, reminded Bathsheba who also knew of it (I Kings 1:13); she in turn reminded the king (I Kings 1:17); and David himself then referred to it (I Kings 1:30).

[52] For all David's strong points, being a stern disciplinarian was not one of them. The sons' actions toward him indicate this, and also the direct statement made concerning Adonijah: "His father had not displeased him at any time" (I Kings 1:6). David's hesitancy to hurt any of his sons could have influenced him not to make the selection public knowledge until after Solomon was grown, and to keep postponing it even then.

[53] Geshur was an Aramaean city, east of the Sea of Galilee. It was allotted to Manasseh, but, according to Josh. 13:13, the Geshurites had never been expelled. Cf. Deut. 3:13-14; Josh. 12:5.

the basis of the eldest son being first in line for the throne, a rule commonly followed in the ancient world and which apparently influenced Absalom's thinking, he was third. But Amnon, the eldest, had been killed at Absalom's own hand. This had occurred following Amnon's humiliation of Absalom's sister, Tamar (II Sam. 13:1-22), for which Absalom had contrived this revenge (II Sam. 13:23-29). The deed was done at a feast Absalom held for the royal princes. The second son, Chileab,[54] son of Abigail (former wife of Nabal the Carmelite), is not mentioned again after the notice of his birth, which suggests that he likely had died while still young. This left Absalom as the next possible claimant.

a. The plot (II Sam. 13:30–15:12). It is difficult to tell at what point Absalom decided to plot for the throne. The idea probably arose gradually and likely was present at least by the time he killed Amnon. Absalom's first act, following this murder, was to flee in fear of David to Geshur, where Talmai, his grandfather (mother's father) ruled. He could do little there in furthering the plan, but he did not dare return to Israel until he was summoned by David. After three years, Joab, probably urged by Absalom,[55] persuaded David to permit the return, but the king would still not see his son (II Sam. 14:1-24). After another two years, David did consent to see him, and then forgave him (II Sam. 14:25-33). Now Absalom was in a position to effect his plan in earnest.

His first step was to curry favor with the people (II Sam. 15:1-6). He was a handsome person which attracted people to him. He created an air of importance by moving through the country with a retinue of chariots and fifty attendants. He took the character of one vitally interested in people by intercepting those with problems, before they could get to the king's appointed officers, and tell them how much better matters would be if only he were king. He was clever and convincing, so that these efforts did bring many people to favor him. After four years,[56] when Absalom believed sufficient good-will had been generated, he took the second step. He went to Hebron[57] with the king's unsuspecting permission,[58] assembled his followers, and had himself anointed

---

[54] Called Daniel in I Chron. 3:1. Apparently he had two names.

[55] Joab likely believed that Absalom would be the next king and here desired to maintain favor with him.

[56] The number given in II Sam. 15:7 is "forty," but this is impossible in that David ruled only a total of 33 years in Jerusalem. This must be a copyist's error and so is better read with the Syriac, Vulgate, Arabic, and others: "four years."

[57] Perhaps Absalom chose Hebron for this anointing since David had been anointed there twice.

[58] Absalom's low state of spiritual maturity is indicated both by his desire

king (II Sam. 15:7-12).[59] With a considerable force of men, he then marched north against his father in Jerusalem, and David, taken unawares, found his only recourse was to flee (II Sam. 15:13-17).

An undercurrent of discontent must have existed in the country to make possible the degree of success thus implied for Absalom. It is clear that some people did have grievances, for these were the persons Absalom specially had worked with in his plotting. Perhaps, too, taxes had become very high, causing unrest. Further, the king's interests had become wider than his own land with the development of the empire, and many may have thought themselves neglected. Still further, any regime loses sympathizers and gains enemies with time; and David was now toward the close of his rule. Absalom was attractive and likely caught the fancy especially of younger people who had not witnessed the marked contrast of what David had achieved for the country with what had existed under Saul. Even some persons close to David were swept along. Ahithophel, long-time adviser to David (I Chron. 27:33), whose very son was one of David's "mighty men" (II Sam. 23:34), came at Absalom's call (II Sam. 15:12). Amasa, close relative of both David and Joab (II Sam. 17:25; I Chron. 2:15-17), became his military commander.

b. David's flight (II Sam. 15:13-17:29). Those who left Jerusalem in flight with David were his personal bodyguard, the Cherethites and Pelethites; his faithful 600; and numerous servants. Also Zadok and Abiathar, the two high priests, desired to follow and bring the Ark; but David sent them back, instructing them to inform him, through their two respective sons, Ahimaaz and Jonathan, regarding the plans of Absalom (II Sam. 15:24-29). David also told his own remaining official counselor, Hushai, to return and seek to counteract whatever advice Ahithophel might give Absalom about pursuing David, and then tell Zadok and Abiathar what Absalom decided to do (II Sam. 15:30-37). Hushai did this and was successful in his effort, and then did inform the two high priests as directed (II Sam. 17:1-23). Vital information thus came to David regarding Absalom's plans, so that the king was able to group his forces at Mahanaim, former capital of Ishbosheth, and make preparation for the attack of his son (II Sam. 17:24-29).

Along the way from Jerusalem to Mahanaim, a distance of more than fifty miles,[60] David experienced varied reactions from people. As

to revolt at all and by his willingness to use the excuse of an unpaid vow (II Sam. 15:7) for obtaining the king's permission to go to Hebron at this time.

[59] It is not directly stated that he was anointed at Hebron, but this follows from the story taken as a whole.

[60] The exact distance depends on the correct location of Mahanaim; cf. *supra*, p. 261, n. 5.

one would expect, most were sympathetic, weeping at the sad scene they witnessed; however, not all were so inclined. One Shimei, a descendant of Saul and still loyal to the former ruler, saw this as an opportunity to bring long awaited reprisal, and met the king at Bahurim[61] to inveigh curses and throw stones. David graciously and remarkably refused to bring action against him (II Sam. 16:5-13). Ziba, appointed servant to Mephibosheth, appeared sympathetic by offering saddled asses and prepared food for the king's family; but he was only seeking to further his own cause as against his master, Mephibosheth (II Sam. 16:1-4; 19:24-30). On arrival at Mahanaim, David received a most gratifying reaction. An Ammonite named Shobi and a Gileadite named Barzillai brought furniture, dishes, and food in large quantity for his weary followers.

c. The battle (II Sam. 18-1–19:29). The battle took place near Mahanaim in an area called the "wood of Ephraim" (II Sam. 18:1-18). Absalom had gathered the general troops of Israel, having taken time to do so as counseled by Hushai. David divided his comparatively small force into three groups, headed respectively by Joab, Abishai, and a Gittite named Ittai. Though fewer in number, David's men were hard-core troops with whom Absalom's hastily gathered soldiers were no match in morale or ability. With the blessing of God, David's men won a decisive victory. Contrary to David's explicit order, however, and with the real battle won, Joab killed Absalom, who had probably become ensnared by his long hair in a tree. When David learned of the deed, as well as the victory, his reaction was to express grief for his son rather than joy at the victory. David's love for his undeserving son is touching, but grief at this time hardly encouraged the loyal men who had fought so hard and well (II Sam. 18:19–19:8). Absalom's death broke the revolt, and what remained was for David to return to Jerusalem.

d. Sheba's revolt (II Sam. 19:9–20:22). Developments at this point led to another revolt, however; though this time it was less serious. This was initiated by Sheba, a Benjamite, who called for secession on the part of northern tribes at the time of David's return across the Jordan.

A general movement had arisen among the northern tribes to bring David back, and David had taken special steps to encourage Judah also to take part, not wishing his own tribe to think that because they had aided Absalom they were now in his disfavor. He even promised to make Amasa, Absalom's general, his own chief commander in place

---

[61] Identified with modern Ras et-Tmim to the east of Mt. Scopus. It was at Bahurim also that Ahimaaz and Jonathan, messengers to David, had to hide from Absalom's pursuers (II Sam. 17:17-21).

of Joab who had killed Absalom. The men of Judah quickly responded that they did wish to take part, and David left for the trip home.

Previous yet to the outbreak of the revolt, David had significant encounters with three different persons as he came to the Jordan River. Shimei, now fearful because of his vindictive actions when David fled, was among the first to meet David there and humbly he pled for mercy, quite in contrast to his former insolence. David granted the mercy, though he really did not forgive him, as shown by his later command to Solomon to take his life (II Sam. 19:17-23; I Kings 2:8-9). Another who met him was Mephibosheth, also seeking mercy in view of the deceitful actions of his servant, Ziba (II Sam. 19:24-30). David then divided Mephibosheth's property equally between Mephibosheth and Ziba, an action certainly unfair in view of Mephibosheth's sincere and truthful words in contrast to those of Ziba.[62] The third person involved was eighty-year-old Barzillai, who had benefited the king so greatly with provisions earlier (II Sam. 19:31-39). Now he crossed the Jordan with David, who urged him to continue to Jerusalem and receive a permanent residence in the palace. But the aged Barzillai refused, desiring instead to return to his own city where he felt more at home.

At this time the trouble started. The men of Judah had been the first on hand to escort the king across the Jordan and on to Gilgal.[63] Only a part of Israel's representatives had yet arrived and, when others came later to Gilgal, jealousies broke out anew as the northern tribes thought they saw favoritism on David's part. Heated words were exchanged, and finally Sheba, particularly vocal, induced the northern tribes to secede from David's kingdom and follow him.[64]

It must have been most disquieting to David, who had just gone through one revolution, to have another break out. He remained undaunted, however; for, upon arrival back in Jerusalem, he immediately dispatched Amasa, his new general, to gather an army from Judah to put down the outbreak (II Sam. 20:3-22). When Amasa took longer than the three days allotted him, David, believing that haste was important, commissioned Abishai,[65] Joab's brother, to take the hard-core troops instead and quell the rebels. Though Joab was not in charge,

[62] Mephibosheth gave evidence of true sorrow, expressed appreciation for past generosity, showed no bitterness at David's decision, and was willing to let Ziba have all if David so desired.
[63] For location, cf. *supra*, chap. 8, p. 172, n. 12.
[64] Another outbreak of the same deep-seated division that was to flower fully in the day of Rehoboam.
[65] Purposely bypassing Joab here in favor of the brother who had also performed well in leadership before this, and was one of David's five among the "mighty men" (II Sam. 23:18-19).

he accompanied the force; and, when Amasa was encountered along the way, Joab proceeded treacherously to kill him much as he had Abner years before. This was a shocking action, but the troops did not delay because of it, no doubt in part due to their knowledge of Joab and his violent ways. They pressed on in pursuit of Sheba and finally caught up with him far north at Abel of Bethmaacah.[66] A serious battle did not develop, however, as David had feared, for the townspeople, led by a "wise woman," were quite willing to deliver Sheba's severed head to David's army in exchange for their own safety. Apperently, the initial revolt had been hasty rather than deep-seated, and Sheba had soon been left without extensive support. He clearly had not been able to assemble an army of any real strength, and he had fled northward mainly to escape David's forces. Now that he was dead, the revolt was finished.

3. *Solomon's accession (I Kings 1:1–2:9; I Chronicles 22:6–23:1; 28–29).* Solomon was crowned king while David still lived, meaning that a brief coregency existed. Adonijah, fourth son of David, had made an abortive attempt to seize the throne after Absalom had failed, and Solomon was hastily made king in his place.

The attempt of Adonijah to rule likely came soon after David returned to Jerusalem following the brief exile caused by Absalom. This follows from several facts taken together. First, it is known that David ruled a total of no more than forty years, and that Absalom was born after those years began (II Sam. 3:2-3). Then it is clear that Absalom had grown to adulthood by the time of Amnon's crime against Tamar, which places that sad event at least something more than twenty years after David's first anointing at Hebron. Further, ten more years had now elapsed since that crime (II Sam. 13:38; 14:28; 15:7), which means a minimum at this point of more than thirty years. Lastly, we know that David lived a short while after Solomon's accession. These matters together suggest that Absalom's try for the throne may have been made about David's thirty-fifth year, and Adonijah's within two or three years following.

Adonijah's attempt to take the kingship was no doubt influenced by Absalom's. As David's fourth son, he was next in line should Absalom fail. With Absalom dead, and with no public announcement yet given by the king as to his choice of successor, Adonijah made his try (I Kings 1:5-9).[67] He assembled for himself "chariots and horsemen,

---

[66] Probably modern Tell Abil near recently-drained Lake Huleh. Called Abel-maim when later taken by Aramaeans (II Chron. 16:4).

[67] Though both Absalom and Adonijah clearly thought in terms of the eldest living son having right to the throne, neither believed that the king was thinking in these terms or else they would not have tried to seize the crown as they did.

and fifty men to run before him" even as Absalom had done, and also persuaded two key persons of David's official family, Joab and the high priest Abiathar, to support him.[68] When he believed the time was right, he assembled these and other less influential persons at the spring En-rogel, that he might be formally anointed.

But news of this clandestine gathering soon came to the attention of opposition forces, comprised principally of Nathan the prophet, Zadok the other high priest, Benaiah the leader of David's bodyguard in company with that guard, and the elite "mighty men" (I Kings 1:10, 38). These constituted a formidable group, which accounts for Adonijah's secrecy. Nathan, working through Solomon's mother, Bathsheba, took the lead in calling David's attention to the situation (I Kings 1:11-53). When so informed, David finally made his long-overdue announcement regarding Solomon to at least the small number gathered before him, and gave direction for the young man to be anointed immediately at the Spring of Gihon. When the people shouted at the moment of anointing, the sound carried as far as Adonijah's assembled group at En-rogel.[69] These in fright quickly dispersed. Adonijah then submitted to Solomon and civil strife was averted.

David spent the remaining short span of his reign in preparing both the new king and the people for the period of rule before them. He made public proclamation of Solomon's new position (I Chron. 28: 1-8); charged Solomon in turn with the weighty responsibilities that faced him (I Kings 2:1-9; I Chron. 28:9-10), involving especially the building of God's Temple (I Chron. 22:6-19; 28:11-21); and spoke parting encouragement and instruction to the people (I Chron. 29:1-22). Then he died "full of days, riches, and honor," and was buried in Jerusalem (I Kings 2:10-11; I Chron. 29:26-28).

F. ISRAEL'S GREATEST KING

David was Israel's greatest king. People looked back to his reign as the high point in their history. Jerusalem came to be thought of as the "city of David" (I Kings 2:10; 3:1; 8:1; Neh. 3:15), for it had been established by David and was the "city where David dwelt" (Isa. 29:1). He became the measure of righteousness for succeeding

[68] Joab, opportunist that he was, had at first favored Absalom. Now with David's favor being turned from him, he found it easy to follow Adonijah. The reason for Abiathar's action is not apparent, unless it was jealousy of Zadok who seemingly had taken the lead over him under David; this in view of Zadok's being mentioned first and also having charge of the Ark (II Sam. 8:17; 20:25; 15:24, 27, 29, 35, 36). He may have thought he could do better with Adonijah.

[69] En-rogel is about 2,000 feet south of Gihon and hidden from it by an intervening hill, thus near enough for this sound to have been heard without Adonijah's party having been able to see the anointing ceremony itself.

kings. It was for David's sake that God did not destroy Judah in times of serious sin (II Kings 8:19). Most important, the coming Messiah was to be the descendant of David. For this reason, Christ is called the "son of David" (Matt. 1:1), and the people praised Christ in His triumphal entry to Jerusalem with the words, "Hosanna to the son of David" (Matt. 21:9, 15).

Chapter Twelve

SOLOMON

I Kings 2:12–11:43; II Chronicles 1–9

A marked contrast existed between the kingships of Solomon and David, a contrast caused by the diverse backgrounds of the two rulers. David had been raised in the open, watching sheep, and later had experienced the rigors of a fugitive life. Solomon, however, had known only the ease of the palace, with its attendant luxuries. Accordingly, David became a king of action, aggressive and efficient, who could personally lead armies to victory. Solomon became a king of peace, happy to stay at home and content merely to retain the land his father had gained. David's court never grew larger than the requirements of his government, but Solomon's became lavish to suit his tastes. As a result, Solomon needed greater revenue than David, and he raised taxes accordingly. He also engaged more in foreign trade, showing adeptness, indeed, and enjoying marked success. David was more a man of the people; Solomon was a man of the court. More significant, David maintained a vibrant faith in God as a "man after God's own heart," while Solomon, though beginning well in spiritual devotion, failed to hold this basic relationship before God, fell into sinful ways, and finally came under God's censure.

A. ESTABLISHED AS KING (I Kings 2:12-46; 3:4-28;
II Chronicles 1:1-17)

1. *Consolidation of power (I Kings 2:12-46).* As long as the co-regency between Solomon and David continued, matters went smoothly between Solomon and those who had opposed him; but when David died, the situation changed. Adonijah initiated the change by requesting, through Bathsheba, the mother of Solomon, marriage to Abishag, a beautiful Shunammite girl who had ministered to David in his old age (I Kings 1:1-4). Solomon promptly refused and had this older brother killed for what he believed was a threat to his rule by this

request. Custom of the day required that a man's concubines should become a part of the inheritance of his heir (I Kings 2:22; cf. II Sam. 16:21). It is possible that Solomon's suspicions concerning his brother's true intentions were correct, for Adonijah believed that he held the favor of the people (I Kings 2:15), a condition essential if one is to usurp rulership.

With Adonijah removed as an opponent, Solomon turned to Adonijah's main supporters, Abiathar and Joab. He deposed Abiathar from his office as high priest, banishing him to his private land in Anathoth (I Kings 2:26-27). This left Zadok as sole high priest, solving the thorny problem David had avoided. This development carried ominous overtones for Joab, who now sought refuge for himself "at the horns of the altar,"[1] located at the tent David had erected for the Ark. Solomon, in turn, following his father's instruction (I Kings 2:5-6),[2] directed Benaiah, former chief of the guard under David, to kill Joab at the altar, since Joab refused to leave (I Kings 2:28-34). Thus this man received his due at last. He had killed both Abner and Amasa in his jealousy, while military commander himself; and now he was killed in turn by Benaiah, Solomon's selection to fill that position.

David also had instructed Solomon to take the life of Shimei, who had cursed David when he fled from Jerusalem at the time of Absalom's rebellion (I Kings 2:8-9). At first Solomon merely consigned the man to his home in Jerusalem,[3] but later he did take his life when Shimei left the city to recover two escaped servants (I Kings 2:36-46). If Shimei had been so opposed to David when David was weak, Solomon could know that likely he had not become a friend since; so he killed him in a further move to consolidate power. Solomon's opponents now had been removed, and he properly ceased from taking more lives. The kingdom was firmly established in his hand.

2. *Promise from God (I Kings 3:4-28; II Chronicles 1:1-17).* Shortly

---

[1] Joab here was acting on the basis of Ex. 21:13-14 but apparently only thinking in terms of his involvement in the recent plot. David's charge to Solomon to take his life, however, had been on the basis of his having killed Abner (II Sam. 3:27f) and Amasa (II Sam. 20:8f), which murders were beyond any safety the altar might afford.

[2] David's attitude toward Joab is difficult to assesss. When provoked so many times, why David had not punished the man long before causes one to wonder. One factor certainly was that Joab unquestionably was capable. Also, after the Uriah incident, David was under an embarassing obligation to him for having cooperated in putting this fine soldier in a deadly position. In this instruction to Solomon, he seems to have been taking an easy way out to bring the deserved punishment.

[3] Shimei is described as a man of the family of Saul (II Sam. 16:5), who apparently agitated in favor of a return to the former dynasty. By confining him to Jerusalem, Solomon thought to curtail any insurrection he might attempt.

after this, Solomon received an unsual token of God's favor (I Kings 3:5-15). Commendably recognizing the need of God's blessing, Solomon sacrificed "a thousand burnt offerings" at Gibeon where the tabernacle now stood.[4] Gibeon apparently was selected for this occasion of sacrifice, rather than David's tent in Jerusalem, because the altar there was no doubt larger and more suitable for the extensive sacrificing Solomon proposed.[5] While the king was there, God showed His pleasure by appearing to him in a dream by night,[6] inviting him to make a request. Solomon was pleased at this and humbly requested wisdom in his rule. In further approval, God indicated not only that this request would be granted, but promised Solomon in addition "riches and honor" to the extent that no person of his day would be like him. Solomon's later life portrayed the fulfillment of this gracious word from God. Thrilled at these promises, knowing besides that his opponents had been disposed of and having inherited an extensive and prosperous country from his father, Solomon truly had bright prospects for a happy, successful rule.

B. SOLOMON'S KINGDOM

1. *Defense measures.* A prominent feature in Solomon's manner of rule was effecting significant measures of defense. This was in keeping with his general interest of only maintaining the present boundaries of his country rather than expanding them. His major defense measure was the fortification of key cities which ringed Israel's heartland (I Kings 9:15-19). These were Hazor to the extreme north, Megiddo at the strategic north-south pass into the Esdraelon Valley, and Gezer, Beth-horon, and Baalath guarding the western approaches from Philistine territory. Tadmor[7] is also listed, but if identified with Palmyra, the famous trading center 175 miles northeast of Damascus, it cannot have been an inner defense center. It may have been an outer command point, however, to give early warning of enemy movement from the northeast. Troops quartered in the inner defense cities would have

---

[4] The Tabernacle had been moved from Nob (cf. *supra*, chap. 10, p. 254, n. 54) probably after Saul's tragic slaughter of the priests of Nob (I Sam. 22: 18-19).

[5] This is probably the significance of the phrase in I Kings 3:4, "for this was the great high place." The altar there was likely the great brazen altar still, prescribed by God, 7½ feet square and 4½ feet high (Ex. 27:1-8). David's altar likely was smaller.

[6] A type of dream-vision in which Solomon was awake and conscious to the extent of being able to formulate a rational response to the question posed.

[7] The Kethib reading in I Kings 9:18 is "Tamar." This, however, is not the best reading, in view of II Chron. 8:4 having Tadmor. If the same locality is not intended in both passages, a "Tamar" did exist south of the Dead Sea which would have been a logical defense post toward the south.

provided a wall of protection from foreign attack and could have moved quickly to put down attempts at revolution from within. In Jerusalem itself, Solomon built both a "wall"[8] and the "Millo"[9] to give added strength.

Another significant defense feature was Solomon's employment of the chariot, in which he differed from David (II Sam. 8:4).[10] Canaanites had used this weapon for years, and Solomon now followed their lead, assembling as many as 1,400 chariots and 12,000 horsemen, and maintaining 4,000 stables to house the horses (I Kings 10:26; II Chron. 9:25).[11] Besides Hazor, Gezer, and Megiddo[12] mentioned above, both Tanaach and Eglon[13] have also revealed, through excavation, strong defenses and chariot stables from this same time. To staff these cities with adequate military personnel and maintain such chariot forces, Solomon had to keep a large standing army, calling for enormous amounts of food and other provisions.

2. *Solomon's court.* Solomon's court was larger than David's. Two principal officials are listed besides those in David's government: one named Azariah, who was "over the officers" (*'al hannissabim*), likely meaning over the district officers; and one named Zabud who was a type of prime minister (*'al habbayith*). There were also additional minor officials: twelve who superintended districts (likely under the Azariah just named; I Kings 4:7-28) and as many as 550 supervisors of labor (I Kings 9:23).

Solomon's own family was large. If David felt the influence of other countries for maintaining a large harem, Solomon did more. His wives ultimately numbered 700 and his concubines 300 (I Kings 11:3). The

---

[8] From I Kings 11:27 we learn that David's wall still had a gap (*perets*) somewhere. Solomon probably closed it and added more wall to enclose the new Temple area within the city confines. It probably enclosed his palace too (I Kings 3:1).

[9] The Millo was existent in David's time (II Sam. 5:9), and apparently Solomon added to it. Hezekiah added still more when later fearing an Assyrian invasion (II Chron. 32:5). Its exact identity is uncertain, but clearly was related to defense, perhaps a tower or fortress. Cf. J. Simons, *Jerusalem in the Old Testament* (Leiden: E. J. Brill, 1952), pp. 116-17; 131-44.

[10] Cf. *supra*, chap. 11, p. 270, where David even destroyed enemy chariots rather than keeping them for himself. His fighting was much in the mountains, however, whereas these defense cities of Solomon were largly in flat areas where the chariot could be used.

[11] The 40,000 figure in I Kings 4:26 must be a scribal error in view of the 4,000 figure in II Chron. 9:25 and the fact that 1,400 chariots suggests 4,000 horses, not 40,000.

[12] Stables were found for 450 horses at Megiddo. Recently, however, Yadin has challenged the dating of these to Solomon, believing the time of Ahab more likely; cf. "New Light on Solomon's Megiddo," *BA*, 23 (1960), pp. 62-68.

[13] Cf. Albright, *AP*, pp. 124-25. On Hazor, cf. *supra*, chap. 5, pp. 100-101.

number of his children is not given but must have been sizable. All these ate at court expense. Solomon must have entertained lavishly besides, for his board bill was enormous. One day required no less than thirty *kor*[14] of fine flour, sixty *kor* of meal, ten fat cattle, twenty pasture-fed cattle, one hundred sheep, and other animals (I Kings 4: 22-23).

3. *Financial support.* Fortification of cities, support of a standing army, and provisions for a lavish court called for a very large revenue. Solomon's sources appear to have been of four types.

a. Taxation. There was a program of taxation for which purpose Solomon divided the country into twelve districts.[15] He assigned an officer over each as chief tax collector. Each district was to furnish provisions for the court for one month per year (I Kings 4:7-28). There was need for barley and straw to feed horses, as well as food for the people. Such a burden must have been oppressive and makes understandable the cry for relief given by the people, when Rehoboam later came to the throne (I Kings 12:3-4).

b. Labor conscriptions. Solomon maintained a program of labor conscription. The corvee was common in the ancient world, but it was always intensely disliked. David had used foreign labor, even having a minister of cabinet rank in charge of it toward the close of his reign (II Sam. 20:24), indicating that he came to depend greatly on this labor source. This, too, Solomon did, using large numbers of Canaanites still living in the country (I Kings 9:21-22). But he also resorted to conscription of Israelites themselves (I Kings 5:13). While building the Temple he sent 30,000 (10,000 per month) to Lebanon to help bring the cedar trees he needed. Men so conscripted simply worked for the government without pay, for the length of time designated.

c. Foreign tribute and gifts. A third source of revenue imposed no burden on the Israelites themselves. It consisted of tribute and gifts received from foreign countries. Details on the amounts are not supplied, but the indication is that many countries sent representatives with silver, gold, fine garments, valuable spices, and animals (I Kings 10: 24-25). The Queen of Sheba, whose visit is described at some length

[14] The *kor* or *homer* (same measure) was the largest capacity measure and was probably equal to 58.1 gallons liquid measure or 6¼ bushels dry; cf. R.B.Y. Scott, "Weights and Measures of the Bible," *BA*, 22 (1959), pp. 22-40.

[15] These did not always conform to old tribal boundaries, which may not mean that Solomon deliberately tried to break up old loyalties, but only to divide the country more in keeping with productivity, so that the load would be as equally borne as possible. However, people must have felt emotional alarm that old established lines were not observed.

(I Kings 10:1-13), brought one such gift of 120 talents[16] of gold besides large quantities of spices and precious stones.

d. Trade. Solomon devloped far-flung trade relationships, which also produced considerable revenue. One avenue of trade was through the Red Sea to the south. David's southern conquest had reached to the Gulf of Aqaba, making this sea route accessible. With the aid of Phoenician experts, Solomon constructed and provided crews for a fleet of ships leaving Ezion-geber at the tip of the Gulf (I Kings 9: 26-28; 10:11, 12, 22). The ships went as far as Ophir,[17] no doubt stopping at many ports enroute, for the trip took "three years"[18] (I Kings 10:22). The ships took copper from Solomon's mines near Ezion-geber[19] and returned with gold, silver, hardwood, precious stones, ivory, and animals.

To provide an adequate supply of copper, Solomon maintained an excellent refinery at Ezion-geber. This fact, not mentioned in the biblical record, has been brought to light by excavation.[20] The refinery is believed to have been one of the largest of the day, and probably was constructed by Solomon at the same time as his ships. A good supply of copper ore was available in the Arabah Valley between the Dead Sea and the Gulf.

Solomon also carried on trade involving horses and chariots. He not only purchased many for his own use, but he took advantage of his strategic position along north-south trade routes to buy and sell for others. He bought them mainly from Egypt and Kue (Cilicia),[21] and sold them to Hittites and Aramaeans (I Kings 10:28-29).

[16] The talent weighed about 30 kg, just over 66 pounds. With the present price of gold at $35 per ounce (troy), this makes each talent worth approximately $33,700; 120 talents, $4,044,000.

[17] The identity of Ophir is uncertain. Four sites are suggested: southwest Arabia, southeast Arabia, Somaliland, and Supara in India. In favor of the last is the long time of the journey, that all items imported are from India, and that trade is known to have existed that far away at the time. Albright, however, favors the third suggestion: cf. ARI, pp. 133-35.

[18] "Three years" means all of a middle year and at least some part of the prior and following years.

[19] Solomon's ships are called ships "of Tarshish" (I Kings 10:22). A tarshish was a refinery. Thus, the name of the fleet indicated that it was to carry refinery products; cf. Unger, AOT, pp. 225-26; Albright, BASOR, 83 (Oct., 1941), p. 21.

[20] Discovered by N. Glueck (1938-40); cf. The Other Side of the Jordan (New Haven: American Schools of Oriental Research, 1940), pp. 50-88.

[21] The Hebrew word, miqweh of I Kings 10:28 (translated "linen yarn" in KJV) is best taken in reference to the Asia Minor country, Kue, and so translated "from Kue." Horses were a comparatively late introduction to Egypt, though by Solomon's time they could have had sufficient stock for some export. Asia Minor

C. Foreign Relations

Because he inherited a land area of empire size and conducted such trading operations, Solomon's involvement in foreign affairs became extensive. A clear indication of this is his many marriages to foreign women. Marriages were common seals of foreign alliances. That he had wives of Moabites, Ammonites, Edomites, Zidonians, and Hittites (I Kings 11:1) suggests that he held alliances with all these people.

1. *Alliance with Egypt.* It is directly stated that Solomon made an alliance with Egypt, sealing it with his marriage to the Pharaoh's daughter (I Kings 3:1). Solomon no doubt considered this his most important treaty, for Egypt was a major world power. Indeed, that Solomon should have been so honored by this powerful southern neighbor signifies that he held high standing in the world of his day.[22] The alliance was one of his earlier ones, and the honor accorded by the Pharaoh really must be attributed more to David than Solomon. In keeping with the importance of the alliance, Solomon built a special house for the Egyptian bride (I Kings 7:8). Solomon also gained the city, Gezer,[23] through this marriage. The Pharaoh had previously seized Gezer, slaying its occupants, and now gave it to his daughter, Solomon's wife, as a present (I Kings 9:16). Solomon fortified it as a defense city.

2. *Alliance with Tyre.* Another important alliance was made with the Phoenician king, Hiram I (c. 978-944). Solomon's wife of the "Zidonians"[24] (I Kings 11:1) was likely a daughter of this ruler. Tyre, rebuilt by the Phoenicians in the twelfth century, was now capital of this maritime country, which controlled about 150 miles of the Mediterranean coastline north of the Bay of Acre. Phoenicia held colonies at many points around the Mediterranean, and her trade with them and other countries was widely known. Solomon was particularly interested in her cedar, for which he was willing to trade wheat and

is known to have had fine horses. Egypt had fine chariots, introduced apparently by the Hyksos. For discussion, cf. Albright, *ARI*, pp. 135-36.

[22] At one time Egyptian Pharaohs did not give their daughters even to kings of Babylon or of Mitanni. However, Egypt had slipped in world position by this time. The Pharaoh involved would have been one of the last of the Twenty-first Dynasty.

[23] I Kings 9:16 states that Pharaoh burned Gezer at this time, and it is archaeologically questionable if Gezer here suffered this form of destruction. Some believe that a textual error has crept into the text and that it should read "Gerar." It is also possible that Gezer was already in Israel's hand at this time in view of David's victories in the Philistine area. Cf. Albright, *ARI*, pp. 213f.

[24] The Zidonians were principally inhabitants of Zidon (Sidon), but the term came to be used for Phoenicians generally. Tyre and Zidon were the two principal cities of Phoenicia, with Zidon the older. Tyre, however, had by this time become the more important and the residence of the king. Cf. I Kings 16:31.

fine oil (I Kings 5:2-11). Hiram had already supplied cedar to David in anticipation of the Temple, and now was pleased to continue this with Solomon. He also loaned Solomon 120 talents of gold (I Kings 9:10-14), which indicates that Solomon did not have enough revenue to do all he wished, even though his sources were extensive. At the end of twenty years, when the Temple and other buildings had been completed, Solomon sought to repay Hiram (probably as the completion of these payments) for both the cedar and gold by giving him twenty cities, presumably located near Phoenicia. However, Hiram was not happy with the cities, for apparently they were poor; and he voiced displeasure to Solomon and returned them (I Kings 9:12, 13; II Chron. 8:2). The form Solomon's repayment then took is not stated. At least the incident did not disrupt the treaty between the two countries, for Hiram joined Solomon in the maritime venture from Ezion-geber, already noticed, sometime later. It may be, indeed, that this joint enterprise involved Solomon's repayment; Hiram perhaps receiving a major part of the proceeds for some time.

3. *Visit of the Queen of Sheba (I Kings 10:1-13; II Chronicles 9: 1-12)* Among Solomon's distinguished visitors from foreign lands was a Sabean queen from the southern tip of Arabia, the land of Sheba. This country is roughly identified with the modern state of Yemen.[25] Solomon's ships had likely been stopping at ports of this land. In fact, the Queen's long, arduous journey (some 1,200 miles) may have been motivated in part by mercantile advantages that she saw in personal confrontation with the one who had sent the ships. Southwestern Arabia was well known for trade in spice and incense, and this queen may have felt that her business by caravan route was jeopardized by Solomon's merchant fleet.[26] She came also, as she says, to see Solomon himself, having heard, probably from sailors of the ships, concerning his great wealth and wisdom. She brought a large gift to Solomon of 120 talents of gold, was duly impressed with what she saw at his luxurious court, received in turn all that she desired (perhaps including trade agreements) along with a large gift, and returned satisfied to her country. Significantly, I Kings 10:15 states that part of Solomon's revenue from trading came from spice merchants of the kings of Arabia, indicating that, whatever agreements may have been made with the queen, Solomon continued with his trade in the area.[27]

[25] Regarding Sabean settlement, cf. Albright, *ARI*, pp. 132-35. Modern explorations in Yemen are described by W. Philips, *Qataban and Sheba* (New York: Harcourt, Brace and Co., 1955).

[26] On Sabean trade, cf. Albright, *op. cit.*

[27] A clay stamp from South Arabia was found at Bethel by James Kelso. It dates about the time of Solomon, and shows that trade was existent at the time.

D. BUILDING ACTIVITY (I Kings 5:1–9:9; II Chronicles 2–7)

Besides fortifying defense cities and constructing one of the world's fine copper refineries, Solomon erected several splendid buildings in Jerusalem, the most important of which was the Temple.

1. *Building the Temple (I Kings 5–6; 7:15-51; II Chronicles 2–4).* As noted in the previous chapter, David had wanted to build the Temple, but he was forbidden by God. He did gather extensive material for it, however (I Chron. 22:1-5; 14–16),[28] and also passed along to Solomon written plans which had been revealed to him by the Spirit of God for the structure (I Chron. 28:11, 12, 19).

It has been noted that Solomon contracted with Hiram of Tyre for cedar wood and supplied a levy of 10,000 workers per month to assist in cutting and transporting it. Cedar was considered a fine wood for such building.[29] Hiram took responsibility for conveying the logs by sea to a Palestinian port of Solomon's choosing. He also supplied stonecutters to help prepare the great quantity of stone needed (I Kings 5:18).

Actual building began in the spring of Solomon's fourth year (c. 966 B.C.; I Kings 6:1), and was completed seven years later in the fall (I Kings 6:38). The location was on Mt. Moriah (II Chron. 3:1), the site of Araunah's threshing floor where the plague had stopped in David's day (II Sam. 24:16-25), and most likely the place where Abraham long before had been commanded to sacrifice Isaac (Gen. 22:2). Mt. Moriah was immediately adjacent to David's city on the north.

The plan of the Temple proper called for a building similar to the Tabernacle, but twice the size.[30] It was ninety feet long and thirty feet wide, containing the same two divisions: the Holy Place and the Holy of Holies, occupying two-thirds and one-third of the total respectively. It was built of stone, but paneled with cedar overlaid with gold. The Holy of Holies housed the Ark of the Covenant with its mercy seat and two cherubim. Two additional[31] cherubim were of carved olive

The stamp was originally about 3x4 inches and probably was used to seal bags of cargo. Cf. G. W. VanBeek and A. Jamme, "An Inscribed South Arabian Clay Stamp from Bethel," *BASOR,* 151 (Oct., 1958), pp. 9-16.

[28] The amount David gathered in gold and silver is described as 100,000 talents of gold and 1,000,000 talents of silver. At $35 an ounce (cf. *supra,* n. 16), the gold alone would have been worth $2,780,000,000.

[29] Gudea (c. 2100 B.C.), ruler of Lagash, had acquired cedar from this region already in his day. The Egyptian Wenamon came to Lebanon for cedar for Egypt (c. 1100 B.C.); cf. Barton, *AB,* pp. 449f, 455.

[30] This plan finds close parallel with a temple at Tell Tainat of northern Syria unearthed in 1936. More recently, one discovered at Hazor also bears marked resemblance; cf. Yadin, *BA,* 22 (1959), pp. 3f.

[31] Since the two cherubim of the mercy seat were made of one piece with it (Ex. 25:18-19), these two large cherubim were additional.

wood overlaid with gold and stood fifteen feet high (I Kings 6:23-28; II Chron. 3:10-13). In the Holy Place were the altar of incense or "golden altar" (I Kings 7:48; II Chron. 4:19), ten golden lampstands standing five on each side (I Kings 7:49; II Chron. 4:7), and ten tables of showbread (I Kings 7:48; II Chron. 4:8). A difference from the Tabernacle existed in that before the Holy Place was a porch thirty feet wide and ten feet deep, and on the porch two bronze pillars called Jachin and Boaz (I Kings 7:15-21).[32]

Along the sides and rear of this structure were chambers, three stories high, providing storage area (I Kings 6:5-10). Around the whole building lay a court similar to that which surrounded the Tabernacle. Found in it were the great brazen altar, thirty feet square and fifteen feet high (II Chron. 4:1), a large laver or "molten sea" fifteen feet across the brim (I Kings 7:23-26), and ten small lavers located five on each side of the building. This court, as well as the Temple proper, was restricted to the priests, but around it was the "great court" (II Chron. 4:9) intended for the people.

2. *Dedicating the Temple (I Kings 8:1–9:9; II Chronicles 5–7)*. A building of this grandeur and significance called for appropriate dedication ceremonies. Solomon first had the all-important Ark of the Covenant brought from the tent David had made and placed in the Holy of Holies. Other articles of furniture might be newly made, but not this one. Since it was the same Ark constructed earlier at Mt. Sinai in the time of Moses, it had represented God's presence in the Tabernacle and would continue to do so in the Temple. Significantly, when it was placed in its assigned location, the "cloud" of God's glory filled the building (I Kings 8:1-11; II Chron. 5:1-14), even as it had the Tabernacle. Then Solomon preached a brief sermon to those gathered (I Kings 8:12-21; II Chron. 6:1-11), after which he offered a longer prayer of dedication (I Kings 8:22-53; II Chron. 6:12-42). When he finished, miraculous fire fell from heaven to ignite the burnt-offering placed on the brazen altar (II Chron. 7:1-3).[33] Then Solomon continued with other sacrifices until the enormous total of 22,000 oxen and 120,000 sheep had been offered, during seven days of celebration (I Kings 8:

[32] These pillars seem to have been free standing, being described only as "before the temple" (II Chron. 3:17). They were each 24 feet high, counting their capitals which were topped with "bowls" (*gulloth*). Their names, Joachin and Boaz, may have been the first words in sayings ascribed to them. *Jachin* would fit such a saying as "Yahweh will establish (*yakin*) thy throne forever"; *Boaz* in "In the strength (*beoz*) of Yahweh shall the king rejoice." For discussion of parallels, cf. Albright, *ARI*, pp. 144-48.

[33] Cf. *supra*, chap. 7, p. 153 as to miraculous fire in connection with the Tabernacle. Other instances of special fire from God are recorded in Judg. 6:21; I Kings 18:38; I Chron. 21:26.

62-66; II Chron. 7:4-11).[34] Following this, God showed His favor by appearing to Solomon a second time, once more promising blessing if Solomon would obey God's commandments as David his father had done (I Kings 9:1-9; II Chron. 7:12-22).

3. *Other fine buildings (I Kings 7:1-12)*. Solomon erected several other buildings as well, probably locating them near the Temple in the new part of the city now being added. One of them was his personal residence, the palace. It must have been an elegant structure, for it took thirteen years to build, even six years longer than the Temple. Another was the "House of the Forest of Lebanon," perhaps so named because it was supported by rows of cedar pillars. It was used at least in part to store arms (I Kings 10:16-17; Isa. 22:8). A third was the "Hall of the Pillars," perhaps a sort of splendid passage-building, lined with pillars, between the "House of the Forest of Lebanon" and a fourth building, the "Hall of Judgment." In this last structure, Solomon sat for judgment on a six-step throne of ivory overlaid with gold (I Kings 10:18-20). Next came Solomon's own palace, probably joined to the "Hall of Judgment" for ease of access. Last was the special house made for Solomon's honored wife, the daughter of Pharaoh. The Temple was built first and then these other buildings later, during the thirteen years ascribed for the palace construction, for a total of twenty years (I Kings 9:10). Apparently Hiram continued to help with material, workmen, and gold for all this time, with Solomon then granting in partial payment the twenty cities which, as noticed, were refused.

E. LITERARY AGE

The time of David and Solomon is commonly called Israel's "golden literary age." David had marked ability in fine arts, and Solomon followed him in skill as a writer. Their common interest, in turn, encouraged others to develop like talents. It was a day which lent itself to artistic expression: a day of optimism and prosperity, a day of importance for Israel as a world member, a day of sufficient wealth to give time for leisure and reflection, and especially a day when stress lay on true worship of God.[35]

1. *Historical writing*. The age saw works of history produced. Both David and Solomon had official court scribes, and from their formal records histories of the reigns of both kings were written. Nathan the prophet wrote one which covered the rule of both David (I Chron.

---

[34] Solomon of course did not offer these sacrifices himself. But with the numerous priests and Levites on hand, and likely additional altars temporarily placed conveniently near for this special time, the number of animals indicated could have been offered in the seven days reported.

[35] True worship continued for all David's reign and half or more of Solomon's.

29:29) and Solomon (II Chron. 9:29). Gad, his counterpart, wrote one which covered the reign of David alone (I Chron. 29:29). The history of Solomon given in I Kings seems to have been taken mainly from "the book of the acts of Solomon," whose author is not identified (I Kings 11:41). The prophets Ahijah and Iddo, both of whom continued to live after Solomon, wrote histories which included accounts of his reign (II Chron. 9:29).

2. *Music and psalmody.* Besides history, music and psalmody were written. David, in anticipation of the day when the Temple would be built, gave specific instructions regarding music in worship. Some 4,000 Levites were designated as "singers," and they were divided into twenty-four courses to serve for a week at a time.[36] Instruments were to be played, including lyres, harps, and cymbals (I Chron. 25:1-6), and David designated 288 "singers" to join in a choir (I Chron. 25:7). David himself wrote seventy-three psalms, some of which were to be used in Temple service. He appointed Asaph as chief of choral worship (I Chron. 16:4-5), and this man in turn penned twelve psalms. The sons of Korah seem to have been a particular singing group from the Levites, and ten psalms are ascribed to them, either as authors or performers (cf. I Chron. 6:31f). Ethan and Heman, two men compared for wisdom with Solomon (I Kings 4:31), are credited with one psalm each, and Solomon is ascribed two. It is clear that Solomon, upon completing the Temple, in no way lessened the place of music in service, and may have stressed it even more (II Chron. 5:12-13; 9:11).

3. *Wisdom and dramatic literature.* Thirdly, wisdom and dramatic literature was produced. Some of the psalms are to be classed as wisdom literature, but the finest Old Testament examples are the books of Proverbs and Ecclesiastes. Solomon wrote all of the latter and most of the former.[37] The book of Job too, falls under this classification, but may have been written earlier.[38] Solomon also wrote the Song of Solomon, classed as semi-drama. In summary, most of the third division of the Hebrew Bible, called the "writings" (*Kethubim*), came from this golden age of literature.

[36] Cf. *supra*, chap. 11, pp. 275-76.

[37] Solomon himself excelled in wisdom, of course, and would have encouraged this quality in others. He spoke 3,000 proverbs and composed 1,005 songs, including as subject matter items pertaining to trees, hyssop, beasts, birds, creeping things, and fish (I Kings 4:32-33). Prov. 1-24 is directly ascribed to him (1:1; 10:1) and 25-29 are also, though said to have been compiled by Hezekiah's people. Only 30-31 are given to others namely Agur and Lemuel.

[38] A problem regarding its historical accuracy (in view of its detailed conversational content) arises if written in Solomon's time. It may have come from the hand of Job himself.

F. SPIRITUAL DECLINE AND PUNISHMENT (I Kings 11; II Chronicles 9:29-31)

1. *The decline (I Kings 11:1-8).* Solomon was capable as a king. The country continued strong and prosperous during his rule. For the most part the empire remained intact. The people had never had such a good life as during the reigns of both David and Solomon; though taxes continued to rise which produced dissatisfaction by the close of Solomon's rule.

Religiously, however, Solomon brought upon himself the disfavor of God. He had started well. Divine approval had been uniquely signified by Yahweh's promise of wisdom, riches, and honor. But change came. Solomon did not remain faithful to his early religious commitments. He compromised the fine convictions he had expressed in his prayer at the Temple dedication. When he experienced this spiritual decline himself, his country was influenced as well.

A principal reason for this sad development is found in Solomon's international affairs and the resulting effect upon him. He permitted the thinking and customs of other nations to influence his decisions and manner of living. This situation developed especially as a result of his marriages to foreign women. These marriages, supposedly routine seals of beneficial alliances, became far more than that for Solomon; for the wives "turned away his heart after other gods." The extent of his defection is indicated by the notice that he built a "high place" (*bamah*) to "Chemosh the abomination of Moab," and to "Molech the abomination of the children of Ammon," and apparently also to the false gods "of all his foreign wives" (I Kings 11:7-8).

It is not clear at what point in Solomon's reign this defection began seriously to show itself. No signs of it are evident at the completion of the Temple, eleven years after his inauguration, when he offered his grand sermon and prayer. It may be presumed to have come gradually and perhaps after the midpoint of his reign, when the bad influence of his foreign wives and contacts could have had time to work. Commendably, however, prior to his death Solomon did realize what had happened and turned back to God, as evidenced in his final book, Ecclesiastes, where he concludes that the "whole duty of man" is to "fear God, and keep his commandments" (12:13).

2. *The punishment (I Kings 11:9-43).* Solomon had been warned by God early in his reign against such defection (I Kings 3:14; 9:4-9). Accordingly, divine disapproval was now shown, for God told him that most of his kingdom would be ruled by someone other than his son. Also, during Solomon's reign, three problem areas developed which are described as punishments from God.

a. Jeroboam (I Kings 11:26-40). The first concerned Jeroboam, who later came to be the first king of the northern domain of Israel. Evidently a capable man, Jeroboam had been placed in charge of the work-force from the northern tribes building the Millo for Solomon. One day, when on leave, he was met by Ahijah the prophet who tore his new garment symbolically into twelve parts and gave Jeroboam ten. He explained that these ten pieces represented ten tribes over which Jeroboam would rule when Solomon was dead. He told him the reason for this punishment being meted out to Solomon, and promised Jeroboam rich blessing on his own reign if he would avoid similar defection. Solomon somehow learned of Ahijah's words to Jeroboam, perhaps through an indiscretion of the young man, and immediately sought to take Jeroboam's life, much in the pattern of Saul with David years earlier. But Jeroboam fled, also as David, though in this instance he fled all the way to Egypt, and was given protection by Pharaoh Shishak (Sheshonq I, 940-920). From Egypt Jeroboam eventually returned to Israel after Solomon's death to assume the rule over the northern ten tribes.

b. Hadad of Edom (I Kings 11:14-22). The second problem area concerned Hadad of Edom, whose activity served to diminish Solomon's control over the empire in the south. Hadad had been the sole survivor of the royal family in Edom, at the time of Joab's great slaughter there during David's reign.[39] He had sought asylum in Egypt, as Jeroboam did later. On learning that David and Joab were dead, he returned to Edom and probably became head of his country, which was under Solomon's jurisdiction as a province. But Hadad was a bitter enemy of Israel, remembering Joab's atrocities, and made continual trouble for Solomon. He probably did not succeed in actually removing Edom from Israelite jurisdiction, for Solomon's copper and maritime operations from Ezion-geber apparently continued for all his reign; but certainly he put forth a strong effort to this end and did cause serious difficulty for Solomon's interests. No doubt Hadad's opposition grew greater in Solomon's latter days as God's favor came to be increasingly withdrawn.

c. Rezon of Damascus (I Kings 11:23-25). The third problem area concerned Rezon of Damascus, who served to lessen Solomon's control over the empire in the north. Rezon had been a supporter of Hadadezer, king of Zobah, whom David had defeated early in his reign (II Sam. 8:3-9). Rezon apparently had escaped unharmed from that battle and then formed a small army of his own to further his personal desire for power. His main prize was Damascus, and he succeeded in

[39] *Supra*, chap. 11, p. 270, n. 32.

becoming ruler there. Damascus had not been particularly strong as a center of power before this, but he made it so. He clearly was capable as a military figure and gathered an efficient force behind him. He gradually increased the position and influence of his new center and thus was able to cause serious trouble for Solomon. No indication is given, however, that he was able actually to remove Damascus from provincial status, while Solomon reigned. Indeed, the fact that Solomon saw fit to invest in construction at Tadmor (Palmyra; I Kings 9:18), still far north of Damascus, is quite out of keeping with the idea; though this building activity may have been carried out quite early in Solomon's reign, when Rezon's threat had not yet developed. Toward the close of Solomon's rule, however, this man did create severe opposition to Israel, again in keeping with God's favor being increasingly withdrawn from Solomon. It may be that effective control by Solomon in both Edom and the Damascus region was all but lost by the time of his death.

G. SOLOMON THE KING

Solomon's rule was long, lasting forty years (970-931), as that of David his father. It was a rule of prosperity and peace, and it was a time of genuine accomplishment. Israel became known through all the Near East as a result of extensive building, trading, and international relations. Beside this, the arts were advanced, particularly music and literature. Further, true worship of God at the new Temple assumed a form and dignity in keeping with the regulations of Moses' Law. All this can be said to Solomon's credit. He stands as one of Israel's fine rulers.

However, he could have stood much higher had he remained faithful to God. Few rulers have had greater opportunity or prospects. He had an empire by inheritance, and he had God's particular promise of wisdom, riches, and honor. All the hard work of consolidation and enlargement of country to empire size had been done by David. With excellent groundwork laid and attractive possibilities ahead, Solomon had only to continue his father's efforts to witness the finest of achievements. The greater world powers were not at this time in a position to give him great opposition either. The place Israel might have achieved in world affairs was most significant. But Solomon failed to meet God's standard. He did not remain faithful to God's will and way. Consequently, this great potential for Israel was not realized; but instead there came a gradual diminishing of world position in Solomon's last years. In fact, he had to be informed before his death that only a small part of his realm would be passed on to his son. As he died, he must have felt deep regret that he had not remained faithful, as God had instructed him early in his reign.

CHAPTER THIRTEEN

THE NORTHERN KINGDOM

I Kings 12–22; II Kings 1–17

The division of kingdom that God predicted to Jeroboam through Ahijah had a background in the history thus far studied. The tribes of Judah and Ephraim had been mutually jealous since the days of Egypt. Judah was the largest, and had been honored with the lead position as the tribes moved through the wilderness. Ephraim, in contrast, was one of the smaller tribes,[1] but had descended from Joseph and had been given precedence over Manasseh by Jacob. Also the great leader, Joshua, had been of her number. Ephraim had displayed her sense of importance twice during the Judges Period: once to Gideon (Judg. 8:1-3) and later to Jephthah (Judg. 12:1-6), complaining each time that she had not been properly recognized in doing battle with the enemy.

At the founding of the monarchy the existence of this basic cleavage was recognized in God's choice of Israel's first king from small Benjamin, located between these two rival tribes. The split was accented after Saul's death, when only Judah crowned David and the northern tribes turned to Ishbosheth. It also showed itself following Absalom's rebellion and David's return to rule, when the northern tribes once more went their own way, led by Sheba of Benjamin, though this time only for a few days (II Sam. 19:41–20:22). What Ahijah predicted and what Solomon feared in causing Jeroboam to flee to Egypt, then, was only a new outbreak of an old condition. In view of this, any king coming to Israel's throne should have been careful not to give cause for a new instance of division, especially when discontent already existed, as was true at Solomon's death. Rehoboam, Solomon's son, however, did not exercise this manner of care and so did experience the final cleavage.

---

[1] In the wilderness, the number of Ephraim fell from 40,500 to 32,500 (Num. 1:33; 26:37) making her then larger only than Simeon. In contrast, Judah grew from 74,600 to 76,500 (Num. 1:27; 26:22).

A. THE REVOLT (I Kings 12:1-24; II Chronicles 10)

That Rehoboam was in a measure aware of the difficult situation facing him is indicated by his willingness to go to Shechem to meet with the leaders of the northern tribes. If things had been normal, they would have come to him at Jerusalem, the capital, for the inaugural ceremonies. Shechem was selected now, no doubt, because it was central ground for the discontented tribes, and because of its historical significance.[2] To the meeting, too, came Jeroboam, returning from his place of refuge in Egypt. Apparently he had been summoned by the northern tribes, who somehow had learned of Ahijah's anointing and Solomon's revenge. He was now received by them as their champion to lead in negotiations.

The assembled tribes knew what they wanted from Rehoboam, if they were to accept him as king. Solomon's heavy load of taxation and labor conscription should be reduced. They had suffered long enough and were committed to forcing a change. The demand was voiced, apparently by Jeroboam, and then Rehoboam sought counsel as to how he should respond. He turned first to older men, who had lived through Solomon's harsh years, and later to those his own age. The younger men, no doubt wanting to enjoy a continuing lavish court, counseled refusal, and Rehoboam listened. The ten tribes immediately seceded from the kingdom and set about establishing their own, making Jeroboam the first king, as Ahijah had predicted.

While still at Shechem, Rehoboam made an effort to continue his authority over the North by sending his chief tax collector, Adoram, to demand tax money from the people; but the man was stoned to death for his effort. Rehoboam wisely and hastily then retreated to the safety of Jerusalem. There he assembled an army of 180,000 from his two tribes, Judah and Benjamin,[3] determined still to force his will on the rebels. God, however, through the prophet Shemaiah, forbade the action and Rehoboam properly desisted. The schism would continue, as God had predicted through Ahijah, and Rehoboam would have to be content with ruling only two tribes.

B. THE EARLY YEARS (931–885; I Kings 12:25–16:20)

1. *Jeroboam as king (931–910; I Kings 12:25–14:20)*

a. The new kingdom. As Jeroboam took over as first ruler of the new ten-tribe nation of Israel, he had the challenging task of establishing a new kingdom. It would be interesting to know what steps he

---

[2] *Supra*, chap. 3, p. 49, n. 12; and chap. 8, p. 178, n. 36.

[3] Few of these would have been from Benjamin at this time. Likely Benjamin, which historically had aligned itself with the northern bloc of tribes, only gradually came under Rehoboam's control; cf. *infra*, chap. 14, pp. 335-37.

took to do so, and what the nature of the administration was; but of neither is any information given. A working government was put into operation, however; and it surely took careful thinking and diligent labor on his part, demonstrating that he was a capable person. It is to be presumed that he followed the familiar patterns which had been developed by David and Solomon. In view of the demands made to Rehoboam by the people, we may believe that he tried to keep taxes at a minimum and no doubt avoided labor conscription entirely.

The capital was established initially at Shechem, the place of the meeting with Rehoboam (I Kings 12:25). Since Jeroboam soon directed building activity also at Penuel, across the Jordan on the Jabbok River, he may have had this as an alternate residence. However, he eventually established his permanent capital at Tirzah (I Kings 14:17; 15:21, 33; 16:6, 8, 9; etc.), thought to be modern Tell el-Farah,[4] about six miles northeast of Shechem.

b. Substitute worship. Religiously, Jeroboam committed gross sin in the sight of God by establishing a substitute worship for his northern people (I Kings 12:26-33). He reasoned that if he did not do this the people, in returning to Jerusalem to worship, would be attracted toward a reunion of the two countries. He established new worship centers at Dan in the far North and Bethel in the South.[5] As symbols for the new program, he erected gold images of calves at each center. The intent was still to worship Yahweh, but in a new way.[6] He built a temple ("house of high places"), presumably to house the image and an altar (I Kings 12:31, 33) at each center, and appointed priests of the common people (non-Levites) to serve them. One reason for not using Levites, as required in the Mosaic Law, was that many of them, perhaps most, had left for Judah, evidently in rebellion at these innovations (II Chron. 11:13-14). Jeroboam further made provision for an annual feast, substituting it for the legal Feast of Tabernacles, setting its time of observance just one month later.

2. *Jeroboam rebuked and punished (I Kings 13:1–14:18).* These

---

[4] For discussion of excavation, cf. R. De Vaux, *RB*, 1947-52.

[5] Bethel was located just north of the Benjamite boundary (Josh. 18:13) and so near Judah's territory that Abijam, successor to Rehoboam as king in Judah, was able to take control of it at one time during Jeroboam's reign (II Chron. 13:19). Jeroboam then may have wished he had not placed this center so far south.

[6] Jeroboam apparently wished to parallel the Jerusalem worship of Yahweh in an effort not to offend Jerusalem sympathizers more than necessary. Accordingly, Albright believes these calves were not intended as representatives of Yahweh but only animals on which the people were to think of Yahweh standing in invisible form, a manner of thinking common to Canaanites in reference to Baal or Hadad; cf. Albright, *FSAC*, pp. 203, 229.

acts of Jeroboam constituted a serious offense in the sight of God. They were in direct violation of His Law through Moses, and they introduced a potential syncretism of true worship with the fertility cult of Baal. Without question, Jeroboam's innovation made the later introduction of Baal worship into the land under Ahab and Jezebel (I Kings 16:30-33) much easier. For Canaanites, too, made calves in connection with their religious exercises, thinking of Baal or Hadad as standing on their backs.[7]

Accordingly, God soon sent a messenger to bring, rebuke to Jeroboam. Called merely "a man of God," the messenger came north from Judah, spoke against the Bethel altar, and predicted that a prince of the rival house of David, Josiah by name,[8] would one day burn the bones of Jeroboam's priests upon it (I Kings 13:1-3; II Kings 23:15-16). Jeroboam, angry at the warning, pointed his hand at the messenger and ordered nearby attendants to seize him, but miraculously his hand "dried up." Jeroboam then besought the messenger to ask God to restore it, which the messenger did; and God made the hand well again. The incident must have caused Jeroboam to rethink his program, but no indication is given that he made any changes.

Later, through Jeroboam's wife, Ahijah the prophet spoke against this false worship (I Kings 14:1-18). The queen had come to Ahijah disguised to inquire if her son would recover from a serious illness. Ahijah, told by God beforehand that she would do so, took the occasion not only to inform her that the boy would die, but also to denounce the royal family for its gross sin and predict the destruction of the entire household. Jeroboam, in sending his wife to inquire of the prophet, had thought that because Ahijah had favored him once in predicting his rule, he would do so again. He discovered, however, that God's prophets are not in the business of courting royal favor but of proclaiming God's truth whatever the effect might be. The child did die, as Ahijah foretold, and the entire family was destroyed later by a successor, Baasha.

3. *Loss of territory.* Jeroboam did not fare well either in maintaining all the land that he had received on becoming king. It may be assumed that the entire area Solomon had controlled, apart from that retained by Judah, came under his jurisdiction at the inauguration. If it did, significant sections were lost during the early reigns of Israelite kings, and much during that of Jeroboam. One such section was in the North, the Damascus region. Substantial loss in degree of control

[7] For pictures of gods so represented standing on the backs of animals, cf. *ANEP*, figs. 500, 501, 522, 534, 537.

[8] One of the remarkable "name" prophecies of the Old Testament, made here nearly three centuries before the man named began to rule.

had occurred there already while Solomon reigned, because of the vigorous opposition of Rezon. But during Jeroboam's rule, the region itself was lost; a matter known from the fact that, when Rezon died, he left Damascus as capital of an independent Aramaean state.[9] Another section was in the Southwest, where the Philistines now became active again, reclaiming some of their lost territory. Nadab, Jeroboam's son and successor, found it necessary to try and regain Gibbethon from them in his reign, though without success (I Kings 15:27). In the East, at least Moab was lost, for the Moabite Stone[10] records her reconquest by Omri, Israel's sixth king.

Besides loss of such territories, Jeroboam's country suffered at least one serious invasion by a foreign enemy into its heartland. This came at the hands of Shishak (Sheshonq I), king of Egypt, who had earlier given asylum to Jeroboam when he fled from Solomon. Now, however, after first effecting severe loss on Judah to the south, Shishak marched into and through Jeroboam's territory, inflicting widespread destruction of life and property.[11]

4. *Jeroboam's death (I Kings 14:19-20; II Chronicles 13:20).* Jeroboam himself did not die at the hand of an assassin, an aspect of God's punishment which was reserved for his son, Nadab. Jeroboam died a natural death after twenty-two years of rule. He had shown ability but forfeited God's blessing because of sin. He gave the new country its start, but he fell short of moving it on to being a strong, vigorous state. Indeed, he left the country with seeds of discontent which were to sprout in royal assassinations, rapid succession of kings, and serious weakness of rule.

5. *Nadab (910–909; I Kings 15:25-31).* Nadab[12] succeeded his father, reigning at Tirzah two years. His only recorded endeavor was his siege of Gibbethon[13] in Philistine territory, noted above. While maintaining this siege, he was assassinated by one of humble origin (I Kings 15:27-28), Baasha, who then ruled in his stead. Baasha pro-

---

[9] For evidence, and general discussion of Aramaean history at this time, cf. M. Unger, *Israel and the Aramaeans of Damascus* (London: James Clarke & Co., Ltd., 1957), pp. 38-57. Unger believes that this Rezon was likely the Hezion of I Kings 15:18, who is listed also on the votive stele of Benhadad I.

[10] Cf. *infra*, p. 309.

[11] For discussion of this invasion, cf. *infra*, chap. 14, pp. 339-40.

[12] Nadab may have been Jeroboam's second son, depending on whether Abijah, who died of illness, was the eldest or not. This is not made clear, but is likely.

[13] Gibbethon is best identified with modern Tell el-Melat, three miles east of 'Aqir (likely Ekron) and three miles west of Gezer. Though small in area, it must have been considered important; for 26 years later Omri, then general under King Elah, besieged it again (I Kings 16:15-17). Cf. J. Simons, *GTT*, pp. 201, 337, 359, 510.

ceeded to destroy all the house of Jeroboam according to Ahijah's prediction.

Religiously, Nadab followed in the footsteps of his father. Particularly he is said to have continued in the sin "wherewith" his father "made Israel to sin" (I Kings 15:26). This descriptive phrase, repeated with variations in respect to most of Jeroboam's eighteen successors (cf. I Kings 15:34; 16:19, 26, 31; 22:52; etc.), refers to the sin of worship at the golden calf centers. All eighteen continued this substitute form of worship, and God held it against each as serious sin.

6. *Baasha (909–886; I Kings 15:32–16:7; II Chronicles 16:1-6).* Baasha ruled for a long period, twenty-four years. Little, however, is recorded of his reign except that he continued in conflict with Judah to the south. One particular episode is described. Baasha sought to fortify Ramah, just four miles north of Jerusalem and well within Benjamite territory. His intention was to control north-south traffic above Judah's capital, clearly a tactic more economic than military. Asa, king of Judah, retaliated by persuading Benhadad I (c. 896-874), king of the rising Aramaean power at Damascus, to attack Baasha's northern cities. Benhadad did so, likely not needing much excuse, and Baasha had to cease his efforts at Ramah to protect his own land. The degree of Benhadad's success against him at this time is not indicated. At least Baasha was not able to accomplish all that he had intended against Judah.

Religiously, Baasha continued in the way of his two predecessors and accordingly was warned through Jehu, the prophet, that his house would suffer a fate similar to that of the house of Jeroboam (I Kings 16:1-7).

7. *Elah and Zimri (886–885; I Kings 16:8-22).* Elah succeeded his father and ruled two years. The Philistine city Gibbethon was attractive also to him, and he sent his general, Omri, to lay siege to it once more. While Omri was there, Zimri, another military figure, conspired against and killed Elah. Zimri proceeded to destroy all the house of Baasha, according to Jehu's words, and proclaimed himself king. Meanwhile Omri, at Gibbethon, learning of the assassination, had himself declared king by his army and returned to Tirzah to put down Zimri's rebellion. This was accomplished, and Zimri committed suicide, burning the palace over him, after a rule of only seven days.

With Zimri dead, Omri's claim to the throne was still not unchallenged, however. A certain Tibni, otherwise unknown, was now set up as ruler by a part of Israel. A divided rule existed during four years,[14]

[14] Omri ruled 12 years (I Kings 16:23), from Asa's 27th (I Kings 16:15) to Asa's thirty-eighth year (I Kings 16:29). The notice of his beginning to reign in Asa's thirty-first year (I Kings 16:23), then, must be in reference to his sole rule.

before Omri, with the backing of his army, was able to emerge victor and establish Israel's fourth ruling family.

C. DYNASTY OF OMRI (885–841; I Kings 16:23–22:53; II Kings 1–8)

1. *Political situation.* With Omri, the political situation in Israel became stabilized once more. It may be presumed that this pleased the people. Omri represented the third ruling family in three years. Elah had ruled only two years and Zimri but seven days; and the faction between Omri and Tibni had been disturbing to all. But with this division settled, Omri began a family rule that was to last three generations.

Stabilization came none too soon. The Aramaean state to the north, with capital at Damascus, was rapidly rising in power. Asa of Judah had already asked assistance from her king, Benhadad I, against Baasha. Benhadad was aggressive. A stele left by him near Aleppo shows that he was able to make his power effective as far as northern Syria by c. 850 B.C.[15] Had Israel remained weak much longer, she would have had little chance of competing with a ruler so strong. Ahab, Omri's son, was to find matters difficult as it was.

In addition to Damascus, a greater source of danger was rising further east. Assyria, which had been bidding to become a world power for some decades, but had been contained by the Mittanians and Hurrians and later by Aramaean groups of the upper Euphrates region, was now breaking out from her confinement.[16] This came particularly under Ashur-nasir-pal II (883-859), who was known for extreme cruelty and ruthless methods.[17] With him the period of the Assyrian empire is said to have begun, as he marched his army across the Euphrates and occupied land as far west as Byblos, Sidon, and Tyre on the Mediterranean.[18] Omri ruled in Israel at the time; and, though his country was not yet touched by this conqueror, it was by his successor, Shalmaneser III.

2. *Omri's reign (885–874; I Kings 16:23-28).* Omri was a strong ruler, easily the most capable and aggressive Northern Israel had yet known. Marked testimony of this is provided by an unexpected source.

---

[15] For discussion of this stele, cf. Albright, *BASOR,* 87 (1942), pp. 23-29; Albright and Della Vida, *BASOR,* 90 (1943), pp. 30-34. For text, notes, and picture, cf. *DOTT,* pp. 239-41; text and notes, *ANET,* p. 501.

[16] For brief discussion, cf. *supra,* chap. 10, p. 237.

[17] He boasts of his cruelty even in his annals; cf. Finegan, *LAP,* p. 202-203 for sample quotations, taken from Luckenbill, *Ancient Records of Assyria and Babylonia,* I sec. 443, 447; also *ANET,* pp. 275-6, or Barton, *AB,* p. 457.

[18] Cf. his inscription, *ANET,* pp. 275-76.

Assyrian rulers, living over a century later, still referred to Israel as the "land of Omri."[19] Though the biblical record says little about him, his exploits must have been remarkable to so impress rulers of this strong state. Three accomplishments are especially noteworthy.

a. New capital, Samaria (I Kings 16:24). The biblical account does tell of one achievement. Omri built a new capital for Israel, the city of Samaria. Tirzah had been capital from the time of Jeroboam. Omri continued residence there while still in conflict with his rival, Tibni, but two years later he purchased a new site, the hill of Samaria, where he built an entirely new city.[20] A decisive move of this kind bespeaks a man of vision and courage. Inevitable opposition must be over-ridden and careful planning implemented. His motivation lay clearly in making a capital more easily defended against military attack. History witnesses to his wisdom in choice of site, for Samaria proved to be an almost impregnable stronghold. Excavation has revealed too, that excellent workmanship characterized the building activity.[21] The city Samaria, named after the hill purchased, continued as capital until Israel's fall to the Assyrians in 722 B.C.

b. Conquest of Moab. A second accomplishment is known from the inscribed Moabite Stone.[22] This valuable monument was found lying on the ground near the Arnon River by a German missionary in 1898. Written by Mesha, king of Moab (II Kings 3:4), it states that "Omri, king of Israel" had conquered Moab in the days of Mesha's father. Mesha's point is to say that, under the pleasure of his god Chemosh, he was able to throw off the tribute that Omri had imposed.[23] Omri, then, was capable of raising a sufficient army from his country, so recently weakened by insurrection, to defeat a land of the standing of Moab. This means that he was an able person; not only in meeting the challenge of maintaining the land he had, but of enlarging it. From this it follows, too, that he must have experienced some measure of success over the Aramaeans of Damascus, for it is not likely that he would save chanced this attack on Moab, to the southeast, if he had then greatly feared Damascus to the north.

[19] For instance, Adad-nirari III (810-782), cf. *ANET*, pp. 281-82; Tiglath-pileser III (745-727), *ANET*, pp. 283-84; Sargon II (721-705), *ANET*, pp. 284-85.

[20] The hill of Samaria, named after its owner, Shemer, is located 7 miles north-west of Shechem and stands 300 feet high, quite by itself, though ringed by other mountains, so that attackers had to charge uphill from any side. It was strategically located also in that it commanded north-south trade routes.

[21] Cf. A. Parrot, *Samaria, the Capital of the Kingdom of Israel* (Eng. tr., London: S.C.M. Press, Ltd., 1958).

[22] For text and discussion, cf. *ANET*, p. 320; for the same and a picture, cf. *DOTT*, pp. 195-99.

[23] Cf. II Kings 3:4-27 for the story of Mesha's rebellion and Israel's attempt to force continued payment. Cf. *infra*, pp. 316-17.

c. Phoenician alliance. Still a third accomplishment is implied in the marriage of his son, Ahab, to the Phoenician princess, Jezebel. It is likely that he made a treaty with her father, King Ethbaal;[24] for, as observed earlier, such marriages were normal seals of formal alliances. A pact between Israel and Phoenicia would have been mutually advantageous too: Israel gaining cedar from Lebanon and fine imported merchandise from maritime Phoenicia; and Phoenicia gaining grain and olive oil from Israel, besides valuable trade routes to customers further south. In addition, each would have experienced additional strength against the rising Aramaean power in Damascus.[25] This alliance and resulting marriage, however, though seeming to be wise at the time, proved instead to be a terrible mistake; for it opened the way for the entrance of Baal worship into Israel.

3. Ahab and Jezebel (874–853; I Kings 16:28-34; 20:1–22:40)

a. Introduction of Baal worship. Probably the two most familiar names in the history of Northern Israel are King Ahab and Queen Jezebel. But they are known because the biblical record says they did evil in the sight of God more than all before them (I Kings 16:30). The main reason for this indictment is that they introduced Jezebel's native religion, the cult of Baal-Melqart,[26] to Israel.[27] Worship of Baal, the Canaanite deity, had been observed among Israelite tribes in pre-monarchial days, and Samuel had found it necessary to fight vigor-

[24] In I Kings 16:31, Ethbaal is called "king of the Zidonians," when actually his capital was Tyre. Cf. *supra*, chap. 12, p. 293, n. 24.

[25] It is possible, however, that Benhadad of Damascus had already himself made alliance with Tyre. His stele found near Aleppo (cf. *supra*, n. 15) is dedicated to the Tyrian god, Baal-Melqart, suggesting that at least a friendly relation existed between the two countries, if not a treaty. If so, the political advantage of Omri's treaty with Tyre lay mainly with Israel.

[26] This Tyrian god is called Melqart. Melqart, however, corresponds to the older Canaanite Baal in idea. Really, Melqart was the Tyrian counterpart to Baal and so quite properly called "Baal" in the biblical account.

[27] Actually this introduction was due primarily to Jezebel rather than Ahab. Ahab permitted it, and so was responsible; but Jezebel mainly effected it. The Baal prophets were those who ate "at Jezebel's table" (I Kings 18:19); she was the one who ordered the "prophets of Yahweh" killed (I Kings 18:4); and she sent the threatening note to Elijah (I Kings 19:2). As for Ahab, he called for prophets of Yahweh when he wanted advice (I Kings 22:6-12) and named his children with Yahweh-type names: Athaliah, Ahaziah, Jehoram. Baal names became common now, however, as suggested by names listed on ostraca found at Samaria: cf. J. W. Jack, *Samaria in Ahab's Time: Harvard Excavations and Their Results* (Edinburgh: Clark, 1929), p. 37. Though these ostraca have now been dated by Albright in the reign of Jeroboam II, about one century after Ahab, the names they show likely had been used for many years. Cf. for commentary and text, *ANET*, p. 321; also *DOTT*, pp. 204-208.

ously against it. David, however, had finally succeeded in ridding the land of the foreign, degraded religion. Now it was brought back in this worship of the Tyrian god, Baal-Melqart.

Jezebel, persistent and dominant as she was, was not content with having her religion merely co-exist with that of Yahweh worship. She wanted it to supplant what had been before and lent every effort that it would. She came near to accomplishing her purpose, too, as is indicated especially by her vicious slaughter of the native prophets of Yahweh (I Kings 18:4), something she, being the foreigner, would not have dared undertake unless she had already been well in command of religious matters.[28] The earlier sin of Jeroboam, establishing the golden calf worship, had been serious enough; but this introduction of the Baal cult was much worse. It involved an outright substitution of deity—even polytheism for montheism—and degrading, licentious observances, including religious prostitution.

b. Capable rule. Apart from these serious religious faults, however, Ahab was a capable ruler, seeking to follow the pattern of his father. For one thing, Ahab continued building activity. Excavation at Samaria has revealed that he built an inner and outer wall of fortification (five feet and nineteen feet thick, respectively) around the general court area. Imposing foundations of a large structure located near those of Omri's palace have been identified with those of Ahab's "ivory house" (I Kings 22:39; cf. Amos 3:15; 6:4). The walls of this structure were faced with white marble, thus giving the appearance of ivory; and more than two hundred real ivory figures, plaques, and small relief panels, likely used to decorate furniture and walls, were found in a store-room.[29] It is stated further that Ahab built cities for the people (I Kings 22:39).

c. Experiences in warfare. Militarily, Ahab was generally effective, due to the gracious blessing of God in spite of the religious defection. On two occasions he defeated Aramaean forces in accordance with predictions of "a prophet" of Yahweh (I Kings 20:1-34). In the second instance, the advisors of Benhadad[30] instructed him to attack Israel in a valley, rather than a mountain as the first time; for Yahweh, Israel's

---

[28] People normally react more quickly at native clergy being harmed by an outsider than almost anything else. Jezebel must have felt very confident even to attempt it. With them killed, too, it meant more than ever that she had things her own way.

[29] Cf. Finegan, *LAP*, pp. 187-88.

[30] This must be Benhadad II, son of the Benhadad whom Asa had employed to attack Baasha long before; because in I Kings 20:34 he speaks to Ahab of his father having privileges in Samaria, and the father of Benhadad I was Hezion who died long before Samaria was built. Unger, *Israel and the Aramaeans of Damascus* (James Clark & Co., Ltd., 1947), pp. 59-61 takes the opposite view.

God, was a God only of the hills and not of the valleys. Benhadad did so but found that the place made no difference. Ahab was enabled this time to inflict an even greater defeat than in the first instance, and the Damascus ruler was forced to sue for mercy. Benhadad was surprised at the leniency of Ahab's terms of surrender,[31] however, as was also Yahweh's prophet, who was then instructed to bring rebuke (I Kings 20:35-43).

Ahab's motive in this leniency may be found in a threat then posed by the great Shalmaneser III (859-824), king of Assyria. If Benhadad were to be helpful to Ahab and other rulers of the West in resisting this greater and common foe, he should not be deprived of his army. It is significant, indeed, that not many months later, in 853 B.C., both Ahab and Benhadad did join in a northern coalition to stop Shalmaneser's mighty army at Qarqar on the Orontes River. To this coalition, Ahab was able to contribute 2,000 chariots and 10,000 soldiers, and Benhadad 1,200 chariots, 1,200 horsemen, and 20,000 soldiers.[32]

Still the same year[33] Ahab again fought with Benhadad, this time at Ramoth-gilead,[34] and was killed, thus fulfilling a prediction and warning by the fearless prophet Micaiah (I Kings 22:13-39). Jehoshaphat, king of Judah, had allied himself with Ahab for the battle, and was nearly killed himself when mistaken for Ahab by the enemy forces. Ahab had disguised himself in view of Micaiah's prediction but was killed in spite of the precaution.

d. Alliance with Judah. That Jehoshaphat was with Ahab in this battle was almost certainly due to an alliance between Israel and Judah. Ahab's daughter Athaliah had been married to Jehoshaphat's son Jehoram, the normal seal of such a pact (II Kings 8:26). Peaceful conditions, conducive to a mutual agreement, had now existed between the two countries since the beginning of Omri's rule. Also, other times of assistance by Jehoshaphat to Ahab's sons were to follow, which further indicate this formal relationship.[35] Though likely producing benefit economically, the alliance was harmful religiously for

[31] Cities formerly taken from Israel were to be restored and Ahab was to have certain "streets" (probably places of trade) assigned him in Damascus, as Damascus had enjoyed formerly in Samaria. But no surrender or reduction of army or arms was required, certainly most unusual.

[32] For the text from Shalmaneser, cf. Barton, AB, p. 458; also ANET, pp. 278-79; DOTT, pp. 46-49.

[33] Cf. Thiele, MNHK, p. 66, n. 7 for an explanation of both battles occurring the same year.

[34] Best identified, according to N. Glueck's suggestion (BASOR, 92 [Dec.,1943]), with Tell-Ramith, some 28 miles east of the Jordan and 15 miles south of the Sea of Galilee.

[35] Very likely the significance too of I Kings 22:44 and II Chron. 18:1.

Judah. The influence of Baal worship from Israel—the result especially of the marriage involved—brought serious corruption to the religious life of Judah.

4. *The prophet Elijah (I Kings 17–19; 21; II Kings 1:1–2:11)*. During the reign of Ahab, one of Israel's outstanding prophets ministered. This was Elijah. Without the extensive record of this man's activities, far less would be known about Ahab and Jezebel.

a. Famine and fire. (I Kings 17–19). Elijah came from backward Gilead across the Jordan and dressed simply in camel's hair clothing (II Kings 1:8). He demonstrated outstanding courage and faith in opposing Jezebel's introduction of the Baal-Melqart cult. His first act was to announce to Ahab that God was about to send a dreaded famine upon the country, because of this displeasing religious innovation (I Kings 17:1).[36] Then Elijah hid from Ahab during the resulting forty-two months of the famine (Luke 4:25; James 5:17):[37] first at the brook Cherith and then in foreign Zarephath between Tyre and Sidon (I Kings 17:2-24), much to the displeasure of Ahab who looked for him even in foreign countries (I Kings 18:10). Following this, he reappeared to Ahab at God's direction and persuaded the king to co-operate[38] in arranging a contest on Mt. Carmel for the purpose of demonstrating which God was true, Yahweh or Baal-Melqart (I Kings 18:17-20). When the contest was held, Yahweh alone sent fire on the altar (I Kings 18:38), the determining sign indicated beforehand; and Elijah succeeded in persuading the influential spectators[39] not only to acclaim Yahweh as true God orally but to do so actively by helping to slay the opposing prophets of Baal (I Kings 18:39-40).[40]

[36] Baal-Melqart, god of storm and good crops, was directly challenged in this prediction of no rain. Could Baal bring rain when Yahweh said none would fall? For forty-two months the people were to learn the answer as a way of preparation for the climaxing contest for fire on Mt. Carmel.

[37] It was necessary for Elijah to remain secluded until the full impact of the reality of Yahweh over Baal might be impressed upon the people, in anticipation of the fire contest on Mt. Carmel.

[38] Royal cooperation was necessary to insure that the Baal prophets, who had nothing to gain by such a contest, would be on hand; also to reassure potential spectators, who otherwise had reason to fear reprisal by the vindictive Jezebel, that no harm would result for them.

[39] These spectators must have approximated 1,500 in number to be able to keep 450 Baal prophets from escaping (I Kings 18:40). They would also have been important, influential persons. Elijah's purpose was to influence all Israel, and so he would have wanted Ahab to invite those whose word to others would carry weight.

[40] This action, repulsive in itself was necessary, as the first act in ridding the land of the foreign cult. It was an act of obedience to God's own order (Deut. 13:6-9; 17:2-7) and a device by which these spectators might commit themselves, by act, to the religious change desired.

b. Failure and renewal. At this point, prospects for national revival of true Yahweh worship were excellent; but Elijah himself, in a moment of weakness, spoiled them. He ran from the country when threatened by Jezebel (I Kings 19:1-3), an act which could only have shocked and disillusioned those who so recently had committed themselves to religious change on Mt. Carmel.[41] Accordingly, when Elijah reached Mt. Horeb sometime later, he was reprimanded by God; but then he was given instructions for a new and different type of ministry, and sent back to Israel (I Kings 19:8-18).[42] An aspect in the new instructions was to acquire a helper, one Elisha, which he did. The two worked together for about ten years[43] in continued resistance to the religious and moral decadence of the regime of Ahab and Jezebel.

c. Three later episodes. From these later years of service, three incidents are recorded. In one, Elijah rebuked King Ahab for his unjust seizure of a vineyard near his alternate palace in Jezreel (I Kings 21:1-29). Jezebel led in arranging for the death of the owner, Naboth, by means of a staged court trial, and Ahab took possession. But Elijah met him at the vineyard, rebuked him, and warned him of coming destruction on his household. In a second episode, Elijah rebuked Ahab's son and successor, Ahaziah, for sending to Baal-zebub, god of the Philistine city Ekron,[44] to receive information relative to Ahaziah's chance of recovery from wounds suffered in a fall (II Kings 1:2-16). Elijah intercepted the messengers and sent them back to the king with the information that Ahaziah would die, and included a rebuke for sending outside Israel for such information, as though there

[41] Jezebel would have taken full advantage of this fact and spread her version of Elijah's flight rapidly all through the country. It would be in keeping with her other actions if she even went further and killed those who had helped in slaying her Baal favorites. Many of the "1500" may have died in the next few days.

[42] This time of reprimand and instruction came in the form both of an object lesson (wind, earthquake, and fire, followed by a still, small voice) and a spoken word. The new type of ministry indicated was to be of the "still, small voice" variety, in contrast to the preceding dramatic measures.

[43] The figure, ten years, is not given, but can be estimated. A few years had to elapse for Israel, ravaged by famine, to regain sufficient strength to do battle again with the Aramaeans; then at least two years for the two battles described in I Kings 20; then the Qarqar battle of 853 B.C. allied with Benhadad, followed by the Ramoth-gilead battle in which Ahab was killed; then the two years (not necesarily twenty-four months, however) of rule by Ahaziah; and finally the year or so involved of Jehoram's reign until Elijah's translation to heaven (II Kings 2:1-13).

[44] Most commonly identified with 'Aqir, ten miles northeast of Ashdod. It was near the boundary between Philistine and Israelite lands and often changed hands (Judg. 1:18; I Sam. 5:10; 7:14; 17:52). Whether it was in Israelite or Philistine control at this time is unknown.

were no God in Israel. Involved in the incident was the destruction by fire of two companies of fifty men each, sent successively by Ahaziah to summon Elijah, and Elijah's own appearance before, and further rebuke of, the king. In the third incident, Elijah was taken to heaven by special provision of God, as his fellow prophet and assistant, Elisha, watched (II Kings 2:1-11). This was a great honor bestowed on Elijah and implies unusual approval by God on his ministry. Elisha took up Elijah's mantle, which had fallen from the great man's shoulders as he was being taken, and wore it himself as a symbol of God's anointing now upon him.

Elijah's main impact on Israel lay, as intended, in his vigorous opposition to the cult of Baal-Melqart promoted by Jezebel. His total effect is hard to assess, but certainly was considerable. As noted, it would have been much greater had he not run when Jezebel threatened him; but still the overall influence of the famine, the contest on Mt. Carmel, and the later faithful ministry conducted with Elisha must have left lasting results. The entrenchment of Baal worship in Israelite life would have become far deeper had not Elijah lived and worked as he did.

5. *Ahaziah (853–852; II Kings 1:2-18)*. Two sons of Ahab succeeded him: first Ahaziah, then Jehoram. Ahaziah ruled only two years and died without sons to succeed him, thus giving opportunity for the second son, Jehoram. Ahaziah died from wounds received in a fall, apparently through an upper, latticed window. As noted, messengers were sent to Ekron's Baal-zebub to inquire as to his chance for recovery but were intercepted by Elijah and then returned with rebuke by the prophet. Two other matters from his reign are recorded. One is that Mesha, king of Moab, revolted from under heavy tribute imposed by Jehoram's grandfather, Omri.[45] Results of this uprising were experienced later in Jehoram's rule as well. The other is that Ahaziah entered into a joint maritime venture with Jehoshaphat, doubtless in keeping with the alliance his father had made with Judah (II Chron. 20:35-37). The venture proved disastrous, however, when the ships built were all destroyed, apparently even before their maiden voyage. The destruction was in accordance with the prophet Eliezer's prediction, which pronounced God's displeasure at this second instance[46] of Jehoshaphat aligning himself with the wicked kings of Israel.

6. *Jehoram (852–841; II Kings 3)*. Jehoram ruled longer than his brother, a total of twelve years (II Kings 3:1). The many incidents told from his reign make it seem more significant than twelve years

---

[45] *Supra*, p. 309.

[46] The first instance was when Jehoshaphat went to aid Ahab in his battle at Ramoth-gilead and was nearly killed; *supra*, p. 312.

would suggest. Two matters account for this degree of notice: first, during his time the Aramaeans of Damascus were especially active in respect to Israel; and second, the great prophet Elisha was then at the height of his ministry.

a. Religious viewpoint. Concerning Jehoram's attitude toward the Baal cult, it is stated that he removed an image of Baal made by his father (II Kings 3:2); and so one might think that he banned Baal worship, or at least was unsympathetic to it. Other matters, however, show that this was not so. At a later time, for instance, he was ironically bidden by Elisha to seek help from the prophets of his father and mother in a time of need, implying that this was his normal practice (II Kings 3:13). Also, Jehu, his successor, later found it necessary to slay Baal prophets of the land when he came to the throne (II Kings 10:19-28). That Jehoram could be expected to have continued the Baal cult follows from the fact that his domineering mother, Jezebel, still lived throughout his reign (II Kings 9:30-33). The image in Samaria which Jehoram removed may have been particularly objectionable to a population segment that he wished to appease.

b. Revolt of Moab (II Kings 3:4-27). Another item to notice from Jehoram's reign relates to the recent revolt of neighboring Moab, as noticed above in connection with Ahaziah's reign. Mesha, Moab's king, refused to send the tribute imposed years earlier by Omri, no doubt encouraged by Ahab's death at the hand of the Aramaeans. But Jehoram missed the economic advantage the tribute had afforded his father and took steps to force its continuance, seeking the aid of Jehoshaphat. By agreeing, Jehoshaphat began a third joint-venture with Ahab's house, in keeping with the alliance made with Ahab, but adding to his sin before God. Consequent trouble came to Jehoshaphat when the combined armies,[47] on their way to attack Moab, found themselves facing death in an arid land for lack of water. Only by Elisha's timely intervention were they spared.[48] The armies then moved into the land of Moab and inflicted severe devastation before Mesha could retaliate; this because they had traveled by an unexpected southern route and taken Mesha by surprise.[49] But Mesha recovered in time to save his

[47] By this time, three armies, for Jehoram and Jehoshaphat had been joined by the king of Edom as they rounded the southern end of the Dead Sea (II Kings 3:9).

[48] This was a significant occasion: three kings able to do nothing to help themselves had to go to one of Yahweh's prophets! Yahweh's instruction through Elisha was for ditches to be dug in the valley where they were encamped. Rain was then sent which flowed down the valley, filled the ditches, and so supplied the armies with ample, clear water.

[49] With Israel located northwest from Moab, Mesha would have expected an attack from the north. By circuiting the southern end of the Dead Sea, Jehoram

country from complete destruction and was finally able, through a dramatic sacrifice of his eldest son, to effect full withdrawal of the enemy forces. The exact connection between this sacrifice and the withdrawal is not made clear. The biblical account, however, does support Mesha's boast on the Moabite Stone[50] that deliverance from Israel's dominance was achieved in his day.

7. *Aramaean episodes in Jehoram's reign (II Kings 5–7; 8:28-29).* Though contacts between Israel and the Aramaeans continued from the reign of Baasha through most of Israel's history, more is related about them during the rule of Jehoram than during the reigns of all the other kings combined.[51] These particular contacts were significant from the biblical point of view because they involved Elisha, great prophet that he was.

a. *Naaman, Aramaean general (II Kings 5).* The first episode recorded concerns the military general of the Aramaean armies, Naaman, who served under Benhadad II. It is likely that Naaman had held this position for some time, and had led in the battles with Ahab noted earlier. But now he sought help from Israel, for he had become afflicted with leprosy, and had been told by a captive Israelite girl that a prophet in Israel could heal him. Benhadad, willing to find such assistance for his valuable officer anywhere, sent appropriate official letters with Naaman to Jehoram in Samaria; but the immediate reaction of the Israelite king was to believe that war was somehow being instigated. Elisha, however, hearing of the situation, asked that the foreign commander be sent to him, thus easing Jehoram's mind. Naaman, who expected due recognition of his high position, then felt insulted when told by Elisha merely to wash seven times in the Jordan River for his recovery, and so nearly missed the physical healing available. Counsel by a wise servant, however, persuaded him to comply, and he then did experience a remarkable restoration. By this he became convinced of the supremacy of Israel's Yahweh and promised henceforth to worship Him alone.[52]

and Jehoshaphat were able to move into the southern section of Moab before Mesha was aware of their presence.

[50] *Supra,* p. 309, n. 22.

[51] This assumes that the stories in II Kings 5-8 all relate to his reign, which is likely. With no time indications given, some scholars have suggested that these may have come from the reign of Jehu or even Jehoahaz. The placing and order of the stories, however, argue that all occurred in the reign of Jehoram.

[52] Naaman even asked to take "two mules' burden of earth" (II Kings 5:17) back to Damascus, to the end of worshiping Yahweh. Heathen ideas related deity and land; and Naaman here thought that he had to have some of Yahweh's land if, even in this unusual manner, he was to worship Him. This showed his heathen ignorance, but it also showed his sincerity; and Elisha apparently agreed to the request.

b. Blinded Aramaeans (II Kings 6:8-23). Sometime later an entire military contingent was sent by the Aramaeans to capture Elisha, but they suffered blindness for their trouble. This unusual episode was occasioned by Elisha's informing Jehoram more than twice (II Kings 6: 10) of when and where Aramaean attacks on Israel were to be directed.[53] When Benhadad's advisors informed him as to this secret of Jehoram's success against him, the Aramaean king sent troops to capture the prophet at Dothan where he was residing. Elisha's servant was terrified on seeing the besieging host, but Elisha reassured him and asked God to open his eyes that he might see the greater protective hosts of God. Elisha then requested God to smite this army with blindness and, when God did, led them like sheep the ten miles south to the capital, Samaria. Here their eyes were reopened to see their dangerous situation, but Elisha instructed Jehoram to treat them kindly by supplying food and permitting their return to Damascus.

c. Siege of Samaria (II Kings 6:24-7:20). Several months later the Aramaeans returned to Israel in greater force and laid siege to Samaria. Being maintained for an extended period of time, the siege brought starvation conditions to the city, with some people driven even to eat their own children (II Kings 6:28-29). Elisha was blamed by Jehoram, likely due to some earlier warning that such a siege might happen as a punishment for sin, but the prophet then revealed that everyone would have all the food he desired on the following day. This came true when the Aramaeans fled in the night at the imagined sound of chariot wheels, which they took to indicate a relief force of Egyptians. Panic prompted them to leave food and all else behind. Starving lepers, in desperation resorting to the Aramaean camp, learned of the flight. They brought to the city the good news of available food in the abandoned camp, and all the people did in truth have the nourishment they needed the following day.

d. Wounded by Aramaeans (II Kings 8:28-29). A final contact with the Aramaeans led to Jehoram's death. Like Ahab his father, he met the Aramaeans in battle at Ramoth-gilead, and like him, too, he had help in the encounter from a king of Judah, now Ahaziah, suggesting that the formal alliance between the two countries still existed. Jehoram was seriously wounded, and returned to Jezreel, alternate capital of the Omride rulers, to recover. Later Ahaziah, who had returned to Judah after the battle, came to Jezreel to visit him, and while there became involved in a storm of destruction brought by Jehu, which resulted in the death of both kings.

---

[53] It would be interesting to know whether Naaman, recently converted to the worship of Yahweh, led in these battles. No indication, however, is given.

8. *The prophet Elisha*

a. Background information. Elisha's work as a prophet was basically the same as Elijah's: resistance to the cult of Baal-Melqart. He requested, at Elijah's translation to heaven, that he might have a double portion of Elijah's spirit (II Kings 2:9), so that he might have divine enablement for his task as Elijah had. Elisha may have come from a wealthy family, for when he was first called by Elijah (I Kings 19:19) he was plowing with a team of oxen in a field where twelve other teams also worked, presumably all owned by his father. If so, he contrasted sharply on this count with his master, Elijah, who had been raised in the poor area of Gilead near the desert. But Elisha's decision to follow Elijah had been final and decisive. He killed his own oxen to prepare a farewell feast for relatives and friends, and he used the wood from his tools as fuel for the fire (I Kings 19:21).

Elisha's period of ministry lasted much longer than Elijah's. He began in Jehoram's early years, continued through the reigns of Jehu and Jehoahaz, and died sometime while Jehoash ruled (II Kings 13:20), a period of about fifty years (c. 850-800). Though having the same objectives in his ministry as Elijah, his manner in reaching them was somewhat different. In keeping with his contrasting background, Elisha was more at home in cities and even at the palace and was often in the company of kings. Also, Elijah had been more a man of moods, either strongly courageous or despairing to the point of death; but Elisha was self-controlled and even-tempered, found neither in dramatic staged contests nor sulking in a desert. It may be, too, that Elisha was more interested in the needs of people; for many of his miracles, again in contrast to Elijah, were to aid, heal, and give relief to persons he encountered.

b. Elisha's experiences. The biblical record tell of Elisha in a series of eighteen separate episodes. This is in contrast to Elijah's story, which is found mainly in three consecutive chapters (I Kings 17–19). The narratives regarding Elisha fall mostly in Jehoram's reign, and so are not separated greatly in time, but still they do not constitute one continuous account. Several of these episodes have already been noticed. The others need only be listed: the making of foul water sweet for drinking (II Kings 2:19-22); rebuking children who mocked him (2:23-25); supplying oil that a widow's debts might be paid (4:1-7); praying that a woman of Shunem, who had been kind to him, might give birth to the child she so much wanted, and later restoring that child to life (4:8-37); making food edible in which a poisonous herb had been mistakenly mixed (4:38-41); multiplying food in time of famine to feed a hundred young prophets (4:42-44); pronouncing leprosy on his servant Gehazi for telling a falsehood (5:20-27); recovering an axhead lost in the Jordan (6:1-7); arranging for restoration by the king, of property belonging to the woman of Shunem, after she had left the land due to famine at Elisha's advice (8:1-6); anointing one Hazael as king in Damascus, and Jehu, captain under Jehoram, as king to succeed Jehoram in Samaria (8:7-15; 9:1-10); and much later, in the reign of Jehoash, predicting three victories by him over the Aramaeans (13:14-19).

One of Elisha's main interests was training young prophets for service (II Kings 2:3-7, 15-18; 4:38-41; 6:1; 9:1).[54] Elijah likely had started the program, establishing schools at Gilgal, Bethel, and Jericho; but Elisha continued and expanded it. He is seen frequently in the company of the students, called "sons of the prophets." His purpose was to provide dedicated, trained men to do the work of true prophets in the manner of Elijah and now himself. Sinful, Baal-worshiping Israel needed them desperately.

D. DYNASTY OF JEHU (841–753; II Kings 9:11–10:36; 13; 14:16-29)

The two strongest ruling families of Israel reigned consecutively: first, the family of Omri, just considered; and second, that of Jehu. Jehu's dynasty ruled longer than Omri's—eighty-nine years as against forty-four—and it included five generations (Jehu, Jehoahaz, Jehoash, Jeroboam II, and Zechariah), in comparison with Omri's three. Jehu's dynasty, however, was not as strong in rule as Omri's, for during its time Israel experienced heavy loss to both the Aramaeans and the Assyrians. Religiously, each dynasty was seriously deficient, but at least that of Jehu did not foster Baal worship as had that of Omri.

1. *Jehu's destruction of the house of Omri (II Kings 9:11–10:28).* Jehu, first king in this fifth ruling dynasty, is best known for his slaughter of the fourth family. God had foretold through Elijah twenty years before (I Kings 19:15-17; 21:21-24) that such a time of punishment would come to this house. With the urging of Elijah and Elisha, Omri's family had been given opportunity enough to repent of its sin in Baal worship and wanton destruction of life. Now came the hour of retribution.

Elisha himself applied the torch to the conflagration, which Jehu then effected. Elisha sent one of the "sons of the prophets" to anoint Jehu as king in Jehoram's place and to instruct him regarding the purging (II Kings 9:1-10). Jehu, Jehoram's military captain, was still at Ramoth-gilead, the site of the last battle, and readily accepted the

---

[54] An interest similar to that of Samuel years before. Whether schools had continued during intervening years is not indicated, but probably they had not.

honor. His men were pleased as well, and all moved quickly across the Jordan to Jezreel to carry out instructions.

First slain was King Jehoram himself, still recovering from wounds.[55] Ahaziah, Judah's king who was visiting, fled for his life from Jezreel, but was later caught and killed by pursuers sent by Jehu.[56] Jehu rode into Jezreel and ordered the attendants of Jezebel to throw her from an upper window from which she was looking. They readily complied, and hungry dogs ate her flesh as Elijah had predicted long before (I Kings 21:23). A letter from Jehu to political leaders in Samaria resulted in the severed heads of Ahab's seventy sons being delivered to Jehu in Jezreel. He had them laid in piles at the gate for all to see. Then he slew all the court officials in Jezreel. After this he left personally for Samaria, and on the way met and killed forty-two relatives[57] of Ahaziah coming to visit the two kings, already dead. Soon after he met one Jehonadab, son of Rechab,[58] who, on profession of sympathy and support for Jehu's cause, was taken along in Jehu's own chariot to assist in the revolution. Jehu arrived at the capital and killed all the officials there as well, presumably including the men who had earlier sought favor by killing Ahab's sons. Lastly, Jehu called all the prophets and priests of Baal to their temple in Samaria, as if to extend favor to them, but then sent eighty of his men into the temple to kill them to the last man. Seldom has history witnessed a more thorough blood purging of a previous royal family and favored religious order than this.

2. *Jehu as king (841–814; II Kings 10:29-36).* Jehu's zeal to rid the land of Omri's house was not matched by his capacity to rule. His twenty-eight years as king were marked by unrest and turmoil, with serious social and economic abuses rife among the people.[59] Nei-

[55] Jehoram's body was cast into the field of Naboth, taken by Ahab years before, in fulfillment of Elijah's prediction (I Kings 21:19). The judgment had been stayed in respect to Ahab himself because of his repentance (I Kings 21:27-29), but now fell upon Jehoram, his son.

[56] Apparently Ahaziah fled toward Megiddo, with Jehu's men smiting him at Gur (unknown), but he reached Megiddo before dying. II Chron. 22:9 indicates that at some point Ahaziah hid in Samaria, perhaps going there first and later moving northwest to Megiddo. The detail is not clear.

[57] These could not have been immediate brothers of Ahaziah, for they had been killed before this by an attack of Philistines and Arabians (II Chron. 21:16-17).

[58] Jehu's attitude toward this man indicates respect for him. Jehonadab was loyal to Yahweh and strict in his manner of life. He became tribe-father of the Rechabites, an ascetic group whose faithfulness to regulations prompted admiration by Jeremiah years later (Jer. 35:1-19; cf. I Chron. 2:55 for identity of Rechab).

[59] This fact is evidenced especially by the writings of Amos and Hosea, both prophets to Israel who wrote about one-half century after Jehu's rule. The abuses of which they speak had existed during his time.

ther was he able to prevent his land from inroads and severe humiliation at the hands of both the Aramaeans and Assyrians.

Religiously, Jehu received God's commendation at the beginning of his rule because of obedience in destroying the house of Omri (II Kings 10:30), but then he failed to follow the path he had started. God's approval was given of the blood purge—even though certainly Jehu killed more than divinely intended—for this constituted the punishment forewarned against the wicked family years before, and it dealt a shattering blow to the cult of Baal-Melqart. Accordingly, God promised that four generations of Jehu's family would succeed him on the throne. Jehu, however, then chose to perpetuate Jeroboam's God-displeasing worship at Dan and Bethel (II Kings 10:29) and so forfeited the divine approval after all, and consequently experienced difficult times.

a. Hazael's havoc in Israel (II Kings 10:32-33). Humiliation of Israel at the hands of foreign powers was especially pronounced during Jehu's reign. This came mainly from the Aramaeans, led by Hazael, in further fulfillment of God's prediction through Elijah (I Kings 19: 15-17).

The fulfillment was first begun when Elisha went north to Damascus to anoint Hazael as the Aramaean king (II Kings 8:7-15). Elisha wept when he did so, for he knew the havoc this man would bring on Israel. The anointing took place shortly before that of Jehu.[60] Though there is no record of how Hazael brought about this havoc, the extent of it is evidenced. He succeeded in seizing from Israel all Transjordan, including the tribal territories of Manasseh, Gad, and Reuben (cf. Amos 1:3). Then, though it is not directly stated, he must have made serious inroads into Israel also west of the Jordan; for a notation from the time of Jehoahaz, son of Jehu, states that Hazael by then was able even to dictate how many horses, chariots, and footmen Israel's king could have in his army (II Kings 13:7).[61] Still a further indication from Jehoahaz' time comes from a comment regarding King Joash of Judah. It says that Hazael was able to advance as far south as Gath in the Philistine area,[62] seize the city, and force Joash to pay tribute,

[60] The time here is evidenced by inscriptions from Shalmaneser III. In one from his fourteenth year (845 B.C.), he mentions Hadadezer (Benhadad II) as still king in Damascus, and in another from his eighteenth year (841 B.C.) he mentions Hazael. This means that Hazael came to the throne between 845 and 841, and probably just before 841 in view of the manner of notice made regarding him.

[61] He was permitted only 50 horsemen, 10 chariots, and 10,000 footmen, a marked contrast to the 2,000 chariots Ahab had brought to Qarqar!

[62] Gath formerly belonged to the Philistines, but Rehoboam included it in a list of cities which he fortified, indicating that it then, and probably still at this

so that the same would not be done to Jerusalem (II Kings 12:17-18). If Hazael could impose his will to this extent as far south as Gath and Jerusalem, he had surely brought Israel already to a position of extreme humiliation; a process no doubt begun as early as the reign of Jehu.

b. Humiliation before Assyria. Israel also suffered during Jehu's rule at the hands of Assyria. In fact, the Assyrian invasion came prior to that of Hazael, and brought even greater harm to Hazael's land than to Israel. The occasion is known only from Assyrian records.[63]

Shalmaneser III, the great Assyrian ruler of the time, was the same man against whom Ahab and Benhadad had combined in a twelve-member coalition at Qarqar a dozen years before. Now for the six-teenth time he crossed the Euphrates in military campaign. He succeeded in leading his large army all the way to Damascus, effecting extensive damage on the city, though without actually capturing it; and then went on to force Jehu in Israel to pay heavy tribute.[64] On his famous Black Obelisk,[65] found in 1846 at Nimrud, Shalmaneser lists the tribute and depicts the Israelite king in bas-relief bowing low in submission presenting his payment. Though Shalmaneser does not claim to have wrought destruction in Israel, the heavy tribute he demanded was humiliating and economically oppressive. Shalmaneser made one more attack in the general area three years later,[66] claiming success once more, but nothing is known of the details. No Assyrian army came again for a generation, which permitted Hazael to regain his strength with which to inflict the aforementioned harm on Israel.

c. Reasons for Jehu's weakness. Some factors which entered into Jehu's inability to defend his country better are suggested by the over-all story. One of the more important certainly was his slaughter of able leaders in the blood purge of Omri's house. Jehu went beyond what God had intended in this purge and unnecessarily killed many who might have helped him, particularly court officials in both Jezreel and Samaria. One does not quickly replace men of experience. Another reason was that some of his people no doubt refused to cooperate

time, belonged to Judah (II Chron. 11:8). Hazael may have acted as an ally of the Philistines in now seizing Gath from Judah, for the city appears to have been in Philistine hands again by the time of Uzziah (II Chron. 26:6).

[63] Left by Shalmaneser III. For all his inscriptions, cf. ANET, pp. 276-81.
[64] Shalmaneser also lists Tyre and Sidon as paying tribute.
[65] This four-sided black limestone pillar stands 6½ feet high, with 5 rows of bas-reliefs and explanatory cuneiform inscriptions on all sides. In the second row on one side appears Jehu, the only extant representation of an Israelite king. The Obelisk resides in the British Museum. For text, cf. ANET, p. 280; for pictures, cf. ANEP, figs. 351-55.
[66] Text in ANET, p. 280. This was Shalmaneser's twenty-first year.

with him, in view of his ruthlessness during the purge. He may have had to work with quite a segment of dissident people. Still another was that the alliances which had been held with Judah and Phoenicia would now have ceased, as a further result of the purge. Judah would have broken relations because of the death of King Ahaziah and his kinsmen,[67] and Phoenicia because of the slaughter of the priests of Baal-Melqart. But perhaps most significant, Jehu himself clearly lacked necessary ability. He must have been qualified in military science, for he had been captain under Jehoram; but he lacked in diplomacy and in a sense of judgment, as made evident by his reckless slaughter of the former regime. All these factors, of course, were under God's control, as He permitted the country to experience punishment in accordance with His announcement to Elijah long before (I Kings 19:15-17).

3. *Jehoahaz (814–798; II Kings 13:1-9).* Jehoahaz succeeded Jehu his father and reigned seventeen years. Little is related regarding his rule, apart from a further degree of subjection to Hazael. The only item stated in addition is that he sought help from God against Hazael and was given a "deliverer" (II Kings 13:5). This "deliverer," strange to say, must have been the Assyrian emperor, Adad-nirari III (810-783), who came to the throne during Jehoahaz's reign. He did serve as "deliverer" to Israel in that he attacked and crushed Damascus in 803 B.C.,[68] thus bringing relief to Israel from the Aramaean oppression. It is true that Israel, too, along with Tyre, Sidon, Edom, and Philistia, was forced to pay tribute, but it did not experience the devastation wrought on Damascus. The Aramaean state was hurt sufficiently so that Israel was now able to start on a long road toward a new position of strength.

4. *Jehoash (798–782; II Kings 13:10-25; 14:15-16).* At Jehoahaz's death, his son Jehoash assumed the throne. During his rule, Israel made rapid strides on this road of recovery. Soon after assuming office, Jehoash was promised a resurgence in military position by Elisha. Elisha, an old man now, called the new king to him and predicted victory over Damascus. He instructed Jehoash to smite the ground with arrows. The king did so, but only three times; and Elisha rebuked him for not smiting it more, explaining that he would have defeated Damascus a corresponding number of times. He would, however, still be victorious on three occasions. Succeeding years saw Je-

---

[67] Athaliah, daughter of Ahab, who had married Jehoram, now ruled in Judah, having seized the throne by treachery. Actually it was good for Judah to be free from this alliance, but Israel no doubt was hurt both economically and militarily.

[68] For the text of Adad-nirari III, cf. *ANET*, pp. 281-82; also *DOTT*, pp. 50-52. By the time of this attack, Benhadad III, son and successor of Hazael, had ascended the throne in Damascus.

hoash experiencing the fulfillment of this prediction, enabling him to recover all the cities Damascus had earlier taken from Israel (II Kings 13:25).

Jehoash also became strong enough to withstand an attack by Amaziah, king of Judah (II Kings 14:8-14). In fact, he was able to inflict a serious defeat upon him, a matter to be treated more in the following chapter.

An item of further significance is that Jehoash appointed his son as co-ruler. Jeroboam II became co-regent when Jehoash had ruled only five of his sixteen years.[69] The reason likely is to be found in the war of Jehoash with Judah. Before engaging in the conflict, he placed his son on the throne to rule while he was away, apparently anticipating a prolonged effort.[70]

5. *Jeroboam II (793-753; II Kings 14:23-29)*. Jeroboam II was the third successive descendant of Jehu to occupy the throne, and he proved to be one of Israel's most capable rulers. Under him, Israel rose to a position of remarkable influence, becoming actual leader along the Mediterranean coast. No description of Jeroboam's battles in accomplishing so much is given, but the end achievement is made clear: Jeroboam was able to establish roughly the same boundaries on the east and north which had existed in the empire days of David and Solomon. It is stated that he placed Israel's northern limit at the "entering of Hamath" (II Kings 14:25), the same phrase used to describe Solomon's northern boundary (I Kings 8:65). It is also stated that "he recovered Damascus and Hamath" which had belonged "to Judah" (II Kings 14:28), the last no doubt a reference to David and Solomon's time, since these cities had not belonged to Israel since. It may be observed, too, that this comparative form of reference implies the restoration of the same general relationship between these cities and Israel as had then existed. Still further, by gaining this control over Damascus, he must also have recovered all Transjordan whic'1 Hazael had seized. With these former extensive boundaries restored,

[69] Evidenced by comparison of certain passages. According to II Kings 14:23, Jeroboam II came to the throne in the fifteenth year of Amaziah of Judah, 782 B.C. But II Kings 15:1 indicates that Azariah, successor of Amaziah in Judah, began to reign in Jeroboam's twenty-seventh year, which year is known to have been 767 B.C. If this was Jeroboam's twenty-seventh year, then he must have begun to reign in 793 B.C., the fifth year of Jehoash's reign. This means that II Kings 14:23 dates from his first year of sole ruler. Cf. Thiele, *MNHK*, pp. 77-81.

[70] Not only does the time of Jehoash's war with Judah fit this beginning of coregency, but so does an unusual second reference to the close of Jehoash's rule in II Kings 14:15-16 (first one given in II Kings 13:12-13). This second statement falls immediately after the account of this war (II Kings 14:8-14), as though the war occurred during the coregency and was a cause for it. For discussion, cf. Thiele, *MNHK*, pp. 84-85.

Israel was the largest and most influential country along the eastern Mediterranean. The name of Jeroboam II must have come to be widely known and respected.

At least three factors would have contributed to this marked change of status for Israel. The first, already noticed, is that rival Damascus, formerly the leading country, had been weakened by the attack of Adad-nirari III. The second is that Jehoash, and especially Jeroboam II, were capable rulers; demonstrated in reference to the former by his successful encounter with Judah (II Kings 14:8-14; II Chron. 25:17-24), and in reference to the latter by the accomplishments just noted. The third is that Assyria, who might have interfered if able, was now like Damascus experiencing a period of marked weakness, a degeneration caused by the rising menace of northern Urartu people, internal dissension within Assyria itself, and a succession of weak rulers.[71] During their reigns, Assyria lost nearly all her foothold west of the Euphrates and could not hinder the expansionist designs of far-away Israel.

6. *Eighth-century prophets.* Prophets had existed in Israel from the time of Moses.[72] Among these, Samuel, Nathan, Gad, Ahijah, Elijah, and Elisha were only the more significant. Many others lived, and their influence was considerable. They addressed themselves mainly to particular sins of individuals, especially kings because of their positions of influence. In the eighth century, however, a change came in the methods employed.[73] While continuing the same basic message of necessary obedience to Yahweh's Law, the prophets came to address it to the people collectively, on a national level. Also, the sins rebuked were the sins of the nation, rather than those of individuals. Still further, many prophets now began to write their messages as well as speak them. As a result, prophetic literature came into existence, which forms an important part of the Old Testament.

Three of these writing prophets ministered during some part of the reign of Jeroboam II. One was Jonah (II Kings 14:25), sent on a mission to Nineveh, the great city of Assyria. His time of arrival there, with the consequent repentance of the inhabitants, is best located at the period of Assyrian weakness just noted. Such a period is more conducive to repentance than one of prosperity and strength. Not only was there military and political weakness at the time, but a series of

---

[71] They were Shalmaneser IV (783-773), Asshur-dan III (773-754), and Asshur-nirari V (754-746).

[72] Moses called himself a prophet and predicted that others like himself would arise (Deut. 18:15-22).

[73] Likely both Obadiah and Joel ministered already in the last half of the ninth century, though as prophets of Judah.

epidemics had swept through the land, bringing death to large numbers. Besides, a total eclipse of the sun, June 15, 763 B.C., added to a widespread fear complex.[74] In this atmosphere, Jonah's message of impending doom for Nineveh would have carried great effect, thus making the remarkable repentance demonstrated understandable.

The two other prophets are Amos and Hosea, mentioned earlier. Amos, a herdsman of Tekoa, was a citizen of Judah, but was sent north to Israel to bring God's warning in the "days of Jeroboam" (Amos 1:1). Hosea, a citizen of Israel, also prophesied in the "days of Jeroboam" (Hos. 1:1). Hosea may have begun his ministry slightly after Amos, for he says that he continued during the reigns of Uzziah, Jotham, Ahaz, and Hezekiah, kings of Judah,[75] while Amos mentions only Uzziah. Prosperity, such as characterized Jeroboam's rule, leads to luxury, idleness, and sin, all three of which were condemned by these prophets.[76] Much of Hosea's message was based on his own sad experience in marriage, having been left by his profligate wife. He likened her unfaithfulness to that of Israel with God.[77]

7. *Zachariah (753 B.C.; II Kings 15:8-12)*. Jeroboam's son, Zachariah, succeeded him, making Zachariah the fourth successive descendant of Jehu to sit on the throne. He did not rule long, however, for he was assassinated within six months by his successor, Shallum.[78] Nothing else is indicated regarding Zachariah except that he continued Jeroboam's false worship at Dan and Bethel. He probably was not as capable as his father, one reason why an assassination plot could be successfully planned and perpetrated.

E. DECLINE OF ISRAEL (752–722; II Kings 15:13–17:41)

The reign of Jeroboam II was Northern Israel's one period of brilliance. With the death of his son, the nation rapidly declined in strength and position. This period of decline closed with the fall of Samaria to the great Assyrian war machine in 722 B.C.

1. *Shallum (752 B.C.; II Kings 15:13-15)*. Shallum killed Zachariah and set himself up as ruler, thus instituting Israel's sixth ruling family.

[74] Cf. A. T. Olmstead, *History of Assyria* (Chicago: University of Chicago Press, 1923), pp. 169-74.

[75] This means a minimum duration of twenty-five years to an impossible maximum of just over a century, depending on how soon in Uzziah's reign he began and how long in Hezekiah's he continued.

[76] Amos 2:6-8; 5:10-12; 6:1-8; 8:4-6; Hosea 2:14-23; 4:1-6, 13-19; 7:4.

[77] Hosea 2:2-13; 3:1-5. Israel's unfaithfulness to God receives testimony also in the Samaritan Ostraca, which are now dated from this time (cf. *supra*, p. 310, n. 27). A high percentage of names on these ostraca are compounded with "Baal," showing that significant allegiance was still directed toward this pagan deity which Jehu had supposedly driven from the country.

[78] In keeping with a prediction of Amos (7:9).

He reigned only one month, however, when Menahem, possibly a military leader under Zachariah, retaliated by killing him. Nothing further is recorded regarding Shallum.

2. *Menahem (752–742; II Kings 15:16-22)*. Menahem now set himself up as Israel's ruler, instituting Israel's seventh ruling family. He ruled for a total of ten years. He is said to have come "from Tirzah" (II Kings 15:14) at the time he killed Shallum in Samaria. The implication is that he had held authority in Tirzah,[79] probably by appointment of Jeroboam II. In killing Shallum, consequently, he may have been avenging Zachariah's death, as well as furthering his own interest in assuming the throne. It is possible that he experienced opposition in this, however, from the city of Tiphsah,[80] for on becoming king he proceeded to kill many of the people there.

During Menahem's rule, the power of Assyria was once more experienced by the Mediterranean countries. Tiglath-pileser III (745-727), perhaps Assyria's strongest ruler (in marked contrast to his immediate predecessors), had now come to the throne and restored Assyria's empire status. He had achieved success first to the south in Babylonia, and also north against the Urartu, before coming again into the West across the Euphrates. He was successful in this direction too, and as he conquered he instituted policies differing from those of prior rulers. Former kings had been satisfied merely with nominal control and a reception of tribute, but this had resulted in constant revolt. Tiglath-pileser incorporated conquered land as Assyrian provinces and deported native leaders who might instigate revolution. The policy proved effective and was copied by successors.

Tiglath-pileser's campaign of 743 B.C.[81] reached all the way to Israel and involved Menahem.[82] He was not yet able to incorporate the area as a province, but he did exact tribute from Menahem.[83] The imposed sum of 1,000 talents of silver was raised by Menahem through a head tax, assessed against all "men of wealth" in the country at the rate of

---

[79] *Supra*, p. 304.

[80] Location uncertain. Possible identification with a city, Thapsacus, located on the west bank of the Euphrates, has been made, but this would hardly fit the story. This city was not far from Samaria.

[81] The date of this campaign is often given as 738 B.C., but Thiele makes a strong case for 743 B.C. on the basis of a careful study of records of Tiglath-pileser III. Cf. Thiele, *MNHK*, pp. 94-115; M. Unger, *Israel and the Aramaeans of Damascus* (London: James Clark & Co., Ltd., 1957), p. 97.

[82] In this same year Tiglath-pileser met a northwest coalition, of which Uzziah (Azariah), king of Judah, was leader. Cf. discussion in the next chapter.

[83] Tiglath-pileser lists several other kings who also paid tribute, including Kishtashpi of Hummuh, Rezin of Damascus, Hiram of Tyre, Urikki of Kue, Pisiris of Carchemish, Tarhulara of Gurgum, and Sulumal of Melid. For text, cf. *ANET*, p. 283; *DOTT*, pp. 54-55.

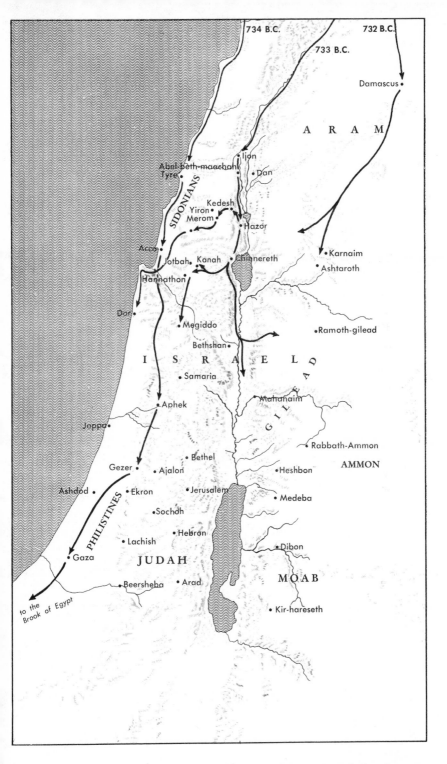

Map 11. The Campaigns of Tiglath-pileser III

fifty shekels each.[84] By this payment, Menahem was able "to confirm the kingdom in his hand," but in doing so became another vassal to the Assyrian ruler (II Kings 15:19-20).

3. *Pekahiah 742–740; II Kings 15:23-26) and Pekah (752–732; II Kings 15:27-31).* At the death of Menahem, Pekahiah, his son, succeeded him. He ruled only two years, however, when Pekah, one of his military leaders, assassinated him at the palace in Samaria, and set himself up as king, thus instituting Israel's eighth ruling family. Pekah is said to have ruled twenty years. Chronological correlations, however, require that these twenty years include the prior years when both Menahem and Pekahiah ruled. Pekah's last year clearly was 732 B.C.,[85] which means that his twenty-year period began in 752 B.C., the year of Menahem's accession. This leaves only eight years for Pekah's sole reign. Thiele suggests the explanation that Pekah had ruled before this across the Jordan in Gilead as a rival to Menahem and Pekahiah, before gaining sufficient courage and support to cross the Jordan with fifty Gileadites, kill Pekahiah, and seize the throne.[86] If this is correct, the first twelve years of his rule were over Gilead only, with sovereignty acknowledged successively to Menahem and Pekahiah. This explains how he could have been called "captain" under Pekahiah (II Kings 15:25). Unger points out that an anti-Assyrian party may have de-

---

[84] With one talent equal to 3,000 shekels, 60,000 persons would have been assessed. The total amount was well over $1,000,000; cf. M. Unger, *op. cit.*, p. 175, n. 58.

[85] Indicated by the fact that II Kings 15:30 and II Kings 17:1 establish that the last year of Pekah, the first year of Hoshea, the twelfth year of Ahaz of Judah and the twentieth year of Jotham of Judah were all the same year, thus giving a correlation with Judean kings, which makes that year to have been 732 B.C. It is determined also by Tiglath-pileser's notice (cf. *DOTT*, p. 55) that he deposed Pekah, establishing Hoshea in his place, which came during his western campaign of 734-32. Cf. the dating indications for Ahaz and Jotham of Judah in the following chapter.

[86] Thiele, *MNHK*, p. 124f; cf. also H. G. Stigers, "The Interphased Chronology of Jotham, Ahaz, Hezekiah, and Hoshea," *BETS*, 9 (Spring, 1966), pp. 84-86. Reasons favoring this suggestion are: (1) that Pekah had a band of Gileadites with him when he killed Pekah (II Kings 15:25); (2) Shallum, killed by Menahem, was a "son of Jabesh" (II Kings 15:13), which suggests a background in Jabesh Gilead, which area, when Shallum was killed by Menahem, would have given support to such a rival as Pekah instead of Menahem; (3) that Menahem, in giving tribute to Tiglath-pileser, is said to have done so "to confirm the kingdom in his hand," which suggests that he had such a rival as Pekah, who desired to take it out of his hand; (4) that Pekah had not dared to seize the throne in Samaria earlier would follow in view of the support of Tiglath-pileser which Menahem had gained by the tribute given; and (5) that Pekah appears in friendly relation with Rezin, king of Damascus, shortly after his seizure of Samaria (Isa. 7:1f) finds ready explanation in an earlier Gileadite-Damascus league, when Pekah ruled only in Gilead near Damascus.

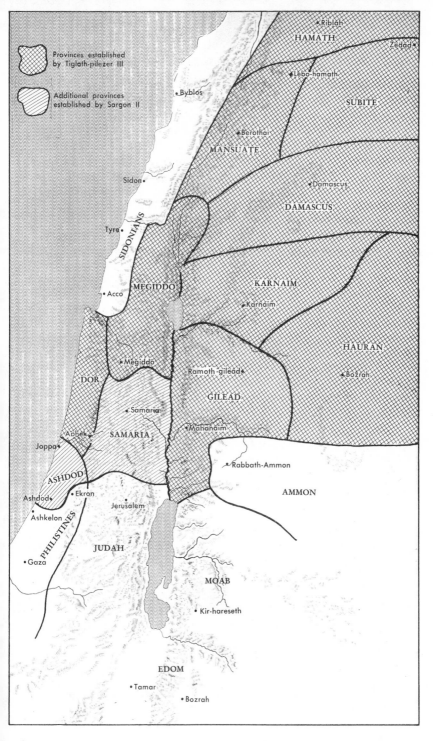

Map 12. The Assyrian Provinces in Palestine

veloped in Israel as a result of Menahem's head-tax program, which paved the way for Pekah's revolution.[87] This suggestion would fit the fact that Pekah did take a strong anti-Assyrian position when he became king in Samaria, then aligning himself with Rezin of Damascus against the great eastern power.

In Pekah's sixth year of sole rule, 734 B.C., Tiglath-pileser III returned to the West to put down this rebellious alliance. He had come at the request of Ahaz, king of Judah, who had been besieged in Jerusalem by Pekah and Rezin (II Chron. 28:5-8; Isa. 7:1f). The two allies had hoped to force Ahaz to join their rebellion, but Ahaz would not and instead asked for aid from the Assyrian ruler.[88] Tiglath-pileser readily complied by conducting his well-known campaigns of 734-732.[89] He first (734) moved down the Mediterranean coast as far as Philistia and subdued cities there, especially Gaza, apparently to cut off possible Egyptian assistance to the coalition. Later (probably 733) he marched into Israel, destroying cities all across Galilee[90] and taking many people captive (II Kings 15:29). Finally (732) he moved against Damascus, likely his prime target from the beginning, devastating the country, capturing the capital city, and executing Rezin the king. Tiglath-pileser himself did not kill Israel's King Pekah, because Hoshea, who succeeded Pekah, did it for him, doubtless in concert with the Assyrian conqueror, however, who claims to have placed Hoshea on Israel's throne (II Kings 15:30).[91]

4. *Hoshea (732–722; II Kings 17:1-6).* Having slain Pekah, Hoshea assumed rule, thus instituting Israel's ninth and last royal family. Israel, at the time of Hoshea's accession, was no longer large. The Assyrians had taken both the North (Galilee) and Transjordan, incorporating these areas as Assyrian provinces,[92] leaving Hoshea only hill country west of the Jordan. Hoshea himself was merely a vassal. Little of the glory that had been Israel's under Jeroboam II longer remained. Even so, Hoshea soon turned in revolt once more against the hated Assyrians, to whom apparently he had submitted only for the sake of expediency.

---

[87] M. Unger, *op. cit.*, p. 99.

[88] Cf. *infra*, chap. 14, pp. 355-56.

[89] For inscription, cf. *ANET*, pp. 283-284. More complete inscriptions in Luckenbill, *Ancient Records of Assyria and Babylonia* (Chicago: University of Chicago Press, 1926), I, secs. 777-779.

[90] Excavation has revealed this devastation, particularly at Megiddo, level III (cf. Wright, *BAR*, p. 164) and at Hazor, level V, where one sherd was found bearing the name Pekah, *pqh*, (cf. Yadin, *BA*, 19 [Feb., 1956], pp. 2-11; 20 [May, 1957], pp. 34-47; 21 [May, 1958], pp. 30-47; 22 [Feb., 1959], pp. 2-20).

[91] Cf. *ANET*, p. 284 for text.

[92] The Damascus territory had also been similarly incorporated; cf. Bright, *BHI*, pp. 257-58, for discussion and references.

The insurrection came soon after Tiglath-pileser was succeeded by his son Shalmaneser V (727-722). Hoshea foolishly made a pact with Egypt, now weak, divided, and therefore unable to give the assistance Hoshea needed. So allied, he refused longer to pay the annual tribute to Assyria.

In 724 B.C., Shalmaneser V marched on Israel (II Kings 17:3-6). Hoshea went to meet him, now bringing his overdue tribute, but this no longer satisfied the Assyrian monarch. Hoshea was immediately taken captive and Shalmaneser moved on to Samaria, placing the capital under siege. He expected it to fall quite readily, no doubt, since the king had already been imprisoned; but it stubbornly resisted. The siege lasted from 724 to 722.[93] Finally, however, the inevitable happened and Samaria fell, bringing the days of Israel as a sovereign nation to a close.[94]

F. An Assyrian Province

After Samaria's fall, an Assyrian governor was placed over the land, thus incorporating Israel west of the Jordan also as a province. Many Israelites were taken captive by Assyria,[95] either prior to the final collapse or at that time, and in place of these a foreign upper class of people was imported.[96] This manner of mixing populations had also been instituted by Tiglath-pileser III, as a means of diminishing chances of rebellion among subjugated peoples. No doubt it served that purpose here in Israel, but it also worked religious havoc. The foreigners

[93] Indicated as from Hoshea's seventh year to his ninth (II Kings 17:6; 18: 9-10). Put more precisely, taking Hoshea's year of accession as 732/731, this places the siege at 725/724-723/722. Cf. Thiele, *MNHK*, pp. 141f. The "three years" indicated (17:5; 18:10) means all of one year and some part of both the preceding and following. This means that the siege lasted a minimum of fourteen months.

[94] Though Sargon II, successor of Shalmaneser V, claims to have been the ruler when Samaria fell (cf. *ANET*, pp. 284-85, or *DOTT*, pp. 58-63 for texts), several reasons argue that this was an empty boast and that Shalmaneser still reigned: (1) II Kings 17:1-6 implies that Shalmaneser took Samaria; (2) Sargon's early notices say nothing of taking Samaria but only the Khorsabad texts from his fifteenth and sixteenth years, which were intended to display his feats; (3) Sargon did not begin to reign until December, 722 B.C., too late to qualify as Hoshea's ninth year which would have closed nine months before. For discussion, cf. A. T. Olmstead, "The Fall of Samaria," *AJSL*, 21 (1904-05), pp. 179-82; Thiele, *MNHK*, pp. 141-47; Unger, *op. cit.*, pp. 106-08; H. Tadmor, "The Campaigns of Sargon II of Assur: A Chronological-Historical Study," *JCS*, 12 (1958), p. 39.

[95] Sargon lists 27,290, which, if correct, must have been taken following the fall of Samaria proper. Many more had been taken by Tiglath-pileser and probably Shalmaneser.

[96] According to II Kings 17:24, these were brought from "Babylon, Cuthah, Avva, Hamath, and Sepharvaim," areas widely scattered in the Assyrian domain.

brought with them their own native ideas of deity and manner of worship. This resulted in a syncretized religion, in which both these false deities and the true Yahweh were revered (II Kings 17:29-41). This mixing of population resulted also in inter-marriage between the Israelites left in the land, of which there were many, and the new foreign people, fewer in number. The descendants of these marriages came to be called Samaritans.

G. SUMMARY

Israel continued as a nation for just over two centuries, 931 to 722 B.C. Nineteen kings reigned, representing nine ruling families. Eight kings were either assassinated or committed suicide. Not one of the nineteen was considered good by God, because each followed either the substitute worship at the golden-calf centers or the more evil cult of Baal. For this reason, God's blessing was withheld. Through Elijah and Elisha, warning was given to the house of Omri concerning the excessive sin of turning to Baal-Melqart. When no heed was given, punishment was meted out, first in the destruction of the Omriad family by Jehu, and then in the abject humiliation of all Israel before the Aramaeans of Damascus. Once again warning came through Amos and Hosea to the house of Jehu, during the prosperous days of Jeroboam II, for gross wickedness related to the material affluence then existent, but again the people would not hear. A second time God permitted major national humiliation; in this instance before mighty Assyria. This occasion did not end until Samaria had fallen and Israel ceased to exist as a sovereign power. Israel had been given opportunity to repent, but would not. God's wrath fell upon her.

CHAPTER FOURTEEN

THE KINGDOM OF JUDAH

I Kings14:21–15:24; 22:41-50; II Kings 8:16-29; 11–25;
II Chronicles 10–36

Judah's history paralleled that of Israel, but ran nearly a century and a half longer.

A. A PERIOD OF CONFLICT WITH ISRAEL (931–870; I Kings 14:21–15:24; II Chronicles 10–16)

The nation left to Rehoboam, following the secession of the northern tribes, consisted primarily of the tribe of Judah. Rehoboam held basically the same area that David did when he was initially made king at Hebron. When Ahijah first spoke to Jeroboam concerning the division, he mentioned only one tribe as remaining loyal to Solomon's descendant (I Kings 11:31). At the time, however, he gave Jeroboam only ten of the twelve pieces of the rent garment in symbol of the tribes he would rule, implying that another tribe would be added to Judah. Benjamin was that added tribe, though at first her loyalty was likely with the seceders (I Kings 12:20). Historically, Benjamin had always aligned herself with the northern group.[1] But now she came to follow Rehoboam[2] and was soon referred to regularly as part of the southern nation.[3] How this change came about is not indicated, but likely Re-

[1] Listed with the tribes over which Ishbosheth ruled (II Sam. 2:9). Also the revolt at the time of David's return to Jerusalem, following Absalom's death, was led by a Benjamite, Sheba (II Sam. 20:1-22).

[2] Perhaps Rehoboam's control never extended over all of Benjamite territory, however. Bethel, made religious center by Jeroboam, was on the border between Benjamin and Ephraim (Josh. 18:13) though in Ephraimite territory (I Chron. 7:28); and later Baasha was able to fortify Raamah, only four miles north of Jerusalem, well within Benjamite land (II Chron. 16:1). Probably the actual border shifted from time to time.

[3] For instance, I Kings 12:21-23; II Chron. 11:1, 3, 10, 12, 23; 14:8; 15:2, 8, 9; etc.

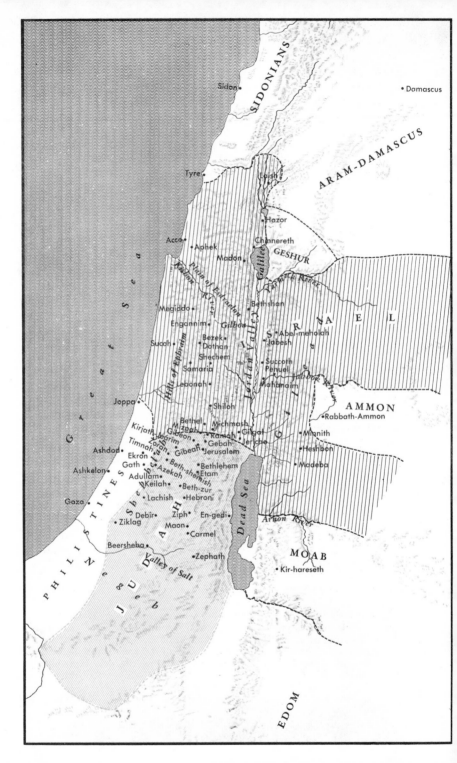

Map. 13. The Kingdoms of Israel and Judah Shortly After the Division

hoboam simply brought pressure to bear on her leaders to switch loyalty, employing ominous threats and/or attractive inducements. Jerusalem, after all, lay directly on the Benjamite border, and a buffer zone was sorely needed between it and the new northern kingdom.

A question arises regarding the tribe of Simeon, to whom Joshua had allotted eighteen cities within the area of Judah (Josh. 19:1-9; I Chron. 4:28-33). Why were her people not included in the southern nation? The answer is best found in an apparent movement of many (perhaps most) Simeonites, some time prior to the division of the kingdom, north to the region of Ephraim and Manasseh, perhaps more specifically northern Manasseh. In both II Chronicles 15:9 and 34:6 Simeon is mentioned along with Ephraim and Manasseh in a way suggesting that all three tribes were then (time of Asa and following) geographically linked together.[4]

1. *Rehoboam (931–913; I Kings 14:21-31; II Chronicles 10–12).* Rehoboam became king at the age of forty-one and ruled for seventeen years. He did evil in the sight of God, not following the pattern of his grandfather, David. He was influenced too much by the religious failures of Solomon's latter days. Rehoboam built high places (*bamoth*), images (*masseboth*), and Asherim poles (*'asherim*), and also permitted male prostitutes (*qadesh*) in the land (I Kings 14:23-24). These infractions represent a return in some part to the Canaanite religion, which David had largely put out of the country. That Rehoboam was now restoring it came probably as a result of pressure by continuing adherents, who had remained silent until this more sympathetic reign of Rehoboam. Because of the existence of Canaanite worship during the Judges Period, God had withheld His blessing then, and Rehoboam should have recognized that He would do so again.

a. Success against Jeroboam (I Kings 14:30; II Chronicles 11:5-13). Rehoboam had military encounters with two main enemies, Jeroboam of Israel and Shishak of Egypt. With the first he was generally successful, but with the second he suffered tragic loss, said to have been God's punishment for the religious defection.

It is stated that Rehoboam had continual conflict with Jeroboam (I Kings 14:30). There is no indication that this was in violent, open warfare, however; in fact, this manner of conflict had been directly

---

[4] II Chron. 34:6 suggests the location as being more specifically northern Manasseh, in that Naphtali, still farther north, is associated with Simeon. Rationale for Simeon's move lies in Simeon's humbled situation in being assigned only cities when all other tribes had been assigned territories. This humbled status was no doubt related to Jacob's prediction that Simeon woud be scattered in Israel (Gen. 49:5-7) and Simeon's small number upon entering Canaan (only 22,000, the smallest tribe). Cf. L. J. Wood, "Simeon, the Tenth Tribe of Israel," *Theolog,* 4 (Fall, 1966), pp. 6-10.

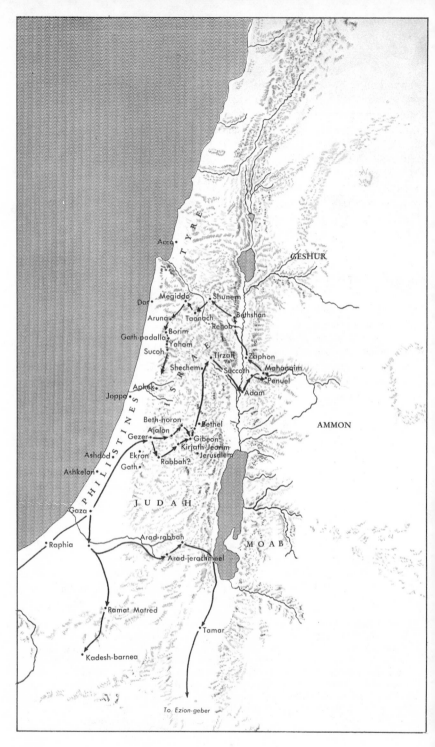

Map 14. The Campaign of Shishak

forbidden by God (II Chron. 11:1-4). The strife likely centered in repeated border disputes, especially involving the Benjamite area. Rehoboam felt that he needed Benjamin as a buffer zone, and Jeroboam naturally would have wanted it too. In that Benjamin does come to be listed with Judah, it follows that Rehoboam won in these disputes more often than Jeroboam. The victories would have concerned both military clashes in defeating Jeroboam's border guards and psychological persuasions in bringing Benjamites to want to be with the southern nation. Rehoboam needed both the land and good will of the people.

In keeping with Rehoboam's success in Benjamin are his endeavors in building the defenses of his nation. He demonstrated an aggressive spirit in fortifying no less than fifteen cities (II Chron. 11:5-10), located in both Judah and Benjamin.[5] Since they are all either to the south or west from Jerusalem, it appears that they were mainly in defense against Egypt and Philistia, rather than Israel to the north. If so, this fortification likely was undertaken following the invasion of Shishak from Egypt in Rehoboam's fifth year.

b. Defeat by Shishak of Egypt (I Kings 14:25-27; II Chron. 12: 2-12). The Egyptian king, Shishak (Sheshonq I, c. 945-924), before whom Rehoboam suffered the loss, was a native of Libya and founder of Egypt's Twenty-second Dynasty. He had earlier given asylum to Jeroboam in his flight from Solomon (I Kings 11:40). Now in Rehoboam's fifth year he made a strong attempt to reassert Egyptian supremacy in Palestine. Shishak lists no less than 150 cities which he overran in this campaign.[6] Many are located in southern Judah and still farther south in Edom, where Shishak may even have destroyed Solomon's copper works at Ezion-geber. Though unlisted by Shishak, Debir and possibly Beth-shemesh, in that they give some evidence of having been destroyed about this time, may have felt his might. No cities of central Judah, however, are mentioned by the conqueror, which is strange, in that the biblical record speaks of Shishak taking vast treasures from Jerusalem itself (I Kings 14:26; II Chron. 12:9). It may be that Rehoboam simply gave this treasure as tribute to Shishak to keep him

---

[5] The two most northern were Zorah and Aijalon, originally allotted to Dan (Josh. 19:41-42). Since II Chron. 11:10 indicates that the fifteen cities were from Benjamin as well as Judah, it must be that these two cities (the nearest to Benjamite territory) had been absorbed by Benjamin after the Danite migration (Judg. 18).

[6] Carved on the exterior of the south wall of the Amon temple at Karnak. Shishak is pictured smiting the Asiatics as the god Amon presents to him ten lines of captives which symbolize the cities listed. Cf. *ANEP*, fig. 349 for a picture; for translation, discussion, and bibliography of publications, cf. J. Simons, *Handbook for the Study of Egyptian Topographical Lists Relating to Western Asia* (Leiden: E. J. Brill, 1937), pp. 90-101, 178-86.

from destroying Judah proper. This would be in keeping with a promise given by God through the prophet Shemaiah to the Judean king. The prophet had come to the king, warning him of the impending punishment from God at the hand of Shishak due to Rehoboam's sin; and Rehoboam had repented, with the result that God had promised to give "some deliverance" (II Chron. 12:6-7). For all central Judah to have been spared serious damage would have constituted a meaningful form of this "deliverance."

In the North, Israel too felt Shishak's power, as noted in the prior chapter. Numerous cities listed by Shishak are from Israel. Megiddo, one of them, gives testimony of the destruction in the form of a part of a victory monument bearing Shishak's name. The Egyptian army even crossed the Jordan into Gilead, and numerous cities from there are listed. All this means that Shishak covered a wide area in the campaign and was remarkably successful. His country at home, however, apparently was too weak for him to maintain a permanent hold. His design of establishing Egyptian authority in Palestine was not realized.[7]

As mentioned above, it was probably after this campaign that Rehoboam fortified his fifteen cities, for Shishak does not seem to have been hindered by them at the time. The effort could well have been made later to forestall a repetition of what had been experienced.

2. *Abijam (913–911; I Kings 15:1-8; II Chronicles 13:1-22)*. The son and successor of Rehoboam was Abijam,[8] who ruled for three years. He continued in the sin of his father. He also continued his father's struggle with Jeroboam, and with still greater success. At one time a major battle broke out between the two sides (II Chron. 13:3-19) in the area of Ephraim near Mt. Zemaraim (likely east of Bethel). Abijam, though having a smaller force, was victorious and gained control even over Bethel, the important southern religious center of Israel. In addition, he took less important Jeshanah and Ephron nearby. This advance did not last long, however, for Asa, his son[9] and successor,

---

[7] Shishak may have maintained a fortification at Sharuhen (modern Tell el-Farah), southeast of Gaza for a time, however. A formidable brick wall, twenty-three feet wide, found there has been ascribed to him, which, if correct, would show an intention to remain at least in this one city, affording a foothold in the land. Cf. Wright, *BAR*, pp. 149-50.

[8] Called Abijah in II Chron. 13:1f. Abijam means "father of the sea," and Abijah, "father is Yahweh." Apparently he was called by both names.

[9] Because Abijam and Asa are said to have had mothers and grandmothers of the same name (I Kings 15:2, 10; II Chron. 15:16), some scholars believe they were brothers and not father and son, as indicated in I Kings 15:8 and II Chron. 14:1; cf. Abijam's short reign of only three years. But Abijam was old enough to have sons (indeed, according to II Chron. 13:21 he had 22 sons and 16 daughters from 14 wives). It is likely that the mother, Maacah, and

was hard pressed again by Baasha, who even moved for a time as far south as Ramah, just four miles from Jerusalem, with an occupying force.

3. *Asa (911–870; I Kings 15:9-24; II Chronicles 14–16)*. Asa ruled forty-one years and was the first of the religiously good kings of the southern kingdom. Eight of Judah's total nineteen kings are said to have been good in God's sight, which is in marked contrast to none out of Israel's nineteen, all of whom are described as evil. This does not mean that all eight in Judah's history pleased God to the same degree, but only that each intended to conduct himself and the kingdom according to the Mosaic Law and carried out this desire to a meaningful extent.

a. Religious activities (I Kings 15:11-15; II Chron. 14:2-5; 15:8-18). Several good acts of Asa are mentioned. He put male prostitutes (*qe-deshim*) and idols (*gillulim*) out of the land. He removed his (grand) mother from being queen mother because she had made an idol to the goddess Asherah. In his fifteenth year, following a victory over an Egyptian army (noted below) and consequent encouragement by the prophet Azariah (II Chron. 15:1-7), he called for an assembly of people from Judah and Benjamin, including also defected Israelites from the tribes of Ephraim, Manasseh, and Simeon, to renew their covenantal promises with God. Sacrifices were offered of the 700 oxen and 7,000 sheep taken as spoil in the recent conflict. He also added some newly dedicated furnishings to the Temple and in some way renewed the altar of God. One thing he did not do, however, was to remove the old Canaanite high places.

In the latter days of his life, sad to say, Asa did not do as well in God's sight. He seems to have become proud and self-reliant. This is evidenced by his imprisonment of Hanani, a prophet, for a rebuke Asa deserved. It is witnessed also by his trust in physicians rather than God when he became diseased in his feet (II Chron. 16:12).

b. Victory over Egypt (II Chron. 14:9-15). Asa experienced two instances of major foreign conflict. The first was with Egypt and it ended in a splendid victory. The Egyptian force was led by one Zerah from Ethiopia, likely a military leader under Osarkon I (c. 914-874),[10]

grandmother, Abishalom, were really grandmother and great-grandmother to Asa. Because of Abijam's short reign, Maacah had carried over as queen mother and was the one deposed by Asa for worshiping a false idol (I Kings 15:13; II Chron. 15:16). Cf. Albright, *ARI*, p. 158.

[10] Some have identified Zerah with O(serak)hon, but the identification is not likely: due to a basic change in spelling for the two; Zerah not being called a Pharaoh; and Osarkon being of Libyan descent and not Ethiopian, as indicated for Zerah. Cf. G. Ricciotti, *The History of Israel* (2d. trans. ed.; Milwaukee: Bruce Publishing Co., 1958), I, p. 359.

king of Egypt. He may have been already serving as commander at an Egyptian outpost, possibly left at Sharuhen by Shishak. Approximately thirty years had elapsed since Shishak's attack, assuming that Zerah's campaign came in Asa's fifteenth year, which is likely.[11] Zerah's attack was launched in the general region of Sharuhen, involving specifically Mareshah[12] and Gerar. Asa looked to God for assistance and received it, enabling him to defeat the larger force and take much spoil for Israel.

c. Self-reliance in respect to Israel (I Kings 15:16-22; II Chron. 16:10). Perhaps this success in Egypt was in part the cause or reason for Asa's now becoming too self-reliant and turning from the commendable trust in God he had been demonstrating. At least it was the very next year, Asa's sixteenth,[13] that the second foreign conflict ensued when he displayed this change of spirit.[14] The new struggle was with Baasha, king of Israel; and its nature was more economic than military. Baasha had penetrated the northern border of Judah for the purpose of fortifying Ramah, only four miles north of Jerusalem, that he might establish control over north-south Jerusalem traffic. In retaliation, Asa, rather than seeking guidance from God, relied on his own judgment and sent for help from Benhadad I of Damascus. Benhadad, just rising to a position of power, was happy to comply and test his strength against Israel. He attacked certain northern cities of Baasha, and the Israelite king was forced to desist at Ramah and protect his own interests. Asa in turn appropriated supplies which Baasha had collected at Ramah and used them to strengthen defenses at Geba and Mizpah.[15] Thinking himself wise in this maneuver, Asa was quite

[11] So argues Thiele, *MNHK*, pp. 57-62. His argument hinges on his belief that the chronological notation of "the 36th year," in II Chron. 16:1, is in reference to the duration at that time of Judah's history rather than to Asa's sole reign. He has convincing arguments as against Albright, "The Chronology of the Divided Monarchy," *BASOR*, 100 (Dec., 1945), pp. 16-22.

[12] Mareshah has been identified with Tell Sandahannah, near Keilah and Achzib (Josh. 15:44; Mic. 1:14-15). Less than two miles north is modern Beit Guvrin.

[13] On the basis of Thiele's chronology; *MNHK*, pp. 59-60.

[14] It should be realized that between the two conflicts, however, Asa's fine assembly for the renewal of the covenant with God was called in Jerusalem. In fact, the 700 oxen and 7,000 sheep then offered were largely from the spoil taken, and no doubt the whole occasion was prompted by a spirit of thanksgiving for God's favor then shown. For all this good result, however, Asa could still have subconsciously been affected with a proud spirit, as a consequence of the success.

[15] Asa likely reestablished the boundary near Benjamin's northern limits. Geba, which he fortified, is mentioned in Josiah's reign later as then having been near the northern border (II Kings 23:8). For location, cf. *supra*, chap. 10, p. 244, n. 24; for Mizpah, chap. 9, p. 227, n. 82.

taken aback and then angered when Hanani, the prophet, did not praise him but brought stern rebuke for trusting in himself rather than God. The prophet told him that what he had really accomplished was to bring Judah under obligation to a foreign power and to set the stage for further conflict, rather than to achieve true benefit as Asa had thought. Hanani implied that had Asa trusted in God, he would have gained a genuine victory over Baasha, even as he had over Zerah of Egypt the prior year (II Chron. 16:8-9), and he would not have involved his country in these detrimental relationships.

B. A PERIOD OF ALLIANCE WITH ISRAEL (873-835; I Kings 22: 41-50; II Kings 8:16-29; 11:1-16; II Chronicles 17:1–23:15)

The next period is marked by good relations with Israel to the north. The fighting which had characterized the prior period ceased. This was the day of the house of Omri in Israel, and peace reigned between the two countries. As noted in the prior chapter, even a treaty—though working religious ill for Judah—was likely signed between them. Athaliah, the last to rule over Judah in this time, was actually the daughter of Ahab, son of Omri.

1. *Jehoshaphat (873–848; I Kings 22:41-50; II Chronicles 17–20)*. Asa's son and successor was Jehoshaphat, who ruled for thirty-five years beginning at the age of twenty-five. Three of these years were as co-regent with his father.[16] Asa developed a serious disease in his feet and may have become sufficiently incapacitated to require his son to act for him. He proclaimed him actual king along with himself. This was the first instance of coregency in either Judah or Israel, following the brief co-rule of Solomon with David. Israel's employment of the idea came more than a century later.[17]

a. Good religious activity (I Kings 22:43, 46; II Chron. 17:3-9; 20: 3-33). Religiously, Jehoshaphat was the second good king of Judah. He followed in his father's footsteps by further ridding the land of Baal's cultic features, even removing the high places (*bamoth*) now to some degree.[18] Further, he gave special orders to Levites and others to teach the "Book of the Law" throughout all Judah. A prime task of the priests and Levites from the beginning had been this teaching,[19] but apparently they had been lax in recent years. Jehoshaphat cor-

[16] Cf. Thiele, *MNHK*, pp. 64-66 for evidence.
[17] At the close of Jehoash's reign; cf. *supra*, chap. 13, p. 325.
[18] Both I Kings 22:43 and II Chron. 20:33 state that the high places were not removed, while II Chron. 17:6 says that they were. The situation likely was that the better known high places were, while those in which many of the common people worshiped (I Kings 22:43) were not.
[19] *Supra*, chap. 8, p. 196.

rectly recognized that, if the people were to obey God's Law, they needed first to be instructed in it.

An illustration of Jehoshaphat's commendable faith in God is seen in connection with an attack made against him by an alliance of Moab, Ammon, and Edom (II Chron. 20:1-30). Learning of the invasion, Jehoshaphat did not despair but called for a time of fasting and prayer in Jerusalem. God responded to the prayer, voiced by the king himself through an attendant prophet, and promised victory. When Jehoshaphat's troops, led by singing Levites, came to where the enemy was located, they found that inter-army rivalry had led to strife and death among them; and the only task of the Judean force was to collect the booty of the dead opponents.

b. Strong ruler (II Chron. 17:10-19). It should not be thought, in view of this instance, that Jehoshaphat was a weak ruler with a weak army. He had, in fact, a strong army consisting of five divisions, three from Judah and two from Benjamin. Perhaps he was caught off guard somewhat by the suddenness of the above attack. Jehoshaphat also gave attention to strengthen the defenses of his country, building both fortresses and store cities. His might became known abroad, and other countries feared to make war against him, perhaps accounting for the tripartite nature of the invading enemy referred to above. Both the Philistines and Arabians sought to maintain his good will by bringing valuable presents.

c. Judicial provisions (II Chron. 19:4-11). Jehoshaphat took steps to improve juridical procedures in the land. In view of the nature of the changes he made, it appears that laxity had arisen relative to matters already spelled out in the Mosaic Law. Jehoshaphat now called for the divinely ordained regulations to be reinstated. He appointed judges in important cities, thus making more local courts (legally prescribed: Deut. 16:18; 19:12; 21:18f; 22:13f), and he urged that those appointed be fair in all decisions. He also appointed certain priests, Levites, and recognized leaders to serve in a central court in Jerusalem (prescribed Deut. 17:8-13). When the matter to be considered at this court involved religion, Amariah, the high priest, was to act as chairman; when it involved a civic question, Zebadiah, a civic leader was to officiate. In these provisions, Jehoshaphat displayed a true heart towards God and towards the people, as well as commendable ability in statesmanship.

d. Alliance with Israel (I Kings 22:44, 48, 49; II Kings 3:4-27; II Chron. 18:1–19:3; 20:35-37). Jehoshaphat's alliance with the house of Omri has already been noticed.[20] That he made it demonstrated

---

[20] *Supra*, chap. 13, pp. 312-13.

further the statesmanlike qualities he possessed; and, in terms of economic and military values, it may have made some contribution to his country. In terms of God's all-important approval, however, great loss was suffered. For one thing, it involved the tragic marriage of his son Jehoram to Ahab's daughter Athaliah, who followed in the ways of her mother Jezebel.[21] Jehoshaphat had abundant reason to regret this marriage many times in years to come.

Other problems arose from this alliance. These resulted from the three specific times that Jehoshaphat aided Israelite kings, in keeping with the pact, as noticed briefly in the prior chapter. He helped Ahab in his battle with Benhadad at Ramoth-gilead, and was nearly killed for his trouble (I Kings 22:29-33; II Chron. 18:29-34). He joined Ahab's eldest son, Ahaziah, in ship building at Ezion-geber on the Gulf of Aqaba; and every ship was destroyed before its maiden voyage (I Kings 22:48-49; II Chron. 20:35-37). He allied himself with Ahab's second son, Jehoram, in a military offensive (wrong in itself) against Moab to coerce tribute-paying to Israel, and nearly perished, along with the attendant armies, for lack of water (II Kings 3:4-27). Prophets of God were involved each time: Micaiah in warning that the Ramoth-gilead battle would be lost, which should have stirred Jehoshaphat to withdraw immediately;[22] Eliezer, less known, in warning that Jehoshaphat's ships would be broken due to God's displeasure at the alliance; and Elisha, in revealing God's way of deliverance for the allied kings in their dire need for water. Jehoshaphat should have learned a lesson the first time, but he did not.

2. *Jehoram (853–841; II Kings 8:16-24; II Chronicles 21).* Jehoshaphat, following the pattern of his father, appointed his son, Jehoram, as coregent for the last four years of his reign.[23] Since the time of the appointment coincides with the year of Jehoshaphat's assistance to Ahab at Ramoth-gilead, Jehoshaphat's incentive in this may have been to have a son ruling at home while he was away for what might be a prolonged war. During these years of coregency, Jehoram should have learned from his father; and perhaps he did in secular matters, but not in religious. Jehoshaphat had been one of Judah's best kings in God's sight, but now Jehoram did evil. A contributing reason surely was his marriage to the wicked Athaliah (II Kings 8:18). He ruled alone eight years after his father's death (II Chron. 21:5), and five unhappy events marked the time.

[21] She is not specifically stated to have been Jezebel's daughter (II Kings 8: 16-24), but this is extremely likely.

[22] Also, following this near miss with death, Jehoshaphat was directly rebuked for the alliance by another prophet, Jehu, son of Hanani (II Chron. 19:1-3).

[23] Cf. II Kings 1:17 and 3:1. For argumentation, cf. Thiele, *MNHK*, pp. 64-68.

The first was his slaughter of six brothers, all sons of Jehoshaphat, to whom the father had previously given gifts of gold, valuable articles, and fortified cities (II Chron. 21:2-4). Jehoram's purpose was to insure his own rule against rivals. Because he was the only king in all Judah's history to commit such a misdeed, other than his own wife when she later seized leadership (II Kings 11:1), it is probable that Athaliah's hand was in this crime.

The second and third concerned two successful instances of revolt against his rule. One was by Edom (II Kings 8:20-22; II Chron. 21: 8-9), who earlier had helped Jehoram and Jehoshaphat against Moab (II Kings 3:4-27). The submission of Edom to Judah likely dated from Jehoshaphat's still earlier triumph over a coalition of which Edom had been a part (II Chron. 20:1-29).[24] It may also have been at that time that an Edomite deputy was installed as ruler in place of a king (I Kings 22:47). Jehoram fought to put down the revolt at this time but was not successful. The other revolt was by a city, Libnah (II Kings 8:22).[25] Apparently this one, too, was successful, for no indication is given that Jehoram even tried to retaliate.

The fourth was an invasion of his country by Philistines and Arabians[26] in which Judah suffered substantial loss. Material goods were seized, and Jehoram's own wives and every son with the exception of Ahaziah, the youngest, were captured (II Chron. 21:16-17).[27] Little could be more tragic and humiliating for a king than this.

The fifth was the gruesome death of Jehoram himself. He died of a fearful disease of the intestines, in accordance with a warning from Elijah[28] in view of his sin (II Chron. 21:12-15, 18-20). In all, one must say that Jehoram's reign was distressing and unsuccessful.

3. *Ahaziah (841 B.C.; II Kings 8:25-29; 9:27-29; II Chronicles 22: 1-9).* Ahaziah succeeded his father and ruled less than one year. The

[24] The control in Edom gained by David had been lost by the time of Rehoboam's reign. The new conquest by Jehoshaphat was of prime importance because it reopened the vital trade route to the South.

[25] Libnah is sometimes identified with Tell es-Safi, four miles west of Azekah at the head of the Elah Valley, but probably better with Tell Bornat, six miles south; cf. Albright, *BASOR*, 15, p. 19.

[26] Philistines and Arabians were the ones who had earlier feared and even paid tribute to Jehoshaphat (II Chron. 17:11).

[27] This son is called Jehoahaz in II Chron. 21:17 (cf. 22:1). Jehoahaz and Ahaziah are basically the same names, with the compound elements "Ahaz" and "Jah" simply transposed.

[28] Elijah probably died about 850 B.C., shortly after the accession of Jehoram in Israel in 852 B.C. Jehoram of Judah began his reign as coregent in 853, which means this letter came early in his reign, likely while Jehoshaphat still lived.

youngest son of the family,[29] he alone had survived the Philistine-Arabian raid. Ahaziah followed his father's wicked ways, strongly influenced by his mother, Athaliah, "who was his counsellor to do wickedly" (II Chron. 22:3).

Though Ahaziah had escaped the hands of the Philistines and Arabians, he was not able to escape Jehu. As observed in the prior chapter, he traveled north to visit his wounded uncle, Jehoram; and Jehu killed both in his destruction of the house of Omri. Ahaziah had earlier helped his uncle in a battle against the Aramaeans, when Jehoram had received his wound. Ahaziah did escape the initial blow of Jehu at Jezreel but was later caught and killed by Jehu's men, dying finally at Megiddo.[30] His servants brought his body back to Jerusalem for burial.

4. *Athaliah (841–835; II Kings 11:1-16; II Chronicles 22:10–23:15)*

a. Cruel, wicked rule (II Kings 11:1-3; II Chron. 22:10-12). Athaliah, mother of Ahaziah, was a true daughter of her mother, Jezebel. She pursued the same goals and displayed the same hard, vindictive character.[31] The two women stand quite alone in biblical history for their forwardness and cruelty. Athaliah had already demonstrated the kind of person she was prior to Ahaziah's death. As noted, she had influenced her husband to kill his rival brothers. She also had sought to install the cult of Baal in Judah as her mother had in Israel (II Kings 8:18, 27; 11:18), though fortunately with less success, due likely to greater opposition. With her son dead, however, she perpetrated a crime still worse. She had Ahaziah's children (her own grandchildren) slaughtered so that she might herself seize the throne, which rightfully belonged to the eldest male of those killed. Human decency, apart from a normal grandmother's love, called for her to go into mourning and seek to comfort and render care for her son's offspring, but this was not Athaliah's way. All the children died with the exception of a baby, Joash, who was rescued by an aunt, a sister of Ahaziah, named Jehoshabeath. Because Ahaziah's brothers had already been killed in the Philistine-Arabian attack, the power-hungry woman did not have

[29] His age of 22, given in II Kings 8:26, is correct and not 42 as given in II Chron. 22:2. His father, Jehoram, was only 40 when he died (II Kings 8:17). A copyist's error, confusing the letter numeral *kaph* (twenty) with the *men* (forty), may be responsible.

[30] *Supra*, chap. 13, p. 321, n. 56.

[31] This was true of Athaliah in spite of almost unparalleled catastrophe that she had experienced: the body of her mother had just been eaten by dogs; her brother, Jehoram of Israel, had been killed at the same time by Jehu in the blood purge of Omri's house; her husband Jehoram had recently died of a fearful disease of the bowels; her son Ahaziah had just been killed by Jehu's pursuing men; and her other sons had shortly before been captured by raiding Philistines and Arabians.

to take their lives. It may be, indeed, that their earlier deaths were what prompted Athaliah first to think of trying for the throne. With all sons now dead, and the grandchildren really too young[32] to give any challenge, the way apparently seemed open to the place of power she wanted.

After this initial, ignominious deed, Athaliah ruled for six years. Seemingly none wished to withstand her, either in the first seizure of power or during the following years, for no report is given of any challenge. We are not told either of any of her activities during these six years, but we may be sure that she did all she could to foster Baalism. The fact that Jehu had dealt a serious blow to the cult in Israel by his well-known blood purge probably motivated her to do even more in Judah to perpetuate it, but it may also have contributed to greater opposition against her.

b. Crowning of Joash (II Kings 11:4-16; II Chron. 23:1-15). The baby Joash, rescued by Ahaziah's sister, reached the age of seven during Athaliah's sixth year of rule. This was old enough for Jehoiada, high priest and husband of Jehoshabeath, who had waited and planned for Athaliah's overthrow, to take action in placing the young boy on the throne in her place. Military and religious leaders were brought into the plan, the effectuation of which was made easier by a widespread discontent with her rule. All went well as the seven-year-old was brought forth from his hiding place and crowned. A large number of assembled people clapped their hands and shouted, "Long live the king." Athaliah heard the shout, came to see the cause, cried in despair, "Treason, treason," and fled for her life. Jehoiada ordered her execution, and this was promptly carried out.

C. Four God-approved Kings (835–731; II Kings 12–15; II Chronicles 23:16–27:9)

Four successive kings, called good in the sight of God, now ruled. These, plus Asa and Jehoshaphat, and two others, Hezekiah and Josiah, yet to come, make a total of eight so described. None of the present four receive so high a commendation as either of the last two or Jeshoshaphat of the first two; but still, together, they gave Judah her longest span of God-approved rule, a period of over one hundred years.

1. *Joash (835–796; II Kings 12; II Chronicles 23:16–24:27).* Joash, who ruled forty years, led the way. The young king needed an advisor; and the aged, pious high priest, Jehoiada, who had already protected and anointed him, served in this capacity. To Jehoiada must go most of the credit for the fine record of Joash's early years.

---

[32] Ahaziah himself was only 23 at his death (II Kings 8:26).

a. Religious reformation (II Kings 12:2-16; II Chron. 23:16–24:14). After the apostate innovations of Athaliah, religious reform was needed in Judah. Joash, through Jehoiada, set about the task. Religious articles imported by Athaliah were destroyed, including the Baal-Melqart temple, its altars and images. The Baal priest, Mattan, was killed, and the personnel and offerings prescribed in the Mosaic Law were re-instituted. True worship of Yahweh was again observed, though some of the high places still continued to be used. Many years later, when Joash had come to an age to act for himself, he gave orders for the Temple to be repaired of damage done to it by Athaliah's sons (II Chron. 24:7). The priests and Levites were slow, however, in collecting funds for the purpose, which prompted Joash, in his twenty-third year, to suggest a new method of raising the necessary money. A box was placed at the side of the altar for people to give when they came with their sacrifices. They did so enthusiastically. Workers were hired and the required repairs made, with money enough left over to provide new furnishings. A high spirit of true worship prevailed in the land.

b. Declension and punishment (II Kings 12:17-21; II Chron. 24: 15-27). So long as Jehoiada continued as high priest, Joash remained a true follower of God; but when he died, the king changed. This development came sometime after Joash's twenty-third year, for it was then that he gave the fine order relative to offerings for Temple repair just noted, but how long after is not indicated. Jehoiada died at the age of one hundred and thirty (II Chron. 24:15),[33] which was sometime in the latter part of Joash's reign. Following the great man's demise, the king began to listen to new advisors, who were more sympathetic to the deposed cult of Baal-Melqart (II Chron. 24:17-18). In fact, he was so influenced that he had Jehoiada's own son, Zechariah, stoned to death for rebuking him for sinful actions (II Chron. 24:20-22).

The close of the year in which Zechariah was stoned saw great loss for Joash at the hands of Hazael, king of Damascus.[34] Having brought a crushing defeat on Israel, Hazael marched south as far as Gath in Philistia and seized it. Then he turned toward Jerusalem. He brought destruction through Judah generally, and took many lives, including those of a number of princes (II Chron. 24:23-24). Only by giving

---

[33] This was much above the average for the day. Jehoiada had been born while Solomon yet reigned, and so likely served as high priest for some of Asa's rule and all of Jehoshaphat's. He probably had been responsible in part for their good records. He would have been about 100 years old when he anointed Joash. His wife, Jehoshabeath, granddaughter of Jehoshaphat, was obviously much younger.

[34] *Supra*, chap. 13, pp. 322-23.

Hazael large tribute[35] did Joash succeed in persuading him to spare Jerusalem from complete devastation (II Kings 12:17-18).

As a further punishment, Joash died by assassination at the hands of conspirators (II Kings 12:19-21; II Chron. 24:25-27). Even his own servants took part, prompted by their disapproval of his reversal in policy after Jehoiada's death. To die in this manner was a bitter close to Joash's life, especially when for years his reign had been a cause for rejoicing in Judah.

2. *Amaziah (796–767; II Kings 14:1-20; II Chronicles 25).* Amaziah succeeded his father — the assassination not bringing change in family rule — and he ruled twenty-nine years, though the last twenty-four were in coregency with his son, Uzziah. Amaziah stood approved of God in life and reign as his father, but, also like him, he did not remove all the high places. One of Amaziah's first actions was to punish his father's conspirators by having them all killed (II Kings 14:1-6).

a. Victory over Edom (II Kings 14:7; II Chron. 25:5-16). Two major battles were fought by Amaziah, the first of which was with Edom and ended in complete victory. Edom, lost by revolt under Jehoram, continued to be attractive to Judah because of the southern trade routes to which it gave access. Amaziah made ambitious plans to regain control there, even hiring soldiers from Israel for one hundred talents of silver to support his own troops. He was rebuked by a "man of God" for securing them, however, and so sent them back home much to their displeasure.[36] He later found he did not need them anyway, for he was able to achieve victory alone. He killed 10,000 of the enemy and took another 10,000 captive, only to slay them later by casting them from the top of a high rock. Following the victory, however, he greatly displeased God by bringing images of Edom's false gods back to Judah and worshiping them. A prophet bringing rebuke pointedly asked, "Why hast thou sought after the gods of the people, which could not deliver their own people out of thine hand?"

b. Defeat by Israel (II Kings 14:8-14; II Chron. 25:17-24). The second battle was with Israel. Amaziah, made proud and self-confident by his Edomite victory, challenged Jehoash of Israel. Israel recently had suffered extensive harm before the might of Hazael of Damascus,

---

[35] Described as all the "sacred treasures" of his fathers and of himself, plus all the gold deposited in the Temple treasury and that of the palace.

[36] This displeasure was demonstrated in their attack, whether in taking an indirect route home or some time later, on cities of northwest Judah in the area of Bethhoron. They killed 3,000 people and took much spoil at the time (II Chron. 25:13).

but by now was experiencing a resurgence, which Amaziah apparently did not realize. Jehoash, commendably, tried to dissuade the Judean ruler,[37] but Amaziah insisted and war did ensue near Beth-shemesh, west of Jerusalem. Judah was defeated, and Jehoash then proceeded to Jerusalem, destroying some 600 feet of city wall and seizing substantial booty and many captives. It is likely that among these captives was even Amaziah himself (II Kings 14:13), which, if so, was a humiliation of the gravest kind. The chronicler states that all this came in punishment for Amaziah having "sought after the gods of Edom" (II Chron. 25:20). If Amaziah was taken captive, which fits significantly with the beginning of his son's coregency, he likely was kept in Israel as long as Jehoash of Israel lived (II Kings 14:17) and was then allowed to return to resume the rule of Judah.[38]

c. Death (II Kings 14:18-20; II Chron. 25:26-28). No information is given regarding Amaziah's rule after he returned except the unhappy note that he too, as his father, saw a conspiracy formed against him. He tried to escape death by flight to Lachish, but was followed and killed there. His body was returned to Jerusalem for burial.

3. *Uzziah (Azariah; 791-739; II Kings 14:21-22; 15:1-7; II Chronicles 26).* Amaziah's son and successor is called by two names, Uzziah and Azariah, names closely associated in meaning and perhaps used interchangeably.[39] Uzziah was one of Judah's most capable rulers. He followed the life-patterns of his two predecessors; and God, in approval, used his native ability to restore a high status for Judah in the world. This improvement in Judah's position came at approximately the same time as Israel's enlargement under the able Jeroboam II. Between the two men, the total land-area finally controlled came to rival even that of the days of David and Solomon.[40]

a. Coregencies. Uzziah ruled longer than any prior king of either Judah or Israel—fifty-two years (II Kings 15:2; II Chron. 26:3). The

[37] Jehoash showed better sense than Amaziah, though in attempting dissuasion he used an allegory which belittled the Judean king and may have incensed him rather than served to change his mind.

[38] Thiele, *MNHK*, pp. 83-87, argues to this conclusion: (1) in that II Kings 14:13 seems to mean that Amaziah was taken captive; (2) that II Kings 14:17 unexpectedly says that Amaziah lived for 15 years after Jehoash died, a rationale for which could well be that Amaziah was so released after Jehoash's death and then returned to reign in Judah for these 15 years; and (3) that Uzziah's becoming coregent at this time thus finds good explanation.

[39] The name, Uzziah, is used in II Kings 15:13, 30, 32, 34; II Chron. 26:1, 3, 11, etc.; Isa. 1:1; 6:1; Hos. 1:1; Amos 1:1; Zech. 14:5. Azariah is used in II Kings 14:21; 15:1, 6, 8, 17, 23, 27; I Chron. 3:12. Azariah (*'azaryah*) means "Yahweh has helped"; Uzziah (*'uzziyah*), "Yahweh is my strength."

[40] Cf. *supra*, chap. 13, pp. 325-26.

first twenty-four were in coregency with his father, and the last twelve were similarly served with his son Jotham, leaving only sixteen years of solitary rule.[41] Uzziah would have been sixteen years of age (II Kings 15:2) at the time of his father's likely captivity to Jehoash of Israel. He would have ruled as supreme head the nine years [42] his father was captive, and then in a secondary capacity, as long as his father lived after returning to be head ruler again. The occasion for Uzziah installing his son Jotham as coregent for his last twelve years is almost certainly related to Uzziah's becoming a leper at the beginning of that period. The disease was inflicted as punishment from God for intruding into the priest's office (II Chron. 26:16-21). Uzziah attempted personally to offer incense in the Temple, though warned against doing so by eighty-one priests. The chronicler states that from the time of this affliction the king had to live in a separate house and that Jotham was then "over the king's house, judging the people" (II Chron. 26:21; II Kings 15:5).

b. Expansion of territory (II Chron. 26:6-16). Uzziah assumed sole rule of Judah some fifteen years after Jeroboam II became supreme head of Israel. Equally talented, he was able to follow the example set by Jeroboam in land acquisition and even, after the demise of Jeroboam, to attain a role yet more influential in the world.

Toward the south, Uzziah maintained the control his father Amaziah had gained over Edom and in addition built port facilities at Elath on the Gulf of Aqaba for the purpose of trade (II Kings 14:22; II Chron. 26:2). Toward the east, he accepted gifts from the Ammonites, indicating a domination imposed on them. Toward the west, he warred successfully with the Philistines, seizing several cities, among which was Gath, taken earlier by Hazael from Amaziah at the time of his captivity. Uzziah also made his own country stronger through additional fortification, particularly at Jerusalem. He installed ingenious engines for shooting arrows and catapulting large stones from the walls. He seems also to have reorganized the army, thus likely increasing its effectiveness. In summary, besides strengthening home base, Uzziah established or maintained effective control east of the Dead Sea, south to the important Gulf of Aqaba, and southwest to the river of Egypt. This, with the extensive holdings of Jeroboam II to the east and north, made the total territory now by far the largest of any time following the king-

[41] Cf. Thiele, *MNHK*, pp. 81-83 for arguments as to a coregency with Amaziah, and pp. 120-23 for argument as to the same with Jotham.

[42] The number, 9, is determined from chronological correlations showing that Jehoash of Israel ruled until 782 B.C., which is 9 years after Uzziah's first accession in 791 B.C.

dom's division and, in truth, approximately that of the united monarchy period.

c. Zenith of influence. It was following the death of Jeroboam II, however, that Uzziah reached the zenith of his influence. By 743 B.C., the year of the first western campaign of Tiglath-pileser III of Assyria, Uzziah had become the strongest ruler along the Mediterranean coast. Since the defeat of Damascus by Adad-nirari III a half century earlier, Jeroboam II had been the strongest; but following his death Israel had become seriously weakened by inner turmoil and a rapid succession of kings.[43] Syrian states north of Damascus had long been kept weak by continued Assyrian aggression and could not lead in resisting Tiglath-pileser. Consequently, Uzziah, who had become known because of his success in the south, was now recognized by these others and given leadership of a coalition to withstand the coming Assyrian conqueror. Tiglath-pileser himself gives record of this coalition and encounter, indicating definitely that it was led by one "Azriau of Yaudi," which can only mean Azariah (Uzziah) of Judah.[44] Uzziah was no longer young at the time, for this was the forty-eighth year of his rule, when he was sixty-four.[45] It would have been a memorable occasion to find himself thus honored by fellow rulers.

4. *Jotham (750–731; II Kings 15:32-38; II Chronicles 27).* Jotham succeeded his father, Uzziah, and reigned twenty years,[46] though the first twelve, as noted, were as coregent with his father. If his father was able to lead in the northern coalition just mentioned, it follows that he was not seriously incapacitated by his leprosy during these years; so Jotham may have been installed co-ruler mainly as a "front" man, to meet people and convey orders worked out and given by the capable Uzziah.

[43] *Supra,* chap. 13, pp. 327-32.

[44] Some scholars, because of alleged chronological difficulties and the fact that this encounter transpired far north of Judah, have suggested that this Azariah was a king of some northern Syrian state. However, it is extremely coincidental that there could have been two kings of the same name, from states of the same name and at the same time. For discussion, cf. Thiele, *MNHK,* pp. 93-94; Unger, *Israel and the Aramaeans of Damascus* (London: James Clark & Co., Ltd., 1957), pp. 96-98. For text, cf. *ANET,* p. 282; or DOTT, pp. 53-56.

[45] Uzziah would already have been a leper eight years, but evidently not greatly impaired in military skill or leadership ability. Tiglath-pileser claims a victory over the coalition.

[46] II Kings 15:30 gives him 20 years, and correlations with other kings require it. The sixteen years mentioned in II Kings 15:33 and II Chron. 27:1 must concern his rule until terminated at the insistence of Ahaz; with Jotham, however, yet living four more years to make the full twenty. Cf. H. G. Stigers, "The Interphased Chronology of Jotham, Ahaz, Hezekiah, and Hoshea," *BETS,* 8 (Spring, 1966), pp. 86-88.

Jotham in turn installed his son, Ahaz, as his coregent. Correlations show that this was done twelve years before Jotham died,[47] which means surprisingly that coregencies here overlapped. That is, Jotham made his son Ahaz his coregent while he was still coregent with his father Uzziah. During four years,[48] Judah had Uzziah as chief ruler, Jotham as his coregent, and Ahaz as Jotham's coregent. The year of Ahaz's accession as Jotham's co-ruler works out to have been 743 B.C., the same year that Uzziah went north to lead in the coalition. The most likely explanation for this unusual situation is that Jotham, now left alone in Jerusalem, fearful of the consequences for his father in this battle, and probably thinking that Tiglath-pileser would bring vengeance on Uzziah's own country if he won victory over the coalition, sought strength by making Ahaz co-ruler with him.[49] He may have doubted seriously that his father would return.

Jotham was the fourth successive God-approved king of Judah. Accordingly, he continued to experience blessing in his reign and was able to maintain his country's strong position. Only one military engagement is mentioned, that with the Ammonites, which battle he won. As a result, Israel received payment of tribute[50] from Ammon for three years. Jotham also carried on extensive construction activity. In Jerusalem he built an important Temple gate and added to the "wall of Ophel." Elsewhere he enlarged cities and erected "forts and towers" as means of fortification.

But prosperity often leads to religious neglect, and it did here in Judah. This is evidenced by the words of the outstanding prophet, Isaiah, who rose to ministry at this time.[51] He speaks much of the sin of a people made proud and selfish through comfort. He warns that punishment would come if change were not made. Indeed, punishment was already at hand at the time of Jotham's death. Pekah, king of Israel, and Rezin, king of Damascus, were at the gate of Jerusalem, laying siege to force Judah to cooperate in a revolt against Assyria (II Kings 15:37). Ahaz had this distressing situation to face as he took over as chief ruler.

[47] For discussion, cf. Stigers, *op. cit.*, pp. 86-88.

[48] Of Jotham's total twenty years, he co-ruled with his father the first twelve and with his son the last twelve, making the middle four the years of overlap.

[49] Since Ahaz presented a pro-Assyrian policy when he became head ruler, it may be that a pro-Assyrian party in Judah was influential in forcing this early coregency. If so, this would have been a second reason for the unusual situation.

[50] It consisted of 100 talents of silver, 10,000 measures of wheat and 10,000 of barley.

[51] Isaiah received his call (or recommissioning) in the year King Uzziah died (Isa. 6:1-8), and may have started ministering a short time before. He continued into the reigns of Jotham, Ahaz, and Hezekiah (Isa. 1:1).

D. Years of Assyrian Dominance (743–640; II Kings 16–21; II Chronicles 28–33)

The might of Assyria now came to be experienced in Judah much more directly and seriously than at any time previous. Until this period, Damascus and Israel had served as terminating points for Assyrian campaigns, but now their resistance was waning and soon was to cease entirely. Ominously, Judah was next in line.

1. *Ahaz (743–715; II Kings 16; II Chronicles 28).* Ahaz ruled for a total of twenty-eight years, though only sixteen[52] were as supreme head (II Kings 16:2; II Chron. 28:1). Twelve years were spent while his father yet lived, and thirteen after his son, Hezekiah, was made co-regent with him, leaving only three years of independent rule.

From the beginning of his reign, Ahaz was pro-Assyrian in his policies. There is reason to believe that he was able to assume headship in power over his father while Jotham yet lived.[53] If so, the reason must be that the Jerusalem nobles believed they were better off in submitting to Tiglath-pileser of Assyria than in resisting him, and accordingly supported the sympathetic Ahaz in grasping the throne.

a. Siege of Pekah and Rezin (II Kings 16:5-9; II Chron. 28:5-21). Because of the pro-Assyrian feeling in Jerusalem, Pekah, king of Israel, and Rezin, king of Damascus, had joined as allies to besiege Jerusalem and force Judah to support a revolt against Assyria. The siege came in Jotham's closing years, as noted, but since Ahaz had already assumed leadership, the task of resistance was mainly his. Recognizing his inability to meet the combined foe in combat, and wishing to keep in the good favor of Assyria, he sought help from Tiglath-pileser III, the same conqueror against whom his grandfather, Uzziah, had led the northern coalition only nine years before. Ahaz now asked this one by letter to enter the region and attack both Damascus and Israel, and so force the two besiegers to return home. He gave the Assyrian monarch considerable gold and silver as an inducement. Ahaz' plan worked, for Tiglath-pileser did come,[54] and Pekah and Rezin were forced to return to their respective countries. Before they did so, however, they wrought extensive damage in Judah, killing 120,000 people and taking

---

[52] From 735 B.C., when he took over as head ruler (Jotham yet living four years), until 719 B.C., when his son, Hezekiah, in turn took over from him (while Ahaz yet lived four years). Cf. Stigers, *op. cit.*, pp. 88-89 for discussion. Admittedly, the dating of Ahaz and Hezekiah is difficult. Cf. Payne, *BS*, 126 (1969), pp. 40-52 for a treatment of the main problems. The dates here set forth seem to fit the scriptural evidence best.

[53] For reasons; cf. Stigers, *op. cit.*, pp. 87-88.

[54] In his famous campaign of 734-32; cf. *supra*, chap. 13, p. 332.

200,000 captives.[55] These captives, however, were permitted to return home to Judah almost immediately, as a result of admonition by God's prophet, Oded.[56]

Ahaz received a rebuke from God for his manner of finding relief from the siege. Isaiah brought it at the time that Ahaz was considering sending his letter and gift to Tiglath-pileser (Isa. 7–8). The prophet told him that his real enemy was not these smaller, neighboring kings, but the mighty Assyrian host whose assistance he was about to seek. The truth of Isaiah's statement is borne out by the havoc Tiglath-pileser then did inflict in the general region during the next three years, apparently even forcing Ahaz, himself, to pay tribute, in addition to the initial gift (II Chron. 28:20-21). It is borne out, too, by the further devastation in Judah of succeeding Assyrian rulers, in years immediately following.

b. Religious defection (II Kings 16:2-4, 10-18; II Chron. 28:1-4, 22-25). Religiously, Ahaz ceased to follow in the way of the four kings who had preceded him. He did evil in the sight of God. He made images of Baal, observed infant sacrifice in the Valley of Hinnom, and worshiped in the high places. While meeting with Tiglath-pileser in Damascus, at the close of the conqueror's devastating campaign, Ahaz saw and admired a certain pagan altar there and sent a plan of it home to Urijah the priest to copy for Jerusalem. When he later returned, he established this altar as the official place of sacrifice at the Temple, in place of the brazen altar prescribed in the Mosaic Law. Besides this, he intentionally damaged several of the sacred vessels of the Temple and even closed the doors of the Temple, thus forcing people to worship where and as he wanted.

c. Military reverses (II Chron. 28:16-19). In view of this manner of conduct, it is not surprising to read of military reverses being soon experienced. The first reverse was with Edom, who once again revolted, even carrying captives from Judah, in the pattern of Amaziah's previous treatment respecting Edom. The important port of Elath on the Gulf of Aqaba was lost once again to Judah. At some time Rezin of Damascus seized Elath for his country (II Kings 16:6), and it may have been shortly after this occasion when Judah lost it. Another reverse occurred when the Philistines once again invaded Judah and inflicted

---

[55] To account for this loss of life, certainly large battles were fought sometime during this general time of siege. From Isa. 7:6 it is clear that the alliance had intended actually to replace Ahaz with one, ben Tabeel; cf. Bright, *BHI*, p. 256, n. 11.

[56] Oded met the host at Samaria and the captives were then taken to Jericho where they were released, some embarrassment evidently being spared in not returning them directly to Jerusalem.

severe destruction, even seizing several cities, which are listed. The chronicler implies that Ahaz, in his letter to Tiglath-pileser, had requested that the great Assyrian press an attack on both Edom and Philistia, besides Israel and Damascus. For this reason, an indication by Tiglath-pileser that he did smite the Philistines and receive tribute from Edom, as well as from other countries, is significant.

2. *Hezekiah (728–686; II Kings 18–20; II Chronicles 29–32).* Hezekiah succeeded his father and ruled a total of forty-two years, though the first thirteen, as noted, were as coregent. There is reason to believe that he assumed chief rule, however, some four years before his father died,[57] likely at the insistence of a growing anti-Assyrian party who objected to further pro-Assyrian actions by Ahaz. It is probable, indeed, that this first accession as co-ruler had been at the insistence of this group, though then Ahaz was still permitted to keep the top position.[58]

a. Approved of God (II Kings 18:4-7; II Chron. 29:2-31:21). Hezekiah was one of Judah's finest kings in the sight of God. He is given the high accolade of having acted as David his father,[59] and also of being the peer of all Judah's kings in trusting God (II Kings 18:5). After the deliberate idolatry of Ahaz, drastic reform was necessary, and Hezekiah effected it. The doors of the Temple were again opened, and the priests and Levites were instructed to remove all foreign cult objects. Then they were to clean and restore all the proper items, that true worship might be reinstated. A grand time of sacrificing and celebrations marked the return of the true Mosaic ceremonies (II Chron. 29:20-36). Further, Hezekiah ordered the Passover to be

[57] Evidenced as follows: (1) II Kings 18:13 says that it was in his fourteenth year that Sennacherib attacked, which attack, according to Assyrian records, came in 701 B.C., which sets the beginning of his reign as 715 B.C. But (2) II Kings 16:1-2 states that Ahaz reigned only sixteen years after Pekah's seventeenth year (735 B.C.) which would be to 719 B.C., some four years prior to 715 B.C. The answer must be that Hezekiah took over as head in 719, with Ahaz still living to 715, from which date Hezekiah's sole rule is figured in II Kings 18:13. Cf. Stigers, *op. cit.*, pp. 86-90. Thiele does not recognize this coregency for Hezekiah and so does not account for chronological notations in II Kings 18:1, 9, 10.

[58] Hezekiah would have only been about twelve years old at the time, too; cf. Stigers, *ibid.*, p. 83. Note that the chronological indications of II Kings 18: 1, 9-10 are in terms of Hezekiah and not Ahaz who yet lived.

[59] This was said also of Asa (I Kings 15:11) and Jehoshaphat (II Chron. 17:3), and is again of Josiah (II Kings 22:2), but not of Joash, Amaziah, Uzziah, or Jotham, the four good kings who immediately preceded Ahaz. In fact, of Amaziah it is stated that he did not measure up to David's standard (II Kings 14:3). David's conduct continued to be a measure for later rulers.

observed once more. Apparently this had been neglected for many years, even before the rule of Ahaz. Hezekiah invited Israelites from Beersheba to Dan to take part in the festal occasion (II Chron. 30: 1-27).[60] Many responded and a time of feasting and worshiping was experienced such as had not occurred since the reign of Solomon (II Chron. 30:26). This in turn led to a cleansing of the land generally, so that high places (*bamoth*), images (*masseboth*), Asherah poles (*'asherim*), false altars (*mizbehoth*), and even the brazen serpent, Moses had made in the wilderness centuries before (Num. 21:5-9), were destroyed. Still further, Hezekiah revitalized the organization of priests and Levites and their support by the tithes of the people (II Chron. 31:1-21). Never before had the land undergone so thorough a reformation.

b. Hezekiah and the Assyrians. Hezekiah was anti-Assyrian, in contrast to his father. He did not, however, openly rebel against the eastern power as long as Sargon II ruled (722-705).[61] Sargon, who resettled Israelite territory with persons taken captive from other subjugated countries, was a capable ruler and military figure. Within one year of Samaria's fall, he brought the Assyrian army into the West again to put down a revolt headed by Hamath.[62] He next fought successfully in Asia Minor, and then gave attention to a revolution in Carchemish, whose population he deported. He followed this by finally breaking the power of the hated kingdom of Urartu[63] to the north, which his predecessors had been unable to do. More significantly for Hezekiah, he came in 711 B.C. to the Philistine territory and crushed a revolt led by Ashdod, then the leading Philistine city.[64] Hezekiah

[60] The celebration probably occurred in Hezekiah's first year (II Chron. 29:3), but likely the first year of his sole reign, which means 715 B.C. Samaria had been taken captive six years before, which made proper the general invitation as far north as Dan. This makes it appear that Hezekiah made some effort at reform in Israel as well as Judah. Cf. Keil, *KDC*, Chronicles, pp. 454-62, however, who argues for a later year in Hezekiah's reign.

[61] After Tiglath-pileser III (745-727) came Shalmaneser V (727-722) and then Sargon II; cf. *supra*, chap. 13, pp. 332-33.

[62] Sargon's inscription states that both Damascus and Samaria had a part in this uprising headed by Hamath; cf. Ricciotti, *The History of Israel* (2d ed. Trans.; Milwaukee: Bruce Publishing Co., 1958), pp. 356-57.

[63] Strong, troublesome foe of Assyria for many years; cf. E. A. Speiser, *Introduction to Hurrian* (*AASOR*, 20, 1940-41).

[64] Ashdod apparently had taken the lead following Gaza's devastation by Tiglath-pileser in 734 B.C. The new Twenty-fifth Dynasty in Egypt had promised aid in this rebellion, and (as Sargon indicates) Judah, Edom, and Moab had been invited to enter. When Sargon put down the revolt, the assistance of Egypt did not materialize and the rebel leader, when he fled to Egypt for protection, was even handed back to the Assyrians! Cf. *ANET*, p. 286 for text.

had been asked to join the Ashdod alliance but wisely had refused.[65]

c. Hezekiah and Sennacherib (II Chron. 32:1-8). When Sargon's less able son, Sennacherib (705-681), came to the throne, however, Hezekiah did join such a pact. He apparently believed the time was now more propitious. This alliance was composed of more members than before, with Tyre the leading city;[66] and a new Egyptian king, Shabaka (c. 710-696), who gave promise of lending more support, having come to the throne. Hezekiah made thorough preparations for an expected retaliation by Sennacherib, however(II Chron. 32:1-8). He constructed further fortifications, made new weapons, and reinforced his military strength. He gave special attention to stopping the water supplies that the enemy might use. At the same time he provided a more convenient access to water for his own people by digging the now-famous Siloam Tunnel from the Spring of Gihon, through the hill of Ophel to a place within the city lower than the starting point; a truly remarkable piece of engineering.[67]

d. Sennacherib's invasion (II Kings 18:13–19:37; II Chron. 32:9-21; Isa. 36–37). During Sennacherib's first four years of rule, he was occupied with Assyrian control of Babylon; but in 701 B.C., he came to put down this revolt in the west.[68] He dealt first with Tyre, the leading city, by crushing resistance there, and Tyre's King Luli fled to Cyprus. At this point, many of the coalition's less enthusiastic members capitulated, including the kings of Byblos, Arvad, Moab, Edom, and Ammon. Then Sennacherib moved south along the Mediterranean and punished another leading city, Ashkelon, deporting her king, Sidqia, to Assyria. It was probably at this point, with the coastline in his control, that Sennacherib moved inland toward the third leading city, Jerusalem. On the way he stopped to lay siege to Lachish.[69] While

---

[65] That he did not was likely due in large part to the advice of Isaiah; cf. Isa. 20:1-6.

[66] Leadership now swung to Tyre because Gaza and Ashdod had been terribly hurt in 711 B.C., and were slow to join any new coalition. Ashkelon and Ekron did join, however. Ekron's king, Padi, who refused to join, was removed from his position. Cf. ANET, p. 287, for text.

[67] An inscription found near the mouth of the tunnel (cf. ANET, p. 321 for text) states that diggers worked from both ends. Their place of meeting shows a slight jog but the degree of skill in maintaining the right slope and direction is incredible. The inscription says that the tunnel was 1,200 cubits long. Measurement today reveals the distance in feet to be 1,777 (others give 1,749), which indicates the length of the cubit to have been just under 18 inches. Cf. II Kings 20:20; II Chron. 32:30.

[68] Sennacherib left a record of this campaign on a prism, called the Taylor Prism, now in the British Museum. Cf. ANET, pp. 287-88; DOTT, pp. 64-68.

[69] Sennacherib does not speak of this move toward Jerusalem nor of the Lachish siege on the prism, though he pictures the Lachish siege in his palace at

here, he received tribute from Judah, indicating Hezekiah's recognition that the cause of the revolt was lost (II Kings 18:14-16).[70] About this time, too, Hezekiah released Padi, the former king of Ekron, who had been deposed by the coalition and imprisoned in Jerusalem when he refused to cooperate in the rebellion.[71] But Sennacherib was not satisfied with this show of submission by Hezekiah, and now sent three lieutenants[72] and a large force of men to pursue psychological warfare against Hezekiah and his people (II Kings 18:17-37; II Chron. 32:9-16; Isa. 36:1-21). Their threats were effective in causing the people to fear, and in prompting Hezekiah to consult with Isaiah from whom the king received a comforting word from God. At this juncture, Sennacherib heard that the Egyptian army, led by Tirhakah,[73] was coming to the aid of the coalition, and turned to meet it rather than continuing on immediately to Jerusalem. He sent a letter to Hezekiah at the time,

Nineveh (cf. *ANEP*, figs. 371-74). For a description of this picture and of evidence from excavation at Lachish, including a pit where as many as 1,500 people were buried in mass, cf. Wright, *BAR*, pp. 167-72.

[70] Sennacherib lists this tribute as 30 talents of gold and 800 of silver, while the Bible mentions 30 of gold and 300 of silver (II Kings 18:14). For discussion relative to the difference in silver talents, cf. Robinson, *The Bearing of Archaeology on the Old Testament* (New York: The American Tract Society, 1941), p. 100. Sennacherib claims that the tribute included also precious stones, inlaid couches and chairs, elephant hides, Hezekiah's own daughters, concubines, and musicians.

[71] The biblical record does not mention this king of Ekron, but Sennacherib does.

[72] Names given for them (II Kings 18:18) were titles of high Assyrian officials: Tartan (*turtannu*) meaning "second in rank," Rabsaris (*rabushareshi*) meaning "chief eunuch," and Rabshakeh (*rab shaqu*) meaning "chief officer"; cf. M. Burrows, *What Mean These Stones?* (New Haven: American Schools of Oriental Research, 1941), pp. 43f.

[73] Because Tikhakah was not yet king of Egypt in 701 B.C. (became king in 689 B.C.), and because some believe he was not even born until 709 B.C., numerous scholars hold that two campaigns by Sennacherib are represented in the biblical story: one in 701 B.C. and one after 689 B.C. Sennacherib's own inscriptions are lacking for his last eight years and do not help. The biblical record, however, gives no hint of a second campaign, and implies in II Kings 19:8-9 (Isa. 37:8-9) that Sennacherib's encounter with Tirhakah followed immediately the siege of Lachish. Therefore, it is better to accept only one campaign. As to the problem regarding Tirhakah, perhaps this army commander was someone other than the later king of Egypt. He is called in the text "king of Ethiopia" rather than king of Egypt, which might be a clue, though Egyptian kings at this time were Ethiopian in lineage. The view that Tirhakah, king of Egypt, was born only in 709 B.C., put forth by M. Macadam, has also been challenged, making it possible that proleptic speech is used in II Kings 19:9, when it calls Tirhakah, "king of Ethiopia"; cf. Kitchen, *AOOT*, p. 83. Albright, for instance, advocates the two-campaign view: cf. *BASOR*, 130 (1953), pp. 8-11; *BASOR*, 141 (1956), pp. 23-27.

however, in which he restated the threats already made by the lieutenants. With this letter in hand, Hezekiah sought further reassurance from God, which was given through Isaiah. This time the prophet told the king that Sennacherib would not capture Jerusalem, nor even come near it (II Kings 19:8-34; Isa. 37:8-35).

From Sennacherib's report, we learn that he did encounter an Egyptian force and defeat it in the plain of Eltekeh, near Ekron.[74] He also speaks of making conquest of the nearby cities of Eltekeh, Timnah, and Ekron, and reinstalling in the latter her former king, Padi, establishing him now as ruler over the whole general region. Sennacherib further states that he conquered a total of forty-six strong cities of Hezekiah, besides numerous villages, and seized over 200,000 prisoners. The biblical record gives the final note, however, in stating that all this activity was suddenly brought to an end by the slaying of no less than 185,000 troops of Sennacherib by the "angel of Yahweh."[75] Of this Sennacherib says nothing, as one might expect. His account, however, indirectly corroborates the fact, because he does not claim to have captured Jerusalem, which would be most unusual otherwise, since Jerusalem was certainly one of his prime objectives from the first. His own words speak only of shutting Hezekiah in Jerusalem "like a bird in a cage."[76]

e. Hezekiah's illness and fame (II Kings 20; II Chron. 32:22-33; Isa. 38-39). Two other episodes in Hezekiah's life, both related to this Assyrian campaign, are recorded. One concerns a severe time of illness from which the king recovered only because of God's gracious hand of healing. The time was during, or just prior to, Sennacherib's invasion of the land.[77] Hezekiah prayed to God that he might recover; and God answered through Isaiah, promising the king fifteen more

---

[74] This encounter with the Egyptians may have preceded the Tirhakah battle, however. If so, Sennacherib fought the Egyptians twice.

[75] An account by Herodotus has led some scholars to suggest a way in which God destroyed these soldiers. Herodotus says that Sennacherib's host was attacked by field mice swarming over the camp and devouring quivers, bows, and shield handles. The suggestion is that the plague, which is carried by rats and mice, was the method God used. This explanation may be doubtful, but at least Herodotus' story provides an indirect confirmation of the biblical miracle, for his account is what might be expected in view of such a miracle. Cf. Herodotus, II, 141; Finegan, *LAP*, pp. 213-14.

[76] *DOTT*, p. 67.

[77] This is indicated not only by the promise to Hezekiah (Isa. 38:6), but also chronological considerations. Hezekiah ruled a total of 29 years as supreme king (II Kings 18:2), and so, subtracting fifteen (the years of life now added to him) from this, the year of his illness results as the fourteenth, the same as the year of Sennacherib's attack (II Kings 18:13).

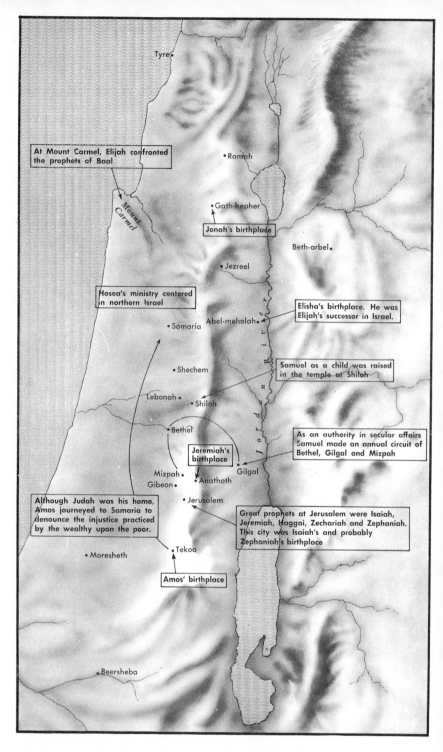

At Mount Carmel, Elijah confronted the prophets of Baal

Jonah's birthplace

Hosea's ministry centered in northern Israel

Elisha's birthplace. He was Elijah's successor in Israel.

Samuel as a child was raised in the temple at Shiloh

As an authority in secular affairs Samuel made an annual circuit of Bethel, Gilgal and Mizpah

Jeremiah's birthplace

Although Judah was his home, Amos journeyed to Samaria to denounce the injustice practiced by the wealthy upon the poor.

Great prophets at Jerusalem were Isaiah, Jeremiah, Haggai, Zechariah and Zephaniah. This city was Isaiah's and probably Zephaniah's birthplace

Amos' birthplace

Tyre

Ramah

Gath-hepher

Beth-arbel

Jezreel

Samaria

Abel-meholah

Shechem

Lebonah

Shiloh

Bethel

Mizpah

Gibeon

Anathoth

Gilgal

Jerusalem

Moresheth

Tekoa

Beersheba

Mount Carmel

Jordan River

Map 15. Cities of the Prophets

years of life, as well as deliverance from the Assyrian power. It is likely that Hezekiah's concern over his sickness was accented by his anxiety for the country (if it was now left without a leader). In consideration with his emotional distress, God gave Hezekiah a remarkable sign as evidence that the promise would be fulfilled: the return of the sun-dial shadow ten degrees.

The other episode concerns the visit to Jerusalem by messengers from Merodach-baladan, king of Babylon. This occurred shortly after Hezekiah's recovery from illness (Isa. 39:1).[78] While the group came ostensibly to congratulate the Judean king on his recovery, the true reason no doubt lay in the anti-Assyrian cause common to both Babylon and Judah. Babylon had long been in a power struggle with Assyria, and Merodach-baladan had been personally involved for a least twenty years. Help was desired from whatever source it might be found. The messengers brought lavish gifts to Hezekiah, and Hezekiah in turn showed them his wealth. For this, however, he was severely rebuked by Isaiah, who told him that the homeland of these men would one day come and seize all this treasure for itself. This did occur one century later, when the great Nebuchadnezzar II came to power.

3. *The prophets Isaiah and Micah*

a. Isaiah. It has already appeared that the prophet, Isaiah, was important to his country. He has been seen remonstrating with Ahaz over his alliance with Assyria, and advising and comforting Hezekiah. It is likely, too, that these episodes only represent many more of similar nature. For instance, Isaiah must have had contact with the pious Jotham earlier, and have had much to do with the God-pleasing reforms effected by Hezekiah. Even with Ahaz, who outwardly scorned him, Isaiah's influence could not have gone unnoticed. Probably, indeed, Isaiah had much to do with the establishment of Hezekiah's co-regency with Ahaz, when Hezekiah was only a lad of twelve. When Hezekiah ruled alone, Isaiah was heard to speak strongly against alliance with Egypt (Isa. 30:1-7; 31:1-3), which certainly influenced Hezekiah's refusal to join the pact of 711 B.C. In this, however, Isaiah was opposed by false prophets (Isa. 30:8-11); and their influence, in turn, may have had a part in Hezekiah's change of mind regarding the coalition of 701 B.C. When Hezekiah, however, turned again to Isaiah for help in the trouble that resulted, the prophet did not react against him but cooperated freely. He understood the king's difficult

---

[78] Merodach-baladan ruled Babylon 721-710 and again 703-702. After 702 he continued his opposition to Assyrian control as a refugee in Elam. It was likely during this time that he sought the support of Judah by means of this embassy.

position and saw genuine sincerity, which was enough to prompt his support.

b. Micah. Another active prophet of the time was Micah. He ministered during the reigns of Jotham, Ahaz, and Hezekiah (Micah 1:1), evidently beginning shortly after Isaiah and continuing contemporaneously with him. Micah came from the village of Moreshath in southwest Judah. He is never depicted at the court as is Isaiah, but Jeremiah (26:17-19; cf. Micah 3:11-12) does speak of him as carrying influence, especially with Hezekiah. Micah's main message concerned the sinfulness of the people. Social abuses and unfaithfulness to Yahweh were particularly denounced. This emphasis and his pointed warning of coming punishment, underscored similar words of Isaiah.

4. *Manasseh (697–642; II Kings 21:1-18; II Chronicles 33:1-20).* Manasseh succeeded his father, Hezekiah, and ruled fifty-five years, the longest of any king in either Judah or Israel. The first eleven, however, were as coregent with his father,[79] making him the fifth consecutive Judean prince to begin reigning in this manner.

a. Religious defection (II Kings 21:2-16; II Chron. 33:2-10). Manasseh did not learn from his godly father in religious matters, but followed the pattern of his Law-defying grandfather, Ahaz, in doing evil in the sight of God. He restored the offensive cultic objects which Hezekiah had destroyed, placed altars of Baal throughout the land and even in the Temple, and recognized the Ammonite deity, Molech, by sacrificing children in the Valley of Hinnom. He approved various forms of pagan divination, and even erected an image of the Canaanite goddess, Asherah, in the Temple. Those who protested, he killed, thus shedding much innocent blood. It may be that Isaiah was among these, as tradition testifies. In all this, the combined influence of current Assyrian practices in religion and of the older Phoenician worship of Baal-Melqart may be discerned. Manasseh is said to have caused the people to do more evil than nations whom God had dispossessed from the land centuries before (II Kings 21:9). Prophets of God duly warned the king concerning his ways, but he did not take heed.

b. Punishment and repentance (II Chron. 33:11-20). Punishment from God was not long in coming,[80] taking the form of Manasseh's

---

[79] Thiele argues for this coregency on the basis that it is the most logical way to account for an extra eleven years, which result when the reigns of the remaining kings of Judah are fitted into the total number of years left until the captivity; *MNHK*, pp. 156-59.

[80] Later and still greater punishment came in the form of Judah's captivity to Babylon. II Kings 23:26 explicitly states that even all of Josiah's reform could not offset the provocations of Manasseh in God's sight.

personal captivity[81] by an Assyrian king.[82] Little is known relative to this captivity. It was brought about by either Sennacherib's son, Esarhaddon (681-669), or grandson, Ashurbanipal (669-633), in the successive reigns of whom Assyria reached the zenith of her power. Both rulers campaigned with success as far south as Egypt, for the first time in Assyrian history; and Ashurbanipal made significant conquest even in the treacherous mountains of Elam to the east.

In favor of Esarhaddon being the one who took Manasseh is this ruler's specific mention of Manasseh, along with twenty-one other kings, as his vassal, stating that all these were required personally to bring valuable building materials to Nineveh in 678 B.C.[83] The language used, however, hardly characterizes the occasion as one of captivity, though it may have been. In favor of Ashurbanipal is the fact that he put down a revolt of southern Mediterranean states in which Manasseh probably was involved,[84] an occasion when such a captivity could easily have resulted. The revolt was widespread, coming to include even Babylon to the east, and it lasted over a period of five years (652-648). Since the biblical record speaks only of "captains" (*sare*) of the host effecting the captivity, it may be that the Assyrian king himself was not present, which may explain why no official notice was entered in the Assyrian record. Furthermore, the latter view better correlates with the biblical story, which implies that Manasseh's captivity came toward the close of his reign, following his many years of idolatrous practice. With the earlier occasion, he would have reigned only seventeen of his fifty-five years when taken; while with the latter, about forty-six.

Manasseh was permitted eventually to return to Judah, as a result of God's favor gained by Manasseh's repentance while a captive. On being restored to the throne, he commendably sought to make amends for his earlier wickedness. He removed the foreign cultic items and

---

[81] Described (II Chron. 33:11) as being taken in hooks and fetters. The practice was to bind the prisoner with fetters and place a hook in his lips by which to lead him in abject submission; cf. Ricciotti, *The History of Israel* (2d ed. trans.; Milwaukee: Bruce Publishing Co., 1958), pp. 389-90 for discussion and evidence.

[82] II Chron. 33:11 states that he was taken to Babylon. Some scholars believe that an error in location exists here; Babylon being substituted for Nineveh. Esarhaddon, however, rebuilt Babylon, after its devastation by his father, Sennacherib, and made it an integral part of the Assyrian domain once again. Manasseh may well have been held captive there. For texts, cf. Lukenbill, *Ancient Records of Assyria and Babylonia* (Chicago, 1927), secs. 646, 647.

[83] Inscribed on Prism B of Esarhaddon; cf. *ANET*, p. 291 for text.

[84] Ashurbanipal lists Manasseh along with 21 other kings as submitting before him as he marched against Egypt (cf. *ANET*, p. 294 for text). There is no direct indication, however, that he was then taken back to Assyria as captive.

reestablished true worship at the Temple. How many years of this manner of rule remained for him after the return is not revealed, but perhaps four or five.[85]

5. *Amon (642–640; II Kings 21:19-26; II Chronicles 33:21-25).* Amon succeeded his father but ruled only two years. He reverted to the idolatrous practices his father had pursued for the major part of his rule, apparently not being impressed by the reform of the closing years. Perhaps his own servants came to be repulsed by his actions, for some of them banded together in conspiracy and killed him in his own house. The people at large, not approving assassinations in any case, took the lives of the conspirators. Amon's eight-year-old son, Josiah, became king.

E. BABYLON BECOMES DOMINANT (640–586; II Kings 22–25; II Chronicles 34–36)

With the accession of Josiah, Judah entered her closing period of history. No longer was there reason to fear Assyria, for Ashurbanipal's last years witnessed little military activity and only weak rulers followed him until Nineveh's fall in 612 B.C. Babylon, however, soon took over as world leader, bringing in the period known as Neo-Babylonian. This shift of power came at the close of Josiah's thirty-one year reign. His time of rule, then, was relatively free from foreign interference and dangers, but those of his three successors were much involved with the new great power, by whom Judah was finally taken captive.

1. *Josiah (640–609; II Kings 22:1–23:30; II Chronicles 34–35).* The three decades of Josiah's reign were among the happiest in Judah's experience. They were characterized by peace, prosperity, and reform. No outside enemies made war, the people could concentrate on constructive activity, and Josiah himself sought to please God by reinstituting matters commanded in the Mosaic Law.

Josiah was made king when he was merely a boy of eight. Religious idolatry was rampant as a result of Amon having reverted to Mannasseh's earlier practices. But apparently the lad had God-fearing advisors who offset any influence of his father, for Josiah returned to following the way of Yahweh. At the age of sixteen, he began of himself "to seek after the God of David his father" (II Chron. 34:3). At the age of twenty he began to cleanse Jerusalem and Judah of the idolatrous objects his father and grandfather had brought into the land

---

[85] There is no way to know how long Manasseh was held captive. It is stated only that during this time he did repent and God did give him deliverance. If he was taken in his forty-sixth year, he could have been there four or five years and still have had four or five after returning to Jerusalem.

(II Chron. 34:3-7). Successful in his own land, he even pursued similar activity to the north in Israel, where Assyria now held nominal control, removing altars and images of false deities.[86]

a. Josiah's reformation (II Kings 22:3-23:25; II Chron. 34:8-35: 19). At the age of twenty-six (622 B.C.), Josiah, pleased at what had been accomplished but seeing much more that needed to be done, put forth still greater effort to bring about what is called the most thorough reform in Judah's history. This special endeavor was prompted in particular by the discovery[87] of "the book of the law of Yahweh by the hand of Moses" (II Chron. 34:14).[88] The discovery was made by Hilkiah, the high priest, while workmen repaired the Temple.[89] Shaphan, a scribe, brought the book to Josiah's attention and read to him from it. Josiah was disturbed at the deviation he recognized between the requirements it set forth and the actual practices in the land. The counsel of Huldah, a prophetess, was sought; and she warned that punishment was inevitable for the country because of this deviation, but added that it would not come in Josiah's day since he sought to do what God desired. Josiah then had this law read to the people and issued orders for the reform.

All foreign cult objects were removed from the Temple, the city of Jerusalem, and throughout the land. The idolatrous priests were removed from their positions, and houses of religious prostitution were destroyed. Child-sacrifice to Molech in the Valley of Hinnom was abolished. Horses dedicated to the sun were removed from the entrance to the Temple, and their chariots were burned with fire. Finally, high places to false deities erected by Solomon just outside Jerusalem, apparently still in use, were razed (II Kings 23:4-14).

Josiah, not content to effect this reform merely in Judah, gave orders

[86] That he could do this in spite of Assyrian control is no doubt tied in with the growing Assyrian weakness of the day.

[87] Manasseh may have destroyed all copies of the Law that he could find, which prompted someone to hide this one so well that it became lost to knowledge. It is possible, too, that this copy had been placed in the Temple cornerstone by Solomon, a practice not uncommon for the day.

[88] Probably a copy of the five books of Moses. Josiah's detailed keeping of the Passover at this time requires it to have been more than merely Deuteronomy, as many hold (cf. G. Wright, Interpreter's Bible, II, pp. 311-330). It should be observed also that nothing in the record suggests that this book had recently been written, as negative criticism has long believed. Indeed, Josiah had already been effecting reforms, as well as Hezekiah earlier, showing that they knew what God desired in His Law without having to find this particular copy. The discovery here added detail to Josiah's knowledge.

[89] As in the former time of Athaliah, the wicked reigns of Manasseh and Amon had led to Temple neglect and even purposeful changes through pagan innovations.

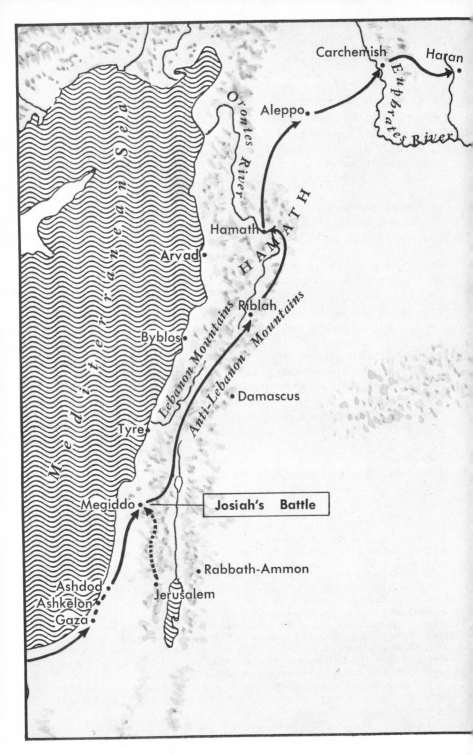

Map 16. Necho's Route and Josiah's Battle

respecting the North as well, taking advantage of Assyria's general period of weakness. A particular place of interest was Bethel, long the center of golden-calf worship. According to a prophecy given over three hundred years before,[90] Josiah burned the bones of the false priests on the altar, which Jeroboam I had erected, and then destroyed the altar and its high place.

Perhaps the most significant feature of Josiah's reform was the observance of the Passover (II Kings 23:21-23; II Chron. 35:1-19). The record states that a Passover had not been kept as carefully since the days of Samuel the prophet.[91] The original command of God had been to observe the feast with care annually, but the people had not obeyed. Josiah made sure the feast was kept properly this year.

b. Josiah's death (II Kings 23:28-30; II Chron. 35:20-27). Josiah was an able king. The sweeping reforms he instituted, in spite of opposition which no doubt arose, could not have been brought about by one of mediocre leadership qualities. He made his authority felt even in the erstwhile provinces of Israel, as noticed, thus enlarging Judah's sphere of influence. However, when he attempted to shape, in some part, world developments, he exceeded himself and brought about his own death.

The occasion involved his endeavor to stop a northward march of Pharaoh Necho II of Egypt in 609 B.C. Necho was moving to the aid of Assyrians in an attempt to stop Babylonia from becoming the new world leader. Assyria's two main cities, Assur and Nineveh, had fallen in 614 and 612 B.C., respectively, to attacks by the Medes and Babylonians;[92] and the remants of Assyria's army, under Ashur-uballit II, had fled westward to Haran.[93] In 610 B.C., Haran had fallen to Nabopolassar, king of Babylon, which all but finished the Assyrians. Now, in 609 B.C., Necho, who had just succeeded Psammetichus I as

[90] Brought by the "man of God" to Jeroboam just after the establishment of the false worship of the calves; supra, chap. 13, p. 305.

[91] This means that it was observed now with yet greater care and detail than in Hezekiah's reforms; cf. supra, pp. 357-58.

[92] The barbaric Scythians from northern Mesopotamia also had some part. These people had been making their presence felt in recent years. They had passed through Philistia about 627 B.C., in Josiah's early years (cf. Jer. 6:22-26), creating fear in Judah; had been stopped by Psammetichus I of Egypt by prayers and presents (Herodotus, I, 105), had defeated Cyaxares of Media in 624 B.C., and now had switched sides, to aid Media and Babylonia against Assyria.

[93] A fragment of the "Babylonian Chronicle," dealing with events of the years 616-609, discovered in the British Museum by C. J. Gadd, has thrown considerable light on this period; cf. ANET, pp. 303-305 for text; DOTT, pp. 75-83 for text and discussion; and D. J. Wiseman, Chronicles of Chaldean Kings (London: The British Museum, 1956) carries a full treatment.

king of Egypt,[94] and who wanted Egypt to regain world prominence instead of Babylonia, was marching northward to help Assyria's few remaining forces. Josiah, in a probable indication of favor toward Babylonia, attempted to stop the Egyptians at strategic Megiddo, and was killed in the effort. His body was returned to Jerusalem for burial.

2. *Seventh-century prophets.* Josiah's day was one of outstanding prophets. Jeremiah began to minister in Josiah's thirteenth year (Jer. 1:2), 627 B.C., and continued until after Jerusalem's fall to Babylonia in 586 B.C. Zephaniah also dates his book to Josiah's reign (1:1) and likely began his ministry about the time that Jeremiah did, at least prior to Josiah's reforms; for he speaks of foreign cults yet existing in the land (1:4). Nahum does not date his book to the reign of a king, but is best placed in Josiah's time too; for the main theme he pursues concerns the fall of Nineveh which came in 612 B.C., three years before Josiah's death. Habakkuk's prophecy as well must be located either at the close of Josiah's rule or during the succeeding reign of Jehoiakim, for he speaks of the Babylonian invasion being near at hand (1:5-6).

At no other time in the history of either Israel or Judah is such a concentration of writing prophets witnessed. The significance must be that God was giving Judah one last intensive warning of impending punishment. No doubt, too, much of the credit for the reform Josiah effected must go to these stalwart men. The king had to lead the way, but these prophets could have aided greatly, both encouraging his movement and prompting the people to accept it. Jeremiah, for instance, speaks harshly of the inexcusable idolatry filling the land (2: 5-13), warning of punishment if repentance were not forthcoming (3:1-5, 19-25). Zephaniah predicts severe punishment for Judah's sin (2:4–3:7). Nahum's warning was more indirect, telling of Nineveh's coming destruction; but the message that God brings punishment on all who do wickedly could not have been missed. Habakkuk again speaks directly of the Babylonians coming against Judah as an instrument of God's justice (1:1-11).

3. *Jehoahaz (609 B.C.; II Kings 23:31-33; II Chronicles 36:1-3).* Josiah had three sons, and each in time ruled over Judah. No other king in either Israel or Judah had this distinction.[95] Yet all three failed to follow their father in obeying God.

The first to rule was the middle son, Jehoahaz. The people by-

[94] Psammetichus had already shown favor toward Assyria, even having taken an army in 616 B.C. to assist in checking Nabopolassar in Mesopotamia. Necho was following his lead.

[95] Ahab in Israel came the nearest, having two sons to rule: Ahaziah and Jehoram.

passed the eldest in selecting him as Josiah's successor at the age of twenty-three. He had ruled only three months, however, when Pharaoh Necho, now in authority over Judah since the defeat of Josiah, ordered his replacement by the older brother, Eliakim, whose name was now changed to Jehoiakim.[96] Apparently, Necho had reason to believe that Jehoahaz would not cooperate with him, and thought the older son would.[97] At this time, too, Necho demanded tribute·from Judah, requiring one hundred talents of silver and a talent of gold. Jehoahaz was taken prisoner to Egypt, where he died as predicted by Jeremiah (22:11-12).

4. *Jehoiakim (609–597; II Kings 23:34–24:7; II Chronicles 36:4-8).* Jehoiakim was twenty-five, two years older than his deposed brother, when he was placed on the throne. Jehoiakim did evil before God and was incapable of efficient rule. He may have already shown his failings when the people earlier chose his younger brother as his father's successor. Jeremiah shows disdain for him by declaring that Jehoiakim would be "buried with the burial of an ass" (22:13-19). The particular act of Jehoiakim which prompted this remark was his construction of a new palace. Apparently he was dissatisfied with that of his father and squandered state funds and used forced labor to build it. Jehoiakim also foolishly cut and burned Jeremiah's book written at the direction of God, apparently thinking that this would in some way offset its dire warnings (Jer. 36:23). Measures of this kind, along with a hated head tax imposed to pay Necho's tribute (II Kings 23:35), would have aggravated the people and stirred a deep unrest. Contributing further to unsettled conditions were great world changes of the day, with Babylonia now emerging as the new world power.

5. *Babylon's rise to power.* Babylon's dominance in the Mediterranean countries had not come as yet in 609 B.C., when Necho marched to meet the Babylonians. The Egyptian Pharaoh was unsuccessful at the time in retaking Haran from Nabopolassar, but he did keep the Babylonians from pressing their claim further. Egypt remained dominant in the West for another three years.[98] Nabopolassar and his talented son, Nebuchadnezzar, had to remain content to strengthen their present holdings in anticipation of another day.

[96] Eliakim means "God has established," and Jehoiakim, "Yahweh has established." Since the meaning is basically the same, Necho, who seems to have ordered also the name change, must have wanted only to demonstrate his authority to do so.

[97] At the time, Necho was at Riblah on the Orontes River, where he had established his camp for the encounter with Babylonia. Jehoahaz was summoned there to receive the news of his dismissal.

[98] Necho's authority in Judah to replace one king by another was only representative of control in all these Mediterranean countries.

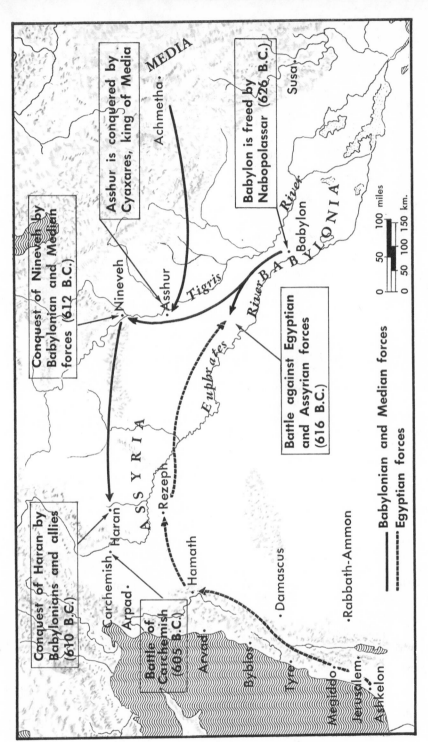

Map 17. Fall of Assyria and Rise of Babylonia

Early in 605 B.C., that day came, when the two sides clashed in the world-changing Battle of Carchemish on the Euphrates. Nebuchadnezzar now led the Babylonians, for his aged father was confined with illness at home. The young Babylonian displayed his genius by sending the Egyptians reeling in headlong defeat. Necho fell back to Hamath on the Orontes River, hoping to regroup; but Nebuchadnezzar gave him no opportunity as he followed hard after him and all but annihilated what remained of the Egyptian force.[99] Thus, Nebuchadnezzar won the control his father had desired, and Babylonia became the new world leader. The "whole of the land of Hatti,"[100] meaning all Syria and Palestine to the border of Egypt, now lay exposed to the new conqueror. All he had to do was assert control, which he began doing immediately, moving as far south as Jerusalem, where he forced the submission of Jehoiakim and other kings of the area.

As Nebuchadnezzar moved through the newly-won country, he desired not only the submission of leading cities but also the procurement of able young men, whom he might relocate in Babylon as prospective government personnel. It is likely that each city was forced to give him their finest. Among those from Jerusalem[101] were Daniel and his three friends, Hananiah, Mishael, and Azariah.[102] While involved in this activity, Nebuchadnezzar was suddenly interrupted by the death of his ailing father, Nabopolassar, in August of 605 B.C., and quickly returned to Babylon to receive the crown as Nebuchadnezzar II. The following fall saw him back in the West again, however, continuing the work. Mentioned by him as a major prize during the summer of 604 B.C. was the Philistine city of Ashkelon, taken after a fierce struggle (cf. Jer. 47:5-7).[103] In 601 B.C., Nebuchadnezzar moved against

[99] Besides references in note 93, see for details, Thiele, *MNHK*, pp. 22-27; D. N. Freedman, *BA*, 19 (1956), pp. 50-60; Albright, *BASOR*, 143 (1956), pp. 28-33); H. Tadmor, *JNES*, 15 (1956), pp. 226-30; J. P. Hyatt, *JBL*, 75 (1956), pp. 277-84.

[100] Nebuchadnezzar's own designation; cf. *DOTT*, p. 79.

[101] This was the third year of Jehoiakim (Dan. 1:1) on the basis of Tishri reckoning, but the fourth year (Jer. 46:2) on Nisan reckoning; cf. Thiele, *MNHK*, pp. 165-66.

[102] The 70-year captivity of Judah (Jer. 25:11-12; 29:10) is figured from this time of Daniel's deportation rather than that of either 597 or 586 B.C., when many more people were taken. The return occurred in 538-37 B.C. Many young men were taken at this time (Dan. 1:1-6). This instance of captivity is commonly called the first aspect of the total captivity, with those of 597 and 586 B.C. called the second and third aspects.

[103] Cf. *DOTT*, pp. 79-80 and H. L. Ginsberg, *BASOR*, 111 (1948), pp. 24-27, who discuss the probability of an Aramaic letter, discovered in Egypt pleading for help from the Pharaoh, having been written by the king of Ashkelon at this time.

Egypt and was met by Necho near the border. Both sides lost heavily in the engagement, and neither could claim victory. At least Nebuchadnezzar was repulsed and had to return to Babylon.

6. *Jehoiachin and the capture of Jerusalem in 597 B.C. (II Kings 24:8-16; II Chronicles 36:9-10).* Nebuchadnezzar's withdrawal gave only brief respite to the region, however; for in 597 B.C. he returned to bring severe devastation. The cause was rebellion on the part of Jehoiakim, who now looked once again to Egypt for support (II Kings 24:1).[104] For a time the Babylonian Monarch sent only contingents of his army, reinforced by Aramaean, Moabite, and Ammonite troops (II Kings 24:2; Jer. 35:11) to keep the revolt in check; but he finally saw the need of a major campaign and came himself.

In December, 598 B.C., Nebuchadnezzar left Babylon, and the same month Jehoiakim died in Jerusalem.[105] Jehoiakim's eighteen-year-old son,[106] Jehoiachin, replaced him on the throne and received the blow of the Babylonian attack the following March, 597 B.C. Egyptian support hoped for by Jehoiakim did not materialize. Jehoiachin was taken captive to Babylon, along with the queen mother, princes, servants, and booty. The outstanding prophet Ezekiel was taken at this time, too (Ezek. 1:1-3), and with him 10,000 leading citizens, including a thousand craftsmen and smiths (II Kings 24:11-16).

7. *Zedekiah and the captivity of 586 B.C. (II Kings 24:17–25:21; II Chronicles 36:11-21; Jeremiah 39:1-10).* Nebuchadnezzar installed Jehoiachin's uncle, Mattaniah, Josiah's third son, on the throne. He was twenty-one at the time, fifteen years younger than Jehoiakim, the oldest of the three sons. Nebuchadnezzar changed his name to Zedekiah, after the pattern of Pharaoh Necho regarding Jehoiakim. The people of Judah seem never to have accepted Zedekiah as their true king, however, probably because he had been appointed by the foreign Nebuchadnezzar. Instead, they ascribed this honor still to Jehoiachin, though in captivity.[107] As a result, and because of Zedekiah's own poor

---

[104] Cf. D. J. Wiseman, *op. cit.*, pp. 26-28.

[105] The exact time is established by comparing the Babylonian Chronicle with II Kings 24:6, 8. Jeremiah's scathing predictions, as to the nature of Jehoiakim's death and burial (Jer. 22:18-19; 36:27-32), suggest that he was killed in a battle with one of the marauding bands and in a situation which prevented a normal, honorable burial.

[106] II Kings 24:8. II Chron. 36:9 gives only eight years, but this must be due to a copyist's error, simply omitting a *yodh,* which as a number designated "ten."

[107] Evidence exists from the discovery of jar handles, both at Tell Beit Mirsim (possibly Debir) and Tell er-Rumeileh (probably Beth-shemesh), stamped with the words, "Eliakim, steward of Jehoiachin," which indicates that royal property was still in Zedekiah's time thought to belong to Jehoiachin. Then, in Babylon, documents bearing the title for Jehoiachin, "king of Judah," have been found in the palace, showing that he was resident there, in keeping with II Kings 25:

judgment and general inability, his term of reign was beset by continual agitation and unrest. Furthermore, rebellion against Babylon came to be strongly urged by Zedekiah's advisors, to whom he finally gave ear. In view of Nebuchadnezzar's earlier harsh treatment of Jerusalem, one would think that the Judean people now would have remained docile, but they did not.

a. Revolt against Babylon (II Kings 24:20; II Chron. 36:13). A strong anti-Babylonian group in Jerusalem brought pressure for the revolt and urged Zedekiah to look again to Egypt for help. A new coalition was being formed of Edom, Moab, Ammon, and Phoenicia (Jer. 27:1-3); and this Jerusalem group wished Judah to join. False prophets aided their cause in declaring that God had already broken the yoke of Babylon and that within two years Judah's captives would return home to Jerusalem (Jer. 28:2-4). In opposition, Jeremiah denounced this manner of speaking, declaring it false and urging continued acceptance of Babylonian lordship (Jer. 27:1-22). Two other developments outside Judah helped fan revolutionary flames in Zedekiah's fourth year: Psammetichus II succeeded Necho in Egypt, and a minor rebellion was staged in Babylon itself. Still, however, Zedekiah was not persuaded to listen to the anti-Babylonians. Instead, he showed good judgment in sending a representative to Nebuchadnezzar in Babylon (Jer. 29:3; 51:59)—perhaps even going himself—to express Judah's loyalty.

But five years later, Zedekiah was persuaded. He then did choose to revolt, and he looked to Egypt for support. Details of possible mutual defense agreements with allied countries are not revealed, but some type of pact was made with Egypt at the time. Hophra succeeded his father, Psammetichus II, as Pharaoh of Egypt in 588 B.C., and he was even more aggressive in furthering a policy of Asian intervention. As a result, early in 588 B.C., Nebuchadnezzar once more marched to the West,[108] and his army laid siege to Jerusalem. The siege was lifted temporarily when the Egyptians sought to honor their alliance by sending troops, but apparently the Babylonians had little trouble in meeting and inflicting defeat on the force before it was able to reach those besieged. Nebuchadnezzar's army was soon back outside Jerusalem's walls.

27-30, and suggesting that he was still considered Judah's king. For text, cf. ANET, p. 308. For discussion, cf. H. G. May, AJSL, 56 (1939), pp. 146-48; Albright, "King Jehoiachin in Exile," BA, 5 (1942), pp. 49-55.

[108] He established headquarters at Riblah on the Orontes River, north of Palestine. He may have sent army contingents in various directions from there. He besieged Tyre from the years 587 to 574 B.C. The Lachish Letters indicate devastation all through Judean cities; cf. DOTT, pp. 212-17. Ammon may have been a target, too; cf. Ezek. 21:18-32.

b. Jeremiah's suffering at the hands of his countrymen. During these months, Jeremiah suffered great hardship at the hands of his fellow Judeans. At the time of the temporary lifting of the siege, he gave due warning that the Babylonians would soon be back and was promptly imprisoned by the Jerusalem princes (Jer. 37:11-16). The worried Zedekiah visited him there, received further prediction that Jerusalem would fall to the enemy, and released the prophet to the freedom of the court of the guard (Jer. 37:17-21). But the princes were not happy with this and once more forced his confinement, only this time in a miry cistern (Jer. 38:1-6). How long he was held in this wretched place is not stated, but finally the king permitted one of his servants, Ebed-melech, to draw him out (Jer. 38:7-13). Despite the persecution, however, Jeremiah faithfully continued to give God's warnings and advice.

c. Fall of Jerusalem (II Kings 25:1-21; II Chron. 36:17-20; Jer. 39:1-10). In accordance with Jeremiah's warning, the city fell to the Babylonians in July, 586 B.C.[109] Zedekiah tried to flee but was captured near Jericho and brought to Nebuchadnezzar's headquarters at Riblah. Zedekiah's sons were slain before his eyes, and then his own eyes were put out. He, with many of the people,[110] was taken captive to Babylon, while Jerusalem suffered severe damage at the hands of Nebuzaradan, an officer of Nebuchadnezzar. Included was the complete destruction of the great Temple built by Solomon, which had stood for four centuries.

Testimony is given by the Lachish Letters[111] that devastation was experienced also through all Judah at this time. In one of the letters, an officer stationed at an observation post writes to the Lachish commander that the signal of Azekah can no longer be seen, which suggests that this city had just fallen to the Babylonian forces. Jeremiah indicates that Azekah and Lachish were two of the last cities to remain before the fearful onslaught (Jer. 34:6-7). The Babylonian Monarch intended that Judah should not again raise her head in revolt.

---

[109] Siege began in the tenth month of Zedekiah's ninth year (Jan., 588 B.C.) and continued until the fourth month of his eleventh year (July, 586 B.C.), a total of eighteen months.

[110] Jeremiah gives the figure of only 832 persons (52:29), but cf. *infra,* chap. 15, p. 385, n. 31.

[111] These are 21 ostraca, dating from this time, which were found in the gate of Lachish. They apparently constituted evidence in a court trial, which may have been in process at the time Lachish fell to the Babylonians. Besides the reference included in note 108, cf. Albright, *BASOR,* 82 (1941), pp. 18-24 for discussion.

CHAPTER FIFTEEN

EXILE AND RETURN

II Kings 25:22-30; II Chronicles 36:22-23; Ezra; Nehemiah; Esther; Jeremiah 40–44; Daniel 1–6

The fall of Jerusalem and the exile of her leading citizens brought an abrupt change in the history of Judah. The Temple, which had been the center of religious activity, was now destroyed. Jerusalem had served as the center of civic life but now lay in ruins. The more able and influential persons had been deported to Babylon, which left less capable people to make decisions and form policies. But though life patterns did change, Judah's history continued. The deportation was only partial, and a populace, made up of the common people, carried on.

A. DEVELOPMENTS IN JUDAH (II Kings 25:22-26; Jeremiah 40–44)

1. *General situation.* The idea of taking influential persons of a conquered nation as captives was copied by the Babylonians from the Assyrians. The latter had found the policy effective in minimizing chances of revolution, and Nebuchadnezzar desired the same benefit. He does not seem to have intermixed populations, however, as the Assyrians, who not only deported Israelites in 722 B.C. but imported strangers to take their place. That Nebuchadnezzar did not was of significant benefit to Judah; for it eliminated the danger of inter-marriage with heathen gentiles, a development which had come to reality in Israel.[1]

Judah was now a province of Babylon. She no longer had her own king, but was ruled by a governor appointed by the foreign authority. The first governor was Gedaliah, son of Ahikam,[2] grandson of Sha-

---

[1] The Samaritans descended from mixed marriages in Israel. As for Judah, some intermarriage had come into existence by the time of Ezra's return to Jerusalem (458 B.C.); but this was with neighboring peoples, not imported foreigners (Ezra 9:1-2).

[2] He had once saved Jeremiah from death (Jer. 26:24).

phan[3] (II Kings 25:22). With Jerusalem destroyed, Gedaliah established a new capital at Mizpah.[4] He may have been active earlier in the court of Judah during the reign of Zedekiah. A seal found at Lachish and bearing the inscription, "Belonging to Gedaliah who is over the house,"[5] is archaeologically dated to the time of the general destruction of 586 B.C. If reference is to the same Gedaliah, the man had filled a supervisory position in Zedekiah's palace.

The people governed by Gedaliah are called "the poor of the land" and were left to cultivate the soil (II Kings 25:12). Their number had been greatly reduced,[6] both by the captivity and death from the wars. Many had died in the war of 597 B.C., and Jehoiachin and 10,000 captives (II Kings 24:14) had then been deported. Many more had perished in the long siege of 588 to 586 B.C., and again a large number had been taken to Babylon. Excavation has revealed that the Babylonian destruction reached all across Judah, for numerous cities show evidence of being burned at this time. Lachish, for instance, gives evidence of devastation at both 597 and 586 B.C. The land, both in size of population and general appearance, little resembled what it had been only a few years before.

2. *Assassination of Gedaliah (II Kings 25:23-26; Jeremiah 40:7–41:18).* Gedaliah had been governor for only two months[7] when he was treacherously murdered by Ishmael, a member of the royal family. Ishmael was among a number who had fled from Judah at the first approach of the Babylonian army and taken residence in Ammon. When Gedaliah was made governor in Mizpah, Ishmael with others returned to Judah and professed loyalty to the new regime. Gedaliah was warned by his military aide, Johanan, that this profession was false, but Gedaliah refused to believe him. Then Ishmael, with the backing of Baalis, king of Ammon (Jer. 40:14), both of whom were apparently jealous of Gedaliah, successfully plotted Gedaliah's death and also killed a small garrison of Babylonians at Mizpah and some Judean assistants. So secretly was the treachery carried out that it remained unknown outside the governor's house for two days. On the second day, Ishmael and his men found it necessary to kill also a visit-

[3] Probably the same as Josiah's scribe, who was active in the reformation movement of Josiah's time (II Kings 22:3).

[4] For location, cf. *supra*, chap. 9, p. 227, n. 82.

[5] For discussion, cf. H. G. May, *AJSL*, 56 (1939), pp. 146-48.

[6] Albright's figure of less than 20,000 must be too low, however; cf. Albright, *BP*, pp. 49, 59f, 62f.

[7] Killed in the seventh month (II Kings 25:25). Though the year is not given, the implication is strong that this was the same year in which the destruction had taken place, 586 B.C. Jerusalem had fallen in the fifth month (II Kings 25:8).

ing group of pilgrims after which they fled in haste for Ammon, apparently fearing now that news of the bloody action might become known. Ishmael took a number of hostages, including daughters of Zedekiah, who had been entrusted to Gedaliah's care and whom Ishmael for some reason had not killed. At this point, Johanan, the military leader, who had earlier warned Gedaliah, became aware of the atrocity and gave pursuit. He caught Ishmael's force at Gibeon, where he succeeded in liberating the hostages; but Ishmael' and eight of his men made good their escape to Ammon.

3. *Jeremiah gives counsel (Jeremiah 40:1-6; 42:1-43:3).* Jeremiah had been left in the land at his own request by the Babylonian general. Given his choice of going to Babylon or remaining in the land, he had decided to stay. He took up residence in Mizpah, where he could be near the new governor, Gedaliah. Upon the assassination of the governor, Jeremiah was consulted by Johanan and his companions, who needed advice now that apparent cause had been given for retaliation by the Babylonians. The people feared further reprisal, which they believed would come as a result of this slaying of the Babylonian appointee and soldiers left to keep order. They asked Jeremiah to seek word from God and promised to follow whatever the word might indicate.

Ten days later Jeremiah received God's revelation, which instructed the people to remain in the land and not to fear, for the Babylonians would not retaliate. Jeremiah communicated this good information to the people, warning particularly against seeking shelter in Egypt. The people, however, now broke their promise and refused to accept the word which he brought. Instead, they accused him of speaking falsely, followed the dictates of their own hearts, and did exactly what he told them not to do. They made plans to go to Egypt.[8]

4. *Descent to Egypt (Jeremiah 43:4-44:30).* The number of Judeans who made the journey was large. Jeremiah 43:5-6 speaks of the group as those who had returned from surrounding countries, as had Ishmael, and those who had been placed under Gedaliah's charge. Jeremiah went as well, certainly against his will, but likely in an effort to keep God's Word before the people as best he could. The land of Judah may have been quite depopulated after the group had left. The migrators came to Tahpanhes,[9] in the eastern Delta of Egypt,

[8] Trust had been placed in Egypt before, always with disappointment, but never had there been a mass flight there. Perhaps the scarcity of numbers contributed to the unwise decision.

[9] Identified as Tell Defenneh, located 27 miles south southwest of Port Said. The same consonantal spelling, *thpnhs,* has been found in a Phoenician letter in Egypt of the sixth century (cf. A. Dupont-Sommer, *PEQ,* 81[1949], pp. 52-

where apparently all took up residence for a time. There Jeremiah, at God's direction, hid stones in the pavement at the entry of a royal palace, and he delivered God's prediction that Nebuchadnezzar of Babylon would one day conquer and establish his pavilion on that very place (Jer. 43:8-13).[10]

From Jeremiah 44:1, 15, it appears that this group of Judeans gradually scattered to various cities of Egypt. Jeremiah warned them that, because of continuing unfaithfulness to God, none would be permitted to return to Judah (vss. 12-14). An extra-biblical source indicates that some Jews, whether descendants of this number or not, later lived in a military settlement on the island of Elephantine, at the first cataract of the Nile in southern Egypt. This evidence comes from the well-known Elephantine papyri found on the island. The papyri date from near the close of the fifth century.[11]

B. The Babylonian Period (605–539)

The time when the Judeans were taken captive was that of the great Neo-Babylonian Empire, when Babylonia reached its zenith of world influence. Empire status was achieved by Nebuchadnezzar at the onset of his rule; and it continued until 539 B.C., when Persian forces under Cyrus the Great brought about its defeat. Judean captives were present from near the beginning of this time and remained until after the Persian conquest.

1. *Nebuchadnezzar (605–562)*. Nebuchadnezzar ruled forty-three years and maintained his country's supreme position as long as he lived. For good reason the image dream interpreted by Daniel depicted him as the "head of gold" (Dan. 2:38), for he stands as one of the great rulers of ancient time. Those who succeeded him were less capable; and the country decayed from within, climaxed by the fall to Cyrus.

a. Military activity. Nebuchadnezzar was proficient in warfare. His conquests through the time of Jerusalem's destruction have been noticed, but he did more. The siege of Tyre, begun apparently during

---

57). Petrie excavated the site in 1883-84 and discovered the foundation of a castle, perhaps the one before which Jeremiah buried the stones; cf. Barton, *AB*, p. 28.

[10] The prediction was fulfilled. A British Museum tablet tells of a successful campaign by Nebuchadnezzar in his thirty-seventh year (568-567) against Pharaoh Amasis. Amasis had replaced Pharaoh Hophra who had been defeated by Nebuchadnezzar in 572 B.C. Now when Amasis rebelled, Nebuchadnezzar marched into Egypt and inflicted a further defeat. Cf. Wiseman, *Chronicles of Chaldean Kings (626–556 B.C.) in the British Museum* (London: Trustees of the British Museum, 1956), p. 94; also Finegan, *LAP*, p. 131.

[11] For discussion and references, cf. *infra*, pp. 409-11.

the same campaign in which Jerusalem fell, was continued for thirteen years. At the close, he received the city's acknowledgment of Babylonian suzerainty, though he does not appear to have actually taken the strong island fortress.[12] Jeremiah (52:30) states that in 582 B.C. he again forced a deportation from Judah, though of this no other information is given.[13] The same year he campaigned successfully in Coele-Syria, Moab, and Ammon.[14] Then in 568 B.C. he invaded Egypt shortly after Pharaoh Amasis had replaced Pharaoh Hophra.[15] The time was one of weakness and confusion in Egypt, and the Babylonian ruler took advantage of it. Nebuchadnezzar's goal does not seem to have been permanent conquest, however, but only punitive action for Egypt's past interference in Syria-Palestine. He was successful, for peaceful relations existed between the two great powers in ensuing years.

b. Building activity. Nebuchadnezzar was an active and successful builder. The words of Daniel 4:30 are apt, as the Babylonian ruler is quoted as saying, "Is not this great Babylon, which I have built by my mighty power?" He constructed an intricate system of fortifications, including Babylon's own defenses and a chain of fortresses both north and south of the capital city. He built temples, palaces, canals, and streets. A processional avenue leading to the city's sacred area was lined with brightly-colored, enameled brick, adorned with rows of bulls and dragons in bas relief. The street led through the famous gate of Ishtar, similarly decorated.[16] In the sacred area proper was the grand ziggurat which Nebuchadnezzar rebuilt from a former day,[17] and the great temple of Marduk, likewise restored. Most famous of all were the hanging gardens, built in terraces by Nebuchadnezzar to please his Median queen, who missed her native mountains. The Greeks were so impressed by the gardens that they classed them as one of the seven wonders of the world.

[12] A prediction by Ezekiel (26:1-14) finds partial fulfillment in this Babylonian campaign. The complete fulfillment came later, however, when Alexander the Great of Greece drew the remains of old Tyre into the Mediterranean to make a causeway out to the fortress on the island offshore.

[13] Jeremiah states that 745 persons were taken this time, probably along with others from Syria, Moab, and Ammon, whom Nebuchadnezzar also defeated the same year.

[14] Cf. Josephus (Antiq. X, 9, 7). An undated text of Nebuchadnezzar, speaking of a campaign into the Lebanon mountains, may refer to the same time; cf. ANET, p. 307.

[15] Cf. supra, n. 10.

[16] Cf. ANEP, figs. 760-62 for pictures.

[17] A. Parrot reconstructs this ziggurat as 298 feet square and 300 feet high, rising in seven stages. Parrot, The Tower of Babel (London: SCM Press, 1955), pp. 46-51.

2. *Nebuchadnezzar's successors (562–539).*[18] None of the successors of Nebuchadnezzar could match his achievements, and Babylonia's glory began to fade soon after his death. His son, Amel-marduk, succeeded him, but ruled only two years (562-560). The Bible mentions him (Evil-merodach) as the one who released Jehoiachin from prison and gave the deposed Judean king a place of privilege at the Babylonian court (II Kings 25:27-30; Jer. 52:31-34). Amel-marduk was murdered by his brother-in-law, Neriglissar (Nergal-shar-usur), who was then enthroned in August, 560 B.C. The identity of this man with the Nergal-sharezer of Jeremiah 39:3, 13, who, as the official (*rab mag*) under Nebuchadnezzar, had played a part in releasing Jeremiah from prison in 586 B.C., is generally accepted. If correct, he was at least middle-aged at the time of his accession. As king, he is known mainly for building activity and a major military venture across the Taurus Mountains. In the latter, he was successful at first, but then suffered defeat and withdrew to Babylon in 556 B.C., shortly before his death. He was succeeded by his young son, Labashi-Marduk, who was assassinated only a few months later by a group of courtiers, including Nabonidus, who now seized the throne.

3. *Nabonidus (556–539).* Nabonidus (Nabu-na'id), the son of an Aramaean nobleman from Haran,[19] was probably the most capable ruler following Nebuchadnezzar.[20] Of priestly lineage and a devotee of the moon god, Sin, he gave himself to antiquarian religious interests. He rebuilt the temple of Sin in Haran, excavated temple sites in Babylonia, and restored long abandoned rites. He did not hesitate to innovate religious practices, many of which were not pleasing, however, to the establishment of the Marduk priesthood. His favoritism of Sin, rather than Marduk, indeed, caused marked irritation and finally outright opposition. Though not given to military activity, Nabonidus did make two campaigns early in his reign: one against Cilicia (554 B.C.) and another against Syria (553 B.C.). An unusual act was his transfer of residence to Tema, southeast of Edom in the Arabian desert. The

[18] For details of this chronology, cf. R. A. Parker and W. H. Dubberstein, *Babylonian Chronology, 626 B.C.–A.D. 45* (Chicago: University of Chicago Press, 1942).

[19] His mother may have been Nitocris, widowed wife of Nebuchadnezzar, cf. Sidney Smith, *Babylonian Historical Texts* (London: 1924), pp. 37, 43 for discussion. Another view is that he may have married this Nitocris, who was either the widowed wife of Nebuchadnezzar or his daughter, cf. Dougherty, *Nabonidus and Belshazzar* (New Haven: 1929), pp. 59f. Either view would explain how Nebuchadnezzar could be called the father of Belshazzar (Dan. 5:2).

[20] Herodotus states that he had been the Babylonian representative in 585 B.C. when a peace treaty between the Medes and Lydians had been drawn (Herodotus, I, 74; cf. R. P. Dougherty, *Nabonidus and Belshazzar* (New Haven: 1929), p. 36.

reason is obscure, though it likely had to do with his religious interests again. He remained in Tema for a period of ten years, leaving the kingdom in the hands of his able son, Belshazzar (Bel-shar-uzur). Actual kingship was entrusted to the young man, which coincides with Belshazzar's portrayal in the book of Daniel.[21] In Babylon, with Nabonidus absent, the annual New Year celebrations were suspended for several years. Always of great importance to the people, their omission stirred serious discontent among more than just the Marduk priests. In 539 B.C., Nabonidus returned to Babylon and ordered the festivities reinstated but apparently too late to offset the harm already done. By this time, Nabonidus was considered by many people as unfit to rule. This prompted a spirit of revolt and made the time ripe for the conquest of Cyrus.

C. Captive Judah

1. *Daniel (Daniel 1–6).* The most significant of the Judean captives was Daniel, who wrote the biblical book bearing his name.

a. Daniel's honor. Daniel, along with his three friends,[22] and others of his age,[23] was taken to Babylon in the summer of 605 B.C. Nebuchadnezzar's reason was not to inflict hardship but to educate these young men, that he might pick from them the most capable to staff various offices of his kingdom (Dan. 1:4). Before three years[24] had passed, Daniel, as a result of interpreting a dream for Nebuchadnezzar (Dan. 2:1-45), was elevated to the important position[25] of chief of the "wise men," upon whom the king depended for counsel.[26] Daniel

---

[21] Dan. 5:1-31 tells the story of Daniel's reading the miraculous writing on the palace wall for Belshazzar. For this he was made "third ruler in the kingdom" (5:29), suiting the fact that Belshazzar was himself the second ruler. For pertinent texts of Nabonidus, cf. *ANET*, pp. 312-15; *DOTT*, pp. 89-91.

[22] All four were given Babylonian names: Daniel, Belteshazzar; Hananiah, Shadrach; Mishael, Meshach; and Azariah, Abed-nego.

[23] Probably in their middle teens, in view of the purpose for which they were brought and the advanced age to which Daniel lived (at least until 536 B.C.).

[24] During Nebuchadnezzar's second year (Dan. 2:1). Since Nebuchadnezzar was crowned in September, 605 B.C., immediately after his return to Babylon, his first year would have begun in the spring (Nisan), 604, and his second, the spring, 603. Daniel's elevation came, then, sometime between spring, 603 and spring, 602 B.C.

[25] The plan had been for the young men to be educated for a minimum of three years (Dan. 1:5), but apparently Daniel was awarded his position prior to that time. However, training may have continued.

[26] Divination was a highly practiced art, and many methods were employed; cf. A. Guillaume, *Prophecy and Divination Among the Hebrews and Other Semites* (London: Hodder & Stoughton, 1938); A. Leo Oppenheim, *The Interpretation of Dreams in the Ancient Near East* (Philadelphia: Transactions of the American Philosophical Society, 1956). That Daniel, in becoming head of these

apparently retained this position for a long time, because years later Nebuchadnezzar still referred to him as "master of the magicians" (Dan. 4:9).[27] Change came for Daniel, however, by the time of Belshazzar's rule, for this king needed to be reminded that Daniel was indeed available to interpret the miraculous writing on the palace wall (Dan. 5:10-12). But by this time sixty-three years had elapsed since Daniel's first appointment, and he may have held numerous positions since. At the time of the Persian conquest of Babylon, when Daniel could not have been less than eighty years,[28] he was still retained by the new regime in a position of high responsibility. In fact, he was made one of the three presidents who superintended the respective governors of Persia's 120 provinces (Dan. 6:1-2).[29]

b. Daniel's influence. With Daniel holding these high positions at the Babylonian court, it is reasonable to assume that he was able to play a significant role in securing pleasant conditions for his captive countrymen. It will be observed shortly that their situation was indeed surprisingly free from hardship. Daniel may also have exerted influence to bring about the elevation of Jehoiachin to a place of honor by King Amel-marduk (II Kings 25:27-30). This type of act toward a captive king suggests the interests of a special friend working in his behalf. Further, Daniel may have had much to do with the decree which permitted Jews to return to Palestine.[30] He held his highest position at the time of this return and could have exerted his greatest influence. It is certain that he desired this permission to be granted, for he specifically included it as a request in prayer (Dan. 9:1-19). One can imagine him broaching the idea to the Persian king and doing all that he could to encourage its realization.

wise men, did not himself practice their arts is clear from the story over-all and particularly from Nebuchadnezzar's consultation with him separately when the king dreamed again in chapter 4 (vss. 7-9 especially).

[27] Since it was shortly after the dream of chapter 4 that Nebuchadnezzar, in fulfillment of the dream, became apparently demented (Dan. 4:28-37), the date must have been toward the conclusion of his 43-year reign.

[28] It is not likely that the age of those taken captive with Daniel was less than an average of 15 years, which would have made him no less than 81 in 539 B.C.

[29] That Daniel was so retained is most remarkable in the light of a change in government and also his own advanced age. It speaks highly of Daniel's ability, but even more of God's particular blessing on him and God's desire that he continue in this place of influence.

[30] The decree was issued in Cyrus' first year (II Chron. 36:22; Ezra 1:1) when Daniel was yet active. The fact that Cyrus permitted other captive peoples to return to their homelands also (cf. ANET, p. 316 for inscription) need not militate against this possibility. The Jews may have been the first to receive this permission, which privilege was then accorded to others as well.

2. *Captives generally*

a. Number. The number of persons taken captive from Judah to Babylon is difficult to determine. Only regarding the second deportation (597 B.C.) is a definite figure given: 10,000, which included 7,000 men of might and 1,000 craftsmen (II Kings 24:14-16). Concerning the first deportation (605 B.C.), all that can be said is that at least some other young men besides Daniel and his three friends were involved. Respecting the third deportation (586 B.C.), when Jerusalem as a city was devastated, those seized are designated as all but "the poor of the land" (II Kings 25:11, 12, 21), and no doubt included the largest number.[31] That a total of many thousands were taken is indicated also by the sizable number of persons who returned from the captivity in 538 B.C., namely 42,360 (Ezra 2:64; Neh. 7:66).[32]

b. Ezekiel. The most illustrious of the captives, other than Daniel and King Jehoiachin, was the prophet Ezekiel. Nothing is revealed regarding him prior to the captivity, but he played a significant role as one of those taken. He was God's messenger among the captives, rebuking them for sin and comforting them with promises of deliverance. His preaching made them realize that their captivity was in no way the result of limitation in God's power to protect them but solely a punishment permitted by Him for their sin. He also cheered them by declaring that God would yet vindicate His sovereignty in working their deliverance and bringing retribution on their captors. Ezekiel was given a better hearing than some of his predecessors, for official elders came to him to seek counsel and hear the word of God (Ezek. 8:1; 14:1; 20:1). During the years of captivity, the people did favorably change in spiritual outlook and personal relationship to God, and in this Ezekiel was certainly a main influence.

3. *Life in Babylon.* Evidence exists that life for the Judean captives was comparatively pleasant; much different, surely, than the condition of bondage experienced by their ancestors in Egypt.

a. Institutions maintained. One aspect of this evidence is that some of Judah's own institutions were maintained. For instance, elders, long employed in the local government of Judah, were still active. As just noted, elders came to Ezekiel, acting as representatives of the people,

---

[31] Jeremiah 52:30 mentions a fourth deportation as occurring in Nebuchadnezzar's twenty-third year (582 B.C.); cf. *supra*, p. 381, n. 13. The smallness of the total number of captives Jeremiah lists (52:28-30) may be explained in terms of possible copyist's errors, or in terms of Jeremiah desiring to list only particular classes or groups of captives; cf. Keil's discussion, *KDC*, Jeremiah, II, pp. 327-331.

[32] Not all returned either, as indicated by the large number still living in the East in Esther's day; cf. *infra*, pp. 407-408.

to seek counsel. Also, the institutions of the prophets and priests (in their respective teaching ministries) were retained; for when Jeremiah addressed a letter to the captives, he mentioned first the elders, then both prophets and priests, and finally the people generally (Jer. 29:1).

b. Freedom of movement. The captives enjoyed freedom of movement in the land. Ezekiel did, even having his own house (Ezek. 8:1). Also, the elders were at liberty to visit him there. The freedom accorded Jehoiachin, after liberation from prison by Amel-marduk, testifies similarly. He was given food and other provisions at the court for the remainder of his life and may even have been granted some authority to rule, for it is stated that he was given a "seat" (throne?) above that of other kings with him in Babylon (II Kings 25:28). Cuneiform tablets found by Weidner[33] in Babylon agree with these biblical notations. They identify Jehoiachin as "King of the land of Judah," and indicate that he and his five sons received liberal allowances of oil and food. They state further that the sons were in the care of an attendant, suggesting that servants were actually provided for the family.[34]

c. Correspondence privileges. Further, the Judeans had correspondence privileges, for they could write letters to friends back in Judah. Jeremiah speaks of such letters (29:25) and also wrote to the captives in Babylon himself (29:1). That communication of this kind must have been carried on is evidenced also by people in Judah knowing of Jehoiachin's status, so that they were able to hope for his return as king (Jer. 28:3-4).

d. Employment opportunities. Perhaps the most significant evidence comes from indications of favorable employment opportunities being open to the captives. One is found in the type of person Nebuchadnezzar chose to deport. He took craftsmen and artisans, particularly in the captivity of 597 B.C. (II Kings 24:14-16). Apparently Nebuchadnezzar planned to put them to work in skilled trades. The other is found in the many business tablets, discovered at Nippur on the canal Kabari, which contain Jewish names in a context showing that they were active in business: renting, buying, and selling.[35] The tablets

---

[33] E. F. Weidner, *Jojachin, Konig von Juda, in babylonischen Keilschrifttexten* (Melanges syriens offerts a Monsieur Rene Dussand, II, Paris, 1939). The texts date from the 10th to the 35th year of Nebuchadnezzar. Three texts are reproduced in *ANET*, p. 308.

[34] For discussion, cf. W. F. Albright, "King Joiachin in Exile," *BA*, 5 (1942), pp. 49-55.

[35] Found in the ruins of a business house, Murashu Sons. Many are in the form of contracts, showing names of participants in business transactions. Cf. H. V. Hilprecht and A. T. Clay, *Babylonian Expedition of the University of*

date from the fifth century[36] and so represent the Jewish situation after the exiles had been in Babylonia for more than a hundred years, but they imply that similar conditions had existed for some time.

e. Fertile land on which to live. Still further, Jews were permitted to live on fine, fertile land. Many resided along or near the river Chebar (Ezek. 1:1, 3; 3:15, 23; etc.), which is likely the same as the canal Kabari (*nari kabari,* meaning "great river"), known from one of the texts just mentioned. It flowed out of the Euphrates above Babylon, passed Nippur, and then entered the Euphrates again. The city Tel-abib, where Ezekiel at one time remained with resident captives for seven days (Ezek. 3:15), was on this canal. Modern Tilabub, near which Israelite pottery has significantly been discovered, likely marks the site. The canal supplied irrigation for a rich farming area,[37] which means that Jews were favored by an advantageous land for farming, whether for themselves or in working for others.

f. Still a punishment. That the captivity was intended as a punishment from God need not militate against the pleasantness of this picture. The experience did serve as a punishment, if only because the people had been uprooted from their homes and were forced to endure the kind of humiliation that comes with captivity under the best of conditions. This sense of humiliation would have been felt most keenly at the beginning of the period, probably the time when Psalm 137 was written, speaking as it does of weeping by the rivers of Babylon. The false prophets, who urged rebellion against the Babylon masters (Jer. 29:4-10), likely were more vocal in the earlier years as well. Jeremiah urged them, and the captives generally, to accept their status and make their lives as pleasant as possible—in keeping with the apparent ease that did result.

D. The Persian Period

The Old Testament prophets had predicted not only this captivity of Judeans but also their return home. Their time of punishment would be completed after seventy years of foreign domination (Jer. 25:11-12; 29:10). A look at the history involved shows that before that time of return arrived, however, a change came in world leadership. Babylonia was defeated by Persia, who then took command. The return of Judah and her subsequent history would be under this new power.

Pennsylvania, Series A. vols. IX-X, 1898, 1904; *ANET,* pp. 221-222; *DOTT,* pp. 95-96.

[36] During the reigns of the Persian kings Artaxerxes I (464-423) and Darius II (423-404).

[37] Cf. G. Contenau, *Everyday Life in Babylon and Assyria* (Eng. trans.; London: 1954), pp. 41-43.

1. Conquest of Babylon

a. Preliminary victories of Cyrus. Persia's conquest of Babylonia climaxed a period of rapid rise in Persian power, brought about primarily by the genius of Cyrus the Great (559-530).[38] His father was the Achaemenian, Cambyses I, king of Anshan, an Elamite region. At his father's death, Cyrus took the throne and soon added the nearby province of Persia (Parsua). When Nabonidus of Babylon saw in Cyrus a potential ally against his rival Astyages (585-550), king of Media, he supported Cyrus, little realizing that the latter was soon to be his great enemy. By 550 B.C., Cyrus had dethroned Astyages and assumed rule of the large domain of Media. Nabonidus now began to fear Cyrus and sought Amasis of Egypt (569-525) and Croesus of Lydia (c. 560-546) as allies. Cyrus, vying for world leadership, reacted by marching his army across northern Mesopotamia to encounter the rich Croesus. He moved almost unhindered, for none were able to withstand him. Surprising Croesus in his capital, Sardis, by crossing the Halys River in the dead of winter (547-546 B.C.), and cleverly using camels so that their scent made Croesus' cavalry horses unmanageable, Cyrus routed the foe and established his western border at the Aegean Sea.

b. Fall of Babylon. With Nabonidus' one ally defeated, and the other inactive,[39] Babylon was soon to fall before the mighty conqueror. At first, after returning from the western sweep, Cyrus spent time enlarging his eastern boundary, advancing it as far as India.[40] But in 539 B.C. he marched on the main prize, Babylon, which now stood alone against him. Babylon at this time was suffering deep unrest, as has been noted. Nabonidus' people, influenced by the disgruntled priests of Marduk, were ready for a change, even if effected by a foreigner. Cyrus was quite ready to oblige them, though how much of the discontent was known to him is uncertain. In any case, his task was remarkably easy.[41] The decisive engagement was not fought

[38] Predicted by name a century and a half earlier by Isaiah (44:28; 45:1) as one who would conquer rapidly and would be God's "servant" in effecting deliverance for the Jews.

[39] It is likely that the agreement with Egypt now failed, Pharaoh Amasis wanting no part of it any longer.

[40] Cf. A. T. Olmstead, *History of the Persian Empire* (Chicago: University of Chicago Press, 1948), pp. 45-49; R. Ghirshman, *Iran from the Earliest Times to the Islamic Conquest*, trans. from French (Baltimore: Hammondsworth, Penguin Books, 1954), p. 131.

[41] Important inscriptions describing the occasion exist from both Cyrus (Cyrus cylinder) and from Nabonidus (Nabonidus Chronicle), and they agree in basic facts. For Cyrus' record, cf. *ANET*, pp. 315-16 and *DOTT*, pp. 92-94; for Nabonidus record, cf. *ANET*, p. 306 and *DOTT*, pp. 81-83.

at Babylon but at Opis on the Tigris to the north, where Cyrus was victorious. His officer, Ugbaru,[42] was then able to take Babylon itself without a fight. This was in October, 539 B.C. Nabonidus himself, who had earlier fled before the oncoming Persian force, was taken prisoner shortly after. Cyrus personally entered Babylon a few weeks later, and was actually welcomed as liberator by the Marduk priests and the people generally.[43] The Persian monarch used tact in treating the populace with consideration. The city was not looted, nor were the religious or civil institutions greatly changed. The result was that a transfer of allegiance to him was brought about with a minimum of resentment or disturbance. With this all-important conquest of Babylonia completed, Cyrus held sway over more land than any ruler before him: from the Aegean Sea to India.

2. *Persian rulers.*[44] Cyrus ruled as supreme monarch for nine years following this Babylonian victory.[45] He appears to have been as skillful in rule as in conquest, knowing when to be firm and when to be charitable, so that friend and foe alike admired him. Finally, in 530 B.C., while leading his army into the far North, he was fatally wounded. His body was returned to the Persian capital, Pasargadae, for burial.

a. Cambyses (530–522). Cyrus was succeeded by his son, Cambyses II, who had acted as deputy to his father in Babylon. Cambyses did away with his brother Smerdis (Bardiya), whom he considered a rival, in establishing himself on the throne. Cambyses' great claim to fame was his conquest of Egypt, which he added to his already huge territory in 525 B.C. He first met the Egyptian army at

[42] J. Whitcomb finds reason for distinguishing between the Ugbaru who, in Nabonidus' inscription, took Babylon for Cyrus and the Gubaru whom Cyrus appointed governor of Babylon sometime later. Many scholars equate the two under the general name, Gobryas. But, in this same inscription of Nabonidus, Ugbaru is said to have died on the eleventh day of the month, Arahshammu, which was only a matter of days after the fall of Babylon, whereas Gubaru is mentioned in numerous other texts as ruling as governor in Babylon for several years. Whitcomb identifies this Gubaru (Gobryas) with Darius the Mede, mentioned several times in the Book of Daniel (5:31; 6:1, 2, 3, 6, 7, etc.). Cf. Whitcomb, *Darius the Mede* (Grand Rapids: Wm. B. Eerdmans Pub. Co., 1959). Another view, suggested by D. J. Wiseman, states that Darius may have been Cyrus himself; cf. Wiseman, "The Last Days of Babylon," *Christianity Today*, 2 (Nov., 1957), pp. 7-10.

[43] Neither Cyrus nor Nabonidus mention Belshazzar in their reports to help us know how to fit the story of Daniel 5 into this conquest. Belshazzar's death may have come when Gobryas first entered Babylon in October, 539 B.C., or it may have come somewhat later when the sacred citadel fell.

[44] For details, cf. A. T. Olmstead, *op. cit.*, or R. Ghirshman, *op. cit.*

[45] Whitcomb argues that Gubaru (Gobryas) ruled the province of Babylon all during Cyrus' nine years and even during the first five years of Cambyses; Whitcomb, *op. cit.*, pp. 15-16, 23-24.

Pelusium[46] and won a clear victory. He was significantly aided by the defection of the commander of Greek mercenaries, whom Pharaoh Amasis had hired. At this time Amasis died and was succeeded by his son, Psammetichus III. But the new ruler had little more success against the Persians, and they now moved on into the rich Delta region. Soon Cambyses held control of the entire country,[47] organizing it as a satrapy[48] of the empire. He was not successful, however, in his attempt to extend his control further, either westward toward Carthage or southward to Nubia and Ethiopia. When enroute home in 522 B.C., encamped near Mount Carmel in Palestine, Cambyses received news that one Gaumata had seized the Persian throne, masquerading as Smerdis, the brother whom Cambyses had secretly assassinated.[49] For some reason, which is not clear, Cambyses at this point committed suicide.

b. Darius Hystaspes (522–486). One of Cambyses' officers, Darius I, son of the satrap, Hystaspes, and a collateral descendant with Cyrus from the royal line of Persia, now assumed command of the army and marched home to put down the insurrection and seize the throne. He was successful in both, putting the pretender to death. He found the empire generally in foment, however, with some areas in open rebellion. He showed himself equal to this challenge also and, within two years, had matters well in hand. He considered the overall triumph sufficiently important to have a record made of it for future generations high on a mountain cliff beside the road to Ecbatana. This inscription, which has come to be called the Behistun Inscription, was written in three languages, and has proven invaluable in modern times for providing the key to reading old Akkadian.[50]

[46] Located near the Mediterranean, twenty miles east of modern Port Said, at the mouth of the most easterly (Pelusiac) branch of the Nile, long since filled with silt.

[47] Cambyses followed the same policy as his father in respecting native religious customs and institutions. He lacked his father's consideration for people and buildings, however, working cruelty and senseless destruction. The Elephantine papyri indicate that the Jewish temple on the island of Elephantine was left intact but that the temples of the Egyptian gods were pulled down; cf. *ANET*, p. 492; and *DOTT*, pp. 262-63 for Elephantine texts.

[48] Persia divided her many provinces into twenty larger divisions called satrapies, the viceroys of which were called satraps.

[49] Olmstead, however, argues that Smerdis had not been killed prior to this time and that this person really was Smerdis, Cambyses' brother; cf. Olmstead, *op. cit.*, pp. 107-16.

[50] Written in Persian, Elamite, and Akkadian, this inscription can be seen on a mountain side some 350 feet above the main road between old Babylon and Ecbatana. Primarily through efforts of H. C. Rawlinson, who in 1835 scaled the cliff and made copies and squeezes, this inscription was made to yield the secret for reading the cuneiform characters. More recently, detailed study of the in-

Darius went on to become one of Persia's most capable rulers. He demonstrated skill in reorganizing the empire. Cyrus had added conquered kingdoms without changing established boundaries; but Darius, now, having just suffered effects of serious revolt, changed boundaries by dividing all into newly designed satrapies. Judges with fixed circuits were appointed, and an intricate postal system for effective communication was established. Darius made good use of his early experiences in war, too, by directing his armies to repeated successes. He suffered a humiliating defeat at the hands of the Greeks, however, in the famous battle of Marathon, 490 B.C. He planned revenge, but a revolt in Egypt demanded his attention for a time, and his own death came in 486 B.C. before being able to effect the retaliation.

c. Xerxes I (486–465). Xerxes I succeeded his father. His first two years were occupied in quelling further revolutions, especially in Babylon which he finally incorporated with Assyria.[51] Then in his third year he planned his greatest military campaign, which he hoped would avenge his father's defeat by the Greeks. His plans were thorough, and the number of troops assembled was enormous. At first he was victorious, even capturing Athens and burning the Acropolis. But then his fine fleet of ships was routed at Salamis, and his army, left in charge of his general, Mardonius, was cut to pieces at Plataea the following year (479 B.C.). Xerxes, who had returned to his capital following the defeat at Salamis, now entered into a vigorous building program.

d. Artaxerxes Longimanus (465–425). The last Persian ruler of note is Artaxerxes Longimanus. He succeeded to the throne at his father's assassination, a deed perpetrated by one Artabanus, head of the palace guard. Artaxerxes' first task was to dispose of all rival aspirants to the throne. Then, in 460 B.C., he faced serious revolution in Egypt, which was put down only after several years of fighting by his satrap of Abarnahara[52] (Syria and Palestine), Megabyzus. Difficulty with the Greeks resulted in further humiliation for the Persian monarch, as he signed a treaty (449 B.C.) permitting Greek cities in Asia Minor to be free to join in league with Athens. Neither Artaxerxes

scription has been made by George C. Cameron. Cf. Cameron, *JNES*, 2 (1943), pp. 115f; also Cameron, *National Geographic Magazine*, 98 (1950), pp. 825-44.

[51] Cf. Olmstead, *op. cit.*, pp. 236-37. For Xerxes' own list of countries ruled and those where a condition of revolution existed at his accession, cf. *ANET*, pp. 316-17.

[52] This is the Aramaic form of the Persian '*Ebirnari*'. It means "beyond the river." It was the district created by Darius in his reorganization which, according to Herodotus (*Historiae*, III, pp. 89-97), included "All Phoenicia, Palestine, Syria and Cyprus." Cf. M. Avi-Yonah, *The Holy Land* (Grand Rapids: Baker Book House, 1966), pp. 11-12.

nor Xerxes attained the stature of their predecessor, Darius. The rulers succeeding them were still less talented, and, at the coming of Alexander, the empire was taken by the Greeks.

E. THE FIRST RETURN TO JUDAH (Ezra 1–6)

During these years of Persian history, significant events transpired for the Jews.[53] Principal among these were three separate returns from captivity. The first came shortly after the Persian conquest of Babylon (538 B.C.; Ezra 1:1), led by Sheshbazzar. The second came eighty years later, in the seventh year of Artaxerxes Longimanus (458 B.C.; Ezra 7:7), led by Ezra. And the third came thirteen years after the second, in the twentieth year of Artaxerxes Longimanus (444 B.C.; Neh. 2:1), led by Nehemiah.

1. *Edict of Cyrus (II Chronicles 36:22-23; Ezra 1:1-4; 6:3-5)*. The considerate attitude of Cyrus toward his subjects included permission for people, who had been taken captive to Babylon, to return to their homelands.[54] It is surprising that Cyrus extended this permission to a people from as small a country as Judah, and this already in his first year;[55] but, as suggested earlier, this may have been due to the influence of Daniel.[56]

Cyrus' edict in reference to the Jews is recorded twice in Scripture: Ezra 1:2-4 and 6:3-5.[57] The accounts are not identical, which suggests that the original edict was longer than either and contained the items which both together possess. In summary, they give orders that the Jerusalem Temple be rebuilt, with the cost defrayed from Cyrus' own treasury; that certain specifications be met in this rebuilding; that all Jews who wished could return to their homeland, with those Jews who remained in Babylon being urged to assist with financial contribution; and that the gold and silver vessels taken by Nebuchadnezzar be returned to Jerusalem. The degree of favor for the Jews shown in this edict is remarkable,[58] and causes one to wonder if it may not have been originally penned by Daniel himself.

[53] From this point in time it is common to speak of "Jewish" history. Most of those who returned from captivity were of the tribe of Judah, which gave rise to the name.

[54] Cyrus himself states this policy on his famous cylinder; cf. *ANET*, p. 316; *DOTT*, p. 93.

[55] Cf. Noth, *NHI*, pp. 307-08; Bright, *BHI*, pp. 343-44.

[56] Cf. *supra*, p. 384.

[57] The first is written in Hebrew and has the form of a royal proclamation. The second is in Aramaic and has the form of a *dikrona*, which is a memorandum of an oral royal decision. Cf. Bright, *BHI*, pp. 342-43; E. J. Bickerman, "The Edict of Cyrus in Ezra I," *JBL*, 65 (1946), pp. 244-75; and R. A. Bowman, *Interpreter's Bible*, III (1954), pp. 570-73, 613-16.

[58] That Cyrus speaks highly of "Yahweh, God of heaven" (Ezra 1:2) is not

2. *The return (Ezra 1:5–2:70).* Presumably the return occurred soon after the issuance of the decree, likely in 538 or 537 B.C. It was led by Sheshbazzar, called a "prince of Judah" (Ezra 1:8).[59] Those who made the journey are listed in Ezra 2, with their number indicated as 42,360, besides 7,337 servants (Ezra 2:64-65). This is a substantial number, but it did not include all the Jews who lived in the East. In fact, it probably did not include a majority; for, just over a half century later, in the time of Esther,[60] enough Jews yet lived there to kill as many as 75,000 of their enemy neighbors in two days of fighting (Esther 9:16). As has been noted, Jews had been living in the East under surprisingly pleasant conditions, with many having established themselves in lucrative businesses. They did not find it easy now to leave; and a large number did not. Those who did choose to return made the trip, apparently, without serious incident.

3. *Building the Temple (Ezra 3–6).* A prime order of business on arriving in the homeland was the rebuilding of the Temple. That it be constructed soon was imperative for restoration of the Mosaic ceremonies in worship to God, and also as a witness to neighboring peoples of Jewish devotion to Yahweh.

a. A good beginning. Construction on the Temple did begin soon after arrival in the land. Ezra 3:8 states that the people were led in this by Zerubbabel and Joshua (Jeshua), the high priest,[61] though apparently Sheshbazzar was in general charge (Ezra 5:16). They first erected the altar and reinstated the prescribed sacrifices, in the seventh month of the first year of their return. Shortly after, in the middle of the same month, the people observed the Feast of Tabernacles, since

so surprising in itself, however, for he speaks similarly of Marduk; cf. *ANET*, pp. 315-16. To speak this way of foreign deities was in keeping with his conciliatory policy.

[59] Sheshbazzar may be the same as Zerubbabel. Both are called "governor" of Judah (Ezra 5:14; Hag. 1:1), and both led in building the Temple (Ezra 5:16; 5:2). However, since both names are Babylonian (Zer-Babel and Shin-ab-usur), there is little reason for them differing unless they refer to different men. Cf. Albright, "Recent Discoveries in Bible Lands," in *Young's Concordance*, p. 36. Apparently, Sheshbazzar was succeeded by Zerubbabel, who likely was in the group who came under Sheshbazzar and may already have then been active. If Sheshbazzar is the same as Shenazar (I Chron. 3:18), which is likely since both make good abbreviated forms of the Babylonian Sinabusur ("May Sin protect the father"), then Zerubbabel was his nephew; cf. Wright, *BAR*, pp. 203-05; Albright, *JBL*, 40 (1921), pp. 108-10. Both were descendants of Jehoiachin (I Chron. 3:16-19; Matt. 1:11-13).

[60] Esther married the Persian ruler, Xerxes I (Greek name for the Persian, *Khshayarsha*, an equivalent to the Hebrew, Ahasuerus, Esth. 1:1), who reigned 486-465.

[61] Joshua was son of Jehozadak (Josadak), who was among those taken into captivity, a descendant of Eleazar through Zadok (I Chron. 6:15).

its prescribed time was then at hand. Later, in the second month of the second year, they began work on the Temple proper.

The first step was laying the foundation, which seems to have been accomplished rather quickly. When it was completed, the people celebrated. Many rejoiced, but others, who could remember the glory of the former Solomonic Temple, openly wept (Ezra 3:8-12). They could see that the new Temple would be more modest than the former. At this point, trouble began. Opposition was experienced from Samaritans to the north (Ezra 4:1-5).[62] The Samaritans seem to have thought that the territory of Judah was theirs to control, though this was not legitimate on their part.[63] Besides, the Jewish workers on the Temple began to use more of their time for rebuilding their own houses and farming their own lands (Hag. 1:3-11).[64] It was not long before all work ceased, with the result that the Temple remained little more than a foundation until the second year of Darius (520 B.C.; Hag. 1:1), a period of about sixteen years.

b. Construction resumed. In Darius' second year, the prophets Haggai and Zechariah urged that building operations be resumed. They addressed the people generally, and specifically Zerubbabel and Joshua, who were still in command, Zerubbabel now having held Sheshbazzar's former position for some time. Their prophetic efforts were fruitful and work did begin the sixth month of this year (Hag. 1:15; Ezra 5: 1-2). Again opposition arose, this time more official. It came from the satrap of Abarnahara himself, Tattenai by name, but it does not seem to have been as serious. He first asked the Jews regarding their authority to do this building and then wrote directly to Darius for his confirmation. When he received reply that the Jews did have official Persian approval, he ceased opposition and even lent assistance, according to Darius' order (Ezra 5:3–6:14). Four years later, in the sixth year of Darius (March, 515 B.C.; Ezra 6:15), the Temple was completed.

F. THE SECOND RETURN (Ezra 7–10)

Fifty-eight years elapsed between the completion of the Temple and the second return of Jews to Judah. Only a few clues exist concerning the history of those years.

---

[62] These Samaritans first asked to assist and were properly refused (their worship of God being mixed with foreign deity worship, II Kings 17:29-41) by Zerubbabel, and then they openly opposed.

[63] Cf. Discussion, M. Avi-Yonah, *op. cit.*, p. 13.

[64] Likely these workers were composed almost entirely of those who had returned from captivity. Jews who had continued to live in Judah during the captivity may not have been very cooperative, for now they would have to share their housing and lands, which may have led to some friction. Strife of this kind could have contributed also to the failure in Temple building.

1. *Intervening years.* Darius ruled Persia until 486 B.C., followed by Xerxes I until 465 B.C. It was during the rule of Xerxes that the story of Esther transpired, which shall be noticed presently. Then came Artaxerxes Longimanus, during whose seventh year the second return occurred. It was led by Ezra, a descendant of Aaron, skilled in teaching the Law (Ezra 7:6, 10).[65] Ezra was known to Artaxerxes, for this Judean had attained a position of some standing at the court. He may have held an office like Minister of Jewish Affairs. In some undisclosed manner he persuaded the king to permit him to travel to Judah for the purpose of effecting needed reforms.

Three matters give indication as to life in Judah during these intervening years. From Haggai's indictment of the people for failing to complete the Temple earlier (Hag. 1:3-11), we know that they were rebuilding comfortable houses and farming their land. Indeed, they had become so occupied that they had failed in their prime task of completing God's Temple. From the fact that Nehemiah found it necessary much later (444 B.C.) to come and build Jerusalem's walls, it is clear that little was done in reconstructing the capital city apart from erecting private homes. From Ezra's confession of the people's sin in intermarriage with surrounding pagans (Ezra 9:1-15), we know of interaction with neighboring peoples, which no doubt led to wrong religious practices as well as to the improper marriages.

Politically, Judah was a part of the large Persian satrapy of Abarnahara, which included land southwest of the Euphrates to the border of Egypt, principally Syria and Palestine. In this larger unit, Judah constituted one province over which normally a governor (*tirshatha,* meaning "He who is to be feared"; Ezra 2:63; Neh. 8:9; 10:1) ruled.[66] It may be that at times Judah did not have its own governor and was ruled directly by the district satrap. In any event, the satrap had authority to intervene at any time, as Tattenai did in connection with the renewal of Temple construction in 520 B.C.

2. *The royal letter (Ezra 7:11-26).* Like Sheshbazzar eighty years before, Ezra too received notable privileges from the Persian monarch in connection with his return. These privileges included authority to take as many of his countrymen with him as desired the opportunity; to receive from Jews in Persia, as well as from Artaxerxes himself and

---

[65] Some scholars hold to a date for Ezra as the seventh year of Artaxerxes II (398 B.C.), and others to the thirty-seventh year of Artaxerxes I (428 B.C.). Both must be rejected; but for discussion, cf. Rowley, "The Chronological Order of Ezra and Nehemiah," in *The Servant of the Lord and Other Essays on the Old Testament* (London: Lutterworth Press, 1952, pp. 131-59; Bright, *BHI,* pp. 375-86; or J. S. Wright, *The Date of Ezra's Coming to Jerusalem* (2d. ed.; London: Tyndale Press, 1958).

[66] Cf. M. Avi-Yonah, *op. cit.,* p. 12.

his court counsellors, gold and silver for the Jerusalem Temple; to draw upon the royal treasury of the satrapy of Abarnahara for needs that might arise; to purchase animals for sacrifice at the Temple; to exempt Temple personnel from Persian taxation; and to appoint civil magistrates in the land of Judah to enforce the laws of Yahweh, with power of life and death over the guilty. Ezra's interest and assigned task was thus not to build the country materially, as it had been with the first return and would be again with the third, but to build the people socially and spiritually. Reform was needed that the people might live more pleasingly in the sight of God.

3. Return and work (Ezra 7:27–10:44)

a. The journey (Ezra 8). Ezra assembled those who wished to return at the river Ahava (unknown, but probably near Babylon). The size of the group is indicated by the number of men, approximately 1,500, a number much smaller than that of the first return. When no Levites were found in the group, Ezra delayed while 38 Levites were persuaded to join, and they were accompanied by 220 Nethinim[67] as helpers. Final departure occurred the twelfth day of the first month (458 B.C.) and arrival in Jerusalem the first day of the fifth month (Ezra 7:9; 8:31), a journey of just over three and one-half months.

b. Problem of intermarriage (Ezra 9). The main area of reform which confronted Ezra was the intermarriage of a number of Jews with surrounding peoples. Jewish people had permitted their sons to marry heathen daughters of neighboring nations, and even the priests, Levites, and civil leaders were involved. Ezra was told of this defection from the Law soon after his arrival and reacted with remorse. He rent his clothing, pulled hair from his head, and sat confounded until the evening. Then he offered a prayer of confession. When he finished, those standing by were deeply moved and expressed their conviction that the marriages should be dissolved. Ezra agreed and solicited approval from certain of the more sympathetic religious and civil authorities as well. Details were worked out as to how this difficult and grievous task might be carried out.

c. Dissolving the marriages (Ezra 10). Decision was made that

---

[67] The term "Nethinim" ("given ones") is used outside of Ezra and Nehemiah only in I Chron. 9:2. With Sheshbazzar, 392 persons so named returned to Jerusalem (Ezra 2:58), and with Ezra, 220 (Ezra 8:20). They probably were descendants of foreign prisoners, such as the Gibeonites (Josh. 9:27), who had such duties as drawing water and carrying wood for the Levites in Temple service. David had assigned Nethinim to serve in this way (Ezra 8:20); the names ascribed to Nethinim in Ezra 2:43-58 are foreign in type; and both I Esdras 5:29 and Josephus (Antiq. XI, 5, 1) call them "temple slaves."

each case be judged separately. To insure justice, it was determined that judgments should be passed by elders and appointed judges from the villages of the respective parties. They would know the situations better than someone unacquainted. Judging began as soon as arrangements could be made and was completed within three months (Ezra 10:16-17). Without question, such large scale separation of marriage partners worked hardship and heartbreak in many cases, but the issues were serious. From the time of Moses, God's Law had demanded that separation from foreign peoples be maintained, lest Israelites be influenced away from God to a worship of pagan deities. If intermarriage had occurred already, and to this extent, so soon after the return from captivity, the situation could soon lead to serious consequences. Ezra recognized the hard fact and took the unpleasant but appropriate action. It may be, indeed, that news of the condition had reached him even in Babylon and had particularly prompted him to make the journey to Jerusalem in the first place.

G. The Third Return (Nehemiah 1–13)

The third return, that of Nehemiah, came in the twentieth year of Artaxerxes (444 B.C.; Neh. 1:1). No indication is given regarding the number of Jews who went along in this return, but likely there were some to warrant the Persian king providing "captains of the army and horsemen" (Neh. 2:9) to act as guards. Nehemiah himself, of course, was the principal person. Nehemiah's purpose lay in the rebuilding of Jerusalem's walls. Strange to say, the walls of the city had not been restored though the people had been back in the land nearly a century.

1. *A thwarted attempt at wall building (Ezra 4:6-23).* One abortive attempt at wall building likely had been made, however; though only a few years before Nehemiah's return. Knowledge of this comes from a letter written to Artaxerxes by the Samaritans,[68] recorded in Ezra 4:6-23. The letter urges the Persian king to require that the Jews, who were already building "walls" and "foundations" in Jerusalem, be stopped. Artaxerxes responded by an order to this effect, and the work did cease.

The date during Artaxerxes' reign,[69] to which this instance is best

[68] Quite likely Judah did not have her own governor at this time (cf. *infra*, note 72), and so the Samaritans felt free to interfere in this manner.

[69] Ezra 4:6-23 was placed where it is by Ezra for some reason other than chronological, such a reason as the grouping of similar subject matter. Chronologically, the passage is out of place because: (1) the two kings named in it, Ahasuerus (Xerxes, 486-465) and Artaxerxes (465-425), ruled much later than the time of Temple building described elsewhere in the chapter; (2) the type of building activity set forth in the letter concerns "walls" and "foundations" of

assigned, falls during the thirteen-year interval between the returns of Ezra and Nehemiah (458-445).[70] It is not likely that it came in the short seven-year span preceding Ezra's return, for then one would expect him to have mentioned it in its proper historical context in his book.[71] If it came, however, following Ezra's return, and shortly before that of Nehemiah, it could have had a part in motivating Hanani to journey to Persia to seek the help of his brother, Nehemiah, for this rebuilding, as set forth in Nehemiah 1:1-4. In turn, it may have augmented Nehemiah's own desire to heed Hanani's request. Someone directly from the capital, armed with authority,[72] apparently was needed to counteract Samaritan opposition, if Judah's capital was to have her walls rebuilt.[73]

2. *Nehemiah (Nehemiah 1:1–2:10).* Nehemiah held a responsible position at the Persian court, as cupbearer to King Artaxerxes. In this he was more than merely a domestic servant, as is shown by his access to the king to speak intimately regarding a return to Jerusalem, by the king's considering him able enough to act as Judah's governor when he went there, and by the king's requesting Nehemiah to return to his present position when the new task had been completed (Neh. 2:4-6). Furthermore, Nehemiah was granted unusual privilege, like Sheshbazzar and Ezra before him, in connection with the return.

the city, not the Temple; and (3) the Persian king was unable to find Cyrus' original edict when this letter was received, but he did when a letter sent in 520 B.C. (Ezra 5:7–6:5) came, which makes better historical sense if this letter of Ezra 4 came after that of 520 B.C., rather than before.

[70] For discussion, cf. H. H. Rowley, "Nehemiah's Mission and Its Background," *BJRL*, 73 (Mar., 1955), pp. 528-61. Rowley dates this opposition just prior to Nehemiah's return of 445 B.C. He places Ezra's return, however, after that of Nehemiah.

[71] Ezra returned in Artaxerxes' eighth year. That Ezra did not mention it in a historical context coming after his return is understandable, for he did not treat history after 458 B.C. He completed his book with the account of marriage separations, which were concluded within eight months (cf. Ezra 7:9; 10:17) of his first arrival. This means that, if Ezra was to include this letter at all, it had to be placed out of historical context. Ezra's mention of "wall" in Ezra 9:9 can hardly be taken as a reference to the abortive instance of wall-building.

[72] In that no prior governor was displaced by Nehemiah on arrival in Judah, it is probable that none immediately preceded him. Ezra, though still living and active, did not serve as governor.

[73] This means, of course, that Artaxerxes must have changed his mind between replying to the Samaritan letter and giving Nehemiah permission to go. Conditions of unrest in the West, known both from secular history (cf. note 74) and from Ezra 4:6-23, could have prompted this change. A governor in Judah of Nehemiah's stature, loyal to the throne, could be a significant stabilizing force; and to have him rebuild the walls of his city could add to the prestige he would need.

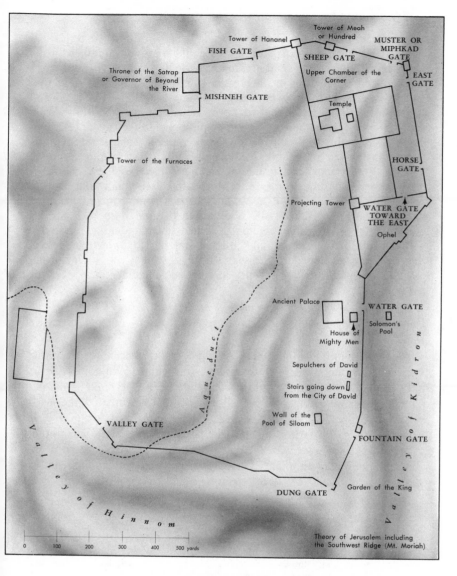

Map 18. Jerusalem in Nehemiah's Time

It was in the month Chisleu (December), 445 B.C., that Hanani came to his brother, Nehemiah, at Susa, the Persian capital, with his sad report concerning matters in Jerusalem. Nehemiah was grief-stricken and spent days in intercession for his people. Not until four months had passed, however, did he ask the king if he might go and render assistance. He seems to have waited for an opportune time, desiring every advantage when the request would be given. Perhaps he was remembering Artaxerxes' earlier refusal, voiced through the Samaritans, as to rebuilding Jerusalem's walls. But in the spring of 444 B.C., the opportunity came. The king noticed sadness on Nehemiah's part one day and asked the reason. Nehemiah told him of Jerusalem's plight, asked if he might journey there to help, and even requested letters to officials in Abarnahara to grant him safe passage and material aid for the rebuilding. The Persian monarch responded with an affirmative answer and granted him all for which he asked, thus cheering and encouraging his faithful servant's heart. He further assigned army officers and cavalry to convey Nehemiah safely over the many miles of travel.[74]

3. *Nehemiah builds the wall (Nehemiah 2:11–6:19).* On arrival, Nehemiah set himself quickly to the task of rebuilding Jerusalem's walls.

a. Preparation. Within three days he made a secret,[75] nocturnal inspection of the walls[76] to determine their exact condition. Apparently he wanted firsthand knowledge, that he might make the most effective plan of action. With facts assembled, he gathered the Jerusalem leaders and presented his ideas. Whatever opposition may have existed among the group, due to the previously thwarted attempt or to possible disinterest, was overcome by the force of Nehemiah's enthusiasm and care in plan. Good response was forthcoming and a positive decision made. Workers were quickly recruited, both from

[74] Though matters were now better in Abarnahara than they had been (cf. *supra*, pp. 391-92), still unrest continued. From the first of his rule, Artaxerxes had been bothered by Grecian attacks on Cyprus, and in 460 B.C., had encountered a serious rebellion in Egypt supported by Greece. This rebellion had continued until 454 B.C., when Megabyzus, satrap of Abarnahara, had finally brought it to an end. But five years later, Megabyzus himself had rebelled, and Artaxerxes had only recently achieved control once again. These matters no doubt influenced the king to provide this military guard for Nehemiah and his group.

[75] No doubt in order to keep any word of his intentions from leaking to the opposition. Apparently Nehemiah anticipated that trouble would come, probably in view of that experienced earlier.

[76] For description of topography encountered, cf. J. Simons, *Jerusalem in the Old Testament* (Leiden: E. J. Brill, 1952), pp. 432f.

Jerusalem and outlying cities; and all were assigned particular sections of the wall on which to labor.

b. Opposition. The work moved forward with surprising rapidity, but only under severe opposition from the outside. Nehemiah held full authority from the king for the task, in contrast to the aborted earlier attempt; but enemies still did their best to hinder. Apparently neighboring provinces, especially Samaria, had benefited from Judah's weakness and did not wish to lose this advantage. Heading the opposition was the governor of Samaria, Sanballat the Horonite (of Beth-horon; Neh. 2:10).[77] His daughter later married into the family of Eliashib, high priest in Jerusalem (Neh. 13:28). He was helped by Tobiah, called "the Ammonite servant" (Neh. 2:10), who may have been governor of Ammon.[78] A third opponent was Geshem (Gashmu) the Arabian (Neh. 2:19; 6:6), often identified with a powerful chieftain of Kedar in northeastern Arabia.[79] With so much opposition, many men would have lost heart, but not Nehemiah.

At first these adversaries were content merely to mock (Neh. 2:19-20; 4:1-3). Then plans were laid to attack Jerusalem, with Arabians and Ashdodites, in addition to Ammonites, to take part (Neh. 4:7-8). News of this intention terrorized the Jews, but Nehemiah responded by dividing the builders into two groups, one to continue building and the other to bear arms. In this way the work progressed, though more slowly. A schedule was kept from dawn until dark to achieve as much speed as possible. During the night, a heavy guard was posted to protect what had been accomplished. All this was effective and resulted in the main attack being called off, though smaller raids were conducted on outlying districts. Josephus tells of these, stating that in them many Jews lost their lives (*Antiq.* XI, 5, 8). The opponents tried four times to lure Nehemiah away from Jerusalem and the work, but he saw through their schemes and did not go (Neh. 6:1-4). Then they threatened to bring to the Persian king an accusation of disloyalty on Nehemiah's part (Neh. 6:5-9). Still further they attempted to

[77] He is called governor of Samaria in the Aramaic papyri from Elephantine; *ANET*, p. 492; DOTT, p. 264. Sanballat (Sinuballit) is a Babylonian name, but his two sons were given Jewish names, Delaiah and Shelemiah.

[78] It is likely that he was an ancestor of the Tobiads, who governed Ammon for generations following this time, as indicated by the Zeno papyri (third century) and by palace and tomb remains at 'Araq el-Emir near present Amman, Jordan. An inscription at the family burial site, bearing the name, Tobiah, may come from the very time of this Tobiah. For discussion of the Tobiads, cf. C. C. McCown, *BA*, 20 (1957), pp. 63-76; R. A. Bowman, *Interpreter's Bible*, III, (1954), pp. 676f.

[79] Mentioned in a memorial inscription from ancient Dedan (modern el-'Ula) and an Aramaic dedication on a bowl in the Egyptian delta; cf. F. M. Cross, *BA*, 18 (1955), pp. 46f; I. Rabinowitz, *JNES*, 15 (1956), pp. 2, 5-9.

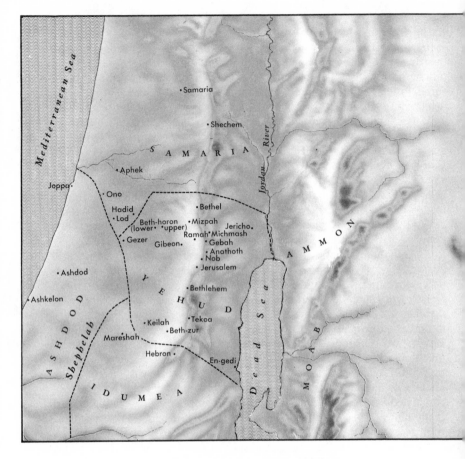

Map 19. Post-exilic Judah

bring reproach on Nehemiah in the sight of his own people through a false prophet Shemaiah (Neh. 6:10-14). But Nehemiah was equal to all the strategy they devised. The work of rebuilding was completed in only fifty-two days,[80] amazing in view of the opposition, and much to the consternation and displeasure of the enemies.

4. *Nehemiah as governor (Nehemiah 7–12).* After completion of the wall, Nehemiah continued as governor of the province, according to Artaxerxes' appointment.

a. Size of Judah. The size of Judah in this post-exilic time was substantially smaller than it had been prior to the captivity. This was the result mainly of a change in the southern boundary, which now seems to have run only at an approximate east and west line just north of Hebron,[81] well north of Beersheba, the former southern limit. The northern boundary apparently was about the same, including such cities as Gibeon (Neh. 3:7) and Mizpah (Neh. 3:15, 19); also the eastern, including at least Jericho (Neh. 3:2); and the western, though of this more question exists.[82] The whole was roughly rectangular in shape, extending north and south about 25 miles and east and west about 32, including approximately 800 square miles. This area seems to have already been divided into districts when Nehemiah arrived, for he used them in assigning people to work on the walls (Neh. 3:2-27).[83]

b. Remission of debts (Neh. 5:1-19). One of Nehemiah's first actions was to remit the debts of poor people. This he did likely during the early time of building the wall, for record of it is included along with the story of that great effort. The province of Judah was in dire economic straits, as a result of high Persian taxes and successive poor crops. In this situation, some of the more wealthy had taken advantage of the poor by bringing them into debt and dispossessing them of property. Nehemiah appealed to the consciences of these people, urging them to stop the practice and restore what they had taken, even exacting an oath before God. Nehemiah himself set a fine ex-

---

[80] Because 52 days is a short time, some scholars (for instance, Albright, *BP*, p. 52, or Bright, *BHI*, p. 365) favor the indication of Josephus (*Antiq.* XI, 5, 8) that the period was really two years and four months. There was, however, great urgency, many workers, and only a portion of the total wall to be rebuilt.

[81] South of Judah the province of Idumaea (Diodorus XIX, 95, 2; 98, 1) had been established. It was inhabited by Edomites and included Hebron to the north and Beersheba to the south, minus the coastal plain. Cf. M. Avi-Yonah, *The Holy Land* (Grand Rapids: Baker Book House, 1966), pp. 25-26.

[82] The question concerns whether a strip reaching into the coastal plain, containing the three cities, Lod, Hadid, and Ono, was included. Since, however, it was near Ono that Sanballat proposed to meet Nehemiah (Neh. 6:2), desiring likely a neutral area, it is not probable that this strip was a part of Judah.

[83] For discussion, cf. M. Noth, *NHI*, pp. 325-26; M. Avi-Yonah, *op. cit.*, pp. 14-22.

ample by refusing the customary gubernatorial remuneration for his services.

c. Security measures (Neh. 7:1-4; 11:1-36). With the wall completed, it was necessary to take security measures. Placed in general charge were Hanani, the brother of Nehemiah, who had made the trip to Susa to request aid, and one Hananiah. Singers and other Levites were recruited to help the gatekeepers in watching the gates and walls. Apparently the population in Jerusalem proper remained small, for Nehemiah now required that one-tenth of the population from other cities, chosen by lot, move to the capital.[84] This action involved an inspection of registrations, and by it Nehemiah came across an old list of those who had returned to Judah under Sheshbazzar. This list is repeated in Nehemiah 7:6-73 almost without variation from that in Ezra 2:1-70.

d. Reading God's Law (Neh. 8-10). Nehemiah, interested in the religious life of the people, encouraged all to assemble for the reading of God's Law. This was in the fall of 444 B.C., shortly after the wall's completion. Ezra, still active thirteen years after his arrival, did the reading.[85] He was joined by other Levites in explaining the meaning, perhaps dividing the people into smaller discussion groups for this purpose. When that part of the Law prescribing the Feast of Tabernacles (Lev. 23:39-43) was read, the people expressed desire to keep it immediately, since it was then the time of year for it. This was done, and in careful detail. All this in turn was followed by a public confession of sin by the people and a further separation from pagan influence.[86] Finally a covenant to keep faithfully all that God required in the Law was signed by both Nehemiah and numerous representatives of the people (Neh. 10:1-39). A fine spirit of renewed commitment to God was demonstrated, which augured well for days to come.

e. Dedication of the walls (Neh. 12:27-47). Formal dedication of the walls was now made. The time was likely still 444 B.C., though at the close of the year. Civil and religious leaders were assembled from all parts of the province. They formed two processions, marching in opposite directions around the walls, meeting together at the

---

[84] The register of names given in Neh. 11:3-36 represents the population as existent in this time of Nehemiah. The register of priests and Levites in Neh. 12:1-26 represents those from the time of Zerubbabel on to this time of Nehemiah.

[85] Since Nehemiah was not a priest, he properly gave room to Ezra who was. Surprisingly, Ezra is not mentioned often by Nehemiah. Apparently he was not greatly involved in the civil matters which occupied Nehemiah's attention.

[86] Perhaps more in other areas than mixed marriages, now that Ezra had dealt with that problem just thirteen years before; though Nehemiah did have to face it again by 430 B.C., cf. *infra*, pp. 405-406.

Temple. The people raised their voices in enthusiastic singing heard at great distance. The dedication proper was followed by a further organization of priests and Levites; this especially regarding the collection and care of the tithes and contributions of the people (Neh. 12:44-47).

5. *Nehemiah's second term (Nehemiah 13)*.   Nehemiah served in Jerusalem during two periods of time. He remained as governor the first time twelve years, from the twentieth to the thirty-second years of Artaxerxes (444-443; Neh. 1:1; 13:6). Then he went back to his former position in the Persian court, no doubt according to the original agreement (Neh. 2:6), but was permitted to return to Jerusalem after an interval probably of only a year or two. The exact time of the interval is not indicated, nor the circumstances of his being permitted to go again to Jerusalem. Probably he simply was unhappy about being away from his people in Judah, and the king allowed him to return to where his interest lay.

a. Reforms.   Upon arriving the second time, Nehemiah was grieved at an increased laxity toward God's Law, which had arisen during his brief absence. Most shocking was the fact that Eliashib, the high priest, had allowed Nehemiah's old enemy, Tobiah the Ammonite, to live actually in a room of the Temple intended for the storage of the tithes of the people. Nehemiah, without hesitation, ordered the room cleared of all Tobiah's effects and restored to its original purpose (Neh. 13:4-9). Then he commanded that the collection of tithes be carried out with greater care, which would have as a side benefit the insurance that all such rooms would be necessarily used (Neh. 13:10-14). Apparently the directives of but twelve years before (Neh. 12:44-47) were already being neglected.

Nehemiah next gave attention to a laxity respecting the Sabbath (Neh. 13:15-22). Not only did Jews themselves desecrate the holy day by working and doing business, but they permitted resident Tyrians to bring in merchandise and conduct trade. Nehemiah closed the city gates and posted guards to enforce his prohibition of all such merchandising.

Nehemiah's reform also concerned mixed marriages again (Neh. 13:23-28). In spite of Ezra's earlier efforts in 458 B.C., and his own in 444 B.C., here in c. 430 B.C. the sin once more existed. Nehemiah found children who could not even speak Hebrew, because Jews had married foreign partners, especially from Ashdod, Ammon, and Moab. Apparently the marriages were not dissolved this time, as in Ezra's reform, but the people were made to swear that no more would be contracted. When Nehemiah found that one of the grandsons of Eliashib, the high priest, had married none other than a daughter of his former enemy, Sanballat, he expelled him from Judah.

b. Duration unknown. How long Nehemiah remained in Judah this time, or whether he ever went back to the Persian capital, is not indicated. He may have remained in Jerusalem until his death, the time of which also is unknown. There is evidence that he was no longer governor of Judah at least in 407 B.C., for an Elephantine papyrus gives the governor's name then as Bagoas.[87]

6. *Malachi, the last Old Testament prophet.* The last of the writing prophets, Malachi, probably ministered during Nehemiah's time. Nehemiah does not refer to him, but certain references made by Malachi show the probability. He implies that the Temple had been in existence for some time (Mal. 1:7-10; 3:8), which means that the date was well after that of Haggai and Zechariah, who only urged rebuilding to continue. He speaks of a governor (Mal. 1:8) as being familiar to the people, which locates his day generally in the Persian period. But, more particularly, he writes of sins of his time, which are identical to those Nehemiah encountered: absence of personal piety, especially among the priests (Mal. 1:6-8); existence of foreign marriages (Mal. 2:10-12); and laxity in paying tithes for Temple support (Mal. 3:7-10).

H. THE STORY OF ESTHER (Esther 1–10)

Many Jews lived outside of Judah during the post-exilic time. The Old Testament supplies information regarding those who continued to live in the East at one important juncture. This was the time when Esther was appointed queen in the Persian court and was providentially instrumental in delivering the Jews from terrible slaughter. The story, recorded in the book of Esther, covers the third to the twelfth years of Xerxes' rule (483-471; Esther 1:3; 3:7).

1. *The story.* The narrative begins in the third year of Ahasuerus (Xerxes).[88] While an extended feast was in progress,[89] Ahasuerus demanded that his queen, Vashti, display her crown and beauty before his festive, drunken guests; and, when she refused, he deposed her in a burst of anger. This, he said, was to provide a proper example, so that all wives would henceforth honor their husbands (Esther 1:1-22).

The situation called for the selection of a new queen, and a contest

---

[87] For text and discussion, cf *DOTT*, pp. 260-65.

[88] Not only is "Ahasuerus" a good Hebrew equivalent for Xerxes' Persian name "Khshayarsha" (cf. *supra*, n. 60), but the history reflected in the book of Esther fits well the history involving Xerxes, and the temperament of Ahasuerus as reflected in Esther suits that of Xerxes in secular history.

[89] Likely the feast when Xerxes planned his famous campaign against the Greeks.

was arranged for doing so. Maidens were brought from all parts of the empire to provide a choice for the king. Among these was a Jewish orphan, Esther,[90] descendant of Kish, who had been among the captives brought years before from Jerusalem. She had been brought up in the home of her cousin, Mordecai,[91] who held an office in the palace at Susa.[92] Beautifying preparations lasted a full year. The contest was finally held, and the king chose Esther as the most attractive. She was made queen in his seventh year.[93]

Shortly after this selection, Haman, the leading member of Ahasuerus' court, conspired to kill all Jews. Mordecai, whose identity he knew, had been refusing to do him the homage he thought was due. Haman persuaded Ahasuerus to sign a decree that on the thirteenth of Adar (twelfth month) all Jews should be executed. He argued that these people were dangerous to the empire and that the king would receive a significant gain in the confiscation of their property. At the time Ahasuerus did not know that Esther was one of their number. Mordecai informed Esther of the decree, and she courageously went to the king, without benefit of normal summons, to request an additional decree that the Jews be permitted to fight back against their executioners. The request was presented at a special banquet at which Haman was present. When the king demanded to know who had plotted against Esther's people, she identified Haman. Ahasuerus was angry at his subordinate and ordered his immediate execution on the very gallows that Haman had prepared for hanging Mordecai. Also he granted Esther's request regarding the further decree. In the fighting that followed between Jews and their would-be executioners, 75,000 of the latter were killed (Esther 9:16).[94]

2. The Significance

a. Number of Jews. This story implies that a surprisingly large

---

[90] Her Hebrew name was Hadassah (Esther 2:7), meaning "myrtle." Esther probably refers to the Babylonian "Ishtar," the name of an important goddess.

[91] Babylonian name based on the name of the deity Marduk.

[92] Susa was located on the Karkheh River in southwest Persia, about 150 miles north of the Persian Gulf. It was the capital of Elam in earlier years. Under the Achaemenids, it served as one of three capitals. Darius I built a fine palace here covering more than two acres. Apparently Esther lived in this palace. French excavators, under the leadership of M. Dieulafoy, worked here between 1880 and 1890. The excellent objects found are housed in the Louvre in Paris. Cf. R. Ghirshman, *Iran from the Earliest Times to the Islamic Conquest* (Baltimore: Penguin Books, 1954).

[93] Intervening time since the third year had been occupied with the Grecian campaign. Cf. *supra*, p. 391. Esther was chosen queen late in 478 B.C.

[94] When the Jews were highly successful on the one day in slaying opponents, Esther requested that a second day be given for the same activity, and the king agreed. The 75,000 were killed over the two days.

number of Jews yet lived in the East, for the slayers must have out-numbered the 75,000 who were slain. These Jews were probably centered in a few particular areas of the empire.[95] The main concentration no doubt was near Babylon, where they had early established themselves in businesses, as noted. It could be expected, too, that after Persia took control, a significant group had moved to important Persian centers, such as Susa where Esther was queen. Pockets of them would still have been found also in cities of old Assyria, where captives had been taken from Israel in 722 B.C. These would have been the chief localities where fighting transpired and the 75,000 died. As for the province of Judah itself, the decrees would have been valid there too; but no indication is given of fighting. Very likely Jews were simply too strong in their home country for any opponents to dare to attempt an execution.

b. Freedom.   Another fact demonstrated is that Jews continued to enjoy freedom to live and work as they pleased.[96] Mordecai was prominent in a court position and later was raised even to Haman's former place of honor. Esther was elevated even to the place of queen. That she could have entered the "beauty contest" as candidate in the first place, and have been chosen by the king without his knowing her nationality, gives signal witness that Jews were not a marked people. They were permitted to live and move about as other people, apparently without discrimination.

c. Jewish enemies.   A third matter of note is that Jews did have enemies, however, as they have had continually since that day. Haman was a leader in this. He knew of the Jews as a distinct people in the empire and identified them collectively as an object of hatred. So strong was his feeling that, when irritated by one of them, he wanted to destroy all. Probably he was not alone in this, so one must believe that Jews of the day were considered by a number of people to be an undesirable social element. Anti-semitism, wrong as it is, is not modern.

d. Providential care.   A fourth significance is that God's special care was being extended toward these Jews of the East, even though they had chosen not to return to the homeland when given opportunity. This care, evidenced particularly in the precise timing of events for the Jews' benefit, is in fact the outstanding feature of the story.[97]

---

[95] The king did send the decree to all 127 provinces (Esther 3:13; 8:9), but this does not necessarily mean that Jews were found in all 127. All decrees likely were sent to every part of the empire.

[96] Tablets found at Nippur mentioned earlier (*supra,* pp. 386-87) actually come from this time. They show clearly that Jews were active in business.

[97] This fact makes the presence and interest of God real in the book, which otherwise does not mention Him by name.

Esther became queen just in time to lead in thwarting Haman's plot. Mordecai's attention was called to a previous plot against the king just in time to give the king reason to honor him at a most opportune moment. The king, experiencing insomnia, had court records read to him, one of which concerned this good and unrewarded deed of Mordecai, the very night before Haman arrived to ask that Mordecai be hanged. This resulted in the king honoring Mordecai, in a manner most humiliating to Haman, just before Haman could make his own request to hang Mordecai. These crucial time sequences led to some remarkable reversals in expected happenings. The honor which the Jew-hating Haman believed was designed for himself came to be given to the Jew Mordecai. The gallows that Haman had made for Mordecai came to be used for himself. The edict that was designed by the Jew-hating Haman for doing away with all Jews became instead the instrument for slaying Jew-haters generally. Only God's special providence could account for such astonishing developments.

e. Feast of Purim. A fifth significance is that this occasion gave rise to the Jewish feast of Purim. The name "Purim" comes from the word "pur," meaning "lot."[98] Haman cast lots for determining the particular day on which the Jewish slaughter should take place (Esther 3:7).[99] Since this event turned to the good of Jews, the feast was instituted and named accordingly. It has long been one of the more popular Jewish observances.

I. THE ELEPHANTINE COLONY

Another area of Jewish occupation outside Judah was that on the island of Elephantine in the Nile River of Egypt. The island is located at the lower end of the first cataract, about 500 miles south of the Mediterranean. Numerous papyri written in Aramaic were found there, most of them in 1903.[100] They date from the fifth century.

---

[98] M. Dieulafoy, who excavated at Susa, discovered a quadrangular prism which has the numbers one, two, five, and six engraved on its sides. This no doubt was the type of die used in this determination. The word "pur" is derived from the Assyrian *puru*, meaning a "pebble" or "small stone."

[99] Further providential influence is seen in the result of the lot casting. It was cast in the first month of Ahasuerus' twelfth year, and the lot selected the twelfth month, giving ample time for the new order permitting the Jews to retaliate.

[100] The early finds were published by A. Cowley, *Aramaic Papyri of the Fifth Century, B.C.* (Oxford: Clarendon Press, 1923); cf. *ANET*, pp. 491-92, and *DOTT*, pp. 256-69 for selections. A later group was published in America; cf. E. G. Kraeling, *The Brooklyn Museum Aramaic Papyri* (New Haven: Yale University Press, 1953). Still another group was published by G. R. Driver, *Aramaic Documents of the Fifth Century, B.C.* (Oxford: Clarendon Press, 1954; abridged and revised, 1957).

As suggested earlier, this group of Jews may have descended from those who took Jeremiah with them when they fled from Judah, years earlier, in fear of Babylon. The colony served as a southern military garrison for the Persians stationed in Egypt. It appears to have ceased existence shortly after the beginning of the fourth century.

The contents of the papyri are varied in character. One gives a copy of the famous Behistun Inscription, placed by Darius II high on a mountain side near Ecbatana, Persia.[101] Another is a marriage document. Still another, dated c. 419 B.C., surprisingly instructs the Elephantine Jews, by the authority of the Persian government, to keep their own Passover Feast, according to the practice of the Temple in Jerusalem.

A matter of major significance is. that these Jews had a temple to Yahweh (*Yahu*). This means that, though far from Jerusalem, they had not forgotten the one true God. The worship of Yahweh was not pure, however; for the names of at least three other deities, who were worshiped by some of the residents, have been found.[102] In 410 B.C., a revolt broke out, led by Egyptian priests of Khnum in cooperation with the Persian commander, and the temple to Yahweh was destroyed. This prompted a letter to be sent by the Elephantine Jews to Johanan, high priest in Jerusalem, asking that help be given to rebuild it; but no answer was forthcoming. Then, in 407 B.C., a further letter was sent to Bogoas, governor at this time of Judah, and one also to Delaiah and Shelemiah, sons of Sanballat governor of Samaria. This led to the matter being brought to the attention of the satrap, Arsames, who apparently gave assistance; for recently published papyri indicate that the temple was rebuilt at least by 402 B.C.[103]

Certain matters of historical significance also call for notice. One is that regular communication existed between this Egyptian group and the Jews in Judah. Another is that this group expected,, and at times received, financial help from the motherland. A third is that correlating information is given regarding certain persons mentioned also in the biblical record. One such person is Sanballat, governor of Samaria, spoken of as father of Delaiah and Shelemaiah,[104] and no doubt the same as the opponent of Nehemiah. Another is Johanan, mentioned as high priest in Jerusalem,[105] said in Nehemiah 12:10-11, 22-23 to be grandson of Eliashib who was high priest in Nehemiah's time (Neh.

[101] *Supra*, p. 390.

[102] For text, cf. *ANET*, p. 491; for discussion, *DOTT*, p. 257.

[103] Cf. E. G. Kraeling, *op. cit.*, p. 63.

[104] Mentioned in line 29 of the letter addressed to Bogoas, governor of Judah, asking help to rebuild the temple; cf. *ANET*, p. 492; *DOTT*, p. 264.

[105] Line 18 of the letter addressed to Bogoas.

3:1). A third is Hananiah, writer of the so-called Passover Papyrus of 419 B.C.[106] who may be the same as the man Nehemiah made superintendent over Jerusalem along with Nehemiah's brother Hanani (Neh. 7:2).[107]

J. THE CLOSE OF OLD TESTAMENT HISTORY

The Old Testament is silent regarding history after the time of Nehemiah. Approximately four centuries are passed over without any biblical notice, until the New Testament era breaks. By Nehemiah's day, seventeen centuries had elapsed since the birth of Abraham. In man's reckoning, this is a long time. It is particularly long when compared with the one century of New Testament history, for which it was preparatory. The fact reminds us that God is above time and man's view is limited. God does not waste time, and each of the seventeen centuries witnessed respective purposes being effected.

---

[106] Line 2 of this papyrus, cf. ANET, p. 491; DOTT, p. 259.

[107] For enlargement of Elephantine significances, cf. Price, Sellers, Carlson, The Monuments and the Old Testament (Philadelphia: The Judson Press, 1958), pp. 320-32.

BASIC FURTHER READING

HISTORY

Albright, W. F. "The Biblical Period," *The Jews, Their History, Culture, and Religion,* pp. 3-65. Edited by L. Finkelstein. New York: Harper & Bros., 1949. Reprinted, The Biblical Colloqium, 1950.
————. "The Old Testament World," *The Interpreter's Bible,* I, pp. 233-71.
————. "The Role of the Canaanites in the History of Civilization," *The Bible and the Ancient Near East,* pp. 328-62. Edited by G. E. Wright. Garden City: Doubleday & Co., 1961.
Breasted, J. H. *A History of Egypt.* 2d ed. New York: Chas. Scribner's Sons, 1912.
Erman, A. *The Literature of the Ancient Egyptians.* Trans. by A. M. Blackman. New York: E. P. Dutton Co., 1927.
Frankfort, Henri. *Ancient Egyptian Religion.* New York: Columbia University Press, 1948.
————. *The Birth of Civilization in the Near East.* Garden City: Doubleday & Co., Anchor Books, 1956.
Gordon, Cyrus. *The Ancient Near East.* 3d. ed. New York: W. W. Norton Co., Inc., 1965. Formerly issued as *The World of the Old Testament.* Garden City: Doubleday & Co., Inc., 1958.
Guillaume, A. *Prophecy and Divination Among the Hebrews and Other Semites.* London: Hodder & Stoughton, 1938.
Gurney, O. R. *The Hittites.* 2d ed. Hammondsworth: Penguin Books, 1954.
Hayes, W. C. *The Scepter of Egypt.* Cambridge: Harvard University Press; Part I, 1953; Part II, 1959.
Hitti, Philip K. *History of Syria, Including Lebanon and Palestine.* New York: Macmillan Co., 1951.
Hooke, S. H. *Babylonian and Assyrian Religion.* London: Hutchinson's University Library, 1953.
Mendenhall, George. *Law and Covenant in Israel and the Ancient Near East.* Pittsburgh: The Biblical Colloqium, 1955.
Moscati, S. *Ancient Semitic Civilizations.* Eng. trans. London: Elek Books, Ltd., 1957.
O'Callaghan, R. T. *Aram Naharaim.* Rome: Pontifical Biblical Institute, 1948.

413

Olmstead, A. T. *History of Assyria.* New York: Chas. Scribner's Sons, 1923.
————. *History of Syria and Palestine.* New York: Chas. Scribner's Sons, 1931.
Oppenheim, A. Leo. *The Interpretation of Dreams in the Ancient Near East.* Philadelphia: Transactions of the American Philosophical Society, 1956.
Steindorff, G. and Seele, K. *When Egypt Ruled the East.* Revised ed. by K. Seele. Chicago: University of Chicago Press, 1957.
Unger, Merrill F. *Israel and the Aramaeans of Damascus.* London: James Clarke & Co., Ltd., 1957.
Van Seters, John. *The Hyksos.* New Haven: Yale University Press, 1966.
Wilson, John. *The Burden of Egypt.* Chicago: University of Chicago Press, 1951.

Archaeology, Geography, Texts

Aharoni, Yohanan. *The Land of the Bible.* Trans. by A. F. Rainey. Philadelphia: The Westminster Press, 1962, 1967.
Albright, W. F. *Archaeology and the Religion of Israel.* 3d ed. Baltimore: Johns Hopkins Press, 1953.
————. *The Archaeology of Palestine.* Revised ed. Hammondsworth: Penguin Books, 1956.
Avi-Yonah, Michael. *The Holy Land.* Grand Rapids: Baker Book House, 1966.
Baly, Denis. *The Geography of the Bible.* London: Lutterworth Press, 1957.
Barton, G. A. *Archaeology and the Bible.* 7th ed. Philadelphia: American Sunday School Union, 1937.
Burrows, M. *What Mean These Stones?* New Haven: American Schools of Oriental Research, 1941.
Childe, Gordon. *New Light on the Most Ancient East.* London: Routledge, Kegan, and Paul, 1952.
DeVaux, Roland. *Ancient Israel, Its Life and Institutions.* Trans by J. McHugh. New York: McGraw Hill Book Co., 1961.
Finegan, Jack. *Light From the Ancient Past.* 2d ed. Princeton: Princeton University Press, 1959.
Garstang, John and Garstang, J. B. E. *The Story of Jericho.* Revised ed. London: Marshall, Morgan & Scott, Ltd., 1948.
Glueck, Nelson. *The Other Side of the Jordan.* New Haven: American Schools of Oriental Research, 1940.
Kenyon, Kathleen. *Digging Up Jericho.* New York: Frederick A. Praeger, 1957.
McCown, C. C. *The Ladder of Progress in Palestine.* New York: Harper & Bros., 1943.
Owen, G. F. *Archaeology and the Bible.* Westwood, N.J.: Fleming H. Revell Co., 1961.
Pfeiffer, C. F. *Baker's Bible Atlas.* Grand Rapids: Baker Book House, 1961.
————. *The Biblical World.* Grand Rapids: Baker Book House, 1966. This is a dictionary of biblical archaeology.
Pritchard, J. B. *The Ancient Near East in Pictures.* Princeton: Princeton University Press, 1954.

―――― (ed). *Ancient Near Eastern Texts Relating to the Old Testament.* Revised ed. Princeton: Princeton University Press, 1955.

Thomas, D. Winton. *Archaeology and Old Testament Study.* Oxford: At the Clarendon Press, 1967.

―――― (ed). *Documents From Old Testament Times.* New York: Harper & Bros., 1958.

Thompson, J. A. *The Bible and Archæology.* Grand Rapids: Wm. B. Eerdmans Publishing Co., 1962.

Unger, Merrill F. *Archaeology and the Old Testament.* Grand Rapids: Zondervan Publishing House, 1954.

Wiseman, D. J. *Illustrations From Biblical Archaeology.* Grand Rapids: Wm. B. Eerdmans Publshing Co., 1958.

Wright, G. E. *Biblical Archaeology.* Philadelphia: The Westminster Press, 1957.

――――. *Shechem.* New York: McGraw-Hill Book Co., 1965.

Wright, G. E. and Filson, F. V. *The Westminster Historical Atlas to the Bible.* Revised ed. Philadelphia: The Westminster Press, 1956.

HISTORY OF ISRAEL

Albright, W. F. *From the Stone Age to Christianity.* 2d ed. Garden City: Doubleday & Co., Anchor Books, 1957. Liberal.

Anderson, G. W. *The History and Religion of Israel.* London: Oxford University Press, 1966. Liberal.

Archer, Gleason. *A Survey of Old Testament Introduction.* Chicago: Moody Press, 1964. Conservative.

Bright, John. *A History of Israel.* Philadelphia: The Westminster Press, 1959. Liberal.

Bruce, F. F. *Israel and the Nations.* London: The Paternoster Press, 1963. Conservative.

Eichrodt, Walther. *Theology of the Old Testament.* Trans. by J. A. Baker. Philadelphia: The Westminster Press, 1961. Liberal.

Eissfeldt, Otto. *The Old Testament, An Introduction.* Trans. by P. R. Ackroyd. New York: Harper & Row, 1965. Liberal.

Free, J. P. *Archaeology and Bible History.* 8th ed. Wheaton: Scripture Press Publications, Inc., 1964. Conservative.

Garstang, John. *Joshua, Judges.* London: Constable & Co., 1931. Liberal.

Harrison, R. K. *A History of Old Testament Times.* London: Marshall, Morgan & Scott, 1957. Conservative.

――――. *Introduction to the Old Testament.* Grand Rapids: Wm. B. Eerdmans Publishing Co., 1969. Conservative.

Hunt, Ignatius. *The World of the Patriarchs.* Englewood Cliffs: Prentice-Hall, Inc., 1967. Liberal.

Kaufmann, Yehezkel. *The Biblical Account of the Conquest of Palestine.* Trans. by M. Dagut. Jerusalem: Hebrew University Press, 1953. Liberal.

Kitchen, K. A. *Ancient Orient and Old Testament.* Chicago: Inter-Varsity Press, 1966. Conservative.

Maly, Eugene. *The World of David and Solomon.* Englewood Cliffs: Prentice-Hall, Inc., 1966. Liberal.

McKenzie, John. *The World of the Judges.* Englewood Cliffs: Prentice-Hall, Inc., 1966. Liberal.

Merrill, Eugene. *An Historical Survey of the Old Testament.* Nunley, N.J.: The Craig Press, 1966. Conservative.

Noth, Martin. *The History of Israel.* 2d ed. London: A. & C. Black, 1958. Liberal.

Payne, J. Barton. *An Outline of Hebrew History.* Grand Rapids: Baker Book House, 1954. Conservative.

————. *The Theology of the Older Testament.* Grand Rapids: Zondervan Publishing House, 1962. Conservative.

Ricciotti, G. *The History of Israel.* 2 vols. 2d ed. Milwaukee: Bruce Publishing Co., 1958. Liberal.

Rowley, H. H. *From Joseph to Joshua.* London: Oxford University Press, 1950. Liberal.

————. *The Faith of Israel.* London: SCM Press, Ltd., 1956. Liberal.

————. *The Servant of the Lord and Other Essays on the Old Testament.* London: Lutterworth Press, 1952. Liberal.

Schultz, Samuel. *The Old Testament Speaks.* New York: Harper & Bros., 1960. Conservative.

Simons, J. *The Geographical and Topographical Texts of the Old Testament.* Leiden: E. J. Brill, 1959. Liberal.

Thiele, E. R. *The Mysterious Numbers of the Hebrew Kings.* Revised ed. Grand Rapids: Wm. B. Eerdmans Publishing Co., 1965. Conservative.

Whitley, Charles. *The Exilic Age.* Philadelphia: The Westminster Press, 1957. Liberal.

Young, Edward J. *An Introduction to the Old Testament.* Grand Rapids: Wm. B. Eerdmans Publishing Co., 1949.

CHRONOLOGICAL CHART

2150 B.C.

2100 B.C.

2050 B.C.

2000 B.C.

2166

ABRAHAM — 175 years

2091 2080

Entered
Canaan

Ishmael
Born

2066 2056?

Mt. Moriah
Sacrifice

2030 2020? 1991

Sarah
Died

Married
Keturah

2026

ISAAC — 180 years

Marries
Rebekah

2006

JACOB — 147 years

UR III (Middle date)

2130

2022

ISIN-LARSA

MIDDLE KINGDOM
1991

Amenemhet I

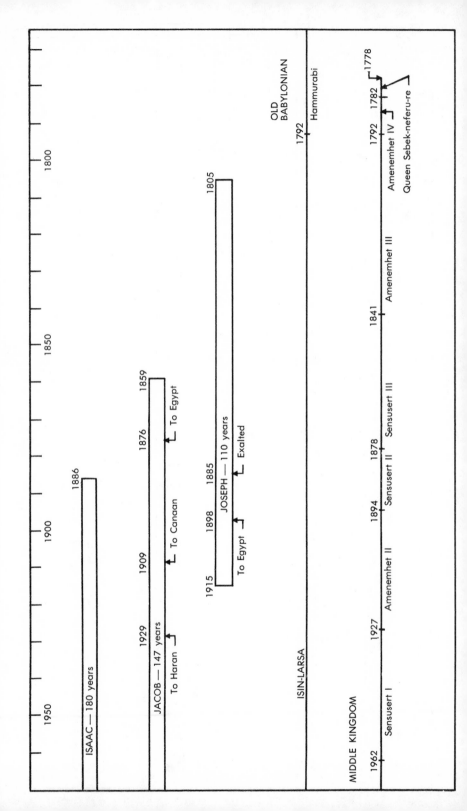

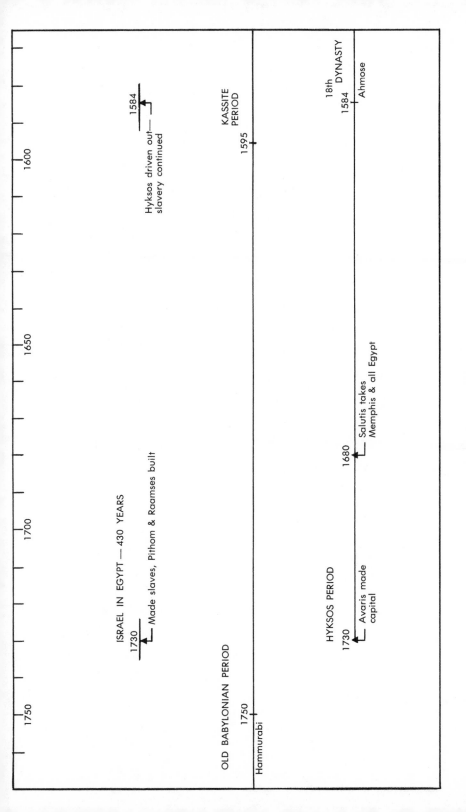

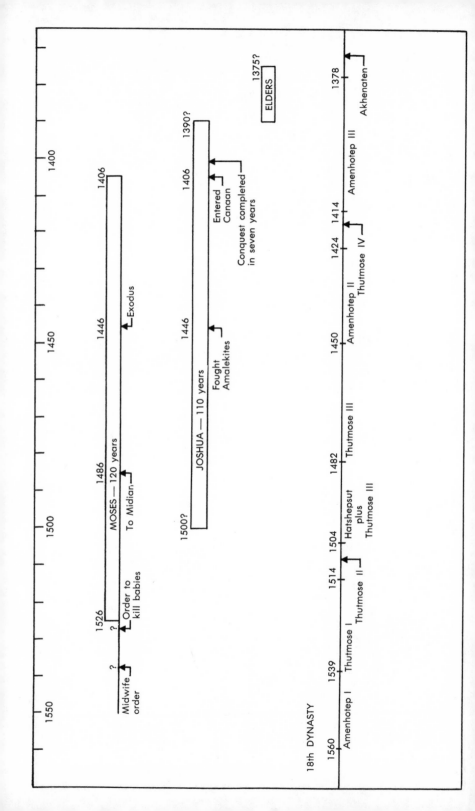

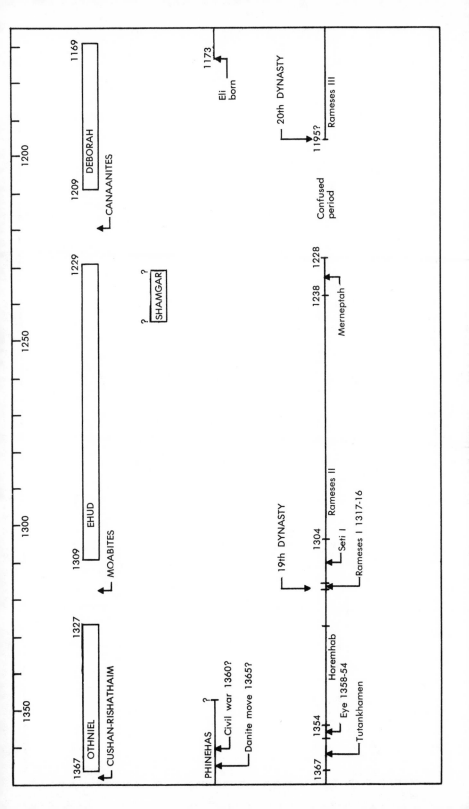

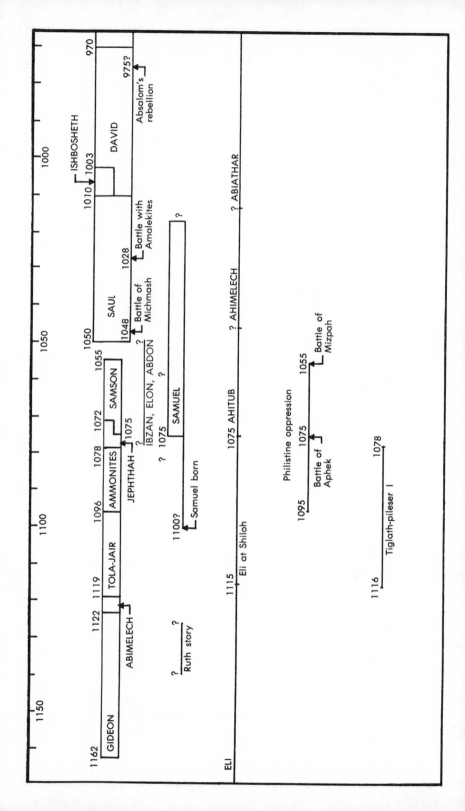

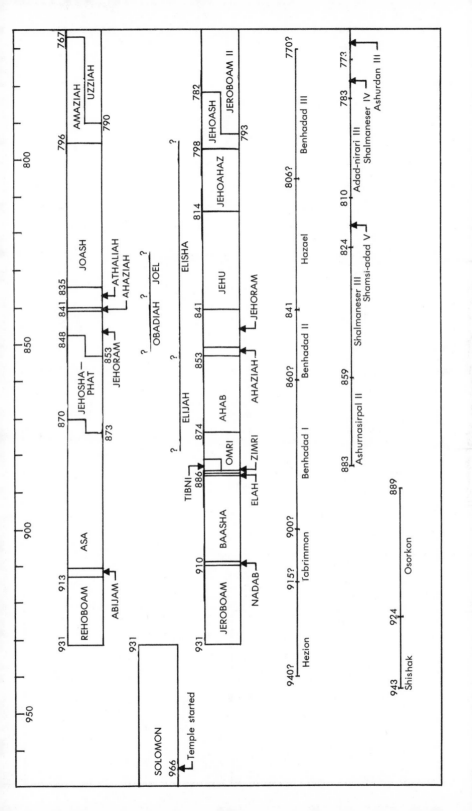

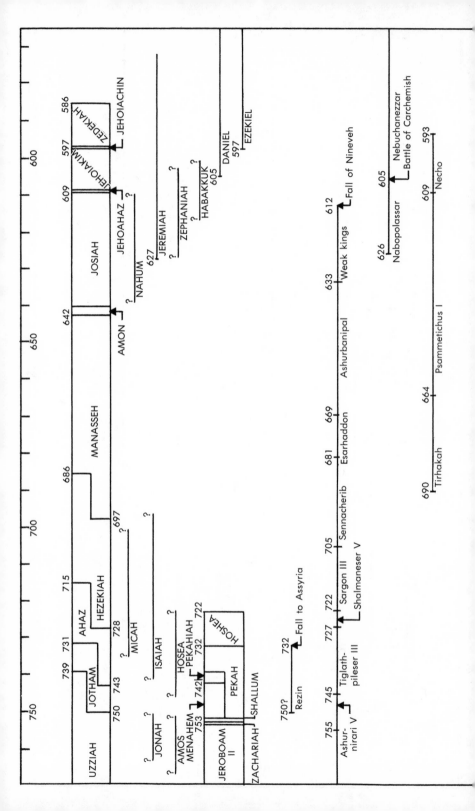

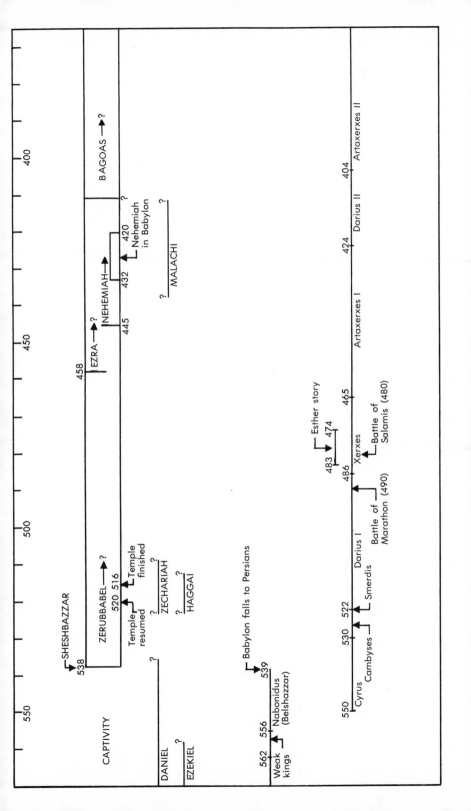

SUBJECT INDEX

Aaron, 117, 122f., 146f., 158
Abar-nahara, 391, 394-396, 400
Abdi-Hiba, 106n.
Abdon, 206, 224
Abed-nego (Azariah), 373, 383n.
Abel, 82n.
Abel-beth-maacah, 284
Abel-meholah, 220
Abiah, 235
Abiathar, 255, 267, 274-275, 288
Abigail, 256, 280
Abihu, 146, 153-154
Abijah, 306n.
Abijam, 340
Abimelech
King of Gerar, 59f., 67
Son of Gideon, 206, 221
Abinadad, 252
Abiram, 160
Abishag, 287
Abishai, 256, 282f.
Abner, 243, 256, 261f.
Abraham (Abram), 27, 30-33, 38-39, 41-46, 47f., 84f.
Abrahamic Covenant, 57
Absalom, 269, 279-283
Acco, 106, 211
Achan, 175, 197n.
Achish, 255, 257-258
Achshaph, 184
Achsib, 211
Acropolis, 391
Adad-nirari III, 309n., 324, 326
Adam (city), 171
Adam (first man), 18
Adonijah, 279, 284f., 286-287
Adoniram (Adoram), 274, 278, 303
Adoni-zedec, 106n.
Adriel, 277n.
Adullam, 255, 265

Aegean Sea, 388
Agag, 245-246
Agade, 40
Ahab, 310-314
Aharoni, 21, 162n.
Ahava (river), 396
Ahasuerus (see Xerxes I)
Ahaz, 332, 354-357
Ahaziah (Israel King), 314-315, 345
Ahaziah (Judah King), 318, 321, 346-347
Ahijah, 298, 300, 305
Ahikam, 377
Ahimaaz, 281
Ahimelech (Priest), 229n., 251, 254
Ahishalom, 340n.
Ahithophel, 274, 281-282
Ahitub, 251n.
Ahlab, 211
Ahmose, 34f., 111, 116
Aholiab, 150
Ai, 175-177
Aijalon (Ajalon), 180, 245, 339n.
Ain Qudirat, 156
Ain Qudeis, 156
Akhenaton (Amen-hotep IV), 94, 104f., 113
Akkad (see Agade)
Akkadian Period, 30, 40
Akkadian Language, 41n., 104n., 390
Alalakh, 105n.
Albright, W. F., 31n., 39n., 155, 176n., 292n., 294n., 304n., 308n., 342, 376n., 378n., 386n., 393n., 403n.
Aleppo, 308
Alexander the Great, 169n., 381n.
Altar of Incense, 151, 296
Amalek, Amalekites, 138, 141-142, 159, 218, 245-246, 257, 258
Amanus Mountains, 41

Amariah, 344
Amarna Letters, 47, 104-107
Amar-sin, 40
Amasa, 281, 283-284
Amasis, 380n., 381, 388, 390
Amaziah, 325, 350-351
Amel-Marduk, 382, 384, 386
Amenemhet III, 114
Amen-hotep I, 116
Amen-hotep II, 103-104, 123f., 134
Amen-hotep III, 94, 104f., 134n., 168
Amen-hotep IV (see Akhenaton)
Amenmose, 118
Amman, 102, 401n.
Ammon (country), 102, 271, 344, 378, 381, 405
Ammonites, 55n., 206, 222-223, 240, 245, 352, 354, 359, 374, 401
Amnon, 280
Amon, 366
Amon, Cult of, 339n.
Amon (god), 113
Amorites, 28n., 31n., 48, 184
Amos, 327
Amphictyon, 193-194
Amram, 86, 117
Amraphel, 53
Anakim, 185, 187
Anath, 208
Anathoth, 288
Anatolia, 21
Aner, 51
Angel of Yahweh, 55, 73, 122, 174, 225, 361
Angels, 55
Anshan, 388
Anubis, 77n.
Aphek, 231f., 252
Aphik, 211
Apiru (see Habiru)

427

SCRIPTURE INDEX

437

Wherever differences in the following maps, and the maps in the body of the book, exist, the line-drawing maps in the body of the book are recommended.

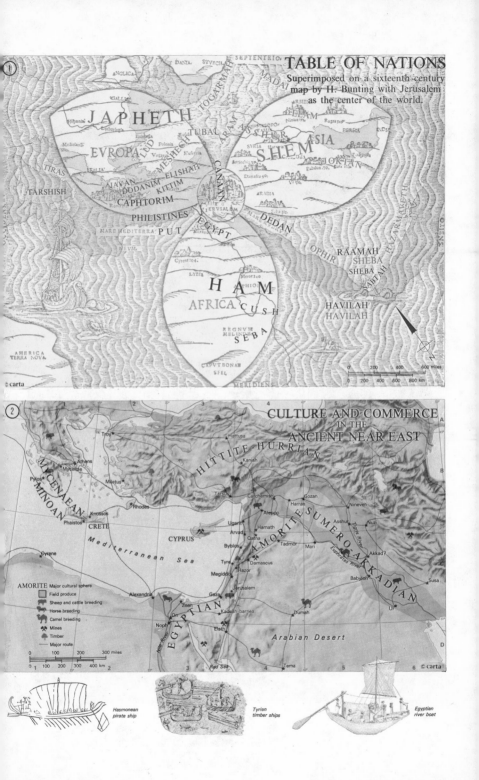

Hasmonean pirate ship

Tyrian timber ships

Egyptian river boat

ANCIENT NEAR EAST
IN THE
SECOND MILLENNIUM B.C.

Black Sea

MYCENAEANS

Mycenae

Troy

Gordium

Knossos

MINOANS

ARZAWA

Kanish

Hattusa

CYPRUS

Mediterranean Sea

HURRIANS

Carchemish

Harran

Gozan

Aleppo

Alalah

Ugarit

ASSYRIA

Hamath

Qatna

Kedesh

Ullaza

Byblos

Sidon

Damascus

Tyre

AMORITES

CANAAN

Megiddo

Joppa

Hazor

Jerusalem

Gaza

Sharuhen

Zoan

On

Noph

Washshukanni

MITANNI

Tirqa

Mari

Euphrates River

Tadmor

Tuttul

Tigris River

Nineveh

Asshur

Nuzi

Arrapha

Eshnunna

Sippar

Babylon

Nippur

Lagash

Erech

Ur

Larsa

Susa

ELAM

BABYLONIA

Persian Gulf

Red Sea

Akhetaton

Nile River

No-amon

Rameses II in his war chariot

PALACE AT MARI
(18th century B.C.)

Great
Courtyard

Old Palace

Throne-
room

Chapel

Storerooms

Workshops

Royal quarters

Scribal School

0   20   40   60 yards

0   20   40 meters

Empire of Hammurabi,
early 18th cent. B.C.

Egyptian sphere
of influence

Empire of Thutmose III,
c.1468 B.C.

Minoan–Mycenaean
sphere

Hittite sphere

Invasion of Sea Peoples,
12th cent. B.C.

Noph — City of importance

0   100   200   300 miles

0   100   200   300   400 km

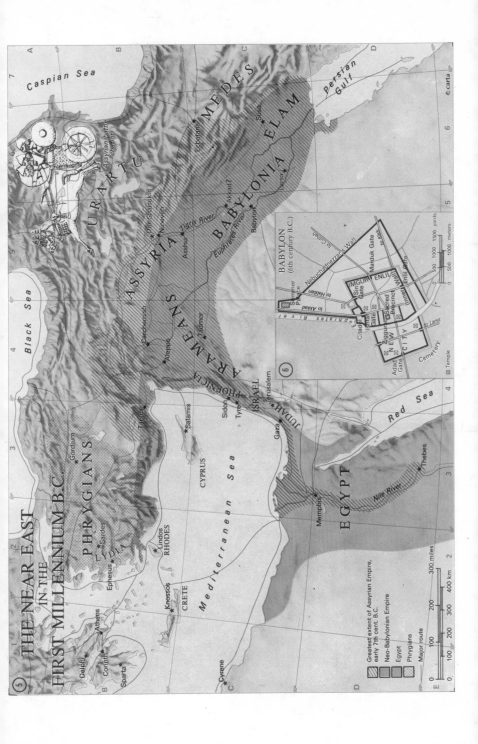

THE NEAR EAST
IN THE
FIRST MILLENNIUM B.C.

Caspian Sea

Black Sea

PHRYGIANS

Gordium

Delphi
Athens
Corinth
Sparta

Ephesus
Sardes
LYDIA

Lindos
RHODES

Knossos
CRETE

CYPRUS

Salamis

Mediterranean Sea

URARTU

M E D E S

Assyrian battle
chariot

Ecbatana

Dûr-Sharrukin
Nineveh

Asshur

Tigris River

ASSYRIA

Akkad?
Babylon
Euphrates River

BABYLONIA

Susa

ELAM

Persian Gulf

Carchemish

Aleppo

Tadmor

ARAMEANS

Tarsus

Sidon
Tyre

PHOENICIA

Jerusalem
ISRAEL
JUDAH

Gaza

Memphis

EGYPT

Nile River

Thebes

Red Sea

Greatest extent of Assyrian Empire,
early 7th cent. B.C.
Neo-Babylonian Empire
Egypt
Phrygians
Major route

0   100   200   300 miles
0   100 200 300 400 km

© carta

BABYLON
(6th century B.C.)

to Opis

to Kish

Nebuchadnezzar's Wall
Marduk Gate

Summer
Palace

to Habban

IMGUR ENLIL

Sin
Gate

Sacred
Precinct

Inner Wall

Ishtar
Gate

Zababa
Gate

Enlil Gate

Euphrates River

Citadel

Shamash
Gate

N E W   C I T Y

to Larsa

Adad
Gate

Cemetery

0   500   1000   1500 yards
0   500   1000 meters

⊠ Temple

THE LAND OF CANAAN

⑦

1 — 2 — 3 — 4

Arvad

Sumur

Arqa

Kedesh
1286 B.C.

Ullaza

Ardata

Zedad

Ziphron

Batruna

Mt. Hor

Hazar-enan

Byblos

Lebo

Khashabu

Hazi

Litani River

Migdal

Sidon

Mt. Hermon

Damascus

Ijon

Tyre

Abel

Usu

Laish

Kedesh

Hazor

Acco

Sea of Chinnereth

Ashtaroth

Mishal

Hannathon

Achshaph

Mt. Carmel

Shimon

Mt. Tabor

En-anab

Kenath

Dor

Yanoam

Yarmuk River

Megiddo
1468 B.C.

Shunem

Beth-shean

Bezer

Salecah

Taanach

Migdal

Pehel

Ramoth-gilead

Gath-padalla

Jordan River

Zaphon

Shechem

Zarethan

Jabbok River

Joppa

Aphek

Lod

Rabbah

Gezer

Beth-horon

Jericho

Aijalon

Gibeon

Beth-haram

Heshbon

Ashdod

Jerusalem

Mt. Nebo

Ashkelon

Keilah

Gath

Gaza

Eglon

Lachish

Hebron

Dibon

Yurza

Arnon River

Sharuhen
c. 1570 B.C.

Beersheba

Arad

Hormah

Kir-moab

Negeb

Zoar

Zered River

Tamar

Bozrah

Punon

Mt. Seir

Battle

Mediterranean Sea

Dead Sea

□ Mentioned in the Execration Texts, 20th–19th cent. B.C.
■ Mentioned in the el-Amarna Letters, 15th–14th cent. B.C.
⊗ Egyptian garrison city
Battle

0 — 20 — 40 — 60 miles

0 — 20 — 40 — 60 — 80 km

Kadesh-barnea

Canaanite priest

THE WALLS OF JERICHO
(7th to late 2nd millennia B.C.)

⑧

Cemetery area

Modern road

later Canaanite walls

Early Canaanite walls

Neolithic tower

Spring

Middle Canaanite buildings

0 — 20 — 40 — 60 yards

0 — 20 — 40 meters

c. carta

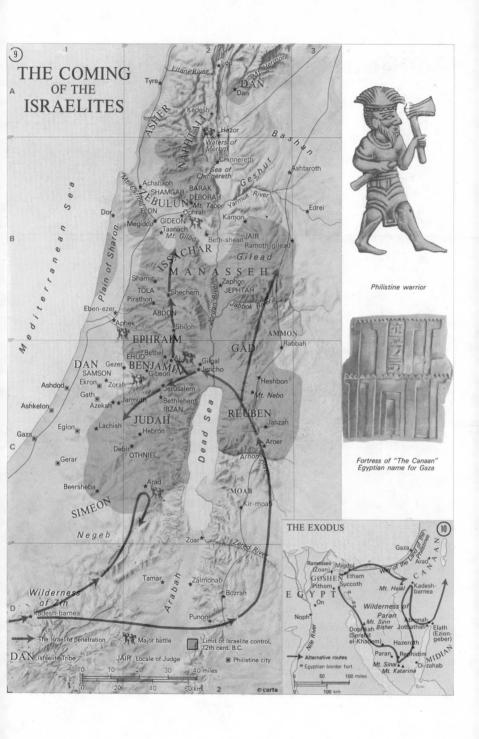

THE COMING
OF THE
ISRAELITES

⑨

A

Litani River
Tyre
Ijon
Mt. Hermon
DAN
Dan
ASHER
Kedesh
Hazor
NAPHTALI
Waters of Merom
Bashan
Chinnereth
Sea of Chinnereth
Geshur
Ashtaroth
Achshaph
SHAMGAR
BARAK
DEBORAH
Mt. Tabor
Yarmuk River
Edrei
ELON
Ophrah
Kamon
GIDEON
Megiddo
Taanach
Beth-shean
JAIR
Mt. Gilboa
Ramoth-gilead
Dor
Mt. Carmel
ZEBULUN
Shamir
ISSACHAR
Gilead

B

Mediterranean Sea

MANASSEH
TOLA
Pirathon
Shechem
Zaphon
JEPHTAH
Eben-ezer
ABDON
Jabbok River
Plain of Sharon
Aphek
Shiloh
EPHRAIM
AMMON
Bethel
Ai
GAD
Rabbah
DAN
Gezer
EHUD
BENJAMIN
Gilgal
SAMSON
Gibeon
Jericho
Ashdod
Ekron
Zorah
Jerusalem
Heshbon
Gath
Jarmuth
Bethlehem
Mt. Nebo
Ashkelon
Azekah
IBZAN
REUBEN
Eglon
Lachish
JUDAH
Jahzah
Gaza
Gerar
Debir
OTHNIEL
Hebron
Aroer
Arnon River
Beersheba
Arad
Dead Sea
MOAB
Kir-moab

C

SIMEON
Negeb
Zoar
Zered River

D

Wilderness of Zin
Tamar
Arabah
Zalmonah
Bozrah
Kadesh-barnea
Punon

Jordan River

Philistine warrior

Fortress of "The Canaan"
Egyptian name for Gaza

→ The Israelite penetration
⚔ Major battle
▨ Limit of Israelite control, 12th cent. B.C.
DAN Israelite Tribe
JAIR Locale of Judge
▨ Philistine city

0   10   20   30   40 miles
0   20   40   60 km

© carta

THE EXODUS
⑩

Gaza
Ramesses (Zoan)
Migdol
Arad
GOSHEN
Etham
Way of the Land of the Philistines
CANAAN
Pithom
Succoth
Mt. Halal
Kadesh-barnea
EGYPT
On
Wilderness of Paran
Abronah
Elath (Ezion-geber)
Noph
Dophkah (Serabit el-Khadem)
Mt. Sinn Bisher
Jotbathah
Hazeroth
Nile River
Paran
Rephidim
Mt. Sinai
Mt. Katarina
MIDIAN
Di-zahab

→ Alternative routes
⊕ Egyptian border fort

0   50   100 miles
0   100 km

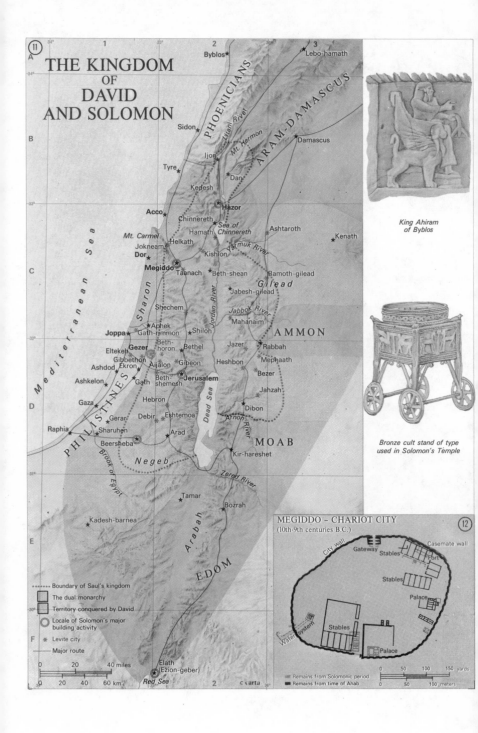

THE KINGDOM OF DAVID AND SOLOMON

11

A

Byblos★

Lebo-hamath

PHOENICIANS

ARAM-DAMASCUS

Sidon★

B

Litani River

Mt. Hermon

Damascus★

Ijon

Tyre★

Dan★

Kedesh★

Hazor★

Acco★

Chinnereth

Sea of Chinnereth

Ashtaroth★

Kenath★

Mt. Carmel

Hamath

Jokneam★

Helkath

Kishion

Yarmuk River

Dor★

Megiddo★

Taanach★

Beth-shean

Ramoth-gilead

Gilead

Mediterranean Sea

Sharon

C

Jabesh-gilead★

Shechem★

Jabbok River

Aphek★

Gath-rimmon

Shiloh★

Mahanaim★

AMMON

Joppa★

Gezer

Beth-horon

Bethel★

Jazer★

Rabbah★

Eltekeh

Gibeon★

Heshbon★

Mephaath★

Gibbethon

Aijalon

Bezer★

Ashdod

Ekron

Beth-shemesh

Jerusalem★

Ashkelon★

Gath★

Jahzah★

D

Gaza★

Hebron★

Dibon★

Dead Sea

Gerar★

Debir★

Eshtemoa★

Arnon River

Raphia★

Sharuhen★

Arad★

MOAB

Beersheba★

Kir-hareseth★

Negeb

Brook of Egypt

Zered River

Tamar★

Bozrah★

Kadesh-barnea★

Arabah

EDOM

E

F

★ King Ahiram of Byblos

Bronze cult stand of type used in Solomon's Temple

····· Boundary of Saul's kingdom

▭ The dual monarchy

▭ Territory conquered by David

◯ Locale of Solomon's major building activity

★ Levite city

— Major route

0   20   40 miles

0   20   40   60 km

Elath (Ezion-geber)

Red Sea

© Carta

MEGIDDO – CHARIOT CITY
(10th-9th centuries B.C.)

12

City wall

Gateway

Stables

Casemate wall

Fort

Stables

Palace

Water System

Stables

Palace

▦ Remains from Solomonic period

■ Remains from time of Ahab

0   50   100   150 yards

0   50   100 meters

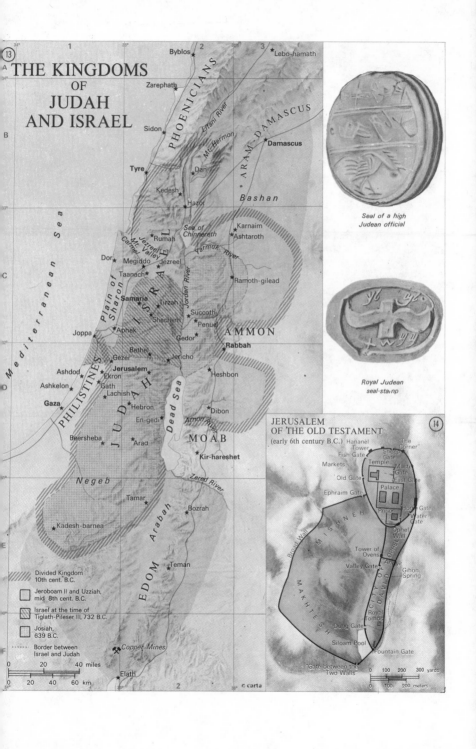

THE KINGDOMS OF JUDAH AND ISRAEL

13

A

1 • 2 • 3

Byblos
Lebo-hamath

Zarephath

PHOENICIANS

Litani River

Sidon

Mt. Hermon

B

ARAM-DAMASCUS

Damascus

Tyre

Dan

Kedesh

Bashan

Hazor

Sea of Chinnereth

Karnaim
Ashtaroth

Rumah

Mt. Gilboa/Carmel

Jezreel Valley

Dor

Megiddo

Jezreel

Yarmuk River

Mediterranean Sea

Taanach

Ramoth-gilead

Plain of Sharon

I S R A E L

Samaria

Tirzah

Jordan River

Shechem

Succoth

Penuel

AMMON

Joppa

Aphek

Gedor

Rabbah

Bethel

Jericho

Gezer

Jerusalem

PHILISTINES

Ashdod

Ekron

Heshbon

Ashkelon

Gath

Lachish

J U D A H

Gaza

Hebron

Dead Sea

En-gedi

Dibon

Beersheba

Arad

Arnon River

MOAB

Kir-haresheth

Negeb

Zered River

Tamar

Bozrah

A r a b a h

Kadesh-barnea

E D O M

Teman

Divided Kingdom 10th cent. B.C.

Jeroboam II and Uzziah, mid 8th cent. B.C.

Israel at the time of Tiglath-Pileser III, 732 B.C.

Josiah, 639 B.C.

Border between Israel and Judah

Copper Mines

Elath

0   20   40 miles
0   20   40   60 km

© carta

Seal of a high Judean official

Royal Judean seal-stamp

JERUSALEM OF THE OLD TESTAMENT
(early 6th century B.C.)

14

Hananel Tower

"The Corner"

Sheep Gate

Fish Gate

Markets

Temple

Muster Gate

East Gate

Old Gate

Palace

Ephraim Gate

Prison

Horse Gate

Water Gate

MISHNEH

Ophel Wall

Broad Wall

Tower of Ovens

Valley Gate

Amal

CITY OF DAVID

Gihon Spring

MAKHTESH

Royal Tombs

Dung Gate

Siloam Pool

Fountain Gate

"Gate between the Two Walls"

0   100   200   300 yards
0   100   200 meters

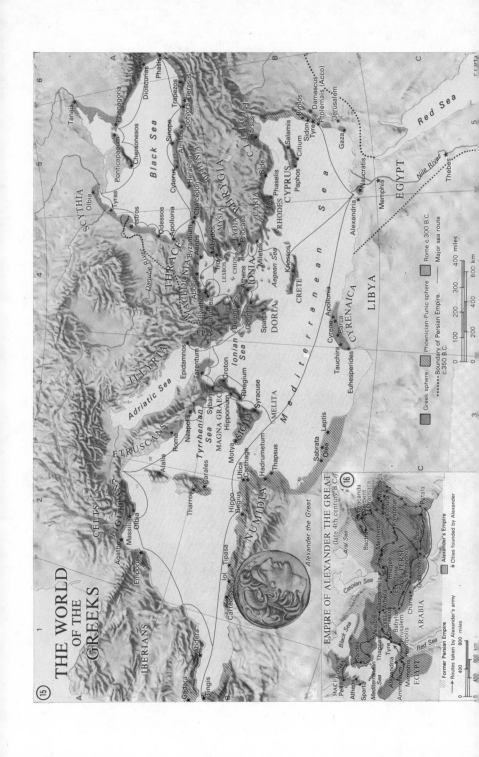

THE WORLD
OF THE
GREEKS

Alexander the Great

EMPIRE OF ALEXANDER THE GREAT
late 4th century B.C.

Former Persian Empire

→ Routes taken by Alexander's army

★ Cities founded by Alexander

0   400   800 miles
0   400   800 km

Greek sphere

Phoenician-Punic sphere

Rome c.300 B.C.

Boundary of Persian Empire
c.350 B.C.

Major sea route

0   100   200   300   400 miles
0   200   400   600 km

Alexander's Empire

CELTS
IBERIANS
LIGURIA
ILLYRIA
SCYTHIA
THRACE
MACEDONIA
EPIRUS
MAGNA GRAECIA
SICILY
NUMIDIA
LIBYA
CYRENAICA
EGYPT
MYSIA
PHRYGIA
LYDIA
CARIA
IONIA
DORIA
BITHYNIA
CILICIA
CYPRUS
RHODES
CRETE
ETRUSCANS

Gades
Tingis
Carteia
Kidera
Emporiae
Agathe
Massilia
Olbia
Alalia
Rome
Neapolis
Carales
Tharros
Tipasa
Iol
Hippo Regius
Utica
Carthage
Hadrumetum
Thapsus
Sabrata
Oea
Leptis
Tarentum
Epidamnos
Croton
Sybaris
Hipponium
Rhegium
Syracuse
MELITA
Euhesperides
Tauchira
Barca
Cyrene
Apollonia
Motya
Naucratis
Alexandria
Memphis
Thebes
Gaza
Jerusalem
Ptolemais (Acco)
Tyre
Sidon
Byblos
Damascus
Citium
Salamis
Paphos
Phaselis
Side
Tarsus
Miletus
Phocaea
Knossos
Chios
LESBOS
Troy
Abydos
Aenos
Byzantium
Chalcedon
Heraclea
Cyteros
Apollonia
Odessos
Istros
Tyras
Olbia
Tanais
Phanagoria
Dioscurias
Phasis
Trapezos
Cotyora
Kerasus
Sinope
Amisos
Ponticapaeum
Chersonesos
Abdera
Olynthos
Potidaea
Delphi
Corinth
Athens
Sparta

Black Sea
Red Sea
Nile River
Danube River
Aegean Sea
Adriatic Sea
Ionian Sea
Tyrrhenian Sea
Mediterranean Sea

EMPIRE OF ALEXANDER THE GREAT (inset)
MACEDONIA
Pella
Athens
Sparta
Mediterranean Sea
Ammonium
Memphis
Heliopolis
EGYPT
Red Sea
ARABIA
PERSIA
Tyre
Damascus
Jerusalem
Alexandria
Thapsacus
Nisibis
Gaugamela
Babylon
Susa
Ecbatana
Persepolis
Charax
Pasargadae
Sogdiana
Marocanda
Bactra
Nautaca
Merops
Cabura
Kandahar
Alexandria
Massaga
Taxila
Bucephala
Patala
Gedrosia
Aral Sea
Caspian Sea
Black Sea

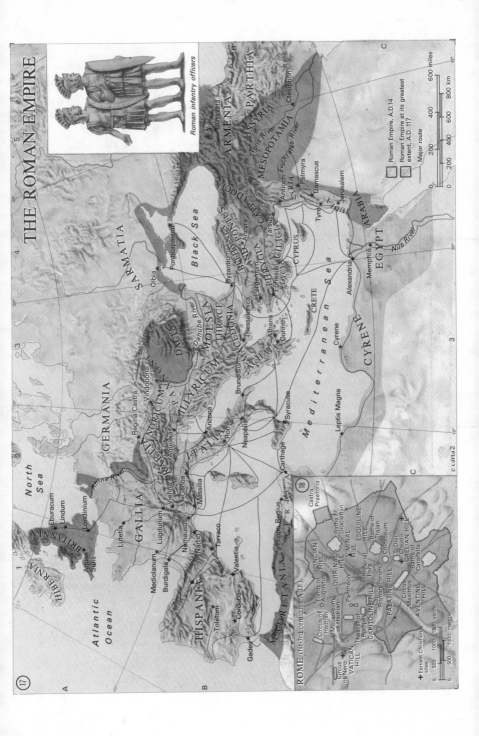

THE ROMAN EMPIRE

Roman infantry officers

Roman Empire, A.D.14

Roman Empire at its greatest extent, A.D. 117

Major route

0   200   400   600   miles
0   200   400   600   800   km

c.carta 2

North Sea

Atlantic Ocean

HIBERNIA

BRITANNIA
Eburacum
Lindum
Londinium
Aquae Sulis

GERMANIA
Lutetia
Burdigala
Mediolanum
GALLIA
Lugdunum
Vienna
Namausus
Genua
Massilia
Narbo
Tarraco

HISPANIA
Toletum
Corduba
Gades

MAURETANIA
Valentia

Rhine River

SARMATIA

Regina Castra
Vindobona
RAETIA
NORICUM
AQUILEIA
PANNONIA
Aquileia
ILLYRICUM
ITALIA
Ancona
Rome
Neapolis
Brundisium

DACIA
Danube River

MOESIA
MACEDONIA
THRACE
Byzantium
Thessalonica
Athens
ACHAIA
Corinth

Olbia
Panticapaeum

Black Sea

CAPPADOCIA
BITHYNIA
PONTUS
Ancyra
PHRYGIA
Pergamum
Ephesus
LYCIA
CILICIA
Tarsus

ARMENIA
Artaxata

ASSYRIA
MESOPOTAMIA
Tigris River
Euphrates River
PARTHIA
Ctesiphon

SYRIA
Antioch
Palmyra
Damascus
Tyre
Jerusalem

CYPRUS
CRETE

Mediterranean Sea

AFRICA
Carthage
Hippo Regius
Leptis Magna
CYRENE
Cyrene

Syracuse

EGYPT
Alexandria
Memphis
Nile River

ARABIA

ROME (1st–3rd centuries A.D.)

Castra Praetoria
PINCIAN HILL
Circus of Nero
VATICAN HILL
Tomb of Augustus
Mausoleum of Hadrian
QUIRINAL HILL
Baths of Diocletian
VIMINAL HILL
ESQUILINE HILL
Baths of Trajan
Pantheon
Theatre of Pompey
Theatre of Marcellus
Tiber Ford
CAPITOLINE HILL
Roman Forum
PALATINE HILL
Il Divo
Claudii
Colosseum
CAELIAN HILL
Circus Maximus
Baths of Caracalla
AVENTINE HILL

✝ Earliest Christian sites

0   500   1000   1500   yards
0   500   1000   meters

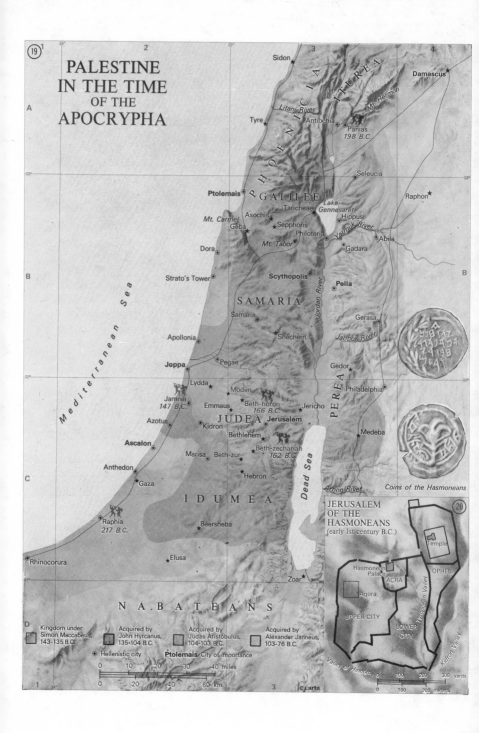

PALESTINE
IN THE TIME
OF THE
APOCRYPHA

Sidon
Damascus

PHOENICIA
ITUREA

Litani River
Tyre
Antiochia
Mt. Hermon
Panias
198 B.C.

Seleucia
Raphon

Ptolemais
GALILEE
Lake
Gennesaret
Hippus

Asochis
Taricheae
Mt. Carmel
Sepphoris
Geba
Philoteria
Yarmuk River
Abila
Dora
Mt. Tabor
Gadara

Strato's Tower
Scythopolis
Pella

SAMARIA
Gerasa
Samaria
Jabbok River
Shechem

Apollonia
Jordan River
Joppa
Pegae
Gedor
Philadelphia

Lydda
Modiin
Jamnia
147 B.C.
Beth-horon
166 B.C.
Emmaus
Jericho
Azotus
JUDEA
Jerusalem
Kidron

Ascalon
Bethlehem
Beth-zechariah
162 B.C.
Marisa
Beth-zur
Medeba

Anthedon
Hebron
Gaza

IDUMEA
Dead Sea

Raphia
217 B.C.
Beersheba
Arnon River

Rhinocorura
Elusa
Zoar

Mediterranean Sea
PEREA

Coins of the Hasmoneans

JERUSALEM
OF THE
HASMONEANS
(early 1st century B.C.)

Temple
Hasmonean
Palace
ACRA
OPHEL
Agora
Tyropoeon Valley
UPPER CITY
LOWER CITY
Kidron Valley
Valley of Hinnom

NABATEANS

Kingdom under
Simon Maccabeus,
143-135 B.C.
Acquired by
John Hyrcanus,
135-104 B.C.
Acquired by
Judas Aristobulus,
104-103 B.C.
Acquired by
Alexander Janneus,
103-76 B.C.

Hellenistic city Ptolemais City of importance

0   10   20   30   40 miles
0   20   40   60 km.

© Carta

0   100   200   300 yards
0   100   200 meters

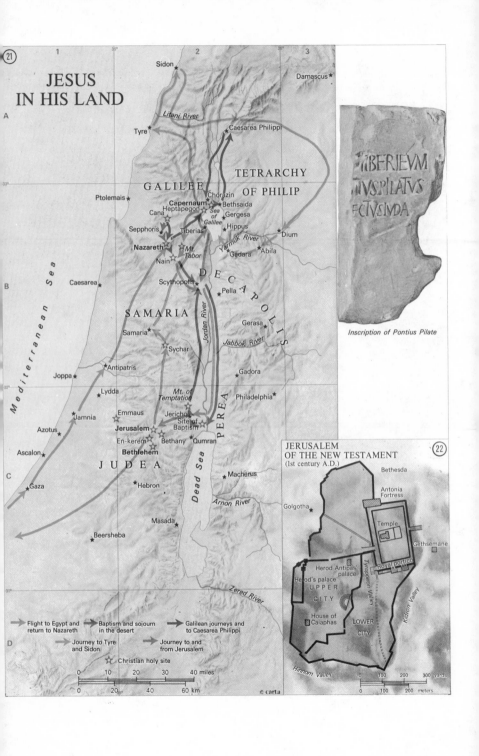

JESUS IN HIS LAND

(21)

Sidon ★

Damascus ★

Litani River

Tyre ★

Caesarea Philippi ★

GALILEE

TETRARCHY OF PHILIP

Ptolemais ★

Chorazin

Capernaum
Heptapegon ★ Bethsaida

Cana ★

Sea of Galilee

Gergesa

Sepphoris ★

Tiberias ★

Hippus

Dium ★

Nazareth ★ Mt. Tabor

Yarmuk River

Abila ★

Nain ★

Gadara ★

D E C A P O L I S

Caesarea ★

Scythopolis ★

Pella ★

SAMARIA

Jordan River

Samaria ★

Gerasa ★

Sychar ★

Jabbok River

Joppa ★

Antipatris ★

Gadora ★

Lydda ★

Mt. of Temptation

Philadelphia ★

Jamnia ★

Emmaus ★

Jericho

Site of Baptism

P E R E A

Azotus ★

Jerusalem ★

Ascalon ★

En-kerem ★

Bethany

Qumran ★

Bethlehem

J U D E A

Gaza ★

Hebron ★

Macherus ★

Dead Sea

Arnon River

Masada ★

Beersheba ★

Zered River

Mediterranean Sea

→ Flight to Egypt and return to Nazareth

→ Baptism and sojourn in the desert

→ Galilean journeys and to Caesarea Philippi

→ Journey to Tyre and Sidon

→ Journey to and from Jerusalem

☆ Christian holy site

0   10   20   30   40 miles

0   20   40   60 km

© carta

Inscription of Pontius Pilate

JERUSALEM OF THE NEW TESTAMENT
(1st century A.D.)

(22)

Bethesda

Golgotha ★

Antonia Fortress

Temple

Gethsemane

Herod Antipas' palace

Royal portico

Herod's palace

UPPER CITY

Tyropeion Valley

House of Caiaphas

LOWER CITY

Kidron Valley

Hinnom Valley

0   100   200   300 yards

0   100   200 meters

㉓ JESUS IN GALILEE

Early preaching
Revisiting central Galilee
Journeys to the north
Transfiguration
Major road

Mediterranean Sea

Sidon
Sarepta
Ladder of Tyre
Ecdippa
Ptolemais (Acco)
Sycaminum
Mount Carmel
Geba
Besara

PHILIP
Kefar-dan
Caesarea Philippi
Thella
Jordan River
Gischala
Cadasa
Bacca
Cana
TYRE
UPPER GALILEE
LOWER GALILEE
HEROD ANTIPAS
Sepphoris
Garis
Gath-hefer
Nazareth
Japhia
Exaloth
Nain
Japhia
Capercotnei
Esdraelon

Chorazin
Bethsaida
Capernaum
Gennesaret
Magdala
Arbela
Tiberias
Sennabris
Philoteria
Sea of Galilee
Gergesa
Hippus
HIPPUS
Gadara
GADARA
Jordan River
Agrippina
Mt. Tabor

Pagan triad worshipped in Syria

© Carta

㉔ THE JOURNEYS OF THE APOSTLES

Tarsus
CYPRUS
Mediterranean Sea
Seleucia
Antioch
Orontes River
Arvadus
Tripolis
Berytus
Sidon
Tyre
Ptolemais
Dor
Caesarea
Joppa
Azotus
Gaza

SYRIA
Damascus
PHOENICIA
GALILEE
Scythopolis
Gadara
Samaria
Neapolis
Lydda
Jamnia
Jerusalem
Beersheba

Jewish community
Pagan center
Paul's journeys A.D. 46–48
Paul's journeys A.D. 49–52
Paul's journeys A.D. 53–58
The journeys of Peter A.D. 36

ANTIOCH (1st century A.D.)

㉕

Orontes River
Mt. Staurin
Mt. Silpius
EPIPHANIA
SELEUCID TOWN
Agora
Hippodrome
Theater
Colonnaded Street
Amphitheater
Seleucid Wall
Wall of Tiberius

CAESAREA MARITIMA

㉖

Roman-Byzantine city wall
Crusader City wall
Herodian City wall
Aqueduct
Hippodrome
Amphitheater
Temple of Augustus
Harbor
Theater

THE GROWTH OF CHRISTIANITY

Eburacum
Lindum
Londinium
Colonia Agrippina
Lugdunum
Vienna
Arelate
Massilia
Corduba
Carthage
Roma
Puteoli
Syracuse
Nicopolis
Samos
Athens
Aegina
Knossos
Cyrene
Alexandria

Black Sea

Ancyra
Amastris
Sinope
Amisus
Constantinople
Nicomedia
Nicaea 325
Chalcedon
Bithynium
Ephesus
Sinus
Tarsus
Laodicea
Paphos
Salamis
Tyre
Caesarea
Jerusalem
Apamea
Dura Europos
Nisibis

ARMENIANS
COBITES

Tigris River
Euphrates River

COPTS

Mt. Sinai

Red Sea
Nile River

Mediterranean Sea

Christian victims in the arena

- Extent of Christian church, A.D. 1st cent.
- Extent of Christian church, A.D. 2nd cent.
- ✴ Major church council 431 (with date)
- ✦ Notable early church
- IV Century of conversion to Christianity
- ---- Boundary of Roman Empire
- COPTS Monophysite church after 431
- |||||| Split of Latin (western) and Greek (eastern) churches, A.D. 5th cent.

```
0    200    400    600 miles
0  200  400  600  800 km
```

© carta

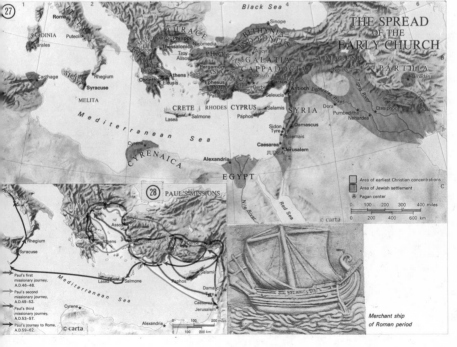

THE SPREAD OF THE EARLY CHURCH

Black Sea

Roma
SARDINIA
Carales
Puteoli
Carthage
Rhegium
Syracuse
MELITA
Cyrene
CYRENAICA

THRACE
Philippi
Thessalonica
Nicomedia
Troy
Assos
Pergamum
Sardis
Athens
Corinth
Eleusis
Ephesus
Patara
CRETE
Lasea
Salmone
RHODES
CYPRUS
Salamis
Páphos

PHRYGIA
GALATIA
CAPPADOCIA
Iconium
Derbe
Tarsus
Seleucia
Antioch
SYRIA
Dora
Sidon
Tyre
Ptolemais
Damascus
Caesarea
JUDEA
Jerusalem
Alexandria
EGYPT

BITHYNIA AND PONTUS
Sinope
Ancyra

DIABENE
PARTHIA
Nisibis
Hamadan
Pumbeditha
Nehardea
Ctesiphon
Susa

Euphrates River
Tigris River

Mediterranean Sea

Nile River
Red Sea

- Area of earliest Christian concentrations
- Area of Jewish settlement
- ✦ Pagan center

```
0   100   200   300   400 miles
0    200    400    600 km
```

© carta

PAUL'S MISSIONS (28)

Roma
Puteoli
Rhegium
Syracuse
Philippi
Troy
Assos
Athens
Corinth
Lasea
Salmone
Paphos
Salamis
Damascus
Caesarea
Jerusalem
Alexandria
Cyrene

- → Paul's first missionary journey, A.D. 46–48.
- → Paul's second missionary journey, A.D. 49–52.
- → Paul's third missionary journey, A.D. 53–57.
- → Paul's journey to Rome, A.D. 59–62.

Mediterranean Sea

```
0    100    200 miles
0    100    200 km
```

© carta

Merchant ship of Roman period

PALESTINE
IN THE TIME
OF THE
OLD TESTAMENT

30

★ Damascus

Zarephath ★

Litani River

Ijon ★

Tyre ★

Abel-beth-maacha ★

Mt. Hermon

Kanah ★

Beth-anath ★

Dan ★

Yiron ★ Kedesh ★

Achziv ★ Abdon ★

Merom ★

Hazor ★

Janoah ★

Beth-emek ★

Ramah ★

Acco ★

Cabul ★ Hukok ★

Kishon River

Aphek ★

Chinnereth ★

Karnaim ★

Naveh ★

Libnath ★ Hannathon Rimmon ★

Sea of Chinnereth

Golan ★

Ashtaroth ★

Mt. Carmel Achshaph ★

Adamah ★

Beth-lehem ★

Geba ★

Shimron ★ Aznoth-tabor ★

Beth-shemesh ★

Yarmuk River

Joktheam ★ Shunem ★

Anaharath ★

En-dor ★

Kamon ★

Edrei ★

Dor ★ Megiddo ★

Jarmuth ★

Jezreel ★ Lo-debar ★

Beth-arbel ★

Tob ★

Iron ★

Mt. Gilboa

Beth-shean ★

Jordan River

Pehel ★ Ham ★

Ramoth-gilead ★

Bezer ★

Hepher ★

Gath ★ Dothan ★

Bezek ★

Jabesh-gilead ★

Socoh ★

Geba ★

Abel-meholah ★

Shiphthan ★ Samaria ★ Tirzah ★

Zaphon ★

Shechem ★

Succoth ★ Mahanaim ★

Jabbok River

Arumah ★ Janoah ★

Penuel ★

Zarethan ★

Gath-rimmon ★ Aphek ★

Yarkon River

Tappuah ★ Lebonah ★

Adam ★

Joppa ★ Yehud ★

Zeredah ★ Shiloh ★

Jogbehah ★

Beth-dagon ★ Ono ★

Geba ★

Betonim ★

Nebellat ★

Ophrah ★

Jazer ★ Rabbah ★

Jabneel ★ Gittaim ★ Lod ★

Beth-horon ★ Bethel ★ Ai ★ Gilgal ★

Gezer ★ Ramah ★

Beth-nimrah ★ Abel-keramim ★

Eltekeh ★ Shaalbim ★ Aijalon ★ Gibeon ★ Geba ★

Jericho ★

Gibbethon ★ Zorah ★ Kiriath-jearim ★ Gibeah ★

Heshbon ★

Timnah ★

Beth-hogla ★

Ashdod ★ Ekron ★ Chesalon ★ Jerusalem ★

Beth-jeshimoth ★

Gath ★ Beth-shemesh ★ Bethlehem ★

Medeba ★

Ashkelon ★ Azekah ★ Socoh ★ Etam ★

Baal-maon ★

Libnah ★ Keilah ★ Gedor ★ Tekoa ★

Zereth-shahar ★

Mareshah ★ Beth-zur ★

Eglon ★ Lachish ★ Hebron ★

Jahzah ★

Gaza ★ Beth-tappuah ★

Dibon ★

Carmel ★ En-gedi ★

Aroer ★

Yurza ★ Debir ★

Arnon River

Ziklag ★ Yattir ★ Maon ★ Eshtemoa ★

Sharuhen ★ Moladah ★ Arad ★

Kir-moab ★

Beersheba ★ Kabzeel ★ Aroer ★

Dead Sea

Mediterranean Sea

Zoar ★

Zered River

feet meters
8202 2500
6561 2000
4921 1500
3280 1000
1640 500
820 250
0 0
Below sea level

0 10 20 30 40 miles
0 20 40 60 km

Tamar ★

Zalmonah ★

Sela ★

Bozrah ★

Punon ★

Rekem ★

Column from Isaiah scroll
from Dead Sea Caves

© Carta

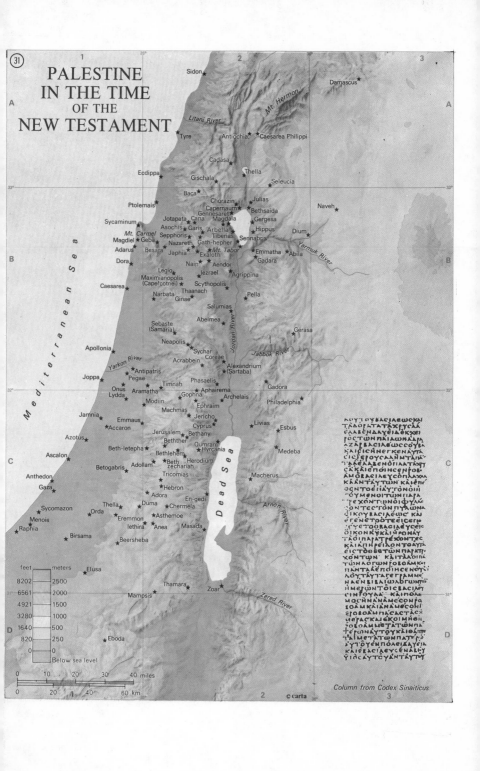

PALESTINE
IN THE TIME
OF THE
NEW TESTAMENT

31

Mediterranean Sea

Dead Sea

Jordan River

Litani River

Yarmuk River

Jabbok River

Yarkon River

Arnon River

Zered River

Mt. Hermon

Mt. Carmel

Mt. Tabor

Sidon
Damascus
Tyre
Antiochia
Caesarea Philippi
Cadasa
Thella
Ecdippa
Gischala
Seleucia
Baca
Chorazin
Julias
Ptolemais
Capernaum
Bethsaida
Naveh
Gennesaret
Sycaminum
Jotapata
Cana
Magdala
Gergesa
Asochis
Garis
Arbella
Hippus
Mt. Carmel
Sepphoris
Tiberias
Sennabris
Dium
Magdiel
Geba
Nazareth
Gath-hepher
Adarus
Besara
Japhia
Emmatha
Abila
Dora
Exaloth
Gadara
Nain
Aendor
Legio
Jezrael
Agrippina
Maximianopolis
(Capercotnei)
Scythopolis
Caesarea
Narbata
Thaanach
Pella
Ginae
Salumias
Abelmea
Sebaste
(Samaria)
Gerasa
Apollonia
Neapolis
Sychar
Acrabbein
Coreae
Antipatris
Alexandrium
Joppa
Pegae
(Sartaba)
Onus
Timnah
Phasaelis
Gadora
Lydda
Aramatha
Aphairema
Modin
Gophna
Archelais
Ephraim
Philadelphia
Jamnia
Machmas
Emmaus
Jericho
Accaron
Cyprus
Livias
Esbus
Jerusalem
Bethany
Azotus
Bethther
Qumran
Medeba
Beth-letepha
Bethlehem
Beth
Herodium
Ascalon
zechariah
Betogabris
Adollam
Tricomias
Macherus
Anthedon
Gaza
Hebron
Adora
En-gedi
Sycomazon
Thella
Duma
Chermela
Menois
Orda
Asthemoe
Raphia
Eremmon
Anea
Masada
Iethira
Birsama
Beersheba
Elusa
Thamara
Zoar
Mampsis
Eboda

© carta

Column from Codex Sinaiticus

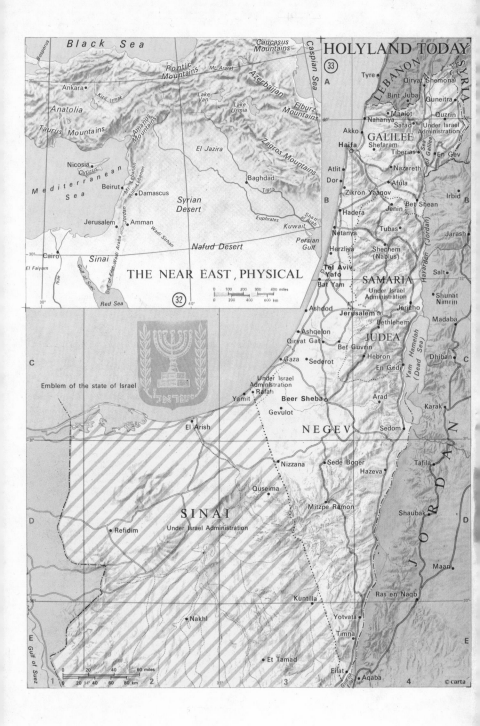

THE NEAR EAST, PHYSICAL

HOLYLAND TODAY

Emblem of the state of Israel